JUDGING RUSSIA

This book is the first in-depth study of the actual role that the Russian Constitutional Court played in protecting fundamental rights and resolving legislative–executive struggles and federalism disputes in both Yeltsin's and Putin's Russia. Alexei Trochev argues that judicial empowerment is a nonlinear process with unintended consequences and that courts that depend on their reputation flourish only if an effective and capable state is there to support them. This is because judges can rely only on the authoritativeness of their judgments, unlike politicians and bureaucrats, who have the material resources necessary to respond to judicial decisions. Drawing upon systematic analysis of all decisions of the Russian Court (published and unpublished) and previously unavailable materials on their (non) implementation, and resting on a combination of the approaches from comparative politics, law, and public administration, this book shows how and why judges attempted to reform Russia's governance and fought to ensure compliance with their judgments.

Alexei Trochev is Adjunct Professor for the School of Policy Studies of Queen's University in Ontario. He received his BA in Russian law from Syktyvkar State University in 1995, master's in public administration from the University of Kansas in 1997, and Ph.D. in political science from the University of Toronto in 2005. He taught constitutional law at the Pomor State University Law School in Arkhangelsk, Russia. Trochev's writings have been published in the *Law and Society Review*, *American Journal of Comparative Law*, *East European Constitutional Review*, and the *International Journal of Constitutional Law*, and he has contributed several book chapters on postcommunist judicial politics.

Judging Russia

CONSTITUTIONAL COURT IN RUSSIAN
POLITICS, 1990–2006

Alexei Trochev

Queen's University

CAMBRIDGE UNIVERSITY PRESS
Cambridge, New York, Melbourne, Madrid, Cape Town,
Singapore, São Paulo, Delhi, Tokyo, Mexico City

Cambridge University Press
32 Avenue of the Americas, New York, NY 10013-2473, USA

www.cambridge.org
Information on this title: www.cambridge.org/9780521173353

© Alexei Trochev 2008

This publication is in copyright. Subject to statutory exception
and to the provisions of relevant collective licensing agreements,
no reproduction of any part may take place without the written
permission of Cambridge University Press.

First published 2008
First paperback edition 2011

A catalog record for this publication is available from the British Library

Library of Congress Cataloging in Publication data

Trochev, Alexei, 1972–
Judging Russia : Constitutional Court in Russian politics, 1990–2006 / Alexei Trochev.
    p.   cm.
Includes bibliographical references and index.
ISBN 978-0-521-88743-4 (hardback)
1. Russia (Federation). Konstitutsionnyi Sud – History   2. Constitutional courts – Russia
(Federation) – History   3. Constitutional law – Russia (Federation) – History   4. Judicial
review – Russia (Federation) – History.   I. Title.
KLB2620.T76   2008
347.47′01 – dc22   2007045634

ISBN 978-0-521-88743-4 Hardback
ISBN 978-0-521-17335-3 Paperback

Cambridge University Press has no responsibility for the persistence or
accuracy of URLs for external or third-party internet websites referred to in
this publication, and does not guarantee that any content on such websites is,
or will remain, accurate or appropriate.

Contents

List of Figures and Tables	*page* viii
Acknowledgments	ix
Abbreviations	xi
Notes on Transliteration	xii

1	Introduction: Three Puzzles of Postcommunist Judicial Empowerment	1
	Judicial (Dis) Empowerment in Context	4
	Why Russia?	10
	The Sources of Data	13
	Overview of the Book	15
2	Nonlinear Judicial Empowerment	19
	Design, Judging, and Compliance: A Trilateral Dynamic of Judicial Review	19
	New Courts in New Polities: Nonlinear Judicial Empowerment	24
	Nonlinearity in Transitional Judicial Politics	38
	Conclusion	52
3	Making and Remaking Constitutional Review, Russian-Style	54
	Creating the USSR Constitutional Supervision Committee: 1988–1990	55
	Designing the 1st Russian Constitutional Court: 1990–1991	61
	Redesigning the Russian Constitutional Court: The 1993 Constitutional Convention	73

v

Contents

	Enacting the 1994 *Russian Constitutional Court Act*	79
	Tinkering with the 1994 *Russian Constitutional Court Act*	85
	Conclusion	90

4 Russian Constitutional Review in Action (1990–1993) 93

Decision Making of the USSR Constitutional Supervision Committee: 1990–1991 95
Decision Making of the 1st Russian Constitutional Court: 1992–1993 99
Defining Separation of Powers 104
Defining Russian Federalism 109
Protecting Constitutional Rights 111
Conclusion 115

5 Decision Making of the 2nd Russian Constitutional Court: 1995–2006 118

Decision-Making Procedures, Decisions, and Caseload 120
Defining Separation of Powers 127
Defining Russian Federalism 139
Protecting Constitutional Rights 158
Creating Rights 166
Scrutinizing Limits on Basic Rights: Proportionality, Russian-Style 168
Constitutional Principles: Written, Unwritten, and Borrowed 173
Constitutional Equality: Formal and Real 177
Elaborating Fairness 179
Conclusion 185

6 The Constitutional Court Has Ruled – What Next? 188

The Failure of the USSR Constitutional Supervision Committee: 1990–1991 189
The Rise and Fall of the 1st Russian Constitutional Court: 1992–1993 191
Implementing Judgments in the "Separation-of-Powers" Cases 191
Implementing Judgments in the "Federalism" Cases 195
Implementing Judgments in Constitutional Rights Cases 200
Conclusion 205

Contents

vii

7	The 2nd Russian Constitutional Court (1995–2007): *Problematique* of Implementation	207
	Enforcing the Separation of Powers	209
	"War of Courts," Russian-Style	214
	Policing Russian Federalism	221
	Rights Revolutions Unfulfilled	228
	Due Process Rights in Criminal Procedure	230
	Rights of Bona Fide Taxpayers	235
	Social Rights: (Not) Compensating the Victims of Stalin's Purges	240
	Regional Defiance: Land, Elections, and *Propiska*	243
	The Public Image of the Russian Constitutional Court	247
	Conclusion	254
8	"Tinkering with Judicial Tenure" and "Wars of Courts" in Comparative Perspective	258
	"Tinkering with Judicial Tenure" in Comparative Perspective	259
	"Wars of Courts" in Comparative Perspective	265
	Conclusion	282
9	Conclusion: Zigzagging Judicial Power	285
	Puzzle 1: Zigzags in Designing Russian Constitutional Review	286
	Puzzle 2: Russian Constitutional Review in Action	287
	Puzzle 3: Successes and Failures in Implementing Russian Constitutional Court Decisions	289
	Puzzle 3.1: The "War of Courts" in the Russian Federation	292
	Summary	294
	Alternative Explanations of Russian Experiments with Constitutional Review	295
	Conclusion	300

Appendix	305
Bibliography	307
Statutes and Decrees	337
Court Decisions	341
Index	353

List of Figures and Tables

FIGURES

2.1	Temporal model of judicial process.	*page* 20
2.2	Dynamic relationship of judicial review.	21

TABLES

1.1	Postcommunist constitutional courts: Creation and access	3
3.1	Making and breaking the Russian Constitutional Court, 1990–1993	65
3.2	Remaking the Russian Constitutional Court, 1993–1995	83
3.3	Tinkering with the tenure of the Russian Constitutional Court	87
5.1	Filings and decisions of the Russian Constitutional Court, 1995–2006	123
7.1	The "War of Courts" in Russia: Constitutionality of regional laws, 1995–2003	216
8.1	Tinkering with the tenure of high courts in comparative perspective	260
8.2	The "War of Courts" in the Czech Republic: Joseph Chodera's case, 1993–1999	279

Acknowledgments

This book could not have been done without the assistance of many people in Canada, the United States, and Russia. In Canada, I owe special thanks to Peter Solomon, for believing in me and inspiring me to study politics. His continuous theoretical guidance and generous practical support were crucial throughout the development of this book. My thanks also go to Peter Russell and Ran Hirschl, for their time, invaluable feedback, and encouragement. I am also indebted to Lawrence LeDuc and Susan Solomon for their intellectual support at the time when the idea for this book was born. I thank William Burnham, Kathryn Hendley, Jeffrey Kopstein, Jacqueline Krikorian, Kim Scheppele, Robert Sharlet, and Gordon Smith, who devoted their time and effort amid other important commitments to read all or portions of the book and provided helpful comments on the draft manuscript. I am grateful to Marc-Antoine Adam, Christian Boulanger, Mirella Eberts, Viktor Gomez, Janet Hiebert, Maria Popova, Dagmar Soennecken, Lavinia Stan, and Elina Treyger for sharing a laugh or two during the fruitful discussions about comparative law and politics. Thanks to John Berger at Cambridge University Press for his generous support and advice throughout the process of publication and to Wayne Cottrell and Joan Montgomery for helping me to edit the early draft of the book.

My friends and colleagues in Russia greatly aided my field research. Unfortunately, I cannot name all of them, in the interest of safeguarding their confidentiality. Thanks to the generous support of the staff at the Russian Constitutional Court, I was able to access unpublished materials about the Court's work. I am grateful to judges, court clerks, government officials, and law professors in Moscow, Arkhangelsk, Novosibirsk, and Syktyvkar for their patience in answering my questions and for providing invaluable insights into the politics of Russian constitutional litigation.

The Institute of Law and Public Policy in Moscow was also extremely helpful throughout my research trips.

I gratefully acknowledge financial support of my research provided by the Centre for Russian and East European Studies and the School of Graduate Studies at the University of Toronto. I also thank the Institute of Intergovernmental Relations at Queen's University, which gave me everything necessary to complete this book.

Koninklijke Brill NV kindly granted the permission to republish the following: Portions of Chapters 3 and 8 appeared earlier in "'Tinkering with Tenure': The Russian Constitutional Court in a Comparative Perspective," in *Russia, Europe, and the Rule of Law*, edited by Ferdinand J. M. Feldbrugge (Leiden: Martinus Nijhoff, 2007), pp. 47–78. Portions of Chapters 5 and 7 appeared earlier in "Russia's Constitutional Spirit: Judge-Made Principles in Theory and Practice," in *Russia and Its Constitution: Promise and Political Reality*, edited by Gordon Smith and Robert Sharlet (Leiden: Martinus Nijhoff, 2007), pp. 51–75.

Most of all, my special thanks go to my family and friends: to my parents, Mikhail and Alevtina, and my sister, Elena, for their unconditional support and faith in me and for their tireless collection of court-related materials from the local press; and to my wife, Catalina, for always finding the time to listen to my rants about judicial politics and for loving and inspiring me every step of the way.

This book is dedicated to the memory of my grandmothers, Uliana and Anna, who raised their families alone after they had lost their husbands in World War II.

Abbreviations

CPD	Congress of People's Deputies – [Sezd narodnykh Deputatov]
CSC	Committee of Constitutional Supervision – Komitet Konstitutsionnogo Nadzora
ECHR	European Court of Human Rights
ICCPR	International Covenant on Civil and Political Rights
ICESCR	International Covenant on Economic, Social, and Cultural Rights
RCC	Russian Constitutional Court – [Konstitutsionnyi Sud Rossiiskoi Federatsii]
RF	Russian Federation
RSFSR	Russian Soviet Federated Socialist Republic
SAPP	Collected Acts of the President and Government of the Russian Federation – [Sobranie Aktov Prezidenta i Pravitelstva Rossiiskoi Federatsii]
SSLC	Legislation Committee of the RSFSR Supreme Soviet – [Komitet po zakonodatelstvu Verkhovnogo Soveta RSFSR]
SZ RF	Collected Legislation of the Russian Federation – [Sobranie Zakonodatelstva Rossiiskoi Federatsii]
USSR	Union of Soviet Socialist Republics
VKS RF	Herald of the Constitutional Court of the Russian Federation – [Vestnik Konstitutsionnogo Suda Rossiiskoi Federatsii]
VSND i VS RSFSR	Official Gazette of the Legislative Agencies of the Russian Federation (and of the prereform Supreme Soviet of the RSFSR) – [Vedomosti Sezda narodnykh deputatov i Verkhovnogo Soveta RSFSR]

Notes on Transliteration

Throughout this book I have used the Library of Congress system of Russian transliteration. However, for well-known names and words, I use the more common spelling (e.g., Yeltsin instead of El'tsin and Chechnya instead of Chechnia).

Moreover, the Russian soft sign, which is represented in transliteration by an apostrophe ('), is generally omitted for the sake of readability, especially in the case of proper names.

I

Introduction: Three Puzzles of Postcommunist Judicial Empowerment

At the beginning of the new millennium, when the dust of the postcommunist transition had settled, the dynamics of judicial empowerment in the area of the former Soviet domination held many a surprise. Whether a democracy or not, each postcommunist country had a functioning constitutional court, a new judicial body armed with the power to revoke laws found to be in violation of constitutional provisions.[1] However, just as political regimes varied in the ex-Soviet world,[2] the young constitutional courts also varied in terms of their real judicial power. Some courts immediately started to rule against the powerful but were eventually tamed by the rulers (Russia in 1993 and Hungary in 1999). Some courts were brave enough to impeach popularly elected presidents (Russia and Lithuania),[3] to bar popular politicians from running for the presidency (Bulgaria),[4] or

---

[1] Only Turkmenistan, a Central Asian state with a sultanistic regime, and Estonia, a consolidated democracy and a member of the European Union, do not have separate constitutional courts. Estonia's Supreme Court has an ad hoc chamber in charge of limited constitutional review.

[2] See Valerie Bunce, "Rethinking Recent Democratization: Lessons from the Postcommunist Experience," *World Politics*, vol. 55, no. 2 (January 2003), pp. 167–192 and notes therein.

[3] In September 1993, the Russian Constitutional Court impeached President Boris Yeltsin for abolishing the legislature. In turn, Yeltsin suspended the Court's operation for 18 months until he finished "packing" the Court in 1995. See Chapters 3 and 4 of this book. In March 2004, the Lithuanian Constitutional Court impeached President Ronald Paksas on corruption charges. Conclusion of the Lithuanian Constitutional Court of March 31, 2004, Case No. 14/04, available in English at http://www.lrkt.lt/dokumentai/2004/co40331.htm, accessed on December 17, 2007.

[4] In 1996, in a 8–4 decision, the Bulgarian Constitutional Court declared highly popular New-York born Foreign Minister Georgi Pirinski ineligible to run in presidential elections. Decision No. 12 of July 23, 1996, *Darzhaven Vestnik*, no. 67, August 6, 1996. In 2001, in a 7–5 vote, the Court barred the exiled King Simeon II from running for the presidency even though about two-thirds of Bulgarians disagreed with this ruling.

2   *Introduction*

to repeal constitutional amendments (Moldova). Others (Serbia, Georgia, Ukraine, and Kyrgyzstan) simply watched, as mass peaceful protests over fraudulent elections overthrew powerful presidents during so-called colored revolutions of 2000–2005. To nobody's surprise, constitutional courts in "autocracies" (Belarus and Uzbekistan) tended to offer nonbinding recommendations to powerful executives.

What is more surprising is that the postcommunist constitutional review appears to stick to nondemocratic polities. Ruling elites in Albania and Belarus, Kazakhstan and Tajikistan, Russia under President Putin and Slovakia under the Meciar government, create these constitutional courts, then, in a matter of a few years, attack them and yet keep these tribunals operating.[5] Even more surprising is the persistence of ***accessible*** constitutional review in nondemocracies. Voters in "hybrid" and authoritarian regimes quickly received the right to sue their governments in these constitutional courts, while new democracies failed to provide their citizens with direct access to constitutional review. For example, since 1992, ordinary Russians have complained to their constitutional courts and have won their cases. Beginning in 1995–1996, citizens in "autocratic" Tajikistan and Uzbekistan have received access to, and successfully used, their constitutional courts. To do the same, Polish citizens had to wait until 1998, and their Latvian counterparts – until mid-2001. These were lucky when compared to individuals in Bulgaria, Estonia, Lithuania, and Romania. These newly consolidated democracies simply disallow their citizens from directly petitioning constitutional courts (see Table 1.1).

What explains this prompt embrace of constitutional review by authoritarian leaders and the "difficult" childhood of postcommunist constitutional justice? Why were the judicial review tribunals unable to prevent the growth of nondemocratic trends in most post-Soviet countries? By illustrating the case of post-Soviet Russia, this book addresses this question by exploring the politics of the origins, the functioning, and the impact of the 16-year-old Russian Constitutional Court (RCC). More specifically,

---

Decision No. 3 of February 8, 2001, *Darzhaven Vestnik*, no. 15, February 16, 2001. For analysis, see Venelin I. Ganev, "The Bulgarian Constitutional Court, 1991–1997: A Success Story in Context," *Europe-Asia Studies*, vol. 55, no. 4 (2003), p. 603; and "Constitutional Watch: Bulgaria," *East European Constitutional Review*, vol. 10, nos. 2–3 (Spring–Summer 2001), p. 9.

[5] Russia's subnational constitutional courts persist in the regions with authoritarian regimes and fail to take root in regions with highly competitive elections. See Alexei Trochev, "Less Democracy, More Courts: The Puzzle of Judicial Review in Russia," *Law and Society Review*, vol. 38, no. 3 (September 2004), pp. 513–548.

TABLE I.I. *Postcommunist constitutional courts: Creation and access*

Country	"Freedom House" ranking 2006	Constitution adopted/amended	Date of enabling legislation – date of the beginning of work	No. of judges	Constitutional complaint
Poland	free	1992/1997	04/1985 – 12/1985	15	yes, since 1998
Hungary	free	1949/1997	10/1989 – 01/1990	11	yes
Bulgaria	free	1991/2003/2005/2006/2007	07/1991 – 11/1991	12	no
Russia	not free	1993	10/1991 – 11/1991	19	yes
Slovenia	free	1991/1997/2000/2003/2004/2006	04/1994 – 05/1993	9	yes
Croatia	free	1990/1997/2000/2001	12/1991 – 01/1992	13	yes
Macedonia	partly free	1991	12/1991 – 01/1992	9	yes
Albania	partly free	1991/1998	04/1992 – 06/1992	9	yes
Romania	free	1991/2003	05/1992 – 07/1992	9	no
Kazakhstan	not free	1993/1995/1998/2007	06/1992 – 07/1992	7	no
Slovakia	free	1992/1998/1999/2001	09/1992 – 03/1993	13	yes
Czech Rep.	free	1992/1997/1998/2000/2001/2002	06/1993 – 07/1993	15	yes
Lithuania	free	1992/2003	03/1993 – 08/1993	9	no
Estonia	free	1992/2003	05/1993 – 05/1993	9	no
Kyrgyzstan	partly free	1993/2003/2006/2007	12/1993 – 09/1995	9	yes
Belarus	not free	1994/1996	03/1994 – 09/1994	12	no
Tajikistan	not free	1994/1999/2003	11/1995 – 01/1996	7	yes
Moldova	partly free	1994/2000/2001/2002	07/1994 – 02/1995	6	no
Uzbekistan	not free	1992/1993/2002/2003	08/1995 – 01/1996	7	yes
Armenia	partly free	1995/2005	12/1995 – 02/1996	9	yes, since 2006
Georgia	partly free	1995/2004/2006	01/1995 – 08/1996	9	yes
Latvia	free	1990/1994/1996/1997/1998/2002/ 2003/2004/2006/2007	11/1989 – 01/1997	7	yes, since 2001
Ukraine	free	1996/2004	06/1992 – 01/1997	18	yes
Azerbaijan	not free	1995/2003	11/1995 – 07/1998	9	yes, since 2004

I analyze three interrelated puzzles of judicial empowerment in postcommunist Russia:

1. Why the same powerful political actors created the judicial review tribunal in 1991, nearly disbanded it after 2 years of its operation, and then revived the court shortly thereafter;
2. How and why the Russian Constitutional Court exercised its broad judicial review powers; and
3. Why government officials, including judges in other courts, promptly carried out RCC decisions in some cases, delayed implementation in other cases, and sometimes simply ignored the RCC's orders.

By cracking these puzzles, this book aims to provide insights into the "black box" of judicial empowerment during the change of nondemocratic political regimes. Taken together, the solutions to these puzzles may reveal *when, how, and why judicial review is likely to flourish or fail.* Perhaps, the evolution of judicial power is far from a linear process, being fraught with twists and turns, while the entrenchment of the rule of law is a by-product of struggles amongst government officials, judges, and the civil society.

JUDICIAL (DIS) EMPOWERMENT IN CONTEXT

A growing number of theories address these questions by linking the establishment of constitutional review to a specific outcome of the regime change – democratization. Some theorists focus on the *international* context of global waves of democratization, while others insist that the *domestic* context is more vital in explaining the success and failures of young constitutional tribunals. One group of scholars argues that postcommunist judicial empowerment is not surprising at all.[6] They view the proliferation of new constitutional review tribunals as an extension of "global diffusion of judicial power" or of a post-World War II hegemony of the human rights agenda. By subjecting their choices to judicial scrutiny, postcommunist rulers demonstrate their commitment to democracy and the rule of law to the voters and to the rest of the world. Constitutional

---

[6] See, for example, John Ferejohn and Pasquale Pasquino, "Constitutional Courts as Deliberative Institutions: Towards an Institutional Theory of Constitutional Justice," in Wojciech Sadurski, ed., *Constitutional Justice, East and West* (The Hague: Kluwer Law International, 2003), p. 21.

Judicial (Dis) Empowerment in Context

courts, then, uphold democratic values, protect individual rights, and serve as a bulwark against a return to the totalitarian past.[7]

Other scholars disagree with this emphasis on international pressures and templates in the process of massive constitutional borrowing and non-borrowing from the West. Instead, they look at the *domestic* context of enormous sociopolitical uncertainty brought about by the change of the political regime. *Institutionalist* approaches to postauthoritarian judicial empowerment examine the need of the rulers to govern new polities and suggest that powerful courts guard separation of powers, resolve disputes among policymakers in a peaceful way, and smooth the functioning of the new regimes. *Strategic* approaches to judicial empowerment in societies as diverse as the United States and Japan, Mexico and Mongolia, and Korea and Bulgaria claim that, in the uncertainty of democratization, politicians who fear electoral loss create a strong and independent judiciary to protect themselves from the tyranny of election winners in the future. When political uncertainty is high, constitution makers are less likely to constrain judicial review bodies. Accessible constitutional courts, then, protect political minorities by providing them with a forum to obstruct majoritarian decision making.[8]

The *public support* theorists go even further in assuming a link between the voters and judicial power. These scholars argue that newly created constitutional courts must gain the support of the citizens by ruling in line with the majority will; otherwise courts will be viewed as illegitimate or redundant government institutions. Over time, the mass of popular judgments

---

[7] See, for example, Catherine Dupre, *Importing the Law in Post-Communist Transitions: The Hungarian Constitutional Court and the Right to Human Dignity* (Portland, OR: Hart Publishing, 2003); Wiktor Osiatynski, "Paradoxes of Constitutional Borrowing," *I-CON: International Journal of Constitutional Law*, vol. 1, no. 2 (April 2003), pp. 244–268; Radoslav Procházka, *Mission Accomplished: On Founding Constitutional Adjudication in Central Europe* (Budapest: Central European University Press, 2002); Herman Schwartz, *The Struggle for Constitutional Justice in Post-Communist Europe* (Chicago: Chicago University Press, 2000).

[8] See, for example, Mark J. Ramseyer, "The Puzzling (In) dependence of Courts: A Comparative Approach," *Journal of Legal Studies*, vol. 23, no. 2 (June 1994), pp. 721–747; Pedro C. Magalhães, "The Politics of Judicial Reform in Eastern Europe," *Comparative Politics*, vol. 32, no. 1 (October 1999), pp. 43–62; Tom Ginsburg, *Judicial Review in New Democracies: Constitutional Courts in Asian Cases* (New York: Cambridge University Press, 2003); Lee Epstein and Jack Knight, "Constitutional Borrowing and Nonborrowing," *I-CON: International Journal of Constitutional Law*, vol. 1, no. 2 (April 2003), pp. 196–223; Jodi Finkel, "Judicial Reform as Insurance Policy: Mexico in the 1990s," *Latin American Politics and Society*, vol. 47, no. 1 (Spring 2005), pp. 87–113.

will create a shield, which constitutional court judges can use later to issue controversial decisions and to compel others to enforce them.[9]

These theories are useful in explaining why democratizing politicians set up powerful constitutional courts. Their explanations are certainly correct in that it is the elites who drive the process of judicial empowerment, and that new constitutional courts provide important benefits for democratizing elites. To be sure, judicial review as "negative" and "positive" law making can certainly assist in democratization: constitutional courts can do a lot "(1) to check arbitrary rulers, (2) to replace arbitrary rules with just and rational ones, and (3) to obtain a share for the underlying population in the making of rules."[10] My study joins these theories in their focus on the political origins of judicial empowerment and draws on the insight that is the political context that ultimately determines the successes and failures of judicial review.[11]

However, my analysis explains why authoritarian politicians, who do not fear losing elections, set up powerful and accessible constitutional courts, and how these courts manage to persist in regimes that do not "transit" toward democracy. My short answer is that authoritarian rulers tolerate constitutional courts as long as the courts: (a) provide important benefits for the new rulers, and (b) do not interfere too much with public policies. However, change of the regime and unstable policy preferences of the new ruling elites complicate a cost–benefit calculus of judicial review.

By exploring the politics of the "birth" and childhood of constitutional review in postcommunist Russia between 1990 and 2006, I place the thorny process of Russia's judicial empowerment within the context of attendant political struggles among the rulers, judges, and the bureaucracies. The struggles between these actors flare up in the course of designing/ destroying, exercising, and (dis)obeying constitutional review. The short-term calculations of political elites and their legal advisers drove the

---

[9] James Gibson, Gregory Caldeira, and Vanessa Baird, "On the Legitimacy of National High Courts," *American Political Science Review*, vol. 92, no. 2 (June 1998), pp. 343–358; Joseph F. Fletcher and Paul Howe, "Public Opinion and Canada's Courts," in Paul Howe and Peter H. Russell, eds., *Judicial Power and Canadian Democracy* (Montreal: McGill University Press, 2001), pp. 255–296; Georg Vanberg, *The Politics of Constitutional Review in Germany* (Cambridge, UK: Cambridge University Press, 2005); and Anke Grosskopf, "A Supranational Case – Comparing Sources of Support for Constitutional Courts" (Ph.D. diss., University of Pittsburgh, 2000).

[10] Barrington Moore, Jr., *Social Origins of Dictatorship and Democracy: Lord and Peasant in the Making of the Modern World* (Boston: Beacon Press, 1966), p. 414.

[11] Carlo Guarnieri and Patrizia Pederzoli, *The Power of Judges: A Comparative Study of Courts and Democracy* (New York: Oxford University Press, 2002), pp. 182–183.

Judicial (Dis) Empowerment in Context

establishment, the suspension, and the renewal of the Russian Constitutional Court between 1990 and 1995. Decisions of this Court also reflect the struggles between judicial preferences and political expediency. And short-term calculations of the bureaucracy and ordinary judges also drove their (un) willingness to implement the rulings of the Russian Constitutional Court. In summary, fluid short-term interests of judges and government officials, rather than their long-term commitments, were more important in expanding and taming judicial power in both Yeltsin's and Putin's Russia.[12]

Strategic accounts of judicial empowerment have also argued that short-term calculations of political actors during the regime change may produce strong constitutional review. My analysis does not assume the inevitability of judicial supremacy. On the contrary, the Russian case shows that momentary considerations in the context of severe diffusion of political power may result in the overthrow of constitutional order and the destruction of judicial review. This means that the successful institutionalization of a constitutional court is not predetermined. It is only one possible outcome of the regime change and, most likely, a by-product of a nonlinear process of postauthoritarian transition.[13]

Frequently changing short-term calculations of the new rulers during the transition may undermine the accountability of elected officials to the voters and the courts, hinder the development of the multiparty system with the vibrant electoral market and ensuing demand for independent courts, destroy state capacity necessary for the implementation of judicial decisions, and may trump institutional rigidity, be it separation of powers or a federalism arrangement, that could produce the need for judicial resolution of interinstitutional rivalries. Moreover, the powerful often pursue their short-term policies through the informal networks of power either by issuing secret orders or doling out funds to their cronies.[14] They use these networks instead of the official channels of public authority both to achieve the maximum benefit and to deprive the opposition (if any) of the

---

[12] For a similar explanation of post-Soviet constitution making, see Michael McFaul, "Institutional Design, Uncertainty, and Path Dependency during Transitions: Cases from Russia," *Constitutional Political Economy*, vol. 10, no. 1 (March 1999), pp. 27–52.

[13] Rebecca Bill Chavez, *The Rule of Law in Nascent Democracies: Judicial Politics in Argentina* (Palo Alto, CA: Stanford University Press, 2004).

[14] On the prevalence of the informal power relations in postcommunism, see, for example, Kathleen Collins, *Clan Politics and Regime Transition in Central Asia* (New York: Cambridge University Press, 2006); and Vladimir Pastukhov, "Law under Administrative Pressure in Post-Soviet Russia," *East European Constitutional Review*, vol. 11, no. 3 (Summer 2002), pp. 66–74.

8   *Introduction*

chance to resist: witness the secret decrees of President Yeltsin to invade Chechnya to avoid the opposition in the Parliament or the redistribution of oil and gas assets in Putin's Russia.

All of these elements of governance are important factors in empowering or weakening courts, but the courts by themselves can achieve little to ensure that these factors work to strengthen judicial review. Regulating the informal power relations by judicial orders is difficult in any society. True, litigation can reveal dealings behind the scenes but courts cannot force the perpetrators to stop making their side deals and cannot destroy subversive informal institutions. Even when judges monitor the formal government institutions they may be not very effective. This is because courts lack the powers of the "sword" and the "purse." Even when constitutional courts have the power to fine or to impeach government officials for noncompliance, for example, in Mexico, Spain, or pre-1994 Russia, they almost never use these punitive measures.[15] Instead, both weak and strong constitutional tribunals around the world tend to rely on political branches and the rest of the judiciary to have their judgments carried out. In the words of the U.S. Supreme Court Justice Stephen Breyer, "the paratroopers and the judges must cooperate."[16] To make this cooperation work, many argue that young and old constitutional courts have to overcome the compliance problem: they have to assert or maintain their own authority yet, lacking enforcement and budgetary powers, they have to please other power holders or the public in order to implement their rulings.[17]

---

[15] Although one-fifth of the Mexican Supreme Court's workload is taken by complaints of alleged noncompliance, this Court removed only two lower-ranking officials from office for noncompliance. Jeffrey K. Staton, "Judicial Activism and Public Authority Compliance: The Role of Public Support in the Mexican Separation-of-Powers System" (Ph.D. diss., Washington University, 2002), p. 273. The Spanish Constitutional Tribunal never used its power to fine officials for noncompliance. Javier Garcia Roca, "Effects, Enforceability, and the Execution of the Decisions of the Spanish Constitutional Court." Paper presented at the Workshop on the Execution of the Decisions of the Constitutional Court. Kyiv, October 28–29, 1999, available at http://www.venice. coe.int/docs/1999/CDL-JU(1999)028-e.asp. Between 1992 and 1993, the 1st Russian Constitutional Court used its power to fine only once: against the editor-in-chief of an official gazette for delaying the publication of its first judgment.

[16] Stephen G. Breyer, "Comment: Liberty, Prosperity, and a Strong Judicial Institution," *Law and Contemporary Problems*, vol. 61, no. 3 (Summer 1998), pp. 3–6. For a similar argument, see Bradley C. Canon and Charles A. Johnson, *Judicial Politics: Implementation and Impact* (Washington, DC: CQ Press, 1999).

[17] On pleasing political branches, or the strategic approach to judicial behavior, see Lee Epstein and Jack Knight, *The Choices Justices Make* (Washington, DC: CQ Press, 1998)

True, the exclusive focus on the jurisdiction of the constitutional court or on the text of its rulings may not be sufficient to assess the role of a court in producing social change if we do not know whether these rulings were carried out. Because constitutional court decisions have a "law-like" effect, for example, they apply to all subnational governments in federalism disputes and to thousands of individuals in individual rights cases, we can understand the role the courts play in governance only if we know how and why public officials react to judicial decisions. In short, to learn how courts can build or undermine their own actual power, and how these courts persist in nondemocratic regimes, we need to study the context in which judges exercise their judicial review powers and see their judgments either enforced or ignored.[18]

To be sure, Russian Constitutional Court judges acutely sense the risk of having their decisions ignored or overruled. However, political turmoil early on in the postcommunist transition made it easy not only to defy court decisions but also to threaten the very institution of constitutional review. This institutional uncertainty also made it nearly impossible to anticipate the reaction of the powerful, whose connection with voters is weak, to judicial decisions. My analysis goes further than many strategic accounts of judicial behavior and examines the actual responses to the decisions of the constitutional court. Instead of presuming that judges strike down laws only when they can secure the compliance of political branches with their judgments, I find that Russia's politicians, bureaucrats, and ordinary judges of all ranks comply with some judgments of the federal Constitutional Court and disobey others. And I also find that voter preferences have played a small role in explaining the choices government officials made in their reaction to judicial review.

In short, my book explores how judicial power grows or fails to grow through the careful examination of the interplay among domestic regime politics, international pressures, and judicial behavior. It explores the

---

and Vanberg, *The Politics of Constitutional Review in Germany*. On enlisting public support, see Grosskopf, "A Supranational Case" and Staton, "Judicial Activism and Public Authority Compliance."

[18] To sample the different approaches to studying this context, see, for example, Ran Hirschl, *Towards Juristocracy: The Origins and Consequences of the New Constitutionalism* (Cambridge, MA: Harvard University Press, 2004); Alec Stone Sweet, *Governing with Judges: Constitutional Politics in Europe* (Oxford: Oxford University Press, 2000); and Kim Lane Scheppele, "Constitutional Ethnography: An Introduction," *Law and Society Review*, vol. 38, no. 3 (September 2004), pp. 389–406.

context(s) of designing and destroying judicial review, of exercising the power of judicial review and eschewing it, and of obeying and defying the decisions of the young constitutional court. Attention to these precepts enables me to explore why and how rulers in postcommunist Russia organized, exercised, and protected their power through judicial empowerment.[19]

WHY RUSSIA?

Although the study of comparative judicial politics seems increasingly to privilege a crossnational analysis, my book describes and explains how and why constitutional review was born and persisted in a single country, namely post-Soviet Russia. More precisely, *Judging Russia* compares the origins, functioning, and impact of three constitutional review bodies: the USSR Constitutional Supervision Committee (1990–1991), the 1st Russian Constitutional Court (1991–1993), and the 2nd Russian Constitutional Court (1995–2006). Intracountry comparisons have been successfully used to study key questions of the body politic,[20] including judicial empowerment in the United States, a premier case of judicial review. Although one should exercise caution in drawing generalizations from a three-case comparison in a single country, I believe that such a methodology may provide several important insights for the study of nascent constitutionalism, in particular, and for comparative politics, in general. In other words, the uniqueness of the politics of Russia's judicial empowerment is often exaggerated, as compared to other times and places, for the following reasons.

First, intracountry comparisons allow control for various background variables, such as historical legacies, the immediate context of postauthoritarian transition, and political leadership. The same rulers in Russia created new constitutional review tribunals, staffed them with apparently

---

[19] For the recent plea "to situate the distinctive stories of judicial politics into a more general set of stories about how regimes organize, exercise, and protect their power," see Howard Gillman, "Elements of a New 'Regime Politics' Approach to the Study of Judicial Politics." Paper presented at the Annual Meeting of the American Political Science Association, Chicago, IL, September 2004.

[20] Just to name a few recent examples, Robert Putnam, *Making Democracy Work* (Princeton: Princeton University Press, 1993); Lavinia Stan, *Leaders and Laggards: Governance, Civicness and Ethnicity in Post-Communist Romania* (New York: Columbia University Press, 2003); and Rebecca Bill Chavez, *The Rule of Law in Nascent Democracies: Judicial Politics in Argentina* (Palo Alto, CA: Stanford University Press, 2004).

Why Russia?

loyal judges, and rendered them ineffective. Similarly, the judges on the bench of these three tribunals behaved radically differently from one another: the first two courts failed while the 2nd Russian Constitutional Court appears to be firmly entrenched. Each of the three tribunals produced a sufficient number of judgments, both published and unpublished, which allows for their systematic comparison along the dimensions of separation-of-power struggles, federalism disputes, and fundamental rights protection. Exploring this zigzagging childhood of Russian constitutional justice, given similar initial starting points for all three tribunals, is hardly possible in a crossnational study, not to mention the large-N quantitative analysis. As Epstein et al. explained, the focus on Russia allows scholars "to exploit the best features of case study and crossnational research designs."[21]

Second, by providing variation of the dependent variable, judicial power, the Russian case allows us to compare both successes and failures of judicial empowerment in similar contexts. Too many recent studies focus on successful judicial empowerment, while only a few examine the failed institutionalization of judicial review.[22] This proliferation of judicial success stories may reflect a global trend toward "juristocracy": there may simply be more successful courts than failed ones in "an age of judicial power."[23] However, political scientists may benefit from studying these "outliers," and single case studies may indicate conditions and relationships neglected by existing research design.[24] In addition, a thorough and

---

[21] Lee Epstein, Jack Knight, and Olga Shvetsova, "The Role of Constitutional Courts in the Establishment and Maintenance of Democratic Systems of Government," *Law and Society Review*, vol. 35, no. 1 (March 2001), pp. 117–164.

[22] See, for example, Tamir Moustafa, *The Struggle for Constitutional Power: Law, Politics, and Economic Development in Egypt* (New York: Cambridge University Press, 2007); Tamir Moustafa, "Law Versus the State: The Judicialization of Politics in Egypt," *Law and Social Inquiry*, vol. 28, no. 4 (Fall 2003), pp. 883–930; and Trochev, "Less Democracy, More Courts."

[23] To name a few recent comparative studies of successful courts, see Ran Hirschl, *Towards Juristocracy*; Peter H. Russell and Kate Malleson, eds., *Appointing Judges in an Age of Judicial Power: Critical Perspectives from Around the World* (Toronto: University of Toronto Press, 2006); Peter H. Russell and David O'Brien, eds., *Judicial Independence in the Age of Democracy* (Charlottesville, VA: University of Virginia Press, 2001); Tom Ginsburg, *Judicial Review in New Democracies*; Schwartz, *The Struggle for Constitutional Justice*; Procházka, *Mission Accomplished*; and Neal C. Tate and Torbjörn Vallinder, eds., *The Global Expansion of Judicial Power* (New York: New York University Press, 1995).

[24] Nancy Maveety and Anke Grosskopf, "'Constrained' Constitutional Courts as Conduits for Democratic Consolidation," *Law and Society Review*, vol. 38, no. 3 (September 2004), p. 468, fn. 3.

comprehensive analysis of judicial politics in a single country may eliminate various factual errors and misunderstandings of foreign politico-legal systems and provide data for building theories of comparative judicial behavior. My study of three constitutional review tribunals in post-Soviet Russia is complex enough to study the conditions and interactions among politicians, judges, and bureaucrats, who both expanded and tamed judicial power within a context of enormous institutional uncertainty.

Finally, the turbulent childhood of Russian constitutional justice attracted the attention of many domestic and foreign scholars.[25] This is hardly surprising given Russia's importance to world politics. Just as many observers quarrel about the dynamics of Russian policies and politics, students of Russian constitutionalism disagree on the impact of constitutional review tribunals in the country. Some criticize these bodies for being too timid, inefficient, and dependent in resolving politically important disputes.[26] Others accuse these tribunals of being both too activist and engaged in a power grab.[27] And yet another group of scholars commends constitutional review for improving the protection of human rights and bringing order and stability to Russian democratization and federalism.[28]

---

[25] See Epstein et al., "The Role of Constitutional Courts..." and sources cited therein.

[26] See, for example, Jeffrey Kahn, *Federalism, Democratization and the Rule of Law in Russia* (Oxford: Oxford University Press, 2002), pp. 176–182; Andrey N. Medushevsky, *Russian Constitutionalism: Historical and Contemporary Development* (New York: Routledge, 2006), p. 235; and Alexandr Belkin, *Kommentarii k resheniiam Konstitutsionnogo Suda Rossiiskoi Federatsii. 1992–1993* [Commentary to the Decisions of the RF Constitutional Court. 1992–1993] (S.-Peterburg: Izd-vo S.-Peterburgskogo un-ta, 1994).

[27] See, for example, William Burnham and Alexei Trochev, "Russia's War Between the Courts: The Struggle over the Jurisdictional Boundary Between the Constitutional Court and Regular Courts," *American Journal of Comparative Law*, vol. 5, no. 3 (Summer 2007), pp. 381–452; William Burnham, Peter Maggs, and Gennady Danilenko, *Law and Legal System of the Russian Federation* (New York: Juris Publishing, 2004), pp. 82–130; and Anton Burkov, "Borba za vlast mezhdu Konstitutsionnym Sudom RF i Verkhovnym Sudom RF: postradaiut li prava cheloveka?" [Struggle for Power Between the RF Constitutional Court and the RF Supreme Court: Will the Human Rights Suffer?], *Grazhdanin i pravo*, no. 5 (2003), pp. 33–38.

[28] See, for example, Epstein et al., "The Role of Constitutional Courts...."; Robert Sharlet, "Russia's Second Constitutional Court: Politics, Law, and Stability," in Victoria E. Bonnell and George W. Breslauer, eds., *Russia in the New Century: Stability or Disorder?* (Boulder, CO: Westview Press, 2001), pp. 59–77; Kim Lane Scheppele, "Constitutional Negotiations: Political Contexts of Judicial Activism in Post-Soviet Europe," *International Sociology*, vol. 18, no. 1 (March 2003), pp. 219–238; and Marie-Elisabeth Baudoin, "Is the Constitutional Court the Last Bastion in Russia against the Threat of Authoritarianism?" *Europe-Asia Studies*, vol. 58, no. 5 (July 2006), pp. 679–700.

These scholarly debates, which, no doubt, are reminiscent of the polemics surrounding the jurisprudence of high courts in advanced democracies, provide important insights into the operation of the Court. For our purposes, the significance of the Russian Constitutional Court lies in its membership in a growing family of constitutional courts around the globe, and it serves as an important model for other post-Soviet constitutional review tribunals. As the rest of this book shows, Russian rulers strive to recruit loyal judges, similar to their counterparts abroad. Just as do high court judges in other countries, Russian judges bravely venture outside of constitutional texts, develop unwritten constitutional principles, and critically apply decisions of foreign and supranational courts. And, not unlike their colleagues in Europe and Asia, judges in Russia are engaged in seemingly never-ending "wars of courts." Finally, similar to the experiences of judicial reform in Latin American countries, Russia's judicial empowerment goes hand in hand with declining levels of public trust in the judiciary.

In short, the first decade-and-a-half of constitutional politics in post-Soviet Russia, tortuous as it was for the Constitutional Court, can hardly be described as idiosyncratic, unique, or exceptional. The systematic study of Russia's experience with constitutional review may have implications for the study of courts in both advanced and recently consolidated democracies, as well as in nondemocratic regimes. More broadly, such a study may provide insights into how courts as institutions shape the processes of regime-building and state formation, and how they develop in hostile political environments without strong legal communities and traditions. This development of courts may not always result in the entrenchment of a rule-of-law regime, as the sobering aftermath of judicial reforms in Latin America has taught us.[29]

THE SOURCES OF DATA

To study the origins, the functioning, and the actual consequences of constitutional review in Russia, I chose to use various kinds of data. For an investigation of the establishment of the three constitutional review

---

[29] Pilar Domingo, "Judicialization of Politics or Politicization of the Judiciary? Recent Trends in Latin America," *Democratization*, vol. 11, no. 1 (February 2004), pp. 104–126; and Linn A. Hammergren, *Envisioning Reform: Improving Judicial Performance in Latin America* (University Park, PA: Pennsylvania State University Press, 2007).

tribunals, the most important sources were the transcripts of the meetings of the 1993 Constitutional Convention and parliamentary sessions, internal memos of parliamentary committees, constitutional drafts, and scholarly proposals about these tribunals. These documents provided both valuable information on the attitudes of constitutional engineers and judicial nominees toward each of the three constitutional courts, and traced the actual dynamics of creating and staffing these courts. Exploring the functioning of the three tribunals required, first of all, the comprehensive and systematic examination of all of their judgments, including dissenting opinions and unpublished decisions. I was able to gain access to these judgments during my 2-month visit to the Russian Constitutional Court in the summer of 2001, as well as during my short annual return trips to Moscow after that. To assess whether Russian constitutional review actually made a difference on the ground, I checked all semiannual implementation reports issued by Russian Constitutional Court staff between 1995 and 2005.

In addition to these written primary sources, interviews were indispensable for my research. Thanks to the generous support of the Court's staff during my stay at the Court in 2001, I had a desk with a phone, a copy machine, and a computer with the database of all judgments.[30] While at the Court, I interviewed fifteen Justices and fifteen Court clerks. These interviews, together with in-person and onsite observation of the Court's public sessions and its everyday operation, not only clarified and expanded upon the data obtained from other sources but also greatly improved my understanding of how the Court as a young yet complex institution worked in practice. To gain a different perspective on the Court's work, I also interviewed fourteen government officials, law professors, judges, legal affairs journalists, and law-enforcement officers, both in Moscow and in the regions, about their perceptions of the Court.

Secondary sources of information also proved helpful in extricating the complicated dynamics of judicial empowerment in Russia. The media, which is not fully independent or impartial, was helpful for studying the background of the litigation, the arguments of the litigants, and the reaction of federal and local politicians and bureaucrats to judgments of the Court. Also, Russian justices gave many interviews and authored a number of books and articles, publicizing their Court, explaining its decisions, and speaking on virtually every aspect of Russian reforms.

---

[30] Access to unpublished judgments of the RCC is no longer a problem because most of them are posted on the Web site of the Court at http://www.ksrf.ru.

OVERVIEW OF THE BOOK

Understanding the persistence of constitutional review tribunals in the late Soviet Union and post-Soviet Russia requires a theory of the power of constitutional review to address the following questions. First, where does this power of constitutional review come from? Second, how does a constitutional court use or choose not to use this review power? Third, does the exercise of this constitutional review power make a difference in a polity? Chapter 2 examines the weaknesses in the "democratization-centered" theories of judicial empowerment, and argues that judicial review power is based on a continuous interplay of perceptions among the judges, politicians, and other government agencies. Thus, this power involves both legal and extralegal factors, which intertwine in complex ways within three processes:

1. designing or dismantling the constitutional review tribunals,
2. hearing and deciding constitutional controversies, and
3. obeying or defying constitutional court judgments.

The rest of the study is organized around the analysis of these three processes, which taken together provide a bigger picture of judicial empowerment. Chapter 3 traces the meandering behavior of constitution makers in the process of designing and fine-tuning constitutional review in the late USSR (1988–1990) and in Russia (1990–2006) (see Puzzle 1 in Chapter 9). This chapter explains why and how an ad hoc coalition of political and legal elites succeeded in making the RCC operational in 1991 in order to overpower USSR authorities. It also shows that the RCC was not abolished in 1993 only because its Justices and some of the presidential advisers managed to convince Boris Yeltsin that his archrivals would resign from the bench. Short-term calculations rather than strategic considerations by ruling elites appeared to be everywhere: in the debates over the powers of the Court and its financial independence, and over the selection of Justices and their tenure. Therefore, a constitutional court emerged as a possible but not an inevitable, and not necessarily efficient, by-product of these political struggles. The uncertain context of a "quadruple" transition to a new mode of governance (and even new statehood for the constituent parts of former socialist federations)[31] permitted politicians to pursue their short-term interests and change them "without notice,"

---

[31] Taras Kuzio, "Transition in Post-Communist States: Triple or Quadruple?" *Politics*, vol. 21, no. 3 (September 2001), pp. 168–177.

16   *Introduction*

that is, to delay the activation of the constitutional courts or to dissolve them and to impeach judges.[32] This meant that a severe diffusion of political power might result in the overthrow of constitutional order, not in the institutionalization of judicial review, particularly given the ease with which new rulers rejected "unjust" laws.

Chapters 4 and 5 address the second puzzle and examine Russian constitutional review in action, tossed by the gigantic waves of political expediency on the tumultuous sea of postcommunist transition. These chapters describe, compare, and explain the extent to which constitutional review tribunals in Russia used their broad prerogatives to judge Russia's rulers, which resulted in markedly contrasting outcomes: the barely noticed "death" of the USSR Constitutional Supervision Committee in 1991, the highly visible near abolition of the 1st Russian Constitutional Court in 1993, and the entrenchment of the 2nd RCC by 2006. The rise and fall of the 1st RCC in 1992–1993 clearly shows that the aspirations of its justices prevailed over the short-term interests of Russian rulers, and eventually provoked a political backlash against the young Court. The slow recovery of the RCC since 1995, however, shows that the Court has been able to restore its own power by catering to the interests of the powers-that-be. The 2nd RCC then used this power to impose its own policy agenda, particularly in areas of criminal procedure, taxation, and federalism reforms. Based on a systematic analysis of judgments in the areas of separation of powers, federalism, and individual rights, these chapters demonstrate that the judicial review tribunals build their power in a nonlinear fashion: partly, by catering to the interests of the powers-that-be, and, partly, by expanding their own jurisdiction under the veils of judicial independence and the rule of law. Which part is to prevail in this conscious judicial strategizing depends on the politico-legal context that surrounds the court, and on the aspirations of the judges.

Chapters 6 and 7 focus on the third puzzle of judicial empowerment, namely, the struggle among judges, politicians, and bureaucrats over the implementation of constitutional court decisions. Both chapters assess and compare the real impact of constitutional review in the areas of separation-of-powers, federalism, and fundamental rights in the context of public distrust for the Russian judiciary. My analysis shows that other powerbrokers do not easily share their power with the constitutional review tribunal. Russian bureaucrats, including law-enforcement officers,

---

[32] For a similar argument about Latin American judicial reforms, see Domingo, "Judicialization of Politics," p. 120.

appear to obey unfavorable Court judgments only when their superiors order them to do so. Similar to the early years of the U.S. Supreme Court,[33] the RCC faced surges of subnational defiance of its judgments, which gradually became accepted by the most recalcitrant regions. The RCC also led the battles against the rest of the Russian judiciary. Moreover, both chapters reveal the chronic incapacity of the new governing bureaucratic apparatus to enforce unfavorable RCC decisions. This is why the impact of Russian constitutional review on the lives of ordinary citizens, who courageously keep suing the state, has been limited.

Chapter 8 judges Russia's experiments with judicial review by comparing them with the experience of other constitutional courts. One of the important controversies in creating both editions of the Russian Constitutional Court was the role of politicians who repeatedly tinkered with judicial tenure attempting to create a friendlier bench. Surveying the experience of the constitutional courts around the world in the past three decades, precisely during "the global diffusion of judicial power," my study reveals many other examples of politicians similarly interfering with judicial tenure. Turning to the less explored dynamics of the institutional struggles between constitutional courts and supreme courts, I survey how and why the "wars of courts" emerge and persist in several countries (Romania and the Czech Republic).

Finally, the Conclusion draws together the arguments of this study, contextualizes Russia's experimentation with judicial review, and suggests insights for future research on the worldwide judicialization of politics. Judicial empowerment has political origins, which means that the powerful, regardless of their democratic or authoritarian pedigree, may perceive a powerful court as a useful tool in securing their governing status. Driven by their short-term power calculations and encouraged by legal elites, the rulers create constitutional review tribunals and staff them with loyal judges. Under certain conditions, judges may choose to rule against rulers, and rulers may defy these adversary rulings and attack the courts. Even if political power holders choose to obey unfavorable rulings, the former may lack the capacity to ensure compliance on the part of bureaucracy. Thus, judicial empowerment does not necessarily result in the entrenchment of the rule of law in nondemocratic regimes: weak and incapable bureaucracies defy constitutional court decisions, while the public perceives judicial review as an inefficacious way to protect individual

---

[33] Leslie Goldstein, *Constituting Federal Sovereignty: The European Union in Comparative Context* (Baltimore, MD: Johns Hopkins University Press, 2001), pp. 22–33.

rights or to challenge public policies. This is why controversial judgments in the area of basic rights result in "unfulfilled" rights revolutions and do not lead to the politicization of the judiciary, as they do in advanced democracies. However, constitutional litigation provides a new arena for political contestation and for public deliberation about the rule of law, and a rule-of-law regime may be one of the by-products of this continuous contestation and deliberation.

2

Nonlinear Judicial Empowerment

The core argument of this book is that rulers – regardless of their authoritarian or democratic pedigree – create and tolerate new constitutional courts as long as the latter: (a) provide important benefits for the new rulers, and (b) do not interfere too much with public policies. However, the enormous uncertainty during the change of political regime, the unstable policy preferences of the new ruling elites, judicial behavior, and the incapacity of the government machinery to obey court decisions – these four factors blended together complicate a cost–benefit calculus of having a strong judicial review and facilitate the unintended *nonlinear* trajectories of judicial empowerment.

To explain why judicial empowerment during the change of political regimes is a nonlinear process, the rest of the chapter consists of three parts. First, it defines judicial empowerment as a dynamic feedback among the three variables: the court design, judicial decision making, and the enforcement of court decisions. Next, it takes a closer look at the benefits provided by the judicial review during the regime change and describes a feedback mechanism that facilitates the nonlinearity of judicial politics. Then, it explores the four factors that exacerbate the nonlinearity in transitional judicial politics and four potential objections to my argument.

DESIGN, JUDGING, AND COMPLIANCE: A TRILATERAL DYNAMIC OF JUDICIAL REVIEW

A traditional way to think of the relationship among the institutional design of courts, their judgments, and compliance with them is to construct it in a temporal linear sequence. First, a court is created and staffed. Next, judges adjudicate. Finally, the rest of the political system enforces judicial orders (Figure 2.1).

19

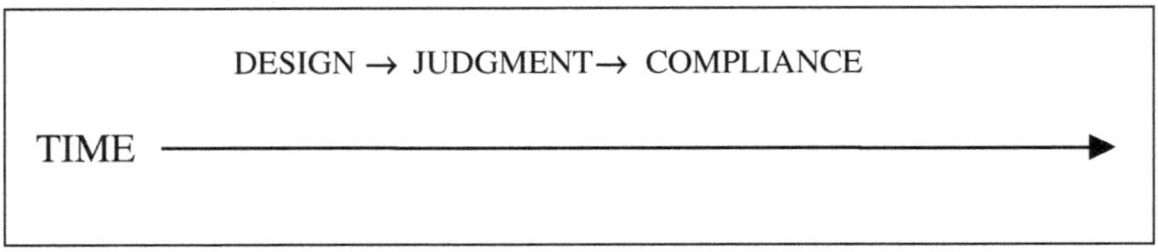

DESIGN → JUDGMENT → COMPLIANCE

TIME ──────────────────────────────────▶

FIGURE 2.1. Temporal model of judicial process.

I argue that judicial empowerment is a dynamic relationship among three variables: the institutional design of the court, the decision making of the court, and the compliance with the decisions of the court.[1] Although the processes of interpreting the constitution and reviewing the constitutionality of public policies are judicial, the outcomes may result in radical changes to the political system. This is because constitutional courts:

1. Break or build operational legal hierarchy by ordering legislatures, government agencies, and regular courts to comply with their rulings;
2. Break or build legal hierarchy "on paper" by placing their decisions above ordinary laws and next to the constitution; and
3. Break or build doctrinal legal hierarchy by legitimizing "judge-made" law in civil-law systems through the usage of the *stare decisis* principle, a necessary step to display principled, apolitical, and impartial decision making.[2]

Whether constitutional courts break established legal hierarchies or build new ones depends on one's stance toward judicial review as a whole. However, regardless of whether a *strong* judicial review destroys or constructs legal hierarchies, it should result in some actual changes in the power structure of a given polity. How much difference the courts make in a political system depends on their origins, their jurisprudence, and the levels of compliance with their decisions. Therefore, those who pay attention to judicial review (politicians, judges, bureaucrats, and legal elites) can attempt to influence the impact of constitutional courts by changing the values of these three variables. Such attempts are not that hard to do in societies, like Russia, where political pressure on the legal system has been the norm. This brings a feedback dynamic to the relationship among

[1] Peter H. Solomon, Jr., "Judicial Power in Russia: Through the Prism of Administrative Justice," *Law and Society Review*, vol. 38, no. 3 (September 2004), pp. 551–553.
[2] Tom Tyler and Gregory Mitchell, "Legitimacy and Empowerment of Discretionary Legal Authority: The United States Supreme Court and Abortion Rights," *Duke Law Journal*, vol. 43, no. 4 (February 1994), pp. 703–815.

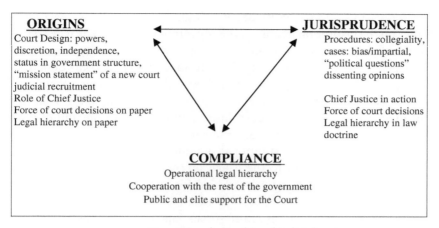

FIGURE 2.2. Dynamic relationship of judicial review.

the three components of judicial power and facilitates *nonlinear* trajectories of judicial empowerment (Figure 2.2). This constant feedback among the institutional setup of the constitutional court, its jurisprudence, and (non) compliance with court decisions brings dynamism and nonlinearity to the process of judicial empowerment.

Consider how the institutional design of a constitutional court affects and is affected by judicial behavior and compliance. Institutional design of the court defines what kind of cases judges can handle and builds in the degrees of discretion, independence, and bias judges possess initially when they adjudicate. Both the design of the court and the actual judicial recruitment process influence how judges perceive their role in the system of governance and how they behave on the bench and outside the courthouse. Court design also affects the degree of compliance by defining the degree of monopoly of the court over judicial review powers, by specifying the legal effect of court decisions and their place in the legal hierarchy "on paper," and by containing sanctions for noncompliance. To see that the matters of designing and redesigning the constitutional courts are important, one only needs to look at the judicial politics in democracies and nondemocracies alike, and at the proliferation of the international multimillion-dollar "rule-of-law" industry full of constitution-making experts, judicial reform consultants, and legal advisers.[3]

---

[3] See, for example, Thomas Carothers, ed., *Promoting the Rule of Law Abroad: In Search of Knowledge* (Washington, DC: Carnegie Endowment for International Peace, 2006).

Nonlinear Judicial Empowerment

Now let us turn to the impact of judicial decision making and compliance on the institutional setup of the constitutional court. The way constitutional judges actually use judicial review powers and the degree of actual independence judges enjoy may differ from the intent of court designers. Judges collectively design the internal procedures of reaching their decisions, define standards of acceptable judicial and extrajudicial behavior of their colleagues and the chief justice, and maximize the authority of their court by lobbying other government agencies. This may lead to rapid changes in the Court's institutional standing. For example, immediately after their appointment to the bench in 1952, German Federal Constitutional Court justices actively lobbied for and gained more budgetary independence of their new Court.[4] Russian Constitutional Court justices, appointed in November 1991, also successfully lobbied for expanding the jurisdiction of their court via a constitutional amendment in April 1992, as I explain in Chapter 3. Or it may take several years of lobbying by the judges to expand the jurisdiction of and access to their Court, as happened in Poland and Georgia. Alternatively, judges in courts with a high degree of discretion may change the design of their courts without asking lawmakers either by way of custom or through constitutional interpretation of judicial review powers.[5] In short, the actual exercise of judicial review may be different from the one enshrined in the constitutional court statute. And growing judicial power may trigger the politicians' desire to curb this power by changing the court design and/or increasing judicial accountability.[6]

How does the level of actual compliance with judicial review output influence institutional design of constitutional courts? High levels of compliance with constitutional court decisions overruling governmental

---

[4] Georg Vanberg, "Establishing Judicial Independence in West Germany: The Impact of Opinion Leadership and the Separation of Powers," *Comparative Politics*, vol. 32, no. 3 (April 2000), pp. 333–353.

[5] See Chapter 5, which explores why, when, and how the Russian Constitutional Court expanded the accessibility and scope of its powers. On Ukraine, see Alexei Trochev, "Ukraine: Constitutional Court Invalidates the 1991 Ban on the Communist Party," *I-CON: International Journal of Constitutional Law*, vol. 1, no. 3 (July 2003), pp. 534–540.

[6] See, for example, Carlo Guarnieri and Patrizia Pederzoli, *The Power of Judges: A Comparative Study of Courts and Democracy* (Oxford: Oxford University Press, 2002); Paul Howe and Peter H. Russell, eds., *Judicial Power and Canadian Democracy* (Montreal: McGill University Press, 2001); and William Lasser, *The Limits of Judicial Power* (Chapel Hill, NC: University of North Carolina Press, 1988).

policies over time lead to broad acceptance of "judge-made" law and judicial supremacy. Low levels of compliance may prompt judges to lobby for amending the constitutional court statute: adding sanctions for disobedience, strengthening the binding force of their judgments, and affirming their monopoly over judicial review power, as happened in Russia and Moldova. For constitutional judges to succeed in the context of any level of compliance, they must possess sufficient authority to convince politicians to approve bills sponsored by the judges. If successful, constitutional courts effectively modify not only the design of their courts but also the structure of all three kinds of legal hierarchies, as discussed above. If unsuccessful, judges risk the survival of the very institution of judicial review, as cases of failed constitutional tribunals in Kazakhstan, Belarus, and Yeltsin's Russia remind us.

How does judicial behavior affect the level of compliance? Tyler and Mitchell have shown that procedural fairness and impartiality increase the likelihood of compliance with judicial decisions.[7] The intensity of disagreement among judges may or may not account for the variation in levels of compliance. Judges can determine the fate of their decisions by dismissing the case, issuing clear decisions with understandable legal reasoning, including precise orders to government agencies, delaying the effect of their rulings, and tracking the implementation of their judgments by other government branches. In societies where courts have traditionally been weak, judges may have to go outside the courtroom to encourage other power brokers to carry out court decisions.

Actual compliance also provides feedback for judicial decision making. High levels of government compliance with unfavorable rulings make judges more confident in their authority, leading them to innovate as well as to preserve the boundaries of judicial power. Judges who are secure in well-institutionalized courts tend to engage less in extrajudicial behavior to avoid the perception of politicization of the court and to maintain the mythical aura of independent and impartial constitutional adjudication. However, judges who are seriously threatened by potential noncompliance may also be isolated within the courthouse, because no serious political force will listen to them. Threats of noncompliance may push judges to search for various ways to defer to legislative or executive branches. Still, low levels of compliance may motivate judges to criticize perpetrators who pose little threat to the viability of constitutional courts.

[7] Tyler and Mitchell, "Legitimacy and Empowerment..."

Astute observers of courts in societies as diverse as Argentina, Germany, and Egypt, have correctly noted that the political origins of judicial empowerment make it a nonlinear process. In her careful analysis of Argentinean judicial politics, Rebecca Chavez argues that the diffusion of political power facilitates stronger courts.[8] But, as the rest of this book shows, the Russian Constitutional Court has barely survived the fragmentation of power under Yeltsin and has improved its authority in the nondemocratic regime under Putin. Exploring the origins and the impact of the German Federal Constitutional Court, Georg Vanberg makes a strong case that judicial empowerment is a curvilinear process due to the varied degrees of the public support for the court.[9] But the Russian Constitutional Court appears to succeed in compelling others to respect its rulings despite the decreasing levels of public support. Tamir Moustafa examines the expansion and contraction of judicial power in nondemocratic Egypt and explains that authoritarian rulers may set up and attack constitutional courts even though these tribunals support the regime's policies and enjoy broad public support. He convincingly argues that nondemocratic leaders face few constraints in creating and destroying independent courts.[10] The next sections in this chapter elaborate how the nonlinearity of judicial empowerment occurs and persists in new states and new political regimes.

NEW COURTS IN NEW POLITIES: NONLINEAR JUDICIAL EMPOWERMENT

How well does my perspective of nonlinear judicial empowerment explain the birth and the childhood of new constitutional courts? Consider the origins of these courts. Establishing constitutional courts in the ex-Soviet world was an entirely elite-driven process because the citizens in these countries simply did not know much about judicial review. In many post-Soviet states that did not "transit" to democracy, new ruling elites were not really "new" but old Communist Party leaders who presented themselves to the public as the "champions of democracy and independence." To entrench their elite status and maximize their power, they established

---

[8] Rebecca Bill Chavez, *The Rule of Law in Nascent Democracies: Judicial Politics in Argentina* (Palo Alto, CA: Stanford University Press, 2004).

[9] Georg Vanberg, *The Politics of Constitutional Review in Germany* (Cambridge, UK: Cambridge University Press, 2005).

[10] Tamir Moustafa, *The Struggle for Constitutional Power: Law, Politics, and Economic Development in Egypt* (New York: Cambridge University Press, 2007).

all the formal attributes of a modern state including new constitutions with bills of rights and powerful constitutional courts. At the same time, these new leaders openly defied Soviet Union laws as unjust and undemocratic. To be sure, they did not want to look like the "old" Soviet-era rulers but they wanted to have as much power as the Soviet rulers had, if not more. By adopting judicial review, based on a Western model, post-Soviet leaders signaled their rejection of the Soviet institutional framework and secured important benefits at home and abroad. The powerful portrayed themselves as "law-abiding" because they were subject to the control of the constitutional court. This enhanced their legitimacy as promoters of a "law-governed" state in the domestic and international arenas. They presented the constitutional court to the nation as an element of modern statehood independent from Communist rule. Ruling elites gained the image of modern and enlightened state builders in society, which was a crucial element for former Communist Party bosses whose only available ideology was one of nationalism and independence. Having a new high court also enabled ruling elites to staff this institution with their supporters, hoping that judges would not alter their policy preferences. Post-Soviet leaders knew Soviet methods of keeping judges in check, of maintaining judicial deference to political authority, and of controlling the resources needed to enforce any court decision (including a decision of the constitutional court). These leaders, most of whom did not know much about judicial review, agreed to have a judicial review because they were sure that they would not lose control over the policy-making process. And the Russian constitutional crisis of 1993, the wholesale resignation of the Belarus Constitutional Court in 1996, and the "taming" of the Hungarian Constitutional Court in 1999 affirmed the belief of postcommunist elites that they ultimately control the fate of constitutional courts.

Legal elites (law professors and judges, government lawyers and members of the Bar, prosecutors and journalists writing on legal topics) who actually designed judicial review strengthened this confidence of the powerful.[11] They sold the idea of a separate constitutional court as an

---

[11] On the need to explore the role of legal elites in Russia, see, for example, Jeffrey Kahn, *Federalism, Democratization, and the Rule of Law in Russia* (Oxford: Oxford University Press, 2002), p. 58; and William M. Reisinger, "Legal Orientations and the Rule of Law in Post-Soviet Russia," in Sally J. Kenney, William M. Reisinger, and John C. Reitz, eds., *Constitutional Dialogues in a Comparative Perspective* (New York: St. Martin's, 1999), pp. 172–192. Beyond Russia, see, for example, Robert A. Goldwin and Art Kaufman, eds., *Constitution Makers on Constitution Making* (Washington, DC: American Enterprise Institute for Public Policy Research, 1988).

indispensable element of modern statehood based on the rule of law.[12] They managed to persuade post-Soviet rulers to create a new and unknown institution – the constitutional court – and designed it according to their perceptions of constitutional review in powerful Western states, such as Germany and France. Even though there was no real and urgent need to establish a separate tribunal unlike other democratic institutions – parliaments, presidency, and free elections – they refused to follow the American model by empowering the already existing Supreme Court to exercise constitutional review. In Russia, authorizing a Supreme Court to conduct constitutional review would run contrary to the image of constitutional review that was introduced during Gorbachev's campaign in 1988 to build a "socialist law-governed state." The USSR Parliament formed a Committee of Constitutional Supervision and urged republican parliaments to create parliamentary committees with similar jurisdiction. Therefore, the path toward a constitutional review body separate from the regular judiciary determined the future establishment of constitutional courts separate from the judicial branch. Post-Soviet ruling elites were convinced (first of all in Russia) by legal elites that the next logical step in establishing the rule of law and independent statehood was to create a constitutional court, not to empower the existing Supreme Court. Court designers gained many benefits from a separate constitutional tribunal – highly paid jobs and respect for their elite status as only they could interpret the meaning of constitutional norms and safeguard constitutional rights and foundations of new statehood. Indeed, a rare postcommunist constitutional court did not have its own creators on the bench. As a result, we have post-Soviet constitutional courts endowed with broad powers (even the power to start proceedings on the Court's own initiative).

Why did these legal elites become so influential? Why did the late Soviet Union turn "to law like a dying monarch to his withered God"?[13] Mikhail Gorbachev's campaign for a "law-based state," the way by which the Soviet president sought to legitimize his reform agenda and transfer the power away from the Communist Party in the mid-1980s, certainly helped.[14] In the 1990s, the need for legalism was even stronger

---

[12] This idea persists beyond the postcommunist world. Both the 2004 Afghanistan Constitution and the 2006 Iraq Constitution set up top judicial review tribunals.

[13] Bernard Rudden, "Civil Law, Civil Society, and the Russian Constitution," *The Law Quarterly Review*, vol. 110, no. 1 (January 1994), pp. 56–84.

[14] Peter H. Solomon, Jr., "Gorbachev's Legal Revolution," *Canadian Business Law Journal*, vol. 17, no. 2 (December 1990), pp. 184–194.

as postcommunist constitution makers struggled to win domestic and international support for their institution-building projects.[15] A few years later, in the mid-1990s, the same leaders revamped original constitutions to suit their momentary interests. And, at the beginning of the new millennium, post-Soviet constitution makers (in Kazakhstan, Ukraine, and Georgia) are still deliberating major constitutional reforms to suit their needs. In short, in the ex-Soviet world, constitution making flourishes but Western-based constitutionalism does not, contrary to the views of those who advocate the primacy of international factors in postauthoritarian transitions.

This rise of legal elites at such a crucial stage of political transformation is neither unique to the late Soviet period nor to the USSR. French and British royal legal advisers played a crucial role in setting up national systems of taxation during the Middle Ages.[16] French *parlements*, judicial tribunals, were also instrumental in toppling the monarchy in the eighteenth century.[17] In the wake of World War II, voters in West Germany also "cherished almost naive belief in the beneficial abilities of law."[18] Traditionally, in civil-law countries, "legal experts have far more influence" over legislative drafting than their colleagues in the United States.[19] But even in the common-law world, legal elites figured prominently in the self-preservation strategies of the ruling elites.[20]

On many occasions, the processes of building a new regime coincided with state building. Arguably, the American Founding Fathers envisioned

---

[15] See, for example, András Sajó, "Rule by Law in East Central Europe," in Volkmar Gessner, Armin Hoeland, and Csaba Varga, eds., *European Legal Cultures* (Aldershot: Dartmouth, 1996), p. 472.

[16] Margaret Levi, *Of Rule and Revenue* (Berkeley, CA: University of California Press, 1988), p. 102.

[17] Barrington Moore, Jr., *Social Origins of Dictatorship and Democracy: Lord and Peasant in the Making of the Modern World* (Boston: Beacon Press, 1966), p. 60.

[18] See Christoph Engel, "The Constitutional Court – Applying the Proportionality Principle – as a Subsidiary Authority for the Assessment of Political Outcomes," *Preprints aus der Max-Planck-Projektgruppe Recht der Gemeinschaftsgüter*, no. 10 (October 2001), p. 2, available at http://www.coll.mpg.de/pdf_dat/2001_10.pdf, as quoted in Peter Krug, "Assessing Legislative Restrictions on Constitutional Rights: The Russian Constitutional Court and Article 55(3)," *Oklahoma Law Review*, vol. 56, no. 3 (Fall 2003), p. 694, fn. 92.

[19] Herbert Jacob, "Courts and Politics in the USA," in Herbert Jacob, Erhard Blankenburg, Herbert M. Kritzer, Doris Marie Provine, and Joseph Sanders, *Courts, Law and Politics in Comparative Perspective* (New Haven, CT: Yale University Press, 1996), p. 20.

[20] Ran Hirschl, *Towards Juristocracy: The Origins and Consequences of the New Constitutionalism* (Cambridge, MA: Harvard University Press, 2004).

a strong judicial review in the process of designing the institutional setup of a new independent state. This association of judicial review with new independent statehood was not unique to the New World. In Europe, the first constitutional courts were created in the new states of Czechoslovakia and Austria in the early 1920s immediately after the collapse of the Habsburg Empire. The West German Constitutional Court was also established immediately after Germany was carved up in two independent states after the fall of the Third Reich. This pattern of creating powerful courts at the onset of state building is repeated in the ex-Soviet world at both national and subnational levels via the "contagion" effect generated by massive emulation of institutional fixes by constitution makers. Post-communist legal elites crystallized this perception: if you want to have a new state, you have to have a constitutional court.[21] And lest we forget, not just courts but many of the democratic institutions in the United States, Britain, and France were by-products of the short-term power needs of self-serving elites and not of their democratic commitment.[22]

Because short-term calculations of power-hungry politicians alone do not determine the fate of the governance structures, let us look at the second element of my feedback perspective on judicial empowerment – the actual exercise of the judicial review power. Here, we need to take into account a combination of law and extralegal factors with both judges and politicians having their various strategies. This combination makes the power of judicial review vary according to changes in law (as written and as practiced), changes in extralegal factors (such as the salience of litigation and intracourt behavior), and changes in interaction between judges and politicians.

Indeed, the power of judicial review is not a material force because courts lack "the sword and the purse." I view judicial review power as a psychological force "that rests on a continuous interplay of perceptions" among the court, politicians, other government agencies, and voters.[23] As

---

[21] Transdniestria, a breakaway region in Moldova, has had its own functioning Constitutional Court since 2002. South Ossetia, a breakaway region in Georgia, established a Constitutional Court in its 2005 Constitution but did not make it operational.

[22] Moore, *Social Origins of Dictatorship and Democracy*, 130; Jack Rakove, *Original Meanings* (New York: Alfred Knopf, 1997); Valerie Bunce, "Comparative Democratization: Big and Bounded Generalizations," *Comparative Political Studies*, vol. 33, nos. 6–7 (August 2000), p. 726.

[23] Richard W. Daniels, *The End of Communist Revolution* (London: Routledge, 1993), p. 54.

Hobbes famously stated in *Leviathan*, "reputation of power is power." And the power of judicial review depends greatly on the reputation of courts and the authoritativeness of their judgments. As Lawrence Baum forcefully argues, a judge's reputation "is based largely on the judgments of lawyers who practice in the judge's court," and the self-esteem of judges "depends heavily on their perceptions of what" other judges, lawyers, and social groups think of them.[24] To be sure, personal predilections of judges have an effect on the judicial power. If judges themselves do not believe in their own authority to speak the truth to power, they are unlikely to constrain the rulers. In many courts, the personality of the Chief Justice, for example, has a significant impact on the internal workings of these tribunals and defines their image to outsiders.[25] Similarly, the ability of a judge to publish a dissenting opinion (if only to lash out at the opponents on the bench) may make a difference in the internal dynamics of judicial decision making and change the perception of the tribunal by outsiders. Finally, some judges are more influential than others. Although standard operating procedures may mitigate the impact of personality in well-established tribunals, such routine procedures may not yet exist in the freshly erected courts, and, therefore, the human factor in new courts is likely to be very important.

On the one hand, judges should cultivate "the perception of principled decision making (and the avoidance of the perception of Court politics or political compromise)," which "is the *sine qua non* of legitimate constitutional adjudication. The maintenance of such legitimacy is crucial because legitimacy is deemed necessary for the voluntary acceptance of Court decisions; voluntary acceptance being the only type of public acceptance of the decision on which the Court formally can rely."[26] On the other hand, citizens and public officials should comply with court decisions, not because these decisions are made by judge-experts and backed by a coercive state, "but because the judge is part of an authority structure

---

[24] Lawrence Baum, *Judges and Their Audiences: A Perspective on Judicial Behavior* (Princeton: Princeton University Press, 2006), pp. 99, 117.

[25] See, for example, "Symposium: The Chief Justice and the Institutional Judiciary," *University of Pennsylvania Law Review*, vol. 154, no. 6 (June 2006), pp. 1323–1930; and Peter H. Solomon, Jr., "Informal Practices in Russian Justice: Probing the Limits of Post-Soviet Reform," in Ferdinand Feldbrugge, ed., *Russia, Europe, and the Rule of Law* (Leiden: Martinus Nijhoff, 2007), pp. 79–91.

[26] Tyler and Mitchell, "Legitimacy and Empowerment," 708. See also Peter Krug, "Assessing Legislative Restrictions on Constitutional Rights: The Russian Constitutional Court and Article 55(3)," *Oklahoma Law Review*, vol. 56, no. 3 (Fall 2003), pp. 694–695.

that is good to preserve."[27] Therefore, constitutional courts are *strong* when they have enough legitimate authority to compel public officials to rewrite statutes or to change their practices of governance. When courts lack such legitimacy, they rarely overrule government policies (high rates of compliance) or officials comply only with favorable judgments (low rates of compliance).

These kinds of perceptions (judicial apolitical decision making and voluntary compliance) are ideal types of attitudes to enhance the legitimacy of judicial power. In reality, neither do all judges appear to avoid the politicization of courts, nor do all politicians and voters believe in the impeccable authoritativeness of judicial institutions. Moreover, in regime transitions, the frequently changing short-term power needs of the rulers and their instrumental use of courts make it nearly impossible for judges to engage in principled decision making. New courts have only the psychological force of their decisions to persuade politicians, but politicians have much stronger material resources to challenge court decisions they dislike.[28] Therefore, young courts are constrained actors that utilize the language of law to instill perceptions of a fair and impartial decision-making process leading to principled, apolitical decisions.

Both political and legal considerations determine judicial behavior – when the court should rule on the merits of a case and when it should dismiss a case. The most difficult legal concern is how to fit court decisions into the legal hierarchy as espoused by law – that is, "the legal hierarchy on paper." Although judges always claim that the constitution is at the top of this hierarchy, what is below the constitution is not so clear. On the one hand, the civil-law tradition does not recognize "judge-made" law and refuses to make constitutional court decisions the equivalent of constitutional rules. On the other hand, court decisions are final and have binding force *erga omnes* – that is, they bind all other governmental branches and private individuals. Moreover, judges engage in creative decision making and issue decisions in forms not mentioned in the court statute.[29] They issue "interpretive" decisions in which they pronounce the constitutionally accepted meaning of a contested legal norm. Judges also write resolutions that formally dismiss a case but at the same time

---

[27] Owen M. Fiss, "Objectivity and Interpretation," *Stanford Law Review*, vol. 34, no. 4 (April 1982), pp. 739, 756.

[28] Alexander Bickel, *The Least Dangerous Branch: The Supreme Court at the Bar of Politics* (Indianapolis: Bobbs-Merrill Co., 1962).

[29] For a useful summary of judicial creativity, see John Bell, *Judiciaries within Europe: A Comparative Review* (New York: Cambridge University Press, 2006), pp. 32–33.

New Courts in New Polities

contain orders to government agencies. This creative decision making can complicate the *ratio decidendi* of court decisions, harm the authoritativeness of legal reasoning, and confuse the structure of legal hierarchy. At the same time, court decisions build this hierarchy of laws (at least its doctrinal version) by interpreting constitutional norms, balancing between constitutional rights provisions, and defining the prerogatives of other governmental branches. This is, of course, where politics, or the authoritative allocation of values, comes into the picture.

Political aspects of judicial decision making are most visible in the exercise of judicial discretion. How courts use these powers, what kinds of cases they choose to hear, and what kinds of decisions they issue – all of these are politically charged questions. The answers to these questions depend on the bias in constitutional rules, judicial preferences, the balance of political forces, and public attitudes. If the constitutional rules in a country favor a strong executive, court decisions are likely to reflect this bias. If most judges agree on a particular issue of public policy, court decisions are likely to contain clear orders to the government on how to enforce them. Young courts may also avoid quarrels with powerful political forces to minimize the danger of assaults by the latter. Finally, judging against the prevailing attitudes among voters may also threaten the legitimacy of young courts if citizens care only about the output of judicial review and can coerce elected officials to abolish constitutional courts.

Politics also figures prominently in the behavior of freshly appointed judges outside their newly minted courts. The early years of the German and Spanish constitutional courts showed that their members actively and frequently bargained with other top policymakers to increase the power and independence of judicial review and to ensure the enforcement of their judgments. The Mexican Supreme Court, after acquiring broad judicial review powers in the mid-1990s, actively shaped media coverage of its exercise of judicial review to advertise its independence in the eyes of Mexican voters.[30] As I will discuss in Chapter 3, the Russian Constitutional Court judges publicly debated the draft of the 1993 federal constitution, "wrote" their own law in 1994, and blocked repeated amendments to the

---

[30] Vanberg, "Establishing Judicial Independence in West Germany"; Heidi Ly Beirich, "The Role of the Constitutional Tribunal in Spanish Politics (1980–1995)" (Ph.D. diss., Purdue University, 1998); and Jeffrey Staton, "Judicial Activism and Public Authority Compliance: The Role of Public Support in the Mexican Separation-of-Powers System" (Ph.D. diss., Washington University, 2002).

constitutional court statute.[31] These judges also quickly set up an active media department to shape media coverage of their Court by arranging access of journalists to its hearings. It did not take long for these judges to realize that, on the one hand, the majority of citizens did not read lengthy judicial decisions or their commentaries in law reviews written in highly legalistic language while, on the other hand, political elites were more worried about the outcomes of constitutional litigation. What motivated the judges to engage in such lobbying and public relations campaigning: personal ambitions, institutional imperatives, or ideological commitments? Because court deliberations are secret, and judges do not tend to disclose them in public, analyzing this kind of extrajudicial behavior, together with judicial opinions, is likely to provide a more complete picture of the values constitutional judges possess, the constraints they face, and the choices they make.[32] However, the actual impact of judicial review on the governance system raises complex theoretical and practical issues of the implementation of court decisions that need to be treated separately. Before I turn to these issues, one caveat is in order.

My thesis analytically separates judicial power from judicial independence. Just like the power of courts, judicial independence is a variable that differs across countries, time, and policy sectors. It is a complex phenomenon that deserves separate study.[33] I treat judicial independence as a mechanism for insulating courts to allow impartial adjudication. More importantly, firm guarantees that courts and judges are free from government and private pressures create the perception of principled and rational judicial decision making among litigants, elites, and the masses. This perception, as it has been argued in this chapter, is crucial for the actual empowerment of courts but it may be absent in informal workings of new regimes.

Judicial independence varies because: (1) it involves relationships between potential sources of pressure (external and internal) and the judge, and (2) it has to be balanced against demands for a greater

---

[31] Alexander Blankenagel, "The Court Writes its Own Law, Roundtable: Redesigning the Russian Constitutional Court," *East European Constitutional Review*, vol. 3, no. 4 (Summer–Fall 1994), pp. 74–79.

[32] Lee Epstein and Jack Knight, *The Choices Justices Make* (Washington, DC: CQ Press, 1998).

[33] See Peter H. Russell and David O'Brien, eds., *Judicial Independence in the Age of Democracy* (Charlottesville, VA: University of Virginia Press, 2001) and Stephen B. Burbank and Barry Friedman, eds., *Judicial Independence at the Crossroads: An Interdisciplinary Approach* (Thousands Oaks, CA: Sage Publications, 2002).

New Courts in New Polities

accountability of judges.[34] Many studies that mix judicial independence with the powers of constitutional courts or equate judicial independence with judicial activism produce poor results.[35] I do not assume that independent courts are necessarily powerful courts and that dependent courts are inevitably powerless. Franco's Spain[36] and Sadat's Egypt,[37] late Tsarist Russia,[38] and Communist Hungary[39] succeeded in creating relatively autonomous, yet powerless, courts. To find out if the courts are actually powerful we need to explore the impact of their decisions on politics separately from their degree of independence.

Exploring this actual impact of court decisions brings us to compliance – a third element of my feedback dynamic of judicial empowerment. The fact that constitutional judges throughout the world – in advanced and nascent democracies, and in "hybrid" and authoritarian regimes – worry about possible noncompliance with their decisions has been amply documented in the opinions they author, the legislation they sponsor, the manuscripts they write, and the speeches they make. This widespread worry is internal to judicial decision making. However, compliance, as it was discussed above, depends on the action/inaction of government officials and institutions as well as on public support for court decisions. This makes compliance external to judicial behavior. Therefore, my study treats compliance with constitutional court decisions as a joint effort on the part of judges, elites, and the public.

The central questions that the "compliance" variable addresses are: what happens after the constitutional court has ruled and why? How do judges go about ensuring the enforcement of their rulings? How do

---

[34] Peter H. Russell, "Toward a General Theory of Judicial Independence," in Russell and O'Brien, *Judicial Independence*, pp. 1–24 and Peter H. Solomon, Jr., "Putin's Judicial Reform: Making Judges Accountable as well as Independent," *East European Constitutional Review*, vol. 11, nos. 1–2 (Winter–Spring 2002), pp. 117–124.

[35] See, for example, Shannon Ishiyama Smithey and John Ishiyama, "Judicial Activism in Post-Communist Politics," *Law and Society Review*, vol. 36, no. 4 (December 2002), pp. 719–741; and Erik S. Herron and Kirk A. Randazzo, "The Relationship between Independence and Judicial Review in Post-Communist Courts," *Journal of Politics*, vol. 65, no. 2 (May 2003), pp. 422–438.

[36] Jose Toharia, "Judicial Independence in an Authoritarian Regime: The Case of Contemporary Spain," *Law and Society Review*, vol. 9, no. 3 (Spring 1975), pp. 475–496.

[37] Tamir Moustafa, *The Struggle for Constitutional Power*.

[38] William Wagner, "Tsarist Legal Policies at the End of the Nineteenth Century: A Study in Inconsistency," *Slavonic and East European Review*, vol. 54, no. 3 (1976), pp. 371–394. See also Peter H. Solomon, Jr., ed., *Reforming Justice in Russia: 1864–1994: Power, Culture and the Limits of Legal Order* (Armonk, NY: M. E. Sharpe, 1997).

[39] András Sajó, "The Judiciary in Contemporary Society: Hungary," *Case Western Reserve Journal of International Law*, vol. 25, no. 2 (Spring 1993), pp. 293–301.

politicians, bureaucracies, and legal communities react to court-mandated policy changes? Answering these questions involves the study of both legal and political elements of postdecisional dynamics, if only to understand why so many constitutional courts – from Spain to Russia to Taiwan to Mexico – have been waging the struggles for compliance after they announce their judgments.[40]

This problem of compliance does not arise every time the government loses a trial because the court may strike down statutes dating back to the *ancien regime*, or policies that governments are unwilling or incapable of implementing, or the laws that the government wanted the Court to invalidate. In such cases, the values that the Court majority espouses roughly coincide with the prevailing priorities of incumbent governments. Although formally losing its case, the government complies and acts on its own preferences by letting the Court decide "hot potatoes" even if compliance means massive spending or reduction of governmental powers. Whether such support for specific court decisions translates into diffuse support for strong judicial review as an institution is unclear.[41]

The compliance problem arises mainly when court judgments threaten the vital interests and top priorities of powers that be, or order government spending on politically unprofitable items, or run counter to the values of the majority of citizens. How far courts can go depends not only on their formal powers alone but also on the degree of their institutional independence, on the public policy area, and on the popularity of other policymakers. Some political scientists argue that judges would be most successful in enforcing procedural rights because due process rights guarantee a constant supply of work for judges, thus contributing to the social perception of the necessity of judicial institutions.[42] Other theorists assert that judicial review will be obeyed if judges focus on the protection

---

[40] A focus on postdecisional dynamics may not capture well the phenomenon of *autolimitation*, when the government reverses its policy under the mere threat of potential constitutional court interference. Alec Stone Sweet, *Governing with Judges: Constitutional Politics in Europe* (Oxford: Oxford University Press, 2000).

[41] James Gibson, Gregory Caldeira, and Vanessa Baird, "On the Legitimacy of National High Courts," *American Political Science Review*, vol. 92, no. 2 (June 1998), pp. 343–358; Joseph F. Fletcher and Paul Howe, "Public Opinion and Canada's Courts," in Paul Howe and Peter H. Russell, eds., *Judicial Power and Canadian Democracy* (Montreal: McGill University Press, 2001), pp. 255–296.

[42] David S. Yamanishi, "Rule of Law, Property Rights, and Human Rights: An Informal Theory of the Effects (and Non-Effects) of Legal Institutions." Paper presented at the annual meeting of the American Political Science Association, Washington, DC, September 2000.

New Courts in New Polities

of all individual rights, rather than on the cases of political heavy-lifting, such as vertical or horizontal separation-of-powers, to avoid the wrath of dissatisfied politicians.[43] Others disagree by claiming that constitutional courts affirming individual rights face a state apparatus that lacks the incentives to comply,[44] and that successful judicial review emerges from providing the services that economic elites want or from not interfering with key interests of these elites.[45] Finally, few existing studies expect disobedience from regular courts, even though the decisions of these courts may be the main targets of constitutional review in nondemocratic settings.[46] This is because constitutional courts will avoid challenging the rulers and will expand their jurisdiction at the expense of less powerful actors, like other courts.

Whatever the truth on this point, my analysis assumes that other powerbrokers do not easily share their power with the new constitutional review tribunal. Although constitutional courts have legal powers to fine or reprimand for noncompliance with their decisions, judges prefer to rely on ethical claims to the authoritativeness of their decisions. As Justice Hans G. Rupp of the German Constitutional Court explained, "The only marshal there is to enforce the court's ruling is its moral authority, the conscience of the parties concerned, and in the last resort, the people's respect for law and good government."[47] Writing half-a-century later,

---

[43] Lee Epstein, Jack Knight, and Olga Shvetsova, "The Role of Constitutional Courts in the Establishment and Maintenance of Democratic Systems of Government," *Law and Society Review*, vol. 35, no. 1 (March 2001), pp. 117–164.

[44] Martin Shapiro, "The Success of Judicial Review and Democracy," in Martin Shapiro and Alec Stone Sweet, *On Law, Politics, and Judicialization* (Oxford: Oxford University Press, 2002), pp. 149–183.

[45] See, for example, Martin Shapiro, "Some Conditions for the Success of Constitutional Courts: Lessons from the U.S. Experience," in Wojciech Sadurski, ed., *Constitutional Justice, East and West* (The Hague: Kluwer Law International, 2003), pp. 37–59; and Venelin Ganev, *Preying on the State: The Transformation of Bulgaria After 1989* (Ithaca, NY: Cornell University Press, 2007).

[46] See, for example, John H. Merryman and Vincenzo Vigoriti, "When Courts Collide: Constitution and Cassation in Italy," *American Journal of Comparative Law*, vol. 15, no. 4 (1967), pp. 665–686; Lech Garlicki, "Constitutional Courts Versus Supreme Courts," *I-CON: International Journal of Constitutional Law*, vol. 5, no. 1 (January 2007), pp. 44–68; William Burnham and Alexei Trochev, "Russia's War between the Courts: The Struggle over the Jurisdictional Boundary between the Constitutional Court and Regular Courts," *American Journal of Comparative Law*, vol. 55, no. 3 (Summer 2007), pp. 381–452; Stone Sweet, *Governing with Judges*; and Ginsburg, *Judicial Review in New Democracies*.

[47] Hans G. Rupp, "Some Remarks on Judicial Self-Restraint," *Ohio State Law Journal*, vol. 21, no. 4 (Autumn 1960), pp. 503–515, at p. 507.

Stephen Breyer of the U.S. Supreme Court agreed that compliance is best assured in an "orderly society, in which people follow the rulings of courts as a matter of course, and in which resistance to a valid court order is considered unacceptable."[48]

But, as the number of observers argues, the key problem for post-Soviet states is to ensure the routine obedience of government officers to laws and the compliance of administrative regulations with the statutes.[49] Due to Soviet authoritarian legacy, much government business is done via executive decrees and regulations, which technically remain on the books even after they have been found unconstitutional. Due to the civil-law tradition that does not recognize "judge-made" law, such regulations can be repealed only by the agencies that issued them; thus bureaucrats continue to apply "unconstitutional" norms until their superiors rescind the offending rules.[50] Therefore, new constitutional courts face a daunting task of fitting their doctrines into the operational legal hierarchy that lacks automatic compliance with court declarations of unconstitutionality. In the transition from one constitutional regime to another, although constitutional doctrine demands automatic invalidation of all preexisting legal rules that contradict newly adopted constitutional standards, the operational legal hierarchy does not purge itself of them because it could paralyze governance. This is important because the de facto hierarchy of laws tells us about the actual distribution of power in a given political system. The jurisprudence of the Spanish Constitutional Tribunal and Italian Constitutional Court shows that these courts spent a lot of their time balancing between invalidating preconstitutional norms and building the structure of a new legal hierarchy.[51] In young federations, like Russia, the hierarchy of law on the ground has a complicated power structure – the degree of asymmetry in the relationship among constituent

---

[48] Stephen G. Breyer, "Judicial Independence in the U.S.," *Issues of Democracy*, vol. 1, no. 18 (December 1996), p. 11, available at http://usinfo.state.gov/journals/itdhr/1296/ijde/breyer.htm.

[49] See, for example, Martin Shapiro, "The Success of Judicial Review," in Sally J. Kenney, William M. Reisinger, and John C. Reitz, eds., *Constitutional Dialogues in Comparative Perspective* (New York: St. Martin's Press, 1999), pp. 208–209; and Kathryn Stoner-Weiss, *Resisting the State: Reform and Retrenchment in Post-Soviet Russia* (New York: Cambridge University Press, 2006).

[50] Alexei Trochev, "Implementing Constitutional Court Decisions," *East European Constitutional Review*, vol. 11, nos. 1–2 (Winter–Spring 2002), p. 95.

[51] See Beirich, "The Role of the Constitutional Tribunal in Spanish Politics" and Mary L. Volcansek, *Constitutional Politics in Italy: The Constitutional Court* (New York: St. Martin's Press, 1999).

New Courts in New Polities

parts and the federal center feeds the ability of some of these parts to disobey the Constitutional Court.[52] Thus, building a new legal hierarchy in a new state is even more daunting because it aims at the construction and maintenance of power within the governance structure. Yet we know little of the actual role of courts in state formation. As Charles Tilly reminded us, "it is easy to forget how large a part certain kinds of courts played in the day-to-day construction of Western states."[53] My study aims to fill this void and to examine how a federal constitutional court attempted to compel other powerholders to respect its vision of building Russia as a modern state.

In summary, what happens after the constitutional court issues an antigovernment decision depends on the authoritativeness of the judgment and of the court itself in the "power map" of a polity. The authoritativeness of judicial decisions or the readiness of government officials and members of the public to comply stems from a mixture of ingrained attitudes toward courts and short-term calculations.[54] These attitudes and calculations do not exist in a vacuum. They shape and are shaped by the structure of informal sanctions and incentives in political branches of government and the rest of the judiciary. Just like the infrastructure of public governance, this informal structure is not court-friendly by default.[55] Instead, it may promote obedience to bureaucratic bosses or other important actors, who frequently change their preferences, as I have discussed earlier in this chapter. Thus, street-level bureaucrats may obey the constitutional court because their superiors or other powerful figures tell them to do so (coercive power) but not because of voluntary acceptance of judicial authority (legitimate power of the court).[56] Such selective implementation

---

[52] Kathryn Stoner-Weiss, *Resisting the State: Reform and Retrenchment in Post-Soviet Russia* (Cambridge, UK: Cambridge University Press, 2006), p. 58.

[53] Charles Tilly, "Reflections on the History of European State-Making," in Charles Tilly, ed., *The Formation of National States in Western Europe* (Princeton: Princeton University Press, 1975), p. 6.

[54] Solomon, "Judicial Power in Russia," p. 553.

[55] For a similar argument to treat courts as part of a network of a modern administrative state, see Edward L. Rubin, "Independence as a Governance Mechanism," in Burbank and Friedman, *Judicial Independence at the Crossroads*, pp. 56–100.

[56] For the distinction between "coercive" power, contingent on external negative outcomes, and "legitimate" power, internalized by the voluntary acceptance of the legitimate authority, see John R. P. French, Jr. and Bertram H. Raven, "The Bases of Social Power," in Dorwin Cartwright, ed., *Studies in Social Power* (Ann Arbor, MI: Research Center for Group Dynamics, Institute for Social Research, University of Michigan, 1959), pp. 150, 156–161, as quoted in Tyler and Mitchell, "Legitimacy and Empowerment," at p. 721, fn. 54.

38 *Nonlinear Judicial Empowerment*

of constitutional court decisions may damage the reputation of the court in the eyes of the citizenry, and create a gap between negative public perceptions of the court and an increased possibility of successful litigation against the state. Therefore, in addition to bills of rights, independent judges, and human rights activists, an effective state apparatus is vital to making the rights revolutions real.[57]

NONLINEARITY IN TRANSITIONAL JUDICIAL POLITICS

The enormous uncertainty during the regime change, the unstable policy preferences of the new ruling elites, judicial behavior, and the incapacity of the government machinery to obey court decisions – these four factors blended together complicate a cost–benefit calculus of having a strong judicial review and exacerbate the unintended nonlinear trajectories of judicial empowerment. My thesis rests on the following assumptions that pertain to the postcommunist world:

1. Effective linkages between the voters and elected officials are lacking;
2. Voters rarely read judicial decisions;
3. A multiparty system that actually aggregates voter preferences is absent;
4. A capable state with usable bureaucracy does not exist and
5. Institutional rigidity (be it separation of powers or federalism) is nonexistent.

Consider how severe institutional uncertainty complicates the judicial empowerment.[58] Many postcommunist countries face enormous challenges brought by a quadruple transition that involves both dismantling the Soviet regime with its planned economy and building new statehood and new nationhood.[59] The turmoil of this transition is hard to overestimate. Edward Walker notes that it involves "fundamental and disjunctive institutional change, rapid attitudinal and behavioral adjustments to an

---

[57] Charles R. Epp, *The Rights Revolution: Lawyers, Activists, and Supreme Courts in Comparative Perspective* (Chicago: University of Chicago Press, 1998).

[58] On uncertainty, see, for example, Valerie Bunce and Maria Csanadi, "Uncertainty in the Transition: Post-Communism in Hungary," *East European Politics and Society*, vol. 7, no. 2 (Spring 1993), pp. 240–275; Kenneth Jowitt, *The New World Disorder: The Leninist Extinction* (Berkeley: University of California Press, 1992); and Mary McAuley, *Russia's Politics of Uncertainty* (Cambridge, UK: Cambridge University Press, 1997).

[59] Taras Kuzio, "Transition in Post-Communist States: Triple or Quadruple?" *Politics*, vol. 21, no. 3 (September 2001), pp. 169–178.

Nonlinearity in Transitional Judicial Politics

ever-changing structure of opportunities, anti-regime mobilization, ethnic violence, and the driving force of intense nationalism."[60] According to Katherine Verdery, it is a "reorganization on a cosmic scale, and it involves the redefinition of virtually everything, including morality, social relations, and basic meanings."[61] The first decade-and-a-half of this transition highlights both political rivalries among top government institutions and the struggles over the very nature of these institutions. In fighting these battles, the new postcommunist rulers do not trust each other, and it is naïve to think that the powerful would defer the resolution of key governance issues to judges in the context of chronic wage and tax arrears, explosion of interenterprise debts, lawlessness, and a surge in crime. This breakdown of rules and authority may destroy judicial power, as the constitutional crises in Russia, Belarus, and Kazakhstan in the mid-1990s demonstrate. Postcommunist constitution making is mostly a result of short-term bargains and reaction to short-range needs, be it the threat of civil war, pressure from the Council of Europe, or a simple power grab. Institutional uncertainty, incomplete information about the effects of the new institutions, and path dependency – all complicate strategic decision making and the translation of the rulers' preferences into institutional design.[62]

Facing the tremendous challenges of governance brought by the collapse of the socialist regime, the new rulers have to rely on their *short-term calculations* to stay in power. These rulers face almost no constraints on changing their policy and institutional preferences in their pursuit of the immediate benefits of governing. There is no well-established system of accountability of governments to the voters: postcommunist politicians appear to remember this notion only during electoral campaigns and tend to forget it shortly after elections. Postcommunist leaders "find it very hard to be accountable when they find it hard to determine either their own interests or the interests of their constituents" because of the extraordinary

---

[60] Edward W. Walker, "Sovietology and Perestroika: A Post-Mortem," in Susan Gross Solomon, ed., *Beyond Sovietology: Essays in Politics and History* (Armonk, NY: M.E. Sharpe, 1993), p. 227.

[61] Katherine Verdery, *The Political Lives of Dead Bodies: Reburial and Postsocialist Change* (New York: Columbia University Press, 1999), p. 35. For a recent exploration of the relationship between changing social norms and legal failures in postcommunism, see Dennis J. Galligan and Marina Kurkchiyan, eds., *Law and Informal Practices: The Post-Communist Experience* (Oxford: Oxford University Press, 2003).

[62] Michael McFaul, "Institutional Design, Uncertainty, and Path Dependency during Transitions: Cases from Russia," *Constitutional Political Economy*, vol. 10, no. 1 (March 1999), pp. 27–52.

fluidity of politics, lacking structure and durable voter attachments.[63] The new rulers are accustomed to making any important policy decision in a closed and informal process.[64] This informal decision-making process is particularly relevant to designing new legislative and executive institutions, and distributing the spoils secretly, out of view of the mass public and former rulers. Therefore, it is reasonable to argue that the short-term calculations of political powerholders and the lack of complete information about the consequences of their institutional choices promote unstable frameworks of public governance and unintended institutional effects.

Another factor that complicates judicial empowerment is judicial decision making: how new constitutional courts behave in this context of uncertainty and respond to the frequently changing short-term power needs of the powerful. Judges acutely sense that the political branches of government expect constitutional courts to deliver tangible and immediate benefits. At the same time, judges have their own ideas of how both to navigate the sea of postauthoritarian transition and to preserve and maximize their judicial power. Accomplishing these three things, namely, serving the rulers, guiding the country, and building the court's power, is no easy task. Institutional disorder and unstable policy preferences of the elites may shift overnight the power balance among political actors, and the postcommunist courts may find themselves together with the weakest party (e.g., parliamentary minority) facing the opposition of several stronger policymakers who would simply ignore constitutional court decisions. Judges may find it difficult to figure out how far they can go if rulers frequently change their preferences. No doubt when judges adjudicate, they are engaged in a cost–benefit analysis that goes beyond solely legal considerations. For example, the Hungarian Constitutional Court chose to pull and push Hungarian rulers closer to Europe. Its Czech and Kyrgyzstan counterparts decided to leave politicians alone and to engage in a prolonged fight with the rest of the judicial system. Meanwhile, the Bulgarian Constitutional Court became a success story by being irrelevant

---

[63] See, for example, Bunce and Csanadi, "Uncertainty in the Transition: Post-Communism in Hungary," pp. 253, 254, 272–273; and Andreas Schedler, Larry Diamond, and Marc F. Plattner, eds., *The Self-Restraining State: Power and Accountability in New Democracies* (Boulder, CO: Lynne Rienner, 1998).

[64] Bunce, "Comparative Democratization: Big and Bounded Generalizations," pp. 703–734; and Teresa Rakowska-Harmstone, "Communist Constitutions and Constitutional Change," in Keith Banting and Richard Simeon, eds., *The Politics of Constitutional Change in Industrial Nations: Redesigning the State* (London: Macmillan, 1985), 203–231.

in the postcommunist struggle for spoils.[65] But the ability of judges to act strategically is limited if the rules of the game are frequently changed, as the rest of this book shows.

Finally, the degree of *the capacity of the state machinery to enforce court decisions* determines the success or the failure of judicial empowerment. It is well known that the courts depend on the rest of the government apparatus to see their judgments carried out. But even if constitutional courts deliver concrete benefits to the powerful, it does not mean that judicial decisions make a real difference in the practice of governance. Both the nature of the postauthoritarian transition and the legacies of the past mitigate the impact of constitutional review on the ground. Recall that the massive restructuring of postsocialist states began with the bureaucrats who both stole from the state and stole the state itself, in the context of a radical breakdown of social norms and ties between the rulers and the ruled.[66] Indeed, the lack of state capacity in public policy implementation is a crucial characteristic of post-Soviet regimes regardless of their authoritarian or democratic orientations.[67] Moreover, those bureaucrats who remained in the public sector could hardly be expected to abandon their tradition of conducting much of government business via executive decrees and regulations just because judges told them to do so. The "Leninist legacy" is responsible for a near total obedience among the bureaucracy to their superiors and the Soviet legal culture of applying ministerial guidelines instead of constitutional rules. Finally, the civil-law tradition does not recognize "judge-made" law and allows these executive decrees to remain "on the books" even after the constitutional court finds them unconstitutional.

In summary, judicial empowerment has political origins: the ruling elites, regardless of their democratic or authoritarian pedigree, may perceive a powerful court as a useful tool in securing their governing status. Driven by their short-term power calculations and encouraged by legal

---

[65] See Radoslav Procházka, *Mission Accomplished: On Founding Constitutional Adjudication in Central Europe* (Budapest: Central European University Press, 2002); Venelin Ganev, "The Bulgarian Constitutional Court, 1991–1997: A Success Story in Context," *Europe-Asia Studies*, vol. 55, no. 4 (June 2003), pp. 597–611.

[66] Steven Solnick, *Stealing the State: Control and Collapse in Soviet Institutions* (Cambridge, MA: Harvard University Press, 1998) and Venelin Ganev, *Preying on the State: The Transformation of Bulgaria After 1989* (Ithaca, NY: Cornell University Press, 2007).

[67] See, for example, Gordon Smith, ed., *State-Building in Russia: The Yeltsin Legacy and the Challenge of the Future* (Armonk, NY: M. E. Sharpe, 1999) and Taras Kuzio, Robert S. Kravchuk, and Paul D'Anieri, *State and Institution Building in Ukraine* (New York: St. Martin's Press, 1999).

elites, rulers create constitutional review tribunals and staff them with loyal judges. Under certain conditions, judges may choose to rule against these elites, and elites may defy these adversary rulings and attack the courts. Even if rulers choose to obey unfavorable judgments, the former may lack the capacity to ensure compliance on the part of bureaucracy. Thus, judicial empowerment does not necessarily result in the entrenchment of the rule of law in nondemocratic regimes: weak and incapable bureaucracies defy constitutional court decisions, while the public perceives judicial review as an inefficacious way to protect individual rights or to challenge public policies. This is why controversial judgments in the area of basic rights result in "unfulfilled" rights revolutions and do not lead to the politicization of the judiciary, as they do in advanced democracies. However, constitutional litigation provides a new arena for political contestation and for public deliberation about the rule of law. A rule-of-law regime may be one of the by-products of this continuous contestation and deliberation.

Consider four possible objections to my theory. First, one might object that the success of constitutional review crucially depends on the prior commitment of ruling elites to democratic ideals and rule-of-law principles.[68] Indeed, the haste with which new postcommunist leaders raced to join or to "return" to Europe, the massive borrowing from the Western constitutional models, and the wholesale adoption of the constitutional courts in the Eastern bloc may seem like evidence of democratic commitments of the ruling elites. The euphoria of early postcommunism, the solemn words of new constitutional texts, and the numerous assurances of "democratizers" charmed many law professors, philosophers, and political scientists who linked the creation and empowerment of postcommunist constitutional courts with the democratic aspirations of postcommunist elites.[69] For example, using crossnational statistical analyses, Lane and Ersson conclude that if a country wishes to introduce democracy, to promote democratic stability and longevity, and to combat corruption "then the best institutional devices it could employ in constitutional

---

[68] See, for example, Gordon Silverstein, "Why Judicial Review Happens? Towards a Theory of Evolution and Acceptance of Judicial Review." Paper presented at the annual meeting of the American Political Science Association, Boston, August 2002; and Jeffrey K. Staton and Mark Strahan, "The Emergence of an Effective Constitutional Court." Paper presented at the annual meeting of the American Political Science Association, Boston, August 2002.

[69] See, for example, Herman Schwartz, *The Struggle for Constitutional Justice in Post-Communist Europe* (Chicago: Chicago University Press, 2000) and Claus Offe, Jon Elster, and Ulrich Preuß, *Institutional Design in Post-Communist Societies: Rebuilding the Ship at Sea* (New York: Cambridge University Press, 1988).

engineering are legal institutions such as strong legal [judicial or constitutional] review . . ."[70] In Donald Horowitz's view, "properly designed" constitutional courts can help prevent the rise of "illiberal democracies" where elected rulers abuse their power and disregard human rights.[71] By subjecting their choices to judicial scrutiny, postcommunist rulers demonstrate their commitment to democracy and the rule of law to the rest of the world. New constitutional courts, then, enforce the principles and values of the Western legal tradition by applying the jurisprudence of European national and supranational courts and legitimize a new postauthoritarian constitutional order in the eyes of the public.[72] To simplify, this emphasis on the international context treats postcommunist constitution makers and judges as children, who receive an exhortation from a wise uncle in the West on how to lead their lives.

To be sure, the studies of constitutional court building must account for the influence of international pressures and opportunities resulting in a certain institutional arrangement.[73] Currently, the international context, as supported by the World Bank, the European Union, and the Council of Europe, favors judicial empowerment. And this context constrains politicians in their attacks on the constitutional courts and provides a crucial leverage for the designers of the constitutional courts in their efforts to persuade the ruling elites of the necessity for having a constitutional court. Also, the international context involves "peer pressure" within the ex-Soviet world: everyone else has a constitutional court, why can't we?

However, the impact of Western institutions and values on postcommunist politics has been exaggerated.[74] As I discussed in Chapter 1, democracy does not flourish in many parts of the former Eastern bloc, and

---

[70] Jan-Erik Lane and Svante Ersson, *The New Institutional Politics: Performance and Outcomes* (London: Routledge, 2000), p. 178.

[71] Donald L. Horowitz, "Constitutional Courts: A Primer for Decision Makers," *Journal of Democracy*, vol. 17, no. 4 (October 2006), p. 127.

[72] See, for example, Sergio Bartole, "Conclusions: Legitimacy of Constitutional Courts: Between Policy Making and Legal Science," in Wojciech Sadurski, ed., *Constitutional Justice, East and West* (The Hague: Kluwer Law International, 2003), p. 425; and Catherine Dupre, *Importing the Law in Post-Communist Transitions: The Hungarian Constitutional Court and the Right to Human Dignity* (Portland, OR: Hart Publishing, 2003).

[73] Procházka, *Mission Accomplished*; Wojciech Sadurski, ed., *Constitutional Justice, East and West* (The Hague: Kluwer Law International, 2003); and Schwartz, *The Struggle for Constitutional Justice*.

[74] For the discussion of successes and failures of foreign legal transplants during the regime change, see, for example, Dupre, *Importing the Law*; and Robert Sharlet, "Legal Transplants and Political Mutations: The Reception of Constitutional Law in Russia and the Newly Independent States," *East European Constitutional Review*, vol. 7, no. 4 (Fall 1998), pp. 59–68.

accessible constitutional review does not exist in several consolidated democracies in this region. All postcommunist countries routinely send their draft legislation for approval to international organizations like the Council of Europe but not all of these countries transit toward democracy, improve their human rights record, and reduce corruption. In fact, it may be useful to view the sprouts of judicial empowerment in many post-Soviet regimes in a context of failed authoritarianism, in which the post-Soviet rulers were too weak to constrain new constitutional courts.[75] Moreover, post-Leninist constitutions do not look like, and do not work like, the Western models, as adapted by local constitutional engineers. Instead, these constitutions resemble eclectic "gardens," but not "traditional French or British parks."[76] Meanwhile, both democratic and authoritarian constitution makers in the region do not hesitate amending the constitutions to suit their power needs. Certainly, there is no limit to perfecting the constitutional rules but the flexibility of postcommunist constitutionalism shows that a rare president or prime minister can stick to the rules of the constitutional game. Similar to the inconsistency of constitutional texts, postcommunist constitutional courts have not developed a coherent body of ideas on the basis of Western liberal democratic principles. To be sure, members of these new tribunals study the work of foreign constitutional courts, particularly in the area of human rights. Yet, the courts in the region come to the opposite conclusions on how to deal with the Communist past, on how to protect welfare rights, and so on. And, as the rest of this book shows, even within a single country, Russia, the constitutional court lacked a coherent and comprehensive proreform ideology in the areas of separation of powers, federalism, and basic rights.[77]

In summary, these idea-based approaches tell us that only the "good guys" can empower courts and ignore the reality in which the "bad guys" – authoritarian rulers – not only create and keep constitutional courts but also make these tribunals more accessible and stronger in the political

---

[75] See Lucan A. Way, "Authoritarian State Building and the Sources of Regime Competitiveness in the Fourth Wave: The Cases of Belarus, Moldova, Russia, and Ukraine," *World Politics*, vol. 57, no. 2 (January 2005), pp. 231–261.

[76] Rett R. Ludwikowski, "'Mixed Constitutions' – Product of an East-Central European Melting Pot," *Boston University Journal of International Law*, vol. 16, no. 1 (Spring 1998), p. 64.

[77] More generally on the inconsistent judicial doctrines in Eastern Europe, see Daniel Smilov, "The Character and Legitimacy of Constitutional Review: Eastern European Perspectives," *I-CON: International Journal of Constitutional Law*, vol. 2, no. 1 (January 2004), p. 181.

system. Those who emphasize ideas in institution building envision judicial review in charge of protecting a new constitutional order based on Western values of pluralism, democracy, and the rule of law. But they ignore the reality in which some consolidated democracies do not allow individual complaints to constitutional courts. Moreover, by failing to separate the ideas of the powerful from their interests, the idea-based approaches appear to underestimate the depth of the institutional disorder in postcommunist politics.

A second potential objection to the argument that the short-term power needs complicate the process of judicial empowerment comes from the insight that the institutional disorder actually helps to strengthen courts. Instead of assuming the commitment of the rulers to liberal democratic values, this view originates from the human need to resolve conflicts in a peaceful manner. It usually follows the classic triad with a judge deciding a dispute between two contesting parties and siding with one of them. This concept of a "triadic dispute resolution" as "two against one" implies that these two together (i.e., the winning party and the judge) are stronger than the losing party.[78] For example, French-style division of power between the president and prime minister in the executive branch is said to produce and maintain the need for judicial review to resolve disputes between these institutions.[79] In the United States, judicial review serves as a "checks-and-balance" arrangement in the system of separate legislative, executive, and judicial branches of government. Courts, then, guard separation of powers by settling various institutional conflicts between and within the elected branches of government and gain power by exploiting these interinstitutional rivalries.[80] In general, the more there are top policy-making bodies, the easier it is for a court to exploit rivalries among them. This is because there is less likelihood of (a) all institutions having the same policy preferences, and (b) serious threats to the court because they can be launched only by a coalition of several institutions. Moreover, the institutional uncertainty during postcommunism appears to cry for more judge-made protections of constitutional bargains and clarifications of constitutional rules and powers of different government bodies. Constitutional court judges, then, act as a team of railroad switchmen, whose

---

[78] Martin Shapiro, *Courts: A Comparative and Political Analysis* (Chicago: University of Chicago Press, 1981).

[79] Bruce Ackerman, "The Rise of World Constitutionalism," *Virginia Law Review*, vol. 83, no. 4 (May 1997), pp. 771–797; and Shapiro, "The Success of Judicial Review," pp. 193–219.

[80] Shapiro, "The Success of Judicial Review."

task is to ensure that the trains, or public policies, designed by the separated branches of government, do not collide, move in a coordinated fashion, and deliver the envisioned results, be it universal suffrage, economic growth, or a social security system. Over time, if constitutional courts are successful, and if political actors respect constitutional principles, the rule of law and democracy strengthen and become "the only games in town."[81]

Naturally, constitutional court judges are among the first to uphold this vision of stable and orderly governance, brought about by judicial review. As Valerii Zorkin, Chief Justice of the Russian Constitutional Court, personally explained to President Putin, the work of the constitutional court is similar to the work of the electrician, whose job is to connect carefully the ends of a malfunctioning electrical network.[82] But the experience of postcommunist constitutional justice raises theoretical and practical challenges to the "interinstitutional rivalries" thesis. First, institutional disorder in postcommunist politics persists despite the active involvement of constitutional courts. Courts are simply not strong enough to bring about orderly governance in the course of the quadruple transition, while the powerful may lack the incentives to ask constitutional judges for help. It is still too early to tell whether constitutional courts were constructive or destructive in the institutional uncertainty of postcommunist transitions. Second, severe interinstitutional rivalries may result in the destruction of judicial review, as the constitutional crises in Russia, Belarus, and Kazakhstan in the mid-1990s demonstrate. Third, the need for judicial review does not explain the timing and the nature of the constitutional review tribunal. Why, for example, did leaders in democratic Latvia delay the activation of the constitutional court for 7 years, while their counterparts in nondemocratic Uzbekistan promptly made their constitutional court accessible and operational? In summary, the need-based vision of judicial review tells us a lot about the role of courts in formal mechanisms of governance but tells little about their role in informal aspects of governance, about the institutional disorder of postcommunist governance, and about the impact of judicial review on the ground. This vision alone cannot explain the zigzagging changes in judicial empowerment in post-Soviet Russia with its bicameral federal parliament and divided executive,

---

[81] Adam Przeworski, *Democracy and the Market* (Cambridge, UK: Cambridge University Press, 1991).

[82] "President Vladimir Putin Met at the Kremlin with Constitutional Court Judges on the Eve of Constitution Day," *Kremlin.Ru*, December 11, 2006, available at http://www.kremlin.ru/text/appears/2006/12/115196.shtml.

Nonlinearity in Transitional Judicial Politics

federalism, and separate branches of the judiciary under a rigid 1993 Constitution. It needs to take the interests of the power brokers more seriously.

A third possible objection to the importance of short-term interests in constructing judicial power might come from the latest *strategic* revolution in the field of judicial politics.[83] Strategic accounts of judicial empowerment suggest that both politicians and judges act strategically instead of pursuing their short-term goals – they forego their short-term benefits in order to maximize their benefits in the long term. Thus, the main concern of strategic approaches is the construction and maintenance of powerful interests in political regimes. Assuming the rationality of actors, who have fixed preferences and act according to institutional constraints, these approaches suggest that strong courts emerge when the rulers want them to be strong enough to secure their property rights,[84] to maximize their profits,[85] to maintain their "hegemonic status" within society,[86] or to control bureaucracy.[87] By paying attention to the timing and context of judicial empowerment, these scholars have strengthened their claim that, in the uncertainty of the regime change, politicians who fear electoral loss create a strong and independent judiciary to protect themselves from the tyranny of election winners in the future. When political uncertainty is high, constitution makers are less likely to constrain judicial review bodies. Accessible constitutional courts, then, protect political minorities by providing them with a forum to obstruct majoritarian decision making.[88]

---

[83] Lee Epstein and Jack Knight, "Towards a Strategic Revolution in Judicial Politics: A Look Back, A Look Ahead," *Political Research Quarterly*, vol. 53, no. 3 (September 2000), pp. 625–661.

[84] Douglass C. North and Barry R. Weingast, "Constitutions and Commitment: The Evolution of Institutions Governing Public Choice in Seventeenth-Century England," in Lee J. Alston, Thrainn Eggertsson, and Douglass C. North, eds., *Empirical Studies in Institutional Change* (Cambridge, UK: Cambridge University Press, 1996), pp. 134–165.

[85] William Landes and Richard Posner, "The Independent Judiciary in an Interest-Group Perspective," *Journal of Law and Economics*, vol.18, no.3 (December 1975), pp. 875–901.

[86] Ran Hirschl, *Towards Juristocracy*.

[87] Matthew McCubbins and Thomas Schwartz, "Congressional Oversight Overlooked: Police Patrols versus Fire Alarms," *American Journal of Political Science*, vol. 28, no. 1 (February 1984), pp. 165–179.

[88] Mark J. Ramseyer, "The Puzzling (In) dependence of Courts: A Comparative Approach," *Journal of Legal Studies*, vol. 23, no. 2 (June 1994), pp. 721–747; Pedro C. Magalhães, "The Politics of Judicial Reform in Eastern Europe," *Comparative Politics*, vol. 32, no. 1 (October 1999), pp. 43–62; Ginsburg, *Judicial Review in New Democracies*; Lee Epstein and Jack Knight, "Constitutional Borrowing and Nonborrowing," *I-CON: International Journal of Constitutional Law*, vol. 1, no. 2 (April 2003), pp. 196–223; and Jodi Finkel, "Judicial Reform as Insurance Policy: Mexico in the 1990s," *Latin American Politics and Society*, vol. 47, no. 1 (Spring 2005), pp. 87–113.

To simplify: the powerful delegate power to independent courts and bind themselves to their judgments, like Ulysses, who survives by tying himself to the boat in order to resist the sweet songs of the deadly Sirens.[89] Constitutional courts, then, are the ropes, which are famous for their reliability and durability, that save the rulers from ultimate self-destruction. The rulers use these ropes only in "life or death" situations and hide them after the crisis has passed to avoid stumbling upon them during their journey. Therefore, judicial review as a saving device is not self-activating and depends on the petitions of political power holders; it is not able to navigate the ship or to set the policy agenda; and it has no magic powers of seeing into the future, of adjusting to danger, or of sticking to Ulysses' skin – courts are just ropes, they are merely strong enough to withstand Ulysses' physical might.[90]

This self-binding Ulysses metaphor is fine except that a postcommunist Ulysses had to rebuild his ship during the storm in an open sea. In other words, postcommunist leaders had to secure their interests, pursue fundamental reforms, and deliver tangible results both at home and abroad – all these had to be done quickly in order to remain in power. Postcommunist constitution making was mostly a result of short-term bargains and reaction to short-range needs of the bargaining actors.[91] Both democratic and authoritarian leaders rarely had the luxury of time to strategize about entrusting their destinies to new and unknown judges. More often, politicians believed in quick institutional fixes and learned from each other how to use constitutional courts to their advantage. This is why nondemocratic rulers in Russia's regions who feared no electoral loss found it beneficial to create accessible constitutional courts.[92] And this is why, for example, it took one weekend to create the constitutional court in Hungary. There, constitution makers had "a vague conception of the functions of a constitutional court" and devoted "very little effort" to place "the court in the context of a balanced arrangement of powers."[93]

---

[89] On self-binding of the rulers, see, for example, Jon Elster, *Ulysses and the Sirens: Studies in Rationality and Irrationality* (Cambridge, UK: Cambridge University Press, 1979); and Jeremy Waldron, "Precommitment and Disagreement," in Larry Alexander, ed., *Constitutionalism: Philosophical Foundations* (Cambridge, UK: Cambridge University Press, 1998), pp. 271–299.

[90] Smilov, "The Character and Legitimacy of Constitutional Review," pp. 190–191.

[91] See, for example, Kataryna Wolczuk, *The Moulding of Ukraine: The Constitutional Politics of State Formation* (Budapest: Central European University Press, 2001).

[92] Alexei Trochev, "Less Democracy, More Courts: A Puzzle of Judicial Review in Russia," *Law and Society Review*, vol. 38, no. 3 (September 2004), pp. 513–548.

[93] László Sólyom, "The First Year of the Constitutional Court," *Acta Juridica Hungarica*, vol. 33, nos. 1–2 (1991), p. 5; and András Sajó, "The Roundtable Talks in Hungary,"

Nonlinearity in Transitional Judicial Politics

Moreover, strategic accounts of judicial empowerment do not view courts as simple ropes in this Ulysses metaphor. Judges also have to be strategic: they have to forego their own policy preferences by pleasing the powerful actors in order to prevent a backlash against their court. Here, judges do not follow existing laws and do not make new law. Instead, they search for the solution, which could be accepted by the powerful, and, hopefully, could expand the power of their court. This is because judges worry about noncompliance with their judgments, and, in the case of judicial review, the state is the one who has to comply. And if judges expect that public officials will not comply, the former refuse to strike down government policies in order to avoid attacks on their tribunal.[94] Thus, the policy preferences of the rulers constrain judicial review tribunals.

Paradoxically, according to strategic accounts, the constitutional courts are strong on paper, weak in adjudicating cases, and again strong in ensuring compliance. Courts have broad judicial review powers but they cannot use them against the wishes of the powerful. And their compliance record is strong because they rarely upset politicians.

Judges surely recognize these constraints. As Justice Gadzhiev of the Russian Constitutional Court bluntly put it, "the constitutional court will cease to exist, if its judges fail to pay attention to the political realities of the day."[95] But these realities of the day are very complicated because the powerful quickly change their minds in the search for frantic solutions to address the challenges of the quadruple transition. Moreover, strategic judicial behavior does not translate into an automatic implementation of court decisions. Just because elected public officials accept court-mandated policies, this acceptance – a sign of the successful constitutional court – does not mean that the state machinery will smoothly carry out these policies. Karen Orren and Stephen Skowronek argue that the governance practice in the United States does not change "because a court... declares that it should."[96] Marc Hertogh and Simon Halliday

---

in Jon Elster, ed., *Roundtable Talks and the Breakdown of Communism* (Chicago: University of Chicago Press, 1996), p. 93.

[94] See, for example, Epstein et al., "The Role of Constitutional Courts"; Vanberg, *The Politics of Constitutional Review in Germany.*

[95] "G. A. Gadzhiev: 'U nas ogromnyi potok zhalob nalogoplatelshchikov, i on vriad li umenshitsia v obozrimom budushchem'" [We Have a Huge Flood of Complaints from Taxpayers, and This Is Unlikely to Change in the Foreseeable Future], *Rossiiskii nalogovyi kur'er*, no. 24 (December 2004), at http://www.rnk.ru.

[96] Karen Orren and Stephen Skowronek, *The Search for American Political Development* (New York: Cambridge University Press, 2004), pp. 125–126.

also claim that in modern governance of well-established democracies, "the full implementation of court decisions usually does not enjoy the highest priority."[97] Bureaucracies may lack the capacity to enforce court decisions simply because they are not used to judicial interventions in their standard operating procedures. Also, bureaucrats usually prefer to obey the concrete orders of their superiors instead of the vague clauses of statutes filled with various judge-made formulas. In short, bureaucratic compliance with court decisions and statutes must be examined and cannot be assumed, as is often the case with the strategic accounts of judicial politics. And in the period of quadruple transition, politicians rarely have the will, time, incentives, and resources to check how bureaucracies carry out court-ordered policies. Meanwhile, due to bureaucratic sabotage, successful litigants may never achieve the tangible benefits from their court victories. This is why my *short-term power needs* approach to judicial review is more adequate in explaining why cautious (and successful, in terms of strategic accounts) constitutional courts fail both to produce rights revolutions and to garner public trust.

A fourth potential objection to my thesis might be that my foci on both the elites and their short-term interests are wrong because the fate of judicial review depends on its acceptance by the broader society, not just by the elites. According to this *public support* approach, which draws on judicial politics in developed democracies, courts, like any other public institution, depend on public support in order to survive. How do ordinary citizens come to support judicial review as an institution? Some argue that the fair and impartial rules and procedures of judicial decision making conquer the hearts of the voters. Others claim that what the court says is more important. Yet others insist that the high probability of winning a court case makes judges more legitimate.[98]

Whatever the truth on this point, a large body of research has shown that by issuing many decisions that pleased the public, the constitutional courts in Germany and Spain and the Supreme Courts in the United States, Canada, and Israel have created a large reservoir of "diffuse" public support for the institution of judicial review. Growing public awareness of and support for the decisions of the constitutional court gradually build

---

[97] Marc Hertogh and Simon Halliday, eds., *Judicial Review and Bureaucratic Impact* (Cambridge, UK: Cambridge University Press, 2004), p. 279.

[98] Tyler and Mitchell, "Legitimacy and Empowerment"; Vanessa A. Baird, "Building Institutional Legitimacy: The Role of Procedural Justice," *Political Research Quarterly*, vol. 54, no. 2 (June 2001), pp. 333–354; and Staton, "Judicial Activism and Public Authority Compliance."

Nonlinearity in Transitional Judicial Politics

this reservoir of institutional legitimacy that the court can draw on. High levels of diffuse support push the governmental branches to respect and comply with the rulings of the judicial review tribunal. Drawing on this reservoir, then, the popular tribunal can issue decisions disliked by the majority of voters and still count on public allegiance. Therefore, the recipe for young constitutional courts is to please the public, preferably various constituencies, and wait.[99] In its extreme form, the *public support* approach suggests that new courts should wait until voters like their rulings so much that they would punish politicians for failure to obey them. For example, if more voters support the constitutional court than, say, the president, the latter should obey the court decisions. Otherwise, the dissatisfied voters will punish the president by voting her out of office.[100]

In short, the core notion behind this *public support* approach is an accountability of governments to the voters and the public knowledge of judicial decisions. Neither of these conditions is easily achieved in postauthoritarian societies. Short-term power needs rather than voter support figured prominently in the calculations of postcommunist rulers when they succeeded or failed in their attacks on the constitutional courts, as described at the beginning of Chapter 1. Even in Hungary, which used to have a powerful constitutional court in the 1990s, voters allowed the government to tame this highly popular tribunal in 1999 and did not know whom to vote for to once again have a strong constitutional court.[101] But even if the voters make politicians really accountable to a strong constitutional court, the ruling elites may lack the capacity to enforce constitutional court decisions. Particularly in the area of human rights, if unelected bureaucrats defy (or forget!) the rulings of the constitutional court, voters lack any real mechanism for compelling officials to obey. True, citizens can ask regular courts to protect their rights against bureaucratic sabotage. But this will work only if the rest of the judiciary agrees with the decisions of the constitutional court. This has rarely been the case, as the "wars of courts" in Spain and Korea, Italy and the Czech Republic, and

---

[99] See, for example, James Gibson, Gregory Caldeira, and Vanessa Baird, "On the Legitimacy of National High Courts" and Joseph F. Fletcher and Paul Howe, "Public Opinion and Canada's Courts."

[100] Vanberg, *The Politics of Constitutional Review in Germany*; Anke Grosskopf, "A Supranational Case – Comparing Sources of Support for Constitutional Courts" (Ph.D. diss., University of Pittsburgh, 2000).

[101] Kim Lane Scheppele, "Democracy by Judiciary. Or Why Courts Can Sometimes Be More Democratic Than Parliaments," in Adam W. Czarnota, Martin Krygier, and Wojciech Sadurski, eds., *Rethinking the Rule of Law After Communism* (Budapest: Central European University Press, 2005), pp. 25–60.

Colombia and Russia demonstrate. Needless to say, voters do not matter much when two (or three, as in Russia, Ukraine, and the Czech Republic) high national courts refuse to respect the judgments of each other. Also, the public support approaches have yet to explain why fewer and fewer voters, in societies as diverse as Russia and Mexico, approve of their high courts despite their groundbreaking jurisprudence in the area of human rights. Should these young courts slow down and retreat after the first decade of assertive decision making?

In summary, *public support* approaches provide an important clue to studying judicial empowerment, namely, that construction and maintenance of the perceptions of judicial objectivity, impartiality, and integrity are crucial for the growth of judicial power. However, these approaches exaggerate the strength of the links among voters, politicians, and judges in the rough waters of postcommunist transformation. Just like *strategic accounts*, these approaches tend to overlook the importance of international pressures and opportunities and to overestimate the capacity of the state to enforce court decisions. Emphasizing accountability to the voters, *public support* approaches seem to suggest that judges, similar to other officials, should race for popularity among the voters. This is dangerous advice that can throw young courts into a race to the bottom instead of the top of judicial independence.

Taken together, the four objections described above correctly focus on the political origins of judicial empowerment during the change of political regimes. All of them center on the new order (or equilibrium): consolidated democracy with successful judicial review that protects new constitutional order, supervises political process, resolves interinstitutional and interelite conflicts, and enhances government accountability. But this fixation on democratic order as a product of the change of the political regime does not explain why postcommunist regimes vary wildly in the "democracy-autocracy" continuum, why the same rulers create and destroy constitutional courts, and why these courts vary in terms of their real power across the region, across time, and across policy areas.

CONCLUSION

This zigzagging judicial empowerment is politically constructed. In post-Soviet quadruple transitions, it occurs and persists due to the enormous challenges of these transitions. Facing these challenges, power-hungry rulers quickly shift their short-term needs. Judges do their best to cope with the unstable policy preferences of the rulers and to deliver tangible

Conclusion

benefits to the powerful: legitimizing their reforms and their ruling status, resolving deadlocks, and dealing with "hot potatoes." Delivering these benefits, however, is a daunting task in the fluid institutional context where the public power is dispersed not only among government agencies but also among the emerging private powerbrokers. Thus, the nonlinearity of judicial empowerment also comes from the varied capacity of judges to compel the rest of the state to obey their rulings. And, if judges do not deliver, politicians face few constraints in rendering courts meaningless in the system of governance. This does not mean that constitutional courts are powerless. Under certain conditions, they can check public policies, set the agenda in public deliberation of crucial reforms, and pull their societies toward common human rights regimes. Chapters 3–7 examine how this dynamic nonlinearity of transitional judicial politics has been working to strengthen and to weaken constitutional review tribunals in the late USSR and post-Soviet Russia.

3

Making and Remaking Constitutional Review, Russian-Style

Institution-building during post-Soviet transformation has been likened to "rebuilding the ship at sea."[1] This metaphor, once qualified that the "sea" was stormy, could also describe well the politics of designing and setting up new constitutional courts in postcommunist Europe. Gigantic "waves" could be imagined as rapid and dramatic changes of constitutional frameworks prompted by the collapse of Communist Party rule, introduction of "true" parliamentary supremacy and later the office of the president, and power struggles over the destiny of the USSR. A "ship" caught in a tumultuous sea in need of repair was no less than a state itself, first – the USSR, and later – independent Russia. Rebuilding this "vessel" quickly to make it modern, democratic, capitalist, and law-based, was crucial for the survival of the state. The ship's "crew," pro-Union elites, anti-Union elites in fifteen Soviet republics, and centripetal forces within the Russian Federation, was naturally divided: some argued for incremental repairs to stay afloat, others searched for radical measures to change the course of the drift; some looked for ways of saving the whole ship, others cared most for their own personal survival; some have found scapegoats and others claimed to have discovered the only correct way to salvation.

What is clear from this metaphor is that the short-time horizons of the "crew" (political elites) dominated post-Soviet state-building, which in itself is a long-term task. Initially, postcommunist political and economic elites heavily discounted the future due to rapid political change and an economic crisis accompanied by the euphoria of institutional fixes that

[1] Claus Offe, Jon Elster, and Ulrich Preuß, *Institutional Design in Post-Communist Societies: Rebuilding the Ship at Sea* (New York: Cambridge University Press, 1998).

Creating the USSR Constitutional Supervision Committee 55

would bring post-Leninist states into the club of prosperous nations.[2] The naïve faith that institutional solutions borrowed from the "civilized West" or the "glorious" precommunist past would virtually guarantee economic progress was supported by appeals to just and universal laws that bound the society and the state. Constitutional review was one such institutional solution; its purpose was to enforce these universal laws and to deliver real justice quickly.

The goal of this chapter is to examine the continuity and change of law and politics during the processes of designing and redesigning constitutional review in the late USSR (1988–1990) and in Russia (1990–2006). I identify which features of constitutional review persisted, which ones were rejected and why. As mentioned in the previous chapter, the important aspects of creating the constitutional review tribunal include its jurisdiction and independence, the judicial recruitment procedure, and judicial discretion and the role of the chief justice. Political struggles determine the timing of the introduction of constitutional review and of the subsequent reforms of constitutional court statutes, the patterns of judicial selection, and the mission of the constitutional review body as envisioned by the politicians, judges, and legal elites. I start with the struggles over the design of constitutional review in the late Soviet period. Then I proceed to examine the importance of the short-term power needs of the rulers when they made, attacked, and remade the constitutional court in Yeltsin's Russia. Finally, I explain how short-term political considerations shaped the tinkering with the status of the Russian Constitutional Court (RCC) in Putin's Russia.

CREATING THE USSR CONSTITUTIONAL SUPERVISION COMMITTEE: 1988–1990

Although the first constitutional review body on Russian soil was the USSR Constitutional Supervision Committee (CSC) established in December 1988, the ideas of an external check on the ruler to prevent her arbitrariness date back to the early nineteenth century. Throughout the nineteenth and first quarter of the twentieth century, Russian scholars debated constitutional reforms and proposed the introduction of constitutional review in treatises and constitutional drafts. Russian constitutionalists

---

[2] For the analysis of this phenomenon in the Czech Republic, see Martin Horak, *Governing the Post-Communist City: Institutions and Democratic Development in Prague* (Toronto: University of Toronto Press, 2007).

56   Making and Remaking Constitutional Review, Russian-Style

discussed the advantages and disadvantages of American-style judicial review, concrete versus abstract review, and *a priori* versus *a posteriori* review. Regardless of their attitudes toward the particular model of judicial review, by the early twentieth century, the majority of Russian constitutional scholars accepted the review of the constitutionality of laws as a "logical and normal function of judiciary, as a basic principle of law."[3]

However, the October 1917 Bolshevik coup suppressed these prejudicial review voices by affirming the supremacy of the Soviets.[4] Under the first USSR Constitution of 1924, the USSR Supreme Court received limited powers to advise the USSR Central Executive Committee on alleged unconstitutionality of acts issued by central and republican executive bodies. With the entrenchment of Stalin's dictatorship and the establishment of the Soviet Procuracy in 1933, the Supreme Court lost its (however limited and weak) oversight powers of the executive.[5] Proposals to introduce some kind of constitutional review in the USSR resurfaced during the constitution-drafting processes in 1964 (thwarted by Khrushchev's ouster) and in 1977, albeit they were never published and received no public discussion.[6]

---

[3] Isaak Gurvich, "Severo-Amerikanskie Soedinennye Shtaty," [The United States of North America] in *Gosudarstvennyi stroi v Zapadnoi Evrope i Soedinennykh Shtatakh. T. 3* [Governance in Western Europe and the United States] (S.-Pb., 1907), p. 107. See also Lev A. Shalland, "Verkhovnyi sud i konstitutsionnoe gosudarstvo," [Supreme Court and Constitutional State] in *Konstitutsionnoe gosudarstvo: Sbornik statei*, 2nd ed. [Constitutional State: Collection of Articles] (S.-Pb., 1905), pp. 412–421; Vsevolod N. Durdenevskii, "Sudebnaia proverka konstitutsionnosti zakona," [Judicial Review of the Constitutionality of the Law] *Voprosy prava. Zhurnal nauchnoi iurisprudentsii*, vol. 11, no. 3 (1912), p. 89; and Sergei A. Kotliarevskii, "Umy i palaty," [Minds and Chambers] *Poliarnaia zvezda*, 1906, reprinted in *Novoe vremia*, nos. 19–20 (1995), p. 59.

[4] See Mikhail Mitiukov, *K istorii konstitutsionnogo pravosudiia Rossii* [On the History of the Constitutional Justice in Russia] (Moskva: ATSO, 2002), pp. 18–46. On the history of constitutional review in the Soviet Union, see Mikhail Mitiukov, *Predtecha konstitutsionnogo pravosudiia: vzgliady, proekty i institutsionalnye predposylki (30 – nachalo 90-h gg. XX v.)* [Forerunner of the Constitutional Justice: Views, Drafts, and Institutional Prerequisites (1930 – Beginning of the 1990s)] (Moskva: Formula Prava, 2006).

[5] Peter H. Solomon, Jr., "The U.S.S.R. Supreme Court: History, Role, and Future Prospects," *American Journal of Comparative Law*, vol. 38 (1990), pp. 127–142. For the best analysis of this period, published in Russian, see Mikhail Mitiukov, *Sudebnyi konstitutsionnyi nadzor 1924–1933 gg.: voprosy istorii, teorii i praktiki* [Judicial Constitutional Supervision 1924–1933: Questions of History, Theory, and Practice] (Moskva: Formula prava, 2005).

[6] Boris Lazarev, "Komitet konstitutsionnogo nadzora SSSR (Podvodia itogi)," [USSR Constitutional Supervision Committee (Arriving at Conclusions)], *Gosudarstvo i pravo*, no. 5 (May 1992), pp. 21–34; Aleksandr Danilov and Aleksandr Pyzhikov, "Neizvestnyi konstitutsionnyi proekt," [Unknown Constitutional Draft] *Gosudarstvo i pravo*, no. 1 (January 2002), p. 88.

Creating the USSR Constitutional Supervision Committee   57

Gorbachev's agenda to "renew Socialism" through stronger legislatures, *glasnost*, and *perestroyka* opened new debates on legal reform.[7] Indeed, Gorbachev started his *perestroyka* by slamming the bureaucracy's arbitrariness and sabotage of Soviet statutes as an impediment to swift economic reforms. This bureaucracy-bashing was directed at those who pursued their narrow departmental interests (*vedomstvennost*) and those who defended the interests of their local constituencies (*mestnichestvo*) at the expense of overarching public interest. The processes of empowering elected legislatures, drafting numerous laws to spearhead political and economic renovation, and overseeing bureaucratic compliance with *perestroyka* laws brought lawyers closer to policy making circles.

Constitutional review of legal acts figured prominently in this agenda. Soviet legal scholars argued that constitutional review could help *perestroyka* laws by "cleansing" the Soviet legal system of executive regulations that violated Soviet laws and international human rights standards and by advising the legislative branch on the constitutionality of proposed statutes. To achieve this mission, some scholars proposed to empower the Supreme Court to exercise constitutional review,[8] some advocated the introduction of a separate quasijudicial Constitutional Supervision Committee following the Hungarian model,[9] and others supported the establishment of a separate Constitutional Court following the Polish and German models.[10] Although disagreeing on a particular institutional arrangement of constitutional review, most scholars during this period agreed that this review power should extend only to the regulations of the executive branch. Professor Iurii Shulzhenko of the Institute of Law and State at the Academy of Sciences summed up this consensus: "The

---

[7] Peter H. Solomon, Jr.," Gorbachev's Legal Revolution," *Canadian Business Law Journal*, vol. 17, no. 2 (December 1990), pp. 184–194.

[8] Vladimir Kudriavtsev, "Pravovaia sistema: puti perestroiki," [Legal System: The Ways of Perestroyka], *Pravda*, December 5, 1986, p. 3; Vladimir I. Terebilov, "Zakon i tolko zakon," [Law and Only Law], *Pravda*, December 12, 1987; Vladimir Tumanov, "Sudebnyi kontrol za konstitutsionnostiu normativnykh aktov," [Judicial Review of Constitutionality of Normative Acts], *Sovetskoe gosudarstvo i pravo*, no. 3 (March 1988), p. 14; Mark Orzikh, Mark Cherkes, and Anatolii Vasilev, "Pravovaia okhrana Konstitutsii v sotsialisticheskom gosudarstve," [The Legal Protection of the Constitution in the Socialist State], *ibid.*, no. 6 (June 1988), p. 10.

[9] Boris Kurashvili, "Novshestva vyzyvaiut somneniia," [Innovations Raise Doubts] *Izvestiia*, November 15, 1988, p. 2; S. Emelianov, "Uchitsia politicheskoi rabote," [To Study Political Work] *Sovetskaia Rossiia*, November 16, 1988, p. 4; Valerii Savitskii, "Mozhno i Komitet, no ..." [Maybe the Committee But ...], *Izvestiia*, November 13, 1988, p. 2.

[10] "Iuridicheskaia nauka i praktika v usloviiakh perestroiki," [Legal Science and Practice under the Conditions of Perestroyka], *Kommunist*, no. 14 (1987), p. 44; P. Lebedev, "Nuzhen sud!" [Court Is Needed!] *Izvestiia*, November 13, 1988, p. 2.

functioning of the separate constitutional review tribunals must be designed in such a way so that the parliament has the supreme role in the sphere of constitutional review and the parliament alone has the power to decide the issue of the constitutionality of legislation."[11]

Constitutional advisers introduced constitutional review into the Soviet power map to police bureaucracy and to affirm legislative supremacy by keeping the statutes out of the purview of the constitutional review body. Gorbachev quickly approved this legal innovation, and the constitutional amendments of December 1988 established the USSR Constitutional Supervision Committee (CSC).[12] The mission of the Committee at that time was to ensure "strict compliance of laws and executive regulations with requirements of the USSR Constitution" in order to guarantee the supremacy of the legislature as a "foundation of socialist statehood and self-government."[13] At the time, the idea of however limited quasijudicial constitutional review was so inspiring that even reformers applauded it. For example, Andrei Sakharov, an eminent Soviet nuclear physicist, dissident and human rights activist, repeatedly said that he wanted to work in the Committee, and that the office of the chair of the CSC was the most important in the country and ought to be occupied by a person with absolute inner freedom and absolute honesty.[14]

Despite such a quick entrenchment of the CSC in the constitution and a noble task of the Committee, it took the USSR parliament – the *Supreme Soviet* – another full year to draft a bill on the CSC and another half-a-year to appoint its members. The 18-month delay reflected the compromises surrounding the creation of a working constitutional review tribunal in the context of radical political reform and the collapsing statehood of the Soviet Union. By that time, centripetal "waves" among Soviet Union Republics seriously threatened not only the "socialist" nature of the USSR but the survival of the Soviet Union as a state. Republics that aspired to

---

[11] Iurii Shulzhenko, "Avtoritet Osnovnogo zakona," [The Authority of Basic Law], *Moskovskaia pravda*, June 14, 1988.

[12] Constitutional amendments specified the status, powers, and the composition of the USSR CSC. See Zakon SSSR of December 1, 1988 "Ob izmeneniiakh i dopolneniiakh Konstitutsii SSSR," *Vedomosti Verkhovnogo Soveta SSSR*, no. 49 (1988), item 727. For the English translation, see "Comparative Text of the 1977 USSR Constitution with Draft and Final Amendments," *Review of Socialist Law*, vol. 15, no. 1 (1989), p. 75.

[13] *Materialy XIX vsesoiuznoi konferentsii Kommunisticheskoi partii Sovetskogo Soiuza* [Materials of the 19th All-Union Conference of the Communist Party of the Soviet Union] (Moskva: Politicheskaia literatura, 1988), pp. 119, 146.

[14] L. M. Batkin, compiler, *Konstitutsionnye idei Andreia Sakharova* [Constitutional Ideas of Andrei Sakharov] (Moskva: Novella, 1990), p. 81.

independence from the USSR simply distrusted another top-level Union body to scrutinize their actions. Other republics hesitated to empower constitutional review before they would gain more rights in the renewed Soviet Union. Conflicts among radical reformers and hardline Communists further slowed down the constitutional engineering in the final years of the USSR. Hardliners could not reconcile constitutional review with the parliamentary supremacy and delayed the introduction of the CSC. Reformers were also divided: some advocated the ratification of a new constitution before the appointment of the Committee, while others called for a separate constitutional court.[15]

When the USSR law on the CSC was finally passed in December 1989, it disappointed legal experts because of the weak constitutional review powers (mainly advisory without any sanctions) it granted to the Committee.[16] Although this law expanded the mission of the CSC to monitor local defiance of Union laws and to assist in drafting the new Union Treaty, the Committee did not receive any binding or suspensive powers on republican noncompliance with Union laws. The Committee received the power to issue *ex officio* final and binding decisions only in cases of Union regulations violating human rights.[17] The drafters of the CSC statute assured parliamentary supremacy by keeping the process of the recruitment of the Committee members under the tight control of the USSR Supreme Soviet chairman.[18]

However, the CSC began its work only in May 1990 after the USSR Supreme Soviet elected the Committee members representing the majority of Soviet Union Republics and several Russian regions without any discussion – a sign that the Communist leadership approved all nominees.[19] Most of the new appointees were law professors – it was alleged that only law professors could be free from the bureaucratic politics of

---

[15] Mitiukov, *Predtecha konstitutsionnogo pravosudia*, pp. 58–108.

[16] Lazarev, "Komitet konstitutsionnogo nadzora SSSR," p. 23. Mikhail Gorbachev also later admitted "a serious error" in not proceeding with a full-blown constitutional court. See his *Life and Reforms. Volume 1* (Moscow: Novosti, 1995), p. 491.

[17] The CSC could not, on its own initiative, review the cases of alleged violations of human rights by the legislation of republics.

[18] D. A. Kerimov and A. I. Ekimov, "Konstitutsionnyi nadzor v SSSR," [Constitutional Supervision in the USSR] *Sovetskoe gosudarstvo i pravo*, no. 9 (September 1990), p. 8.

[19] Herbert Hausmaninger, "From the Soviet Committee on Constitutional Supervision to the Russian Constitutional Court," *Cornell International Law Journal*, vol. 25, no. 2 (Spring 1992), p. 307. Baltic Republics refused to send their representatives to the Committee, and the Latvian Parliament suspended the power of the Committee to review the laws of Latvia.

the executive branch and could apply constitutional norms and international legal rules authoritatively and apolitically, just like in the European constitutional courts. Not surprisingly, the chairman of the CSC Sergei Alekseev, a renowned legal theoretician, in his first interviews announced that the Committee would stay away from politics and would focus on the human rights cases to demonstrate that constitutional review in the collapsing federation under the flexible and outdated constitution could improve the protection of individual rights. Chairman Alekseev insisted that the Committee could achieve this by combining international human rights standards with reformed constitutional norms, and by considering cases on its own initiative in the absence of a constitutional complaint.[20] He used his office successfully enough: the majority of the USSR CSC decisions, which will be examined in Chapter 4, were issued on the Committee's initiative and struck down federal and local administrative acts violating human rights.[21] Still, the majority of legal elites, including the CSC members, perceived the Committee as a temporary measure that would give way to a constitutional court with broad powers to issue final and binding decisions.[22] In fact, the drafts of the Union Treaty published until the August 1991 coup d'etat had already contained provisions for the new full-blown Constitutional Court of the USSR. However, following the failure of the August 1991 coup, during which Communist hardliners attempted to stop Gorbachev's reforms of the Soviet federation, the authority of the Union's institutions drastically deteriorated. Constituent parts of the USSR gained more bargaining power and deleted any mentioning of the Constitutional Court in the last draft Union Treaty published in November 1991. They envisioned a loose confederation and

---

[20] See, for example, Sergei Alekseev, "What Is the Constitution?" *Moscow News*, May 6–13, 1990, p. 6; and Iurii Feofanov, "Interviu s S. S. Alekseevym," *Izvestiia*, June 17, 1990, p. 2.

[21] The USSR CSC functioned until December 23, 1991, and produced a total of twenty-nine decisions and statements. See, for example, Lazarev, "Komitet konstitutsionnogo nadzora SSSR"; Hausmaninger, "From the Soviet Committee"; Peter B. Maggs, "Enforcing the Bill of Rights in the Twilight of the Soviet Union," *University of Illinois Law Review*, vol. 4, no. 4 (1991), pp. 1049–1063; William Kitchin, "Legal Reform and the Expansion of Judicial Power in Russia," in C. Neal Tate and Torbjörn Vallinder, eds., *The Global Expansion of Judicial Power* (New York: New York University Press, 1995), pp. 421–40; Cheryl A. Thomas, "The Attempt to Institute Judicial Review in the Former USSR," *ibid.*, pp. 441–459.

[22] See, for example, Kerimov and Ekimov, "Konstitutsionnyi nadzor v SSSR," p. 11; and "Konstitutsionnyi nadzor – shag k pravovomu gosudarstvu," [Constitutional Supervision – A Step toward the Law-Based State], *Kommunist*, no. 4 (1990), pp. 68–76.

proceeded to set up their own constitutional courts. By November 1991, Latvia, Ukraine, and Kyrgyzstan already had established their own constitutional courts in their constitutions, while Russia, as discussed in the next section, managed to both establish its own tribunal and appoint justices.[23] In short, the growing diffusion of political power between the center and republics, the short-term goals of political actors, and the mounting institutional uncertainty about the future of the USSR resulted in discarding the idea of constitutional review at the Union level.

To sum up, the design of the USSR CSC reflected the uncertainties and contradictions of the late Soviet period. The power diffusion within the last years of the USSR produced a very weak form of constitutional review, contrary to the existing theories of judicial empowerment. The Committee was charged with a noble task of guarding constitutional order but its powers were largely advisory and suspensive. Its status within the government and society as an "assistant to the legislature" was low while the expectations of strong constitutional review were high. Moreover, growing power dispersion resulted in the rejection of constitutional review at the Union level by the fall of 1991 both in the draft Union treaties and in practice. Faced with the establishment of constitutional courts across the collapsing USSR and Russian regions, the Committee dissolved itself at the end of 1991.

DESIGNING THE 1ST RUSSIAN CONSTITUTIONAL COURT: 1990–1991

Although the 1978 Russian constitution was "automatically" amended in October 1989 to establish a Russian clone of the USSR CSC, a few members of the superlegislative Congress of People's Deputies (CPD) elected in May 1990 in Russia's first competitive elections were in a hurry to make the Committee operational.[24] At that period, which signified a "romantic" phase of Russian constitutional reforms (1990), most lawmakers insisted

---

[23] Mitiukov, *Predtecha konstitutsionnogo pravosudia*, p. 122.

[24] The 1,068-member Congress of People's Deputies had broad legislative, appointment and impeachment powers. It met 2–3 times a year and sat for 2–3 weeks at a time. When the Congress was not in session, the 252-member Supreme Soviet performed its legislative functions. See Thomas F. Remington, *The Russian Parliament: Institutional Evolution in a Transitional Regime, 1989–1999* (New Haven, CT: Yale University Press, 2001); and Josephine T. Andrews, *When Majorities Fail: The Russian Parliament, 1990–1993* (Cambridge, UK: Cambridge University Press, 2002).

on drafting and passing their own laws instead of copying the USSR templates.[25] The Congress set up a Constitutional Commission headed by Boris Yeltsin, who headed the Russian Parliament (*Supreme Soviet*) at the time, to draft a new Russian constitution. This Commission was to work in parallel with the Supreme Soviet that was to draft urgent amendments to the 1978 RSFSR constitution.[26] This division of labor provided three arenas for struggles between proconstitutional review groups and their opponents as well as three points of access for legal elites whose expertise was needed to prepare constitutional amendments: the Constitutional Commission, the Supreme Soviet, and the Congress of People's Deputies. This structure of legislative process simultaneously enhanced and complicated the process of creating and staffing the Constitutional Court because actors whose proposals were defeated at one forum could advance their proposals in the other two law-making arenas.

To overcome these complications, the supporters of the full-blown constitutional court chose to introduce this tribunal in Russia through the back door. They buried several clauses on the federal Constitutional Court in the by-laws (*Reglament*) of the Russian Supreme Soviet that were passed in October of 1990.[27] The opponents of the constitutional court objected that such a court threatened parliamentary supremacy and a unified Russian judicial system. But the author of these clauses, Iurii Rudkin, the Deputy Chairman of the RSFSR Supreme Soviet Legislation Committee (SSLC), managed to convince most of his fellow legislators that a court rather than a quasijudicial committee was needed to effectively safeguard the foundations of Russian federalism.[28] Building on his success, Rudkin together with Mikhail Mitiukov, an MP from Eastern Siberia, quickly proposed to establish the constitutional court through

---

[25] Ilia Shablinskii, *Predely vlasti: borba za rossiiskuiu konstitutsionnuiu reformu: 1989–1995 gg.* [The Limits of Power: The Struggle for the Russian Constitutional Reform: 1989–1995] (Moskva: TsKI MONF, 1997), p. 32.

[26] The work of the Constitutional Commission is documented in the six-volume *Iz istorii sozdaniia Konstitutsii Rossiiskoi Federatsii. Konstitutsionnaia Komissiia: stenogrammy, materially, dokumenty (1990–1993 gg.)* [On the History of Creating the RF Constitution. Constitutional Commission: Stenographic Reports, Materials, Documents (1990–1993] (Moskva: Wolters Kluwer, 2007).

[27] Mitiukov, *K istorii konstitutsionnogo pravosudiia Rossii*, pp. 53–54. Interestingly, some of the supporters came from the Russian regions, which soon proceeded to set up their own regional constitutional courts (Komi Republic, St. Petersburg, and Sverdlovsk Oblast). See Alexei Trochev, "Less Democracy, More Courts: A Puzzle of Judicial Review in Russia," *Law and Society Review*, vol. 38, no. 3 (September 2004), pp. 513–548.

[28] Iurii Rudkin, a law professor from Yaroslavl – a region in central Russia, has been a RCC Justice since 1991.

the constitutional amendments at the 2nd Congress of People's Deputies in December 1990.[29] They lobbied for a thirteen-member tribunal with a detailed list of broad, binding powers of abstract a priori and a posteriori constitutional review over laws and executive regulations.

The Constitutional Commission approved their haste in entrenching the tribunal but it rejected the insertion of the detailed list of these powers in the 1978 constitution because they could undermine the Commission's plans to establish a strong federal presidency in Russia. On the one hand, the Commission shared the vision of a powerful constitutional court. A quick introduction of the Constitutional Court in Russia would set it apart from the USSR with its powerless CSC, from several regions within Russia that planned to set up their own regional CSCs, and from other parts of the Soviet Union that lacked constitutional review tribunals. Having its own Constitutional Court, a tribunal independent from the USSR authorities and in charge of protecting the Russian constitution from them, would be an important symbolic gain in Russia's struggle for sovereignty.[30] Valerii Zorkin,[31] who headed the experts' group of the Commission, favored a U.S.-style presidential republic with institutional guarantees of separation of powers among the legislative, executive, and judicial branches of government. His vision of matching the constitutional framework of Russia with that of the world's superpower paralleled the personal ambitions of Boris Yeltsin, aspiring to circumvent Gorbachev's constitutional reforms at the USSR level. On the other hand, the Constitutional Commission did not want to specify the powers and the status of the Constitutional Court before outlining the contours of the soon-to-be-introduced Russian presidency. It planned to define the powers of the Court in a package with the draft law on the presidency: the president would nominate justices and the CPD would elect them after extensive consultations with the regions and parliamentary blocs; the justices would enjoy life tenure; and the Court would determine the legal grounds for the impeachment of the president and for the repealing of presidential decrees by the Congress. This constitutional design undermined the supremacy of a newly minted Russian legislature because it made the presidency and the Court equal to the

---

[29] Mikhail Mitiukov, a former local judge and a law professor from Khakassiia – a region in Eastern Siberia, represented both Yeltsin and Putin in the RCC in 1996 and between 1998 and 2005. He repeatedly failed to be appointed to the bench of the RCC.

[30] Shablinskii, *Predely vlasti*, p. 52.

[31] Zorkin chaired the Constitutional Court in 1991–1993 and was twice reelected to head the Court – in February 2003 and February 2006. See Chapters 4 and 5 of this book.

Parliament and was highly controversial, making it impossible to establish the presidency right away.

This combination of the Court's prosovereignty and propresidency ties legitimized the quick establishment of the Court in the eyes of a majority of Russian political elites. This included archrivals such as Russian Communists and Boris Yeltsin, who was unbeatable for the president's office, opposed Gorbachev's policies, and aspired to reform "sovereign" Russia. However, propresidency and prosovereignty linkages were not enough for the creation of the Constitutional Court. Its designers also had to persuade the powerful parliament that it could keep this tribunal under control. That they succeeded is reflected in the text of the constitutional amendment passed by the 2nd Congress in December 1990. Amended Article 119 of the constitution had two new short provisions – that "the Constitutional Court shall be elected by the Congress of People's Deputies" and that the Court powers "shall be defined in a separate statute confirmed by the Congress."

Similar to the quick establishment of the USSR CSC in the USSR Constitution, the establishment of the Russian Constitutional Court was achieved quickly and without serious opposition. And similar to the passage of the law on the USSR constitutional supervision, the process of enacting the Constitutional Court statute was a much more complicated matter. As we all know, "the devil is in the details," and the details of creating the first constitutional court in Russia proved to be controversial albeit for different reasons than the creation of the Union's CSC. It took four lengthy legislative sessions to enact the RCC Act and an additional meeting of the Congress to elect the Court (see Table 3.1 for the timeframe of designing the 1st RCC). Unlike in the CSC case, the Russian regions took an active part in drafting the RCC statute and nominating their candidates for the bench of the new court. The binding nature of constitutional review as a real check on other branches of government undermined parliamentary supremacy and the authority of law-enforcement agencies and regular courts. Although the drafters of the RCC statute offered incentives to the increasingly powerful Supreme Soviet and the CPD, they offered nothing to the Procuracy and the Supreme Court.[32] Preventing the potential accusations of too powerful a Court, they urged that the Court would

---

[32] The Procuracy, headed by the Russian Procurator General, is a government agency in charge of supervising the observance of law by all government bodies and public officials and conducting criminal investigations. Throughout 1991, it faced serious threats of being abolished. For more, see Gordon B. Smith, *Reforming the Russian Legal System* (New York: Cambridge University Press, 1996), pp. 104–128.

Designing the 1st Russian Constitutional Court

TABLE 3.1. *Making and breaking the Russian Constitutional Court, 1990–1993*

October 24, 1990	By-law (*Reglament*) of the Russian Supreme Soviet mentions the Russian Constitutional Court (RCC) for the first time.
December 15, 1990	Amendments to the 1978 RSFSR Constitution establish the RCC.
March 25, 1991	First discussion of the bill on the RCC at the Supreme Soviet Legislation Committee.
May 6, 1991	The Supreme Soviet approves the bill on the RCC but rejects the power of the Court to review the constitutionality of the "law-application practice."
May 21, 1991	The RCC Act is published and includes the power of the Court to review the "law-application practice."
May 25, 1991	Boris Yeltsin proposes fifteen judicial nominees to the 4th Congress of People's Deputies for the bench of the RCC. The Congress fails to approve the Court Act despite the fact it was presented with four different versions of the bill and sends it back to the Supreme Soviet.
June 27–28, 1991	The Supreme Soviet discusses and approves the RCC Act and asks the Congress of People's Deputies to decide on the power of the Court to review the constitutionality of the "law-application practice."
July 5, 1991	The Supreme Soviet selects twenty-one judicial nominations to be elected by the Congress of People's Deputies for the fifteen-seat RCC
July 12, 1991	The 5th Congress of People's Deputies approves the bill on the RCC with the power of the Court to review the "law-application practice."
October 28–30, 1991	The 5th Congress of People's Deputies reviews twenty-three judicial nominations and elects thirteen RCC justices in three rounds of voting.
April 1, 1992	The Supreme Soviet fails to approve the bill specifying the sanctions for noncompliance with the decisions of the RCC.
April 21, 1992	Amendments to the 1978 Constitution empower the RCC to resolve jurisdictional disputes between government bodies and to review the constitutionality of political parties and regional laws. The 6th Congress of People's Deputies fails to approve the bill specifying the sanctions for noncompliance with the RCC decisions.
December 9, 1992	Amendments to the 1978 Constitution empower the Supreme Soviet to suspend decrees of the Russian president until the RCC confirms their constitutionality.
October 7, 1993	President Yeltsin suspends the operation of the RCC and proposes to transfer the power of constitutional review to the Russian Supreme Court.

66 Making and Remaking Constitutional Review, Russian-Style

not delve into politics and would deal strictly with questions of law.[33] This focus on legality, of course, meant the invasion of the new tribunal into the traditional domain of the law-enforcement agencies and other courts and created, in these bodies, a strong allergy to the Constitutional Court for years to come.

Following the results of the March 17, 1991 referendum, in which 70 percent of voters favored the introduction of the Russian presidency, the SSLC moved swiftly to draft the bills on the presidency and the Constitutional Court. In a stark contrast with the vague and brief 1989 USSR Law on Constitutional Supervision, the authors of the Court statute prepared a detailed draft with a strong constitutional court.[34] The draft envisioned that the Constitutional Court, staffed with judges appointed for life and acting independently from other branches of government and from the USSR authorities, would determine the constitutionality of both law on the books and law "in action." Thus, the Constitutional Court had the power to check the constitutionality of federal and regional legal acts, international agreements, law-application practice, and actions/decisions of high federal and regional government officers. The Court also had the power to take cases on its own initiative and reject petitions on the grounds of inexpedience. Its judgments were final and binding, and its chief justice had important powers of assigning the cases to the justices, calling the Court meetings, and managing other internal aspects of the Court's work.[35] Importantly, individuals could request the constitutional review of this so-called law-application practice only if this practice was a routine matter, not just an isolated incident, and only after the injured party exhausted all other available venues of redress. This proposed power of the Court to consider individual appeals was a dramatic change from the USSR CSC, which lacked the power to accept constitutional complaints from individuals.

When the authors of the bill on the RCC introduced the bill to the Supreme Soviet on May 6, 1991, they immediately encountered a strong

---

[33] Mitiukov, *K istorii konstitutsionnogo pravosudiia Rossii*, pp. 75–77.

[34] Sergei Pashin, a young lawyer, drafted the original version of the RCC statute at the request of SSLC member Boris Zolotukhin. For Pashin's defense of his draft, which was dramatically changed in subsequent legislative debates, see Sergei Pashin, "Sudia 'sudit' zakony," [Judge "Judges" Laws] *Narodnyi deputat*, no. 12 (1991), pp. 69–72; and Sergei Pashin, "Pora stanovleniia," [Time of Formation] *Iuridicheskaia gazeta*, no. 12 (1993), p. 5.

[35] For a critique of the 1991 RCC Act, see, for example, Alexander Blankenagel, "*Detstvo, otrochestvo, iunost*" *Rossiiskogo Konstitutsionnogo Suda* ["Childhood, Adolescence, Youth" of the Russian Constitutional Court] (Moskva: TsKI MONF, 1996).

Designing the 1st Russian Constitutional Court 67

opposition to such a powerful tribunal. Short-term power needs dominated these debates: how to protect the supremacy of the newly minted parliament against the soon-to-be-introduced presidency and the constitutional court; how to protect the authority of the law-enforcement agencies and regular courts; and finally, how to appoint the "right" justices to the RCC. From the beginning of the debates of the bill the opponents of full-blown constitutional review managed to delete the clause that the RCC decisions were superior to federal statutes.[36] At the 4th Congress of People's Deputies (May 25, 1991) legislators from the left and from the right attacked the Constitutional Court as too powerful. They alleged that a constitutional review power to repeal unconstitutional laws deprived the legislature of its power to make laws and invaded the legislative authority in a "hidden, indirect way."[37] Communist Iuurii Slobodkin, a judge from Moscow Oblast, demanded that the RCC be given only advisory powers similar to the USSR CSC jurisdiction. A full-blown judicial review, in his view, amounted to impermissible "commandeering towards the legislature." Pro-Yeltsin Deputy Mazaev also insisted on the power of the legislature to override RCC decisions.[38] However, pro-Court legislators managed to reject these proposals at the second consideration of the bill in the Supreme Soviet on June 27, 1991 and at the subsequent confirmation of the bill at the 5th Congress on July 12. Another compromise was struck over the role of the Constitutional Court in the legislative-executive disputes. Under the bill, the Congress could impeach the president and repeal his decrees only when the RCC determined that the presidential actions were unconstitutional. Similarly, the Supreme Soviet could repeal presidential decrees only after the RCC found a presidential decree nonconforming with the constitution. These constitutional review powers effectively made the new tribunal equal to if not above the legislature, which drew considerable opposition from various parliamentary groups. The 4th CPD defeated the RCC bill but at the same time amended the 1978 constitution: the Congress received the power to repeal presidential decrees without RCC approval while the Supreme Soviet had to secure an RCC decision regarding the unconstitutionality of presidential acts in order to repeal them. Amended Article 121-10

---

[36] Mitiukov, *K istorii konstitutsionnogo pravosudiia Rossii*, p. 79.

[37] *Ibid.*, p. 85. These politicians were correct in their predictions. European constitutional courts also cannot do their work "without invading the job of the legislature." See Alec Stone Sweet, *Governing with Judges: Constitutional Politics in Europe* (New York: Oxford University Press, 2000).

[38] Mitiukov, *K istorii konstitutsionnogo pravosudiia Rossii*, p. 90.

68   *Making and Remaking Constitutional Review, Russian-Style*

made it impossible to impeach the Russian president without the Court's approval.[39]

A much stronger opposition to the powerful constitutional court came from the representatives of the Procuracy and the regular courts who staunchly objected to the constitutional review of their decisions through the proposed power of the RCC to check the constitutionality of the "law-application practice."[40] They mounted such serious resistance that the SSLC Chairman Sergei Shakhrai, in order to save the bill, promised to delete the jurisdiction of Constitutional Court over "law-application practice" as "inhibiting the freedom of inner conviction of the judges of all courts" and threatening to overload the docket of a new tribunal.[41] But he did not keep his promise and empowered the RCC through the backdoor – the published version of the RCC Act contained the deleted clauses.[42] The law-enforcement lobby struck back 3 weeks later at the 4th Congress of People's Deputies that was due to confirm the Court statute. They complained that the jurisdiction of the new Court intruded into the prerogatives of criminal and civil justice administration, led to "judge-made" law, and overburdened the Court.[43] They defeated the bill in four different versions, resulting in its remission back to the Supreme Soviet where they repeated their major offensive. Masking the nature of their objections to this review power by the concern that the new tribunal would be flooded with individual complaints, left-wing judge Slobodkin and Yeltsin's protégé Valentin Stepankov, the Russian Procurator General, summarized the attitudes of the majority of regular judges, procurators, and the police. Slobodkin insisted that only regular courts should deal with individual complaints. In his view, the RCC jurisdiction in this area would discredit the Supreme Court. Stepankov accused the fifteen-member RCC of usurping the power to determine the constitutionality of the "law-application practice," in soliciting individual appeals of regular court decisions and in replacing the Supreme Court as a court of last resort.[44] They nearly won this debate – the Supreme Soviet approved

---

[39] Zakon RSFSR of May 24, 1991 "Ob izmeneniiakh i dopolneniiakh Konstitutsii (osnovnogo zakona) RSFSR," *VSND i VS RSFSR*, 1991, no. 22, item 776.

[40] Note that the USSR CSC powers were limited to those acts that fell outside the scope of procuratorial supervision. Therefore, the USSR Procuracy was not against the CSC jurisdiction.

[41] Cited in Mitiukov, *K istorii konstitutsionnogo pravosudiia Rossii*, pp. 78–79.

[42] Zakon RSFSR "O Konstitutsionnom sude RSFSR," *VSND i VS RSFSR*, no. 19 (1991), item 621.

[43] Mitiukov, *K istorii konstitutsionnogo pravosudiia Rossii*, pp. 91–92.

[44] *Ibid.*

Designing the 1st Russian Constitutional Court

the bill after voting to deprive the RCC jurisdiction in this matter and to allow a single legislator to petition the Court. But the authors of the RCC bill reopened the debate, fervently lobbied for the inclusion of the power to review the constitutionality of the "law-application practice," and persuaded the legislature to hold another vote. As a result of their efforts, the Supreme Soviet voted to let the next Congress of People's Deputies decide whether to keep this RCC jurisdiction.[45] A week later, after intensive lobbying by the RCC designers, the 5th Congress approved the Court's power to review the "law-application practice," thus subjecting the Supreme Court and the Procuracy to constitutional review, and confirmed the RCC statute.[46]

Unlike this seemingly technical rivalry among the law-enforcement bodies, the debate over appointing judges to the new constitutional tribunal was much clearer for the majority of lawmakers. Once it became clear that the RCC would be activated quickly to overpower the USSR authority and to balance the power of the presidency, most legislators rushed to submit their preferred picks for the bench of the constitutional court. Linking the appointment of the justices to the confirmation of the RCC bill ensured that politicians had to select their nominees quickly and in the process of confirming the statute while candidates to the bench had to impress legislators by ensuring their loyalty to them and to the cause of Russia's independence.[47] Legislators already knew the list of nominees selected by the parliamentary factions when debating the statute, however, and they could tinker with the rules of judicial selection both to appoint their preferred nominees and to block their enemies from gaining a seat at the RCC. This combination of short-term personal affinities with long-term goals of constitutional design ensured that a new Court would be accountable to the legislature, at least at the stage of judicial recruitment. Boris Yeltsin presented a list of fifteen judicial nominations to the Supreme Soviet on May 17, 1991, after extensive discussions in parliamentary committees and 4 days before the opening of the 4th Congress that was due to confirm the RCC statute and to elect justices. This list created a stir among the CPD members, who disagreed with the proposed nominations and suspected that Boris Yeltsin would nominate justices loyal to him as a future Russian president, and they defeated the bill, as was discussed above. The failure to confirm the bill was so unexpected

---

[45] *Ibid.*, pp. 92–93. [46] *Ibid.*, pp. 96–97.
[47] This meant that persons perceived as the members of Gorbachev's team were excluded from the nominations.

70   Making and Remaking Constitutional Review, Russian-Style

that the SSLC Chairman Shakhrai publicly accused legislators of burying the RCC statute, and Boris Yeltsin withdrew his list of judicial nominees.[48] This defeat meant that numerous parliamentary groups rather than one power center controlled the process of judicial recruitment. At the same time, they were busy with bargaining over the rules of selecting judges for the new tribunal. Following the defeat of the RCC bill, the SSLC received more than 180 proposed amendments to the RCC bill – all in a matter of 5 weeks![49] Two-fifths of them dealt with judicial status and recruitment, while other proposals narrowed the powers of the Court, limited the finality and binding force of its judgments, and expanded access to the Court. The SSLC rejected most of these changes as incompatible with judicial independence and persuaded the legislature to approve the RCC bill without them.

On the passage of the RCC statute, three legislative committees[50] discussed thirty-eight judicial nominations, eleven of which were sponsored by the parliamentary blocs. Among them were twenty-nine holders of graduate degrees in law, eleven legislators, seventeen legal scholars, eleven federal government officials, and nine officers of regional government. On July 5, twenty-one candidates were recommended for election to the fifteen-member tribunal. However, the legislature failed to elect the Court right away because the position of the Supreme Soviet chairman remained vacant in the aftermath of Boris Yeltsin's election to the presidency on June 12, 1991. Naturally, the potential candidates for this position did not want to rush and wanted to keep judicial recruitment under their control. Moreover, the legislators were keen to fight for the inclusion of their favorite candidates on the bench. Major disagreements on whether and how to guarantee regional representation on the bench also slowed down the process of appointing judges. All of this led to the politicization of judicial recruitment, which culminated in the election of the justices at

---

[48] Ibid., p. 86.

[49] Jane Henderson, "The First Russian Constitutional Court: Hopes and Aspirations," in Rein Müllerson, Malgosia Fitzmaurice, and Mads Andenas, eds., Constitutional Reform and International Law in Central and Eastern Europe (The Hague: Kluwer Law International, 1998), pp. 105–121, at 116. Henderson notes that age limits for the RCC Justices were almost "the most controversial issue" during the legislative debates. This controversy reflects the efforts of legal elites to expand the pool of eligible candidates for the RCC seats and to overcome the popular rejection of "gerontocracy" of the late Soviet period when old and incapacitated Communist Party leaders ruled the USSR in the early 1980s.

[50] SSLC, Committee on Legality and Combating Crime, and Committee on Human Rights.

Designing the 1st Russian Constitutional Court

the second leg of the 5th Congress of People's Deputies on October 29. The newly elected chairman of the Supreme Soviet, Ruslan Khasbulatov, presented a list of twenty-three nominees to the legislature.[51] Unlike silent Soviet legislators during the elections of the USSR CSC, the Russian lawmakers probed judicial nominees very rigorously. But the key players in this process ensured their control of the confirmation hearings by limiting each of the nominees to a 5-minute question period from the floor. As one judge told the author, "We knew the rules of the game: if you wanted to run for the seat at the RCC, you had to get the approval of the parliamentary factions."[52] According to Mitiukov, who introduced the list of nominees, political blocs captured the nomination process, pushing for their favorites and ignoring the professional qualities of the nominees.[53] Thus, most nominees were asked to outline their political loyalties and views on controversial issues of the time, Yeltsin's ban of the Communist Party and the August 1991 *coup d'etat*.[54] After three rounds of secret voting spread over two days, the 5th CPD managed to fill thirteen out of fifteen seats on the bench of the new tribunal.[55] The legislators from both left and right seemed to avoid electing the little-known candidates from the regions and the openly pro-Yeltsin nominees. Instead, they favored law professors and those who worked closely with the Supreme Soviet and the Constitutional Commission: five of the justices came from the Supreme Soviet, three from the Constitutional Commission, and two consulted the Supreme Soviet on various bills.

As often happens with justices-turned-politicians of newly minted tribunals, they lobbied for the expansion of the powers of their Court. When the 1978 Russian constitution was amended in April 1992 to define Russia as an independent sovereign state in the aftermath of the USSR dissolution, it also authorized the RCC to determine the constitutionality of political parties and public associations, to adjudicate intergovernmental disputes, and to consider any other cases that did not violate the legal

---

[51] Khasbulatov added three nominees from Saratov Province and Sakha-Yakutia and Mari El Republics to the list of twenty names recommended by the Supreme Soviet. *Piatyi (vneocherednoi) Sezd narodnykh deputatov RSFSR: Stenogr. Otchet. T.* 2 (Moskva: Respublika, 1992), pp. 126–137.

[52] Interview with the RCC Justice, May 30, 2001.

[53] Mitiukov, *K istorii konstitutsionnogo pravosudiia Rossii*, p. 100.

[54] The minutes of this session were published in *Rossiiskaia gazeta*, November 1, 1991.

[55] In the course of increasingly hostile legislative–executive confrontation, Russia's rulers could not reach an agreement on the remaining two seats on the bench, which were never filled.

essence of constitutional review.[56] But judges later admitted that this non-exhaustive list of powers contributed to the politicization and eventual demise of the 1st Court in the fall of 1993.[57]

To sum up, the dynamics of a "tug-of-war" between the supporters and opponents of the powerful and independent constitutional court dispel the traditional version of judicial empowerment as a struggle between "pro-strong Court" reformers and "antistrong Court" reactionaries. True, on the surface some left-wing politicians favored a weak and dependent constitutional review. On the other hand, Yeltsin's lieutenants, like Mazaev and Stepankov, repeatedly opposed the powerful Constitutional Court, united with Communist legislators to defend the existing operational legal hierarchy, and refused to subject it to constitutional review. Therefore, both the power considerations and the institutional identities of relevant actors trumped their ideological commitments in the process of designing the Court. This debate about proper limits of constitutional review of judicial decisions has never been closed since 1991, as demonstrated in this book. Russian political elites fiercely bargained over the powers, recruitment procedures, and judicial nominees to ensure that the new constitutional court would protect their interests and that its judges would be loyal to those who elected them. These processes also show that the constitution makers cherished high "hopes and aspirations" for building a new Russian statehood with strong constitutional review. They took the issue of judicial empowerment seriously because legal elites managed to convince Russia's rulers that a powerful constitutional court could and would turn Russia into democratic "rule-of-law" state. This messiah-like vision of the 1st RCC was different from both the creation of the U.S. Supreme Court in the 1790s, a weak judicial body within a nascent federation and a new political regime at the time, and from the creation of the French Constitutional Council in 1958, which was set up to guarantee the supremacy of the executive branch of government.[58]

---

[56] Zakon RSFSR of April 21, 1992 "Ob izmeneniiakh i dopolneniiakh Konstitutsii (osnovnogo zakona) RSFSR," *VSND i VS RSFSR*, no. 20 (1992), item 1084.

[57] Nikolai Vitruk, *Konstitutsionnoe pravosudie v Rossii: 1991–2001 gg.: ocherki teorii i praktiki* [Constitutional Justice in Russia: 1991–2001: Essays on Theory and Practice] (Moskva: "Gorodets-izdat," 2001), p. 15; Boris Ebzeev, *Konstitutsiia. Pravovoe gosudarstvo. Konstitutsionnyi sud* [Constitution, Rule-of-Law State, Constitutional Court] (Moskva: Zakon i pravo "IUNITI", 1997), pp. 148–150.

[58] See, for example, Robert McCloskey and Sanford Levinson, *The American Supreme Court* (Chicago: University of Chicago Press, 1994); and Alec Stone, *The Birth of Judicial Politics in France* (Oxford: Oxford University Press, 1992).

REDESIGNING THE RUSSIAN CONSTITUTIONAL COURT: THE 1993 CONSTITUTIONAL CONVENTION

As it should be clear by now, parliamentary supremacy stood strong when it came to designing and appointing the Russian Constitutional Court. And it also stood strong in undermining the newly coined Russian presidency. President Yeltsin grew increasingly frustrated with the legislators and the RCC in the course of 1992 and early 1993, and eventually asked for voter confidence in his leadership and his policies in a referendum on April 25, 1993. He claimed victory over the legislature when 59 percent of the voters approved his leadership and 53 percent approved of his policies.[59] Yeltsin promptly published a new draft Constitution, which narrowed the powers of the constitutional court to reviewing the constitutionality of international treaties, federal and regional laws, presidential decrees and executive regulations, and settling jurisdictional disputes between federal and regional levels of government.[60] This brief and vague status of the constitutional review powers stood in stark contrast to the elaborate definitions of the RCC powers under the 1978 constitution and all the other constitutional drafts. Limiting the jurisdiction of the RCC was supposed to minimize the involvement of the tribunal in political struggles.

To polish his draft, President Yeltsin convened the Constitutional Convention, an advisory body staffed with his supporters, in the summer of 1993.[61] Yeltsin ordered this body to come up with the draft Constitution ahead of the parliamentary draft to prevent creating a weak federal presidency with a strong parliament. Several RCC judges (Ernest Ametistov, Boris Ebzeev, Tamara Morshchakova, and Nikolai Vitruk) played an active role in this Convention, and by mid-July 1993, this body approved the draft constitution with a relatively strong federal Constitutional Court despite Yeltsin's growing distaste for this tribunal. Preserving the Court would strengthen the Russian democratic statehood in the eyes

---

[59] See Boris Yeltsin, *The Struggle for Russia* (New York: Random House, 1994), pp. 212–215.

[60] "Proekt Konstitutsii Rossiiskoi Federatsii. Predstavlen Prezidentom Rossiiskoi Federatsii" [President Yeltsin's Constitutional Draft], *Moskovskaia pravda*, May 5, 1993.

[61] The minutes of the meetings of the 1993 Constitutional Convention are published in the twenty-volume *Konstitutsionnoe soveshchanie. Stenogrammy. Materialy. Dokumenty. 29 aprelia-10 noiabria 1993 g.* [Constitutional Convention. Stenographic Reports. Materials. Documents. April 29–November 10, 1993] (Moskva: Iuridicheskaia literatura, 1995–1996) and are available at http://www.constitution.garant.ru.

74   *Making and Remaking Constitutional Review, Russian-Style*

of citizens and the international community, according to the drafters.[62] Responding to Yeltsin's concerns, the Constitutional Convention took away the power of the Court to determine the constitutionality of political parties and to initiate impeachment procedures against the top government officers. Regardless of their attitudes toward Yeltsin, the RCC judges disagreed among themselves on whether to keep these powers: Justices Ebzeev, Kononov, and Morshchakova defended the jurisdiction over political parties while Justices Ametistov and Vitruk were against it.[63] But the Convention also empowered the RCC to review the constitutionality of public associations and "law-application practice."[64] Similar to the debates in 1991, the Russian Supreme Court actively lobbied to abandon the power of the RCC to review the constitutionality of "law-application practice" because it "discredited" the work of ordinary courts, completely subordinating the Supreme Court to constitutional review, and left intact the unconstitutional legal norm.[65] The RCC judges disagreed with this view and argued that their Court effectively protected individual rights through this procedure. Justice Morshchakova argued that this constitutional review power allowed the RCC to be a real court dealing with the questions of justice instead of politics and therefore empowered individuals to complain about the unconstitutionality of legal norms. The Convention sided with her arguments to allow constitutional complaints under the condition that the upcoming RCC Act would require individuals to exhaust all remedies prior to launching a constitutional complaint. In addition, Ebzeev and Morshchakova persuaded the majority of the Convention to introduce referrals by regular courts to the federal Constitutional Court.[66]

---

[62] Mikhail Mitiukov and Aleksandr Barnashov, *Ocherki konstitutsionnogo pravosudiia* [Essays on Constitutional Justice] (Tomsk: Izd-vo Tomskogo un-ta, 1999), p. 216.

[63] Mitiukov and Barnashov, *Ocherki konstitutsionnogo pravosudiia*, p. 232; Ebzeev, *Konstitutsiia. Pravovoe gosudarstvo. Konstitutsionnyi Sud*, pp. 8–9.

[64] Article 125 of the draft Constitution of the RF. "Proekt Konstitutsii Rossiiskoi Federatsii, odobrennyi Konstitutsionnym soveshchaniem" [Constitutional Convention draft], *Rabochaia tribuna*, July 21, 1993. Other drafts of the federal Constitution published in the summer of 1993 envisioned the constitutional court with more powers than the Constitutional Convention's draft. For the text of drafts, see Suren Avakian, *Konstitutsiia Rossii: priroda, evoliutsiia, sovremennost* [Russia's Constitution: Nature, Evolution, Contemporaneity] (Moskva: RIuID, 2000), pp. 233–502.

[65] Mitiukov and Barnashov, *Ocherki konstitutsionnogo pravosudiia*, p. 233.

[66] *Ibid.*, p. 234. For a detailed discussion of the debates on these issues at the Convention, see William Burnham and Alexei Trochev, "Russia's War Between the Courts: The Struggle over the Jurisdictional Boundary Between the Constitutional Court and Regular Courts," *American Journal of Comparative Law*, vol. 55, no. 3 (Summer 2007), pp. 397–405.

Redesigning the Russian Constitutional Court

However, the idea of a strong constitutional court lost many of its supporters after the RCC clashed with President Yeltsin in September 1993 when the latter dissolved the Congress of People's Deputies and the Supreme Soviet. In response to the Court's finding that Yeltsin had violated the constitution, Yeltsin shelled the parliament's building and suspended the RCC by decree 1612 of October 7.[67] In this decree, prepared after consulting Nikolai Vitruk, the deputy chairman of the Court,[68] Yeltsin accused the tribunal and its Chairman Zorkin of extreme politicization and asked the Constitutional Convention to review the necessity of keeping a separate Constitutional Court at all and of transferring the constitutional review function to the already existing federal Supreme Court.

Yeltsin's proposal reopened a debate in the Convention on the nature of constitutional review. But he gave the Convention only 4 weeks to draft the new constitution for Russia. This short period effectively limited the deliberations over constitutional engineering and empowered a narrow circle of legal experts close to president.[69] The justices moved swiftly to protect their Court by submitting their proposals to Yeltsin and by taking an active pro-Court stance at the Convention. Their main arguments were that doing away with the Court would seriously threaten the international image of Russia, would affirm legislative supremacy, and would reverse the democratic transition. Recognizing Yeltsin's distaste for his opponents on the bench, the Court proposed to increase the number of judges to eighteen or twenty-one, limit their term in office to 3, 6, or 9 years, and restrict the powers and the tenure of the chair of the Court. Justices vowed to depoliticize the Court by banning its ex officio powers and by relinquishing its power to determine the constitutionality of actions of high federal government officers and of political parties.[70]

By the end of October 1993, the Constitutional Convention achieved near unanimity that a new constitution would preserve a federal Constitutional Court as a separate body from the Supreme Court, contrary to Yeltsin's directives.[71] The Convention also rejected the creation of a higher judicial office in charge of constitutional interpretation and constitutional oversight of the judicial decisions although the RCC judges themselves disagreed about the usefulness of this suprajudicial body.[72]

---

[67] Decree No. 1612 of October 7, 1993, *SAPP*, no. 41 (1993), item 3921.

[68] By that time, the Constitutional Court was already deeply divided between anti-Yeltsin and pro-Yeltsin Justices with the latter group boycotting the Court's meetings.

[69] Avakian, *Konstitutsiia Rossii*, p. 179.

[70] Vitruk, *Konstitutsionnoe pravosudie v Rossii*, pp. 26–31.

[71] Mitiukov and Barnashov, *Ocherki konstitutsionnogo pravosudiia*, p. 218.

[72] *Ibid.*, p. 220.

76 *Making and Remaking Constitutional Review, Russian-Style*

Again, among the most hotly contested issues at the Convention were the questions of judicial recruitment and the powers of the RCC. On the one hand, the Convention agreed with Yeltsin's proposal to follow the U.S. model and have the Federation Council, the upper chamber of the federal legislature, to appoint justices nominated by the president. On the other hand, the Convention disagreed with pro-Yeltsin justices, who lobbied for appointing the whole Court anew in a masked effort to purge anti-Yeltsin justices from the bench. Instead, the Convention kept the life tenure of all sitting RCC judges as a symbolic protection of nascent judicial independence.[73]

This bargaining brought up the question of how many additional justices President Yeltsin should nominate to secure a loyal bench. The proposals at the Constitutional Convention envisioned up to twenty-five seats on the Court, leading to a twenty-one-member tribunal in the final draft constitution.[74] The rationale for a twenty-one-judge Court was that the Court could be easily divided into three, seven-judge chambers to increase the output of the Court and to mitigate the partisan conflicts among justices that plagued the tribunal by ensuring a pro-Yeltsin majority in each chamber and *en banc*.[75] President Yeltsin, who had a final say over the draft's text, thought that twenty-one judges were too many, and he cut their number to eighteen. But his adviser, Sergei Filatov, persuaded Yeltsin to have at least nineteen justices.[76] Adding six judges to a thirteen-member Court would provide a minimal pro-Yeltsin majority on the bench.[77] At the time, Yeltsin's legal advisers and pro-Yeltsin justices also hoped that

---

[73] *Ibid.*, p. 228.

[74] Russia is by no means unique in increasing the size of its constitutional court. Constitutional courts were enlarged in Croatia (from 11 to 13 judges), Estonia (from 5 to 9 judges), Poland (from 10 to 15 judges), and Slovakia (from 10 to 13 judges).

[75] An interview with the RCC staff in Moscow in June 2001. Justices Ametistov, Kononov, Morshchakova and Vitruk were believed to be a pro-Yeltsin minority on the bench. A twenty-one-member Court would then have twelve pro-Yeltsin justices (four of them in each chamber), and nine anti-Yeltsin judges (three in each chamber). See *Moskva. Osen'-93: Khronika protivostoianiia* (Moskva. Autumn of 1993: The Chronicle of Standoff] (Moskva: Respublika, 1995), pp. 10–17, 638.

[76] Pavel Kievskii, "Sergei Filatov: Yeltsin pravil Konstitutsiiu," [Sergei Filatov: Yeltsin Corrected the Constitution] *Trud*, December 10, 2003. See "Proekt Konstitutsii Rossiiskoi Federatsii, vynosimyi na vsenarodnoe golosovanie 12.12.1993" [Constitutional draft to be approved by popular vote on December 12, 1993), *Rossiiskaia gazeta*, November 10, 1993.

[77] Gordon B. Smith, *Reforming the Russian Legal System* (New York: Cambridge University Press, 1996), p. 138. Boris Vishnevskii, "Arbitr, udalennyi s polia," [Umpire That Was Removed from the Field] *Rossiiskaia Federatsiia segodnia*, no. 24 (2001), pp. 24–26, at 26.

Redesigning the Russian Constitutional Court

they could press Justices Zorkin and Luchin to resign from the bench, resulting in two more vacancies at the Court.[78] Not surprisingly, Vladimir Tumanov, the first chairman of the reconstructed Constitutional Court, had to admonish Zorkin in 1995 for going public about this "packing" of the Constitutional Court.[79]

Following the suspension of the RCC in the fall of 1993, Yeltsin's team reversed its stance on having a brief and vague listing of the powers of the Court in the new constitution. Presidential aides pressed the Convention to elaborate the jurisdiction of the Court in greater detail because they distrusted the soon-to-be-elected new federal legislature and because President Yeltsin would lack the power to veto the new RCC statute under the new constitution. The RCC judges also joined this push because they understood that it was much easier to influence the Convention than the new federal legislature, which was widely expected to be hostile to Yeltsin. They felt comfortable in debating fundamental constitutional choices in a narrow circle of lawyers, who dominated the constitutional drafting at the Convention. Moreover, given Yeltsin's preference for a rigid constitution, justices sought to prevent legislative tinkering with their Court. In addition, a detailed constitutionalization of their Court would enhance its institutional standing vis-à-vis other courts and a much more powerful president. Therefore, the interests of the president and the designers of the 2nd RCC coincided much as they did during the drafting the 1991 RCC Act, albeit this time the president had a strong anti-Court bias. Similar to 1991, justices appeared to believe in the ability of constitutional texts to restrain powerful politicians.

This shared interest in enshrining the powers of the reconstituted Constitutional Court directed the work of the Constitutional Convention in October 1993 toward both the enumeration of powers and access to the Court. On the one hand, the Convention narrowed the scope of constitutional review to federal laws and executive regulations, regional laws that fell under the exclusive federal and concurrent federal–regional jurisdiction, federation treaties, and international agreements that have not come

---

[78] See RCC decision 88-R of December 1, 1994 (Ebzeev, dissenting), in Ebzeev, *Konstitutsiia. Pravovoe gosudarstvo. Konstitutsionnyi Sud*, pp. 137–143; presidential decree No. 2289 of December 25, 1993 "O zameshchenii vakantnykh dolzhnostei federalnykh sudei," [On Filling the Vacant Offices of Federal Judges] *SAPP*, no. 4 (1994), item 698.

[79] Zorkin claimed that appointing an additional six Justices was done out of "momentary political expediency." See Nikolai Dorofeev, "Vladimir Tumanov: Ia ne liubliu gromkikh protsessov," [Vladimir Tumanov: I Don't Like Celebrated Cases] *Trud*, June 28, 1995.

78 Making and Remaking Constitutional Review, Russian-Style

into force.[80] Standing in these cases was limited to the federal president and legislative chambers, the parliamentary minority,[81] the federal Cabinet, the high federal courts, and regional governments. In addition, the Convention took away the power of the RCC to determine the constitutionality of political parties, public associations, and the "law-application practice" and rejected giving standing to the Procurator General and the federal Human Rights Ombudsman to ask for abstract constitutional review.[82]

On the other hand, the Constitutional Convention empowered the rest of the judiciary to request concrete constitutional review in addition to a full-blown constitutional complaint from individuals.[83] The RCC also received the power to issue binding interpretation of the federal Constitution at the request of the Russian president, federal Cabinet, the federal parliamentary chambers, and regional legislatures amid objections that this power was not a judicial function and enables the Court to write the constitution.[84] The Convention kept the authority of the Court to settle jurisdictional disputes between federal government bodies, between federal and regional governments, and between top institutions of regional governments. Moreover, the Convention inserted the Constitutional Court in the procedure of impeaching the Russian president. Here, the RCC was to determine the constitutionality of the procedure in bringing charges against the federal president. Instead of enhancing the stature of the Court, this measure clearly aimed at protecting the president from being impeached.[85] Also, the Constitutional Convention did not insert the Court in the process of the dissolution of the State Duma by the president. This made his job of dealing with a recalcitrant legislature easier but, at the same time, allowed the Court to stay out of political crises.[86] Finally,

[80] See Article 125-2 of the Russian constitution. Justice Ernest Ametistov came up with these restrictions on the judicial review of regional laws and international treaties to preserve Russian federalism and to avoid "chaos in international arena" respectively. Mitiukov and Barnashov, *Ocherki konstitutsionnogo pravosudiia*, pp. 235, 237.

[81] *Ibid.*, p. 237. In an effort to depoliticize the Court, the RCC initially rejected the right of a single legislator to petition the Court and proposed to empower one-third of the members of the Russian parliament to launch constitutional litigation. However, presidential aides criticized this "unthinkable number" and proposed to lower it to one-fifth to extend standing at the RCC to any major parliamentary group.

[82] *Ibid.* Justice Ebzeev advocated empowering these two officials to petition the Court.

[83] *Ibid.*, pp. 233–235. Justice Morshchakova actively promoted these constitutional review powers. See Article 125-4 of the Russian constitution.

[84] *Ibid.*, p. 235. See Article 125-5 of the Russian constitution.

[85] *Ibid.*, p. 238. See Article 125-7 of the Russian constitution.

[86] *Ibid.* As Justice Vitruk argued, "the Court should not issue preliminary sanctions for resolving political conflicts."

Enacting the 1994 Russian Constitutional Court Act

the Constitutional Convention granted the Court the right to initiate federal legislation, a key power for the Court, which had been drafting its own statute in the aftermath of its suspension.[87]

In short, the entrenchment of the federal Constitutional Court in the 1993 constitution represented a bargain struck among the federal president, RCC justices, other top federal courts, and regional governments. The fact that the Court remained a formally powerful institution represented the main achievement of that bargaining. Similar to 1991, the RCC designers had to convince politicians of the necessity and usefulness of centralized judicial review by a neutral, apolitical body serving to protect the supremacy of constitutional arrangements. President Yeltsin agreed to keep a separate Court because he seriously weakened the tribunal, muted his opponents on the bench, received the opportunity to staff it with his supporters, and preserved an international image of Russia's commitment to the rule of law.[88]

ENACTING THE 1994 *RUSSIAN CONSTITUTIONAL COURT ACT*

Following the approval of the Russian constitution at the nationwide referendum and the election of both houses of the new legislature – the Federal Assembly – on December 12, 1993, a group of justices and clerks of the RCC quickly drafted the new Constitutional Court bill. Using German constitutional review as a model, they sent their elaborate bill to the 450-member State Duma, the lower house of the Russian parliament, on January 29, 1994. Their haste was justified; judges had to set the agenda for reforming their Court before the politicians could capture the process of revamping the Court.[89] As acting Chief Justice Nikolai Vitruk explained it to the freshly elected legislators, judges prepared the bill

---

[87] See Article 104-1 of the Russian constitution: "The Constitutional Court of the Russian Federation ... shall be entitled to initiate legislation on the matters within their respective terms of reference."

[88] Mitiukov and Barnashov, *Ocherki konstitutsionnogo pravosudiia*, p. 237; Vitruk, *Konstitutsionnoe pravosudie v Rossii*, pp. 30, 32. Just as in 1991, Russia's international image was important for Yeltsin. He wanted neither to be likened to the Nazi regime, which disbanded the Austrian and Czechoslovakia Constitutional Courts in the 1930s, nor to be viewed as the first post-Communist leader to dissolve a new Constitutional Court. Yeltsin sent his draft Constitution to be reviewed by the experts of the Venice Commission "Democracy through Law." The Venice Commission supported a separate court with broad constitutional review powers and easy access.

[89] *Gosudarstvennaia Duma: Stenogramma zasedaniia. Vesenniaia sessiia. T. 4. 6–27 aprelia 1994 g.* (Moskva: Respublika, 1995), p. 37.

80 *Making and Remaking Constitutional Review, Russian-Style*

to "depoliticize" their tribunal through establishing a narrow jurisdiction, stronger collegiality, uniform decision-making procedures, and easier access of individuals to the Court. He emphasized that the bill would prevent the RCC turning into a "team of firefighters" extinguishing the flames of political conflicts and would improve the Court's work, particularly in the area of protecting constitutional rights.[90]

While the RCC judges attempted to maximize the independence of their Court, the presidential side and the legislators aspired to keep the Court accountable to the political branches. It took 5 months to hammer out the compromise among the newly elected State Duma, the presidential administration, and the RCC judges. Fresh memories of the Constitutional Court's entanglement in the confrontation between Yeltsin and the Supreme Soviet made politicians acutely aware of the great potential of judicial power. They did not want to defer to the expertise of the RCC designers and launched fierce attacks on the bill prepared by justices and on Yeltsin himself, thus ensuring anything but a smooth passage of the new RCC Act that required a two-thirds majority.

Judicial recruitment, the implementation of the RCC decisions, and financial independence of the Court stirred the most controversy.[91] Rival political camps understood very well the repeated warnings of Justice Vitruk that the decision making of the Court would depend in many ways on the composition of the Court.[92] Hoping that the Court in its current composition could help them quash Yeltsin's policies, Communist MPs insisted that the Court begin its work immediately, before the passage of the bill.[93] But Yeltsin's supporters in the Duma succeeded in keeping the tribunal inoperative until six new justices were appointed, which was necessary to build a pro-Yeltsin majority on the bench. Just as during the passage of the 1991 RCC Act, federal MPs already knew the nominees that they wanted the president to nominate to the bench and tried to require Yeltsin to choose from the list of nominees sponsored

---

[90] *Ibid.*, p. 44.

[91] These issues resurfaced in 2000 when Vladimir Putin launched his reforms of Russian governance. See Alexei Trochev, "Implementing the Russian Constitutional Court Decisions," *East European Constitutional Review*, vol. 11, nos. 1–2 (Winter–Spring 2002), pp. 95–103.

[92] *Gosudarstvennaia Duma: Stenogramma zasedaniia. Vesenniaia sessiia. T. 4. 6–27 aprelia 1994 g.*, p. 819.

[93] Their proposal vote garnered 40 percent of the votes in the Duma. *Gosudarstvennaia Duma: Stenogramma zasedaniia. Vesenniaia sessiia. T. 4. 6–27 aprelia 1994 g.*, pp. 135–141, 200.

Enacting the 1994 Russian Constitutional Court Act

by the Duma.[94] The presidential side staunchly opposed any limits on the discretion of the federal president in nominating justices. As Justice Vitruk recalls, legislators insisted so strongly on their right to propose their nominees that the bill became hostage to a struggle among parliamentary factions over their favorite candidates on the bench.[95] The resulting compromise is reflected in Article 9 of the 1994 RCC Act, which lists federal MPs, regional legislatures, high federal courts, federal agencies, national legal community bodies, and law schools as having the right to submit their nomination proposals to the Russian president. The president, however, is not required to consider these proposals. This means that the parliament can influence the composition of the Court only at the last stage of judicial recruitment: when the Federation Council, the upper chamber of the parliament, appoints presidential nominees to the Constitutional Court. [96]

Fearing that a propresidential bias of the Court would render the Duma's use of judicial review against Yeltsin's policies toothless, legislators proposed various sanctions for nonimplementation of the RCC decisions. Undoubtedly, the 1st Court faced the problem of nonimplementation of its rulings by federal and regional authorities.[97] Even Vladimir Tumanov, Yeltsin's supporter and soon-to-be chief justice of the reconstituted RCC, agreed with Yeltsin's antagonists on the need to address this problem of widespread disregard for court decisions.[98] However, devising punishment for noncompliance at this time would have damaged the image of the Court as it would both support anti-Yeltsin forces and weaken parliamentary supremacy. In a nutshell, enshrining the sanctions for noncompliance would emphasize the superiority of the RCC over other branches of government, more clearly resulting in a deep controversy and a danger of burying the bill altogether. Therefore, as much

---

[94] By April 6, 1994 (the first day of the debates over the RCC Act in the State Duma), the Russian Congress of Judges and the Justice Ministry had each submitted twelve judicial nominees. Vladimir Kriazhkov and Leonid Lazarev, *Konstitutsionnaia iustitsiia v Rossiiskoi Federatsii* [Constitutional Justice in the Russian Federation] (Moskva: BEK, 1998), p. 117.

[95] Vitruk, *Konstitutsionnoe pravosudie v Rossii*, p. 36.

[96] *Federalnyi konstitutsionnyi zakon "O Konstitutsionnom Sude Rossiiskoi Federatsii." Kommentarii* [Federal Constitutional Law "On the Constitutional Court of the Russian Federation." Commentary] (Moskva: Iuridicheskaia literatura, 1996), p. 64.

[97] See Chapter 6 of this book.

[98] *Gosudarstvennaia Duma: Stenogramma zasedaniia. Vesenniaia sessiia. T. 4. 6–27 aprelia 1994 g.*, p. 77.

as constitutional judges desired to have provisions for the punishment of noncompliance, they could not risk a confrontation with the powerful president, hostile legislature, and vengeful Supreme Court. Moreover, facing strong opposition from the regions towards any attempt to legislate sanctions for non-compliance with the RCC decisions, constitutional judges were afraid that the debate over noncompliance could delay reactivation of their tribunal.[99] As Justice Vitruk told the Duma, the sanctions for noncompliance with the RCC decisions were a complicated theoretical and practical problem, they should be written into the Criminal Code or a separate law, and the level of compliance depended on the legal culture of the society and the state as a whole.[100]

The RCC justices were also prepared to sacrifice safeguards of judicial independence for the sake of the prompt enactment of their bill. Although they initially proposed strong guarantees of financial independence, the justices had to drop it completely from the draft under pressure from the MPs and Yeltsin's team. As Justice Vitruk bitterly complained to the Duma, both pro-Yeltsin and anti-Yeltsin groups accused the Constitutional Court of being "too expensive," and essentially made the Court dependent on the executive branch.[101] The Duma also came close to removing the requirement that the budget of the Court for a given year could not be less than its budget in a previous fiscal year.[102] However, this proposal was rejected as unconstitutional and after several days of bargaining among judges and politicians, the RCC Act was passed on June 24, 1994, and sent for approval to the Federation Council.[103]

As was mentioned earlier, the Federation Council appoints presidential nominees to the Court. It appears that this power was a key bargaining chip in the hands of the RCC judges and the president who insisted that the Federation Council simply approve the Act in exchange for a final say in appointing members of the Court.[104] After legislative

---

[99] Trochev, "Implementing the Russian Constitutional Court Decisions," p. 96.

[100] *Gosudarstvennaia Duma: Stenogramma zasedaniia. Vesenniaia sessiia. T. 4. 6–27 aprelia 1994 g.*, pp. 46–47, 54–55.

[101] *Ibid.*, pp. 55, 813–814.

[102] The Duma vote was 50 percent in favor of removing this requirement (short of required two-thirds-majority vote). *Gosudarstvennaia Duma: Stenogramma zasedaniia. Vesenniaia sessiia. T. 6. 8–24 iuniia 1994 g.* (Moskva: Respublika, 1995), p. 645.

[103] This chamber was initially directly elected for a two-year term. I will refer to its members as "senators" throughout the book.

[104] *Sovet Federatsii. Zasedanie 8. 12–14 iiulia 1994 g. Stenograficheskii otchet* (Moskva: Sovet Federatsii, 1995), pp. 44–79.

Enacting the 1994 Russian Constitutional Court Act

TABLE 3.2. *Remaking the Russian Constitutional Court, 1993–1995*

October 25, 1993	Russian Constitutional Court justices and constitutional scholars vow to save their Court by reforming its powers and decision-making procedures.
October 28, 1993	The Constitutional Convention keeps the RCC as a separate body in the draft constitution.
December 12, 1993	New Russian constitution is ratified in a nationwide referendum establishing the nineteen-member RCC and keeping all thirteen justices from the 1st Court on the bench.
April 8, 1994	The State Duma fails to approve the bill on the RCC in the first reading.
April 16, 1994	Presidential Council on Cadres selects eighteen nominations for President Yeltsin to fill six new seats on the RCC.
April 26, 1994	The State Duma approves the bill on the RCC in the first reading.
June 24, 1994	The State Duma approves the bill on the RCC and sends it to the Federation Council.
July 12, 1994	The Federation Council approves the bill on the RCC and sends it to President Yeltsin.
July 21, 1994	President Yeltsin signs the bill on the RCC into law.
October 24, 1994	The Federation Council appoints three (Olga Khokhriakova, Vladimir Tumanov and Vladimir Iaroslavtsev) out of six Yeltsin nominees for the RCC.
November 15, 1994	The Federation Council appoints one (Iurii Danilov) out of five Yeltsin nominees for the RCC.
December 6, 1994	The Federation Council appoints one (Vladimir Strekozov) out of two Yeltsin nominees for the RCC.
December 16, 1994	The Federation Council fails to appoint Yeltsin's nominee for the last seat on the RCC.
January 17, 1995	The Federation Council fails to appoint Yeltsin's nominee for the last seat on the RCC.
February 7, 1995	The Federation Council fills the last seat on the RCC by appointing Marat Baglai.

maneuvering, the chamber quickly approved the RCC Act by an 82 percent vote but showed its teeth during the judicial appointment process (see Table 3.2).[105] Although the bill required the Federation Council to fill six remaining seats on the bench within a month, the senators managed to

---

[105] President Yeltsin signed the RCC Act on July 21, 1994, and the Act entered into force upon its publication on July 23, 1994. See Federalnyi konstitutsionnyi zakon "O Konstitutsionnom Sude Rossiiskoi Federatsii" of July 21, 1994, *SZ RF*, no. 13 (1994), item 1447.

84   Making and Remaking Constitutional Review, Russian-Style

appoint the last justice only in February 1995. Just as in staffing the tribunal in 1991, the process of selecting these six justices was long and controversial. In addition to two dozen names proposed by the Russian Justice Ministry and the Congress of Judges, the president received another fifty nominations for the bench from academia, public associations, and parliamentary groups by early April 1994. In mid-April, the Presidential Council on Cadres Policy narrowed the list to eighteen nominees. President Yeltsin picked six names from this list and nominated them for judgeships in October 1994. Yet the senators, complaining that Yeltsin did not leave any room for their choices, appointed only three justices.[106] He quickly responded with five nominees for the remaining three seats on the bench only to secure appointment of one justice.[107] Legislative–executive wrangling ensued in the next 3 months with the Federation Council rejecting four Yeltsin nominees and appointing two justices.[108] Even Vladimir Shumeiko, the Speaker of the Council and an open presidential supporter who skillfully manipulated voting procedures, could do little to overcome this senatorial resistance to Yeltsin's nominees for the bench. By April 1997, the Federation Council rejected presidential nominations for the RCC thirteen times.

The protracted appointment of the 2nd Court revealed a clear pattern of conflict between the legislature and the president: the Federation Council repeatedly rejected Yeltsin's staunch supporters on the bench and tended to appoint less known nominees, mainly from academic circles.[109] Yeltsin's aides even had to beg the senators to question the nominees in hope that their answers would shatter their pro-Yeltsin image and

---

[106] Olga Khokhriakova, a Moscow-based labor law professor, Vladimir Iaroslavtsev, a judge from St. Petersburg, and Vladimir Tumanov, a Moscow-based constitutional law professor, were appointed to the bench on October 25, 1994. *Sovet Federatsii. Zasedanie 11. Biulleten no. 1 (38). Chast 1. 24 oktiabria 1994 g. Stenograficheskii otchet* (Moskva: Sovet Federatsii, 1995).

[107] Iurii Danilov, a Deputy Head of the Federal Anti-Monopoly Policy Committee, was appointed to the RCC on November 15, 1994. *Sovet Federatsii. Zasedanie 12. Biulleten no. 1 (42). Chast 1. 15 noiabria 1994 g. Stenograficheskii otchet* (Moskva: Sovet Federatsii, 1995).

[108] Vladimir Strekozov, a Moscow-based constitutional law professor, was appointed to the bench on December 6, 1994. *Sovet Federatsii. Zasedanie 13. Biulleten no. 1 (45). 6 dekabria 1994 g. Stenograficheskii otchet* (Moskva: Sovet Federatsii, 1995). Marat Baglai, also a constitutional law professor from Moscow, was appointed to the bench on February 7, 1995. *Sovet Federatsii. Zasedanie 16. 7–10 fevralia 1995 g. Stenograficheskii otchet* (Moskva: Sovet Federatsii, 1996).

[109] The Federation Council continued to appoint law professors well into 2005 (Nikolai Bondar in 1999, Sergei Kazantsev in 2002, Larisa Krasavchikova in 2003, and Sergei Mavrin in 2005).

Tinkering with the 1994 Russian Constitutional Court Act 85

reinforce their legal qualifications. But all the senators wanted to know was whether the nominee approved Yeltsin's dissolution of the parliament in October 1993. In summary, short-term power needs of both judges and politicians dominated the process of remaking the Russian Constitutional Court: judges wanted to reactivate their tribunal quickly, Yeltsin's team wanted to "pack" the revamped Court, and his opponents wanted the Court to punish Yeltsin as soon as possible. Neither of the political branches wanted too strong of a court. This is why an unusual ad hoc coalition of Yeltsin's enemies and supporters rejected granting financial independence to the tribunal and imposing sanctions for noncompliance with its judgments.

TINKERING WITH THE 1994 *RUSSIAN CONSTITUTIONAL COURT ACT*

This prevalence of the short-term power needs in designing and redesigning was not unique to Yeltsin's rule. Vladimir Putin, who replaced President Yeltsin in 2000, also chose to pursue his short-term goals by tinkering with the RCC Act: reforming the terms of judicial tenure, strengthening the binding force of the court decisions, and relocating the tribunal from Moscow to St. Petersburg. As explained in the previous chapter, this tinkering with the institutional set up of the Court was shaped both by the jurisprudence of the RCC and by the widespread disregard for its judgments. Let me briefly consider each of these three reforms.

When President Putin proposed on August 19, 2000, to extend judicial tenure from 12 to 15 years and remove the mandatory retirement at the age of seventy, he envisioned that these amendments would apply to all sitting justices to "equalize" their status.[110] Recall that in 1991, the mandatory retirement age for judges topped the list of the most controversial issues in the course of designing the Constitutional Court. Under the 1991 RCC Act, judges were appointed for life with the mandatory retirement age of sixty-five, while under the 1994 RCC Act, justices were appointed for 12 years, but they had to retire at age seventy. Naturally, all RCC justices wanted to have the same terms of tenure, and here they were supported by the Russian Supreme Court justices who saw the introduction of 12-year

---

[110] For a detailed analysis of this "reform," see Alexei Trochev, "'Tinkering with Tenure': The Russian Constitutional Court in Comparative Perspective," in Ferdinand Feldbrugge, ed., *Russia, Europe, and the Rule of Law* (Leiden: Martinus Nijhoff, 2006), pp. 47–78.

86   *Making and Remaking Constitutional Review, Russian-Style*

terms as a dangerous attack on the life tenure of all federal judges.[111] For the ten justices from the 1st Constitutional Court who remained on the bench in 2000, Putin's amendments meant that they would either serve 15 years or until the retirement age of sixty-five, whichever term would be longer. These amendments would have the most immediate effect on the tenure of the Chief Justice Marat Baglai, sixty-nine, and his deputy, Justice Tamara Morshchakova, sixty-four. Both would reach retirement age in March 2001. Under the proposed changes, the former would serve 9 more years, and the latter would sit on the bench until 2006. The pressure to meet the March 2001 retirement deadline dictated the prompt passage of these amendments through the legislature where Putin still faced potential resistance in the Duma and in the governor-packed Federation Council. And resistance he did face. Several Justices of the Court were appalled at the very fact that the president had not consulted the Court about these amendments. Sensing that Putin's initiative was aimed at keeping both judges on the bench, the Duma managed to twist his "tenure" amendments in such a way that they would not apply to Justice Morshchakova. Putin gave in, the image of the RCC and its Chief Justice plummeted, and Justice Morshchakova repeatedly slammed legislative tinkering with judicial tenure in the media. To Putin's credit, he did not replace Morshchakova until April 2002 and he tried to repair the damage caused by this tinkering. At the end of 2001, he again vowed to "equalize" the status of the RCC justices by bringing back the mandatory retirement age of seventy for the RCC Justices starting in January 2005 under the condition that this reinstatement applied only to justices appointed under the 1994 RCC Act. The Duma unanimously approved this "tenure" amendment despite the fact that the parliament had lifted this mandatory retirement age several months earlier. Thus, up until the spring of 2005, the nineteen-member Russian Constitutional Court consisted of four groups of Justices according to their length of tenure. To resolve this confusion on the bench, President Putin amended the RCC Act once again in April 2005.[112] This time the amendments provided for the mandatory retirement age of seventy for all sitting RCC judges, thus lengthening by 5 years the tenure of six remaining justices appointed under the 1991 RCC

---

[111] Viktor Zhuikov, "Konstitutsionnyi Sud RF vypolniaet istoricheskuiu rol," [The RF Constitutional Court Performs Historic Role] *Rossiiskaia iustitsiia*, no. 10 (October 2001), p. 18.

[112] Federalnyi konstitutsionnyi zakon No. 2-FKZ of April 5, 2005 [Law on Amending the 1994 RCC Act], *Rossiiskaia gazeta*, April 9, 2005.

Tinkering with the 1994 Russian Constitutional Court Act 87

TABLE 3.3. *Tinkering with the tenure of the Russian Constitutional Court*

Year	Legislative debates	Length of term	Judge must retire at age	Applies to
1991	Four Legislative Sessions	Life Tenure	65	All judges
1994	Four Legislative Sessions	12 years	70	Future judges
1997 (failed)	One Legislative Session	12 years	65	All judges
Winter 2000–2001	Three Legislative Sessions	15 years	None	Judges Elected in 1994–2000
Winter 2001	Unanimous Legislature	15 years	70 (since January 1, 2005)	Judges Elected in 1994–2000
Spring 2005	Unanimous Legislature	Life Tenure	70	All judges

Act (see Table 3.3 for the never-ending "tinkering with the tenure" of the RCC justices). In summary, the short-term preferences of the rulers and clashes over judicial personalities rather than strategic concerns or democratic commitments explain this zigzagging behavior of politicians. And, as I will show in Chapter 8, this tinkering with judicial tenure by the powerful is anything but a unique Russian experience.

Another way in which President Putin chose to improve the status of the Constitutional Court was to strengthen the binding force of its judgments.[113] Unlike Boris Yeltsin, the second Russian president has no wish to tolerate regional violations of federal laws, clearly wanting to secure the regions' overall compliance and thus the Federation's integrity. President Putin held extensive consultations with federal law-enforcement officials and the RCC judges, who discussed various ways of improving compliance with Constitutional Court decisions (see Chapters 6 and 7 for the analysis of compliance with RCC decisions). On May 23, 2001, Putin sent to the Duma a set of amendments to the 1994 RCC Act dealing with implementation. The aim of these amendments was to oblige the regional authorities to repeal or alter legislation found

---

[113] For a detailed analysis of this "reform," see Alexei Trochev, "Implementing Russian Constitutional Court Decisions," *East European Constitutional Review*, vol. 11, nos. 1–2 (Winter–Spring 2002), pp. 95–103.

unconstitutional and to provide sanctions for the failure to implement Constitutional Court decisions. The process of adopting these implementation amendments was complicated and, for the Court, perilous because they provided an opening for the opponents of a strong Court, who then proceeded to introduce two amendments limiting its power. As the changes were being debated in the Duma, a strange ad hoc coalition of left-wing, right-wing, and centrist MPs began attacking the very power of the Court to issue rulings binding upon other branches of government, not to speak of creating legal norms. Some Duma deputies defended the Constitutional Court's prerogatives but the play of politics produced a dangerous situation, whereby in November 2001 the Duma Committee actually approved proposals that would deprive the Court of its essential power and convert it into an advisory body similar to the short-lived USSR Constitutional Supervision Committee, as described at the beginning of this chapter. These amendments were almost approved by the Duma and were dropped only after active resistance by the Court justices. RCC judges were forced to campaign against the threatened changes in both public forums and directly with the president. They complained that any end to the binding force of Constitutional Court decisions would represent the end of constitutional justice in Russia and threatened that the Court could invalidate such changes. This time the judges succeeded, and President Putin signed these amendments into law on December 15, 2001. The amendments as passed set various deadlines for federal and regional governments to change statutes, decrees, and resolutions found unconstitutional. But the new law contains no sanctions in the event of failure by the federal institutions to comply. Only *regional* noncompliance is subject to these sanctions: the regional legislatures can be dissolved and the regional governors can be removed for the failure to comply in a timely manner.[114] In summary, the short-term interest of the powerful president in bringing recalcitrant regions to heel resulted in tinkering with the institutional setup of the constitutional court and in turning judges into lobbyists.

Unlike the hastily adopted "tenure" and "implementation" amendments, the proposal to move the Russian Constitutional Court from Moscow to St. Petersburg did not come from judges. Valentina Matvienko, Putin's pick for the St. Petersburg governor, voiced the idea in early 2003 and proposed to move all three top federal courts (RCC, Supreme Court,

---

[114] Federalnyi konstitutsionnyi zakon No. 4-FKZ of December 15, 2001 [Law on Amending the 1994 RCC Act], *Rossiiskaia gazeta*, December 20, 2001.

Tinkering with the 1994 Russian Constitutional Court Act 89

and Higher *Arbitrazh* Court) to Putin's hometown. Apparently, the president also believed that courts were good condidates for relocation, on the grounds that courts at a distance would be less dependent on federal authorities and that the Germans had placed their Constitutional Court outside the capital. The presidential administration took control of three historic buildings in the downtown of Russia's "second capital," two of which could be redesigned as courthouses. The president decided to start with the Constitutional Court and asked for an estimate of the cost of the move and a test of local public opinion about it. Financial estimates of the relocation hovered around US$1 billion while most residents of St. Petersburg opposed the move. In January 2004, then Prime Minister Mikhail Kasianov asked relevant agencies to discuss an operational plan for the move. He chose not to proceed with the move after receiving a strong rebuttal from both his ministers and judges who complained that the move was too costly and too disruptive to the functioning of the Court. For judges, the worst aspect of the plans to move their Court lay in the way they were developed, among a few politicians without any consultation with the judges! In the spring of 2004, public discussions of the move stopped, perhaps because of the presidential elections, appointment of a new prime minister, and a reshuffling of the Cabinet.[115]

But a few months later, Putin's lieutenants openly insisted that the Constitutional Court would be relocated to St. Petersburg, and late in 2005 the St. Petersburg legislature submitted the "relocation" bill to the State Duma. In early 2006, President Putin approved it, and the Cabinet announced that the bill would cost a meager US$8 million. In March 2006, the Duma approved the bill in the first reading amid fervent opposition from judges and the left-wing MPs who complained about the waste of public funds as a result of the move. Judges, then, proceeded to lobby for better working and living conditions, which raised the cost of relocating their Court to more than US$300 million. By November 2006, they also nearly got the Duma to provide for three conditions of the move: to allow the Court to keep its offices in Moscow, to hold meetings and hearings outside St. Petersburg, and to negotiate the timing of the actual move with president. But the Duma reneged on these promises after pressure from Putin's administration in December 2006. Judges were outraged and publicly complained to the Federation Council and President

---

[115] See Peter H. Solomon, Jr., "Threats of Judicial Counterreform in Putin's Russia," *Demokratizatsiia*, vol. 13, no. 3 (Summer 2005), pp. 325–345.

90 *Making and Remaking Constitutional Review, Russian-Style*

Putin. On December 27, 2006, the Federation Council returned the bill to the Duma but made clear that the relocation of the RCC would occur in early 2008 just before the next presidential elections. Three weeks later, after judges had managed to persuade President Putin to agree to their three conditions, the Duma voted for the version of the law as approved by judges, the Federation Council promptly followed suit, and President Putin signed the bill on February 5, 2007.[116] Putin's administration vowed to complete the move by March 1, 2008, a day before the 2008 presidential elections. However, judges persuaded the president that they needed more time. As a result, Vladimir Putin decreed that the RCC would begin its work in St. Petersburg on May 21, 2008.[117] In summary, Putin's initiative to move the RCC to his hometown confirmed the perceptions that both the internal clashes behind Kremlin walls over large sums of money trumped judicial independence and that judges became hostage to this exercise in routine pork-barrel politics.[118] Similar to other reforms of the 1994 RCC Act, this reflects short-term interests of politicians in dealing with constitutional review.

CONCLUSION

Designing, redesigning, and staffing the Russian Constitutional Court was an arduous political process in which reformers and conservatives simultaneously clashed and cooperated to benefit from constitutional review. The resulting compromise solutions display a relatively strong commitment to some sort of judicial review over conflicts among political branches. The fact that Russia still had a functioning authoritative constitutional tribunal after the bloody October 1993 confrontation between President Yeltsin and the parliament is a sign of maturing political commitment to

---

[116] Federalnyi konstitutsionnyi zakon No. 2-FKZ of 5 February 2007 [Law on Amending the 1994 RCC Act], *Rossiiskaia gazeta*, February 9, 2007.

[117] See interview with Vladimir Kozhin, the Director of the RF President's Business Management Directorate, in Andrei Kamakin, "Kolybel' Konstititutsii," [Cradle of Constitution], *Itogi*, December 2, 2007, available at http://www.itogi.ru/paper2007.nsf/Article/Itogi_2007_12_02_01_4914.html; Decree No. 1740 "O meste postoiannogo prebyvaniia Konstitutsionnogo Suda Rossiiskoi Federatsii," [On the Location of the Permanent Sojourn of the RF Constitutional Court] *Rossiiskaia gazeta*, December 27, 2007, p. 2.

[118] See, for example, Marina Ozerova, "Sekrety dumskoi dressirovki," [The Secrets of the Duma Training], *Moskovskii komsomolets*, February 7, 2007; and Tony Halpin, "Putin the Local Boy Makes £100m Good for Home City," *The Times*, January 25, 2007 available at http://business.timesonline.co.uk/tol/business/markets/europe/article 1296001.ece.

Conclusion

constitutional review. However, the processes of making and remaking the RCC at the beginning of the 1990s demonstrate that politicians primarily pursued their short-term interests: first, to overpower the USSR, then, to strengthen the presidency vis-à-vis the legislature. This pursuit took place initially in a complicated legislative procedure: the 1st RCC had to be created by the two legislatures, while the 2nd Court had to undergo a rebirth at the 1993 Constitutional Convention and in the bicameral federal legislature. This cumbersome legislative structure provided threats and opportunities for both friends and foes of the Constitutional Court and resulted in strange coalitions of Communists and law-enforcement agencies, Yeltsin's aides and his staunch critics. Politicians revealed their short-term goals in their utmost concern with questions of judicial recruitment in designing both of Russia's Constitutional Courts because individuals who staffed the courts mattered as much as (if not more) than the institutional powers of the RCC. Simultaneous passage of the Court statute and the lengthy selection of the justices strongly politicized legislative debates but at the same time provided the necessary public scrutiny of the justices-to-be. This politicization resulted in an ideologically diverse bench but it did not save the 1st RCC from a near-death experience and did not prevent Russia from experiencing a constitutional crisis in the fall of 1993.

That the Russian politicians were asked both to design constitutional review and to select judges for the RCC at the same time was hardly accidental. This simultaneity was due to the fact that the main architects of the Court aspired to sit on the bench of the new tribunal. Most of them had to cater to the short-term interests of politicians in order to convince the latter of the necessity of strong constitutional review. In 1991, they did it in the context of the constitution-making euphoria and in a strong legislature-weak presidency arrangement. In 1993–1994, they redid it under a strong anti-Court bias and in a semipresidential system. In both cases, the designers of the Court succeeded in tailoring foreign constitutional arrangements to the needs of their political superiors, and some of the designers became the RCC justices.[119] The fact that they were

---

[119] This pattern is not unique to the RCC. Constitution makers in the Russian regions that have their own constitutional courts pursued the same course of action. See Trochev, "Less Democracy." The author of the 1996 Ukrainian Constitutional Court Act, Ivan Tymchenko, became the first Chief Justice of the Ukrainian Court. Laszlo Solyom and Geza Kilenyi, designers of the Hungarian Constitutional Court, not only became the Justices but also brought several of their loyal friends to the bench. See John W. Schiemann, *The Politics of Pact-Making: Hungary's Negotiated Transition to Democracy in Comparative Perspective* (New York: Palgrave Macmillan, 2005), pp. 130–135.

agile in building and protecting their Court from the repeated attempts to empower the already existing Supreme Court with judicial review powers also shows their success. My analysis demonstrates that Russia has a separate constitutional court not because of distrust in the ordinary judges or its civil-law tradition. Russia has this tribunal because a narrow circle of defenders of the constitutional court has more influence on the rulers than a 115-member federal Supreme Court.

The Russian Constitutional Court in both its editions surprised many observers by its activism and innovative decision making. How did they attempt to build a new Russia in the tumultuous sea of post-Communist transformation? What was the role of judicial review in the past decade of the Russian transition? Did judges manage to serve the powerful well? The following chapters will demonstrate that the long-term success of post-Soviet constitutional review depends crucially on the extent to which constitutional review fits in the system of governing the post-Soviet polities.

4

Russian Constitutional Review in Action
(1990–1993)

Question: So you are trying to stop the people from falling over the precipice?
Answer: That is the main task of the Constitutional Court. The very existence of this body is a guarantee of public security. We should and must protect the borders of the legal ground beyond which lie the abyss, the precipice, perdition.

— Chief Justice of the Russian Constitutional Court Valerii Zorkin[1]

The Constitutional Court should act as a court of law and should not behave as a crew of firefighters or paramedics.

— Russian Constitutional Court Justice Nikolai Vitruk[2]

This chapter together with Chapter 5 examines judicial behavior, which is the second element of *nonlinear* judicial empowerment, as outlined in Chapter 2. Judicial behavior is a key element in the trilateral dynamic of judicial empowerment because the two other elements – design of judicial review and compliance with court decisions – do not exist without the court decisions. A polity could have a judicial review body that is enshrined in the constitution and is issuing decisions in parallel with the widespread nonimplementation of court decisions (the USSR Constitutional Supervision Committee). One could also think of a polity where the court asserts judicial review powers without explicit constitutional authorization (lacking the design of judicial review), exercises judicial review of laws, and compels the government to obey its judgments (U.S. Supreme

---

[1] Interview with the chief justice of the Russian Constitutional Court, Valerii Zorkin, *Komsomolskaia pravda*, January 15, 1992, p. 1.
[2] See his remarks in *Gosudarstvennaia Duma Federalnogo Sobraniia RF: Stenogramma zasedanii. Vesenniaia sessiia. T. 4, April 6–27, 1994* (Moskva: Respublika, 1995), p. 44.

93

Court). In both cases, court decisions play an important role. Without them, however, one cannot assess the strength of the constitutional court because the exercise of the power of judicial review is unknown, the reaction of the politicians toward the constitutional court is absent, and the interplay between the judges and politicians is not visible.

This chapter addresses the following questions: to what extent did the Russian Constitutional Court use its powers in its first 2 years of functioning and why, and what were the main areas of the Constitutional Court's intervention and why. The turbulent early years of this court attracted numerous scholars who either studied it as a case study or compared it to other postcommunist courts.[3] Most of these studies reflect a sympathetic bias toward these courts because most of the time it was the judges themselves who supplied the data about their courts.[4] My analysis also draws on my interviews with justices and examines the following features of the decision making of the Russian Constitutional Court: how creative judges were in solving political controversies and enhancing the standing of their Court vis-à-vis other political actors, how well judges handled dissent on the bench, and in which policy areas they tended to intervene. More importantly, my analysis focuses both on the decisions on the merits of the case (*postanovleniia*) and unpublished decisions, which dismiss a case without hearing (*opredeleniia*).[5] This chapter begins by exploring the jurisprudence of the short-lived USSR Constitutional Supervision Committee in 1990–1991 and ends with the examination of the success and the failure of the 1st Russian Constitutional Court in 1992–1993. In Chapter 5, I assess how the 2nd Russian Constitutional Court exercised its judicial review powers between 1995 and 2006. Rather than examining each and every judgment, I focus on the major decisions that involve politically important questions and contribute to either success or failure of judicial review in Russia.

---

[3] See, for example, Lee Epstein, Jack Knight, and Olga Shvetsova, "The Role of Constitutional Courts in the Establishment and Maintenance of Democratic Systems of Government," *Law and Society Review*, vol. 35, no. 1 (March 2001), pp. 117–164 and sources cited therein.

[4] In addition to private interviews with scholars, RCC Justices published many interviews in mass media and wrote academic articles and books. Virtually all of the Justices either publicly commented on the judgments or wrote scholarly commentary about the judgments.

[5] For the summaries of its decisions in English, see Ger P. van den Berg, compiler, "Constitution of the Russian Federation Annotated with Summaries of Rulings and Other Decisions of Constitutional (Charter) Courts: 1990–2001," *Review of Central and East European Law*, vol. 27, nos. 2–3 (2001), pp. 175–488.

DECISION MAKING OF THE USSR CONSTITUTIONAL
SUPERVISION COMMITTEE: 1990–1991

As I argued in Chapter 3, the USSR Constitutional Supervision Committee (CSC) had weak judicial review powers and was introduced too late to uphold constitutional order in the disintegrating Soviet Union. And the Committee acted like a constrained tribunal in the cases that mattered to the rulers, providing support to the view that judges are constrained and strategic actors who, first, secure the compliance of political actors with their rulings, and, then, strike down the contested law.[6] Indeed, the CSC tried to be strategic from the start and struck down USSR legal acts only after a favorable move by the Union authorities. Consider the Committee's decision to review the constitutionality of Gorbachev's decree of April 20, 1990, restricting mass meetings and demonstrations in Moscow. According to Chairman Alekseev, by taking up this case "we have set a rather high standard for ourselves, letting everybody know that everyone without exception is obligated to comply with the Constitution."[7] In the decision, announced on September 13, 1990, the CSC declared Gorbachev's decree unconstitutional because the Union Law on Mass Meetings granted the right to local authorities, not to the USSR government, to ban mass rallies and demonstrations under certain conditions. This decision was announced several days after Gorbachev had agreed to repeal the decree although the Committee indicated, in late June 1990, that it would strike down the decree.[8]

Although the CSC Chairman Sergei Alekseev initially hoped that the Soviet government leaders would use his Committee frequently, the majority of the twenty-nine CSC rulings[9] were issued at the initiative of the Committee, a clear indication of the powerlessness of Soviet constitutional review.[10] On the one hand, the Union republics largely distrusted the CSC

---

[6] Georg Vanberg, *The Politics of Constitutional Review in Germany* (Cambridge, UK: Cambridge University Press, 2005).

[7] Anatoly Stepovoi, "Committee Starts Operation," *Izvestiia*, May 18, 1990, p. 2, in *Current Digest of the Soviet Press*, vol. XLII, no. 16 (1990), p. 24.

[8] Herbert Hausmaninger, "From the Soviet Committee on Constitutional Supervision to the Russian Constitutional Court," *Cornell International Law Journal*, vol. 25, no. 2 (Spring 1992), p. 314.

[9] The CSC Deputy Chairman Boris Lazarev cites this figure, which includes six so-called statements by several Committee members, in his "Komitet konstitutsionnogo nadzora SSSR (Podvodia itogi)," [USSR Constitutional Supervision Committee (Arriving at Conclusions)], *Gosudarstvo i pravo*, no. 5 (May 1992), p. 24.

[10] Stepovoi, "Committee Starts Operation."

96   *Russian Constitutional Review in Action (1990–1993)*

as an additional tool of USSR domination. The only Union republics that petitioned the CSC were Russia, Armenia, and Azerbaijan. The Russian parliament in January 1991 asked the Committee to review Gorbachev's decree on joint police-military patrols in the city streets. The Russian Supreme Soviet alleged that the prerogative to maintain public order was beyond the Union's jurisdiction, and that the joint patrols should not follow the Communist Party directives. Although the CSC agreed with the petitioner that police should not carry out the Communist Party directives, it upheld Gorbachev's decree as a whole and removed law-enforcement from Russia's control.[11] Armenia and Azerbaijan asked the Committee to resolve their bloody dispute over the Nagorno–Karabakh territory but the Committee took its time and issued its decision on November 28, 1991, in which it declared all contested acts unconstitutional and called for the respect of the USSR Constitution, USSR laws, laws of Armenia and Azerbaijan, and individual rights. Again, the Committee issued this decision only after the USSR State Council vowed to restore the constitutionality in the Nagorno–Karabakh territory. Moreover, the break-up of the USSR a week after this decision (and the dissolution of the Committee a week after that) precluded both the publication and any effect of this CSC decision on the stances of Armenia and Azerbaijan.[12]

On the other hand, the Union authorities were busy in their struggles against the secessionist strategies of the breakaway republics. Moreover, the USSR constitution (Article 127.3) authorized the Union president to repeal acts of the republics found contradictory to the USSR law. The CSC issued a total of six decisions at the request of President Gorbachev and the USSR Supreme Soviet Chairman Lukianov and upheld all their requests. The USSR top officials challenged Russia's ban on simultaneous holding of state and party offices, Latvia's ban on preferential treatment of the Soviet Army's housing rights, Lithuania's restrictions on republican citizenship and criminal sanctions for subversive activities, and legal obstacles enacted in eight republics to block the Union referendum of September 17, 1991. Although the Committee couched these decisions in legal terms and invoked international human rights law, three of them

---

[11] Peter B. Maggs, "Enforcing the Bill of Rights in the Twilight of the Soviet Union," *University of Illinois Law Review,* vol. 4, no. 4 (1991), p. 1057.

[12] USSR CSC Decision No. 28(2–5) of November 28, 1991, unpublished, available in Mikhail Mitiukov, *Predtecha konstitutsionnogo pravosudiia: vzgliady, proekty i institutsionalnye predposylki (30 – nachalo 90-h gg. XX v.)* [Forerunner of the Constitutional Justice: Views, Drafts, and Institutional Prerequisites (1930 – Beginning of the 1990s)] (Moskva: Formula Prava, 2006), pp. 146–149.

Decision Making of the USSR Constitutional Supervision Committee 97

generated dissenting opinions by three Committee members that were appended to the majority opinions. Moreover, the republics paid little attention to the CSC announcements and flatly refused to comply.

That the CSC heard most cases at its own initiative also indicates the enthusiasm of its leadership toward the exercise of constitutional review powers. As the case law of the Committee shows, the CSC members were most optimistic about civil rights. On May 16, 1990, less than 3 weeks after twenty-one of the twenty-seven CSC members were appointed, the Committee announced that it would review, on its own initiative, the constitutionality of the Union legislation on residence permits, on the right of state employees to sue their employer, and on consumer rights. These issues had long been criticized by the Soviet jurists and did not present a challenge for the Committee: residence permits (*propiska*) restricted mobility rights and a host of social rights; consumers were deprived of the choice of returning defective goods; and about 20 million state employees could not sue the State if they thought they were fired or reprimanded illegally. In 5 weeks, on June 21, 1990, the CSC declared the latter restrictions on judicial access in labor disputes unconstitutional, citing various constitutional guarantees and international human rights acts. Therefore, in its first decision the CSC chose to bring international human rights law into the domestic legal hierarchy and placed international law above domestic legal norms. Whether appropriate or not, this insertion of international law into the domestic legal order was an innovative approach albeit long advocated by the liberal legal elites and it suited Gorbachev's agenda of championing the values of humanity. As we will see, the Russian Constitutional Court continued this struggle to apply international standards of judicial protection in the Russian hierarchy of laws well into 2006.

On October 26, 1990, the CSC ruled that the residence permit (*propiska*) system violated the constitution and international human rights treaties, only after the USSR government began declassifying various restrictions on the freedom of movement, previously held secret. In a series of decisions, the Committee also struck down numerous unpublished government regulations in the area of individual rights and demanded their immediate publication. This insistence of the Committee on publishing legal norms is crucial for developing a legal hierarchy because secret rules cannot trump published laws and should not have a binding force in a rule-of-law state. However, secret government acts persisted well into the 1990s, as I will demonstrate in the rest of this book. The CSC reiterated its opposition to the *propiska* system in October 1991, when it invalidated provisions restricting the property rights of real estate owners and punishing violations of the residence permit rules. Again, this decision came after the CSC received assurances from numerous USSR government agencies that the *propiska* system was no longer useful. As we will see, the Russian Constitutional Court fought the housing permit requirements well into 2003 because the *propiska* system, a cornerstone of the Soviet statehood, introduced by Stalin in 1931, continues to serve as a useful instrument of Russian governance.

The local defiance of the CSC decisions, the persistence of these secret regulations, and the residence permit restrictions show the inadequacy of the thesis that judges are constrained and strategic actors who, first, secure the compliance of political actors with their rulings, and, then, strike down the contested law.[13] Indeed, the CSC tried to be strategic from the start and struck down USSR legal acts only after a favorable move by the Union authorities. However, these judicial strategies of securing compliance did not work most of the time, as I will examine in greater detail in Chapter 6.

To overcome this image of a timid and cautious constitutional review, the CSC members did not feel constrained by the procedure of handling cases, as outlined by the CSC statute. They issued various "statements" about the numerous deficiencies of the Soviet legal system, leaked their views on scheduled cases prior to the actual Committee hearings, held regular news conferences, and gave interviews with commentaries on the Committee decisions, a practice closely followed by the 1st Russian Constitutional Court in 1992–1993. Recognizing that this extrajudicial behavior lacked any binding effect on the rulers, the Committee leaders presented them as initiatives for the consideration of the USSR parliament.[14] For example, the Committee members repeatedly demanded a genuine Constitutional Court with exclusive and broad powers of judicial review. Chairman Alekseev, a civil law professor, actively lobbied for strong presidential power and his view of property rights reform.[15] His extrajudicial behavior was most evident in the last days of the USSR. On December 2, 1991, Chairman Alekseev told journalists that he was offered another important job in academia. On December 11, he publicly sided with Gorbachev on the impossibility of the dissolution of the Soviet Union through an agreement among Russian, Ukrainian, and Belarus presidents.

---

[13] Vanberg, *The Politics of Constitutional Review in Germany.*
[14] Mitiukov, *Predtecha konstitutsionnogo pravosudiia*, pp. 116–117.
[15] Hausmaninger, "From the Soviet Committee," p. 328.

The next day, the CSC announced that international human rights and nuclear nonproliferation treaties were binding on seceding republics. Ten days later, Chairman Alekseev told the press that the Committee dissolved itself as a result of the collapse of the Soviet Union.[16]

Yet the visibility of the Committee on the political scene was extremely low, given that neither the USSR authorities nor the Union republics were prepared to tolerate a strong judicial review of their actions. Conservative political elites recognized the redundancy of judicial review, while liberal political actors distrusted the CSC and demanded a powerful and independent constitutional court. Following the failed August 1991 coup, as the power of the USSR central government began to crumble with overwhelming speed, the Soviet Union authorities lost any interest in using judicial review to persuade the republics to stay in the Union. Meanwhile, the Union republics declared their independence and aspired to have their own constitutional courts. Not surprisingly, some of the CSC members and their staff accepted positions at the new Russian Constitutional Court, which, surprisingly, quickly became a much more powerful institution than its Union predecessor.

DECISION MAKING OF THE 1ST RUSSIAN CONSTITUTIONAL COURT: 1992–1993

The rapid rise to power and no less rapid failure of the 1st Russian Constitutional Court riveted the attention of numerous observers inside and outside of Russia. In almost 2 years of its operation, the Court received about 30,000 petitions, heard thirty cases, and issued twenty-seven decisions on the merits of cases (*postanovleniia*), two findings on the unconstitutionality of President Yeltsin's actions, and eighty-six rulings dismissing cases.[17] Seven justices wrote twenty-five dissenting and concurring opinions.[18] Unlike the USSR CSC, the Court usually acted on petitions from numerous federal and regional political actors, public associations,

---

[16] *Ibid.*, pp. 326–327.

[17] "Deiatelnost Konstitutsionnogo Suda RF v tsifrakh (noiabr 1991 g. – iiul 2001 g.)," *Rossiiskaia iustitsiia*, no. 10 (2001), pp. 43–45. Scholars cite different figures due to the fact that the 1st RCC did not maintain its records in 1992. See, for example, Carla Thorson, "Constitutional Courts as Political Actors: Russia in Comparative Perspective" (Ph.D. diss., University of California at Los Angeles, 2003), pp. 96–100.

[18] Donald D. Barry, "Decision-Making and Dissent in the Russian Federation Constitutional Court," in Roger Clark, Ferdinand Feldbrugge, and Stanislaw Pomorski, eds., *International and National Law in Russia and Eastern Europe: Essays in Honor of George Ginsburgs* (The Hague: Kluwer Law International, 2001), pp. 1–17.

and individuals. The Court struck down in whole, or in part, ten federal executive branch decrees, ten federal laws and legislative enactments, and four legal acts of the Russian regions. Similar to the Union CSC, the Court attached long lists of federal legal acts found in violation of the Russian constitution. But it is not these Court statistics that attracted many domestic and foreign observers. What surprised many was the courage and decisiveness with which this tribunal engaged itself in the settlement of the most serious political controversies inside and outside of the courtroom. The remainder of this chapter examines how this Court struggled to champion the power of judicial review in the areas of separation-of-powers, federalism, and constitutional rights. But first I explain briefly why the judges decided to be proactive and why politicians allowed them the freedom to do so.

To be sure, the easy access to judicial review (even a single federal legislator could petition the Court) and the broad, nonexhaustive list of Constitutional Court powers to review the constitutionality of all acts, decisions, and actions of federal and regional top government bodies, contributed to the involvement of the Court in the heavy power struggles of the time. That the Court was required (Article 58.2 of the 1991 Act) to review the compliance of legal acts with the principle of separation of powers also opened the door for judges to define this principle. More important, however, was the choice of the judges to take an active role in power struggles and to use the power of judicial review to shape the foundations of the new postcommunist Russia. Justices, who represented the newly forming Russian legal elites, were eager to make their Court really powerful and to avoid the image of its timid Union-level predecessor. Moreover, the close ties of many justices with the Russian legislature and the presidential administration allowed them to lobby political branches of government to make their Court operational, although politicians had the choice and necessary resources to delay the start of judicial review.[19]

That the RCC members elected Valerii Zorkin, an accomplished constitutional law expert and an advocate of a strong presidency, to chair the Court is another indication of their aspiration to engage in a powerful judicial review. As Justice Ebzeev put it, the court chairman influences

---

[19] For example, Russian leaders could have followed the example of their Ukrainian and Latvian colleagues who delayed the activation of constitutional courts for 6 years. Mikhail Mitiukov and Aleksandr Barnashov, *Ocherki konstitutsionnogo pravosudiia* (Tomsk: Izd-vo Tomskogo un-ta, 1999), p. 60.

the status that the Court has in the actual practice of Russian governance.[20] Chairman Zorkin, a former head of the expert task force in the Russian Constitutional Commission, had a working relationship with both President Yeltsin and the Supreme Soviet Chairman Khasbulatov and quickly succeeded in getting a separate building and generous funding for the Court with a staff of 247.[21] This was an unprecedented achievement for a judiciary in post-Soviet space because the Russian government bureaucracy initially allocated three small rooms for the whole Court in the building of the Supreme Soviet![22]

Most justices promoted the importance of their Court in the process of rebuilding Russia and insisted that they could work under the heavily amended 1978 Russian constitution. Following the example of the USSR CSC, the Zorkin Court issued numerous nonbinding statements with lists of legal acts of dubious constitutionality. To advertise the usefulness of their Court, they set up a Court press service, which to date remains an effective tool the judges use to communicate their concerns to the media. For example, they quickly signaled to the public their outrage at the omission of 10 million rubles from the 1992 Court's budget and of the threats of physical violence to several justices. At the same time, the judges lobbied for the quick adoption of the new constitution with separation of powers and a powerful Constitutional Court. They partially succeeded in April 1992, when constitutional amendments redefined the Russian Constitutional Court as the "highest body of judicial power in charge of protecting constitutional order" and granted the Court the powers to review the constitutionality of political parties and to settle jurisdictional disputes between the executive and the legislature.[23]

---

[20] Leonid Nikitinskii, "Interview with Boris Ebzeev, Justice of the Constitutional Court of the Russian Federation," *East European Constitutional Review*, vol. 6, no. 1 (1997), pp. 83–88.

[21] Hausmaninger, "From the Soviet Committee," p. 333. German Constitutional Court Justices also had to bargain with politicians over funding of their Court; see Georg Vanberg, "Establishing Judicial Independence in West Germany: The Impact of Opinion Leadership and the Separation of Powers," *Comparative Politics*, vol. 32, no. 3 (April 2000), pp. 333–353.

[22] Interview with an RCC Justice, Moscow, June 27, 2001. The USSR CSC had a staff of thirty clerks.

[23] Zakon RSFSR of April 21, 1992 "Ob izmeneniiakh i dopolneniiakh Konstitutsii (osnovnogo zakona) RSFSR," *VSND i VS RSFSR*, no. 20 (1992), item 1084. See Sergei Pashin, "Pora stanovleniia," [Time of Formation] *Iuridicheskaia gazeta*, no. 12 (1993), p. 5; Mikhail Mitiukov, *K istorii konstitutsionnogo pravosudiia Rossii* [On the History of the Constitutional Justice in Russia] (Moskva: ATSO, 2002), p. 106.

Judges also introduced a new way of publishing their decisions.[24] The Court set up its own Herald (*Vestnik Konstitutsionnogo Suda RF*) and proceeded to publish: (a) a timeline of the constitutional litigation – to show that it could deliver speedy constitutional justice; (b) the excerpts of the testimonies of invited experts and parties to the litigation – to show that judges listened to both sides of the controversy and drew on the expertise of well-respected lawyers; (c) the Constitutional Court interim orders and decisions on the merits – to show that judges followed due process; and (d) the dissenting and concurring opinions of the RCC judges – to show the importance of the voice of each judge on the bench.

Moreover, it was President Yeltsin himself who repeatedly called on the RCC to play a more active role in settling legislative–executive disputes, while the Russian Supreme Soviet Chairman Ruslan Khasbulatov quietly reminded the legislature that "the Constitutional Court does not stand above the President" and the legislature.[25] In December 1992, Chairman Zorkin received public accolades for brokering a deal between Yeltsin and Khasbulatov who agreed to hold a constitutional referendum in March 1993.[26] In March 1993, Zorkin appeared on TV and condemned Yeltsin's decree on the special rule as a threat to the constitutional order. Yeltsin, in turn, accused the Court of politicization and prolegislature bias, and announced that he would stop petitioning the Court. He tried to test the loyalty of the justices by inviting them to a private meeting on May 29, 1993. However, only a minority – six of thirteen justices – met with Yeltsin. That none of them was willing to discuss the details of the meeting[27] indicates that Yeltsin's proposals to them were blatantly illegal. Two weeks later, Yeltsin told Zorkin that he was "worried by the friendship between Zorkin and Khasbulatov." Zorkin insisted that he did not incite Khasbulatov against Yeltsin but to no avail.[28] Together with proactive

---

[24] The USSR courts never published the full texts of their decisions.

[25] Mitiukov, *K istorii konstitutsionnogo pravosudiia*, pp. 115, 119.

[26] Ilia Shablinskii, *Predely vlasti: borba za rossiiskuiu konstitutsionnuiu reformu: 1989–1995 gg.* [The Limits of Power: The Struggle for the Russian Constitutional Reform: 1989–1995] (Moskva: TsKI MONF, 1997), p. 49.

[27] Justices Ametistov, Kononov, Morshchakova, Oleinik, Rudkin and Vitruk attended the meeting. Thorson, "Constitutional Courts as Political Actors," p. 185.

[28] Anna Ostapchuk, "Prezident skazal, chto ego bespokoit 'moia druzhba s Khasbulatovym'. Valerii Zorkin o situatsii v Konstitutsionnom sude," [President Told Me That He Was Concerned about 'My Friendship with Khasbulatov.' Valerii Zorkin on the Situation in the Constitutional Court] *Nezavisimaia gazeta*, November 12, 1993, p. 1.

Decision Making of the 1st Russian Constitutional Court   103

judges, serious legislative–executive confrontation both invited the Constitutional Court into the arena of heavyweight politics and nearly caused its dissolution after President Yeltsin's victory in the fall of 1993.

The caseload of the 1st Constitutional Court also reflects the fundamental choice of its judges to define the constitutional order of the new Russia. According to several justices, Chairman Zorkin controlled the agenda of the Court and selected politically salient cases for consideration.[29] For example, in the infamous 1992 *Communist Party* case, the constitutional petition to examine the constitutionality of the Communist Party came to the Court in May 1992 after the petitioners had "consulted" with Chairman Zorkin. Justice Viktor Luchin openly complained that Zorkin overstepped his authority by consulting the politicians in advance, while Zorkin justified his action by saying that he tried to strengthen Russia's nascent constitutional order.[30]

However, it was the Court majority that determined the case selection and repeatedly avoided undisguised partisan politics. True, the Court promptly accepted the petition against the constitutionality of the Communist Party but, throughout the six-month trial, judges slammed the opposing sides for bringing politics in the courtroom and eventually declined to rule on the merits of the petition.[31] Moreover, the Court dispelled Zorkin's hope to examine the constitutionality of hastily drawn privatization reforms. None of the judges agreed with Justice Luchin's call to review the constitutionality of President Yeltsin's actions to dissolve the USSR in December of 1991.[32] In April 1993, the Court rejected the complaint of the dismissed Lipetsk Province governor against President Yeltsin who had fired him. Even in July 1993, when the Zorkin Court was already divided over the confrontation between Yeltsin and the Russian Supreme Soviet, the majority rejected the petition of the parliament to impeach Yeltsin for his decree of March 20, 1993, on the "special rule of governance." Thus, the 1st Russian Constitutional Court displayed some

---

[29] Thorson, "Constitutional Courts as Political Actors," p. 127.

[30] Jonathan Steele, *Eternal Russia: Yeltsin, Gorbachev, and the Mirage of Democracy* (Cambridge, MA: Harvard University Press, 1995), pp. 348–349. Despite Luchin's criticism, this practice of judges 'encouraging' political actors to bring lawsuits to their Court seems to persist (see the discussion of the taxpayers' litigation in Chapter 7).

[31] RCC decision 9-P of November 30, 1992, *VKS RF*, nos. 4–5 (1993), pp. 37–64 (Ebzeev, Kononov, and Luchin, dissenting). Dissenting opinions are published in *VKS RF*, no. 6 (1993), pp. 1–48.

[32] Viktor Luchin, *Konstitutsiia Rossiiskoi Federatsii: problemy realizatsii* [Constitution of the Russian Federation: The Problems of Realization] (Moskva: IUNITI, 2002), p. 419.

degree of judicial restraint, refused to bring open partisan politics in the courtroom, and attempted to pick its cases with care.[33]

Still, most justices preferred to concentrate on serious political issues, although the pro-Yeltsin minority began to oppose this activist agenda in early 1993 when the rift between the president and the Supreme Soviet began to widen.[34] Not surprisingly, the Zorkin Court involvement in sharp legislative–executive rivalries and federal–regional conflicts generated disagreements on the bench and resulted in twenty-three dissenting opinions. Under the decision-making procedure, dissenters could not really influence the majority opinion because the Court usually announced the result of the litigation shortly after the hearing and presented the judicial reasoning several weeks later. Naturally, the justices who disagreed with the outcome were forced to write their separate opinions, while the majority reportedly ignored the arguments of the dissenters.[35] Throughout 1993, frustrated dissenters, usually a pro-Yeltsin minority, vented their disagreements in the media, and eventually came to boycott the Court sessions. The majority attempted to block the publication of the dissents and insisted that the Court could go on without dissenters on the bench. Finally, in early October 1993, Yeltsin's administration used this split as a pretext to force Chairman Zorkin to resign from his chairmanship in a trade-off to keep the Russian Constitutional Court.

Defining Separation of Powers

The docket of the Zorkin Court reflected the preferences of its chairman for a presidential republic with a strong judicial review: almost half of the Court's judgments dealt with separation-of-powers issues.[36] As Chairman Zorkin repeatedly stressed, his Court would protect Russia's

---

[33] Cf. Alexander Blankenagel, *"Detstvo, otrochestvo, iunost" Rossiiskogo Konstitutsionnogo Suda* ["Childhood, Adolescence, Youth" of the Russian Constitutional Court] (Moskva: TsKI MONF, 1996), pp. 17–24.

[34] Herbert Hausmaninger, "Towards a 'New' Russian Constitutional Court," *Cornell International Law Journal*, vol. 28, no. 2 (Spring 1995), pp. 349–386, at 354.

[35] Blankenagel, *Detstvo, otrochestvo, iunost*, p. 99.

[36] Because many judgments simultaneously involved questions of separation of powers, federalism, and fundamental rights, scholars and RCC Justices disagree on the exact distribution of cases among these three issue areas. See, for example, Boris Ebzeev, ed., *Kommentarii k postanovleniiam Konstitutsionnogo Suda Rossiiskoi Federatsii. T. 1* (Moskva: Iurist, 2000), p. 27; Blankenagel, *Detstvo, otrochestvo, iunost*; Hausmaninger, "Towards a 'New' Russian Constitutional Court"; and Epstein et al., "The Role of Constitutional Courts."

Decision Making of the 1st Russian Constitutional Court   105

constitutional system and prevent the legislature, the executive, and the whole society from falling into the abyss of a violent confrontation.[37] Clarifying what separation of powers meant could place the Court in the position of umpire between the legislature and executive in the name of the supremacy of the constitution.

The very first case heard by the 1st Russian Constitutional Court showed that Zorkin's colleagues on the bench shared his idea of a powerful judicial review. On January 14, 1992, after a daylong hearing followed by 2 hours of deliberations, the Court unanimously declared that Russian President Yeltsin's decree on the merger of the former KGB with the Russian Ministry of Internal Affairs (MVD) was unconstitutional.[38] The Court ruled that the merger violated the constitutional principle of separation of powers because the 1978 Russian constitution granted parliament the power to create ministries and to monitor presidential policy making, particularly in the area of constitutional rights protection. According to the Court, this legislative power was an essential element of checks and balances in the separation-of-powers system. Although this system was introduced in the Russian constitution only three months later, in April 1992, the Court attempted to base the separation of powers on the rule that "any state agency may only adopt such decisions and perform such actions that are within its jurisdiction, determined in conformity with the constitution."[39]

The Constitutional Court applied this rule in several other cases against both the executive and the legislature. The Court repeatedly struck down the Soviet-era tradition of issuing joint executive–legislative decrees, and consistently restricted the Soviet-style authority of the Presidium of the Russian Supreme Soviet to procedural questions, thus deleting two rungs from an already congested legal hierarchy. The Court also banned government ministers from sitting simultaneously as members of parliament, and prohibited the legislature from issuing direct orders to the federal Cabinet. Both the legislature and the executive pulled and pushed the Court to take sides so intensively that already by July 1992, Justice Vitruk confessed:

---

[37] "Valery Zorkin: Russia's President Has His Mandate, Not an Indulgence," *Moscow News*, no. 5 (February 1992), p. 16; "Valerii Zorkin: Glavnaia nasha zadacha – zashchitit konstitutsionnyi stroi," [Valerii Zorkin: Our Main Task – To Protect Constitutional Order] *Rossiiskaia iustitsiia*, nos. 7–8 (April 1992), p. 18.

[38] RCC decision 1-P of January 14, 1992, *VKS RF*, no. 1 (1993), pp. 11–19 (Ametistov, concurring). English translation in *Statutes and Decisions. The Laws of the USSR and its Successor States* {hereinafter *Statutes and Decisions*}, no. 3 (1994).

[39] van den Berg, "Constitution of the Russian Federation Annotated," p. 199.

"We are live human beings, who work in a real political environment, and we cannot be absolutely impartial."[40]

The Court also reviewed several cases on the separation of powers within the legislative and the executive branches. For example, the Court ruled that the federal president, not the federal cabinet, could issue decrees in the absence of a federal law on a matter, a precedent that the majority of RCC justices has been adhering to ever since. The relationship within the legislative branch between the Russian Supreme Soviet and the supralegislative Congress of People's Deputies (CPD) was more complicated because of the remnants of parliamentary supremacy: the heavily amended 1978 constitution (Article 109) still recognized the power of the CPD to decide on any matter within the federal jurisdiction. In the April 1993 *Referendum* case, the Court ruled that the Congress lacked the power to annul federal statutes. A month later, in a dispute between President Yeltsin and the Congress over the control of the electronic mass media, the Court changed its view and found that the CPD could annul a federal statute and could order the Supreme Soviet to amend such statute.[41]

The Zorkin Court also changed its view of presidential powers in the infamous "Communist Party" trial that took place in the second half of 1992.[42] In a skillfully crafted 10–3 majority opinion, the Court upheld the most important clauses of Yeltsin's ban of the Communist Party: ban of the top Communist Party bodies and the transfer of the Party property to the Russian state.[43] Here, the Court found that the president, as the "highest official of the republic and the head of its executive power," could

[40] "Nelzia byt sudiei v sobstvennom dele," [One Cannot Be a Judge in His Own Case] *Rossiiskaia gazeta*, July 29, 1992.

[41] Compare RCC decisions: 8-P of April 21, 1993, *VKS RF*, nos. 2–3 (1994), pp. 33–52 (Ametistov and Morshchakova, dissenting), English translation in *Statutes and Decisions*, no. 5 (1994); and 11-P of May 27, 1993, *ibid.*, nos. 2–3 (1994), pp. 75–95 (Kononov, dissenting), English translation in *Statutes and Decisions*, no. 5 (1994).

[42] The proceedings of this 6-month-long trial are published in the four-volume set *Materialy dela o proverke konstitutsionnosti Ukazov Prezidenta RF, kasaiushchikhsia deiatelnosti KPSS i KP RSFSR, a takzhe o proverke konstitutsionnosti KPSS i KP RSFSR* [Materials of the Case on the Determination of the Constitutionality of the Decrees of the RF President Concerning the Activity of the CPSU and CP RSFSR As Well As on the Determination of the Constitutionality of the CPSU and CP RSFSR] (Moskva: Spark, 1996–1997). For an interesting account of the trial in English, see Kathleen E. Smith, *Mythmaking in the New Russia: Politics and Memory during the Yeltsin Era* (Ithaca, NY: Cornell University Press, 2002), pp. 11–29.

[43] RCC decision 9-P of November 30, 1992, *VKS RF*, no. 4–5 (1993), pp. 37–64 (Ebzeev, Kononov, and Luchin, dissenting). Dissenting opinions are published in *VKS RF*, no. 6 (1993), pp. 1–48, English translation in *Statutes and Decisions*, no. 4 (1994).

Decision Making of the 1st Russian Constitutional Court   107

ban political parties in order to safeguard the state and public security and to protect Russia's sovereignty in the aftermath of the August 1991 *coup d'etat*, even though the Russian constitution did not enumerate this power.[44] Dissenting Justices Ebzeev and Luchin objected to this expansion of presidential powers as an infringement upon the separation-of-powers principle, while Justice Kononov criticized the Court for its refusal to examine the constitutionality of the Communist Party. In fact, the Court's refusal was interpreted by Yeltsin's circle as a sign of a pro-Communist majority on the bench. This perception was strengthened in the February 1993 *National Salvation Front* case when the Court's majority refused to examine the constitutionality of the anti-Yeltsin National Salvation Front. Instead, the Court told Yeltsin that he could no longer ban political parties because the Russian constitution did not enumerate this power of the Russian president and authorized exclusive judicial review of their constitutionality (Article 50, 165–1).[45] At this point, the opposition to Yeltsin's agenda was tightly interwoven into the Court's decision making.

The choice of the Constitutional Court to protect the principle of separation of powers and to oppose presidential policies was most clearly reflected in two findings (*zakliucheniia*) on the unconstitutionality of President Yeltsin's actions. The first finding, of March 23, 1993, was issued on the initiative of the Court and the Russian Supreme Soviet and examined the constitutionality of Yeltsin's announcement on TV that he signed a decree on "special governance regime."[46] Under this regime, according to Yeltsin, no government body could repeal his decrees, and regional governors could not be fired without Yeltsin's permission. Yeltsin also announced a nationwide referendum in which voters would vote on their trust in him, on the new draft constitution and the new federal electoral law draft, all in one question. In a 9–3 decision, the Court declared

---

[44] van den Berg, "Constitution of the Russian Federation Annotated," pp. 205–206. For the analysis of this case in English, see, for example, Robert Sharlet, "The Russian Constitutional Court: First Term," *Post-Soviet Affairs*, vol. 9, no. 1 (January–March 1993), pp. 1–39; Donald D. Barry, "Trial of the CPSU and the Principles of Nuremberg," *Review of Central and East European Law*, vol. 22, no. 3 (1996), pp. 255–262; and Jane Henderson, "The Russian Constitutional Court and the Communist Party Case: Watershed or Whitewash?" *Communist and Post-Communist Studies*, vol. 40, no. 1 (March 2007), pp. 1–16.

[45] RCC decision 3-P of February 12, 1993, *VKS RF*, no. 1 (1994), pp. 12–24 (Kononov, dissenting), English translation in *Statutes and Decisions*, no. 4 (1994).

[46] RCC finding 1-Z of March 23, 1993, *VKS RF*, no. 1 (1994), pp. 47–63 (Ametistov, Morshchakova, and Vitruk, dissenting), English translation in *Statutes and Decisions*, no. 4 (1994).

Yeltsin's TV speech unconstitutional because it "destroyed" the principle of separation of powers, intruded in the jurisdiction of the regions, and violated voting rights. The Court, however, stopped short of declaring grounds for Yeltsin's impeachment, and judges had to defend their position publicly against the fury of the legislators who wanted to impeach the president and the rage of pro-Yeltsin groups who accused the Court of an anti-Yeltsin bias.[47]

The second finding, of September 21, 1993, issued at the Court's initiative, allowed the impeachment of the Russian president for issuing decree No. 1400 "On Step-by-Step Constitutional Reform in the Russian Federation."[48] The most important parts of this decree dissolved the Russian legislature (the Congress and the Supreme Soviet) and instructed the Court not to convene any sessions. Chairman Zorkin immediately called the Court in session and managed to garner a 9–4 majority opinion that the Congress of People's Deputies could either impeach President Yeltsin or terminate his powers automatically. Dissenting Justices Ametistov, Kononov, Morshchakova, and Vitruk pointed out various procedural flaws and inconsistencies in the Court's view of the separation of powers. Chairman Zorkin insisted that the Court was placed in the extreme conflict between Yeltsin and the parliament, and that Yeltsin's destruction of the constitutional order was much worse than the procedural flaws in the Court's finding.[49]

In short, the 1st Russian Constitutional Court attempted to define the principle of separation of powers in the context of the heavily amended Soviet-era constitution with its legislative supremacy. The Court refused to recognize the "implied" powers of the political branches of government and disapproved of their unilateral grabs of power. However, the Court's calls for peace and cooperation between President Yeltsin and the Supreme Soviet increasingly fell on the deaf ears of federal political elites. Ultimately, the involvement of the Zorkin Court in the severe confrontation between the executive and the legislature brought the Court to its 16-month suspension in the fall of 1993. Contrary to the theories that link political fragmentation with stronger judicial review, the

---

[47] On July 12, 1993, the Court refused to examine the text of this decree on procedural grounds. See RCC resolution 70-R of July 12, 1993, unpublished, available at the Web site of the Russian Constitutional Court, http://www.ksrf.ru.

[48] RCC finding 2-Z of September 21, 1993, *VKS RF*, no. 6 (1994), pp. 40–56 (Ametistov, Kononov, Morshchakova, and Vitruk, dissenting), English translation in *Statutes and Decisions*, no. 6 (1994).

[49] Ostapchuk, "Prezident skazal."

Decision Making of the 1st Russian Constitutional Court 109

growing power diffusion in Russia resulted in the demise of strong judicial review.

Defining Russian Federalism

The emphasis of the 1st Russian Constitutional Court on cooperation and negotiation among political forces is clearly displayed in its federalism cases, which made up a quarter of its caseload. In the *Tatarstan Referendum* case (March 13, 1992), the Court refused to recognize the unilateral secession of subfederal units and ruled that the only just and legal way of solving this problem would involve negotiations among all interested Russian regions.[50] But, as will be explained in Chapter 6, both sides in this dispute refused to obey the Court even though some believe that such centralizing decisions of high courts help to entrench judicial power.[51] Following the signing of the Federation Treaty on March 30, 1992, which Justice Ebzeev called "a foundation" of the independent Russian Federation,[52] both the federal and regional political elites had diverging views on the proper boundaries of their jurisdictions. These differences were often intertwined with the conflicts over Yeltsin's reform agenda. As in the separation-of-powers cases, the Zorkin Court attempted to settle these conflicts and to interpret the 1992 Federation Treaty. As Zorkin himself put it, his Court would have to prevent the replication of numerous Yugoslavias and of the USSR collapse on Russian soil.

The accommodation of federal and regional interests was the approach that the Zorkin Court chose to define the nature of Russian federalism. "Accommodation" in the context of Soviet unitary structure and the 1992 Federation Treaty meant the expansion of the jurisdiction of regions and balancing their interests with the federal prerogative. Expanding the jurisdiction of the regions, the Court repeatedly blocked the attempts by the federal president and the parliament to issue direct orders to the Russian regions. For example, the Court persistently declared that the Russian

---

[50] RCC decision 3-P of March 13, 1992, *VKS RF*, no. 1 (1993), pp. 40–52 (Ametistov, dissenting), English translation in *Statutes and Decisions*, no. 3 (1994).

[51] For example, Tom Ginsburg argues that the centralizing decisions in local–national disputes might make sense for a young court because such decisions are largely self-enforcing. See his *Judicial Review in New Democracies: Constitutional Courts in Asian Cases* (New York: Cambridge University Press, 2003), pp. 88–105.

[52] Boris Ebzeev. Speech. *Vserossiiskoe soveshchanie rukovoditelei organov gosudarstvennoi predstavitelnoi i ispolnitelnoi vlasti respublik v sostave Rossiiskoi Federatsii, kraev, oblastei, avtonomnoi oblasti, avtonomnykh okrugov, gorodov Moskvy i Sankt-Peterburga* (Moskva: Respublika, 1992), p. 74.

Russian Constitutional Review in Action (1990–1993)

regions did not need the approval of the federal center to set up and dissolve their government bodies and to schedule elections for public offices.[53] The Court ruled twice that the regional constitutional courts should interpret these powers as well as other matters in the sphere of exclusive jurisdiction of the Russian regions.[54]

In two decisions over the powers of the Moscow City government, the Court ruled that the Russian regions could enact their own laws if there was no federal statute on the matter. Moreover, the federal government had to negotiate with the regions all federal bills in areas of joint jurisdiction.[55] In the *Irkutsk* case, the Court required President Yeltsin to negotiate issues of control over hydropower plants in several regions in order to balance the national and the regional interests.[56] In two judgments over the conflict between two neighboring regions, North Ossetia and Ingushetia, the Court asked both regions to cooperate in solving their territorial dispute and rejected the attempts to introduce segregated refugee settlements in one of them.[57] The Court also affirmed the right of the regions to sign interregional agreements to accommodate various kinds of disputes between the regions.[58] Even in the *Kabardino–Balkaria judges* decision, which struck down fifteen clauses of the Kabardino–Balkaria law on the status of judges, the Zorkin Court urged the federal center to consult with the regions on matters of joint jurisdiction![59]

In short, the 1st RCC consistently dismantled the unitary structure of the Russian state and advocated a flexible federation built on negotiations

---

[53] RCC decisions: 13-P of June 3, 1993, *VKS RF*, nos. 4–5 (1994), pp. 21–36 (Kononov and Vitruk, dissenting), English translation in *Statutes and Decisions*, no. 6 (1994); and 14-P of June 7, 1993, *ibid.*, pp. 40–53 (Kononov, dissenting), English translation in *Statutes and Decisions*, no. 5 (1994).

[54] RCC decisions: 13-P of June 3, 1993, *VKS RF*, nos. 4–5 (1994), pp. 21–36 (Kononov and Vitruk, dissenting), English translation in *Statutes and Decisions*, no. 6 (1994); and 18-P of September 30, 1993, *ibid.*, no. 6 (1994), pp. 29–39.

[55] RCC decisions: 5-P of May 19, 1992, *VKS RF*, nos. 2–3 (1993) (Ebzeev, dissenting), English translation in *Statutes and Decisions*, no. 3 (1994); and 6-P of April 2, 1993, *ibid.*, nos. 2–3 (1994), pp. 8–19, English translation in *Statutes and Decisions*, no. 5 (1994).

[56] RCC decision 15-P of September 10, 1993, *VKS RF*, nos. 4–5 (1994), pp. 64–78 (Kononov and Morshchakova, dissenting).

[57] RCC decisions: 17-P of September 17, 1993, *VKS RF*, no. 6 (1994), pp. 18–25; and 73-O of September 16, 1993, in Tamara Morshchakova, ed., *Konstitutsionnyi Sud Rossiiskoi Federatsii. Postanovleniia. Opredeleniia. 1992–1996* (Moskva: Novyi Iurist, 1997), pp. 652–654.

[58] RCC decision 9-P of May 11, 1993, *VKS RF*, nos. 2–3 (1994), pp. 54–59, English translation in *Statutes and Decisions*, no. 5 (1994).

[59] RCC decision 18-P of September 30, 1993, *VKS RF*, no. 6 (1994), pp. 29–39.

Decision Making of the 1st Russian Constitutional Court 111

and compromise between the federal level and regions, in order to prevent the disintegration of the new Russia. Thus, the Court tolerated the asymmetrical federation (except on the issues of judicial independence), recognized the variety of elected government structures in the regions, and legitimized the place for intergovernmental agreements in the Russian legal hierarchy.[60]

Protecting Constitutional Rights

As I discussed in Chapter 3, the power of the 1st Russian Constitutional Court to review individual petitions was a product of compromise. Individuals could not contest the constitutionality of laws or presidential decrees, while the Court lacked the power to annul the contested legal act – both limitations reflected respect for the political branches of government. On the one hand, individuals could challenge the constitutionality of the practice of application of laws and of other legal acts that violated their rights. On the other hand, individuals could petition the Court only after they had exhausted all other venues, a sign of respect for the executive and regular courts. In addition, individuals bore the burden of proof that alleged violations were so widespread that they constituted the "law-application practice." The Constitutional Court could only strike down this law-application practice, which was a code word for reversing the decisions of other courts.[61] These procedural difficulties together with the preference of the judges to focus on "hot potatoes" resulted in a mere six decisions being issued by the Zorkin Court at the request of individuals. However, the Court frequently cited violations of constitutional rights in the "separation of power" cases and the "federalism" cases. Paradoxically, as one court watcher noted, most of the individual complaints reviewed by the 1st Russian Constitutional Court dealt with the socialist-era restrictions of labor rights, not political freedoms.[62] I examine these "labor rights" judgments below to show the pattern of the Constitutional Court decision making in cases brought by individuals.

According to several justices, the Zorkin Court put numerous individual complaints over criminal procedure on the backburner because most justices shared two basic concerns: (1) that the transition to a market

---

[60] Ebzeev, *Kommentarii*, p. 407.

[61] See William Burnham and Alexei Trochev, "Russia's War between the Courts: The Struggle over the Jurisdictional Boundary between the Constitutional Court and Regular Courts," *American Journal of Comparative Law*, vol. 55, no. 3 (Summer 2007), p. 388.

[62] Blankenagel, *Detstvo, otrochestvo, iunost*, pp. 36–38.

economy would plunge millions of Russians into poverty, and (2) that rising levels of crime and physical insecurity would make the protection of due process rights for the accused unpopular in the eyes of the public. As Chairman Zorkin put it, Russia's retired people were among the most vulnerable social groups in the market economic reforms. And, as we shall see in the next chapter, the 2nd RCC shared this vision of expanding social rights.

On February 4, 1992, the RCC upheld an individual's right to choose when to retire, which was violated by Article 33-1-1 of the Labor Code.[63] Ironically, this Labor Code provision was enacted in 1988 as a part of Gorbachev's "perestroyka" reform to get rid of old Soviet apparatchiks.[64] Although the 1978 Russian constitution did not ban age discrimination explicitly, the Court read this ban into the constitution and struck down the practice of dismissing employees for the sole reason that they had reached retirement age. The Court found that Russia was bound by International Labor Organization Recommendations 162 and 166, which banned age discrimination, as well as by the USSR CSC's decision of April 4, 1991, which declared this practice unconstitutional. Therefore, the Court ruled that infringement on the freedom to choose the time of retirement from the labor force violated both individual labor rights and Russia's international obligations. In this decision, the Court "advised" the Russian Supreme Soviet to delete the offending provisions from the Labor Code and ordered the Russian judiciary to apply constitutional rules in labor disputes.

In its next "labor rights" decision of June 23, 1992, the Court reviewed eight individual complaints regarding the timing of judicial review of illegal dismissal.[65] Complainants alleged that the Russian courts restricted their constitutional right to appeal court decisions in disputes over unjustified dismissals to 1 or 2 years, citing either Article 211-5 of the Russian Labor Code or Article 90-4 of the USSR Labor Act respectively. The Zorkin Court lashed out at the judiciary for following these Soviet-era regulations and ordered them to apply Article 1 of the Civil Procedure Code, which did not impose any time limits for the appeal of labor disputes. Otherwise the Russian judiciary would violate fourteen constitutional

---

[63] RCC decision 2-P of February 4, 1992, *VKS RF*, no. 1 (1993), pp. 29–37 (Gadzhiev, concurring), English translation in *Statutes and Decisions*, no. 3 (1994).

[64] Rozaliia Ivanova, "Kommentarii," in Boris Ebzeev, ed., *Kommentarii k postanovleniiam Konstitutsionnogo Suda Rossiiskoi Federatsii. T. 2* (Moskva: Iurist, 2000), p. 584.

[65] RCC decision 8-P of June 23, 1992, *VKS RF*, nos. 2–3 (1993), pp. 41–52, English translation in *Statutes and Decisions*, no. 3 (1994).

Decision Making of the 1st Russian Constitutional Court   113

provisions on basic rights and international obligations! In effect, the 1st Russian Constitutional Court again ordered the Russian judiciary to follow the rules of the Russian constitution, not the guidelines of the USSR Supreme Court, a task that the Russian Supreme Court failed to do.

The Zorkin Court continued to clash with the Russian Supreme Court, in its decision of January 27, 1993, over the practice of awarding damages in illegal dismissal disputes.[66] Nine individual complainants asked the Constitutional Court to annul judicial decisions that recognized the fact of illegal dismissal, yet failed to award the salary for the whole period a person was out of work. For example, one engineer fought his dismissal in courts for 12 years and eventually won his case. Yet the court awarded him compensation for only 1 year of lost work! Outraged at this injustice, the Russian Constitutional Court judges discovered that these limits were initially set in the Stalin-era regulation of 1938. The Zorkin Court ruled that these limits on damages in the illegal dismissal cases violated the fundamental "principles of fairness, legal equality, state guarantees of individual rights, and just compensation of harm caused by illegal actions of state officials." More importantly, the Court found that these principles had existed in the Russian constitution since 1978, bound courts to award damages in full for the whole period of dismissal, and required the state, not the employer, to adjust the amount of damages according to the inflation rate. In fact, the Zorkin Court repeatedly admonished the legislature and the executive for their failure to honor state monetary obligations to individuals and to protect their savings.[67]

To be sure, the Russian Supreme Court was technically right when it objected to the power of the Russian Constitutional Court to review individual complaints, as shown in the previous chapter. Reviewing constitutional complaints, the Zorkin Court persistently invaded the jurisdiction of the Russian Supreme Court under the guise of unwritten constitutional principles and international legal norms and ordered the Russian Supreme Court to reverse its decisions. However, the 1st Russian Constitutional Court also expanded the jurisdiction of courts by championing the direct binding force of constitutional provisions on the judicial review of administrative actions. For example, the Zorkin Court ordered the regular courts to review the dismissal of the procurators, extrajudicial eviction orders,

---

[66] RCC decision 1-P of January 27, 1993, *VKS RF*, nos. 2–3 (1993), pp. 56–64, English translation in *Statutes and Decisions*, no. 4 (1994).

[67] RCC decisions: 7-P of June 9, 1992, *VKS RF*, nos. 2–3 (1993), pp. 29–36, English translation in *Statutes and Decisions*, no. 3 (1994); and 12-P of May 31, 1993, *ibid.*, nos. 4–5 (1994), pp. 12–16, English translation in *Statutes and Decisions*, no. 5 (1994).

disputes over Communist Party property, and disputes between media owners and journalists. Therefore, individuals obtained the right to sue the federal government and the Russian legislature.

In fact, the Zorkin Court was so optimistic in its ordeal of protecting constitutional rights that it continued to review individual complaints *after* September 21, 1993, when President Yeltsin recommended that the Court not convene its sessions until ratification of the new Russian constitution. According to the late Justice Ernest Ametistov, who supported Yeltsin, the decision making of the Court in the area of individual complaints united his colleagues and allowed them to base their judgment on legal principles, not partisan attitudes.[68] Indeed, "social rights" decisions allowed a broad basis for reaching agreement among the judges and generated only two dissenting opinions.[69] Justices achieved a broad consensus on the bench by combining international human rights provisions with constitutional provisions on the particular right or freedom, on constitutional supremacy, and on Russia's international obligations in order to justify their conclusion that the particular right was violated.[70] The outdated text of the 1978 Russian constitution forced the Court to "discover" numerous unwritten constitutional principles of equality, fairness and legal certainty, which laid the groundwork for the rights jurisprudence of the 2nd RCC, as discussed in Chapter 5. Principled decision making in this area "raised the nation's constitution-consciousness," according to Justice Ametistov.[71]

In summary, however skillfully, the 1st Russian Constitutional Court interpreted the spirit and the letter of the heavily amended 1978 Russian constitution to elevate the status of constitutional rights and to champion their judicial protection. Because this Court lacked the power to strike down any offending legal rule at the request of individuals, justices chose to order the legislature to pass an appropriate statute because

---

[68] Ernest Ametistov, "Zashchita sotsialnykh prav cheloveka v Konstitutsionnom Sude Rossiiskoi Federatsii: pervye itogi i dalneishie perspektivy," [Protection of Social Rights in the Constitutional Court of the Russian Federation: First Conclusions and Subsequent Perspectives] *VKS RF*, no. 4 (1995), p. 31.

[69] Gadzhiev dissented in RCC decision 2-P of February 4, 1992; Morshchakova dissented in RCC decision 7-P of April 16, 1993.

[70] See Jane Henderson, "Reference to International Law in the Decided Cases of the First Russian Constitutional Court," in Rein Müllerson, Malgosia Fitzmaurice, and Mads Andenas, eds., *Constitutional Reform and International Law in Central and Eastern Europe* (The Hague: Kluwer Law International, 1998), pp. 59–77.

[71] Reported in Herman Schwartz, *The Struggle for Constitutional Justice in Post-Communist Europe* (Chicago: University of Chicago Press, 2000), p. 143.

Conclusion

they determined that only federal laws, not governmental directives, could restrict individual rights. The Zorkin Court placed its decisions above Russian Supreme Court decisions and ordered the Russian judiciary to apply constitutional rules and even international legal norms to protect basic rights. As we will see, the 2nd Russian Constitutional Court continued to insist on the supremacy of constitutional rights in the Russian legal hierarchy, and to compete for the supremacy of its judgments vis-à-vis the other two high national courts.

CONCLUSION

The infancy of the Russian Constitutional Court clearly shows that judges have to fight for judicial review power both by issuing judgments and by lobbying politicians. Judges fought too much outside of the bench and brought the 1st RCC to its demise, according to the by now well-known story, which was popularized by Yeltsin's circle, the winners of Russia's 1993 constitutional crisis. This story blames the judges themselves, and particularly Chairman Valerii Zorkin, for his active involvement in heavyweight politics and his anti-Yeltsin stance.[72] True, it was a conscious choice of the majority of justices to plunge into political negotiations between the executive and the legislature and between the federal center and the regions. Certainly, it is difficult to blame the judges for trying to resolve the stalemate between the president and the legislature and to prevent the disintegration of the Russian Federation. But the efficacy of the "peacemaking" efforts of the 1st RCC should also be viewed in the context of the explicit invitation by political branches and further attacks on the Court. It was President Yeltsin who asked the Court to be more active in settling the separation-of-powers disputes and accused the Court of overstepping the boundaries of judicial prerogative. The standard story of the "anti-Yeltsin" Zorkin Court also ignores the fact that the heavily amended 1978 constitution tipped the balance of power in favor of the legislature, and that it was the Court that championed the principle of separation of powers in order to uphold presidential prerogatives.

By placing this story in a comparative context, one also could not predict the failure of the 1st Court. Critics argue that the politicization of its bench was the result of judicial appointments being made on the basis

---

[72] For a detailed overview and rebuttal of this point of view, see Kim Lane Scheppele, "Guardians of the Constitution: Constitutional Court Presidents and the Struggle for the Rule of Law in Post-Soviet Europe," *University of Pennsylvania Law Review*, vol. 154, no. 6 (2006), pp. 1757–1851.

of deals among political factions in the Russian legislature. However, this is the way of staffing constitutional courts in Germany, Hungary, Spain, and Portugal, where political parties control the appointment process. In any event, the selection of the RCC members was much more transparent, democratic, and competitive (Chapter 3) than that of the highly activist Hungarian Constitutional Court, where the legislature did not have a say in appointing five out of ten justices.[73]

Those who criticize the Zorkin Court for too much politicking outside of the bench tend to forget that the powerful German Constitutional Court (created by the 1949 Basic Law during Konrad Adenauer's term as the first chancellor of West Germany) also started its own institutionalization by fighting against the executive. The early years of this court saw its judges fighting for budgetary independence of their court, blocking the appointment of the federal justice minister, and even leaking their decisions to the public before their official announcements. In turn, some officials in Adenauer's government threatened to "blow up the entire constitutional court," to "pack" it, and to amend the Court Act. Moreover, this bitter confrontation between the court and Adenauer revolved around the ratification of the EC General Treaty and the European Defense Community Treaty, an explicit foreign policy issue, which many high courts would refuse to rule on! Just as their Russian colleagues in the separation-of-powers cases, the German judges insisted on their own contribution in determining the nature of their polity. Eventually, Adenauer backed down, fearing public backlash in the upcoming elections, and aimed at constitutional amendments to ensure the constitutionality of this treaty.[74] In summary, comparing the involvement of high courts in political conflicts between branches of government should focus on the "structure–agency" relationship, namely the power-maximizing strategies pursued by politicians and judges under certain institutional arrangements: flexible constitutions, easy access to the court, and a low degree of judicial discretion. In other words as Przeworski and Teune have argued, such comparisons would replace place names with variables.[75]

The rapid success and no less rapid failure of the Russian Constitutional Court also shows that rival political elites are happy to use the

---

[73] John W. Schiemann, *The Politics of Pact-Making: Hungary's Negotiated Transition to Democracy in Comparative Perspective* (New York: Palgrave Macmillan, 2005), pp. 130–135.

[74] Vanberg, *The Politics of Constitutional Review in Germany*, pp. 67–77; and Vanberg, "Establishing Judicial Independence in West Germany."

[75] Adam Przeworski and Henry Teune, *The Logic of Social Inquiry* (New York: John Wiley, 1970).

Court as long as they believe that they can get favorable judgments. In turn, judges do their best to meet the short-term needs of the rulers. Thus, political diffusion provides a demand for judicial review, which may serve as an "insurance" mechanism for electoral losers.[76] However, the severe political fragmentation and the "all or nothing" war between President Yeltsin and the legislature resulted in the temporary demise of constitutional review and the suspension of the constitutional court because deadlocked political elites were prepared to destroy the institutional framework in order to win this war. In the context of electoral uncertainty and severe political contestation, politicians chose to suspend judicial review contrary to the predictions of *strategic* theories of judicial empowerment. Russia reminds us that rulers always have the option of abolishing the Constitutional Court on the grounds of its redundancy or "countermajoritarian difficulty." This may be extreme in today's era of "global diffusion of judicial power," but this option cannot be ruled out, if the degree of political pluralism is high and the popularity of the Court is low. In short, politicians and judges share responsibility for the crisis of the Zorkin Court. On the one hand, embattled politicians expected too much from the Court and punished it when the justices failed to meet their expectations. On the other hand, judges overestimated the degree of their own influence on politicians. Although the psychological power of judicial review failed to work in times of severe political crisis, the judges still managed to persuade President Yeltsin to keep their Court alive and refrain from impeaching his opponents from the bench. How the RCC fared in its second edition is the subject to which I turn in Chapter 5.

[76] Ginsburg, *Judicial Review in New Democracies.*

5

Decision Making of the 2nd Russian Constitutional Court: 1995–2006

*Like corals, throughout centuries, build coral reefs, so do courts, by apply-
ing and reviewing laws against higher legal values, reveal the rich content
of constitutional principles.*

    – Russian Constitutional Court Justice Gadis Gadzhiev[1]

*Constitutional Court is not a painter, whose task is to cover the canvas with
pre-selected color; it is an artist who must paint a picture on this canvas.*

    – Russian Constitutional Court Justice Boris Ebzeev[2]

*Constitutional Court has no right to substitute itself for the people who
ratified the Constitution . . . and has no right to rewrite the Constitution at
its discretion.*

    – Russian Constitutional Court Justice Viktor Luchin[3]

This chapter examines the jurisprudence of the 2nd Constitutional Court
to see whether political elites succeeded in having the Court comply
with their objectives, how they used judicial review, and what the Court
did with its broad judicial review powers. The Russian Constitutional
Court resumed its work in February 1995, after the Federation Council
appointed its last Justice, Marat Baglai. At that time, the Court was in
a difficult position: the new 1993 constitution took away certain powers
from the Court and expanded the powers of the president; some regions

---

[1] Gadis Gadzhiev, *Konstitutsionnye printsipy rynochnoi ekonomiki* [Constitutional Principles of Market Economy] (Moskva: Iurist, 2002), p. 8.
[2] Boris Ebzeev, ed., *Kommentarii k postanovleniiam Konstitutsionnogo Suda Rossiiskoi
Federatsii. T. 1.* [Commentary to the Decisions of the Constitutional Court of the Russian
Federation. Vol.1] (Moskva: Iurist, 2000), p. 24.
[3] Viktor Luchin, *Konstitutsiia Rossiiskoi Federatsii. Problemy realizatsii* [Constitution of
the Russian Federation. Problems of Realization] (Moskva: Unity, 2002), p. 569.

118

Decision Making of the 2nd Russian Constitutional Court   119

boycotted the tribunal for being too centralist; Yeltsin's supporters blasted the Court for its antipresidential bias in the 1993 constitutional crisis; and Yeltsin's arch rivals hoped to use the reconstituted Court to revenge the president. Moreover, the Court itself was split between the supporters and opponents of the Russian President. Yeltsin's camp understood this and disallowed the Court from starting earlier in order to ensure a propresidential bench. As I argued in Chapter 3, "packing" the Court with Yeltsin's nominees was one of the crucial tactics in the political game of preserving the tribunal. Having a propresidential majority was particularly important because ex-Chairman Zorkin and Justice Luchin remained on the bench and because the justices preserved the power to elect their chair, vice-chair, and the judge-secretary. The plan of Yeltsin's legal advisers to ensure a loyal bench worked in the sense that both chambers of the reconstituted tribunal sustained a pro-Yeltsin majority and the judges loyal to President Yeltsin headed the tribunal well after Yeltsin's resignation on December 31, 1999. Chairman Tumanov, who led the RCC between 1995 and 1996, criticized the Zorkin Court for its anti-Yeltsin bias, represented Yeltsin at the 1993 Constitutional Convention, and approved broad presidential powers in the 1993 Russian constitution.[4] Tumanov's successor, Chairman Marat Baglai, who authored the controversial *Chechnya* decision, headed the RCC until February 2003. Justice Tamara Morshchakova, who openly dissented from some openly anti-Yeltsin decisions of the Zorkin Court in 1993, served as the vice-chair of the Court from 1995 until her retirement in early 2002. But in February 2003, the Court surprised many by electing Valerii Zorkin to the position of chairman.[5] Zorkin competed with Baglai, the incumbent, and won 10–9. He won despite the efforts of the presidential administration to raise judicial salaries and to influence the composition of the Court on the eve of the election.[6] Chairman Zorkin strengthened his position in

---

[4] Chairman Tumanov was elected in an 11–8 vote. For his biography and political views, see M. S. Balutenko, G. V. Belonuchkin, and K. A. Katanian, *Konstitutsionnyi Sud Rossii. Spravochnik* [Constitutional Court. Glossary] (Moskva: IEG "Panorama," 1997), available at http://www.panorama.ru/ks/tumanov.shtml.

[5] The RCC is the only federal court that elects its own chairperson. With the exception of the chairs of the Russian Supreme Court and the Higher *Arbitrazh* Court, who are appointed by the Federation Council, chairs of all other federal courts are appointed by the Russian president.

[6] On February 12, 2003, the Federation Council appointed Tiumen *arbitrazh* court judge Mikhail Kleandrov and civil law professor Larisa Krasavchikova to replace Justices Tiunov (Zorkin's supporter in 1993) and Vitruk (Zorkin's opponent in 1993). New justices were hastily dispatched to the Court to take part in the election of the Court's

February 2006 when he was reelected in a 14–5 vote to lead the Court for another 3 years.

However, as I will explain, having a loyal bench did not translate into a pliant constitutional court: President Yeltsin did not always win; and his supporters on the bench often opposed expanding his powers. Moreover, the RCC was able to regain some degree of the public trust and the legitimacy of the power holders both at the federal and regional levels. The Court did so by expanding its own jurisdiction precisely when President Putin began to concentrate his political power. Thus, growing judicial power went hand in hand with the concentration of power in the hands of the popular president. This is an unexpected outcome for the theories that link judicial empowerment with the fragmentation of power in the political system. Why does the Constitutional Court appear to be bolder in less-democratic Russia under Putin rather than in the more-democratic Russia under Yeltsin? This chapter addresses this question by exploring the impact of the Constitutional Court in the areas of separation of powers, federalism, and individual rights. But first, it is useful to learn more about the decision making and caseload of the tribunal.

DECISION-MAKING PROCEDURES, DECISIONS, AND CASELOAD

In a marked contrast with the 1st Russian Constitutional Court, its successor does not tend to make decisions overnight in a hasty manner.[7] Partly, this is the result of the 1994 Act, which now limits the jurisdiction of the Court to the review of legal rules instead of actions of government officials,[8] does not allow the Court to review cases on its own initiative, restricts the role of the chair, and enhances collegiality in decision making.

---

chair but to no avail. Former Justice Morshchakova criticizes this incident in Leonid Nikitinskii, "...I suda net. Diagnoz doktora Morshchakovoi," [...And No Court. The Diagnosis of Doctor Morshchakova] *Novaia gazeta*, July 19, 2004.

[7] The 2nd RCC under both Baglai and Zorkin appeared to hasten the review of certain controversies, when judges felt that their judgments would gain the support of political branches or would prevent wholesale violations of constitutional rights. However, it still took the RCC several weeks after public hearings to announce these hasty decisions. Interview with the RCC Justice, Moscow, June 20, 2001.

[8] The courts of general jurisdiction and the *arbitrazh* courts handle the judicial review of administrative action. For the analysis of their work, see, for example, Peter H. Solomon, Jr., "Judicial Power in Russia: Through the Prism of Administrative Justice," *Law and Society Review*, vol. 38, no. 3 (September 2004), pp. 549–581 and Kathryn Hendley, "Suing the State in Russia," *Post-Soviet Affairs*, vol. 18, no. 2 (April–June 2002), pp. 148–181.

Decision-Making Procedures, Decisions, and Caseload 121

This also reflects the view of the majority of the judges that their Court should refrain from playing the role of a rescue team in charge of preventing constitutional crises.[9] In politically charged cases, the time lag of several months allows litigants to allay their passions and judges to engage in collective decision making.

Strong disagreements among judges tend to delay the announcement of Constitutional Court decisions even further. Following the German model, the judge-rapporteur has to draft an opinion of the Court even if she opposes the majority opinion.[10] Dissenting opinions are attached to the text of the judgment and published. Between 1995 and 2006, there were 134 dissenting opinions attached to 82 decisions on the merits and an additional 32 dissenting opinions attached to rulings dismissing cases – a clear sign of the institutionalization of the young tribunal.[11] Since 2002, dissenting opinions are published only in the bimonthly *Russian Constitutional Court Herald* with a circulation of 2,500 copies, thus

---

[9] According to then Acting Chairman of the Russian Constitutional Court Nikolai Vitruk, "The Court should act as a court of law and should not behave as a crew of firefighters or paramedics." See his remarks in *Gosudarstvennaia Duma Federalnogo Sobraniia RF: Stenogramma zasedanii. Vesenniaia sessiia. T. 4, April 6–27, 1994* (Moskva: Respublika, 1995), p. 44. See also an interview with Justice Tumanov, "Delo suda – ne politika, a pravo," [The Job of the Court Is Not Politics but Law] *Rossiiskie vesti*, August 2, 1995; interviews with Justice Baglai, "Dva goda nazad nachala deistvovat Rossiiskaia Konstitutsiia. Marat Baglai," [The Russian Constitution Went in Force Two Years Ago] *Nezavisimaia gazeta*, December 26, 1995; and "Sud – ne pozharnaia komanda. Marat Baglai," [Court Is Not a Fire Rescue Team] *Vremia MN*, August 16, 2002; and an interview with Justice Strekozov, "Zhizn posle zhizni. Vladimir Strekozov," (Life after Life) *Ogonek*, no. 23 (June 1995), p. 38.

[10] When a dissenting judge refuses to write the opinion for the Constitutional Court, this task is assigned to the court clerks. In contrast, both the Russian Supreme Court and the Higher *Arbitrazh* Court follow the Soviet tradition of discouraging dissenting opinions and usually force the dissenters to rewrite the judgments according to the majority opinion. For an interesting analysis of dissenting opinions, Russian-style, see Alexander Vereshchagin, "Dissents in Russian Courts," in Natalia Iu. Erpyleva, Mayann E. Gashi-Butler, and Jane E. Henderson, eds., *Forging a Common Legal Destiny: Liber Amicorum in Honour of William E. Butler* (London: Wildy, Simmonds, and Hill Publishing, 2005), pp. 314–326. For the views of judges of the Russian Constitutional Court, who authored many dissents, on the matter, see Gadis Gadzhiev, "Publikatsiia osobogo mneniia sud'i, Ili Istoriia normy, kotoraia iavliaetsia kamertonom sudebnoi reformy v Rossii," [Publication of Dissenting Opinion of a Judge, Or the History of the Norm That Serves As a Tuning Fork of the Russian Judicial Reform] *Zakonodatelstvo i Praktika Mass-Media*, no. 12 (December 2005), available at http://www.medialaw.ru/publications/zip/136/5.htm; and Anatolii Kononov, "Pravo na Osoboe Mnenie," [Right to Dissenting Opinion], *Zakon*, no. 11 (November 2006).

[11] For a similar argument, see Tom Ginsburg, *Judicial Review in New Democracies: Constitutional Courts in Asian Cases* (New York: Cambridge University Press, 2003), p. 226.

making them less accessible to the average Russian.[12] However, dissenting opinions are available in all legal databases as well as at the Web site of the Russian Constitutional Court.

Just like the German Federal Constitutional Court, its Russian clone functions both in *en banc* sessions and in two chambers. The *large* chamber has ten Justices and the *small* one has nine. Both chambers hear constitutional complaints and have equal authority to strike down offending statutes by a simple majority of votes. In theory, this means that six votes in the large chamber and five votes in the small one are sufficient to overturn federal or regional pieces of legislation. In practice, however, some judges may be sick while the others may be away on official business, and both chambers often hear cases without a full complement of judges. For example, there were cases in which the small chamber had only seven judges, which means that only four votes were necessary to strike down a statute.

In terms of issued decisions, the 1994 RCC Act gives the Court two options when judges accept a case: to uphold or to invalidate the contested legal norm. But, following the example of their German and Italian colleagues, the Russian judges went beyond the letter of the Act and invented other kinds of decisions with orders to the government and other courts. Starting in 1997, the Court has been increasingly declaring contested legal norms as "noncontradictory to the constitution," interpreting them and making these interpretations binding on government bodies. In these "interpretative" decisions, the constitutional court did not strike down the law on its face but offered its own binding interpretation of the contested norm and, as a rule, ordered other courts and government agencies to enforce this judge-made interpretation.[13] As the RCC judges told me, they chose this approach to prevent a legal vacuum arising from the invalidation of the norm and to show respect for the legislative authority to make laws. Arguably, judges made this choice to interpret statutes instead of voiding them in order to preserve the independence, influence,

---

[12] Prior to 2002, dissents were published together with RCC decisions in *Rossiiskaia gazeta* and *SZRF* with a total circulation of 500,000 copies. The sponsors of the move to restrict their publication alleged that dissents hampered the implementation of RCC decisions. See Alexei Trochev, "Implementing Constitutional Court Decisions," *East European Constitutional Review*, vol. 11, nos. 1–2 (Winter–Spring 2002), p. 101.

[13] The Court calls this binding statutory interpretation a "constitutional-legal meaning of the legal norm" [*konstitutsionno-pravovoi smysl pravovoi normy*].

Decision-Making Procedures, Decisions, and Caseload

TABLE 5.1. *Filings and decisions of the Russian Constitutional Court,*
1995–2006

Petitions and decisions	1995–April 2000	May 2000–2005	2006	Total
Petitions submitted	55,993	79,998	14,989	150,980
Individual complaints	55,392	79,285	14,926	149,603
Petitions by federal institutions	60	31	9	100
Petitions by parliamentary minorities	16	27	0	43
Petitions by regional governments	113	147	22	282
Referrals by courts	93	229	25	347
Reviewed by the RCC in public sessions	2,997	989	80	4,066
Decisions on merits	113	95	10	218
Declarations of unconstitutionality	84	54	3	141
Interpretative decisions	5	31	7	43
Dismissed by the RCC in closed sessions	798	2,405	643	3,846
Rulings with "positive" content	146	814	145	1,105
Interpretative rulings	8	95	38	141
Published rulings	68	492	90	650

and prestige of their tribunal.[14] In short, the constitutional court in Russia increasingly acts as a "positive" legislator – one-third of its decisions on the merits issued during the first 5 years of Putin's presidency contained binding statutory interpretation (see Table 5.1). Clearly, the growing non-democratic tendencies of Putin's regime did not prevent the Constitutional Court from expanding this unwritten judicial power and from supplanting the will of the political branches with judge-made rules.

[14] Anders Fogelklou, "Interpretation and Accommodation in the Russian Constitutional Court," in Ferdinand Feldbrugge, ed., *Russia, Europe, and the Rule of Law* (Leiden: Martinus Nijhoff, 2007), p. 31.

But a more clear display of the activism of the Russian tribunal is evident in the dramatic increase in the number of rulings with so-called positive content, in which the Court formally dismisses the case in a closed hearing (see Table 5.1). These rulings (1,105 issued between 1995 and 2006) involve cases where the petitioner's claim is successful in the sense that the petitioner generally gets what she or he is asking for, but the Court justifies the absence of a decision on the merits because the *ruling with positive content* appears to simply extend a previous – and still valid – decision of the Court. "Positive content" here means good news for the petitioner most of the time because the Court elaborates a constitutional right or a government prerogative, orders government bodies to enforce this right, and even declares contested laws unconstitutional.[15] Initially, the Court refused to publish these rulings to avoid accusations of invading the domain of political branches. As a result, Russian and Western scholars started to pay attention to these rulings only recently.[16] But lawyers routinely rely on these rulings in litigation, while Russia's regular courts also increasingly apply the key holdings of these rulings.[17] All of the 15 RCC justices in their interviews insisted on treating these rulings as "minidecisions of the Constitutional Court" because they always had something *new* in them and reflected the debates among judges.[18] Indeed, some of the rulings with "positive content" have even gone beyond the

[15] Kim Lane Scheppele, "Constitutional Negotiations: Political Contexts of Judicial Activism in Post-Soviet Europe," *International Sociology*, vol. 18, no. 1 (March 2003), pp. 229–230.

[16] See, for instance, Scheppele, "Constitutional Negotiations"; Ger P. van den Berg, compiler, "Constitution of the Russian Federation Annotated with Summaries of Rulings and Other Decisions of Constitutional (Charter) Courts: 1990–2001," *Review of Central and East European Law*, vol. 27, nos. 2/3 (2001), pp. 175–488; Carla Thorson, "Constitutional Courts as Political Actors: Russia in Comparative Perspective" (Ph.D. diss., University of California at Los Angeles, 2003).

[17] Interview with Dmitri Bedniakov, a member of the Federation Council and a commercial lawyer, Toronto, 4 November 2002. Also, see the report by Viacheslav Lebedev, the Russian Supreme Court Chairman, "Praktika primeneniia reshenii Konstitutsionnogo Suda Rossiiskoi Federatsii sudami obshchei iurisdiktsii pri osushchestvlenii pravosudiia," [The Practice of Enforcing Decisions of the RF Constitutional Court by the Courts of General Jurisdiction in the Course of Adjudication] in Mikhail Mitiukov, Sergei Kabyshev, Vera Bobrova, and Sergei Andreev, eds., *Problemy ispolneniia federalnymi organami gosudarstvennoi vlasti i organami gosudarstvennoi vlasti subektov Rossiiskoi Federatsii reshenii Konstitutsionnogo Suda Rossiiskoi Federatsii i konstitutsionnykh (ustavnykh) sudov subektov Rossiiskoi Federatsii* (Moskva: Formula prava, 2001), pp. 46–49.

[18] Interviews with the RCC justices, June 2001. For a collection of key rulings, see Leonid Lazarev, *Pravovye pozitsii Konstitutsionnogo Suda Rossii* (Moskva: Gorodets, 2003).

Decision-Making Procedures, Decisions, and Caseload 125

holdings of previous decisions of the Court in interpreting the Russian constitution or the statutes and generated thirty-two dissenting opinions between 1995 and 2006.[19] According to some judges, drafting these rulings is often more difficult than the decisions on the merits of the case because the Court has to walk a fine line by simultaneously dismissing the claim and ordering government agencies to reopen the case of the petitioner. This difficulty, however, did not prevent the Court from issuing ninety-five "interpretative" rulings between 2000 and 2005. In most of them the RCC cited its previous judgments, defined the "constitutional meaning" of contested norms, and required government agencies to comply with these precedents. However, some of such "interpretative" rulings did not refer to any precedent.[20] Note that this expansion of judicial power took place in parallel with the concentration of political power in the hands of President Putin.

Thus, in most cases, the Court determines the constitutionality of a contested rule in its plenary session without a public hearing, a strategy advocated by many RCC justices.[21] Chairman Zorkin favors this trend as a way of dealing with the overloaded docket of the Court, of accelerating the disposition of cases, and of complying with the "speedy trial" requirement imposed by the European Court of Human Rights.[22] But this strategy also allows the Court to be off the political radar because there is no public hearing and media coverage. As the last row of Table 5.1 shows, judges chose to publish only about 60 percent of their rulings and to post the remaining rulings of the Court on its Web site and in legal

---

[19] See, for instance, RCC decisions: 144-O of November 26, 1998, *VKS RF*, no. 2 (1999), pp. 2–8 (Kononov, dissenting), English translation in *Statutes and Decisions. The Laws of the USSR and its Successor States* {hereinafter *Statutes and Decisions*}, no. 6 (2001); 92-O of June 27, 2000, *ibid.*, no. 6 (2000), pp. 10–12 (Luchin, dissenting); 33-O of February 8, 2001, *ibid.*, no. 3 (2001), pp. 70–78 (Khokhriakova and Zhilin, dissenting); 284-O of December 10, 2002, *ibid.*, no. 3 (2003), pp. 68–71 (Gadzhiev, dissenting); and 137-O of July 17, 2006, *ibid.*, no. 5 (2006) (Bondar, Ebzeev, and Kononov, dissenting).

[20] See, for example, RCC decisions: 134-O of June 8, 2000, *VKS RF*, no. 6 (2000), pp. 26–29; 33-O of February 8, 2001, *ibid.*, no. 3 (2001), pp. 70–78 (Khokhriakova and Zhilin, dissenting); and 26-O of February 21, 2002, *ibid.*, no. 4 (2002), pp. 70–73.

[21] See, for example, Boris Ebzeev, "Konstitutsionnyi Sud Rossiiskoi Federatsii: stanovlenie, iuridicheskaia priroda, pravovye pozitsii," in Boris Ebzeev, ed., *Kommentarii k postanovleniiam KS RF. T. 2* [Commentary to the RF Constitutional Court Decisions. Volume 2] (Moskva: Iurist, 2000), p. 19. Vladimir Tumanov, "Piat let konstitutsionnoi iustitsii v Rossii: uroki, problemy, perspektivy," [Five Years of Constitutional Justice in Russia: Lessons, Problems, Perspectives] *VKS RF*, no. 6 (1996), p. 13.

[22] Internet press-konferentsiia s Valeriem Zorkinym, *Garant-Internet*, November 26, 2003, available at http://www.garweb.ru/conf/ks/20031126/index.htm, accessed December 17, 2007.

databases. Thus, judges minimize the public visibility of their rulings in order to prevent backlash against their rulings. It makes sense for a less popular tribunal that issues unpopular rulings, like protecting due process rights of the accused in the context of surging crime rates or championing the rights of the taxpayers in times of a severe fiscal crisis. Although these rulings may have a limited impact beyond the daily life of a successful litigant, they show both the areas of public policy in which the Court decided not to intervene and the policy areas in which the Court insisted on its involvement. However, the lack of visibility and of official publication undermines the binding force of these rulings with positive content, as I explain in Chapter 7.

Finally, in terms of the caseload of the RCC, Table 5.1 clearly shows that individual constitutional complaints dominate the docket of the tribunal, a pattern not unfamiliar to the constitutional courts in Germany and Spain. Both under Yeltsin and Putin, thousands of Russians continue to ask the constitutional court to judge Russia's powers-that-be. On average, the Court reviews fewer than 5 percent of them, and the Court's Secretariat considers the rest to be inadmissible. Between 1995 and 2006, 1,377 petitions came from government bodies (including courts), and 772, a half, received the attention of the Russian Constitutional Court.[23] On the one hand, the sheer number of reviewed individual petitions and the more liberal approach to the petitions from the government bodies show the dramatic departure of the 2nd RCC from its predecessor: the petitions from government bodies made up 10 percent of the caseload between 1995 and 2006. On the other hand, the 50-percent success rate of government bodies in getting the attention of the Court indicates that justices had to repair its reputation and show its usefulness to the political branches of government. For example, the Court refused to examine only two out of eleven petitions by the Russian president (18-percent failure rate). Compare this with the Court's dismissal of one-half of petitions brought by the federal MPs, and three-quarters of referrals by other courts and petitions of regional governments. On the one hand, this ranking approximates the hierarchy of political power in Russia crowned by the federal presidency. On the other hand, the Russian president may be more successful because he has more resources and better lawyers than other government agencies do. The strategies these lawyers pursue in constitutional litigation may also influence the success rate. For example, Sergei Shakhrai who served as President Yeltsin's representative at the Russian Constitutional

---

[23] Vladimir Strekozov, ed., *Konstitutsionnyi Sud Rossiiskoi Federatsii. Postanovleniia. Opredeleniia. 2006* (Moskva: Norma, 2007), pp. 720–722.

Court in 1997–1998, repeatedly recalled presidential petitions when the chances of losing the case were high, and when the president settled the dispute outside of the Court.[24] For other political actors, pursuing constitutional litigation could, in itself, bring political dividends regardless of the likelihood of winning the case.[25] For example, as Table 5.1 makes clear, Russian regions continued to use the RCC more actively under Putin's centralizing regime (147 petitions) than under Yeltsin's presidency (113 petitions). And they did so despite the fact that the pro-Putin party, "United Russia," controlled both the federal parliament and most regional legislatures and governorships. The same pattern is visible in the petitions of the parliamentary minorities: sixteen petitions during Yeltsin's era versus twenty-seven petitions during the first 6 years of Putin's presidency. The growth of judicial referrals to the Constitutional Court also shows the growing popularity of the tribunal within the judicial community. What is important here is that Russian politicians and legal elites recognize the legitimacy of Constitutional Court decisions and rulings in legal doctrine, in "law on the books" and in "law in action." And this growth of the legitimacy of judicial review goes hand in hand with the growth of the authoritarian trends in Russia's governance, contrary to the theories that link judicial empowerment with the dispersion of political power.

To explain why the authority of the Constitutional Court grows at the same time as the Russian democracy weakens, let us now examine what the Court did in three areas: separation of powers, federalism, and constitutional rights. My focus here is on the Court's attempts to define the key principles of the Russian constitutional order rather than on individual cases or constitutional review procedures because any constitutional litigation may involve all of these issues at once and petitioners may use various constitutional review procedures to settle their disputes.

DEFINING SEPARATION OF POWERS

In contrast with the 1978 Russian Constitution, which attempted to implant the presidency in the system of parliamentary supremacy, the 1993 Russian Constitution entrenched the system of separation of powers,

---

[24] Balutenko et al., *Konstitutsionnyi Sud Rossii. Spravochnik*, available at http://www.panorama.ru/ks/hr97.shtml.
[25] Constitutional litigation in Israel exhibits this pattern. See Yoav Dotan and Menahem Hofnung, "Legal Defeats – Political Wins: Why Do Elected Representatives Go to Court?" *Comparative Political Studies*, vol. 38, no. 1 (2005), pp. 75–103.

128   Decision Making of the 2nd Russian Constitutional Court

with the federal president at its apex. This system, according to Justice Morshchakova, aspires to secure some sort of stable cooperation between the legislative and the executive branches instead of limiting the state for the sake of individual liberties.[26] But Justices Gadzhiev and Luchin argue that this stability through super-presidentialism overburdens the executive, limits its capacity, and endangers democratization.[27]

Not surprisingly, Yeltsin's opponents chose to mitigate this pro-presidency bias in the Russian Constitution via various constitutional review procedures immediately after the reactivation of the RCC. But the justices rebutted most of these attacks on the Russian presidency not because they favored Yeltsin's policies but because they tried to ensure the survival of their Court. The reconstituted Court started its work in the spring of 1995 by terminating the anti-Yeltsin petitions pending on the docket of its predecessor. In contrast with the Zorkin Court, its successor repeatedly upheld the implied powers of the president, which fell under the vague constitutional status of a "head of state" and a "guarantor of the Constitution."[28] In July 1995, bitterly split, the Tumanov Court introduced "hidden" presidential powers in its decision in the *Chechnya* case. In a 10–8 vote, the Court ruled that the federal president not only had the right but also was required to use military force inside Russia unilaterally (without the approval of the Federation Council) to suppress armed rebellion against the federal government. According to the Court, the federal president could bypass the martial law procedure in

---

[26] Tamara Morshchakova, "Rol Konstitutsionnogo Suda RF v protsesse demokraticheskikh preobrazovanii," [The Role of the RF Constitutional Court in the Process of Democratic Transformation] *Konstitutsionnoe pravosudie*, no. 2 (1998), p. 26.

[27] Gadis Gadzhiev, "Power Imbalance and Institutional Interests in Russian Constitutional Engineering," in Jan Zielonka, ed., *Democratic Consolidation in Eastern Europe* (New York: Oxford University Press, 2001), pp. 269–292 and Viktor Luchin, *Konstitutsiia Rossiiskoi Federatsii. Problemy realizatsii* (Moskva: Unity, 2002), pp. 447–483.

[28] Article 80 of the Russian constitution:

   1. The President of the Russian Federation shall be the head of the State.
   2. The President of the Russian Federation shall be guarantor of the Constitution of the Russian Federation, of the rights and freedoms of man and citizen. According to the rules fixed by the Constitution of the Russian Federation, he shall adopt measures to protect the sovereignty of the Russian Federation, its independence and state integrity, ensure coordinated functioning and interaction of all the bodies of state power.
   3. According to the Constitution of the Russian Federation and the federal laws the President of the Russian Federation shall determine the guidelines of the internal and foreign policies of the State.

Defining Separation of Powers

extraordinary situations, such as Chechnya's violent secession attempts, as long as his orders complied with the constitution and international law, and did not impose undue limits on basic rights.[29]

In April 1996, the Tumanov Court created the new "implied" power of the president "to return federal bills without consideration" back to the legislature. According to the Court, the federal president as "guarantor" of the federal constitution has, in addition to the veto power, the power to send federal bills back to the legislature when the legislative chambers violated constitutional procedures for enacting federal laws. In the Court's view, the president may use this "implied" power to return federal bills by providing specific reasons and listing violations of constitutional norms by the legislature.[30] In a series of decisions, the Court restricted this unwritten "soft" veto power to cases when the legislators agreed that they had violated the constitutional procedures for adopting the federal legislation. In all other cases, the Court ordered the Russian president to challenge the constitutionality of parliamentary procedures exclusively in the Russian Constitutional Court.[31] As a result, Yeltsin grudgingly obeyed the Court after publicly complaining to Chairman Baglai in 1998 that the justices gave the president "a slap in the face" and that "something was not working properly" in his relations with the Constitutional Court.[32] According to Thomas Remington, this judge-made presidential veto power, "Russian-style," faces the same limitations as that of the U.S. president: he cannot veto portions of a bill, and he must sign a bill when his veto has

---

[29] RCC decision 10-P of July 31, 1995, *VKS RF*, no. 5 (1995), pp. 3–64 (Ametistov, Ebzeev, Gadzhiev, Kononov, Luchin, Morshchakova, Vitruk, and Zorkin, dissenting), English translation in *Human Rights Law Journal*, no. 3–6 (1996). See Robert Sharlet, "Transitional Constitutionalism: Politics and Law in the Second Russian Republic," *Wisconsin International Law Journal*, vol. 14, no. 3 (Summer 1996), pp. 495–540 and William Pomeranz, "Judicial Review and the Russian Constitutional Court: The Chechen Case," *Review of Central and East European Law*, vol. 23, no. 1 (1997), pp. 9–48.

[30] RCC decision 10-P of April 22, 1996, *VKS RF*, no. 3 (1996), pp. 5–14, English translation in *Statutes and Decisions*, no. 6 (1999). For a critique of this view, see V. A. Chetvernin, ed., *Konstitutsiia Rossiiskoi Federatsii: Problemnyi kommentarii* (Moskva: MONF, 1997), pp. 464–466.

[31] RCC decisions: 11-P of April 6, 1998, *VKS RF*, no. 4 (1998), pp. 11–20 (Ametistov, dissenting), English translation in *Statutes and Decisions*, no. 4 (2000); and 12-P of July 20, 1999, *ibid.*, no. 5 (1999), pp. 57–80, English translation in *Statutes and Decisions*, no. 1 (2001).

[32] See, for example, Alexander N. Domrin, "'Trophy Art Law' as an Illustration of the Current Status of Separation of Powers and Legislative Process in Russia," in Norman Dorsen and Prosser Gifford, eds., *Democracy and the Rule of Law* (Washington, DC: Congressional Quarterly Press, 2001), pp. 283–288.

Decision Making of the 2nd Russian Constitutional Court

been overridden by two-thirds' majorities in the Duma and the Federation Council.[33]

In addition to the unwritten right to "return federal bills to the legislature," the Baglai Court found that the Russian president could issue normative decrees if a federal statute on the matter was absent or "where the entire system of legal norms was in disharmony."[34] In a series of decisions, the Court ruled that such decrees in both exclusive federal jurisdiction (land law) and joint federal–regional jurisdiction (regional electoral law) were a legitimate exercise of presidential power as long as they were temporary, and would lose their validity with the passage of a federal statute on the matter.[35] As one justice put it, the RCC was forced to approve this presidential rule making in order to secure the direct applicability of the 1993 Constitution in the context of a slow or deadlocked federal parliament. Justices hoped that the pressure of presidential rule making would encourage the parliament to pass the necessary legislation and replace presidential decrees with proper laws.[36] However feeble, these limits on the "implied" powers of the Russian president mitigate the abuse of these powers and introduce some sort of balance in the law-making process.[37]

On the other hand, the 2nd Court did not hesitate to use politically charged controversies in order to define the legislative process. In fact, the first two cases of the Tumanov Court in the spring of 1995 resolved the dispute between the Federation Council and the State Duma over law-making powers and a controversy between the majority and the opposition in the

---

[33] Thomas F. Remington, "Taming Vlast: Institutional Development in Post-Communist Russia," in Donald R. Kelley, ed., *After Communism: Perspectives on Democracy* (Fayetteville, AR: University of Arkansas Press, 2003), p. 103.

[34] *Ibid.*, p. 112. RCC decision 9-P of June 25, 2001, *VKS RF*, no. 6 (2001), pp. 6–21.

[35] RCC decisions: 23-O of February 4, 1997, (unpublished), as summarized in Berg, "Constitution of the Russian Federation Annotated," p. 270; 133-O of July 6, 2000, in Tamara Morshchakova, ed., *Konstitutsionnyi Sud Rossiiskoi Federatsii. Postanovleniia. Opredeleniia. 2000* (Moskva: Iurist, 2001), p. 420; 7-P of April 30, 1997, *VKS RF*, no. 4 (1997), pp. 24–54 (Ebzeev, Gadzhiev, and Vitruk, dissenting), English translation in *Statutes and Decisions*, no. 5 (1999); 11-P of April 30, 1996, *VKS RF*, no. 3 (1996), pp. 15–28 (Luchin, dissenting), English translation in *Statutes and Decisions*, no. 4 (1999); and 2-P of January 27, 1999, *VKS RF*, no. 3 (1999), pp. 5–11.

[36] Interview with RCC Justice, Moscow, June 25, 2001. See also the interview with former Chairman Tumanov in *Pravo i Ekonomika*, no. 9 (September 1999), p. 4.

[37] In support of the view that the Russian constitution constrains President Putin's rule making, see Moshe Haspel, Thomas F. Remington, and Steven S. Smith, "Lawmaking and Decree Making in the Russian Federation: Time, Space, and Rules in Russian National Policymaking," *Post-Soviet Affairs*, vol. 22, no. 3 (July 2006), pp. 249–275. For the rejection of this view, see Katharina Pistor, "The Demand for Constitutional Law," *Constitutional Political Economy*, vol. 13 (2002), pp. 81–85.

Russian parliament over the minimum number of votes necessary to pass a bill.[38] In the first case, in a 14–4 vote, the Court upheld nascent bicameralism by requiring the State Duma to wait until the review of certain federal bills by the Federation Council, on the condition that the upper chamber would begin to review them within the 14-day period set by the constitution. In the second case, in a 16–2 vote, the Constitutional Court protected the rights of the opposition when it ruled that both chambers of the Russian parliament should use the total number of seats for each house (450 for the Duma and 178 for the Council), regardless of whether they were all filled, to meet the quorum and other vote-counting rules in the legislative process. In a 13–1 decision, the Tumanov Court also affirmed the rigidity of the 1993 Russian Constitution by laying out several stages for adopting constitutional amendments and bound the federal legislature to adopt a "law on the constitutional amendment," an act that was not mentioned in the federal constitution.[39] In total, by 2006, about thirty decisions of the Court elaborated rights and obligations of the Duma, the Federation Council, and the president in core stages of the federal legislative process.[40]

Policing the boundaries of the legislative prerogative, judges could not help tackle the rule making of the executive branch. Recall that under Article 125 (2a), the Constitutional Court had the power to check the constitutionality of the enactments of the federal Cabinet at the request of various political actors (but not individuals). Consider how the judges tried to limit the fiscal powers of the federal executive. In April 2004, 1 month after Vladimir Putin was reelected as Russian president, the RCC enhanced government accountability by overruling the practice of the federal Cabinet to suspend the authority of the federal Audit Chamber, an arm of the Russian parliament, to review federal spending. This case was brought by a group of senators who were furious that the Cabinet repeatedly denied the constitutional prerogative of the legislature to monitor the implementation of the federal budget through the Audit Chamber.

---

[38] RCC decisions: 1-P of March 23, 1995, *VKS RF*, nos. 2–3 (1995), pp. 3–16 (Gadzhiev, Luchin, Morshchakova, and Rudkin, dissenting), English translation in *Statutes and Decisions*, no. 4 (1995); and 2-P of April 12, 1995, *VKS RF*, nos. 2–3 (1995), pp. 17–31 (Ebzeev and Gadzhiev, dissenting), English translation in *Statutes and Decisions*, no. 4 (1995).

[39] RCC decision 12-P of October 31, 1995, *VKS RF*, no. 6 (1995), pp. 10–17 (Morshchakova, concurring), English translation in *Statutes and Decisions*, no. 6 (1999).

[40] See, for example, Mikhail Mitiukov and Aleksandr Barnashov, *Ocherki konstitutsionnogo pravosudiia* (Tomsk: Izd-vo Tomskogo universiteta, 1999), pp. 240–264.

132 *Decision Making of the 2nd Russian Constitutional Court*

The Cabinet argued that it had specific constitutional authorization to spend federal funds, and therefore, its own reports on spending were sufficient, no additional monitoring from the Audit Chamber was necessary. The Constitutional Court disagreed and ruled that parliamentary control of federal spending was an inalienable constitutional power of the legislature and an essential element of the separation of powers.[41]

In the revenue-raising area, the Court examines the nature of the payment to state coffers in every case to determine whether the executive branch interferes with the constitutional power of the legislature to set federal taxes. On the one hand, in a series of decisions, the Court ruled that only a federal statute, not federal Cabinet edicts, should establish federal taxes.[42] In the Court's view, the Russian Constitution assigns the power to set taxes exclusively to the legislature as "one of the principles of a democratic law-based state, aimed at protecting the rights of taxpayers against arbitrariness ... on the part of the executive power."[43] To be sure, the Court did not shy away from requiring the legislature to be specific in setting new taxes, levies, and standards in order to minimize the danger of their arbitrary and undue application on the part of the executive.[44] On the other hand, the Court upheld the power of the federal government to set, unilaterally, various nontax fees and payments to the federal and regional budgets, such as highway truck user fees,[45] payments for animals taken out of their habitat,[46] automobile safety inspection fees,[47]

---

[41] RCC decision 9-P of April 23, 2004, *VKS RF*, no. 4 (2004), pp. 30–49 (Bondar, concurring).

[42] RCC decisions: 3-P of February 18, 1997, *VKS RF*, no. 1 (1997), pp. 43–53 (Morshchakova, dissenting), English translation in *Statutes and Decisions*, no. 1 (2000), p. 77; 6-P of April 1, 1997, *ibid.*, no. 4 (1997), pp. 13–17, English translation in *Statutes and Decisions*, no. 1 (2000), p. 89; 16-P of November 11, 1997, *ibid.*, no. 6 (1997), pp. 9–22 (Kononov and Vitruk, dissenting), English translation in *Statutes and Decisions*, no. 2 (2000), p. 56; 14-P of October 28, 1999, *ibid.*, no. 6 (1999), pp. 8–15, English translation in *Statutes and Decisions*, no. 1 (2001); 258-O of December 14, 2000, *ibid.*, no. 2 (2001), pp. 46–49.

[43] RCC decision 16-P of November 11, 1997, *VKS RF*, no. 6 (1997), pp. 9–22 (Kononov and Vitruk, dissenting), English translation in *Statutes and Decisions*, no. 2 (2000).

[44] RCC decisions: 15-P of November 22, 2001, *VKS RF*, no. 1 (2002), pp. 12–23 (Kononov and Vitruk, dissenting); 2-P of February 28, 2006, *VKS RF*, no. 3 (2006), pp. 15–36 (Kleandrov, dissenting).

[45] RCC decision 22-P of July 17, 1998, *VKS RF*, no. 6 (1998), pp. 58–67 (Kononov, dissenting), English translation in *Statutes and Decisions*, no. 5 (2000).

[46] RCC decision 14-O of February 8, 2001, in Tamara Morshchakova, ed. *Konstitutsionnyi Sud Rossiiskoi Federatsii. Postanovleniia. Opredeleniia.* 2001 (Moskva: Iurist, 2002), pp. 239–242.

[47] RCC decisions: 88-O of May 14, 2002, *VKS RF*, no. 6 (2002), pp. 75–80; and 94-O of May 14, 2002, *VKS RF*, no. 6 (2002), pp. 81–88.

patent registration fees,[48] and environmental protection payments.[49] Thus, the Constitutional Court attempted to balance fair taxation with the need to fill up the state coffers.

Finally, the judicial branch of government received the greatest protection from the RCC. When, in 1998, the Russian government cut the courts' financing by 26.2 percent, using the provision in the 1998 federal budget law that allowed the executive to cut all spending proportionally in the case of a federal budget deficit, the Constitutional Court promptly declared this measure unconstitutional. The RCC ruled that neither the federal legislature nor the federal executive could cut federal funding of the judicial branch without the approval of the judicial self-government bodies (the Russian Council of Judges and the All-Russian Congress of Judges), otherwise, cuts in funding threaten both judicial independence and constitutional freedoms.[50] Also, political branches cannot, in the view of the RCC, reduce the size of the allowance for retired judges or modify the conditions for receiving such allowance.[51]

In addition to protecting the financial independence of the judiciary, the Constitutional Court also defined the nature of courts in the federal system of separation of powers. In the Court's view, the separation of the judiciary from the legislature and the executive means that: (1) no state agency other than a court of law can administer justice, and (2) a court of law cannot be charged with performing functions incompatible with administering justice.[52] According to Justice Morshchakova, courts have to balance the prerogatives of the legislative and executive branches with the protection of individual rights.[53] Therefore, the Constitutional Court repeatedly declared unconstitutional various criminal procedures that empowered courts to carry out the tasks of the prosecution: to initiate criminal cases and formulate accusations,[54] to return criminal cases to the prosecution

---

[48] RCC decision 283-O of December 10, 2002, *VKS RF*, no. 2 (2003), pp. 57–66.

[49] RCC decision 284-O of December 10, 2002, *VKS RF*, no. 2 (2003), pp. 66–79 and no. 3 (2002), pp. 68–71 (Gadzhiev, dissenting).

[50] RCC decision 23-P of July 17, 1998, *VKS RF*, no. 6 (1998), pp. 68–73, English translation in *Statutes and Decisions*, no. 5 (2000).

[51] RCC decision 5-P of February 19, 2002, *VKS RF*, no. 3 (2002), pp. 40–51. Actually, the complainants (seven retired judges) asked the Constitutional Court to overrule the practice of the Russian Supreme Court, which disallowed payment of retirement allowance to certain categories of retirees. Pavel Aptekar, "Byvshim sudiam povezlo," [Former Judges Got Lucky] *Vremia novostei*, February 20, 2002.

[52] RCC decision 19-P of November 28, 1996, *VKS RF*, no. 5 (1996), pp. 15–21, English translation in *Statutes and Decisions*, no. 3 (2001).

[53] Morshchakova, "Rol Konstitutsionnogo Suda RF," pp. 26–31.

[54] RCC decisions: 11-O of January 26, 1999, *VKS RF*, no. 2 (1999), pp. 62–63; 1-P of January 14, 2000, *VKS RF*, no. 2 (2000), pp. 49–64 (Ebzeev and Vitruk, dissenting);

for supplementary investigation,[55] to convict the accused when the prosecution has dropped the charges,[56] and to initiate a civil claim in a criminal case.[57] Moreover, the Constitutional Court repeatedly admonished the legislature for delays in enacting the judicial reform legislation[58] until finally, in March 2002, the Court ordered the Russian parliament to introduce "immediately" a judicial arrest and "search and seizure" warrant.[59] This March 2002 decision, which was described by many as "sensational" and "revolutionary," effectively transferred the power to approve arrests and searches from the Procuracy to regular courts, and overcame the previously successful lobbying by the law-enforcement agencies to keep these powers.[60] In other cases, the Constitutional Court consistently expanded judicial oversight of administrative action, required courts to apply constitutional norms directly in the absence of federal law on a matter, and protected judicial discretion.

However, the federal Constitutional Court staunchly guarded its own monopoly over the judicial review of legislation and repeatedly clashed with the other two high national courts, the Supreme Court and the Higher *Arbitrazh* Court, over issues of jurisdiction.[61] These intercourt clashes arose on several fronts. The first front involves the power of statutory interpretation. Similar to the Italian and German Constitutional Courts,

176-O of June 23, 2000, in Tamara Morshchakova, ed., *Konstitutsionnyi Sud Rossiiskoi Federatsii. Postanovleniia. Opredeleniia. 2000* (Moskva: Iurist, 2001), p. 375.

[55] RCC decisions: 7-P of April 20, 1999, *VKS RF*, no. 4 (1999), pp. 41–49, English translation in *Statutes and Decisions*, no. 4 (2001); 9-O of February 3, 2000, *ibid.*, no. 3 (2000), pp. 57–59; 2-P of March 4, 2003, *ibid.*, no. 3 (2003), pp. 10–16.

[56] RCC decisions: 7-P of April 20, 1999, *VKS RF*, no. 4 (1999), pp. 41–49, English translation in *Statutes and Decisions*, no. 4 (2001); 150-O of July 5, 2000, *ibid.*, no. 6 (2000), pp. 46–49.

[57] RCC decision 297-O of December 6, 2001, *VKS RF*, no. 2 (2002), pp. 77–80.

[58] RCC decision 3-P of February 2, 1999, *VKS RF*, no. 3 (1999), pp. 12–24, English translation in *Statutes and Decisions*, no. 4 (2001). In this case, the Russian Constitutional Court banned criminal courts from handing out death penalty sentences until the federal legislature authorized jury trials all across Russia.

[59] RCC decision 6-P of March 14, 2002, *VKS RF*, no. 3 (2002), pp. 51–56.

[60] Iurii Feofanov, "Otlagatelnyi uklon," *Vremia MN*, March 27, 2002, p. 7.

[61] William Burnham and Alexei Trochev, "Russia's War between the Courts: The Struggle over the Jurisdictional Boundary between the Constitutional Court and Regular Courts," *American Journal of Comparative Law*, vol. 55, no. 3 (Summer 2007), pp. 381–452. See also two articles by Peter Krug, "Departure from the Centralized Model: The Russian Supreme Court and Constitutional Control of Legislation," *Virginia Journal of International Law*, vol. 37, no. 3 (1997), pp. 725–787 and "The Russian Federation Supreme Court and Constitutional Practice in the Courts of General Jurisdiction: Recent Developments," *Review of Central and East European Law*, vol. 26, no. 2 (February 2000), pp. 129–146.

the Russian Constitutional Court "discovered" that it had the monopoly to interpret statutes and to require all other government agencies, including domestic courts, to follow its interpretation. A typical boilerplate statement at the end of an "interpretative" decision or a ruling of the RCC, which contains the "constitutional-legal meaning" of the contested norm, is this: "[T]he Court's revealed constitutional meaning of the legal norm is binding on the legislator and those applying the law, and may not be contradicted or overridden by legislative or law-application practice.... Thus, neither the courts of general jurisdiction deciding criminal cases, nor the agencies implementing sentences in carrying out their powers may give the provisions of Art.... any different meaning that departs from its constitutional-law meaning elucidated by the Constitutional Court...in this decision."[62] Showing how the Russian constitution compelled its own statutory interpretation has been the key challenge for the RCC in such decisions. On the other hand, the Constitutional Court is uncertain whether to recognize the binding force of the statutory interpretations given by the Russian Supreme Court and the Higher *Arbitrazh* Court,[63] and encourages lower courts to challenge them via referrals to the Constitutional Court. As a clerk at the Constitutional Court told me: "We view judges who refer cases to us as true heroes!"[64]

In addition to interpreting statutes, the Constitutional Court discovered that it had jurisdiction over subconstitutional conflicts, arguing that they are really constitutional issues: conflicts between federal laws, conflicts between a federal law, on the one hand, and statutes or other laws of regions, on the other, and conflicts between a federal statute and a federal regulation. Under Russian law, courts of general jurisdiction and *arbitrazh* courts resolve all three categories of conflicts. And, initially, the Constitutional Court followed the letter of the law and repeatedly

---

[62] See, for example, RCC Decision 1-P of February 27, 2003, *VKS RF*, no. 3 (2003), pp. 3–9 (case on counting time served in detention).

[63] Compare RCC decisions: 103-O of February 19, 2004 (unpublished), in which the RCC ruled that the Presidium of the RF Supreme Court lacked the power to interpret statutes; and 351-O of October 20, 2005 (unpublished), in which the RCC refers to the decision of the Presidium of the RF Supreme Court as law in force. See also RCC decision 200-O of July 4, 2002, *VKS RF*, no. 1 (2003), pp. 77–81. The initial draft of this decision abolished the binding force of the statutory interpretations of the Higher *Arbitrazh* Court. However, the published version of the judgment did not contain this strong proposition. See also T. Abova, "Vysshii Arbitrazhnyi Sud Rossiiskoi Federatsii. Sistema arbitrazhnykh sudov," [Higher *Arbitrazh* Court. The System of the *Arbitrazh* Courts] in Igor Petrukhin, ed., *Sudebnaia vlast* (Moskva: Prospekt, 2003), pp. 376–377.

[64] Interview with the clerk of the Russian Constitutional Court, May 2001.

Decision Making of the 2nd Russian Constitutional Court

refused to resolve such subconstitutional conflicts by sending the petitioners to other courts.[65] However, in February 1999, the RCC ruled, "When the conflict between legal rules causes a conflict with constitutional rights that are based on them, the issue of resolving such a conflict takes on a constitutional aspect and, therefore, falls within the jurisdiction of the Constitutional Court."[66] As for regional and federal law conflicts, the Court asserted in April 2002: "Based on the direct stipulation of the Constitution...the Constitutional Court...plays the role of the court that is empowered to decide in the final instance public law disputes on the consistency of normative acts of subjects with the Constitution...or federal statutes.... This is due to the fact that the evaluation of consistency of an act of a region...with a federal act is always constitutionally based on the division of powers between the federation and its regions secured by the Constitution..." As Judge Vitruk pointed out in his dissenting opinion in this case, this job is assigned to the regular courts, not the Constitutional Court.[67] Finally, in December 2002, the Constitutional Court twice asserted that the conflict between the edicts of the federal Cabinet and federal law was also a constitutional question "since the Constitution of the Russian Federation, in establishing the delimitation of competence among the federal bodies of state power, directly grants the Cabinet of the Russian Federation corresponding powers, including the power to issue normative decrees."[68] Both cases involved disputes between the federal Cabinet and the Russian Supreme Court, which repeatedly annulled Cabinet edicts on patent fees and environmental protection payments at the request of several corporations. The RCC accepted the appeal by the Cabinet and affirmed its own exclusive jurisdiction over such disputes. The Constitutional Court ruled that its judgments in such cases, unlike those of the Supreme Court, are final and binding, and that the

---

[65] See, for example, RCC decisions: 23-O of February 4, 1997 (unpublished); 13-P of October 8, 1997, *VKS RF*, no. 5 (1997), pp. 49–56, English translation in *Statutes and Decisions*, no. 2 (2000), p. 29; 30-O of February 6, 2003 (unpublished).

[66] RCC decision 4-P of February 23, 1999, *VKS RF*, no. 3 (1999), pp. 49–56, English translation in *Statutes and Decisions*, no. 6 (2000). The Court confirmed this view in its decision 8-P of May 14, 2003, *ibid.*, no. 4, pp. 12–23 (Kononov, dissenting).

[67] RCC decision 8-P of April 4, 2002, *VKS RF*, no. 5 (2002), pp. 3–37 (Gadzhiev, Iaroslavtsev, Morshchakova, and Vitruk, dissenting).

[68] RCC Decisions: 283-O of December 10, 2002, *VKS RF*, no. 2 (2003), pp. 57–66; and 284-O of December 10, 2002, *VKS RF*, no. 2 (2003), pp. 66–79 and no. 3 (2002), pp. 68–71 (Gadzhiev, dissenting). Dissenting Judge Gadzhiev argued that the Constitutional Court in this case lacked the power either to resolve such subconstitutional conflicts or to reverse the judgments of the Supreme Court in which the Supreme Court declared federal regulation void.

Defining Separation of Powers 137

federal Cabinet had constitutional power to set these fees. Moreover, the RCC required the federal legislature to comply with these conclusions in fiscal reforms.[69] In January 2004, the Constitutional Court went further and struck down the provision of the newly adopted Russian Civil Procedure Code that authorized the Supreme Court to review the legality of the edicts of the federal Cabinet. The RCC declared this power of the Supreme Court unconstitutional on the grounds that the issue of whether "a normative act of the Government of the Russian Federation contradicts a federal statute" comes within the exclusive jurisdiction of the RCC.[70] As a result of this decision, individuals received the right to complain against the federal Cabinet to the Constitutional Court although neither the 1993 constitution nor the 1994 RCC Act can authorize such complaints.

The final front of expansion of the jurisdiction of the RCC at the expense of other courts concerns judicial review of decisions of the top courts and other top-level government bodies. Recall that the 1993 Constitutional Convention took away the RCC powers to review the constitutionality of both judicial decisions, that is, law-application practice, and the actions of high government officials. However, in a 2004 decision just discussed, the Constitutional Court declared:

> "The decision of a court of general jurisdiction that a normative act of the Cabinet of the Russian Federation contradicts a federal statute and is inoperative... provides the grounds [for an] application to the Constitutional Court... [under Art. 125(2)] if the applicant considers that the normative act is valid notwithstanding such decision. In this way, the Constitutional Court... operates as a court of final resort in resolving such public law disputes."[71]

In effect, this means that the Constitutional Court officially declared its superappellate function of reviewing the Supreme Court's decisions. Prior to this ruling, the RCC repeatedly found judicial mistakes in the decisions of other courts and ordered them to rehear the cases of petitioners according to the guidelines of the RCC.[72]

But the most remarkable expansion of the jurisdictional power of the RCC came in March 2007 in the case brought by three Communist Party members who in vain tried to call a nationwide referendum

---

[69] *Ibid.* Justice Zorkin authored both rulings.
[70] Decision 1-P of January 27, 2004, *VKS RF*, no. 2 (2004), pp. 3–21 (Kononov, dissenting).
[71] *Ibid.*
[72] Burnham and Trochev, "Russia's War between the Courts," pp. 428–431.

against President Putin's policies. The Central Election Commission did not approve the proposed referendum questions, saying they violated the requirements of federal constitutional law on referenda, and the Russian Supreme Court upheld this decision. The petitioners complained to the RCC against both decisions and challenged the constitutionality of the law on referenda. The RCC partly agreed with petitioners that it was constitutional to place spending questions on the ballot but it stopped short of ordering the Supreme Court and the Central Election Commission to reopen the case of the petitioners. At the same time, the RCC found that Supreme Court review of decisions of the Central Election Commission was an unconstitutional invasion of its exclusive power to decide constitutional disputes. It observed: "[A]ll disputes that are constitutional in their legal nature, character or effects must be decided according to the constitutional mode of judicial procedure, which is coextensive with the assignment of constitutional judicial review – otherwise, the principles set out in the Constitution ... that lie at the base of the organization and administration of justice, the boundaries of different types of judicial jurisdiction, and the judicial securing of rights and freedoms of the citizen would be destroyed...." Consequently, the Court directed the legislature to amend the statute and to provide for review by the Constitutional Court instead of the Supreme Court.[73] Judge Kazantsev dissented in this case by warning that this expansion of the jurisdiction ran against the letter of the Russian constitution, contradicted the exhaustive lists of powers of other constitutional courts abroad, and made the powers of the RCC unlimited.[74] Indeed, it is very easy to imagine that the RCC could start reviewing actions of any other government officers and institutions.

In sum, the conventional accounts that the Russian Constitutional Court is somehow weaker (or has fewer powers) than its predecessor of 1992–1993 are no longer true because the Court has effectively regained almost all of the powers it lost during the 1993 constitutional crisis. The growing authoritarian trends in Putin's Russia did not prevent the expansion of its judicial power. True, the 2nd Court was initially much more cautious than its predecessor in defining the constitutional scheme of the separation of powers. Still, through a lively debate among the justices, the Constitutional Court settled various disputes among and

---

[73] RCC decision 3-P of March 21, 2007, *Rossiiskaia gazeta*, March 30, 2007 (Kazantsev, dissenting).
[74] *Ibid.*

within the legislative, executive, and judicial branches of federal government. This expansion of judicial power paved the way for the growing role of the 2nd RCC in defining Russian federalism and protecting basic rights.

DEFINING RUSSIAN FEDERALISM

According to the official statistics published by the RCC, between 1995 and 2006 the Court received 627 petitions "on the issues of federalism" and issued over a hundred judgments accompanied by numerous dissents. As Table 5.1 shows, regions petitioned the Constitutional Court during Putin's presidency more often than they did during Yeltsin's era: on average, the Court receives two petitions per month from each of the regions. By itself, this figure does not say much because regions do not always advance federalism-based claims in their petitions to the RCC and because they settle federalism disputes outside of the court. What is remarkable is that the Constitutional Court seems to have regained the trust of the regions, which, in the mid-1990s, boycotted this tribunal, suspended its jurisdiction on their territory, and accused it of being "hostage to political questions." How did the RCC achieve this respect from regional elites? I argue that the Court achieved this by remaining one of the most "region-friendly" federal institutions despite the fact that many of its judgments undercut vital regional interests and enhanced federal supremacy.

But before I proceed with the analysis of these judgments, three caveats are worthy of note. First, judges rarely have the capacity to resolve center-regional, interregional, and intraregional disputes.[75] As Pomeranz argues, the federal Constitutional Court is just one player among many in the complex, ongoing debate on the future of Russian federalism and its judgments alone are not sufficient to build and maintain a healthy federation.[76] The key question is how successful the Court has been in structuring this debate and setting up the framework of managing conflict within the nascent Russian Federation. Second, the 1993 constitution preserved

---

[75] See, for example, Irina Umnova, "Konstitutsionno-pravovye aspekty biudzhetno-finansovogo federalizma," [Constitutional-Legal Aspects of the Budgetary-Fiscal Federalism] *Federalizm*, no. 1 (1999), pp. 135–146; William Pomeranz, "The Russian Constitutional Court's Interpretation of Federalism: Balancing Center-Regional Relations," *Parker School Journal of East European Law*, vol. 4, no. 4 (1997), pp. 401–443.

[76] Pomeranz, "The Russian Constitutional Court's Interpretation of Federalism," p. 403.

140 *Decision Making of the 2nd Russian Constitutional Court*

unique Soviet and Tsarist legacies of a hierarchical and multiethnically structured Russia.[77] Russia's regions, or "subjects of the Federation," vary in their constitutional status. Although all regions possess equal constitutional rights, ethnic republics have the most power, while nine autonomous districts are also included in the composition of six provinces and one territory (so-called *matryoshka* federalism). The 1993 constitution defines republics as states (Article 5.2), and they are free to establish an official "state language" (Article 68.2) and to choose the way to adopt their own constitutions, while the rest of the regions have to adopt their charters exclusively through their legislatures (Article 66). Finally, although there are these interregional contradictions, the 1993 Russian constitution is similar to many other federal constitutions: it is vague and ambiguous on the division of powers between the Federation and the regions. This constitutional ambiguity allowed both President Yeltsin to champion asymmetrical and bilateral federalism in 1994–1997 and President Putin to denounce any asymmetry in center-regional relations in 2000–2005. Federal–regional conflicts over judicial appointments in the 1990s, for example, clearly show that the federal center lacked any coherent strategy in staffing federal courts in the regions.[78] This inconsistent behavior of the federal and regional political actors coupled with the vagueness, vacillation, and incoherence of the constitutional provisions pertaining to federalism make it nearly impossible for judges to identify the "tolerance intervals" of powerful elites, contrary to the *strategic* explanations of judicial politics.[79] Because of the changing preferences of politicians and of the rules of the federal–regional game, justices were often at a loss to predict the responses of the rulers to their judgments.

Following the passage of the 1993 Russian constitution, the revamped federal Constitutional Court of 1995 changed its "accommodation" approach to a vision of "unification" within Russian federalism. Recalling the weaknesses of Gorbachev's presidency in handling the USSR breakup, most judges agreed that the federal center had to be stronger to save

---

[77] Zhanna Ovsepian, *Stanovlenie konstitutsionnykh i ustavnykh sudov v subektakh Rossiiskoi Federatsii (1990–2000 gg)* [The Formation of Constitutional and Charter Courts in the Subjects of the Russian Federation] (Moskva: IKTs 'MarT', 2001), pp. 12–13.

[78] Alexei Trochev, "Judicial Selection in Russia: Towards Accountability and Centralization," in Peter H. Russell and Kate Malleson, eds., *Appointing Judges in an Age of Judicial Power: Critical Perspectives from Around the World* (Toronto: University of Toronto Press, 2005), pp. 375–394.

[79] Cf. Epstein et al., "The Role of Constitutional Courts," explaining the decision making of the Court between 1992 and 1996 through these "tolerance intervals."

Defining Russian Federalism 141

Russia from political, economic, and territorial collapse even if it meant the widespread use of coercion, commandeering, and near-total federal preemption of regional autonomy. Disillusioned by the inconsistency of the federal government in enforcing its judgments, and disappointed by the unwillingness of regional governments to comply voluntarily (see Chapters 6 and 7), the Constitutional Court steered toward a stronger federal center.[80] This was a tragic choice between authoritarianism and territorial breakdown, but as some have argued, federalism is closely related to the tragic aspect of politics. As Malcolm Feeley and Edward Rubin have noted, federalism "belongs to a world where there are no optimal solutions, where conflicts are irreconcilable, where political conditions are more likely to get worse than better. It is a grim expedient that is adopted in grim circumstances, an acknowledgment that choices must be made among undesirable alternatives."[81]

In the Russian case, a strong authoritarian federal center was less of an evil than the "former Russia" was, according to judges. Chairman Zorkin, who also chaired the Court between 1991 and 1993, repeatedly expressed his fear of Russia disintegrating into a multitude of microstates as the USSR had broken up earlier. He spoke of this frequently and usually in apocalyptic terms like the need to "save Russia" from the abyss, catastrophe, chaos, disaster, perdition, or the "brink of a precipice," which he darkly predicted would be a hundred times worse than the ongoing Yugoslav wars. During the summer of 2004, in one of his many public interviews, Zorkin was still referring to the collapse of the USSR and Yugoslavia and in that mindset commented "from the mouths of certain regional leaders from time to time one hears talk about the necessity of building a federation on 'divided sovereignty.'" He added, indignantly, "And this in spite of decisions adopted by the Constitutional Court."[82] Disgusted by the flourishing bilateralism during Yeltsin's reelection campaign in 1996, Zorkin and his colleagues openly called for a "dictatorship

---

[80] The RCC is not unique in this regard. Case law of the Spanish Constitutional Tribunal also exhibits a similar tendency to favor the central government in resolving center-periphery conflicts. John M. Long, "The Geography of Spain's Constitutional Court" (Ph.D. diss., University of South Carolina, 2001). The U.S. Supreme Court also tends to strike down far more state statutes as compared to federal ones. See David O'Brien, *Storm Center* (New York: Norton, 2000), p. 30.

[81] Malcolm M. Feeley and Edward L. Rubin, *Federalism: Political Identity and Tragic Compromise* (Ann Arbor: University of Michigan Press, 2008), chapter 2.

[82] Quoted in Robert Sharlet, "The Russian Constitutional Court's Long Struggle for Viable Federalism," in Gordon B. Smith and Robert Sharlet, eds., *Russia and Its Constitution: Promise and Political Reality* (Leiden: Martinus Nijhoff, 2007), pp. 23–50.

142 *Decision Making of the 2nd Russian Constitutional Court*

of law" as a necessary element of a strong democratic federal statehood, and have been eager to assert the supremacy of the federal constitution over regional laws.[83] In October 1999, Justice Gadzhiev, who authored many of the RCC opinions in taxation cases, advocated consistent restrictions on the regional fiscal policy space in order to secure common market and economic freedoms.[84] And it was the majority of the Tumanov Court who insisted on reviewing the constitutionality of Yeltsin's war in Chechnya in 1995, even though Chairman Tumanov did his best to avoid accepting this case. In short, most judges were ready to become the messiahs to save Russia and to ensure that their Court remained on the political scene. This is why they chose to steer toward a stronger federal center, just like young constitutional (supreme) courts did in other federations: the U.S. Supreme Court in the early nineteenth century, the Australian High Court since 1920, the Supreme Court of Canada in the 1950s, and the Spanish Constitutional Tribunal in the 1980s.[85]

However, federal political actors made the job of the RCC very difficult. Both under Yeltsin and under Putin, federal elites were selective in launching constitutional litigation, making the process look more like Stalin-era "show trials" to undermine regional governors whom the Kremlin did not like, rather than a struggle to build the rule of law.[86] For example,

---

[83] President Putin would begin his presidency with the "dictatorship of law" agenda in 2000. See "Poslednii shans – diktatura zakona: interviu s Valeriem Zorkinym," [Last Chance – Dictatorship of Law: Interview with Valerii Zorkin] *VEK*, no. 43 (October 1996); "Diktatura Chubaisa ili zakona? Interviu s Gadisom Gadzhievym," [Dictatorship of Chubais or Dictatorship of Law? Interview with Gadis Gadzhiev] *Patriot*, no. 50 (December 1996), p. 11; "Interview with Justice Boris Ebzeev," *East European Constitutional Review*, vol. 6, no. 1 (Winter 1997), pp. 86–87.

[84] Gadis Gadzhiev, "Osnovnye konstitutsionno-pravovye problemy ekonomicheskoi reformy v Rossii," [Basic Constitutional-Legal Problems of the Economic Reform in Russia] in N. Varlamova and T. Vasileva, eds., *Rossiiskii federalizm: konstitutsionnye predposylki i politicheskaia realnost* (Moskva: MONF, 2000), p. 114.

[85] On the early years of the U.S. Supreme Court, which continues to strike down far more state statutes as compared to federal ones, see Leslie Goldstein, *Constituting Federal Sovereignty: The European Union in Comparative Context* (Baltimore and London: Johns Hopkins University Press, 2001). On Australia, see Mikhail Filippov, Peter C. Ordeshook, and Olga Shevtsova, *Designing Federalism: A Theory of Self-Sustainable Federal Institutions* (New York: Cambridge University Press, 2004), pp. 200–201. Case law of the Spanish Constitutional Tribunal also exhibits a similar tendency to favor the central government in resolving center-periphery conflicts. See Long, "The Geography of Spain's Constitutional Court."

[86] Alexei Titkov, "Konstitutsionnyi sud v otnosheniiakh Tsentra s regionami," [Constitutional Court in Center-Regional Relations] in Nikolai Petrov, ed., *Regiony Rossii v 1999 g.: Prilozhenie k "Politicheskomu almanakhu Rossii"* (Moskva: Carnegie Center, 2001), p. 261.

Defining Russian Federalism   143

by December 1995, Yeltsin's legal team had prepared briefs to challenge the constitutionality of laws passed by seventy-five regions.[87] However, President Yeltsin targeted the laws of only a few regions (Khakassia and Kalmykia). Instead, he chose to negotiate with most regions instead of suing them in order to secure both his own reelection in June 1996 and the election of regional governors loyal to him.[88] In 2000, a group of federal MPs, in an effort to target some, but not other, entrenched governors, asked the RCC to invalidate six republican constitutions containing clauses on citizenship, sovereignty, and control of natural resources.[89] Moreover, as I will show in Chapter 7, the federal center, including the Russian Supreme Court, proved inconsistent in requiring regions to obey the Constitutional Court decisions and to repeal regional statutes that violated the federal constitution.

How did the RCC push its federalism agenda? Between 1995 and 2006, the Court rarely supported any expansion of the rights of the regions vis-à-vis the federal center, while consistently trying to protect the symmetrical nature of the Federation from the encroachment of republics, which claimed a privileged status, and from the arbitrary policies of the federal government toward selected regions. Thus, the Court upheld most of the challenges to regional electoral laws and fiscal policies brought by President Yeltsin, the members of the federal parliament, and the federal courts.[90] Justices refused to engage in controversies over personalities (federal appointees in the regions) and over concrete pieces of property by

---

[87] V. A. Vinogradov, "O konstitutsionnoi deliktnosti zakonodatelstva subektov Rossiiskoi Federatsii," [On Constitutional Delicts of Laws of the Subjects of the Russian Federation] in Suren Avakian, ed., *Konstitutsionnoe zakonodatelstvo subektov RF: problemy sovershenstvovaniia i ispolzovaniia v prepodavanii* (Moskva: Izdatelstvo MGU, 1999), p. 269.

[88] Something similar happened in December 1998: the Russian Procurator-General asked the federal Cabinet to challenge five regional laws in the Russian Constitutional Court but no litigation ensued. See I. V. Mikhalevich, "O praktike prokurorskogo reagirovaniia na nesootvetstvie federalnomu zakonodatelstvu pravovykh aktov subektov Rossiiskoi Federatsii," [On the Practice of the Procuratorial Responses to the Nonconformity of Legal Acts of the Subjects of the Russian Federation with Federal Legislation] in Suren Avakian, ed., *Konstitutsionnoe zakonodatelstvo subektov RF: problemy sovershenstvovaniia i ispolzovaniia v prepodavanii* (Moskva: Izdatelstvo MGU, 1999), p. 255.

[89] RCC decision 92-O of June 27, 2000, *VKS RF*, no. 5 (2000), pp. 59–80 and no. 6 (2000), pp. 10–12 (Luchin, dissenting).

[90] Tatiana Vasileva, "Razreshenie pravovykh kollizii mezhdu Federatsiei i subektami Federatsii," [Resolution of Legal Collisions between the Federation and the Subjects of the Federation] *Konstitutsionnoe pravo: vostochnoevropeiskoe obozrenie*, no. 1 (2002), p. 109.

144 Decision Making of the 2nd Russian Constitutional Court

forcing federal and regional actors to hammer out compromises in such disputes. Both under Yeltsin and under Putin, the RCC recognized the limits of judicial intervention and repeatedly stayed away from disputes that could shatter fragile interethnic peace in the North Caucasus.[91] Instead, the Court either focused on extraordinary cases (Chechnya – secession, and Udmurtia – abolition of local self-government) or on the cases in which it could define the basic principles of Russian-style federalism (undivided sovereignty, presidential powers to nominate and dismiss governors).

First, in the *Chechnya* case, mentioned above, the Court approved and legitimized the authority of the Russian president to use military force to quell rebellion in the regions and secession from the federation.[92] Many argue that the RCC lost its innocence in this case by upholding the war in Chechnya. Yet, high national courts abroad have a long history of discouraging unilateral secession from a federation, while scholars have not reached a conclusion over costs and benefits of secession.[93]

Second, the Court expanded federal supremacy in the joint federal–regional jurisdiction enumerated in Article 72 of the Russian constitution. The 2nd RCC, unlike its predecessor, required uniformity in the setup of regional governments, which ought to follow the federal model of separation of powers (semipresidential republic).[94] This uniformity makes the job of the Constitutional Court easier because judges would apply the same constitutional principles to both federal and regional levels, and regions would have to follow all of their separation-of-powers judgments,

---

[91] RCC decisions: 103-O of December 26, 1996, unpublished (on the 1996 Peace Accords with Chechnya); 272-O of September 26, 2003 and 229-O of November 20, 2001, both unpublished (on the elections rules in multiethnic Dagestan); 365-O of December 1, 2005, *SZ RF*, no. 5 (2006), item 634 (on the dispute between North Ossetia and Ingushetia).

[92] RCC decision 10-P of July 31, 1995, *VKS RF*, no. 5 (1995), pp. 3–64 (Ametistov, Ebzeev, Gadzhiev, Kononov, Luchin, Morshchakova, Vitruk, and Zorkin, dissenting). See Sharlet, "Transitional Constitutionalism"; and Pomeranz, "Judicial Review and the Russian Constitutional Court."

[93] USA: *Texas v. White*, 74 US 700 (1869); Canada: Reference re Secession of Quebec, 2 S.C.R. 217 (1998). For a summary of scholarly debates about constitutionalizing secession, see Vicki C. Jackson, "Comparative Constitutional Federalism and Transnational Judicial Discourse," *I-CON: International Journal of Constitutional Law*, vol. 2, no. 1 (January 2004), pp. 91–138.

[94] RCC decision 2-P of January 18, 1996, *VKS RF*, no. 1 (1996), pp. 13–30 (Gadzhiev, Rudkin, and Vitruk, dissenting), English translation in *Statutes and Decisions*, no. 3 (1999).

Defining Russian Federalism 145

as explained in the previous section.[95] Although the Court declared unconstitutional the parliamentary system at the regional level, it did allow for some variation between presidential and semipresidential arrangements. The Court declared that the regions were free to choose between a unicameral and a bicameral legislature, to set reserve seats in the legislature for ethnic minorities, and to introduce a system of divided executive.

Third, this Court allowed the federal level to delineate the federal and regional functions by adopting federal statutes instead of signing intergovernmental agreements in the area of joint jurisdiction. Regions, then, had to follow these statutes, and could not require the federal center to sign such agreements.[96] Also, if the region failed to legislate in the area of joint jurisdiction, then the federal center had the power to preempt regional responsibilities.[97] For example, the Court declared that regions could not regulate advertising because only the federal legislature could set up the foundations of a single market, that is, free distribution of goods and fair competition.[98] These foundations, according to the Court, taken together with federal supremacy in fiscal policy, do not permit the expansion of regional and municipal taxes and fees beyond those listed in federal law.[99] This judicial vision of fiscal centralism ran against an earlier ruling of the Court, in which the majority ruled that regions could legislate their own taxes but their rates should be reasonable, be proportional to the public benefit and should not paralyze constitutional rights (freedom of movement in this case).[100] More importantly, this court-ordered fiscal centralization ran against President Yeltsin's 1993 decree, which allowed regional governments to set up their own taxes. Yeltsin promptly repealed

---

[95] Vladimir Kriazhkov, *Konstitutsionnoe pravosudie v subektakh Rossiiskoi Federatsii* [Constitutional Justice in the Subjects of the Russian Federation] (Moskva: Formula prava, 1999), p. 130, fn. 27.

[96] RCC decisions: 13-O of February 4, 1997, summarized in Berg, "Constitution of the Russian Federation Annotated," 269–270; 1-P of January 9, 1998, *VKS RF*, no. 2 (1998), pp. 5–18, English translation in *Statutes and Decisions*, no. 1 (1999).

[97] RCC decision 15-P of November 3, 1997, *VKS RF*, no. 6 (1997), pp. 2–8, English translation in *Statutes and Decisions*, no. 2 (2000).

[98] RCC decision 4-P of March 4, 1997, *VKS RF*, no. 1 (1997), pp. 54–63 (Zorkin, dissenting), English translation in *Statutes and Decisions*, no. 1 (1999).

[99] RCC decisions: 5-P of March 21, 1997, *VKS RF*, no. 4 (1997), pp. 5–12, English translation in *Statutes and Decisions*, no. 2 (1999); and 22-O of February 5, 1998, *VKS RF*, no. 3 (1998), pp. 30–34.

[100] RCC decision 9-P of April 4, 1996, *VKS RF*, no. 2 (1996), pp. 42–61 (Baglai, dissenting), English translation in *Statutes and Decisions*, no. 1 (1999).

146 *Decision Making of the 2nd Russian Constitutional Court*

his decree and chose not to interfere with regional fiscal autonomy.[101] The regions continued to levy their own taxes and set up various trade barriers, particularly in the wake of the August 1998 financial crisis. As a result, it was impossible by the end of the decade to ignore the diversity of the fiscal regimes in the Russian regions.[102] Clearly, the widespread explosion of regional and local taxes, fees, and trade barriers (and even customs duties!) made judges worrisome of the future of Russia's common market and of the federation itself.

Fourth, the RCC attacked the issue of subnational sovereignty in the summer of 2000. The Court chose to do so only after President Putin borrowed a "dictatorship of law" agenda from the RCC justices to rein in autonomy-minded governors, and only after the RCC gave a green light to the Russian Supreme Court in April 2000 to strike down regional statutes found to be in violation of federal standards. To ensure the enforcement of their judgments, the RCC felt the importance of securing the support of the recently elected popular president, who no longer needed the support of governors to gain votes, and the backing of the Supreme Court, which both repeatedly demanded the power to review regional law making and resisted regional "capture" of federal judicial appointments.[103] In a series of decisions, in June 2000, the RCC struck down the "sovereignty" clauses of seven regional constitutions.[104] As one RCC justice told the author, "We struck down the key clauses of seven constitutions of the republics in June 2000 only after President Putin announced his crackdown on recalcitrant regions; we would not have been brave enough to do this under Yeltsin."[105] In the same decisions, the Court

---

[101] See remarks by Justice Gadis Gadzhiev in "My daleko ushli ot vsiakoi tainstvennosti i zakrytosti," [We Went Far Away from Any Secrecy and Reticence] *Rossiiskaia gazeta*, November 1, 2001.

[102] See, for example, Kathryn Stoner-Weiss, *Resisting the State: Reform and Retrenchment in Post-Soviet Russia* (New York: Cambridge University Press, 2006); and Leonid Polishchuk, "Legal Initiatives in Russian Regions: Determinants and Effects," in Peter Murrell, ed., *Assessing the Value of Law in the Economic Transition from Socialism* (Ann Arbor: University of Michigan Press, 2001), pp. 330–368.

[103] Trochev, "Judicial Selection in Russia."

[104] RCC decisions: 10-P of June 7, 2000 (Altai Republic), *VKS RF*, no. 5 (2000), pp. 2–45 (Luchin and Vitruk, dissenting); and 92-O of June 27, 2000 (Adygeia, Bashkortostan, Ingushetia, Komi, North Ossetia, and Tatarstan Republics), *ibid.*, no. 5 (2000), pp. 59–80 and no. 6 (2000), pp. 10–12 (Luchin, dissenting).

[105] Interview with the RCC Justice, Moscow, May 22, 2001. Indeed, ex-Chairman Baglai identified all these regional violations of the 1993 constitution as early as 1997. See his "Problemy ukrepleniia konstitutsionnoi zakonnosti," [Problems of Strengthening

Defining Russian Federalism 147

struck down numerous provisions on regional citizenship, and regional control over land use and natural resources. The Court declared that the units of the federation could not have sovereignty because under the 1993 Russian constitution the "multinational people of the Russian Federation" gave the undivided sovereignty to the federal, not the regional, level. According to the Court, the fact that Article 5.2 of the 1993 constitution labels ethnic republics as "states" does not mean that republics have state sovereignty and, thus, this "statehood" has no legal consequences. Similarly, the fact that ethnic republics have their symbols, like a flag, a coat of arms, and an anthem, does not empower republics much, except for their distinctions from other Russian regions. Finally, and most importantly, the Court ruled that intergovernmental agreements could neither derogate sovereignty from the federal center nor violate constitutional norms. This judicial blow to bilateralism was based on the earlier RCC judgments, described in this chapter, in which the Court "discovered" that the federal center could delineate the functions falling in the joint federal–regional jurisdiction through federal statutes, even though Article 11.3 of the federal constitution did not mention federal statutes – it mentioned only the constitution and intergovernmental agreements.[106] Thus, the RCC demoted intergovernmental agreements to the lowest rungs of the operational legal hierarchy, treated republics as any other units of the federation and demanded that they bargain for their powers in the federal parliament rather than through extraconstitutional side deals with the federal president.

Fifth, the RCC upheld the constitutionality of the federal center to dissolve regional legislatures and to remove regional governors,[107] measures

---

Constitutional Legality] in V. P. Kazimirchuk, ed., *Konstitutsiia i zakon: stabilnost i dinamizm* (Moskva: IGP RAN, 1998), pp. 27–29.

[106] RCC decisions: 13-O of February 4, 1997, unpublished; 1-P of January 9, 1998, *VKS RF*, no. 2 (1998), pp. 5–18, English translation in *Statutes and Decisions*, no. 1 (1999).

[107] These sanctions for regional noncompliance with federal norms were enshrined in July 2000 amendments to the 1999 Federal Law "On the Basic Principles of Organizations of Regional Bodies of State Power." See Federalnyi zakon "O vnesenii izmenenii i dopolnenii v Federalnyi zakon 'Ob obshchikh printsipakh organizatsii zakonodatelnykh (predstavitelnykh) i ispolnitelnykh organov gosudarstvennoi vlasti subektov Rossiiskoi Federatsii'" of July 29, 2000, *SZ RF*, no. 31 (2000), item 3205. These provisions were passed in exchange for allowing certain regional governors to run for a third term. See "Kremliu razreshili uvolniat gubernatorov," [Kremlin Was Permitted to Dismiss Governors] *Gazeta.Ru*, April 4, 2002. The RCC approved this bargain in July 2002 when it upheld the constitutionality of a third and fourth term for incumbent governors.

148   *Decision Making of the 2nd Russian Constitutional Court*

that were key components of Putin's federal reform.[108] In a 13–4 decision, the Court ruled in April 2002 that neither dissolving regional legislatures nor removing governors from office contradicted the constitution.[109] This was a vote of confidence in the president as these sanctions represented a cornerstone of Putin's "vertical power structure" and enabled the federal level to impeach elected regional officials. In the 17 months that it took the judges to decide this case, they devised a complicated and unworkable procedure for punishing recalcitrant regional authorities. The Court ruled that dismissing a governor and dissolving a legislature were possible only after their intentional noncompliance had been confirmed via decisions of three different courts, including the RCC.[110] This RCC decision disallowed any arbitrary use of "implied" presidential powers, and inserted the federal judiciary into the process of solving federal–regional conflicts.[111] But President Putin essentially overruled this decision in 2004 when he sponsored a bill abolishing direct gubernatorial elections and granting the federal president the arbitrary power to nominate and dismiss regional governors. In a 12–6 vote, the RCC upheld the constitutionality of this attack on federalism in December 2005 by overturning its own precedent set in 1996 that regional governors had to be directly elected.[112]

Finally, the RCC was no less centralist in handling disputes over fiscal federalism and the appointments of federal government officials in the field. The Court repeatedly rejected challenges to the power of the federal center to control regional fiscal policies. The RCC ruled that the constitutional requirements of *Sozialstaat* (Article 7) and a single-budget system limited the autonomy of the budgets of the regions and obliged them to provide federally set guarantees of social protection, that is, the federal government could "commandeer" regions to increase salaries and

---

[108] Alexei Trochev and Peter H. Solomon, Jr., "Courts and Federalism in Putin's Russia," in Peter Reddaway and Robert W. Orttung, eds., *The Dynamics of Russian Politics. Volume 2* (Lanham, MD: Rowman and Littlefield, 2005), pp. 91–121.

[109] RCC decision 8-P of April 4, 2002, *VKS RF*, no. 5 (2002), pp. 3–37 (Gadzhiev, Iaroslavtsev, Morshchakova, and Vitruk, dissenting).

[110] Anna Zakatnova, "Tri barera dlia Putina," [Three Hurdles for Putin] *Nezavisimaia gazeta*, April 5, 2002, pp. 1–2.

[111] Except in the case where the federal president has unilateral power to suspend a governor who faces criminal charges.

[112] RCC decision 13-P of December 21, 2005, *VKS RF*, no. 1 (2006), pp. 49–75 (Kononov and Iaroslavtsev, dissenting). For a critique of this judgment, see, for example, Masha Gessen, "The Dear Departed Judiciary," *Moscow Times*, December 29, 2005, p. 7, available at http://www.themoscowtimes.com/stories/2005/12/29/006.html; and Dmitry Babich, "One Decision and Two 'No Comments'," *Russia Profile*, December 22, 2005, available at http://www.russiaprofile.org.

Defining Russian Federalism 149

benefits for public employees.[113] Regions (and municipalities) cannot even pick and choose banks in which to keep their budgetary accounts – they have to keep them in the branches of the Russian Central Bank.[114] The Court further ruled that regional sales, gambling, and transport taxes could not exceed the maximum rate set by federal law. The Court also repeatedly upheld a federal statute ordering the regions to pay for the support staff of 10,000 Justice of the Peace courts, which are legally courts of the regions, even though the JPs' salaries are paid for by the federal government.[115]

In addition to the clashes over fiscal policies, the federal center and the regions continuously dispute the appointment and dismissal of federal government officials in the field, regional governors and legislators, and local mayors. On occasion, one of the parties would ask the Court to resolve such disputes. These kinds of disputes always involved concrete personalities and threatened the peace of the federation, especially given the long-standing importance of personalities in Russian politics. The RCC was active in resolving conflicts between regional governors and local mayors. Since early 1997, the Court has repeatedly overruled regional laws, which abolished the elected local self-government bodies or empowered the governors to nominate and remove the heads of municipalities.[116] In the January 1997 *Udmurtia Republic* case, the Court struck down the abolition of elected local self-government in the republic.[117] This 12–2 judgment, authored by Justice Zorkin, was issued at the request of Yeltsin, Duma members, and several individuals, who took the side of the mayor of Udmurtia's capital city Izhevsk in his fight against the regional legislature. The Court struck down parts of the contested Udmurtia statute but, out of respect for the regional prerogative, did not specify how to restore the elected municipal bodies. In the wake of the verdict, both sides claimed victory, and moved very slowly to obey the Court (as I will explain in Chapter 7). However, the justices were the boldest in those

---

[113] RCC decision 43-O of April 13, 2000, in Tamara Morshchakova, ed., *Konstitutsionnyi Sud Rossiiskoi Federatsii: Postanovleniia. Opredeleniia. 2000* (Moskva: Iurist, 2001), p. 262.

[114] RCC decision 12-P of June 17, 2004, *VKS RF*, no. 4 (2004), pp. 74–91 (Gadzhiev, concurring).

[115] RCC decisions: 182-O of October 4, 2001, *VKS RF*, no. 2 (2002), pp. 30–32; 366-O of November 8, 2005, *VKS RF*, no. 2 (2006), pp. 31–33.

[116] V. D. Karpovich, ed., *Kommentarii k Konstitutsii RF* [Commentary to the Constitution of the Russian Federation] (Moskva: Iurait-M, 2002), pp. 93–94.

[117] RCC decision 1-P of January 24, 1997, *VKS RF*, no. 1 (1997), pp. 2–24 (Gadzhiev and Vitruk, dissenting), English translation in *Statutes and Decisions*, no. 1 (2000), p. 51.

150   *Decision Making of the 2nd Russian Constitutional Court*

cases that did not challenge specific individual appointments. Since 1996, the RCC insisted that neither republics nor other Russian regions could veto appointments of federal judges, regional tax police heads, procurators, and police chiefs, as all such matters were a prerogative of the federal center. The Court ruled that only the federal legislature could allow regional involvement in this process, while the regions could not assert this power themselves. Moreover, the Court gradually discovered that "regional consent" to these appointments did not apply to the outcome; instead, it merely permitted the procedure of allowing the regional government to express its opinion about the appointee.[118] The Court made this "discovery" after President Putin announced a serious crackdown on regional violations of federal laws, including illegal encroachments on the part of the regions in the process of recruiting federal judges and financing federal courts (see Chapter 7 for the reaction of the regions).[119]

In summary, the critics of the Court are right: most RCC judges support Putin's struggles against recalcitrant governors.[120] But this is not a clear sign of judicial dependency in adjudicating center–regional conflicts. Instead, it is a sign of the courts depending on the political branches to see their judgments carried out. As I have shown, judicial preferences for a strong federal center were formed well before Putin's ascendancy to power. And Putin's initiatives largely built on the jurisprudence of the Court developed during Yeltsin's rule. To be sure, Putin's federalism reforms generated the squall of regional complaints, and this may be one of the reasons for the growing attractiveness of constitutional litigation in the eyes of the regions.

As the preceding discussion makes it clear, the RCC appears to be a tribunal in which Moscow is doomed to win against any regional assaults on federal supremacy. Many times, this seems to be the case. But, as the

---

[118] Compare RCC decision 3-P of February 1, 1996, *VKS RF*, no. 1 (1996), pp. 34–47 (Vitruk, dissenting), English translation in *Statutes and Decisions*, no. 3 (1999), in which the Court equates "regional consent" with the veto power of the region, with its decision 10-P of June 7, 2000, *VKS RF*, no. 5 (2000), pp. 2–45 (Luchin and Vitruk, dissenting), where the Court redefines "regional consent" as a right of the regions to express their opinion about an appointee. See also Karpovich, *Kommentarii k Konstitutsii RF*, pp. 580, 913–914.

[119] Vladimir Putin, "Novoi Rossii nuzhna silnaia i nezavisimaia sudebnaia sistema," [New Russia Needs a Strong and Independent Judicial System] *Rossiiskaia gazeta*, January 26, 2000, pp. 1–2.

[120] See, for example, Andrey N. Medushevsky, *Russian Constitutionalism: Historical and Contemporary Development* (New York: Routledge, 2006), p. 235, where the author argues that the Court "demonstrates loyalty to all actions of the authorities, refusing to oppose the presidential decrees on transformation of federalism."

Defining Russian Federalism

court statistics in Table 5.1 show, the Court accepts for review about 15–20 percent of petitions coming from regional governments. Moreover, the Chief Justice or the Judge-Rapporteur routinely meets in person with the petitioners from the regional governments to discuss their cases. To be sure, judges do not rule in favor of each of these complaints. But this proportion is much higher than the share of regional input in federal law making in the areas of joint federal–regional jurisdiction. In the federal political process, in which the Russian president completely dominates the federal legislature, only 4 percent of legislative initiatives coming from the regions become federal laws. Clerks in the federal Cabinet routinely refuse to provide financial estimates of bills submitted by the regions. Such refusals effectively block regional initiatives because the State Duma automatically rejects any bill that lacks such an estimate. At the request of the Tomsk regional legislature, which in vain tried to lobby Prime Minister Fradkov and the Speakers of both chambers of the Russian parliament, the RCC overruled this practice of unfettered discretion by the Cabinet clerks as unconstitutional in November 2006. The Court unanimously held that the standard operating procedures (*Reglament*) of the Cabinet could not encroach on the very essence of the constitutional right to introduce legislation.[121] So, the Constitutional Court remains the only official forum in today's Russia where regional concerns can get full attention at the federal level.

Two areas of intergovernmental disputes, the scope of regional law making and fiscal federalism, illustrate this point. Since 1995, the Constitutional Court has repeatedly allowed regions to legislate in the area of joint jurisdiction "until the adoption of a federal statute on the matter."[122] According to Justice Ebzeev, the Court "discovered" this power of the regions in the constitutional spirit of joint jurisdiction, not in the literal meaning of the constitutional norms.[123] Although the Russian Constitutional Court warned that such regional law making ought to comply with federal jurisdiction, constitutional freedoms, and subsequently

---

[121] RCC decision 9-P of November 26, 2006, *VKS RF*, no. 1 (2007), pp. 26–47 (Bondar and Gadzhiev, concurring, and Kononov, dissenting).

[122] RCC decisions: 16-P of November 30, 1995, *VKS RF*, no. 6 (1995), pp. 42–47, English translation in *Statutes and Decisions*, no. 3 (1999); 3-P of February 1, 1996, *ibid.*, no. 1 (1996), pp. 34–47 (Vitruk, dissenting), English translation in *Statutes and Decisions*, no. 3 (1999); and 9-P of April 4, 1996, *ibid.*, no. 2 (1996), pp. 42–61 (Justice Baglai, dissenting), English translation in *Statutes and Decisions*, no. 1 (1999).

[123] Boris Ebzeev, ed., *Kommentarii k postanovleniiam Konstitutsionnogo Suda Rossiiskoi Federatsii. T. 1.*, p. 472.

adopted federal statutes on the matter, many observers criticized this "discovery" of the Constitutional Court as allowing unfettered regional law making in areas of federal jurisdiction.[124] In fact, the Court simply recognized that "life in the regions goes on outside of legal norms," as Justice Vedernikov put it in early 1995.[125] By allowing all regions (not just republics) not to wait for the approval of the often deadlocked federal center, the 2nd RCC sought to bring more symmetry to Russian federalism and to limit the sporadic intrusion of federal actors in the regional political process. For example, in the spring of 1996, just before the presidential election, the Court did not allow President Yeltsin to appoint governors in those regions that managed to pass necessary electoral laws, disagreed with Yeltsin's attempt to delay the introduction of municipal elections, and refused the request of State Duma members to repeal electoral laws in the Sverdlovsk Region.[126] These judgments might have affected the number of votes by which Yeltsin won his second term. Further, when the federal center under Putin sought to rein in recalcitrant governors by passing a federal law that imposed term limits on governorships, the Court, in July 2002, ruled that it was essentially up to the regions themselves to determine the number of terms that the governors could serve.[127] In summary, these limitations on the power of the federal center to interfere with the electoral process brought some sense of stability to regional political regimes and solidified both nascent political competition in some regions and "creeping authoritarianism" in others.[128]

---

[124] A. N. Lebedev, *Status subekta Rossiiskoi Federatsii* (Status of the RF Subject) (Moskva: IGP RAN, 1999), pp. 137–144.

[125] Valentin Maslennikov, "Khvatit zhdat, pora dogoniat," [Enough Waiting, It Is Time to Catch up] *Rossiiskaia gazeta*, March 16, 1995.

[126] RCC decisions: 11-P of April 30, 1996, *VKS RF*, no. 3 (1996), pp. 15–28 (Luchin, dissenting), English translation in *Statutes and Decisions*, no. 4 (1999); 13-P of May 30, 1996, *ibid.*, no. 3 (1996), pp. 37–47 (Ametistov, dissenting), English translation in *Statutes and Decisions*, no. 3 (1999); and 59-O of May 22, 1996, in Tamara Morshchakova, ed., *Konstitutsionnyi Sud Rossiiskoi Federatsii. Postanovleniia. Opredeleniia. 1992–1996* (Moskva, 1997), pp. 181–184. See also Valentin Maslennikov, "Konstitutsionnyi sud – ne dekorativnyi bantik v rossiiskoi demokratii," [Constitutional Court Is Not a Decorative Bow in Russian Democracy] *Rossiiskaia gazeta*, August 2, 1996.

[127] RCC decision 12-P of July 9, 2002, *VKS RF*, no. 6 (2002), pp. 3–15 (term limits for regional governors).

[128] See, for example, Vladimir Gelman, Sergei Ryzhenkov, and Michael Brie, *Making and Breaking Democratic Transitions: The Comparative Politics of Russia's Regions* (Lanham, MD: Rowman and Littlefield, 2003) and Jeffrey Kahn, *Federalism, Democratization, and the Rule of Law in Russia* (New York: Oxford University Press, 2002).

Defining Russian Federalism 153

The Court, however, continued to defend its own doctrine of avoiding political questions. Facing political squabbles, the RCC consistently refused to tinker with the timing of elections at both the federal[129] and regional[130] levels, to cancel elections,[131] or to question the legitimacy of the already elected legislatures.[132] In short, the Court behaved like a mature tribunal in a well-established political system: it refused to enter the political fray and to change the rules of the electoral game before the winners had been announced.[133]

Under Putin's presidency, the Court continued to provide a forum for regional concerns. In April 2000, the RCC gave a green light to the Supreme Court and its army of lower courts to review the legality of regional law making. As a result, thousands of regional and local legal acts were found to be null and void.[134] However, the RCC kept the power to have a final say in this campaign of "harmonizing" regional law making. In July 2003, the Constitutional Court struck down the provisions of the 6-month-old Civil Procedure Code that authorized other courts to handle challenges against the regional charters and republican constitutions, declared that only the RCC could handle such cases, and discovered that the Procurator General was empowered to bring challenges in the Constitutional Court, despite the fact that Article 125 of the constitution does not mention the Procurator General as one of those high officials who can petition the Constitutional Court.[135] In addition, between 2003 and 2004, the RCC repeatedly confirmed the constitutionality of several

---

[129] RCC decision 77-O of November 20, 1995, *VKS RF*, no. 6 (1995), pp. 22–30 (Ametistov, dissenting), English translation in *Statutes and Decisions*, no. 2 (1996).

[130] RCC decisions: 11-P of April 30, 1996, *VKS RF*, no. 3 (1996), pp. 15–28 (Luchin, dissenting), English translation in *Statutes and Decisions*, no. 4 (1999); 59-O of May 22, 1996, in Tamara Morshchakova, ed., *Konstitutsionnyi Sud Rossiiskoi Federatsii. Postanovleniia. Opredeleniia. 1992–1996* (Moskva, 1997), pp. 181–184; and 216-O of December 7, 2001, *VKS RF*, no. 2 (2002), pp. 87–89.

[131] RCC decisions: 105-O of December 26, 1996 (unpublished), summarized in van den Berg, "Constitution of the Russian Federation Annotated," p. 265; and 93-O of July 1, 1998, *VKS RF*, no. 5 (1998), pp. 67–69.

[132] See, for example, RCC decisions: 9-P of July 10, 1995, *VKS RF*, no. 4 (1995), pp. 2–12 (Vitruk, dissenting); 16-P of May 29, 1998, *ibid.*, no. 5 (1998), pp. 10–13; 4-P of March 23, 2000, *ibid.*, no. 3 (2000), pp. 21–28; and 2-P of January 22, 2002, *ibid.*, no. 3 (2002), pp. 14–23.

[133] For the discussion of the "proper" roles of courts in elections, see, for example, Filippov et al., *Designing Federalism*, p. 77.

[134] Trochev and Solomon, "Courts and Federalism in Putin's Russia," pp. 91–121.

[135] RCC decision 13-P of July 18, 2003, *VKS RF*, no. 5 (2003), pp. 15–29.

regional statutes that the Russian Supreme Court had previously found to be inconsistent with federal law.[136] According to observers, these decisions of the Constitutional Court rendered a serious blow to the authority of the federal center and even ushered in a quiet counterrevolution in the federal system.[137]

And even in fiscal federalism, which has become heavily centralized under Putin, Russian regions benefited from the Court-imposed requirement to "legislate" any kind of taxes. Recall from the previous section that the RCC repeatedly disapproved of the frequent introduction of new taxes and fees by a unilateral declaration of the federal Cabinet. Regional leaders who, until 2001, sat in the Federation Council and controlled the State Duma members from their regions, had a far greater say in making the Russian tax statutes than in influencing the content of federal Cabinet regulations. In fact, throughout 1997, the RCC repeatedly sided with regional petitions on this matter and invalidated alcohol licensing, hydro, and border-crossing fees on these grounds.[138] However, facing the weakening revenue-collecting capacity of the federal center, the Court later changed its position and allowed the federal Cabinet to introduce and regulate certain fees and levies.[139]

Under Putin's presidency, justices continued to balance fiscal federalism in a creative way and allowed certain regional autonomy. For example, the RCC upheld the right of regions to set up extrabudgetary funds and to determine their own revenue bases, even though the Federal Budget Code did not assign this power to the regions and the Russian Supreme Court had earlier ruled that the creation of regional extrabudgetary funds violated federal law.[140] In another decision, the Russian Constitutional Court refused to hear a petition by the federal Cabinet and reiterated that

---

[136] RCC decisions: 103-O of March 6, 2003, *VKS RF*, no. 4 (2003), pp. 81–85; 19-P of December 15, 2003, *ibid.*, no. 1 (2004), pp. 26–37; and 10-P of May 13, 2004, *ibid.*, no. 4 (2004), pp. 50–60.

[137] Stoner-Weiss, *Resisting the State*, pp. 151–152.

[138] RCC decisions: 3-P of February 18, 1997, *VKS RF*, no. 1 (1997), pp. 43–53 (Morshchakova, dissenting), English translation in *Statutes and Decisions*, no. 1 (2000); 6-P of April 1, 1997, *ibid.*, no. 4 (1997), pp. 13–17, English translation in *Statutes and Decisions*, no. 1 (2000); 16-P of November 11, 1997, *ibid.*, no. 6 (1997), pp. 9–22 (Kononov and Vitruk, dissenting), English translation in *Statutes and Decisions*, no. 2 (2000).

[139] RCC decisions: 22-P of July 17, 1998, *VKS RF*, no. 6 (1998), pp. 58–67 (Kononov, dissenting), English translation in *Statutes and Decisions*, no. 5 (2000); 283-O of December 10, 2002, *ibid.*, no. 2 (2003), pp. 57–66; and 284-O of December 10, 2002, *ibid.*, no. 2 (2003), pp. 66–79 and no. 3 (2003), pp. 68–71 (Gadzhiev, dissenting).

[140] RCC decision 228-O of December 6, 2001, *VKS RF*, no. 2 (2002), pp. 71–76.

the delimitation of state property ownership between the federation and its parts should be achieved by balancing federal and regional economic interests through the process of federal legislation.[141] The federal center cannot, in the view of the Court, transfer regional or municipal property without reaching an agreement with the owner and without adequate compensation.[142]

In fact, the Court applied these requirements of consent and adequate compensation to property disputes between the regions and local self-governments. More importantly, the RCC has begun to accept petitions from local self-government units in a clear move to oversee the constitutionality of local government reforms undertaken by President Putin.[143] Neither the 1993 Russian constitution nor any other federal statute grants the municipalities the right to petition the Constitutional Court. And, up until 2002, the Court denied all complaints from the municipalities despite the predictions of the mainstream judicial empowerment theories that the rivalries among power holders or viable electoral market during Yeltsin's era would encourage the expansion of the jurisdiction of the Court. To be sure, in the 1990s, the RCC consistently protected the autonomy of local self-government, like in the 1997 *Udmurtia* case discussed earlier in this chapter.[144] And Justices could continue doing their job without accepting the complaints of municipalities. But the Constitutional Court chose to expand its jurisdiction precisely when the Kremlin moved to concentrate political power both by gaining control of the federal legislature and by strengthening its grip over the regions. For example, the Court repeatedly ruled that the federal center had to compensate the municipalities in full for the cost of providing housing for federal judges, police officers,

---

[141] RCC decision 112-O of May 14, 2002 (unpublished), available at the Web site of the RCC at http://www.ksrf.ru.

[142] RCC decisions: 14-P of November 22, 2000, *VKS RF*, no. 1 (2001), pp. 10–17; 8-P of June 30, 2006, *ibid.*, no. 4 (2006), pp. 24–34; 540-O of November 2, 2006, *ibid.*, no. 2 (2007), pp. 80–88; and 542-O of December 7, 2006, *ibid.*, no. 2 (2007), pp. 123–128.

[143] For an overview of local government reforms in Russia, see Tomila Lankina, *Governing the Locals: Local Self-government and Ethnic Mobilization in Russia* (Lanham, MD: Rowman and Littlefield, 2004); and Tomila Lankina, "President Putin's Local Government Reforms," in Peter Reddaway and Robert W. Orttung, eds., *The Dynamics of Russian Politics, Volume 2: Putin's Reform of Federal–Regional Relations* (Lanham, MD: Rowman and Littlefield, 2005), pp. 145–177.

[144] Since early 1997, the Court has repeatedly overruled regional laws that abolished the elected local self-government bodies or empowered the governors to nominate and dismiss the heads of municipalities. V. D. Karpovich, ed., *Kommentarii k Konstitutsii RF* (Moskva: Iurait-M, 2002), pp. 93–94.

and prison guards.[145] These judgments, if implemented, are likely to strengthen both the judicial protection and financial base of local self-government, given that President Putin's judicial reform involved the hiring of several thousand federal judges during his first term. Finally, in May 2006, the Court ruled that federal and regional governments had to reimburse municipalities for subsidizing the cost of providing childcare to anyone.[146] Clearly, the Court wants to stop the practice of "unfunded mandates" and to become the forum for protecting local self-government, a sure loser in the race to strengthen governance in Russia under Putin.[147] However, it is far from certain whether the federal center will comply with this judicial vision of fiscal federalism.

In summary, the Russian Constitutional Court has earned its place in the game of Russian federalism. Aspiring to avoid federal disintegration and recovering from the wounds inflicted on the Court by President Yeltsin in 1993, judges chose to champion strong federal supremacy even if it meant turning Russia's regions into nothing more than implementing agents of the federal level, partly returning to the Soviet system of subordinating the regional governments to that of Moscow.[148] Three factors indicate the growing role of the Court in "fixing" Russian federalism. First, the RCC carved out its own niche to review Putin's reforms of Russian governance and was not afraid to review virtually all key reforms of the popular president. To be sure, the Court upheld most of them, yet it allowed dissenting judges to criticize Putin's policies in public. For example, Justice Gadzhiev, who had ardently advocated restrictions on regional fiscal policies in 1999, blasted the federal center in 2006 for "usurping" regional autonomy through federal statutes.[149] Second, the RCC managed to earn support from

---

[145] RCC decisions: 132-O of April 9, 2003, *VKS RF*, no. 5 (2003), pp. 65–68; 303-O of July 8, 2004, *ibid.*, no. 1 (2005), pp. 112–115; 58-O of February 15, 2005, unpublished; 224-O of June 9, 2005, unpublished; and 485-O of October 17, 2006, unpublished, all available at the Web site of the RCC at http://www.ksrf.ru

[146] RCC decision 5-P of May 15, 2006, *VKS RF*, no. 3 (2006), pp. 68–81.

[147] On the fiscal independence of local self-governments, see RCC decision 16-P of November 11, 2003, *VKS RF*, no. 6 (2003), pp. 31–45.

[148] Leonid Polishchuk, "Should the Legal Foundations of a Federal State be Flexible or Rigid? Canadian Experience and Russian Dilemmas," in Peter H. Solomon, Jr., ed., *Making Federalism through Law: Canadian Experience and Russian Reform under Putin* (Toronto: CREES, University of Toronto, 2003), p. 59.

[149] "Sudia Konstitutsionnogo Suda zaiavil, chto federatsiia uzurpiruet prava subektov RF," [Judge of the Constitutional Court Said That the Federation Usurps the Rights of

Defining Russian Federalism 157

autonomy-minded regions. If, in the mid-1990s, they simply boycotted the RCC sessions and accused the Court of being "hostage to political questions,"[150] by 2003, the regions continued to petition the Court so much that Chairman Zorkin had to ask some of the regions to postpone submission of their requests.[151] Finally, the federal center under President Putin attempted to incorporate RCC decisions into his reforms of Russia's federalism.[152] As it should be clear by now, using the RCC decisions to prepare federalism reforms was in itself a titanic effort due to the numerous judgments and inconsistent approaches taken by the Court.[153] Yet, the fact that the political branches under Putin were beginning to pay systematic attention to RCC decisions is an indicator of the growing power of the Court.

This growing attractiveness of the RCC to the federal center and the regions (and, increasingly, local governments) comes from a well-established pattern of using court decisions as political resources in their relations among each other, a dynamic not unfamiliar to the students of federalism.[154] As I will explain in Chapters 6 and 7, the challenge ahead is to build a federal government that is capable or willing to enforce judicial decisions that go against its interests. A bigger challenge is to ensure that the strong federal center will restrain itself to avoid a return to a unitary state, which, in turn, may result in secession. And judges will certainly have their opinions on how to address these urgent tasks.

---

the RF Subjects] *RIA 'Novyi Region-Moskva,'* January 27, 2006, available at http://www.nr2.ru/moskow/53983.html.

[150] See, for example, RCC decision 53-O of June 21, 1996, *VKS RF*, no. 4 (1996), pp. 20–22, English translation in *Statutes and Decisions*, no. 5 (2001).

[151] The flood of regional petitions to the RCC continued despite the fact that Justice Nikolai Vitruk, a staunch advocate of regional autonomy, had already left the bench in early 2003. Irina Begimbetova, "V povestku sessii Gossoveta RT vkliucheny 42 dopolnitelnykh voprosa," [The Agenda of the Session of the State Council of Tatarstan Includes Forty-Two Additional Questions] *Intertat.Ru*, May 26, 2003.

[152] On Russian federalism reforms under Putin, see, for example, Peter H. Solomon, Jr., ed., *Making Federalism through Law: Canadian Experience and Russian Reform under Putin* (Toronto: CREES, University of Toronto, 2003), and Peter H. Solomon, Jr., *The Dynamics of "Real Federalism": Law, Economic Development, and Indigenous Communities in Russia and Canada* (Toronto: CREES, University of Toronto, 2004).

[153] Report by Milena Gligich-Zolotareva, in *Analiticheskii vestnik 'Mezdunarodnyi opyt federativnoi demokratii,'* no. 23 (2003), pp. 15–16, available at http://www.council.gov.ru.

[154] Peter H. Russell, "The Supreme Court in Federal–Provincial Relations: The Political Use of Legal Resources," *Canadian Public Policy*, vol. 11, no. 2 (1985), pp. 161–170.

PROTECTING CONSTITUTIONAL RIGHTS

In marked contrast to its predecessors, the 2nd RCC paid much more attention to the protection of individual constitutional rights. Both scholars and justices agree that the focus on such rights simultaneously depoliticizes judicial decision making and brings the top court closer to common citizens, resulting in increased public trust in judicial review. In fact, virtually all successful post–World War II constitutional courts are famous for their tireless championing of human rights, encouraged by the work of the European Court of Human Rights in Strasbourg. For the 2nd RCC, which was emerging after a 16-month suspension, a closer focus on defending and interpreting the elaborate Bill of Rights enshrined in the 1993 Russian constitution was also a way out of the institutional crisis. Chief Justice Tumanov tended to avoid political disputes and preferred to deal with civil rights. Unlike his predecessor, Tumanov actively used the Court's new discretionary powers and rejected most of the complaints that had the potential to disrupt relations between his Court and President Yeltsin.[155] Tumanov's deputy, Tamara Morshchakova, who many place in the pro-Yeltsin camp, also preferred giving a priority to due process rights in criminal procedure. Similarly, Chief Justice Marat Baglai, who headed the RCC between 1997 and 2002, made sure that constitutional rights cases dominated the Court's docket. As he told Russian TV in June 1998, "we, young democrats, go through a difficult transition, during which we cannot simply throw citizens in the waves of the raging sea of liberalism."[156] In August 2002, Baglai insisted that through the focus on constitutional rights his Court was able to build the *Rechtsstaat* without interfering in the political process.[157] His successor, Chief Justice Zorkin, also repeatedly insisted on the primacy of protecting fundamental rights in the work of the Court. His colleagues also repeatedly emphasized that they shared this concern for individual rights, and that the Court had done a great deal in this area.[158]

---

[155] Thorson, "Constitutional Courts as Political Actors," p. 119.

[156] Recall "rebuilding the ship in an open sea" from Chapter 2. Baglai interview with *RTR Vesti*, June 4, 1998.

[157] Konstantin Katanian, "Sud – ne pozharnaia komanda," [Court Is Not a Fire-Rescue Team] *Vremia MN*, August 16, 2002.

[158] See speeches by Chief Justice Zorkin at the RCC Web site, available at http://www.ksrf.ru/news/speech.htm; Anna Zakatnova, "Respublikanskii zakon Dagestana protivorechit Konstitutsii Rossii," [Law of the Dagestan Republic Contradicts the Russian

Protecting Constitutional Rights

Indeed, between 1995 and 2006, the RCC received 37,733 (25 percent of the total) petitions about violations of substantive constitutional rights, 33,393 (22 percent) complaints about violations of due process rights in civil procedure, and 35,155 (23 percent) petitions about violations of due process in criminal procedure.[159] Filing individual complaints is easy and inexpensive, and the Court always allows indigent petitioners to file their constitutional complaints free of charge. This is similar to the experience of the constitutional courts in Germany, Korea, and Spain – Russians flood their Constitutional Court and ask it to judge Russia's authorities.[160]

The RCC contributed to rights litigation in two ways. First, the Court went beyond the literal meaning of the 1994 Act, which allows individuals to bring constitutional complaints only against a "statute." Initially, the Tumanov Court thought that a "statute" referred only to a federal statute, and, as a result, justices repeatedly refused to review regional laws violating individual rights.[161] However, the Baglai Court reversed this position and routinely checked the constitutionality of numerous regional laws at the request of individuals. After prolonged debate, with complaints by sixteen individuals, the RCC further "discovered" that individuals could also challenge the constitutionality of acts of amnesty – acts adopted by the State Duma. In the Court's view, amnesty was a unique act of legislature equal to the force of the federal Criminal Code; yet no other court was authorized to review its constitutionality.[162] A more radical expansion of what the Court could review occurred in January 2004, just a few months before the beginning of President Putin's second term in office. Contrary to the pressure of creeping authoritarianism in the country, the Constitutional Court boldly ruled that individuals

---

Constitution] *Nezavisimaia gazeta*, May 17, 2000, p. 3. Interviews with the RCC Justices, Moscow, May–June 2001.

[159] RCC Web site, http://www.ksrf.ru/contact/review.htm.

[160] To be sure, Russians also increasingly flood the European Court of Human Rights with their complaints against the Russian government. Indeed, in 2006 alone, this court received 12,241 applications against Russia. See its annual report for 2006, available at http://www.echr.coe.int.

[161] Anatolii Kovler, "Interviu Predsedatelia KS RF V. A. Tumanova," *Gosudarstvo i Pravo*, no. 1 (1995), p. 5; and Viktor Luchin and Olga Doronina, *Zhaloby grazhdan v Konstitutsionnyi Sud RF* [Citizen's Complaints to the RF Constitutional Court] (Moskva: Zakon i Pravo. Unity, 1998), p. 63. See, for example, RCC decisions 8-O and 17-O, both of March 11, 1996 (both unpublished).

[162] RCC decisions: 11-P of July 5, 2001, *VKS RF*, no. 6 (2001), pp. 28–41; and 7-P of April 24, 2003, *ibid.*, no. 4 (2003), pp. 3–11.

could file constitutional complaints against the federal Cabinet when the latter acted upon statutory authorization.[163] Until then, the RCC consistently refused to hear any challenge to the acts of the federal executive brought by private citizens, and insisted that other courts had the authority to review individual petitions against presidential decrees, government regulations, and ministerial instructions.[164] This decision, in effect, eliminated the power of the Russian Supreme Court to review almost all federal Cabinet edicts under the new 2002 Civil Procedure Code, and required the Supreme Court to refer such cases to the RCC. Although this may have burdened the RCC and significantly delayed the judicial review of executive law making, this strategic move by the Court prepared the grounds for allowing constitutional complaints against presidential decrees, which had been a taboo for the Tumanov and Baglai Courts.[165] Indeed, on two occasions and acting upon individual complaints, the Constitutional Court hinted that one decree of President Putin's on calculating sick leave benefits was unconstitutional and ordered the federal legislature to bring the rules of calculating these benefits in line with the constitutional principles of fairness and equality.[166] The Court did not strike down Putin's decree. Instead, judges daringly ruled that if presidential decrees were meant to replace the statutes, the RCC would review them at the request of individuals. In short, judges sent a clear signal that the popular president was not above the constitution.

A second way the RCC encouraged rights litigation was through the gradual expansion of access to the Court. The Court went beyond the literal meaning of the 1994 Act and recognized that corporations,[167]

---

[163] RCC decision 1-P of January 27, 2004, *VKS RF*, no. 2 (2004), pp. 3–21 (Kononov, dissenting). Since then, the Court has repeatedly struck down the edicts of the federal Cabinet at the request of individuals. See, for example, RCC decisions: 7-P of April 6, 2004, *VKS RF*, no. 4 (2004), pp. 3–18 (Bondar and Kononov, dissenting); 138-O of March 4, 2004, *ibid.*, no. 5 (2004), pp. 81–85; and 8-P of July 14, 2005, *ibid.*, no. 4 (2005), pp. 46–66 (Bondar, dissenting).

[164] See, for example, RCC decision 56-O of March 19, 1997, *VKS RF*, no. 4 (1997), pp. 2–4, English translation in *Statutes and Decisions*, no. 5 (2001).

[165] Rustem Faliakhov, "Na pravitelstvo zapretili zhalovatsia v sudy," [Complaints to Courts against the Government Are Banned] *Gazeta*, January 28, 2004.

[166] The RCC reviewed the Decree of the RF President No. 508 of March 15, 2000 "On the Amount of the Benefit for the Temporary Work Disability," *SZ RF*, no. 12 (2000), item 1259. See RCC decisions: 138-O of March 4, 2004, *VKS RF*, no. 5 (2004), pp. 81–85; and 16-O of March 2, 2006, *ibid.*, no. 3 (2006), pp. 112–117.

[167] RCC decision 17-P of October 24, 1996, *VKS RF*, no. 5 (1996), pp. 2–10 (Ebzeev, dissenting), English translation in *Statutes and Decisions*, no. 1 (2000).

Protecting Constitutional Rights

foreigners,[168] state-owned enterprises,[169] subjects of the Federation,[170] and local governments[171] effectively have a constitutional right to appear before the Court. This, in effect, means that the RCC finds basic rights everywhere in the 1993 constitution and even in international human rights treaties. And it also means that the growing nondemocratic trends are not strong enough to prevent the expansion of access to the constitutional tribunal.

Moreover, the RCC has routinely heard collective complaints against the state. On February 24, 1998, the Russian Constitutional Court struck down parts of the 1997 federal bill on mandatory contributions to the Pension Fund.[172] This decision was issued at the request of twenty-five "little" persons: attorneys, notaries, and small business owners from all over Russia. Following the nonimplementation of this judgment in federal courts, four of the petitioners asked the Court to "clarify" this decision, and the Court stood firm in its decision of November 26, 1998.[173] The January 1999 amendments to the federal Pension Fund bill still ignored these RCC decisions. Following this defiance, 2,687 citizens (2,057 notaries, 562 small business owners, 61 attorneys, and 7 farmers) and 15 regional public "associations of disabled persons" sued again in the Russian Constitutional Court. The Russian Constitutional Court again agreed with the "little" people and struck down the amended law on December 23, 1999.[174]

---

[168] RCC decisions: 6-P of February 17, 1998, *VKS RF*, no. 3 (1998), pp. 35–40, English translation in *Statutes and Decisions*, no. 3 (2001); and 147-O of June 23, 2000, *ibid.*, no. 6 (2000), pp. 33–38.

[169] RCC decision 24-P of October 12, 1998, *VKS RF*, no. 1 (1999), pp. 10–17, English translation in *Statutes and Decisions*, no. 5 (2000).

[170] RCC decision 14-P of November 22, 2000, *VKS RF*, no. 1 (2001), pp. 10–17.

[171] As I explained in the previous section, the Court initially refused to accept petitions from local self-government bodies. See, for example, RCC decision 20-O of March 19, 1997, unpublished and summarized in Vladimir Kriazhkov and Leonid Lazarev, *Konstitutsionnaia iustitsiia v Rossiiskoi Federatsii* [Constitutional Justice in the Russian Federation] (Moskva: BEK, 1998), p. 286. Following the resolve of Putin's administration to reform local self-government, the Court began to accept petitions from local self-government bodies. See RCC decisions: 7-P of April 2, 2002, *VKS RF*, no. 3 (2002), pp. 57–71 (Vitruk, dissenting); and 132-O of April 9, 2003, *ibid.*, no. 5 (2003), pp. 65–68.

[172] RCC decision 7-P of February 24, 1998, *VKS RF*, no. 3 (1998), pp. 41–57, English translation in *Statutes and Decisions*, no. 3 (2000).

[173] RCC decision 144–O of November 26, 1998, *VKS RF*, no. 2 (1999), pp. 2–8 (Kononov, dissenting), English translation in *Statutes and Decisions*, no. 6 (2001).

[174] RCC decision 18-P of December 23, 1999, *VKS RF*, no. 1 (2000), pp. 2–25. For an analysis of this litigation, see Rozaliia Ivanova, "Kommentarii," in Boris Ebzeev, ed.,

162   *Decision Making of the 2nd Russian Constitutional Court*

Arguably, these creative ways to expand justiciability and access constitute *strategic* self-empowerment behavior on the part of the RCC judges, similar to what other constitutional review tribunals often do.[175] However, their focus on the constitutionalization of due process rights also expanded the jurisdiction of other courts, as I have argued in this chapter in the discussion of the "separation-of-powers" cases. As the 2nd RCC tirelessly insisted, a judicial procedure guarantees constitutional rights, and state authorities could not justify any restrictions on the right to judicial protection.[176] Moreover, in the Court's view, litigants can appeal directly to the European Court of Human Rights (ECHR) in Strasbourg without petitioning the RCC first.[177] To be sure, the extensive catalogue of due process rights in the 1993 constitution helped the 2nd RCC champion their absolute nature, although initially the Court also insisted that any constitutional right could be subject to restrictions.[178] As the 2nd RCC repeatedly argued, the state could justify no limitations on certain rights, including the right to judicial protection, listed in Articles 19.1 (universal equality before the law and courts), 20.2 (right to jury trials), and 46 to 54 (due process rights). According to the RCC, the absolute nature of basic due process rights was an inherent part of the Russian constitutional order, in which the state has to respect human dignity and treat the individual (broadly defined) as a coequal while the latter has the capacity to protect her rights by lawful means and sue the state.[179] Defining judicial protection as a "universal" right of individuals and

---

Kommentarii k postanovleniiam KS RF. T. 2 (Moskva: Iurist, 2000), pp. 471–479, and 564–576.

[175] See, for example, Ginsburg, *Judicial Review in New Democracies*; Radoslav Procházka, *Mission Accomplished: On Founding Constitutional Adjudication in Central Europe* (Budapest: Central European University Press, 2002); and Kim Lane Scheppele, "Declarations of Independence: Judicial Reactions to Political Pressures," in Stephen B. Burbank and Barry Friedman, eds., *Judicial Independence at the Crossroads* (Thousands Oaks, CA: Sage Publications, 2002), pp. 259–262.

[176] See, for example, RCC decisions: 9-P of May 28, 1999, *VKS RF*, no. 5 (1999), pp. 2–13 (Vitruk, dissenting), English translation in *Statutes and Decisions*, no. 6 (2000); and 2-P of February 14, 2000, *ibid.*, no. 3 (2000), pp. 3–12.

[177] Russia accepted the jurisdiction of the ECHR in 1998. See, for example, RCC decisions: 6-O of January 13, 2000, *VKS RF*, no. 2 (2000), pp. 44–48; 233-O of October 27, 2000, *ibid.*, no. 2 (2001), pp. 10–13; and 290-O of December 21, 2000, *ibid.*, no. 2 (2001), pp. 74–77.

[178] RCC decision 17-P of December 20, 1995, *VKS RF*, no. 6 (1995), pp. 48–63 (Kononov and Vitruk, dissenting).

[179] RCC decisions: 4-P of May 3, 1995, *VKS RF*, nos. 2–3 (1995), pp. 42–44; and 11-P of June 27, 2000, *ibid.*, no. 5 (2000), pp. 46–52.

Protecting Constitutional Rights

corporations, the RCC included in it both unfettered access to courts and the duty of courts to render fair and well-grounded decisions.[180]

However, justices were pragmatic in championing due process rights. While the RCC declared that the Article 48 right to "qualified legal assistance" trumped the interest of the state to protect state secrets, thus allowing litigants in any judicial procedure to choose their own lawyers in cases involving state secrets,[181] the RCC, in a 5–4 vote, limited the application of Article 48 to members of the Bar, thus narrowing the circle of eligible defense counsel and enhancing their monopoly on legal representation.[182] In the 1999 *Death Penalty* case, the 2nd RCC used the right to trial by jury (Article 20.2) to outlaw the death penalty and to uphold the constitutional right to life. After a prolonged debate among justices, who initially held diametrically opposing views on this issue, the RCC ruled that courts could not hand out death penalty sentences until jury trials began to operate in every Russian region. Here, the RCC indicated a clear hope that by the time jury trials had been set up across Russia, the political branches would ratify Protocol No. 6 to the 1950 European Convention of Human Rights, which banned the use of the capital punishment in member states.[183]

In short, a lively debate among justices created a hierarchy of constitutional rights with the rights to life, to human dignity, and to judicial protection at the apex. As Justice Ebzeev put it, these absolute rights form the basis of the Russian constitutional order and set necessary limits on the

---

[180] RCC decisions: 67-O of March 1, 2001, *VKS RF*, no. 4 (2001), pp. 36–39; and 3-P of January 24, 2002, *ibid.*, no. 3 (2002), pp. 24–31.

[181] RCC decisions: 8-P of March 27, 1996, *VKS RF*, no. 2 (1996), pp. 34–41; 293-O of November 10, 2002, *ibid.*, no. 2 (2003), pp. 38–41; and 314-O of November 10, 2002, *ibid.*, no. 2 (2003), pp. 45–48. For more on the role of the defense counsel in "espionage" cases, see Pamela A. Jordan, *Defending Rights in Russia: Lawyers, the State, and Legal Reform in the Post-Soviet Era* (Vancouver: University of British Columbia Press, 2005), pp. 152–156.

[182] RCC decision 2-P of January 28, 1997, *VKS RF*, no. 1 (1997), no. 1, pp. 25–42 (Ametistov, Luchin, Oleinik, and Vedernikov, dissenting), English translation in *Statutes and Decisions*, no. 3 (2001). The Ukrainian Constitutional Court came to the opposite conclusion in 2000 albeit Article 59.2 of the 1996 Ukrainian Constitution explicitly charges the Bar with providing defense counsel in criminal proceedings. Decision of the Ukrainian Constitutional Court 13-rp of November 16, 2000, *Visnyk Konstytutsijnogo Sudu Ukrainy*, no. 5 (2000), p. 24. Needless to say, this judgment provoked outrage among the Ukrainian Bar members. See Aleksandr Chernenko, "Budet zashchishchat! Ia skazal!" [Shall Protect! I Said So!] *Iuridicheskaia praktika*, no. 48, November 30, 2000.

[183] RCC decision 3-P of February 2, 1999, *VKS RF*, no. 3 (1999), pp. 12–24.

164   *Decision Making of the 2nd Russian Constitutional Court*

state in order to secure human development and individual freedoms.[184] These absolute rights can trump other basic rights but not to the extent that the latter become a fiction, as the Court put it in the 1999 *Jehovah's Witness* case.[185] Consider how the Court struggled with the Article 24 right to access personal data collected by government agencies. Initially, the 2nd RCC, in an 11–4 vote, upheld the federal statute that allowed law-enforcement agencies to conduct secret surveillance of persons suspected in criminal activities as a legitimate crime-combating function and the authority of regular courts to review the legality of such surveillance. This judgment was a clear compromise with the political branches: voiding even a single norm of this statute would shake the foundations of the Russian law-enforcement system, inherited from the Soviet era and paralyzed by the surge of crime in the 1990s. Dissenting justices argued that the contested federal statute was vague, allowed for the abuse of authority and the violation of fundamental rights, turned judicial review of surveillance activity into a pure formality, and, therefore, was unconstitutional.[186] By 2000, dissenters seemed to persuade the majority that restrictions on access to information should be an exception, adequate enough only to protect constitutional values, such as state security, health, and the morality and rights of other persons. The means the state chose to restrict these "access to information" rights or to allow government agencies to gather personal data had to be proportional, concrete, and necessary to satisfy the state interest and to prevent the abuse of discretion by government agencies.[187] For example, in May 2003, the RCC ruled that an "absolute" right to judicial protection trumped the Article 24 right to personal data privacy: a federal statute could require banks to inform court bailiffs whether an unsuccessful litigant had enough money in her account to pay for the court-awarded damages in order to ensure

---

[184] Boris Ebzeev, "Zashchita prav cheloveka v Konstitutsionnom Sude Rossiiskoi Federatsii," [Protection of Human Rights in the RF Constitutional Court] *Konstitutsionnoe pravosudie*, no. 1 (2003), pp. 93–94.

[185] RCC decision 16-P of November 23, 1999, *VKS RF*, no. 6 (1999), pp. 21–36 (Zharkova, dissenting), English translation in *Statutes and Decisions*, no. 1 (2001).

[186] RCC decision 86-O of July 14, 1998, *VKS RF*, no. 6 (1998), no. 6, pp. 10–57 (Gadzhiev, Kononov, Morshchakova, and Oleinik, dissenting), English translation in *Statutes and Decisions*, no. 5 (2001). See also RCC decision 18-O of February 4, 1999, *ibid.*, no. 3 (1999), pp. 38–48 (Kononov, dissenting).

[187] RCC decisions: 3-P of February 18, 2000, *VKS RF*, no. 3 (2000), pp. 13–20, English translation in *Statutes and Decisions*, no. 1 (2005); 191-O of July 6, 2000, *ibid.*, no. 1 (2001), pp. 35–37; 239-O of December 15, 2000, *ibid.*, no. 2 (2001), pp. 56–58.

Protecting Constitutional Rights 165

timely enforcement of judicial decisions, an essential element of effective judicial remedy.[188]

The RCC quickly discovered that most substantive constitutional rights could be subject to "legitimate and proportional" restrictions by the state.[189] Which rights are these? In the Court's view, they include the rights to private property (Article 35) and to entrepreneurial activity (Article 34),[190] land use (Article 36.1),[191] mobility (Article 27.1),[192] labor (Article 37.4),[193] electoral rights (Article 32.1),[194] and freedoms of speech and mass media (Article 29).[195] To determine when and how the state could limit this group of basic rights, the RCC actively used Article 55.3 of the Russian constitution, which states in full: "Human and civil rights and freedoms may be restricted by federal law only to the extent necessary for upholding the foundations of the constitutional system, morality, or the health, rights, and lawful interests of other persons or

---

[188] RCC decision 8-P of May 14, 2003, *VKS RF*, no. 4 (2003), pp. 12–23 (Kononov, dissenting).

[189] RCC decision 1-P of January 16, 1996, *VKS RF*, no. 1 (1996), pp. 2–12 (Vitruk, dissenting).

[190] RCC decisions: 20-P of December 17, 1996, *VKS RF*, no. 5 (1996), pp. 22–29, English translation in *Statutes and Decisions*, no. 1 (2000); 14-P of May 12, 1998, *ibid.*, no. 4 (1998), pp. 41–50, English translation in *Statutes and Decisions*, no. 4 (2000); and 4-P of April 1, 2003, *ibid.*, no. 3 (2003), pp. 41–53.

[191] RCC decision 387-O of November 6, 2003, *VKS RF*, no. 1 (2004), pp. 95–99.

[192] RCC decisions: 17-P of December 20, 1995, *VKS RF*, no. 5 (1995), pp. 48–63 (Kononov and Vitruk, dissenting), English translation in *Statutes and Decisions*, no. 2 (2001); 9-P of April 4, 1996, *ibid.*, no. 2 (1996), pp. 42–61 (Baglai, dissenting), English translation in *Statutes and Decisions*, no. 1 (1999); 147-O of June 23, 2000, *ibid.*, no. 6 (2000), pp. 33–38. For a good analysis of the judicial interpretation of housing permits, see William Burnham, Peter B. Maggs, and Gennady M. Danilenko, *Law and Legal System in the Russian Federation*, 3rd ed. (New York: Juris Publishing, 2004), pp. 251–257.

[193] More precisely, the right to strike. RCC decisions: 5-P of May 17, 1995, *VKS RF*, nos. 2–3 (1995), p. 45; 318-O of October 16, 2003 (unpublished), available at the RCC Web site, http://www.ksrf.ru.

[194] RCC decisions: 26-P of November 17, 1998, *VKS RF*, no. 1 (1999), pp. 48–67 (Vedernikov, dissenting) (less populated electoral districts), English translation in *Statutes and Decisions*, no. 5 (2000); 10-P of June 11, 2002, *ibid.*, no. 5 (2002), pp. 51–63 (elections with one name on the ballot); and 12-P of July 9, 2002, *ibid.*, no. 6 (2002), pp. 3–15 (term limits for regional governors).

[195] RCC decisions: 62-O and 63-O of May 17, 1995 (both unpublished), available at the RCC Web site, http://www.ksrf.ru; 104-O of December 4, 1995, in Tamara Morshchakova, ed., *Konstitutsionnyi Sud Rossiiskoi Federatsii. Postanovleniia. Opredeleniia. 1992–1996* (Moskva: Iurist, 1997), pp. 498–500; 17-P of December 20, 1995, *VKS RF*, no. 5 (1995), pp. 48–63 (Kononov and Vitruk, dissenting), English translation in *Statutes and Decisions*, no. 2 (2001); 70-O of April 19, 2001, *VKS RF*, no. 4 (2001), pp. 63–65; 15-P of October 30, 2003, *VKS RF*, no. 6 (2003), pp. 3–30 (Gadzhiev, Iaroslavtsev, and Kononov, dissenting).

166   *Decision Making of the 2nd Russian Constitutional Court*

for ensuring the defense of the country and state security." As Peter Krug observed, the Court frequently applies this express statement of "broad proportionality" and has joined a growing family of constitutional courts around the world in developing its own methods of balancing rights with government interests. Let us consider how the Court

1. expanded the meaning of basic rights,
2. allowed the government to interfere with these rights only through federal legislation,
3. treated the list of legitimate state interests in Article 55.3 as exhaustive, and
4. construed these interests narrowly.[196]

Creating Rights

In addition to the aforementioned expansion of due process rights – that even the critics of Russian judicial activism called "revolutionary" – the 2nd RCC expanded numerous political, economic, and social rights through what judges call "constitutionalization" of other branches of the law, a process familiar to the students of Western European constitutional courts.[197] For example, in a series of decisions, the RCC recognized that the 1993 constitution protected the property rights of private corporations, state-owned enterprises, regions, and municipalities. Therefore, the state had to ensure equal treatment of both public and private property and could not discriminate against private property holders in taking title, in bankruptcy proceedings, in imposing punishment for property crimes, and so on.[198]

Moreover, similar to its Korean counterpart, the RCC "constitutionalized" the freedom of contract, which is not found in the text of the Russian constitution, by relying on Article 8's freedom of economic activity.[199] As the Court put it, the state has to regulate property rights and contractual relations of property transfers in order to ensure that contracts "in good

---

[196] Peter Krug, "Assessing Legislative Restrictions on Constitutional Rights: The Russian Constitutional Court and Article 55(3)," *Oklahoma Law Review*, vol. 56, no. 3 (Fall 2003), p. 677.

[197] Gadis Gadzhiev, *Konstitutsionnye printsipy rynochnoi ekonomiki.*

[198] See, for example, Rilka O. Dragneva and William B. Simons, "Rights, Contracts and Constitutional Courts: the Experience of Russia," in Ferdinand Feldbrugge and William Simons, eds., *Human Rights in Russia and Eastern Europe: Essays in Honor of Ger P. van den Berg* (The Hague: Kluwer Law International, 2002), pp. 35–63.

[199] On Korea, see Ginsburg, *Judicial Review in New Democracies*, pp. 226–227.

Protecting Constitutional Rights

faith" are protected.[200] The Court does not view the freedom of contract as an end in itself – this "judge-made" freedom is needed to guard broadly defined property rights, including those of disadvantaged parties.[201] In the 1999 *Bank Accounts* case, the Court ruled that banks could not lower interest rates on term deposits without the consent of the holder of the bank account. According to the Court, the 1993 constitution requires the state to ensure both formal and real equality among contracting parties, so that a weaker party (bank customer) has certain advantages against the stronger party (bank). These advantages – for example, the right to close a bank account at any time – are necessary to balance the economic freedom of financial institutions with that of their clients.[202] The Court further ruled that the contractual freedom of creditors to be protected in bankruptcy proceedings must be analogous to the freedom of minority shareholders in corporations.[203] Similarly, the Court later ruled that health care providers could not arbitrarily cancel contracts to perform health-related services. Here, the Court found that the Article 41 right to health protection trumped the economic freedom of clinics in order to ensure stronger protection of patients' rights.[204] The RCC also expanded the freedom of contract to labor relations by invalidating socialist-era protections of job security and expanding the rights of employers in the private sector while recognizing the constitutionality of keeping certain advantages for vulnerable employees, such as parents with disabled children.[205] The Court further entrenched this freedom in the political domain when it declared that the federal government lacked the authority to transfer the property of local or regional governments without compensating and signing a contract with the latter, as I explained in this chapter in the section on federalism cases. In short, the creation and broad application

---

[200] RCC decision 6-P of April 21, 2003, *VKS RF*, no. 3 (2003), pp. 54–61.

[201] Gadzhiev, *Konstitutsionnye printsipy rynochnoi ekonomiki*, p. 198.

[202] RCC decisions: 4-P of February 23, 1999, *VKS RF*, no. 3 (1999), pp. 49–56, English translation in *Statutes and Decisions*, no. 6 (2000); and 10-P of July 3, 2001, *ibid.*, no. 6 (2001), pp. 15–27 (Ebzeev, dissenting). The Russian Supreme Court came to the opposite conclusion that banks could lower interest rates unilaterally. See Decision of the Presidium of the RF Supreme Court No. 8pvo4 of July 14, 2004, *Bulleten Verkhovnogo Suda RF*, no. 2 (2005), pp. 2–4; and "Review of Judicial Practice of the RF Supreme Court in the 4th Quarter of 2003," *ibid.*, no. 7 (2004), p. 28.

[203] RCC decisions: 9-P of June 6, 2000, *VKS RF*, no. 4 (2000), pp. 46–53; 5-P of April 10, 2003, *ibid.*, no. 3 (2003), pp. 48–53.

[204] RCC decision 115-O of June 6, 2002, *VKS RF*, no. 1 (2003), pp. 61–67.

[205] RCC decisions: 33-O of February 8, 2001, *VKS RF*, no. 3 (2001), pp. 70–78 (Khokhriakova and Zhilin, dissenting); and 3-P of January 24, 2002, *ibid.*, no. 3 (2002), pp. 24–31.

168   *Decision Making of the 2nd Russian Constitutional Court*

of this freedom of contract in a state-centered polity with a fragile market economy is a sign of the growing strength of Russian constitutional review.

Scrutinizing Limits on Basic Rights: Proportionality, Russian-Style

As I have mentioned, the RCC recognized that certain constitutional rights, including the freedom of contract, could be subject to "legitimate and proportional" restrictions by the state. The Court consistently ruled that only a federal statute could impose such restrictions, thus striking down numerous regional laws and federal Cabinet regulations. The Court continued to fight against residency permits, which all regions had kept from the Soviet era, in spite of the rulings of the USSR Constitutional Supervision Committee in 1990, as described in the beginning Chapter 4. The Moscow and Voronezh regions sold their residency permits at exorbitant costs,[206] the Krasnodar region banned any real estate transactions with non-Krasnodar residents,[207] while Moscow, Tatarstan, and Bashkortostan required local residency permits as a basis for holding elected office.[208] The RCC declared these restrictions on mobility rights as unconstitutional by citing the text of Article 55.3 and the exclusive authority of the federal legislature to limit them. In a similar fashion, the Constitutional Court annulled several edicts of the federal Cabinet that limited freedom of movement[209] and freedom of the mass media, and discriminated against private school teachers in their Article 39 rights to a pension.[210] In short, the 2nd RCC is centralist when it comes to the

---

[206] RCC decisions: 9-P of April 4, 1996, *VKS RF*, no. 2 (1996), pp. 42–61 (Baglai, dissenting), English translation in *Statutes and Decisions*, no. 1 (1999); and 10-P of July 2, 1997, *ibid.*, no. 5 (1997), pp. 20–24.

[207] RCC decisions: 116-O of October 7, 1998, *VKS RF*, no. 6 (1998), pp. 74–79, English translation in *Statutes and Decisions*, no. 5 (2001); 41-O of February 3, 2000, *ibid.*, no. 3 (2000), pp. 60–64; 147-O of June 23, 2000, *ibid.*, no. 6 (2000), pp. 33–38; and 204-O of October 5, 2000 (unpublished), available at the RCC Web site, http://www.ksrf.ru.

[208] RCC decisions: 12-P of April 27, 1998, *VKS RF*, no. 4 (1998), pp. 21–35 (Strekozov and Vitruk, dissenting); 2-P of January 22, 2002, *ibid.*, no. 3 (2002), pp. 14–23: and 88-O of July 1, 1998 (unpublished), available at the RCC Web site, http://www.ksrf.ru.

[209] Justice Anatolii Kononov reviews the mobility rights cases in his, "Konstitutsionnyi printsip svobody peredvizheniia i praktika Konstitutsionnogo Suda Rossiiskoi Federatsii," [Constitutional Principle of the Freedom of Movement and the Practice of the RF Constitutional Court] in *Rossiia i Sovet Evropy: perspektivy vzaimodeistviia* (Moskva: IPPP, 2001), pp. 172–181.

[210] RCC decisions: 10-P of July 31, 1995, *VKS RF*, no. 5 (1995), pp. 3–64 (Ametistov, Ebzeev, Gadzhiev, Kononov, Luchin, Morshchakova, Vitruk, and Zorkin, dissenting); 4-P of February 2, 1998, *ibid.*, no. 3 (1998), pp. 3–10, English translation in *Statutes*

Protecting Constitutional Rights 169

protection of basic rights: the regions and the federal executive can only strengthen the protection of basic rights, while only the federal legislature can restrict these rights. Moreover, when the federal parliament delegates authority to regulate basic rights to the executive or to the regions, it has to be precise in order to prevent the abuse of this regulatory authority.[211] As the Court repeatedly ruled, the exercise of constitutional rights should never depend on the discretion of government officials.

More importantly, the bulk of the 2nd RCC efforts to develop its own proportionality doctrine comes from review of federal statutes. Between 1996 and 2005, the Court used proportionality tests in most of its "rights" decisions, the lion's share of which provided a constitutionally acceptable meaning for contested provisions or annulled them. As a rule, the RCC does not approve restrictions that aim at the core of rights, thereby making them meaningless. Also, the Court repeatedly ruled that the governmental interest of "rationalizing" governance could not serve as a sufficient basis for the limitation of basic rights.[212]

Two decisions involving the law on bankruptcy illustrate the Court's application of its proportionality analysis to balance governmental interest and property rights. In the first, the Court found that a provision permitting the transfer of property from a bankrupt estate to a municipality represented a disproportionate interference with the property rights of the debtor because it failed to provide compensation.[213] In the second, the Court examined a legislative grant of power to a bankruptcy trustee to cancel a long-term contract with a creditor.[214] The Court ruled that this constituted interference with freedom of contract grounded in arbitrary criteria that were not "necessary" to meet the legitimate goal of protecting the rights of others. In both cases, the Court emphasized that the proportionality test requires that legislation strike a fair balance between the values of the legitimate interest and the implicated constitutional right.[215]

---

and Decisions, no. 3 (2000); and 310-O of December 6, 2001, ibid., no. 3 (2002), pp. 85–89.

[211] RCC decision 17-P of November 12, 2003, VKS RF, no. 6 (2003), pp. 46–53.

[212] RCC decisions: 2-P of January 15, 1998, VKS RF, no. 2 (1998), pp. 19–27 (Ebzeev and Vitruk, dissenting), English translation in Statutes and Decisions, no. 3 (2000); 3-P of February 18, 2000, ibid., no. 3 (2000), pp. 13–20, English translation in Statutes and Decisions, no. 1 (2005); and 133-O of June 6, 2002 (unpublished), available at the RCC Web site, http://www.ksrf.ru.

[213] RCC decision 8-P of May 16, 2000, VKS RF, no. 4 (2000), pp. 38–45.

[214] RCC decision 9-P of June 6, 2000, VKS RF, no. 4 (2000), pp. 46–53.

[215] Krug, "Assessing Legislative Restrictions," pp. 690–691.

170   *Decision Making of the 2nd Russian Constitutional Court*

The proportionality test, or more precisely, its "excessive burden" version, plays a large role in RCC judgments in the areas of fiscal policy. As Russia has embarked on large-scale privatization and taxation reforms, the Court staunchly defended the judicial protection of property rights by ruling in a series of decisions that no property taking, including fines, is allowed without a court decision. The Court, accordingly, frequently chastised the Russian parliament for imposing "unfair" sanctions on businesses, and invalidated numerous statutes that imposed huge fines for vaguely defined tax code violations and other transgressions. The RCC held that "vaguely defined transgressions" violated the Article 50 ban on "trying a person twice for the same crime" and affirmed the power of the courts to reduce the amount of a fine.[216] As a rule, the RCC is suspicious of the same fines for self-employed individuals and corporations, as the former are presumed to have a weaker ability to pay. Also, a fiscal penalty is "unfair" and unconstitutional when it far exceeds the amount of tax payment and can result in the bankruptcy of the taxpayer.[217] Restraining Russia's predatory fiscal policies, the Court ruled that the "rule of law" requirement in Article 1 of the 1993 constitution banned an excessive tax burden and heavy fiscal penalties, which provoked law-abiding taxpayers to hide their income.[218] Although the RCC repeatedly ruled that fines could be imposed only on malicious perpetrators, that is, on those who knowingly broke the law,[219] the Court also ruled that the 1993 Constitution protects only those who behave "in good faith" and do not abuse their rights.[220] As I will show in Chapter 7, the tax authorities and the judicial branch developed their own – highly questionable from the point of view of the Constitution – understanding of what exactly constitutes "good faith behavior," thus sabotaging "on the ground" the constitutionalization of taxpayers' rights in the law.

---

[216] See, for example, RCC decisions: 20-P of December 17, 1996, *VKS RF*, no. 5 (1996), pp. 22–29, English translation in *Statutes and Decisions*, no. 1 (2000); 130-O of July 5, 2001, *ibid.*, no. 1 (2002), pp. 64–69.

[217] See, for example, RCC decisions: 14-P of May 12, 1998, *VKS RF*, no. 4 (1998), pp. 41–50, English translation in *Statutes and Decisions*, no. 4 (2000); 11-P of July 15, 1999, *ibid.*, no. 5 (1999), pp. 48–56, English translation in *Statutes and Decisions*, no. 1 (2001).

[218] RCC decision 18-P of December 23, 1999, *VKS RF*, no. 1 (2000), pp. 2–25.

[219] See, for example, RCC decisions: 11-P of July 15, 1999, *VKS RF*, no. 5 (1999), pp. 48–56, English translation in *Statutes and Decisions*, no. 1 (2001); 7-P of April 27, 2001, *ibid.*, no. 5 (2001), pp. 46–67 (Kononov, dissenting); 130-O of July 5, 2001, *ibid.*, no. 1 (2002), pp. 64–69.

[220] RCC decision 138-O of July 25, 2001, *VKS RF*, no. 2 (2002), pp. 27–30.

Similar to its substantial involvement in defining the constitutional boundaries of fair taxation, the 2nd RCC has also been active in reviewing the constitutionality of Russia's electoral system. In November 1998, the RCC upheld the constitutionality of a 5 percent electoral barrier for the State Duma elections. At the same time, the Court warned that this barrier would violate electoral rights if only one party met this threshold regardless of how many votes it had received, or if all elected parties received less than half of the votes.[221] Here, the Court reiterated its earlier 1995 decision that the choice of the electoral system is a political question, and that the mixed majoritarian-proportional system does not violate voting rights.[222] Using a proportionality test, the Court strengthened the constitutional protection of the nascent political party system by ruling that the Central Electoral Commission – a federal body in charge of organizing elections, lacked the power to disqualify parties from an electoral campaign merely because the top three candidates on the party list decided not to run in the election.[223]

In a series of decisions, the RCC further expanded the power of the courts to resolve electoral disputes, the majority of which involved refusals of the electoral commissions to register candidates and decisions to cancel registrations already approved. The regular courts tended to defer to the electoral commissions controlled by the regional governors in light of the fact that the federal electoral statutes made it easy to disqualify candidates on technical grounds, including failure to submit any of a long list of documents on time and in the proper form. Courts were also reluctant to set aside elections even when it had been established, after the fact, that candidates had been improperly disqualified. As a rule, judges acted rigorously in refusing to cancel an election unless "the violations of law would not permit the conclusion that the electoral results reflected the will of the electors."[224] In January 2002, however, the Russian Constitutional Court, in a 9–1 decision, declared this tough standard unconstitutional and instructed courts to cancel electoral results more readily.[225] In December 2001, the RCC struck down the ban on appeals against judicial decisions

---

[221] RCC decision 26-P of November 17, 1998, *VKS RF*, no. 1 (1998), pp. 48–67 (Vedernikov, dissenting).

[222] RCC decision 77-O of November 20, 1995, *VKS RF*, no. 6 (1995), pp. 22–30 (Ametistov, dissenting), English translation in *Statutes and Decisions*, no. 2 (1996).

[223] RCC decision 7-P of April 25, 2000, *VKS RF*, no. 4 (2000), pp. 30–37.

[224] Solomon, "Judicial Power in Russia," p. 568.

[225] RCC decision 1-P of January 15, 2002, *VKS RF*, no. 3 (2002), pp. 3–13 (Bondar, dissenting).

in electoral cases to a higher court as an excessive restriction of voting rights.[226] And in February 2004, the RCC declared unconstitutional the power of the Central Electoral Commission to choose which court to use in electoral violation cases.[227] In these and other electoral rights cases, the Constitutional Court sought to raise the stakes for the political manipulation of electoral registrations, deter abuses of power by the electoral commissions, and require courts to award adequate compensation – including damages and annulment of the elections – to the victims of such abuses. In other words, the RCC used proportionality to determine both how far the government could go in limiting constitutional rights and how much the government should pay for the abuse of these rights.

Two electoral rights cases, decided in 2003, also demonstrate another sign of the maturity of the RCC, namely, the use of proportionality to balance countervailing constitutional rights. The first case involved the ban of nationwide referendums during the years of federal elections, which was hastily adopted in the fall of 2002 when the Communist Party began collecting signatures for a referendum against private property on land. Some 110 Communist members of the Duma immediately challenged this ban as an unconstitutional restriction of voting rights, as it placed the popular referendum initiative at the mercy of the lawmakers. Their opponents, the presidential lawyers, argued that the 1993 constitution restricted the timing of the referendum by allowing lawmakers to regulate its timing, questions, and other conditions. In June 2003, in a 17–2 decision, the RCC sided with the presidential camp and ruled that the right to vote in elections and the right to vote in a referendum were equally important and could not impair each other. Therefore, the federal legislature had the authority to balance them, and it did so in a proportional way by allowing a 2-year window to call referendums.[228]

The second decision involved the balance between freedom of mass media and electoral rights. Three journalists and 104 Duma members challenged the vaguely defined ban on electoral campaigning by mass media. The Central Electoral Commission, which drafted and rushed this ban through the federal legislature, fiercely defended it as a legitimate barrier to negative advertising. To the surprise of many observers, the RCC quickly issued a judgment on October 30, 2003, 5 weeks before

---

[226] RCC decision 17-P of December 25, 2001, *VKS RF*, no. 2 (2002), pp. 10–16.

[227] RCC decision 4-P of February 25, 2004, *VKS RF*, no. 2 (2004), pp. 47–56.

[228] RCC decision 10-P of June 11, 2003, *VKS RF*, no. 4 (2003), pp. 30–51 (Iaroslavtsev and Luchin, dissenting).

Protecting Constitutional Rights 173

parliamentary elections. The Court agreed with the petitioners and struck down this ban as an excessive and a disproportionate restriction of freedoms of information and mass media. Justices declared that "only (under conditions of) really guaranteed right to objective information and liberty to express opinions, could elections be regarded as free." Therefore, a federal statute could restrict journalistic freedom of expression during elections so that voters received objective information and made informed decisions at the ballot boxes. However, the proportionality principle required the legislature to ban only premeditated electoral campaigning, and placed the burden of proof on the state authorities.[229] Thus, journalists could freely express their opinions about elections and candidates, and predict their results, as one witnessed during the 2003–2004 federal election campaigns. Ironically, this decision gave virtually a free hand to state-owned TV channels to devote disproportionate coverage to the reelection campaign of President Putin in 2004.

This decision reaffirmed the Court's insistence on malicious intent as the requirement of proportionality and legitimacy of state sanctions. Recall that the RCC ruled that the federal center could fire regional governors and dissolve regional legislatures only for intentional noncompliance with federal laws, and that federal statutes could impose fines and other penalties only on malicious perpetrators. This persistence of the Constitutional Court demonstrates its efforts to develop principled decision making even in politically sensitive cases and its boldness in restricting the arbitrariness of state authorities.

Constitutional Principles: Written, Unwritten, and Borrowed

Crafting these proportionality tests is inextricably linked to fundamental legal principles, some of which lie outside the constitutional text. The RCC has been developing its own hierarchy of both written and unwritten legal principles. "Generally accepted principles of law," such as fairness, equality, proportionality, legal certainty, judicial independence, "behavior in good faith," the inviolability of property rights, freedom of contract, and a ban on the abuse of rights are at the top of this judge-made hierarchy. Most of these principles are hidden in the 1993 Constitution, which refers only to "fairness" in its preamble, to equality under law in Articles 8

---

[229] RCC decision 15-P of October 30, 2003, *VKS RF*, no. 6 (2003), pp. 3–30 (Iaroslavtsev, Gadzhiev, and Kononov, dissenting).

and 19, and to "property" in Articles 8, 34, and 35.[230] This hierarchy of fundamental legal principles is not set in stone. As Justice Gadzhiev pointed out, in the Court's 2000 case involving state subsidies to the mass media,[231] the RCC elevated the constitutional principles of inviolability of property rights and freedom of contract to the top category of "generally accepted" legal principles. The Court "upgraded" these principles in order to declare that the 1993 Constitution protected property rights of municipalities and the regions and required the federal government to observe Article 55.3, which only refers to "human and civil rights."[232] Therefore, the 2nd RCC often departs from a strictly literal interpretive methodology in developing its own vision of "rights as trumps."[233]

According to the Constitutional Court, constitutional clauses express these "hidden" fundamental legal principles, and all courts must apply these principles even if ordinary legislation does not mention them.[234] But where would Russian judges find these principles? Most RCC justices believe that they lie in international human rights law rather than in the spirit of the constitution or in natural law.[235] Between 1995 and 2005, forty-three judgments cited the 1948 Universal Declaration of Human Rights, one hundred ten referred to the 1966 ICCPR, and nine to the 1966 ICESCR, in addition to three dozen judgments that mentioned nonbinding resolutions and declarations of various United Nations bodies.

That the 2nd RCC chose to invoke nonbinding international legal acts and to make them binding on Russian branches of government shows

---

[230] Gadzhiev, *Konstitutsionnye printsipy rynochnoi ekonomiki.*

[231] For commentary, see Peter Krug, "Glasnost as a Constitutional Norm: The Article 29 Jurisprudence of the Constitutional Court and Other Courts in the Russian Federation." Paper presented at the Annual Convention of the American Association for the Advancement of Slavic Studies, Arlington, VA, November 2001.

[232] Gadis Gadzhiev, "Kommentarii," in Boris Ebzeev, ed., *Kommentarii k postanovleniiam Konstitutsionnogo Suda Rossiiskoi Federatsii.* T. 3. (Moskva: Iurist, 2002), p. 243.

[233] Krug, "Assessing Legislative Restrictions on Constitutional Rights," p. 689. "Rights as trumps" is borrowed from Ronald Dworkin, "Rights as Trumps," in Jeremy Waldron, ed., *Theories of Rights* (Oxford: Oxford University Press, 1984), pp.153–167.

[234] Gadzhiev, *Konstitutsionnye printsipy rynochnoi ekonomiki*, pp. 54–55.

[235] RCC decisions: 14-P of July 22, 2002, *VKS RF*, no. 6 (2002), pp. 29–41 and no. 1 (2003), pp. 3–6 (Iaroslavtsev, dissenting); and 228-O of October 1, 2002, *ibid.*, no. 2 (2003), pp. 3–6. Justices Vitruk and Oleinik repeatedly referred to the spirit of the constitution in their dissents. See, for example, RCC decisions: 86-O of July 14, 1998, *ibid.*, no. 6 (1998), pp. 10–57 (Gadzhiev, Kononov, Morshchakova, and Oleinik, dissenting), English translation in *Statutes and Decisions*, no. 5 (2001); 17-P of June 10, 1998, *ibid.*, no. 5 (1998), pp. 28–41 (Vitruk, dissenting), English translation in *Statutes and Decisions*, no. 4 (2000); and 1-P of January 14, 2000, *ibid.*, no. 2 (2000), pp. 49–64 (Ebzeev and Vitruk, dissenting).

Protecting Constitutional Rights 175

another side of the bold court.[236] After prolonged debate among justices on the subject of acceptable international legal norms, the majority of them agreed pragmatically that their Court had "implied" constitutional authority to determine which norms were generally recognized in international law and thus were binding on Russia.[237] Drawing the criticism of international law professors, the 2nd RCC did not wait for political branches to ratify certain international treaties or declarations and resolutions of international organizations. For example, the Court referred thrice to the 1950 European Convention of Human Rights as binding before May 5, 1998, when Russia ratified this Convention.[238] Between that date and 2006, the 2nd RCC mentioned this Convention in more than 200 decisions and cited the judgments of the European Court of Human Rights (ECHR), a judicial body in charge of interpreting this Convention, in some ninety decisions. The reliance of the RCC on ECHR judgments, which involved other countries, shows that Russian justices took these judgments seriously.[239] The ECHR jurisprudence helps Russian judges to find the way out of the conflict between countervailing constitutional principles and, sometimes, serves as "the last straw" in both helping to secure a majority opinion on a divided bench and in

[236] On the hostility towards applying international human rights law in the RCC, see Kim Lane Scheppele, "Constitutional Ethnography: An Introduction," *Law and Society Review*, vol. 38, no. 3 (September 2004), p. 398.

[237] Tamara Morshchakova, "Primenenie mezhdunarodnogo prava v konstitutsionnom pravosudii: itogi i perspectivy," [Application of International Law in Constitutional Adjudication: Conclusions and Perspectives] *Konstitutsionnoe pravosudie*, no. 4 (2001), p. 119; Nikolai Vitruk, *Konstitutsionnoe pravosudie v Rossii (1991–2001 gg.)* (Moskva: Gorodets-izdat, 2001), pp. 125–133.

[238] RCC decisions: 9-P of April 4, 1996, *VKS RF*, no. 2 (1996), pp. 42–61 (freedom of movement in Article 2 of the Protocol No. 4 to the 1950 Convention), English translation in *Statutes and Decisions*, no. 1 (1999); 9-P of March 16, 1998, *ibid.*, no. 3 (1998), pp. 71–78 (fair trial in Article 6 of the 1950 Convention), English translation in *Statutes and Decisions*, no. 3 (2001); and 13-P of April 29, 1998, *ibid.*, no. 4 (1998), pp. 35–40 (fair trial in Article 6 of the 1950 Convention), English translation in *Statutes and Decisions*, no. 3 (2001).

[239] See, for example, Justice Oleg Tiunov, "O roli Konventsii o zashchite prav i osnovnykh svobod i reshenii Evropeiskogo suda po pravam cheloveka v praktike Konstitutsionnogo Suda Rossiiskoi Federatsii," [On the Role of the Convention on the Protection of Rights and Basic Freedoms and of the Decisions of the European Court of Human Rights in the Practice of the RF Constitutional Court] in *Rossiia i Sovet Evropy: perspektivy vzaimod-eistviia* (Moskva: IPPP, 2001), pp. 75–88; and Nikolai Bondar, "Konventsionnaia iuris-diktsiia Evropeiskogo Suda po pravam cheloveka v sootnoshenii s kompetentsiei Konstitutsionnogo Suda RF," [Conventional Jurisdiction of the European Court of Human Rights in the Relation with the Competence of the RF Constitutional Court] *Zhurnal rossiiskogo prava*, no. 6 (2006), pp. 113–128.

176 *Decision Making of the 2nd Russian Constitutional Court*

resisting political pressure.[240] As Justice Ebzeev told his colleagues from abroad, ignoring the jurisprudence of the Strasbourg Court is not acceptable when it comes to the protection of basic rights and societal values that make these rights work.[241]

Indeed, the RCC examines the ECHR judgments in every instance of constitutional-rights litigation; nevertheless, it does not always include references to them in the text of the decision, which is always a result of bargaining among justices. What is more interesting is that the RCC judges routinely study the jurisprudence of high courts from abroad.[242] For example, Justice Kononov, who failed to convince the majority of his colleagues of the unconstitutionality of criminal punishment for "hit-and-run" traffic accidents, referred to the decisions of Croatian, German, Korean, and Spanish constitutional courts, the French Constitutional Council, and the Supreme Court of Canada.[243] In short, the RCC is increasingly active in bringing Russia into what Anne-Marie Slaughter calls a "global community of human rights law."[244] The Court's collegial decision making contributes to the critical assessment of this global exchange of ideas among high courts. Similar to the Italian and Spanish Constitutional Courts, the 2nd RCC has played an important role in incorporating European human rights law into Russia's domestic legal system and warning political branches of potential controversies that could find their way to the Strasbourg Court. The following two sections discuss how the Russian Constitutional Court has dealt with the fundamental issues of equality and fairness.

---

[240] Interview with the RCC Justice, Moscow, 9 December 2005. For more on the impact of the ECHR on RCC decision making, see Alexei Trochev, "Russia's Constitutional Spirit: Judge-Made Principles in Theory and Practice," in Robert Sharlet and Gordon B. Smith, eds., *Russia and Its Constitution: Promise and Political Reality* (Leiden: Martinus Nijhoff, 2007), pp. 55–58.

[241] Boris Ebzeev, "Zashchita prav cheloveka," pp. 95–96.

[242] See, for example, RCC decisions: 10-P of November 14, 2005, *VKS RF*, no. 1 (2006), pp. 3–24 (Bondar, Gadzhiev, Krasavchikova, and Mavrin, dissenting), in which Justice Gadzhiev referred to the decisions of the U.S. Supreme Court and the seventh Circuit Court of Appeals: *Majors v. Abell* 361 F3d 349 (7th Cir. 2004); and *McConnell v. Federal Election Commission* 124 SCt 619 (2003); and 6-P of May 16, 2007, *VKS RF*, no. 3 (2007), pp. 62–77 (Kazantsev, dissenting), in which Justice Kazantsev drew on the decisions of the Spanish Constitutional Tribunal.

[243] RCC decision 6-P of April 25, 2001, *VKS RF*, no. 5 (2001), pp. 31–45 (Kononov, dissenting).

[244] Anne-Marie Slaughter, *A New World Order* (Princeton, NJ: Princeton University Press, 2004).

Constitutional Equality: Formal and Real

As the RCC has relentlessly argued, public policies implicating basic rights have to respect constitutional principles. In the *Rural Teachers Dwellings* case, the Court annulled a federal ban on the privatization of teachers' apartments in villages and boldly declared that the constitutional principle of equality protected both constitutional and statutory rights.[245] Furthermore, the choice of its justices to champion the absolute nature of due process rights (see earlier in this chapter) has resulted in the frequent use of the principle of equality "before the law and the court," which, by the end of 2003, had been invoked in more than 160 judgments and about 30 dissenting opinions. The Court has been suspicious of the vague provisions of federal statutes that allowed government authorities to discriminate against certain groups, or to deprive them of certain basic rights. In the Court's view, constitutional equality requires the legislature to make laws certain, clear, and unambiguous in order for them to be applied in a uniform and consistent manner. Vague and ambiguous legal rules open the door for discretion by the executive authority, and, inevitably, result in arbitrariness and violations of equality and the supremacy of law.[246] For example, the Court struck down or offered its own interpretation of federal statutes that discriminated against suspects, the accused, witnesses, victims, plaintiffs, defendants, and all other parties involved in the judicial procedure. Suspending pension payments to convicts, revoking their housing benefits, and evicting them from their apartments also violated constitutional equality, according to the RCC.[247] In addition to this, the Court also chose to champion formal equality, or "equality of opportunity," in religious freedom. For example, in a series of decisions, the RCC interpreted the highly restrictive 1997 Act "On the Freedom of Conscience and Religious Associations" in such a way that this law could not treat differently and could not impose new requirements on religious groups that were legally functioning before its enforcement.[248] The

---

[245] RCC decision 13-P of October 24, 2000, *VKS RF*, no. 1 (2001), pp. 3–9.

[246] RCC decision 11-P of July 15, 1999, *VKS RF*, no. 5 (1999), pp. 48–56, English translation in *Statutes and Decisions*, no. 1 (2001).

[247] RCC decisions: 8-P of June 23, 1995, *SZ RF*, no. 27 (1995), item 2622 (Danilov, dissenting); 11-P of October 16, 1995, *VKS RF*, no. 6 (1995), pp. 5–9, English translation in *Statutes and Decisions*, no. 6 (1999); and 15-P of November 21, 2002, *ibid.*, no. 1 (2003), pp. 7–12.

[248] RCC decisions: 16-P of November 23, 1999, *VKS RF*, no. 6 (1999), pp. 21–37 (Zharkova, dissenting) (Jehovah's Witness), English translation in *Statutes and*

178   Decision Making of the 2nd Russian Constitutional Court

Russian Orthodox Church criticized the RCC for this approach even though the Court upheld various measures to prohibit the proliferation of sects, "which practice illegal and criminal activities" and use "psychological pressure or threats of violence."[249]

Moreover, the 2nd RCC made inroads to entrench real or substantive equality for disadvantaged groups, or "equality of outcome," as was the case in the constitutionalization of freedom of contract cases discussed above. As Justice Gadzhiev pointed out, formal equality in economic rights is not sufficient to secure "equal opportunities" and may result in grave inequality.[250] Recognizing the disadvantages of the "little" people in the uncharted waters of corporate governance, the Court upheld the federal law "On Joint Stock Ventures," which granted extra protection to minor shareholders in large public corporations.[251] In the area of social rights, the RCC consistently upheld substantive equality of disadvantaged (handicapped) persons. At the request of fifteen regional associations of disabled persons, the Court struck down the federal "social tax" statute, which granted exemptions from social tax payments to nationwide associations of disabled persons but not local associations. In the same decision, the RCC annulled the provision that granted exemptions from these taxes only to self-employed, handicapped recipients of disability pension, as discriminating against other categories of disabled self-employed. Moreover, the Court noted that "special measures aimed at achieving real equality of opportunities for disabled persons could not be considered discriminatory."[252]

Decisions, no. 1 (2001); 46-O of April 13, 2000, *ibid.*, no. 4 (2000), pp. 58–64 (Jesuit Order); and 7-O of February 7, 2002, *ibid.*, no. 4 (2002), pp. 28–34 (Salvation Army).

[249] For further analysis of these issues, see Marat Shterin, "Legislating on Religion in the Face of Uncertainty," in Denis J. Galligan and Marina Kurkchiyan, eds., *Law and Informal Practices: The Post-Communist Experience* (New York: Oxford University Press, 2003), pp. 113–134.

[250] Gadzhiev, *Konstitutsionnye printsipy rynochnoi ekonomiki*, p. 125.

[251] RCC decision 255-O of December 6, 2001, *VKS RF*, no. 2 (2002), pp. 80–83. Protection of stockholders, particularly of minority stockholders, is also of great importance in encouraging investment, since stock is worthless if stockholders' rights are not protected. For an analysis of Russian "judge-made" law in this area, see Burnham, Maggs, and Danilenko, *Law and Legal System in the Russian Federation*, pp. 307–314. For the "historical institutionalist" analysis of Russia's experiments with corporate governance, see David M. Woodruff, "Rules for Followers: Institutional Theory and the New Politics of Economic Backwardness in Russia," *Politics and Society*, vol. 28, no. 4 (2000), pp. 437–482.

[252] RCC decision 18-P of December 23, 1999, *VKS RF*, no. 1 (2000), pp. 2–24.

Protecting Constitutional Rights   179

The RCC also repeatedly struck down federal statutes that limited the amount of disability payments to both the victims and clean-up workers of nuclear plant accidents, including the 1986 Chernobyl disaster, as violating constitutional equality. According to the Court, the state had to use maximum resources to compensate affected individuals for the harmful effects of radiation leaks, to adjust disability payments to the rate of inflation, and to compensate, equally, all those who suffered from radiation in the affected area. In effect, these decisions recognized that the Article 42 right to a "favorable environment," which the Court ruled was both an individual and a collective right of current and future generations, imposed on the state obligations to "take adequate measures to protect the environment and the people from nuclear catastrophes," and to establish a "system of benefits and compensation" that would go beyond the limits of ordinary compensation for harm.[253] What would these "adequate measures" entail, and how much would they cost? The RCC attempted to answer these complicated public policy questions by elaborating the constitutional requirements of fairness and by urging the political branches of government to respect them.

Elaborating Fairness

Reviewing cases on constitutional rights, the 2nd RCC rarely relies on a single principle and usually uses a combination of principles in its judgments. Unlike "equality," which is enshrined in Article 19 of the Russian constitution, the principle of "fairness" belongs to the constitutional preamble: "We, the multi-ethnic people of the Russian Federation,... honoring the memory of our ancestors, who bequeathed to us their love and respect for our homeland and their faith in goodness and fairness,... adopt this constitution of the Russian Federation." This rooting in the constitutional text may partly explain why fairness is, after equality, the second most-often-cited principle in RCC decisions. Six out of ninety judgments, which cited fairness, referred to the preamble of the 1993 constitution,[254] and one decision referred to Articles 1 (rule-of-law state)

---

[253] RCC decisions: 7-P of March 11, 1996, *VKS RF*, no. 2 (1996), pp. 26–33 (Gadzhiev, dissenting), English translation in *Statutes and Decisions*, no. 6 (1999); 18-P of December 1, 1997, *ibid.*, no. 6 (1997), pp. 41–63 (Morshchakova and Vitruk, dissenting), English translation in *Statutes and Decisions*, no. 2 (2000); and 11-P of June 19, 2002, *ibid.*, no. 5 (2002), pp. 64–84 (Vitruk, dissenting).

[254] RCC decisions: 4-P of February 2, 1996, *VKS RF*, no. 2 (1996), pp. 2–11, English translation in *Statutes and Decisions*, no. 2 (2001); 4-P of February 23, 1999, *ibid.*,

180   *Decision Making of the 2nd Russian Constitutional Court*

and 7 (*Sozialstaat*).[255] Thus, already by the end of its first year, the 2nd RCC had chosen to make the constitutional preamble binding on the government and to strike down laws that violated fundamental principles found in the preamble, something that took the constitutional review tribunals of France, India, and Israel more than a decade.[256]

Stemming from the 2nd RCC's focus on due process rights, twenty-four of these judgments demanded "fair" administration of justice from the Russian courts as a fundamental tenet of the 1993 constitution. Just like its predecessor, the 2nd RCC continued to criticize the regular courts for their formalism in adjudication and encouraged them to apply statutes in light of new constitutional principles.[257] Therefore, the RCC consistently voided federal statutes that restricted judicial discretion, in hopes that abstract constitutional principles would restrict judicial arbitrariness.[258] The fact that a dozen dissenting opinions referred to fairness shows that justices have not come to a conclusion about what this notion really means.

Consider how the RCC elaborated constitutionally prescribed limits on the repressive powers of the state. In the 2003 *Recidivism* decision, the Court ruled that fairness in criminal law dictates the imposition of punishment according to the nature of the crime, the degree of harm caused by it, and the extent of guilt of the perpetrator. Facing enormous pressure from law-enforcement agencies and surging crime rates, the majority was unwilling to strike down Criminal Code provisions imposing heavier sentences on recidivists. In a 17–2 decision, the Court ruled that heavier punishment for repeated felonies did not violate either the Article 50 "non bis in idem" ban on "trying twice for the same crime" or "fair" criminal justice, and pushed this "hot potato" back to the legislature. The majority opinion did emphasize that fairness required that first-time

---

no. 3 (1999), pp. 49–56, English translation in *Statutes and Decisions*, no. 6 (2000); 33-O of February 8, 2001, *ibid.*, no. 3 (2001), pp. 70–78 (Khokhriakova and Zhilin, dissenting); 11-P of July 5, 2001, *ibid.*, 6 (2001), pp. 28–42; 3-P of March 19, 2003, *ibid.*, no. 3 (2003), pp. 17–40 (Vitruk and Kononov, dissenting); and 270-O of July 10, 2003, *ibid.*, no. 5 (2003), pp. 91–93.

[255] RCC decision 11-P of June 19, 2002, *VKS RF*, no. 5 (2002), pp. 64–84 (Vitruk, dissenting).

[256] See Scheppele, "Declarations of Independence," pp. 248–251, and references therein.

[257] See, for example, RCC decisions: 244-O of December 14, 2000, *VKS RF*, no. 2 (2001), pp. 50–55; and 48-O of February 20, 2002, *ibid.*, no. 4 (2002), pp. 67–70.

[258] See, for example, RCC decisions: 20-P of July 2, 1998, *VKS RF*, no. 5 (1998), pp. 70–80, English translation in *Statutes and Decisions*, no. 3 (2001); 4-P of March 12, 2001, *ibid.*, no. 5 (2001), pp. 2–19; and 48-O of February 20, 2002, *ibid.*, no. 4 (2002), pp. 67–70.

Protecting Constitutional Rights 181

offenders would not be punished in a similar way as ex-convicts. Dissenters disagreed and argued that heavier sentences for recidivists violated both "non bis in idem" and constitutional fairness, and higher moral principles. Justice Vitruk blasted heavier sentences as an amoral legacy of Tsarist and Soviet regimes, while Justice Kononov appealed to the Aristotelian purpose of fairness as a measure to soften punishment and the Kantian belief in moral sovereignty as the only way to repentance.[259]

Challenges in applying fairness to social rights also abound in the RCC's case law.[260] Although many judges were outraged by the plight of ordinary Russians in what Chief Justice Baglai called the "raging sea of liberalism," they refused to interpret the Article 7 provisions on "a decent life" and "free development of every individual" at the request of the State Duma. In July 1999, the Court ruled that this would involve them in law making. Thus, reviewing social protection bills pending in the Duma was beyond its powers. According to Justice Olga Khokhriakova, who authored most of the social rights judgments, the RCC has not tried to give an overarching definition of the *Sozialstaat*.[261] At the same time, the RCC ordered other courts to be guided by the principle of "social justice" in determining the size of an obligatory share of an estate to balance the Article 35 inheritance rights of all successors and the amount of compensation for taking "public purpose" property, such as daycare centers, boilerhouses, and so on, from bankrupt companies.[262]

Still, one could make several observations on how the RCC responded to 33,080 social rights complaints received by the Court between 1995 and 2006.[263] First, the RCC embraced a "socially oriented" concept of individual freedoms, thus rejecting the neoliberal hegemony of negative rights and a minimalist state.[264] The justices recognized that balancing classic negative rights with positive rights was the only way to maintain

---

[259] RCC decision 3-P of March 19, 2003, *VKS RF*, no. 3 (2003), pp. 17–40 (Vitruk and Kononov, dissenting).

[260] See Nikolai Bondar, "Rossiiskaia Federatsiia," in *Konstitutsionnoe pravosudie i sotsialnoe gosudarstvo: Sbornik dokladov* [Constitutional Justice and Social State] (Moskva: IPPP, 2003), pp. 160–187.

[261] RCC decision 98-O of July 1, 1999 (unpublished), available at the RCC Web site, http://www.ksrf.ru. See Olga Khokhriakova, "Rossiiskaia Federatsiia," *Konstitutsionnoe Pravo: Vostochnoevropeiskoe Obozrenie*, no. 1 (2003), p. 90.

[262] RCC decisions: 209-O of December 9, 1999, *VKS RF*, no. 2 (2000), pp. 41–43; and 8-P of May 16, 2000, *ibid.*, no.4 (2000), pp. 38–45.

[263] This number combines the total of petitions on labor and housing rights, and rights to education, healthcare, and social protection.

[264] For a theoretical justification of constitutionalizing social rights, see Cecile Fabre, *Social Rights under the Constitution* (Oxford: Oxford University Press, 2000).

182   *Decision Making of the 2nd Russian Constitutional Court*

social peace in the course of the historically unprecedented redistribution of property and skyrocketing socioeconomic inequality. Unlike the high courts in well-established democracies, the RCC interpreted social rights as a mechanism to enhance human dignity and to enable a free and fair interpersonal exchange.[265] The constitutional catalogue of social rights (Articles 37–44) together with *acquired* positive rights impose a constitutional duty on the state, and, thus, these rights can be protected through judicial review.[266] Therefore, the real issue before the Court is not whether these rights exist, they do. Instead, the Court sought to reform the social safety net: how to reduce Soviet-era paternalism in the social sphere, on the one hand, and how to protect the disadvantaged, on the other hand.

Realizing that budgetary constraints determine the availability of social services, the justices focused on the welfare of the most vulnerable groups of the population, such as the disabled, orphans, pensioners, and the unemployed, who clearly lacked "equal opportunity" and depended on the state for their survival. For example, in 1997, the RCC struck down the Employment Act, which provided no allowance to temporarily disabled, unemployed persons beyond the first 30 days of their illness.[267] In 2002, the RCC upheld the constitutionality of the Orphans Benefits Act, which limited higher education subsidies to orphans under 23 years of age, yet the judges hinted that universities could provide free education to such students regardless of their age, given the availability of funds.[268] In 2005, the Court scolded President Putin and the State Duma for abolishing the official poverty line as a basis for calculating the minimum amount of old-age pensions. The RCC found that this abolition violated the constitutional principle of human dignity and declared that the constitution required that the minimum amount of old-age pensions could not be set below the official poverty line in each region.[269]

The Court has also tried to apply abstract notions of fairness, equality, and proportionality to resolve a nationwide crisis of nonpayment of wages

---

[265] Ran Hirschl, *Towards Juristocracy: The Origins and Consequences of the New Constitutionalism* (Cambridge, MA: Harvard University Press, 2004).

[266] Bondar, "Rossiiskaia Federatsiia," pp. 160–187.

[267] RCC decision 20-P of December 16, 1997, *VKS RF*, no. 1 (1998), pp. 17–22, English translation in *Statutes and Decisions*, no. 3 (2000). For an analysis of this case, see Kim Lane Scheppele, "A Realpolitik Defense of Social Rights," *University of Texas Law Review*, vol. 82, no. 7 (2004), pp. 1921–1961.

[268] RCC decision 258-O of October 10, 2002, *VKS RF*, no. 2 (2003), pp. 13–16.

[269] RCC decision 17-O of February 15, 2005, *VKS RF*, no. 5 (2005), pp. 13–25 (Gadzhiev, concurring).

Protecting Constitutional Rights

and taxes.[270] In December 1997, the RCC struck down Article 855 of the Civil Code, which gave priority to the payment of wages (and payments to pension, social security, and employment funds, which by law have to be paid at the same time as wages) over payment of taxes. Here, the Court ruled that this priority was unfair and, thus, unconstitutional, because it favored nonstate over public sector employees whose wages depended on the receipt of tax revenues, and it failed to balance constitutional obligations of paying wages and taxes.[271] According to Justice Gadzhiev, this priority of wages over taxes opened a loophole for cash-strapped employers, who could keep high levels of wage arrears and delay payments to pension, social security, and employment funds, resulting in nonpayment of both wages and mandatory contributions to these funds.[272] In another decision, the Court found that the constitutional principles of fairness and equality required the federal government to pay the full amount of pensions to those retirees whose former employers had failed to send contribution payments to the employees' accounts in the Pension Fund.[273]

Generally, however, the RCC has often deferred to the political branches in the areas of social security, unemployment, and housing reforms. The Court agreed with most aspects of these reforms and with the reduction of the scope of acquired social rights. At the same time, the RCC repeatedly argued that a rollback of the welfare state should be carried out in conformity with constitutional principles. In a series of decisions, the RCC ruled that the principles of fairness and equality serve as a basis for the Article 39 right to social security and require legal certainty, predictability of legislation, and clarity of legal provisions so that affected individuals can reasonably expect to receive their pensions and other benefits.[274] Although it approved of the authority of the legislature to regulate the eligibility of recipients of social services and the size of their

---

[270] See Padma Desai and Todd Idson, *Work without Wages: Russia's Non-Payment Crisis* (Cambridge, MA: MIT Press, 2000).

[271] RCC decision 21-P of December 23, 1997, *SZ RF*, no. 51 (1997), item 5878 (Kononov, dissenting), English translation in *Statutes and Decisions*, no. 3 (2000). For the politics of this litigation, see Sarah Ashwin and Simon Clarke, *Russian Trade Unions and Industrial Relations in Transition* (London: Palgrave Macmillan, 2003), pp. 53–55.

[272] Gadis Gadzhiev, "Kommentarii," in Boris Ebzeev, ed., *Kommentarii k postanovleniiam Konstitutsionnogo Suda Rossiiskoi Federatsii. T. 2.* (Moskva: Iurist, 2000), pp. 322–329.

[273] RCC decision 9-P of July 10, 2007, *VKS RF*, no. 4 (2007), pp. 23–37 (Gadzhiev, dissenting).

[274] For a similar meaning of legal certainty in the context of European Union law, see Winfried Brugger, "European Integration and the Ideal of the Common Good," in Vicki C. Jackson and Mark Tushnet, eds., *Defining the Field of Comparative Constitutional Law* (Westport, CT: Praeger, 2002), pp. 95–97.

pension and other social benefits, the RCC insisted that legislative rollbacks could be applied retroactively only if the recipients were offered adequate compensation.[275] To soften the impact of these rollbacks, the RCC encouraged reformers to allow for a transitional period of several years during which the recipients could adjust to the new regulations.

For example, in a judgment that upheld one of the key social policy reforms of President Putin – the 2001 Labor Pensions Act – the RCC allowed existing pensioners themselves to decide whether to switch to the new scheme of calculating pensions.[276] Although the RCC maintained that offering this choice would enhance the trust of pensioners in the legitimacy of pension reform, Justice-Rapporteur Sergei Kazantsev admitted that this decision was the product of a serious compromise among his colleagues, some of whom felt that the contested Act that deleted advantages for hundreds of thousands of workers in the Northern regions, university graduates, and mothers of many children, undermined the trust of the public. According to him, justices had to struggle between their sincere concerns for the plight of retired persons and "progressive" pension reform, the reversal of which would cost Russia 12 billion rubles (US$400 million) annually. Indeed, in the wake of this decision, 335 out of 450 State Duma members, the Sakha and Chukotka Legislative Assemblies, and forty-one outraged pensioners announced that they were preparing to appeal this "unfair" reduction of retirement benefits to the ECHR in Strasbourg.[277]

In summary, the Court's vision of social justice is a complicated and multilayered compromise between private and public interests in which formal and real equality coexist with fairness, and social rights require state action to ensure that the disadvantaged are able to satisfy their minimum basic needs. In the Court's view, by carrying out social policy reforms in a fair and nondiscriminatory fashion, the state would benefit from increased public trust, and the citizens would have their entitlements protected. Although the RCC cannot be accused of "killing welfare reform" as had transpired in Hungary, the Court can certainly be credited with persistent efforts to "constitutionalize" social justice, which is based on a

---

[275] Belgian courts came up with a similar requirement of "adequate compensation" in 1994. See Fabre, *Social Rights under the Constitution*, pp. 162–163.

[276] RCC decision 2-P of January 29, 2004, *VKS RF*, no. 2 (2004), pp. 22–31.

[277] Anna Zakatnova, "Pensii po-novomu," [Pensions in a New Way] *Rossiiskaia gazeta*, January 30, 2004; Irina Nevinnaia, "Ne v polzu pensionerov," [Not in Favor of Pensioners] *Rossiiskaia gazeta*, February 4, 2004; and Svetlana Borozdina, "Budut dengi – budet sotsialnoe gosudarstvo," [Social State Will Be When Funds Are Available] *Gazeta*, January 30, 2004.

Conclusion

notion that the 1993 constitution protects individuals from both the state and other individuals.[278]

CONCLUSION

The conventional accounts that the Russian Constitutional Court is somehow weaker (or has fewer powers) than its predecessor of 1992–1993 are no longer true because the Court has effectively regained almost all of the powers it had lost during the 1993 constitutional crisis. The growing authoritarian trends in Putin's Russia have not prevented the expansion of its judicial power. True, the decision making of the RCC in the past decade confirms the wisdom that judges as political actors are constrained by rules and by the rule-defined positions occupied by the powerful.[279] But it confirms this up to a point. The Russian Constitutional Court is constrained by *some* rules and not others; and *some* power holders constrain the Court more than others do at different points in time and in different areas of public policy. Recall the judge-made discoveries of the implied powers of the president, legislative powers of the regions, access of local governments and the Procurator General to the Constitutional Court, and constitutional complaints against the edicts of the federal Cabinet. This is not to mention the self-empowerment of the Constitutional Court vis-à-vis other courts. In none of these cases did the RCC feel constrained by the rules or the views of the rulers. True, the 2nd Court was initially much more cautious than its predecessor in defining the constitutional scheme of the separation of powers. Yet, the RCC actively set out to shape the fundamentals of Russian governance by focusing on the separation of powers, federalism, and basic rights. Constitutional rights – negative and positive – received the greatest attention from the 2nd RCC. Cautiously rebuilding its own legitimacy in the eyes of the political elites, the Court managed to get over a bitter split on the bench and plunged ahead in reorganizing the Russian political system. That the Court, through a greater tolerance of dissents, gradually developed its own approaches to resolve complicated constitutional questions is a sign of the institutionalization of this tribunal.

As I have shown in this chapter, the RCC has been discovering unwritten constitutional rights and constitutionalizing rights in a "brave, new

---

[278] András Sajó, "How the Rule of Law Killed Hungarian Welfare Reform," *East European Constitutional Review*, vol. 5, no. 1 (1996), pp. 31–41.

[279] Martin Shapiro and Alec Stone Sweet, *On Law, Politics, and Judicialization* (Oxford: Oxford University Press, 2002), p. 10.

world" regarding access to information, the right to a favorable environment, and property rights in corporate governance and bankruptcy proceedings. The RCC boldly chose to create a hierarchy of constitutional rights, something that the German Constitutional Court refused to do.[280] Elaborating hidden fundamental legal principles, such as fairness and proportionality, is also a novel approach for Russian jurists, whose thinking is traditionally rooted in legal positivism. If the 1st RCC was forced to go beyond the text of the outdated and heavily amended 1978 constitution, the 2nd RCC consciously refused to stick to the "letter" of the 1993 constitution and chose to become an active policymaker despite the growing nondemocratic trends in the political system.

On the one hand, political elites and the RCC benefit from the Court-ordered changes in the meaning of a rigid constitution. Recall the growth of the "implied powers" of the federal president, the recentralization of federalism, and the monopolization of judicial review by the RCC. On the other hand, extensive reliance on unwritten constitutional principles has established the framework for the Court's scrutiny of public policy in highly visible cases. Indeed, as my analysis clearly shows, the Court's involvement in public policy reforms intensified during the first term of highly popular President Putin. Between 2000 and 2006, the Court reviewed all his major reforms on separation of powers, federalism, elections, judiciary, land, taxation, social security, and other public policy areas. To be sure, the Court did not strike down the core of these reforms. Yet the justices attempted to subject these wide-ranging reforms to broader constitutional principles, thus taming the authority of the political branches of government. Moreover, many RCC decisions paved the way for Putin's federalism and taxation reforms and reforms of criminal and civil procedure. This pattern of judicial policy making appears to parallel what the French Constitutional Council went through in the 1980s, when the opposition Socialist Party asked the Council to strike down virtually all pieces of reform carried out by the French government.[281] In short, the 2nd RCC has clearly overcome its initial timidity and does not hesitate to review the public policies of a highly popular president who controls a parliamentary majority.

---

[280] On Germany, see Donald Kommers, *The Constitutional Jurisprudence of the Federal Republic of Germany* (Durham, NC: Duke University Press, 1997).

[281] See Alec Stone, *The Birth of Judicial Politics in France* (Oxford: Oxford University Press, 1992).

Less visible is the normative significance of the emphasis the Court has placed on equality, fairness, proportionality, and respect for human rights. Here, the usefulness of the Court to political elites is clear: regardless of how "expensive" they are, constitutional rights cases identify sore spots that could trigger litigation in the European Court of Human Rights and damage Russia's reputation abroad. Appealing to these unwritten constitutional values and allowing litigants to use them as arguments in their legal battles, the RCC deepened their meaning and clearly viewed its constitutional review power as both a legal and a psychological force. Defending real equality and social justice brings the Court closer to ordinary people, who, in turn, respond with an unending stream of constitutional complaints against governmental actions. Frequent collective complaints to the RCC clearly show that petitioners seek both justice and monetary rewards. Yet the RCC lacks the material power to implement its own judgments against the government and has to support its reasoning with both legal and normative arguments. How successful was the RCC in this area during the last decade? What challenges has the RCC been facing in enforcing its rulings? Did successful petitioners get what they wanted? Without answers to these questions, which are the focus Chapters 6 and 7, we will not be able to say if constitutional review has really made a difference in postcommunist Russia.

6

The Constitutional Court Has Ruled – What Next?

Twice, in 1993, the Constitutional Court of the Russian Federation, with its hasty decisions and actions, pushed the country to the brink of the civil war.

– Russian President Boris Yeltsin[1]

Chapters 3–5 explained how and why Russia's politicians designed and redesigned the federal constitutional court, and how and why this court functioned the way it did in its first decade and a half. To be sure, the business of creating high courts and conducting judicial review is never done in a vacuum, devoid of a sociopolitical context. This context involves the extent of compliance with the decisions of the constitutional courts, a third element of the trilateral dynamic of judicial review power, as I argued in Chapter 2. Compliance consists of both judicial foresight (How will the elites and the public react to the court decision?) and the actual reaction of the powers-that-be and society, in general, to the judicial decisions: attacks on the very institution of constitutional review, disobedience and delay, or quiet acquiescence. What accounts for this variation? Without studying the actual patterns of compliance and defiance with the decisions of the constitutional courts, one cannot tell how these courts make a difference outside the courthouse: does judicial review bring about significant social change or do courts produce just another "hollow hope"?[2]

As I discussed in Chapter 2, scholars have not reached a consensus on the best strategy for a young constitutional court to improve compliance. Some suggest that judges should focus on the separation-of-powers

---

[1] Ukaz "O Konstitutsionnom sude RSFSR" No. 1612 ot 7.10.1993 g. [Decree "On the Constitutional Court of the Russian Federation"]. No. 1612 of Oct. 11, 1993, *SAPP*, no. 41 (1993), item 3921.

[2] Gerald N. Rosenberg, *The Hollow Hope: Can Courts Bring About Social Change?* (Chicago: University of Chicago Press, 1991).

The Failure of the USSR Constitutional Supervision Committee   189

conflicts between the legislature and the executive by exploiting interinstitutional rivalries between central government bodies. Others propose to uphold the supremacy of the central government in federalism disputes. Another group of scholars tells new judges to focus on the "rights" cases and to avoid heavyweight political clashes. Yet others advise young courts to wait and please the public. But determining which course of action strengthens or endangers the court is impossible without gauging the actual reaction of the power holders and of the broader society to court decisions. Only by studying the range of actual responses to the decisions of constitutional courts can one tell whether it is easier to enforce judgments on basic rights or federalism or the separation-of-powers issues. In this chapter and Chapter 7, I explore how judges in Russia go about ensuring the enforcement of their judgments and how politicians, bureaucracies, and legal elites react to Court-mandated policy changes. I focus on the cases where the Constitutional Court struck down laws and interpreted them and the constitution in such a way that required governmental action: changes in existing laws, passage of new bills, rehearing in regular courts, and so forth.

The core argument of this chapter is that both the context of institutional uncertainty and the balance of power among major political forces influence the range of responses that political actors can make in case of an unfavorable court decision. I conceive of "institutional uncertainty" as a combination of uncertain rules (confused structure of legal hierarchy) and weakly institutionalized organizations (fragility of new constitutional tribunals as institutions and weak state capacity). These uncertainties are mutually linked with each other and are inevitably present in any radical transition to a new constitutional order. Institutional uncertainty is relevant both for *judges*, who test the limits of judicial review power, and *politicians*, who try their best to maximize the benefits from favorable court decisions and to minimize the damage from unfavorable ones. As I will explore, politicians, just like judges, are adept in responding creatively to judicial review. Studying these "postdecisional" dialogues among judges, politicians, and bureaucrats will help us understand the dynamics of judicial empowerment in postauthoritarian societies.

THE FAILURE OF THE USSR CONSTITUTIONAL SUPERVISION COMMITTEE: 1990–1991

As I have shown in Chapters 3 and 4, the USSR Constitutional Supervision Committee (CSC) was created in an atmosphere of deep suspicion on the part of the Union republics, whose leaders flatly refused to comply with its judgments and statements. In the context of the collapsing Soviet empire, politicians were preoccupied with fundamental problems of sovereignty, and the CSC decisions were only one of the few tools the Union leaders had to keep the USSR from dissolution. Recalcitrant republics, including Russia, were prepared to secede from the Soviet Union, and they would not pay any attention to the objections of the CSC. In short, as with the short-lived Czechoslovakia Constitutional Court and the well-established Yugoslavia Constitutional Court, the Soviet CSC neither prevented the collapse of the Union nor was able to supervise its dissolution in 1991.

The success of the CSC in the area of fundamental rights was slightly better. Recall from Chapter 3 that the CSC struck down laws and regulations only after the federal authorities gave their assurances that they would carry out its judgments. The USSR executive did repeal some of the invalidated regulations. Also, the CSC enthusiastically introduced international human rights standards into the domestic legal hierarchy. This, however, did not help to implement the CSC's rulings on the unconstitutionality of residence permits and secret governmental directives. These two elements still constitute the core of Russia's mechanism of social control, and the political branches of government fiercely opposed dismantling them regardless of numerous court judgments against these elements in the past decade.[3]

In summary, the record of implementing the two dozen decisions of the CSC is poor. Most of them were simply ignored despite the rulers' assuring their implementation.[4] The few successfully implemented decisions did not require even the intervention of the quasijudicial review body because political branches were prepared to repeal regulations prior to the CSC action. Also, the experience of the CSC supports the "judicial heteronomy" thesis developed by Venelin Ganev to explain the politics of judicial review in Bulgaria: the CSC's work did not involve serious political questions, and, thus, its judgments were irrelevant to those who

---

[3] For example, when, in 2007, the Higher *Arbitrazh* Court ruled that individuals could request judicial review of the unpublished letters of the Russian Finance Ministry and the Federal Tax Service, both agencies vehemently opposed this ruling. See Letter of the RF Ministry of Finance No. 03-02-07/2-138 of August 7, 2007, unpublished. English translation is available at http://subscribe.ru/archive/law.kodekseng/200708/16121843.html.

[4] Mikhail Mitiukov, *Predtecha konstitutsionnogo pravosudiia: vzgliady, proekty i institutsionalnye predposylki (30 – nachalo 90-h gg. XX v.)* [Forerunner of the Constitutional Justice: Views, Drafts, and Institutional Pre-requisites (1930 – Beginning of the 1990s)] (Moscow: Formula Prava, 2006), pp. 115, 118.

The Rise and Fall of the 1st Russian Constitutional Court

had the power to destroy it.[5] The problem of nonimplementation of the CSC decisions lay in the contempt for the CSC by the Soviet republics, its irrelevance for much of the Soviet bureaucracy, and the lack of respect among public officials for the primacy for the Soviet Constitution. Conservative legal elites, who advocated parliamentary supremacy or an "iron-hand" rule, recognized the redundancy of judicial review, while the liberal legal elites distrusted the quasijudicial nature of the CSC, and demanded and eventually designed a full-fledged constitutional court with strong enforcement powers.

Indeed, the idea of an independent and powerful constitutional court quickly spread across the collapsing USSR. It aimed to overcome the half-hearted nature of the Soviet CSC and to equip the judicial review bodies with binding and final decisions. Learning from the failure of the CSC, the post-Soviet constitution makers attempted to design their constitutional courts with strong enforcement powers. This is how the "compliance" variable influences the "institutional design" element in my dynamic model of judicial review presented in Chapter 2. Was the Russian Constitutional Court more successful in getting the political actors to comply with its orders and why? This is the subject of the rest of this chapter.

THE RISE AND FALL OF THE 1ST RUSSIAN CONSTITUTIONAL COURT: 1992–1993

In quantitative terms, the 1st RCC and the USSR CSC appear to have many similarities. Both institutions lasted for about 2 years and issued, approximately, an equal number of decisions with long lists of legal acts of dubious constitutionality. Members of both tribunals frequently aired their views on political conflicts in the mass media. However, Russia's first Constitutional Court will stay much longer in public memory as the first judicial body to say "no" to powerful political actors. This section explores the dynamics of the "implementation" game the RCC judges played in resolving legislative–executive rivalries, managing federalism conflicts, and defining fundamental rights.

Implementing Judgments in "Separation-of-Powers" Cases

As I have shown in Chapters 4 and 5, the majority of the RCC judges favored a presidential republic and insisted on their vision of a

---

[5] Venelin Ganev, "The Rise of Constitutional Adjudication in Bulgaria," in Wojciech Sadurski, ed., *Constitutional Justice, East and West* (The Hague: Kluwer Law International, 2002), p. 263.

separation-of-powers doctrine in the context of the heavily amended 1978 constitution. Starting with its first decision on the unconstitutionality of the merger of the KGB with the Ministry of Internal Affairs (see Chapter 4), the RCC succeeded in getting the political branches of the federal government to comply with its judgments.[6] Initially, Chairman Zorkin had to explain the judicial reasoning to political leaders, and, as a result, the latter accepted the Court's role in settling the disputes between the executive and the legislature. Enthusiastic judges, however, overestimated the willingness of embattled political actors to listen to court orders. As the Russian legislature fought harder and harder against President Yeltsin's policies and against his vision of the new post-Soviet constitution in the winter of 1992, the RCC issued its controversial decision in the *Communist Party* case, discussed in Chapter 4.[7] Although the RCC refused to declare the Communist Party unconstitutional and upheld the "unwritten" presidential power to ban political parties in order to safeguard the state and public security and to protect Russia's sovereignty, Yeltsin's circles interpreted this decision as a pro-Communist one. Indeed, the Communists appeared to be the key beneficiaries of the trial: they presented themselves as the "victims" of government repression, as the ardent proponents of freedom of association, as skillful litigators, and as the framers of the debate over the meaning of patriotism for the new Russia.[8] To be sure, the federal and the regional governments also benefited from the Court's judgment: they quickly nationalized the property of the Party. But Russia's law-enforcement agencies allowed the Communist Party to continue its uninterrupted functioning despite the criticism of some of the RCC justices.[9] Why? In part, because both the Court and the Kremlin were too weak to compel the law-enforcement officials to enforce the judgment. All the Court could do was to slap a symbolic fine on the

---

[6] RCC decision 1-P of January 14, 1992, *VKS RF*, no. 1 (1993), pp. 11–19 (Ametistov, concurring). English translation in *Statutes and Decisions. The Laws of the USSR and its Successor States* (hereinafter *Statutes and Decisions*), no. 3 (1994).

[7] RCC decision 9-P of November 30, 1992, *VKS RF*, no. 4–5 (1993), pp. 37–64 (Ebzeev, Kononov, and Luchin, dissenting). Dissenting opinions are published in *VKS RF*, no. 6 (1993), pp. 1–48, English translation in *Statutes and Decisions*, no. 4 (1994).

[8] Kathleen E. Smith, *Mythmaking in the New Russia: Politics and Memory during the Yeltsin Era* (Ithaca, NY: Cornell University Press, 2002), p. 29.

[9] See, for example, justice Ametistov's complaints in Valerii Vyzhutovich, "Doigryvanie otlozhennoi partii," [Resuming the Suspended Party]. *Izvestiia*, February 13, 1993, p. 5; Dmitrii Orlov, "Reshenie po 'delu KPSS' narushaetsia kompartiei i ne vypolniaetsia chinovnikami. Tamara Morshchakova," [Decision in the 'CPSU Case' Is Violated by the Communist Party and Is Not Carried out by the Officials. Tamara Morshchakova]. *Rossiiskie vesti*, July 16, 1996.

The Rise and Fall of the 1st Russian Constitutional Court

perpetrators. Meanwhile, Yeltsin's administration faced both Communist opposition in the federal and regional parliaments and Communist sympathizers within the ranks of the law-enforcement community. Crucially, Yeltsin needed the support of regional leaders, many of whom were still loyal Communists, in his fight against the legislature. The ensuing inability of the rulers to compel compliance or, to use Lucan Way's phrase, "pluralism by default," impeded the enforcement of the Constitutional Court's ruling.[10] In any case, in December 2002, President Putin issued a decree that entitled former Communist Party functionaries – members of those Party institutions with respect to which Yeltsin's ban was declared constitutional by the Court – to higher state pensions.[11] Therefore, only a partial implementation of this most famous decision of the Zorkin Court kept Communist opposition alive and well, and thus promoted pluralism in Russian politics. Yet, without the Court's intervention, Russia might well have ended up in arbitrary purges of ordinary Communists and other opposition parties.

The postdecision "implementation" game in the separation-of-powers cases became more complicated in early 1993 when all three statesmen – Chairman Zorkin, President Yeltsin, and Speaker Khasbulatov – broke their promises to cooperate in good faith to overcome the constitutional crisis. This crisis received a great deal of scholarly attention and will not be reiterated here.[12] A growing perception of the split on the bench between the propresidential minority and the anti-Yeltsin majority fueled the rumors of a biased Court and reduced the level of compliance by political actors. Overruling Yeltsin's TV speech on the introduction of a "special governance regime" in March 1993 in an overnight, hastily assembled session did not improve the Court's image, although it forced the president to delete any mentioning of "special regime" in his call for the referendum

---

[10] Lucan A. Way, "Authoritarian State Building and the Sources of Regime Competitiveness in the Fourth Wave: The Cases of Belarus, Moldova, Russia, and Ukraine," *World Politics*, vol. 57, no. 2 (January 2005), pp. 231–261.

[11] Ukaz "Ob utverzhdenii perechnia dolzhnostei, periody sluzhby (raboty) v kotorykh vkliuchaiutsia v stazh gosudarstvennoi sluzhby dlia naznacheniia pensii za vyslugu let federalnykh gosudarstvennykh sluzhashchikh" [Decree on the List of Positions Eligible for the Pension Calculation of the Federal Government Officers] no. 1413 of December 17, 2002, *Rossiiskaia gazeta*, December 20, 2002.

[12] See, for example, Robert Sharlet, "Russian Constitutional Crisis: Law and Politics under Yeltsin," *Post-Soviet Affairs*, vol. 9, no. 3 (October–December 1993), pp. 314–336; and Kim Lane Scheppele, "Guardians of the Constitution: Constitutional Court Presidents and the Struggle for the Rule of Law in Post-Soviet Europe," *University of Pennsylvania Law Review*, vol. 154, no. 6 (2006), pp. 1757–1851.

on a new constitution to be held in April 1993. The Russian parliament immediately moved to impeach Yeltsin but failed by a narrow margin, while Yeltsin publicly announced that he distrusted the Court and would not petition it anymore. Soon thereafter, rival political leaders complied with the April 1993 decision in the *Referendum* case, which restrained the all-powerful Congress of People's Deputies and saved Yeltsin's agenda in an upcoming referendum. The votes in this referendum, which was held on April 25, 1993, were counted according to Court-ordered rules and returned a vote of confidence in Yeltsin's policies. Yeltsin used this as a pretext to convene a Constitutional Convention, a body in charge of drafting the new Russian Constitution. Zorkin and his supporters on the bench refused to recognize the legitimacy of this Convention while other justices joined it and took an active role in constitution drafting. Naturally, this division only deepened the split on the bench, which culminated in the September 1993 finding regarding Yeltsin's impeachment, discussed in Chapter 4. By that time, the legislative–executive conflict and the crisis on the bench were so severe that nobody could predict the future. The high stakes of political confrontation and the stalled constitutional reform blended the raw power struggles with institutional unpredictability. Yeltsin was determined to get rid of the Constitutional Court and perceived Zorkin as his personal enemy, and only the intervention by the pro-Yeltsin minority on the bench saved the Court from the president's wrath. In October 1993, Yeltsin dissolved the Russian parliament and suspended the RCC until the ratification of the new constitution by popular vote on December 12, 1993. Yeltsin declared that "a number of members of the Constitutional Court have indicated their refusal to attend deliberations and hearings of the Court," found that that "makes any further activities of the Court impossible," and ordered the Court "not to hold any sessions until adoption of a new Constitution of the Russian Federation." The decree further declared that the Court had "made political decisions" and had "placed the country on the brink of civil war." Yeltsin further asserted that the Court had "played a negative role, actually that of an accomplice, in the tragic developments of October 3 and 4, 1993, in Moscow" and "had transformed itself into an instrument of political struggle, posing extreme danger to the state."[13] At the same time, Yeltsin ordered the Court to draft a new Court Act. He was persuaded that a new and improved Constitutional Court without his opponents on the bench

---

[13] Ukaz "O Konstitutsionnom sude RSFSR" No. 1612 ot 7.10.1993 g. [Decree "On the Constitutional Court of the Russian Federation"]. No. 1612 of Oct. 11, 1993, *SAPP*, no. 41 (1993), item 3921.

would not harm him. On the contrary, the tribunal would protect him from the political opposition, while the international community would approve of his keeping the Court.

What this "implementation game" shows is that courts are clearly constrained actors, and that they anticipate the reaction of the political branches of government. At the same time, the federal politicians agreed with some of the RCC decisions and refused to comply with others. Politicians criticized the RCC for being "biased" yet they routinely petitioned the Court to fight against their opponents. Neither the "thick" nor the "thin" political culture approaches that emphasize the "legal nihilism" of Russian elites can explain this variation. The "thick" culturalist theories, which emphasize the centuries-old tradition of flouting the law in Russia, fail to tell us why Yeltsin complied with RCC orders in 1992 and did not do so in 1993. The "thin" culturalist explanations, which focus on the values and belief systems of Russian reformers in the early 1990s, also fare poorly in tackling this puzzle. True, Yeltsinites justified their non-compliance by their appeals to a higher justice and morality.[14] Yet they began to question the legitimacy of the 1978 constitution and the Zorkin Court judgments only in 1993, the second year of the Court's functioning, and only when the RCC ruled against the president. Thus, politicians manipulated their instrumental vision of the law to defend their stances in the raw power struggles against the legislature.

The calculation of costs and benefits of noncompliance greatly influenced the choice of embattled judges and political actors. This calculation, however, was not made in a vacuum. Rapidly deteriorating political confrontation and institutional unpredictability complicated this calculation, as the choice was about the nature of representative institutions and interinstitutional rivalries turned violent, rendering any arbitration or mediation useless to the fighting politicians. A perception of biased judicial decision making appears to have reduced the level of compliance with court decisions yet it did not eliminate the willingness of the parties to use judicial review in their own interests by petitioning the Court.

Implementing Judgments in "Federalism" Cases

Unlike its early successes in separation-of-powers cases, the Zorkin Court decisions in "federalism" cases met with considerable disobedience by the Russian regions. While reformers in Yeltsin's circle and

---

[14] Alexander Lukin, *The Political Culture of the Russian 'Democrats'* (Oxford: Oxford University Press, 2000), p. 204.

196   *The Constitutional Court Has Ruled – What Next?*

the Supreme Soviet tried to incorporate Russia's territorial integrity into a new democratic constitutional order, the Russian regions demanded more rights and contested the supremacy of federal authorities, including that of the young RCC.[15] Consider what happened after the March 1992 *Tatarstan Referendum* case, discussed in Chapter 4. In that case, the Court struck down Tatarstan's Declaration of Sovereignty and the move of this republic, one of the most recalcitrant regions, to schedule a March 1992 referendum on the question: "Do you agree that the Tatarstan Republic is a sovereign state and a party to international law, basing its relations with the Russian Federation as partners? Yes or no?"[16] Justices viewed this referendum as a unilateral secession from Russia that paved the path towards the "balkanization" of Russia. The petitioners in the Tatarstan case, Russian MPs, and judges had all the assurances that this RCC judgment was going to be carried out: President Yeltsin promptly complied with previous RCC decisions; Speaker Khasbulatov promised the judges that Tatarstan leaders would be brought in an iron cage to Moscow like Catherine the Great used to bring peasant rebels to the Red Square; the federal Prosecutor General threatened to arrest Tatarstan leaders if they allowed the referendum to proceed; and the federal defense minister was rumored to be mobilizing troops on Tatarstan's borders. However, once the RCC struck down Tatarstan's sovereignty, the federal center suddenly lost all of its enforcement powers despite the repeated pleas from judges: President Yeltsin chose to negotiate a side deal with Tatarstan; the deadlocked Russian parliament was unable to do anything; and law-enforcement agencies ignored the RCC decision. The only agency that acted was the federal Cabinet: it imposed an economic blockade and denied some goods to Tatarstan. But Moscow was denied taxes from one of the richest regions for several years to come. Moreover, Tatarstan authorities boycotted the court proceedings and held the referendum as if there was no court decision.[17] The neighboring Bashkortostan Republic immediately suspended the jurisdiction of the RCC over its territory, while other republics contemplated the creation of their own constitutional courts in order to protect their autonomy from intrusions of the federal center.[18] Instead of forcing

---

[15] On the tension between the self-determination of ethnic minorities and Russia's territorial integrity, see Lukin, *Political Culture of the Russian 'Democrats,'* p. 204.

[16] Quoted in Schwartz, *Struggle for Constitutional Justice,* p. 122.

[17] 82 percent of the electorate participated, with 61.3 percent of them approving the question. Jeffrey Kahn, *Federalism, Democratization and the Rule of Law in Russia* (New York: Oxford University Press, 2002), pp. 131–132.

[18] Alexei Trochev, "Less Democracy, More Courts: A Puzzle of Judicial Review in Russia," *Law & Society Review,* vol. 38, no. 3 (September 2004), pp. 513–548.

The Rise and Fall of the 1st Russian Constitutional Court 197

Tatarstan to abandon its referendum, Yeltsin attempted to convince Tatarstan to sign the March 1992 Federation Treaty. Tatarstan refused to sign, withdrew from both the April 1993 federal referendum and the June 1993 Russian Constitutional Assembly, and boycotted both the federal elections and the constitutional referendum in December 1993.[19] President Yeltsin continued to negotiate and eventually signed a highly controversial side deal with Tatarstan in April 1994. This bargaining dealt a huge blow to the nascent RCC, as the usually cautious Chief Justice Baglai of the 2nd RCC admitted in late 2001.[20] Paradoxically, Tatarstan and the rest of the autonomy-minded republics enjoyed a high degree of public support. According to a nationwide public opinion survey conducted in November 1992, 8 months after the *Tatarstan Referendum* case, 44 percent of Russians agreed with the right of Tatarstan to secede from Russia, and more than 60 percent of Muscovites agreed to grant independence to Chechnya. Only 7 percent of Russians approved the use of force against separatist regions.[21] Neither the RCC nor the federal center, however, acted upon these wishes of the citizenry. As I discussed in the previous chapter, the RCC struck down Tatarstan's "sovereign" status only in June 2000, when justices received assurances that President Putin was seriously committed to "harmonizing" the regional laws. Still, the Tatarstan saga continued well into Putin's second term. In 2004, the Tatarstan Supreme Court refused to strike down the republic's 1990 Declaration of State Sovereignty, while the Tatarstan leaders managed to persuade President Putin to sign a new bilateral power-sharing treaty, which would solidify Tatarstan's "sovereignty" within Russia.[22]

The fate of the rest of the "federalism" cases heard by the 1st RCC also appears to have been determined by the initiative of the regions, which acted on a call for the "accommodation" of federal and regional interests, repeatedly pronounced by the Zorkin Court. The regional insistence made

---

[19] Kahn, *Federalism, Democratization and the Rule of Law in Russia*, pp. 151–157.
[20] Marat Baglai, "Konstitutsionnoe pravosudie v Rossii: stanovlenie i razvitie," [Constitutional Justice in Russia: Formation and Development]. *Zhurnal rossiiskogo prava*, no. 10 (October 2001), p. 7.
[21] Leontii Byzov, "Rossiiane o khode ekonomicheskikh i politicheskikh reform nakanune VII Sezda," [Russians on the Course of Economic and Political Reforms on the Eve of the 7th Congress]. *Konstitutsionnyi vestnik*, no. 13 (November 1992), p. 220.
[22] Vera Postnova, "Tatarstan uporstvuet v svoei nezavisimosti," [Tatarstan Insists on Its Own Independence]. *Nezavisimaia gazeta*, June 29, 2004; Andrei Smirnov, "Kremlin Signs Power-Sharing Treaty with Tatarstan," *Eurasia Daily Monitor*, November 21, 2006; and Chloe Arnold, "Russia: Federation Council Backs Tatarstan Power-Sharing Bill," *RFE/RL Russia Report*, July 11, 2007.

President Yeltsin's approach to enforcing RCC decisions appear to be haphazard in other federalism cases. Consider Yeltsin's reaction to two RCC judgments, the *Mordovia Presidency* and the *Cheliabinsk Governor*, which explored the limits of federal intrusion in regional elections. Both decisions went against presidential decrees and were issued in June 1993, the peak of Yeltsin's distrust in the Zorkin Court.

Yeltsin complied with the *Mordovia* decision, which upheld the constitutionality of the Mordovia legislature's move to abolish the post of a directly elected president.[23] Yeltsin issued a decree to annul this move in order to keep in power his favorite, the already-elected President Gusliannikov. The RCC ruled that Yeltsin lacked the authority to interfere in this matter, which belonged to the exclusive jurisdiction of Mordovia. Although the federal news agency initially refused to air this judgment, Yeltsin decided not to use force and let the local politicians settle this bitter dispute.[24] A bitter irony of this dispute is that the Mordovian Constitutional Court, which also upheld the constitutionality of the abolition of the presidency in the region, was abolished in early 1994 by the same Mordovian legislature, while the political regime in the republic was among the most antidemocratic ones in the second half of the 1990s.[25]

However, President Yeltsin did not comply with the RCC decision in the *Cheliabinsk Governor* case.[26] Here, the Cheliabinsk regional legislature complained to the Court that Yeltsin appointed the regional governor, Vadim Soloviev, without asking for its consent. To get rid of Yelstin's appointee, the Cheliabinsk legislature scheduled gubernatorial elections, which Yeltsin's appointee was likely to lose. The Court agreed with the petitioners and overruled this unilateral appointment, while the gubernatorial elections produced a victory for Petr Sumin, the preferred choice of the legislators. In return, Yeltsin took away guards from the RCC and refused to recall his appointee. Meanwhile, both governors headed the Cheliabinsk region simultaneously until November 1993, when Yeltsin dissolved the federal and the regional legislatures and confirmed

---

[23] RCC decision 13-P of June 3, 1993, *VKS RF*, no. 4–5 (1994), pp. 21–36 (Kononov and Vitruk, dissenting), English translation in *Statutes and Decisions*, no. 6 (1994).

[24] Yeltsin did not intervene in 1995, when the 2nd RCC refused to rule on Gusliannikov's petition and upheld its *Mordovia Presidency* decision. See RCC decision 99-O of November 2, 1995, in Tamara Morshchakova, ed., *Konstitutsionnyi Sud RF. Postanovleniia. Opredeleniia. 1992–1996* (Moskva: Novyi Iurist, 1997), pp. 658–660.

[25] Trochev, "Less Democracy, More Courts," pp. 518, 526–527.

[26] RCC decision 14-P of June 7, 1993, *VKS RF*, no. 4–5 (1994), pp. 40–53 (Kononov, dissenting), English translation in *Statutes and Decisions*, no. 5 (1994).

The Rise and Fall of the 1st Russian Constitutional Court   199

Soloviev's governorship.[27] But Petr Sumin struck back by winning three consecutive gubernatorial elections in 1996, 2000, and 2004.

The regional impact on enforcing RCC judgments was also visible in the fiscal federalism cases. In the 1993 *Moscow Privatization Program* case, the court struck down Yeltsin's decree granting broad powers to the Moscow mayor in privatizing highly prized state property in the city, but the Russian president rescinded this decree only in 1997, after Mayor Luzhkov gained near total control over the key Moscow industries. However, Yeltsin complied with the RCC decision in the *Irkutsk* case, which was issued in September 1993, about the same time as he contemplated dissolving the Court for its "cozy relationship" with the Supreme Soviet. Recall from Chapter 4 that, in this case, the Court struck down a presidential decree and required Yeltsin to negotiate with the regions about issues of control over the hydropower plants in Siberian regions in order to balance national and regional property interests. Clearly, at that time, the federal center had the resources and the capacity to disobey this judgment, as it did with other regions that were petitioning the RCC.[28] Yet, facing serious resistance from Irkutsk, Yeltsin chose to negotiate with the region. In 1996, he signed a bilateral treaty with the Irkutsk region, a document that was based on the RCC decision and allowed joint federal–regional management of Russia's three largest hydropower plants. Moreover, regional lobbying made this treaty workable in practice. By 1997, the federal center and Irkutsk were equal partners in selling energy to China under a whopping US$1.5 billion contract.[29] However, with the arrival of President Putin, the federal Cabinet filed a series of lawsuits for the transfer of power stations located in the Irkutsk region from regional back to federal ownership. In 2002, the *arbitrazh* courts agreed with the federal government and effectively deleted any regional prerogative in the hydro comanagement scheme.[30] But the federal government failed to succeed in the Russian Constitutional Court, which refused to hear the federal government's petition to reverse its 1993 *Irkutsk* decision.

---

[27] Valeriia Zykova, "O politicheskoi situatsii v Cheliabinskoi oblasti," [On Political Situation in the Cheliabinsk Region]. *Politicheskii monitoring IGPI*, (October 1993). Available at http://www.igpi.ru/monitoring/1047645476/oct_93/1058172872.html.

[28] For a similar case in the Novosibirsk region, see RCC decision 77-O of July 11, 1996 (unpublished). Available at the Web site of the RCC at http://www.ksrf.ru.

[29] Gadis Gadzhiev, "Kommentarii," in Boris Ebzeev, ed., *Kommentarii k postanovleniiam Konstitutsionnogo Suda RF. T. 1* (Moskva: Iurist, 2000), pp. 351–352.

[30] Maksim Shandarov, "Siberian Federal Okrug," in Peter Reddaway and Robert W. Orttung, eds., *The Dynamics of Russian Politics: Putin's Reform of Federal–Regional Relations, Volume 1* (Lanham, MD: Rowman & Littlefield Publishers, 2004), p. 234.

The RCC stood firm and reiterated that the delimitation of state property ownership between the federation and its parts should be achieved by balancing federal and regional economic interests through the process of federal legislation.[31] This prompted Irkutsk's Governor Govorin to lobby the federal center in 2004 for the return of some kind of role for the region in hydromanagement.[32]

These patterns of compliance and noncompliance with RCC decisions show that judicial review rarely resolves federalism disputes once and for all. The federal Constitutional Court is just one of the players in the federalism game, and the implementation of its judgments manages rather than solves conflicts within the Federation. On the one hand, "accommodating" common and local interests inevitably brings politics into the picture and confuses the legal hierarchy by placing bilateral federal–regional agreements above federal statutes. On the other hand, this accommodation approach rejects commandeering by the federal center just as it rejects any unilateral policies on the part of the regions. This provides an opportunity for all affected regions to fight for their interests at the bargaining table and protect their constitutional rights in courts. But even this accommodation approach was not sufficient to pacify the most autonomy-minded regions and make federal judicial review attractive to them. Instead, many of them accused the RCC of being biased towards the federal center and moved to set up their own judicial systems, including their own constitutional courts.[33]

In short, the impact of the judicial settlement of federalism disputes depends on the willingness, resources, and capacity of the federal center and the regions to negotiate over their disagreements. In the case of the 1st RCC, the regions clearly had all of these endowments while the federal center was torn between building a "just and democratic" federation and preventing the secession of recalcitrant regions. Thus, it was the intensity of regional empowerment initiatives that determined whether RCC judgments were implemented or not.

Implementing Judgments in Constitutional Rights Cases

As I have shown in Chapter 4, the 1st RCC chose to focus on social rights. Such an approach, in the words of Justice Vedernikov, "favored little

---

[31] RCC decision 112-O of May 14, 2002 (unpublished). Available at the Web site of the RCC at http://www.ksrf.ru.

[32] Tatiana Egorova, "Irkutskaia oblast: Vernite 'Irkutskenergo'," [Irkutsk Region: Return 'Irkutskenergo']. *Vedomosti*, January 12, 2004.

[33] Trochev, "Less Democracy, More Courts," pp. 513–548.

The Rise and Fall of the 1st Russian Constitutional Court 201

people yet these rulings could ruin the state."[34] This court-ordered generosity was met with resistance from both the executive and the rest of the judiciary. Reviewing the acts of Yeltsin's government, the Court repeatedly required the government to honor its monetary obligations to citizens.[35] These included the government's promises to deliver automobiles to more than 170,000 railway workers and grain producers as a part of the productivity incentive programs, and adjusting rates for inflation in savings accounts in public banks.[36] Although the RCC ruled that the government's delay in fulfilling these promises violated the constitutional property rights of the railway workers, farmers, and bank account holders, Yeltsin's government strongly believed in a laissez-faire approach and refused to comply with the RCC orders. Only in 1995 did Russia nominally recognize these obligations as its internal debt. Yet a year later Justice Zorkin still repeatedly complained that federal officials simply forgot both RCC decisions.[37] In fact, it took another 5 years and the will of President Putin to design a meaningful program for clearing off this debt.[38] This program still fell short of providing compensation to railway workers and farmers in the amount sufficient to buy a car, according to the Russian Ombudsman.[39] Echoing dark predictions by Justice Vedernikov, the federal government complained that compensating the workers and the farmers in full would cause Russia's budget to collapse. Eventually the matter again came before the RCC, which, in December 2000, upheld the constitutionality of Putin's compensation scheme. Here, the 2nd RCC reasoned that the lack of budgetary means justified the restrictions on constitutional property rights because other constitutional rights also required public spending, and that a federal statute had to balance the rights of

---

[34] "Zatovarilis. Nikolai Vedernikov," [Overstocked. Nikolai Vedernikov]. *Rossiia*, February 24–March 2, 1993.

[35] RCC decisions: 7-P of June 9, 1992, *VKS RF*, no. 2–3 (1993), pp. 29–36, English translation in *Statutes and Decisions*, no. 3 (1994); and 12-P of May 31, 1993, *ibid.*, no. 4–5 (1994), pp. 12–16, English translation in *Statutes and Decisions*, no. 5 (1994).

[36] These and many other obligations were an essential part of the Soviet welfare state, which pervaded the lives of ordinary citizens far more than its Western European analogs. See, for example, Linda J. Cook, *Postcommunist Welfare States: Reform Politics in Russia and Eastern Europe* (Ithaca, NY: Cornell University Press, 2007).

[37] "Beseda s Valeriem Zorkinym: Zhit po pravu," [Conversation with Valerii Zorkin: To Live Under the Law]. *Sovetskaia Rossiia*, October 5, 1996, pp. 1–2; "Poslednii shans – diktatura zakona. Interviu s Valeriem Zorkinym," [Last Chance – Dictatorship of Law. Interview with Valerii Zorkin]. *VEK*, no. 43 (22 October 1996).

[38] See Ger P. van den Berg, compiler, "Constitution of the Russian Federation Annotated with Summaries of Rulings and Other Decisions of Constitutional (Charter) Courts: 1990–2001," *Review of Central and East European Law*, vol. 27, no. 2–3 (2001), p. 204.

[39] *Ibid.*, p. 434, fn. 17.

the promised car owners against the rights of all other citizens.[40] In short, similar to the impact of judicial review in postcommunist Hungary, the final social policy in Russia was a compromise between the court and political actors.[41]

Lack of money is the usual excuse of governments around the world when they do not want to carry out a certain policy (not necessarily court-mandated). However, the prevalence of governmental directives in the law on the ground weakened the impact of the 1st RCC's decisions. As I explained in Chapter 2, in the Soviet era, ministerial instructions were de-facto supreme over both the constitution and statutes. Naturally, the post-Soviet bureaucracy has neither been accustomed to citizens suing the state nor to court-ordered policy changes. Apart from this incapacity of the Russian bureaucracy to carry out RCC decisions, the political mood of a laissez-faire government dominated Yeltsin's decision making in the early 1990s. This meant that the spirit of these RCC decisions ran contrary to the prevailing view of Yeltsin's circle that the overblown welfare state should be dismantled. In short, the federal government had neither the economic incentives nor the normative commitments to honor its obligations and carry out court-mandated social policies at that time. Even though such RCC decisions surely pleased the public, their popularity alone was not enough to compel other branches of government to obey the constitutional court – voters lacked the mechanisms to hold the rulers accountable for the nonimplementation of these popular judgments.

Just as the executive branch of the Russian government disobeyed the Zorkin Court on the grounds of lack of funds, the regular courts also did not want to arouse the wrath of powerful or cash-strapped employers by awarding full compensation for wrongful dismissals. As I have shown in Chapter 4, the 1st RCC invalidated numerous socialist-era restrictions of labor rights. Recall that this Court lacked the power to strike down an offending statute at the request of individuals. The Court could only strike down the "law-application practice," which, in reality, meant only the decisions of regular courts. Thus, constitutional complaints pitted the Zorkin Court against the Russian Supreme Court, which routinely issued binding statutory interpretations. And as I demonstrated in Chapter 4, the 1st RCC did not hesitate to lambaste the Supreme Court for the weak

---

[40] RCC decision 251-O of December 15, 2000, in Tamara Morshchakova, ed., *Konstitutsionnyi Sud RF. Postanovleniia. Opredeleniia. 2000* (Moskva: Iurist, 2001), p. 540.

[41] Kim Lane Scheppele, "Constitutional Negotiations: Political Contexts of Judicial Activism in Post-Soviet Europe," *International Sociology*, vol. 18, no. 1 (2003), pp. 219–238.

The Rise and Fall of the 1st Russian Constitutional Court   203

protection of the rights of employees, thus disclosing the falseness of working class hegemony and the faults of the welfare system under the Soviet regime.[42] The Supreme Court, however, defended its own statutory interpretations.

In its first decision of February 1992, which upheld employees' right to choose when to retire, the Zorkin Court "advised" the Russian parliament to delete the offending provisions from the Labor Code and ordered the Russian judiciary to apply constitutional rules in labor disputes. To be sure, the RCC judges themselves did not have a clear vision of how to enforce this judgment *erga omnes*. Justices Morshchakova and Luchin, who disagreed in many other cases, shared the view that all illegally fired individuals had to petition the RCC, which would then automatically rule in their favor. Justice Rudkin believed that such complainants should all work their way up to the Supreme Court, which then would apply this RCC judgment in each individual case. Justices Ametistov and Tiunov warned that petitions of thousands of wrongfully dismissed individuals would overload the RCC. Both advocated granting the power to local courts in such cases in order to speed up the protection of labor rights.[43] Meanwhile, the Supreme Court refused to reopen the cases of the original complainants. This defiance prompted the RCC to make up its mind and to issue a "clarification" decision in September 1992. Pragmatism won, as the RCC required local courts to apply constitutional norms in place of the offending provisions of the Labor Code.[44]

Something similar happened with the judgment in the *Wrongful Dismissals case*, discussed in Chapter 4. Here, the RCC struck down the way that the regular courts applied Article 213 of the Labor Code, which restricted compensation for illegal dismissal to 1 year regardless of the actual length of unemployment.[45] The Court ruled that employers have to pay wages for the total period of unemployment arising from illegal

---

[42] Alexander Blankenagel, *"Detstvo, otrochestvo, iunost" Konstitutsionnogo Suda* ["Childhood, Adolescence, Youth" of the Russian Constitutional Court] (Moskva: TsKI MONF, 1996), p. 38.

[43] "Esli vas uvolili po starosti, otkazalis propisat ili lishili liubimoi gazety...Konstitutsionnyi sud Rossii v gostiakh u 'Literaturnoi gazety': T. Morshchakova, V. Luchin, Iu. Rudkin, O. Tiunov, E. Ametistov, N. Vitruk," [If You Were Sacked on the Grounds of Age, Were Refused a Residence Permit or Were Deprived of Your Favorite Newspaper... The Constitutional Court of Russia is a Guest of 'Literaturnaia gazeta']. *Literaturnaia gazeta*, March 4, 1992, p. 11.

[44] RCC decision 8-R of September 24, 1992, *VKS RF*, no. 1 (1993), pp. 38–39.

[45] RCC decision 1-P of January 27, 1993, *VKS RF*, no. 2–3 (1993), pp. 56–64, English translation in *Statutes and Decisions*, no. 4 (1994).

dismissals. However, the Supreme Court refused to obey and continued limiting the compensation for wrongful dismissals to 1-year's pay. Complainants again asked the RCC to protect their rights, and in June 1995, the latter stood by its previous decision and accused the Supreme Court of violating the constitution and sabotaging RCC decisions.[46] This June 1995 ruling was the first of some six hundred rulings with "positive content" in which the 2nd RCC confirmed the validity of its previous judgments and monitored compliance with them, as I have explored in Chapter 5. The Supreme Court continued to resist, arguing that the RCC could not review the constitutionality of judicial decisions and could not issue orders to ordinary courts under the new 1993 constitution. Finally, the political branches settled this clash between the high courts in favor of the Constitutional Court by amending the Labor Code in March 1997.[47] Still, well into 2000 the 2nd RCC continued to order the regular courts to reopen wrongful dismissal cases and to award full compensation for the period of forced absence.[48] This means that the regular courts defied this RCC decision for more than seven-and-a-half years!

This struggle between high courts may, in part, be explained by the conservative nature of the regular judges, who behaved as career bureaucrats, refused to take basic rights seriously, and waited for explicit legislative authorization to act. However, as I will show in Chapters 7 and 8, intercourt rivalries ought to be expected in constitutional revolutions because all courts gain power to uphold constitutional supremacy, to enforce constitutional norms, and to interpret statutes in light of new constitutional principles. For example, as early as 1991, the Supreme Court chose to review the constitutionality of pretrial detention by invoking the 1966 International Covenant on Civil and Political Rights. This bold move in effect set aside the Russian Criminal Procedure Code, which at the time did not allow courts to conduct a judicial review of pretrial detention orders.[49] My point here is that Russia's regular court judges resisted RCC orders not because the former were "distrusted, conservative career bureaucrats" unable to accept the supremacy of fundamental

---

[46] RCC decision 29-O of June 15, 1995, *VKS RF*, no. 2–3 (1995), pp. 67.

[47] Federalnyi zakon "O vnesenii izmenenii i dopolnenii v KZoT RF" ot 17.03.1997, [Federal Law on Amending the RF Labor Code]. *SZ RF*, no. 12 (1997), item 1382. See Rozaliia Ivanova, "Kommentarii," in Boris Ebzeev, ed., *Kommentarii k postanovleniiam Konstitutsionnogo Suda RF*. T. 2 (Moscow: Iurist, 2000), pp. 611–13.

[48] RCC decision 198-O of October 5, 2000, *VKS RF*, no. 1 (2001), p. 60.

[49] "Viacheslav Lebedev: 'Ot dolzhnosti Genprokurora ia otkazalsia,'" [Viacheslav Lebedev: I Refused to Become the Procurator General]. *Izvestiia*, January 23, 2003.

rights. On the contrary, the high courts engaged in a fierce competition over the power of judicial review because they could use this power to build their jurisdiction.[50] And the benefits of the expansion of jurisdiction determined the intensity of this competition for "judge-made" law. As I will discuss in the next chapter, the experience of the 2nd RCC clearly shows that all three branches of the Russian judiciary shirked their responsibility for reviewing the politically sensitive presidential decrees, while at the same time all courts fought each other for the exclusive power to review regional laws in order to contest regional separatism and champion human rights.

In summary, both the executive and the regular courts blocked and sabotaged the impact of constitutional rights litigation in the 1st RCC. To be sure, the legacies of the past – lack of rule-of-law traditions, supremacy of executive regulations in the law on the ground, and disrespect for basic rights, to name a few – played an important role in the unwillingness and inability to implement Constitutional Court decisions. However, the early years of the postcommunist transition made their own contribution to the problems of obeying the RCC. On the one hand, championing social rights and requiring the state to honor its obligations to citizens ran contrary to the governmental agenda of spontaneous privatization of state assets and dismantling the welfare state. On the other hand, the post-Soviet constitutional revolution empowered all courts, which meant that Russia's high courts would inevitably fight for their jurisdiction in constitutional rights cases.

CONCLUSION

Overall, what impact did the 1st RCC have on the Russian transition? The main achievement of the Zorkin Court is that, for the first time in Russian history, a judicial body became a real veto point in Russian governance and allowed individuals to sue the state. This Court successfully exploited interinstitutional rivalries in its first year of operation, yet it was doomed to failure when the political branches set out to destroy each other in severe struggles over the nature of political institutions. Facing the threat of breakaway regions, this Court banned unilateral secession and disallowed tinkering by the federal center with regional political processes, yet it

---

[50] William Burnham and Alexei Trochev, "Russia's War between the Courts: The Struggle over the Jurisdictional Boundary between the Constitutional Court and Regular Courts," *American Journal of Comparative Law*, vol. 55, no. 3 (Summer 2007), pp. 381–452.

required the federal center to consult with regions in most cases. The shifting short-term power needs of leaders complicated the implementation of the decisions of the Constitutional Court. While the recalcitrant regions, such as Tatarstan and Bashkortostan, seriously questioned the legitimacy of federal constitutional review, other regions, such as Irkutsk and Mordovia, applauded RCC decisions. Finally, the tough stance of the 1st RCC on generous social rights at the expense of the collapsing state budget allowed citizens to sue the state, yet the regular courts and the bureaucracy blocked the implementation of this generosity. The successes and failures of the Zorkin Court clearly show that judicial strategies of focusing on separation-of-powers cases or federalism disputes or human rights issues worked mainly when politicians and the state machinery agreed to comply with judicial decisions. None of these judicial strategies alone brought success to the Constitutional Court.

In short, powerful politicians rather than ordinary citizens felt the greatest impact of this Court. When Yeltsin's circle realized that an active constitutional review repeatedly blocked their constitutional reforms, they initially decided to get rid of the Court and impeach Chairman Zorkin and his allies on the bench. Later, after intensive lobbying by the justices, they softened their position by suspending the Court in hopes of transforming it into a toothless guardian of the 1993 constitution. Did the 2nd RCC mend its wounds and fare better in making its judgments be enforced by political branches and the rest of the judiciary? How so and why? This is the subject of Chapter 7.

7

The 2nd Russian Constitutional Court (1995–2007): *Problematique* of Implementation

Firing two or three officials from the executive branch for ignoring RCC decisions would greatly enhance the enforcement of laws in Russia.
 – Chief Justice of the Russian Constitutional Court Vladimir Tumanov[1]

We have a well-established practice of sham compliance of other courts with the Constitutional Court decisions.
 – Russian Constitutional Court Justice Tamara Morshchakova[2]

Many Constitutional Court decisions containing orders to the legislature are not carried out or are carried out with long delays.
 – Clerk of the Chief Justice of the Russian Constitutional Court
Vladimir Ovchinskii[3]

Unlike its predecessor, the 2nd Russian Constitutional Court has focused its primary attention on developing generally applicable constitutional principles instead of resolving specific political disputes. Badly damaged by Yeltsin's suspension, the 2nd RCC initially turned its attention to individual rights rather than to serious political controversies at both the

---

[1] Maxim Zhukov, "Ob otstavke obiavleno zaranee," [Resignation Is Announced in Advance] *Kommersant'-Daily*, July 25, 1996, p. 3.

[2] Tamara Morshchakova, "Voprosy vzaimodeistviia Konstitutsionnogo Suda Rossiiskoi Federatsii i sudov inykh vidov iurisdiktsii," [Questions of Interaction between the RF Constitutional Court and Courts of Other Jurisdictions] in Mikhail Mitiukov, Sergei Kabyshev, Vera Bobrova and Sergei Andreev, eds., *Problemy ispolneniia federalnymi organami gosudarstvennoi vlasti i organami gosudarstvennoi vlasti subektov Rossiiskoi Federatsii reshenii Konstitutsionnogo Suda Rossiiskoi Federatsii i konstitutsionnykh (ustavnykh) sudov subektov Rossiiskoi Federatsii* (Moskva: Formula prava, 2001), p. 58.

[3] Vladimir Ivanov, "Neuvazhaemyi Konstitutsionnyi sud," [Disrespected Constitutional Court] *Gazeta*, July 19, 2007, available at http://gzt.ru/wallet/2007/07/18/220222.html.

federal and the subnational levels. However, as I have shown in Chapter 5, the RCC became increasingly involved in the core of Russian politics under the first term of President Putin.

Before I discuss how and why the Court continued to face serious challenges in getting its judgments implemented, a caveat is in order. Recall from Chapter 5 that the 2nd Court has gone beyond the letter of the 1994 RCC Act by issuing various kinds of decisions. Several dozen of them do not annul a contested statute but, instead, contain a constitution-conforming interpretation of the statute. Hundreds of other decisions with so-called positive content formally reject petitions, but, at the same time, contain orders to government bodies or courts, including finding statutes unconstitutional. Tracking down these rulings and carrying them out would be a daunting task for the bureaucracy and the judiciary in any country.[4] Monitoring their implementation is also a challenge for the RCC, which remains the only court in the whole country to have a separate department staffed with four officers in charge of monitoring the enforcement of its judgments. This department monitors the publication of the RCC decisions and resolutions in official media, and prepares and circulates among justices semiannual reports outlining the implementation of the Court judgments, including the decisions "with positive content." Thus, tracking of implementation is concentrated in one place at the Court.[5]

A more difficult task is getting information as to whether and how government agencies comply with the RCC decisions. Compliance may involve passing a new law/decree/regulation to replace one annulled by the Court or reopening a case in regular or *arbitrazh* courts *and* following RCC guidelines. This "compliance" information comes to the Court from both private and public sources. Individuals who win constitutional litigation but fail to get government bodies to respect the RCC judgments, routinely complain to the Court, which issues "positive content" decisions to reinforce the binding force of its previous judgments. Government bodies, including the rest of the judiciary, inform the Court regarding the steps they take to carry out its decisions. However, the relationship between the Constitutional Court and other government agencies in the process of enforcing decisions of the tribunal is far from being

---

[4] In an effort to help litigants and other government agencies understand whether an RCC decision has this "positive content," the RCC began in 2007 marking its decisions with the letter O or P where P stands for "positive content."

[5] In 2000, President Vladimir Putin also charged his counsel to monitor the implementation of judgments of the Russian Constitutional Court.

institutionalized.[6] In summary, monitoring the implementation of RCC judgments is not easy for Russian voters, contrary to the "electoral punishment" thesis. As I explore at the end of this chapter, Russian citizens distrust the political parties far more than the judiciary, and, paradoxically, they approve of landmark RCC judgments, while disapproving of the work of the Court, in general. More important, the Court faces both the purposeful noncompliance of elected officials, bureaucrats, and judges, and lack of knowledge of the Court among the masses in the context of waning public support for the judicial system as a whole. Judgments, however, vary in the degree of their public visibility. The most visible decisions of the RCC may be those in the separation-of-powers cases, the implementation of which I discuss next.

ENFORCING THE SEPARATION OF POWERS

As I discussed in Chapter 5, the 2nd RCC was the most active in defining the legislative process at the federal level, expanding the law-making powers of the federal president, and protecting the independence of the judiciary. Defining the legislative process required judicial interference in the relationship among the State Duma, the Federation Council, and the president. This interference both set limits on the law-making prerogatives of each of the three actors, and it called for cooperation in "good faith." Overall, each legislative chamber and the president gradually learned to obey the RCC decisions. Initially, the anti-Yeltsin majority in the Duma refused to recognize the 1993 constitution and repeatedly criticized any formal guarantees of expanded presidential powers. Not surprisingly, Yeltsin's opponents viewed the reconstituted RCC with suspicion, even though they flooded the tribunal with challenges directed against Yeltsin's policies. At the same time, both legislative chambers use the Court-ordered quorum to pass legislation and respect most Court

---

[6] On the problematic nature of this relationship in cases of the constitutionality of social insurance taxes and small business fines, see Anatolii Pershutov, "Problemy vzaimodeistviia Federalnogo Sobraniia i Konstitutsionnogo Suda RF v protsesse zakonotvorchestva," [Problems of Interaction of the Federal Assembly and the RF Constitutional Court in the Legislative Process] *Pravo Sibiri*, nos. 1–2 (2001); and in cases of the constitutionality of compensations to victims of Stalin's purges, see Khiil Sheinin, "Problemy ispolneniia reshenii Konstitutsionnogo Suda Rossiiskoi Federatsii," [Problems of Enforcing the Decisions of the RF Constitutional Court] in Mitiukov et al., *Problemy ispolneniia . . .*, pp. 107–113.

decisions regarding law-making procedures.[7] Following the 1995 RCC decision on Article 136 of the Russian constitution, the political branches passed the 1998 Act on the constitutional amendment procedure, which copied, word-for-word, the Court's interpretation.[8] This judgment thus set the initial framework for constitutional reforms, something that both the anti-Yeltsin lobby in the federal parliament and the regional governors have been pushing for since the passage of the 1993 constitution.[9]

The Duma, however, repeatedly defied a Court-imposed ban on introducing fundamental changes to a bill in its second reading.[10] Most federal bills go through three readings: during the first reading the Duma votes on the concept of the bill; during the second one, the Duma votes on the amendments proposed by MPs and Duma committees; and during the third reading, the Duma votes on the final version of the bill that goes then to the Federation Council. The fact that the Duma introduced fundamental changes to various bills during the second reading of the legislative process is not a symptom of a postcommunist "mess." Instead, it clearly shows both the prevalence of the changing short-term needs of the ruling elites under Yeltsin and under Putin and the weakness of the Constitutional Court to impose any meaningful punishment on the politicians. Here, the Court could not exploit interinstitutional rivalries and draw on the support of the executive branch to compel the Duma to follow through because both the president and the federal Cabinet wanted to preserve the flexibility of the law-making process as much as the Duma did. They wanted this flexibility in order to advance their

---

[7] Until 2002, the Federation Council, the upper house of the Federal Assembly, consisted of regional governors and speakers of regional legislatures, who sometimes could not be present in Moscow, causing a delay in the federal legislative process. This delay is no longer a problem following Putin's reform of the way the Federation Council members get their seats: regional governors and legislatures appoint one full-time member each. See V. D. Karpovich, ed., *Kommentarii k Konstitutsii Rossiiskoi Federatsii* (Moskva: Iurait-M, 2002), pp. 772–773. For a summary of Putin's reform of the Federation Council, see, for example, Robert W. Orttung, "Key Issues in the Evolution of the Federal Okrugs and Center-Region Relations under Putin," in P. Reddaway and R. W. Orttung, eds., *The Dynamics of Russian Politics. Volume 1*, (Lanham, MD: Rowman and Littlefield, 2004), pp. 27–30.

[8] Federalnyi zakon "O poriadke priniatiia i vstupleniia v silu popravok k Konstitutsii Rossiiskoi Federatsii" of March 4, 1998, [Federal Law on the Procedure of Adopting and Entering into Force the Amendments to the RF Constitution] *SZ RF*, 1998, no. 10, item 1146.

[9] See Robert Sharlet, "Russia in the Middle: State Building and the Rule of Law," in Donald R. Kelley, ed., *After Communism: Perspectives on Democracy* (Fayetteville, AR: The University of Arkansas Press, 2003), pp. 143–159.

[10] Para. 7 of RCC decision 11-P of July 5, 2001, *VKS RF*, no. 6 (2001), pp. 28–41.

Enforcing the Separation of Powers

frequently changing power needs through legislative maneuvering in the Duma. And they did not want the courts to interfere with this ability. Moreover, the ability of the Duma to change the original concept of any bill during the law-making process is a potentially powerful weapon in the passage of federal constitutional statutes, which are not subject to the presidential veto. Ironically, the 2nd RCC repeatedly suffered from this maneuvering in the Duma when President Putin introduced his "tenure" and "implementation" amendments to the 1994 RCC Act, as I discussed in Chapter 3.

Both Russian presidents actively used their quasiveto and law-making prerogatives, all allowed by the RCC, and vetoed bills on the grounds of their noncompliance with RCC decisions.[11] Both Yeltsin, who faced strong opposition in both legislative chambers, and Putin, who dominated both the Duma and the Federation Council, had accepted the Court-ordered scheme of the separation of powers, which rests on the propresidential bias of constitutional rules.

Unlike their superiors, lower-ranking federal government officials initially ignored the RCC. Already by mid-1996, the federal bureaucracy's sabotage of RCC decisions led then Chairman Tumanov to exclaim: "Firing two or three officials from the executive branch for ignoring RCC decisions would greatly enhance the enforcement of laws in Russia."[12] As I discussed in Chapter 5, the Court repeatedly invoked the separation-of-powers arguments in reviewing fiscal policies and defended the exclusive authority of the legislature to set taxes. This was not easily done, however. By 1998, Russia had only twenty statutes on taxation as compared to 100 presidential decrees, 100 federal Cabinet directives, and more than 1,000 ministerial instructions in the fiscal area. Moreover, these instructions violated federal laws while the parliament lacked any meaningful oversight over this bureaucratic rule making.[13] Therefore, the federal executive clearly dominated fiscal policies and wanted to share this taxing power neither with the legislature nor with the Constitutional Court, particularly in the context of a chronic failure to collect taxes in the 1990s.

---

[11] See Mikhail Mitiukov, "Voprosy parlamentskogo prava v resheniiakh Konstitutsionnogo Suda Rossiiskoi Federatsii," [Issues of Parliamentary Law in Decisions of the RF Constitutional Court] in Mikhail Mitiukov and Aleksandr Barnashov, *Ocherki konstitutsionnogo pravosudiia* (Tomsk: Izd-vo Tomskogo universiteta, 1999), p. 263.

[12] Maxim Zhukov, "Ob otstavke obiavleno zaranee," [Resignation Is Announced in Advance] *Kommersant'-Daily*, July 25, 1996, p. 3.

[13] Sergei Pepeliaev, "Kommentarii," in Boris Ebzeev, ed., *Kommentarii k postanovleniiam Konstitutsionnogo Suda RF. T. 2* (Moskva: Iurist, 2000), p. 540.

212 The 2nd Russian Constitutional Court (1995–2007)

The Court attempted to break this actual supremacy of executive law making for the first time in February 1997. Here, the RCC struck down the federal Cabinet directive on license fees for the production and sale of alcoholic beverages as unconstitutional interference with legislative authority. Judges allowed this directive to stay in force for 6 months, until September 1997. The Cabinet, however, attempted to enact a "temporary" directive on the matter with the clear intent to keep charging alcohol license fees the old way. The Court objected informally, and the required legislation was passed in January 1998.[14] At the same time, the federal Cabinet persistently ignored another case involving its own directive establishing hydro fees to be paid by enterprises. After numerous reminders by the justices, the Cabinet sent the required documentation but its representative still failed to show up at the Court's session in March 1997. The Cabinet lost the case the following month, as outraged justices declared the Cabinet in contempt of the Court, while Prime Minister Chernomyrdin quietly reprimanded a couple of his subordinates.[15]

This lack of penalties for noncompliance also encouraged the federal government to defy RCC decisions when setting its spending priorities. Consider the dispute between the federal Cabinet and the judicial branch over the repeated underfinancing of courts, which culminated in a July 1998 RCC decision, as discussed in Chapter 5. When the Cabinet, headed by the liberal economist Sergei Kirienko, chose to cut the 1998 budget of the already underfunded federal judiciary by 26 percent, the chairs of the Russian Supreme Court and the Higher *Arbitrazh* Court petitioned the RCC to annul this cut. The RCC agreed with them and struck down the cuts to the court budget. The Constitutional Court unanimously ruled that neither the federal legislature nor the federal Cabinet could cut federal funding of the judicial branch, including the allowance of retired judges, without the consent of the judicial self-government bodies (the Russian Council of Judges and the All-Russian Congress of Judges).[16] Finance Minister Mikhail Zadornov, however, immediately tried to get around this verdict and asked the Russian Council of Judges to consent

---

[14] RCC decision 3-P of February 18, 1997, *VKS RF*, no. 1 (1997), pp. 43–53 (Morshchakova, dissenting), English translation in *Statutes and Decisions*, no. 1 (2000), p. 77. See Ger P. van den Berg, compiler, "Constitution of the Russian Federation Annotated with Summaries of Rulings and Other Decisions of Constitutional (Charter) Courts: 1990–2001," *Review of Central and East European Law*, vol. 27 (2001), p. 271, fn. 15.

[15] RCC decision 16-O of April 1, 1997, *VKS RF*, no. 4 (1997), pp. 18–19.

[16] RCC decision 23-P of July 17, 1998, *VKS RF*, no. 6 (1998), pp. 68–73, English translation in *Statutes and Decisions*, no. 5 (2000).

Enforcing the Separation of Powers

to the cuts. But the Council of Judges naturally refused, and, after hearing nothing positive from the Cabinet, asked the Procurator General to launch criminal proceedings against Zadornov. Procurator General Skuratov, for his part, confined himself to issuing a "toothless" letter to the prime minister about the need for better funding and more secure funding for the courts. Around the same time, the Duma officially asked President Yeltsin to oblige the Cabinet to pay the federal judges in full. In February 1999, the Russian parliament passed a law on court financing, which did not provide new money for the courts, but authorized judicial bodies to take the money directly from the government accounts without special authorization.[17] And only in 2001, President Putin promised and delivered a revolution in court financing – a 5-year program that called for annual new expenditures of seven to ten billion rubles (US$230 to US$330 million), totaling almost 44 billion rubles.[18]

To ensure that the president meets his funding commitments to the judiciary, the RCC, in early 2002, demanded a faster transfer of the power to approve pretrial detention from the Procuracy to courts.[19] Invoking Article 22-2 of the Russian constitution,[20] the RCC struck down provisions of the Criminal Procedure Code that authorized the Procuracy to detain the accused, and ordered the Russian parliament to transfer this power to the courts immediately. This bold move overcame the resistance of the law-enforcement agencies, who, in 2001, succeeded in delaying the transfer of this power until 2004.[21] In a nationwide survey, the majority (52 percent) of Russians supported this March 2002 judgment with 30 percent disapproving of it and 18 percent having no opinion on the matter.[22] Needless to say, this judgment required a significant increase in the

---

[17] See Peter H. Solomon, Jr. and Todd S. Foglesong, *Courts and Transition in Russia: The Challenge of Judicial Reform* (Boulder, CO: Westview Press, 2000), pp. 16–18.

[18] See Peter H. Solomon, Jr., "Putin's Judicial Reform: Making Judges Accountable as well as Independent," *East European Constitutional Review*, vol. 11, nos. 1–2 (2002), pp. 117–124.

[19] RCC decision 6-P of March 14, 2002, *VKS RF*, no. 3 (2002), pp. 51–56.

[20] Article 22-2 of the 1993 Russian constitution: "Arrest, taking into custody and holding in custody shall only be authorized by a judicial decision. Without a judicial decision no person may be subjected to detention for a period of more than 48 hours."

[21] For the analysis of judicial review of arrests in Russia in the 1990s, see Todd S. Foglesong, "*Habeas Corpus* or 'Who Has the Body?' Judicial Review of Arrests and Detention in Russia," *Wisconsin International Law Journal*, vol. 14 (1996), pp. 541–78; and Solomon and Foglesong, *Courts and Transition in Russia*, pp. 71–73.

[22] "Rossiianam nravitsia pravo ubivat radi samooborony," [Russians Like the Right to Kill for the Sake of Self-Defense] *Lenta.Ru*, April 4, 2002, available at http://lenta.ru/russia/2002/04/04/arrest.

spending on courts (hiring several hundred judges just to handle arrests, building jails at the courthouses, and so on). However, this decision was implemented in a matter of 2 months: President Putin sponsored the bill, the parliament quickly passed it according to the RCC guidelines, and Russian judges started to approve detention on July 1, 2002, eight-and-a-half years after the 1993 Russian constitution enshrined the monopoly of courts to detain.[23] Did this transfer of power to judges to approve detention make a difference in practice? Not much. Although the number of detentions slightly decreased (249,300 judge-ordered detentions in 2006), judges tend to approve 91 percent of arrests – as many as procurators used to do prior to the introduction of the Criminal Procedure Code.[24]

"War of Courts," Russian-Style

While the 2nd RCC fiercely defended judicial independence from the intrusions of the political branches at the federal level, the Court also frequently defined the separation of powers within the judicial system. As preceding chapters make clear, the relationship among the three high courts in Russia is far from amicable. Although disagreements between courts occur in any judicial system, I focus on the cases in which the domestic courts refused to obey Constitutional Court guidelines and objected to the jurisdiction of the Constitutional Court. Both the Russian Supreme Court and the Higher *Arbitrazh* Court have questioned the power of the RCC to order the reopening of cases. Consider the objections of the Higher *Arbitrazh* Court, a new court created and staffed in 1992 with civil law professors, judges, and lawyers that still refuses to rehear cases according to RCC guidelines. The Higher *Arbitrazh* Court judges resisted by arguing that reopening a case could reveal nothing new, and, therefore, their initial decision would not be changed.[25] They complained that their court was overloaded with appeals for review on the grounds

---

[23] Federalnyi Zakon "O vnesenii izmenenii i dopolnenii v Federalnyi Zakon 'O vvedenii v deistvie Ugolovno-protsessualnogo kodeksa Rossiiskoi Federatsii'" of May 29, 2002 [Federal Law on Amending the Law on the Introduction of the RF Criminal Procedure Code], *Rossiiskaia gazeta*, June 1, 2002.

[24] Official court statistics are available at the Web site of the Judicial Department of the Russian Supreme Court, available at http://www.cdep.ru. See also Peter H. Solomon, Jr., "The Criminal Procedure Code of 2001: Will It Make Russian Justice More Fair?" in William Pridemore, ed., *Ruling Russia: Law, Crime, and Justice in a Changing Society* (Lanham, MD: Rowman and Littlefield, 2005), pp. 77–98.

[25] "Spravka ob ispolnenii reshenii Konstitutsionnogo Suda Rossiiskoi Federatsii, priniatykh v oktiabre-dekabre 2001 goda," April 3, 2002, unpublished document.

Enforcing the Separation of Powers 215

of judicial error, a new remedy granted by a February 1998 RCC decision. If the review was not granted, the appellants would complain and petition to fire the *arbitrazh* judges.[26] In the spring of 2001, this Court openly proposed to forbid the RCC from reviewing the constitutionality of its decisions and objected to the exclusive power of the RCC to produce binding statutory interpretations.[27]

In return, the Russian Constitutional Court attempted to declare the binding force of the "guiding explanations" of the Higher *Arbitrazh* Court to be unconstitutional. These explanations, a legacy of the Soviet regime, contain statutory interpretations and direct lower courts in their adjudication. The 1995 Act on *Arbitrazh* Courts authorizes the Higher *Arbitrazh* Court to issue binding explanations, while ordinary courts obey the explanations of the Supreme Court as a matter of custom. In July 2002, the Constitutional Court attempted to strike down this provision of the 1995 *Arbitrazh* Courts Act. The RCC initially ruled that these explanations prevent judicial errors but lack the force of a precedent to predetermine judicial decisions in concrete cases. However, the published text of the RCC decision did not contain this declaration of unconstitutionality.[28] In short, unlike their Latvian colleagues, most RCC justices are not prepared to declare these guiding explanations as nonbinding on lower courts.[29] Indeed, it may be a wise move to preserve the domain of "judge-made" law, the proper boundaries of which remain a subject of debate among Russian jurists.

Consider how Russia's top courts fought over the power to review regional statutes as acts of less political importance (see Table 7.1 for the chronology of this saga). Initially, these courts even avoided scrutinizing the laws of the regions where powerful governors controlled the judiciary and the procuracy, while the federal political elites used these courts selectively to punish their opponents in the regions. In October 1995, the Supreme Court declared that ordinary courts had the power to

---

[26] Oleg Boikov, "Postanovleniia Konstitutsionnogo Suda Rossiiskoi Federatsii v deiatelnosti arbitrazhnykh sudov," [Decisions of the RF Constitutional Court in the Activity of the *Arbitrazh* Courts] in Mitiukov et al., *Problemy ispolneniia . . .*, pp. 50–55, at 51.

[27] *Ibid.*, p. 54.

[28] Compare para. 4 of the original version of RCC decision 200-O of July 4, 2002 (*Energomash* case), available online at http://www.businesspravo.ru/Docum/DocumShow_DocumID_29416.html, with para. 4 of the official text in *VKS RF*, no. 1 (2003), pp. 77–81.

[29] Latvian Constitutional Court decision 2002–06–01 of February 4, 2003, available on the court's Web site, at http://www.satv.tiesa.gov.lv/Eng/spriedumi/06–01(02).htm (in English).

TABLE 7.1. *The "War of Courts" in Russia: Constitutionality of regional laws,*
1995–2003

October 31, 1995	– The Supreme Court declares that where Article 120 of the Russian constitution states "judges shall be subject only to the Russian constitution and federal law" it means that courts have the *right* to set aside regional laws deemed unconstitutional, to apply the constitution directly, and to refer such cases to the Constitutional Court.
June 16, 1998	– The RCC disallows the power of regular courts to invalidate regional laws and *requires* them to refer such cases to the Constitutional Court.
August 4, 1998	– The Supreme Court rules that Constitutional Court decisions are not binding on regular courts.
November 5, 1998	– The RCC allows regular courts to strike down regional laws analogous to those found unconstitutional.
February 10, 1999	– The Supreme Court denies the Procuracy the right to contest regional laws in the regular courts and sponsors a bill empowering the regular courts to strike down regional laws.
March 4, 1999	– The RCC refuses to reverse its position at the request of the Procurator-General and insists on the binding force of its judgments on all Russian courts.
November 24, 1999	– The State Duma adopts a bill empowering the regular courts to strike down regional laws.
December 22, 1999	– The Federation Council vetoes the bill on empowering the regular courts to strike down regional laws.
April 2, 2000	– The Higher *Arbitrazh* Court introduces a bill on the power of *arbitrazh* courts to strike down regional laws.
April 10, 2000	– The RCC allows regular courts to annul regional laws *except* regional constitutions/charters. Regions may protest against such annulment in the Constitutional Court.
May 25, 2000	– The Supreme Court orders regular courts to strike down all regional laws including regional constitutions/charters.
September 19, 2000	– The Supreme Court introduces a bill giving administrative courts the power to strike down regional laws.
November 22, 2000	– The Russian parliament passes a bill (first reading) granting the administrative courts the power to strike down regional laws.
February–April 2001	– In a number of decisions, the RCC protests against the power of regular courts to annul regional constitutions/charters.
July 18, 2003	– The RCC disallows challenges to regional constitutions/charters in the regular courts.
September 18, 2003	– The Higher *Arbitrazh* Court withdraws the bill on the power of *arbitrazh* courts to strike down regional laws.

Enforcing the Separation of Powers

set aside regional laws deemed to violate the 1993 constitution.[30] The Supreme Court treated regional constitutions/charters the same as ordinary regional laws, which could be reviewed to determine their compliance with federal law. The regular courts had gradually increased their role in harmonizing regional laws: in 1996, they struck down 1,203 regional legal acts, in 1997, 1,654 acts, and in 1998, 2,016 acts.[31] In June 1998, the RCC prohibited regular courts from invalidating regional laws and ordered them to ask the RCC to check the constitutionality of these acts.[32] In November 1998, however, the RCC allowed regular courts to strike down regional laws analogous to those found unconstitutional, thus relinquishing its monopoly over the exercise of constitutional review.[33] It should be noted that the RCC made this move away from a rigid, centralized judicial review system well before comparative constitutional scholars recommended a less centralized judicial review system.[34] However, the regular courts, starting with the federal Supreme Court, initially refused to use this power and enraged the RCC justices.[35] Instead, the Supreme Court unwillingly ordered the lower courts to stop reviewing regional laws and engaged in a sophisticated campaign to get back judicial review power through lobbying the presidential administration and sponsoring a federal bill on administrative courts.

---

[30] See William Burnham and Alexei Trochev, "Russia's War between the Courts: The Struggle over the Jurisdictional Boundary between the Constitutional Court and Regular Courts," *American Journal of Comparative Law*, vol. 55, no. 3 (Summer 2007), pp. 408–412, and two articles by Peter Krug, "Departure from the Centralized Model: The Russian Supreme Court and Constitutional Control of Legislation," *Virginia Journal of International Law*, vol. 37, no. 3 (1997), pp. 725–87 and "The Russian Federation Supreme Court and Constitutional Practice in the Courts of General Jurisdiction: Recent Developments," *Review of Central and East European Law*, vol. 26, no. 2 (February 2000), pp. 129–146.

[31] These figures include regional laws and edicts of regional executive and legislative bodies. Svetlana Sukhova, "Zakonnyi disput," [Legal Dispute] *Segodnia*, February 16, 2000, p. 2.

[32] RCC decision 19-P of June 16, 1998, *VKS RF*, no. 5 (1998), pp. 51–66 (Gadzhiev and Vitruk, dissenting), English translation in *Statutes and Decisions*, no. 5 (2000). The Spanish Constitutional Tribunal holds a similar view on the duty of ordinary judges to refer statutes for constitutional review. See its decisions 23/1988, 158/1993, 18/2003.

[33] RCC decision 147-O of November 5, 1998, *VKS RF*, no. 1 (1999), pp. 35–40.

[34] For instance, Victor Ferreres Comella argues that "ordinary judges should also be authorized to actually set aside a statute when the constitutional precedents set by the 'constitutional' court make it relatively clear that this statute is invalid." See his "The European Model of Constitutional Review of Legislation: Toward Decentralization?" *I-CON: International Journal of Constitutional Law*, vol. 2, no. 3 (2004), pp. 461–491, the quote is on p. 474.

[35] RCC decision 19-O of March 4, 1999, *SZ RF*, no. 15 (1999), item 1928, English translation in *Statutes and Decisions*, no. 6 (2001).

218   *The 2nd Russian Constitutional Court (1995–2007)*

On April 10, 2000, at the start of President Putin's campaign to harmonize regional laws with federal ones, the RCC allowed regular courts to check the constitutionality of regional legislation, partially reversing its own decision of June 1998.[36] The Constitutional Court cautioned that this new power of regular courts was not final[37] and did not extend to the republics' constitutions and regional charters. But the Procuracy and the regular courts actively used this power to uphold the supremacy of federal law especially vis-à-vis regional statutes analogous to those already found unconstitutional by the RCC. Between August 2000 and June 2001, the regular courts invalidated about 4,000 pieces of regional legislation.[38] Still, the regular courts continued to hear procuratorial challenges to regional laws and local government enactments, although at a slower pace, well into 2003.

As I have shown elsewhere, the regional clones of the RCC (i.e., the constitutional/charter courts) in fifteen Russian regions fell victim to this "harmonization of laws" campaign.[39] From 2000 to 2003, the federal courts in all regions struck down constitutional/charter court acts that granted constitutional review powers beyond federal authorization. Article 27 of the 1996 Federal Act on the Russian judicial system allows regions to have constitutional/charter courts reviewing regional laws and municipal by-laws, and interpreting regional constitutions/charters. Initially, the RCC interpreted this list of powers as exhaustive, and ruled that only the federal legislature could expand it.[40] The federal Supreme Court applauded this approach because the narrow powers of the regional constitutional/charter courts would not interfere with the jurisdiction of the soon-to-be introduced federal administrative courts. In 2000, the Supreme Court introduced a bill on administrative courts, authorizing them to hear individual complaints against violations of regional charters and

---

[36] Gennadii Zhilin, "Problemy povysheniia effektivnosti konstitutsionnogo sudoproizvodstva v Rossiiskoi Federatsii," [Problems of Raising the Effectiveness of the Constitutional Justice in the Russian Federation] *Konstitutsionnoe pravosudie*, no. 4 (2000), pp. 14–22.

[37] Regional authorities could ask the RCC to confirm the constitutionality of regional laws invalidated by regular courts. See RCC decision 6-P of April 10, 2000, *VKS RF*, no. 4 (2000), pp. 15–29 (Zhilin, dissenting).

[38] Ekaterina Grigoreva, "Piat tysiach nesootvetstvii," [Five Thousand Irregularities] *Izvestiia*, June 30, 2001, p. 2.

[39] Alexei Trochev, "Less Democracy, More Courts: The Puzzle of Judicial Review in Russia," *Law and Society Review*, vol. 38, no. 3 (September 2004), p. 538.

[40] Para. 5 of RCC decision 14-P of October 16, 1997, *VKS RF*, no. 5 (1997), pp. 57–64, English translation in *Statutes and Decisions*, no. 2 (2000), p. 38.

constitutions, a measure that would drastically narrow the jurisdiction of regional courts.[41] Although the Supreme Court judges promised that the new administrative courts would not encroach upon the jurisdiction of the regional constitutional judiciary,[42] the regional judges still opposed the idea of sharing their already narrow jurisdiction with one more judicial branch.[43] The RCC, in turn, reversed its position on the powers of the regional constitutional/charter courts. In March 2003, the Bashkortostan and Tatarstan legislatures succeeded in a case against the Russian Supreme Court and the Procuracy over the powers of the regions to expand the competence of their courts beyond federal regulations. In this case, the RCC ruled that the regions could expand the powers of their constitutional/charter courts to matters not authorized in the 1996 Federal Act on the judicial system as long as the additional powers do not encroach upon the jurisdiction of the federal judiciary.[44] Moreover, in July 2003, the RCC disallowed challenges to regional constitutions/charters in the regular courts and empowered the Procurator General to challenge these regional acts only in the federal Constitutional Court.[45] The regional governments, victims of the "harmonization of laws" campaign, can now appeal Russian Supreme Court decisions to the Russian Constitutional Court, straining the relations between these courts even more.[46]

These struggles between the high courts over the division of labor indicate the intense interinstitutional competition for the power of judicial

---

[41] Gosudarstvennaia Duma FS RF, "Postanovlenie no. 824-III GD 'O federalnykh admnistrativnykh sudakh v Rossiiskoi Federatsii,'" [On Federal Administrative Courts in the Russian Federation] November 22, 2000 (published in the legal database "SPS Konsultant Plius: Zakonoproekty").

[42] Vladimir Radchenko, "Kompetentsiia administrativnykh sudov nam poniatna," [We Understand the Jurisdiction of the Administrative Courts] *Rossiiskaia iustitsiia*, no. 6 (2001), pp. 9–11.

[43] Valerii Rudnev, "Administrativnye sudy: byt ili ne byt?" [Administrative Courts: To be or not to be?] *Rossiiskaia iustitsiia*, no. 9 (2002), p. 20; Abdullakh Geliakhov, "Pozitsii Konstitutsionnogo Suda Kabardino–Balkarskoi Respubliki po sovershenstvovaniiu zakonodatelstva v sfere konstitutsionnoi iustitsii," [Positions of the Constitutional Court of Kabardion–Balkaria Republic on the Improvement of Laws in the Spere of the Constitutional Justice] in Mitiukov et al., *Problemy ispolneniia . . .*, pp. 211–217.

[44] RCC decision 103-O of March 6, 2003, *VKS RF*, no. 4 (2003), pp. 81–85.

[45] RCC decision 13-P of July 18, 2003, *VKS RF*, no. 5 (2003), pp. 15–29, English translation in *Statutes and Decisions*, no. 2 (2005). For a review of this case in English, see Igor Rabinovich, "Bashkortostan, Tatarstan Weaken Putin's Reforms," *Russian Regional Report*, vol. 8, no. 13, July 23, 2003.

[46] Iurii Kolesov, "Tretia vlast na troikh," [Third Power for the Three] *Vremia Novostei*, November 5, 2003.

review. The Russian Supreme Court defended its position by drawing on the U.S. model of decentralized judicial review, in which the lower courts can strike down statutes violating the federal constitution.[47] The Russian Constitutional Court and its regional "clones" espoused the German centralized model with a single court in charge of constitutional review. Note that these struggles would not arise if the ordinary judges were "conservative, career bureaucrats" unwilling to overrule the legislature. In summary, the 2nd RCC fared much better than its predecessor in addressing heavyweight political controversies. This Court survived both the serious legislative–executive clashes of the Yeltsin era and the much-improved relations between President Putin and the Russian parliament. More importantly, both political branches have tended to accept the Court-ordered rules of the political process, and, under Putin's first term in office, a weak parliamentary opposition routinely asked the Court to review the constitutionality of his governance reforms. This acceptance of the Court clearly shows that it has earned the reputation of an authoritative arbiter of public policy even if this leads to more dialogue between political actors and the Court. However, the federal government bureaucracy still has few incentives to obey RCC orders and far more incentives to follow the instructions of the government bosses. Similarly, the Russian judiciary continuously blocks the implementation of RCC decisions. Taken together with unfinished "wars of courts" in Romania and the Czech Republic, discussed in Chapter 8, the experience of constitutional courts clearly demonstrates that these young tribunals have to fight for their judicial review power against the rest of the judiciary.[48] This is true in both politically salient cases as well as individual rights litigation, which I will explore in detail after assessing the successes and failures in carrying out RCC judgments in federalism disputes.

[47] See, for example, Determination of the Russian Supreme Court No. 53-G01–9 of August 17, 2001, unpublished, available at the Web site of the Russian Supreme Court at http://www.vsrf.ru/vs_docs.php (declaring the provision of the federal law on the immunity of the regional legislators as violating the constitution); and Ruling of the Presidium of the Tiumen Regional Court of November 15, 2002, *Biulleten Verkhovnogo Suda RF*, no. 4 (2003) (declaring the provision of the Russian Family Code as unconstitutional).

[48] Tom Ginsburg, *Judicial Review in New Democracies: Constitutional Courts in Asian Cases* (New York: Cambridge University Press, 2003), p. 256; Renate Webber, "The Romanian Constitutional Court: In Search of Its Own Identity," in Wojciech Sadurski, ed., *Constitutional Justice, East and West* (The Hague: Kluwer Law International, 2002), pp. 283–308; and Radoslav Procházka, *Mission Accomplished: On Founding Constitutional Adjudication in Central Europe* (Budapest: Central European University Press, 2002), pp. 159–167.

POLICING RUSSIAN FEDERALISM

As I have discussed in Chapter 5, the 2nd RCC dealt with a variety of federal–regional, interregional, and intraregional disputes over government structure and elections; appointments in the judicial and the executive branches; fiscal revenues and local self-government. This Court gradually chose to spearhead a symmetrical federation with strong federal supremacy. According to my analysis, between 1995 and 1999, the Court was disappointed by the inconsistency and hesitancy of the federal center to enforce federal supremacy, and by extension, the decisions of the RCC. In that period, the Court rarely delved into key questions facing any federation: the nature of regional autonomy and the boundaries of a constitutionally allowed asymmetrical federalism. Justices chose to be shy in that period because they faced accusations of having a "pro–central government" bias from the autonomy-minded regions, because they did not know how the federal authorities would react to their judgments, and because they hesitated to question the core federalism policies of President Yeltsin. Thus, after approving the use of federal troops to quell secessionist attempts by Chechnya in 1995, then RCC Chairman Vladimir Tumanov admitted, "no serious changes occurred in Chechnya after our judgment."[49] Yet the Constitutional Court repeatedly refused to deal with this hotly contested issue, even though Prime Minister Viktor Chernomyrdin publicly admitted "mistakes" in handling the crisis in Chechnya and Yeltsin's envoy General Alexandr Lebed signed peace accords with Chechnya.[50]

The federal center, as expected, responded differently to the Court decisions, upholding some and ignoring others. As an example of "successful" compliance, consider the aftermath of the January 1997 judgment in the *Udmurtia* case, which struck down the abolition of local self-government in the republic.[51] This 12–2 judgment, authored by Justice Zorkin, was issued at the request of Yeltsin, Duma members, and several individuals,

---

[49] Maksim Zhukov, "Vladimir Tumanov: 'Nyneshnee izbiratelnoe zakonodatelstvo ne adaptirovano k rossiiskim usloviiam,'" [Valdimir Tumanov: Current Elections Laws Are not Adapted to Russian Conditions] *Kommersant'-Daily*, October 20, 1995, p. 3.

[50] See, for example, Maksim Zhukov, "'Mladenets iz probirki' stal polnopravnym chlenom semi," [Baby from the Test-Tube Became a Full-Fledged Member of the Family] *Kommersant'-Daily*, December 27, 1995, p. 3 and Oleg Zhirnov, "Konstitutsionnyi sud predlagaet zabyt Konstitutsiiu?" [Constitutional Court Proposes to Forget the Constitution?] *Moskovskaia pravda*, September 17, 1996, p. 1.

[51] RCC decision 1-P of January 24, 1997, *VKS RF*, no. 1 (1997), pp. 2–24 (Gadzhiev and Vitruk, dissenting), English translation in *Statutes and Decisions*, no. 1 (2000), p. 51.

who took the side of the mayor of Udmurtia's capital city Izhevsk in his fight against the regional legislature. The Court struck down parts of the contested Udmurtia statute but, out of respect for the regional prerogative, did not specify how to restore the elected municipal bodies. In the wake of the verdict, both sides claimed victory, and the regional legislature moved slowly to obey the Court. After repeated complaints from the justices, Yeltsin swiftly ordered Udmurtia Republic to obey this RCC judgment and warned that he would impeach the Udmurtia leaders if they failed to heed the Court's decision and restore the elected local self-government bodies.[52] As a result of this showdown, which the dissenting Justice Vitruk labeled as a "public whipping of the Udmurtia authorities," the region quickly began to amend its laws to restore local self-government in March 1997, according to the presidential directives but not the RCC guidelines. Although Boris Yeltsin approved of Udmurtia's compliance a few months later, the Udmurtia Supreme Court struck down the same contested law as a whole in January 1998, and the Russian Supreme Court confirmed this in September 1998.[53] By 2002, however, local self-government in Udmurtia still remained in an embryonic stage.[54]

What the "implementation" game in this case clearly shows is that both the will and the capacity of the federal center to compel the recalcitrant regions to obey judicial decisions were present. But it also shows that the judicial decisions by themselves did not matter much. They acquired real binding force only after President Yeltsin issued a decree and closely monitored their implementation. As then RCC Chairman Marat Baglai exclaimed in June 1998, the Russian president was "the only trump card" his Court had in implementing its judgments.[55] Moreover, once the federal executive took the matter in its hands, it imposed its own vision of how to carry out the judgment of the Constitutional Court. In other words, it was Yeltsin and his advisers, instead of the Court, who framed the issue and provided solutions. Not surprisingly, following this showdown, the RCC learned to provide clearer guidance on how to comply

---

[52] Decree No. 193 of March 10, 1997, *SZ RF*, no. 10 (1997), item 1130.

[53] Nikolai Vitruk, *Konstitutsionnoe pravosudie v Rossii (1991–2001 gg.)* [Constitutional Justice in Russia (1991–2001)] (Moskva: Gorodets-izdat, 2001), pp. 480–487.

[54] Timur Molotov, "Poslednii oplot," [Final Stronghold] *Udmurtskaia pravda*, January 24, 2002, p. 3.

[55] Mikhail Mitiukov, "Konstitutsionnye sudy postsovetskikh gosudarstv: problemy ispolneniia reshenii," [Constitutional Courts in Post-Soviet States: Problems of Implementation of Decisions] in *Ispolnenie reshenii konstitutsionnykh sudov: sbornik dokladov* [Implementation of Constitutional Court Decisions: Collection of Reports] (Moskva: IPPP, 2003), p. 218.

Policing Russian Federalism 223

with its decisions, so that both winners and losers follow the vision of the Court and not their own ideas on how to carryout the Court's rulings.[56] The regions that had their statutes invalidated, in an effort to delay implementation of the RCC orders, still complained that these orders were not specific enough and demanded that the Court "clarify" them.[57]

As an example of a less successful (for the RCC) implementation game, consider the federal–regional struggles over judicial appointments.[58] Recall from Chapter 4 that the 1st RCC, in the *Kabardino-Balkaria judges* decision, already dealt a serious blow to the participation of regions in appointing federal judges. That decision was issued in 1993 and struck down fifteen clauses of the republic's statute on the status of judges that, among other things, were contrary to the federal requirement of life tenure for all judges and authorized the reappointment of all the judges in the region to 5-year terms subject to compulsory retirement at age sixty. The Zorkin Court held this to be unconstitutional and ruled that judicial appointment procedures belonged to an exclusive federal jurisdiction.[59] It took 4 years for Kabardino–Balkaria to implement this ruling by adopting a new constitution in September 1997.[60] Meanwhile, other regional

---

[56] See, for example, RCC decision 3-P of January 15, 1998, *VKS RF*, no. 2 (1998), pp. 28–43, English translation in *Statutes and Decisions*, no. 3 (2000), in which the Court struck down the local government reforms in the Komi Republic. Here, the Court issued detailed instructions to the regional legislature, local government bodies, and federal courts on how to carry out its judgment. The Komi governor, however, defied the ruling by arguing that these local government reforms were constitutional under the bilateral treaty between Russia and the Komi Republic. See van den Berg, "Constitution of the Russian Federation Annotated," p. 301.

[57] See, for example, Larisa Chetverikova, "Resheniia Konstitutsionnogo Suda Rossiiskoi Federatsii: kak ikh ispolniat?" [Decisions of the RF Constitutional Court: How to Carry Them Out?] *Zakonodatelnye (predstavitelnye) organy vlasti subektov RF. Praktika, mneniia, problemy*, no. 1 (1999), pp. 49–52. See also Boris Ebzeev, ed., *Kommentarii k postanovleniiam Konstitutsionnogo Suda RF. T. 1* (Moskva: Iurist, 2000), p. 500.

[58] On the politics of judicial recruitment in Russia, see Solomon and Foglesong, *Courts and Transition in Russia*, pp. 92–110; Todd Foglesong, "The Dynamics of Judicial (In) Dependence in Russia," in Peter H. Russell and David O'Brien, eds., *Judicial Independence in the Age of Democracy: Critical Perspectives from around the World* (Charlottesville, VA: University Press of Virginia, 2001), pp. 62–88; and Alexei Trochev, "Judicial Selection in Russia: Towards Accountability and Centralization," in Peter H. Russell and Kate Malleson, eds., *Appointing Judges in an Age of Judicial Power: Critical Perspectives from around the World* (Toronto: University of Toronto Press, 2005), pp. 375–394.

[59] RCC decision 18-P of September 30, 1993, *VKS RF*, no. 6 (1994), pp. 29–39.

[60] Vladimir Kriazhkov, "Kommentarii," in Boris Ebzeev, ed., *Kommentarii k postanovleniiam Konstitutsionnogo Suda RF. T. 1* (Moskva: Iurist, 2000), p. 511.

The 2nd Russian Constitutional Court (1995–2007)

and even local governments attempted to appoint judges to regular and *arbitrazh* courts and passed legislation restructuring their judiciaries, contrary to this RCC decision and Article 71 of the federal constitution.[61] Facing regional resistance, Yeltsin tolerated a great deal of regional involvement in recruiting federal judges. But, as I discussed in Chapter 5, between 1996 and 2000, the RCC consistently narrowed the role of the regions in selecting federal judges to the simple notification of the federal authorities about particular judicial nominees.[62] In the Constitutional Court's view, the opinion of the region about a judicial applicant binds neither the Supreme Court chairman in nominating her nor the president in appointing her.[63] Needless to say, the Russian Supreme Court joined the efforts of the RCC to root out a regional veto over judicial appointments. Thus, between 1998 and 2000, the Russian Supreme Court invalidated several hundred cases appealed to it from courts in Bashkortostan and Tatarstan on the grounds that some of their judges had been appointed illegally, that is, those judges had begun their work without waiting for presidential approval.[64] But President Yeltsin responded to these regional encroachments through diplomacy rather than with harsh measures against recalcitrant regions. For example, even after the Russian Supreme Court declared illegal the attempts of Ingushetia's governor to hold a

---

[61] Igor Naidenov, "Sudiam daiut srok," [Judges Are Given Term] *Obshchaia gazeta*, November 30, 2000, p. 1. According to the Russian Ministry of Justice, at least seven regions (North Ossetia, Voronezh, Samara, Arkhangelsk, Irkutsk, Tiumen, and Omsk) passed such legislation. Kathryn Stoner-Weiss, *Resisting the State: Reform and Retrenchment in Post-Soviet Russia* (New York: Cambridge University Press, 2006), p. 57.

[62] Unpublished RCC decisions: 20-O of April 1, 1996; 1-O of January 23, 1997; 32-O of April 19, 1996, available at http://www.ksrf.ru. See also RCC decisions: 3-P of February 1, 1996, *VKS RF*, no. 1 (1996), pp. 34–47 (Vitruk, dissenting), English translation in *Statutes and Decisions*, no. 3 (1999), p. 53; 32-O of March 12, 1998, *ibid.*, no. 3 (1998), p. 66–70, English translation in *Statutes and Decisions*, no. 2 (1999); 10-P of June 7, 2000, *ibid.*, no. 5 (2000), pp. 2–45 (Luchin and Vitruk, dissenting); 91-O of June 8, 2000, *ibid.*, no. 5 (2000), pp. 53–58; and 92-O of June 27, 2000, *ibid.*, no. 5 (2000), pp. 59–80; and no. 6 (2000), pp. 10–12 (Luchin, dissenting).

[63] RCC decisions: 20-O of April 1, 1996; 32-O of April 19, 1996; and 1-O of January 23, 1997 (all unpublished); 217-O of October 27, 2000, *VKS RF*, no. 2 (2001), pp. 8–10; 252-O of December 21, 2000, *ibid.*, no. 2 (2001), pp. 62–65.

[64] "Nepravilnye sudi Tatarstana," *Novosti Instituta Prav Cheloveka*, September 22–October 4, 2000, available at http://www.hrights.ru/hrights/archnews/archnews22_09_4_10_2000.htm; Midkhat Kurmanov, "Judicial System in Russia: A Perspective from Tatarstan," in Thomas Fleiner and Rafael Khakimov, eds., *Federalism: Russian and Swiss Perspectives* (Kazan: Kazan Institute of Federalism, 2001), pp. 66–67; and Alexei Trochev and Peter H. Solomon, Jr., "Courts and Federalism in Putin's Russia," in Peter Reddaway and Robert W. Orttung, eds., *The Dynamics of Russian Politics. Volume 2* (Lanham, MD: Rowman and Littlefield, 2005), pp. 91–121.

March 1998 referendum on the establishment of a regional court system, President Yeltsin appointed a conciliatory commission to allow Ingushetia a greater say in judicial recruitment.[65] President Putin, however, chose to listen to the judges instead of the governors. He agreed that regional consent in selecting the federal judges was redundant, time-consuming, and harmful for his appointment powers. In late 2001, Putin succeeded in removing regional consent in judicial selection over vocal opposition from several regions.[66] In December 2003, the RCC upheld the exclusive authority of the federal center to regulate judicial recruitment.[67]

Still, even under Putin, some regions found ways to defy RCC rulings or to delay their implementation. Consider what happened in June 2000 after the RCC struck down the "sovereignty" clauses of seven regional constitutions.[68] On the one hand, Tyva and Kalmykia, the regions that were not named in the cases before the RCC, quickly announced that they had amended their constitutions to follow the Court's decision.[69] On the other hand, the affected regions openly ignored these rulings, and one of them (Bashkortostan) even refused to publish the rulings because – it was alleged – they would spoil the fall 2000 celebration of the 10-year anniversary of their "sovereign" status within Russia.[70] This open non-compliance enraged the RCC judges, yet they managed to confirm their stance only in April 2001, when Putin's administration petitioned them to "clarify" their June 2000 ruling. Facing pressures from the Kremlin to streamline regional laws, and facing regional defiance of federal policies in Tatarstan and Bashkortostan, Putin's team asked the Court to find

[65] Sergei Shakhrai, Speech at the meeting of the Political Consulting Council. Moscow, February 20, 1998. *Materialy zasedaniia Politicheskogo konsultativnogo soveta 20.02.1998 g.* (Moskva: PKS, 1998), p. 26. For the text of the Russian Supreme Court decision of February 17, 1998, see *Bulleten Verkhovnogo Suda RF*, no. 6 (1998), pp. 1–2, English translation in *Statutes and Decisions*, no. 4 (1999), pp. 21–25.

[66] See Kurmanov, "Judicial System in Russia: A Perspective from Tatarstan," p. 66 and "Podgotovleny izmeneniia v zakon o statuse sudei RF," *IA Finmarket*, December 20, 2000, available at http://www.infoport.ru/main_popup.php?ID=233075.

[67] RCC decision 428-O of December 4, 2003, *VKS RF*, no. 3 (2004), pp. 20–23.

[68] RCC decisions: 10-P of June 7, 2000 (Altai Republic), *SZ RF*, no. 25 (2000), item 2728 (Luchin and Vitruk, dissenting); 92-O of June 27, 2000 (Adygei, Bashkortostan, Ingushetia, Komi, North Ossetia, and Tatarstan Republics), *ibid.*, no. 29 (2000), item 3117 (Luchin, dissenting).

[69] Both regions have entrenched sultanistic political regimes. Jeffrey Kahn, *Federalism, Democratization, and the Rule of Law in Russia* (New York: Oxford University Press, 2002), p. 251.

[70] See Trochev, "Implementing Constitutional Court Decisions," p. 96 and Igor Rabinovich, "Bashkortostan Ignores Court Ruling," *EastWest Institute Russian Regional Report*, vol. 5, no. 36 (2000), October 4.

a way to carry out its decisions and punish the regional leaders who refused to obey them. The justices reacted unusually promptly: it took them 1 week to issue an official clarification.[71] The Court stated that the regional heads were obliged to change their unconstitutional statutes according to the orders of the Court. Failure to comply could result in an official warning from the Russian president, the first step in the procedure for the removal of regional governors or the dissolution of regional legislatures. Such a quick reply by the Court showed a nearly unanimous bench prepared to use the opportunity provided by Putin's support of the Court to assert the finality and binding force of its decisions and to affirm the supremacy of the federal constitution over regional statutes.[72] According to one poll, the majority of Russians (59 percent) supported this latter judgment, although many, including dissenter Justice Vitruk, criticized its "unworkability."[73]

Regional leaders criticized this clarification and engaged in various tactics to delay its implementation.[74] For example, the Adygei Republic continued to uphold its 1991 Declaration of Sovereignty well into 2004.[75] In addition to the informal bargaining with the federal center, political elites in Bashkortostan, Dagestan, and Tatarstan repeatedly asked their own constitutional courts to reaffirm republican sovereignty.[76] These three courts walked a fine line between defending the sovereignty

[71] RCC decision 65-O of April 19, 2001, *Rossiiskaia gazeta*, May 16, 2001, p. 10.

[72] Trochev, "Implementing Constitutional Court Decisions," pp. 97–98.

[73] 36 percent of those surveyed disagreed with the RCC. See "59% oproshennykh ABN polozhitelno otsenivaiut pravo prezidenta otstraniat gubernatorov ot dolzhnosti," [59 percent of People Polled by the ABN Assess Positively the Right of the President to Remove Governors from Office] *Agentstvo Biznes-Novostei*, April 11, 2002.

[74] On Tatarstan reaction, see Lev Ovrutskii, "Zvuki pu," [Sounds Poo] *Moskovskii komsomolets v Tatarstane*, no. 21, May 24–31, 2001, available at http://www.mkt.ru/article/179/1.html; Shamil Idiatullin, "Prezident ne dast v obidu Gossovet i 'Bolshoi Dogovor,'" [President Will Stand up for the State Council and the Big Treaty] *Tatarskie kraia*, no. 22 (June 2001), available at http://www.tatinfo.ru/news/TK/22tk.html; on Bashkortostan, see Natalia Pavlova, "Bashkortostan ne mozhet vypolnit rasporiazhenie Konstitutsionnogo suda RF," [Bashkortostan Cannot Carry out the Order of the RF Constitutional Court] *Strana.Ru*, July 19, 2001, available at http://www.strana.ru/text/topics/153/01/07/19/51701.html.

[75] Vasilii Salnikov and Svetlana Turialai, "Adygeiskii suverenitet voshel v istoriiu," [Adygei Sovereignty Entered History] *Kommersant'-Iug*, November 29, 2004.

[76] Bashkortostan Constitutional Court decisions: 14-P of October 4, 2000, and 17-P of December 28, 2001. For their summaries in English, see van den Berg, "Constitution of the Russian Federation Annotated," pp. 494–497. Dagestan Constitutional Court decision of October 3, 2000, *Digest 'Akty konstitutsionnogo pravosudiia subektov Rossiiskoi Federatsii,'* no. 10 (2000), p. 44. Tatarstan Constitutional Court decisions: 10-O and 11-O both of November 28, 2001 and 8-P of February 7, 2003, *Respublika Tatarstan*, February 14, 2003.

of their republics and rejecting the "proindependence" clauses of their constitutions. Although these courts offered their own vision of republican sovereignty, the RCC did little to quarrel with its regional clones and approved of their "aspiration to follow the spirit of the Russian constitution."[77] Facing continuous pressure from the federal authorities, Dagestan deleted "sovereignty" provisions from its constitution in July 2003.[78] Bashkortostan did the same in December 2002, after its governor, Rakhimov, failed to punish the Bashkortostan Supreme Court, which annulled thirty-three provisions of the republican constitution.[79] Prior to this deletion of sovereignty provisions, both the Bashkortostan legislature and the governor petitioned the RCC in vain to allow for some regional sovereignty.[80] And, as I discussed in the previous chapter, Tatarstan's Supreme Court still refused to invalidate the republic's 1990 Declaration of Sovereignty in June 2004, even after striking down the sovereignty clauses in the Tatarstan constitution a few months earlier.[81] In summary, persistent regions still could find their way around the "implementation" amendments to the 1994 RCC Act, which gave the regions 6 months to "correct" laws that the Court found unconstitutional.

In short, unlike the 1st RCC, with its uncertain legitimacy in the eyes of autonomy-minded regions, its successor managed to earn support from these same regions by the end of 2003. If, in 1996, they simply boycotted RCC sessions and accused the Court of being "hostage to political questions,"[82] by 2003, the regions continued to petition the Court, although one of the most ardent supporters of regional autonomy, Justice Nikolai Vitruk, retired from the bench in March 2003.[83] The shifting short-term power needs of the regional elites explain this paradoxical

---

[77] Igor Rabinovich and Sergei Fufaev, "Respublika Bashkortostan," *Konstitutsionnoe pravo: vostochnoevropeiskoe obozrenie*, no. 4–1 (2000–2001), p. 198.

[78] The text of the new Dagestan constitution was published in *Dagestanskaia pravda*, July 26, 2003.

[79] On Bashkortostan, see Trochev and Solomon, "Courts and Federalism in Putin's Russia." Governor Rakhimov eventually succeeded when the federal center did not reappoint Marat Vakilov, the chief justice of the Bashkortostan Supreme Court, in 2007.

[80] RCC decisions: 249-O of December 6, 2001, *SZ RF*, no. 4 (2002), item 374; and 250-O of December 6, 2001, unpublished, available at http://www.ksrf.ru.

[81] Irina Smirnova, "Tataria lishilas suvereniteta," [Tataria Lost Sovereignty] *Kommersant*, April 1, 2004, p. 4; "V Tatarstane zakryli 'delo o suverenitete,'" [Case on Sovereignty Is Closed in Tatarstan] *IA Rosbalt*, June 17, 2004, available at http://www.rosbalt.ru/2004/06/17/166045.html.

[82] See, for example, RCC decision 53-O of June 21, 1996, *VKS RF*, no. 4 (1996), pp. 20–22, English translation in *Statutes and Decisions*, no. 5 (2001).

[83] Irina Begimbetova, "V povestku sessii Gossoveta RT vkliucheny 42 dopolnitelnykh voprosa," [42 Additional Items Are Included in the Agenda of the Session of the State Council of Tatarstan] *Intertat.Ru*, May 26, 2003.

228   *The 2nd Russian Constitutional Court (1995–2007)*

pattern: the regions simultaneously use constitutional litigation to attack
the federal center and defy unfavorable Constitutional Court judgments.
Under Putin's presidency, the regions tended to obey the RCC out of fear
of punishment by the federal center, which was gaining more and more
power over the regions. If political actors obeyed the Court out of respect
for the abstract rule of law, we would surely see such respect in their
reaction to judgments on individual rights. Was this the case? This is the
focus of the following section of this chapter.

RIGHTS REVOLUTIONS UNFULFILLED

As I have explored in Chapter 5, the biggest achievement of the 2nd RCC
was in resolving disputes between individuals and the state. Learning from
the near-death experience of its predecessor, this Court preferred to focus
on protecting individual rights in order to avoid serious confrontations
with other branches of government. Indeed, many argue that such a focus
helps the constitutional courts to build their legitimacy, to gain popularity among voters, and even to contribute to democratization.[84] This is
because individual rights jurisprudence does not run against policy preferences of elected actors, who allegedly already achieved a substantial
agreement on the supremacy of fundamental rights. Recent court-ordered
"rights revolutions" around the globe largely support this view: national
and supranational constitutional courts spend most of their time dealing with individual rights cases. Increasingly, transnational "rights talk"
among high courts gets attention in the media and academic analysis.[85]

Russia is no exception to this globalization of rights. As I have discussed in Chapter 5, the RCC judges routinely study the decisions of their
colleagues from abroad, and particularly those of the European Court
of Human Rights in Strasbourg. In fact, Russia's accession to the Council of Europe in 1998 has seriously affected the decision making of the
RCC. On the one hand, this Court – like its counterparts in Europe – has
been the locomotive that pulled the Russian legal system toward European human rights standards. The RCC judges were also concerned about

---

[84] See, for example, Lee Epstein, Jack Knight, and Olga Shvetsova, "The Role of Constitutional Courts in Establishment and Maintenance of Democratic Systems of Government," *Law and Society Review*, vol. 35, no. 1 (2001), pp. 117–164 and Anna Jonsson,
"The Constitutional Court of the Russian Federation, 1997–2001," *Uppsala University
Working Papers*, no. 73 (October 2002).

[85] Anne-Marie Slaughter, *A New World Order* (Princeton, NJ: Princeton University Press,
2004).

Rights Revolutions Unfulfilled

the way they would be perceived by the European legal epistemic communities,[86] with the Conference of European Constitutional Courts and the "Venice" Commission for Democracy through Law of the Council of Europe being the most important ones.[87] On the other hand, Russia's rulers also wanted to impress their European colleagues by sharing their values of the rule of law and respect for human rights. As President Putin remarked in November of 2001:

> We do not consider the European Human Rights Court as a competitor of our judicial system. On the contrary, this is the most important element of European values in the modern world and in Russia if we take into account its integration into the world community.

He added that Russia "counts on constructive work" with the Strasbourg Court and expressed the hope that possible "imperfections of the Russian judicial system will be [noted] delicately and professionally." Russia, he said, will correct these mistakes and "this will be useful for our country."[88] These were not empty promises. Facing threats of constitutional litigation, Putin abolished military detention centers in June 2002 and did the same with detention centers for the homeless in February 2004.[89]

"Correcting" these mistakes, however, requires the cooperation of unelected actors: bureaucrats (federal, regional, and local) and judges in other courts. Having a lawyer from the moment of arrest and exercising one's right to vote as well as implementing all other negative and positive rights, as defined by the constitutional court, is impossible if the law-enforcement agencies, electoral commissions, and judicial branch defy the orders of the Constitutional Court. This defiance is normal in a time of transitional uncertainty, which among other things includes both institutional chaos and a weak state capacity. Coupled with the economic crisis of the early 1990s and the short-term horizons of the policymakers,

---

[86] For a succinct summary of the relationship between legal epistemic communities and constitutional courts in the West, see Martin Shapiro, "The Success of Judicial Review and Democracy," in Martin Shapiro and Alec Stone Sweet, *On Law, Politics, and Judicialization* (Oxford: Oxford University Press, 2002), pp. 170–176.

[87] See, for example, Vitruk, *Konstitutsionnoe pravosudie v Rossii*, pp. 30, 32, 37.

[88] "Putin Calls for Cooperating with European Human Rights Court," *ITAR-TASS News Agency*, November 1, 2001, as quoted in Peter Krug, "Strasbourg Review: Russia and the European Court of Human Rights." Paper presented at Annual Convention of the American Association for the Advancement of Slavic Studies, November 2003, Toronto, p. 7.

[89] These detention centers held individuals arrested without judicial warrant, contrary to the 1993 constitution. See presidential decree no. 671 of June 30, 2002, *Rossiiskaia gazeta*, July 3, 2002, and no. 151 of February 6, 2004, *SZ RF*, 2004, no. 6, item 412.

230 *The 2nd Russian Constitutional Court (1995–2007)*

the capacity of the Russian state to deliver public services became paralyzed. In this chaotic situation, the RCC individual rights jurisprudence was acknowledged but not enforced. Although the capacity of state institutions to resolve disputes in a fair and impartial manner has increased substantially in post-Soviet Russia, their capacity to carry out public policies is weak, "largely due to inadequate resources and insufficient coercive means to enforce state policies."[90] But this implementation capacity is crucial to the legitimacy of new postcommunist regimes because the voters expect that a good government "actually gets things done."[91]

Due Process Rights in Criminal Procedure

Consider the fate of RCC judgments in the area of criminal procedure. As I have shown in Chapter 5, the 2nd RCC "revolutionized" due process rights and paved the way for criminal procedure reform in post-Soviet Russia. On the one hand, federal lawmakers codified this reform in the 2001 Criminal Procedure Code and succeeded in incorporating many RCC decisions in this area in the Code.[92] The fact that the 2001 Code did not overrule important RCC decisions is a clear sign of the Court's strength. On the other hand, the political branches failed to incorporate several judgments of the Court in the 2001 Code:

1. Contrary to RCC decisions that held the unlimited duration of pretrial detention to be unconstitutional, the Code sets no limit for extending custody as a punishment for the accused who delay reviewing the materials of the criminal cases against them. Ironically, the previous version of the Criminal Procedure Code, as amended according to RCC guidelines in 1996 after a scandalous attempt by the State Duma to override them,[93] was closer to the European human rights standards in setting a 6-month cap on extending pretrial detentions.[94]

---

[90] Gordon B. Smith, "State-Building in a New Russia: Assessing the Yeltsin Record," in Gordon B. Smith, ed., *State-Building in Russia: The Yeltsin Legacy and the Challenge of the Future* (Armonk, NY: M.E. Sharpe, 1999), p. 11.

[91] Robert D. Putnam, *Making Democracy Work: Civic Traditions in Modern Italy* (Princeton: Princeton University Press, 1993), p. 63.

[92] Ugolovno-protsessualnyi kodeks RF of December 18, 2001 no. 174-FZ, *SZ RF*, no. 52 (Part I) (2001), item 492 [Criminal Procedure Code].

[93] Vitruk, *Konstitutsionnoe pravosudie v Rossii*, pp. 458–460.

[94] RCC decisions: 14-P of June 13, 1996, *VKS RF*, no. 4 (1996), pp. 2–13 (Vitruk, dissenting), English translation in *Statutes and Decisions*, no. 2 (2001); and 167-O of December 25, 1998, *ibid.*, no. 2 (1999), pp. 40–47. See Igor Petrukhin, ed., *Sudebnaia vlast* [Judicial Power] (Moskva: Prospekt, 2003), pp. 168, 634.

Rights Revolutions Unfulfilled

2. Contrary to RCC decisions that struck down the discretionary power of superior courts, including the Russian Supreme Court, to transfer cases among lower courts and to take away cases from them, Article 31-4 of the 2001 Code kept this power for the Russian Supreme Court.[95]
3. Chapter 52 of the Code codifies Putin's judicial reform with its emphasis on rooting out judicial corruption and impunity by authorizing three-judge panels to bring criminal charges against judges from lower courts. This innovation violates RCC decisions that declared unconstitutional the power of regular courts to launch criminal proceedings.[96]

These failures to incorporate RCC decisions in the reform of criminal procedure cannot be explained by the ignorance of politicians. On the contrary, Russian lawmakers were aware of these judgments and had enough time to enshrine them in the 2001 Code, as most decisions were issued in the 1990s. Who are the main beneficiaries of this purposive noncompliance with these RCC decisions? They appear to be law-enforcement officers, who can manipulate the timing of pretrial detention of accused persons who are uncooperative, and the Russian Supreme Court, which kept the power to move politically sensitive criminal cases around. As Elena Mizulina, who authored the 2001 Criminal Procedure Code, complained in early 2001, "law-enforcement agencies, including the Procuracy, have gigantic influence in the State Duma and may block any bill containing legitimate attempts to enforce a Constitutional Court decision."[97] In addition to having a powerful lobby in the federal legislature, the seven competing law-enforcement agencies routinely disobey or ignore

---

[95] RCC decisions: 9-P of March 16, 1998, *VKS RF*, no. 3 (1998), pp. 71–78, English translation in *Statutes and Decisions*, no. 3 (2001); and 3-P of February 2, 1999, *ibid.*, no. 3 (1999), pp. 12–24, English translation in *Statutes and Decisions*, no. 4 (2001). See Petrukhin, *Sudebnaia vlast*, p. 257.

[96] RCC decisions: 19-P of November 28, 1996, *VKS RF*, no. 5 (1996), pp. 15–21, English translation in *Statutes and Decisions*, no. 3 (2001); and 1-P of January 14, 2000, *ibid.*, no. 2 (2000), pp. 49–64 (Ebzeev and Vitruk, dissenting). See Petrukhin, *Sudebnaia vlast*, pp. 330, 643.

[97] A former member of the Russian parliament, Mizulina currently represents the State Duma at the RCC. Elena Mizulina, "Problemy realizatsii reshenii Konstitutsionnogo Suda Rossiiskoi Federatsii v deiatelnosti Gosudarstvennoi Dumy Federalnogo Sobraniia – parlamenta Rossiiskoi Federatsii," [Problems of Enforcing Decisions of the RF Constitutional Court in the Work of the State Duma of the Federal Assembly – RF Parliament] in Mitiukov et al., *Problemy ispolneniia...*, p. 69.

RCC judgments, even if Russia's rulers support the judgments.[98] Indeed, it is naïve to expect a timely compliance with RCC decisions concerning procedural rights, because each of these law-enforcement agencies has different and competing priorities. Only if RCC decisions allow these agencies to achieve their priorities quickly will compliance follow.

The regular courts have the capacity to monitor the compliance of law-enforcement bodies only to the extent that the prosecution, in addition to conducting the criminal-case investigation, shares the materials of the case with defense counsel and provides opportunities for the suspect or the victim to request judicial review. If the prosecution is unwilling or incapable of performing these duties, no appeal is lodged, and it is impossible to know whether the RCC decision protecting due process rights has been enforced. Few of Russia's law-enforcement agencies have benefited from such RCC decisions because they impose tremendous costs on the prosecution and delay the investigation of the background of surging crime levels. But blocking an appeal from judicial scrutiny goes unpunished due to low levels of transparency in prosecutorial procedures. Thus, as one local procurator told me in an interview, the street-level law enforcers face no punishment for noncompliance with RCC decisions.[99] For example, according to one observer, law-enforcement officials tried to avoid enforcing the July 1998 RCC decision that allowed more of the approximately 275,000 people who were then under pretrial detention to appeal for their release from jail.[100]

But what about the enforcement of due process rights during a trial? The Russian Supreme Court repeatedly defied RCC decisions on criminal procedure that touched upon the powers of lower courts and the Supreme Court itself.[101] In particular, the Supreme Court failed to enforce the following RCC decisions:

---

[98] The Procuracy, Ministry of Internal Affairs (MVD), Ministry of Justice, Federal Security Service (FSB), Federal Service of Controlling Narcotics Turnover (FSKN), State Customs Committee (GTK), and Financial Monitoring Committee (KFM).

[99] Interview with the city procurator, Syktyvkar, Russia, July 2001. A similar phenomenon of noncompliance has been observed among the police force in the United States. See Jerome H. Skolnick, *Justice Without Trial: Law Enforcement in Democratic Society* (New York: Wiley, 1966). I am grateful to Peter Russell for bringing this to my attention.

[100] Pamela Jordan, *Defending Rights in Russia: Lawyers, the State, and Legal Reform in the Post-Soviet Era* (Vancouver: University of British Columbia Press, 2005), p. 144.

[101] Tamara Morshchakova, "Voprosy vzaimodeistviia Konstitutsionnogo Suda Rossiiskoi Federatsii i sudov inykh vidov iurisdiktsii," [Questions of Interaction between the RF Constitutional Court and Courts of Other Jurisdictions] in Mitiukov et al., *Problemy ispolneniia . . .* , pp. 56–62.

Rights Revolutions Unfulfilled

- Banning the power of criminal courts to bring criminal charges[102]
- Requiring courts to acquit defendant after the prosecution drops the charges[103]
- Limiting the discretion of the superior courts to transfer criminal and civil cases among the lower courts[104]
- Ordering the Supreme Court to reopen its cases and solve them according to the Constitutional Court's guidelines[105]

In short, the Supreme Court often defied RCC decisions both in the everyday administration of justice and in lobbying the State Duma during the passage of the 2001 Criminal Procedure Code. In return, RCC Justice Morshchakova repeatedly accused the Supreme Court of persistent "sham" compliance with the decisions of her Court.[106]

Finally, the Supreme Court and the Higher *Arbitrazh* Court refuse to enforce the January 2001 RCC decision on Article 1070-2 of the Russian Civil Code. In this case, the Constitutional Court cited Articles 6 and 41 of the 1950 European Convention of Human Rights and allowed individuals to sue judges for damages arising from red tape, falsified documents, and other illegal actions in handling court cases.[107] However, the rest of the federal judiciary routinely nixes such complaints against dishonest judges.[108] Courts act only after such judges have received criminal

---

[102] RCC decisions: 19-P of November 28, 1996, *VKS RF*, no. 5 (1996), pp. 15–21, English translation in *Statutes and Decisions*, no. 3 (2001); and 88-O of October 7, 1997, *ibid.*, no. 5 (1997), pp. 44–48, English translation in *Statutes and Decisions*, no. 5 (2001).

[103] RCC decision 7-P of April 20, 1999, *VKS RF*, no. 4 (1999), pp. 41–49, English translation in *Statutes and Decisions*, no. 4 (2001).

[104] RCC decisions: 9-P of March 16, 1998, *VKS RF*, no. 3 (1998), pp. 71–78, English translation in *Statutes and Decisions*, no. 3 (2001).; and 3-P of February 2, 1999, *ibid.*, no. 3 (1999), pp. 12–24, English translation in *Statutes and Decisions*, no. 4 (2001).

[105] RCC decisions: 4-P of February 2, 1996, *VKS RF*, no. 2 (1996), pp. 2–11, English translation in *Statutes and Decisions*, no. 2 (2001); 59-O of June 6, 1997, *ibid.*, no. 5 (1997), pp. 7–10, English translation in *Statutes and Decisions*, no. 5 (2001); 21-P of July 6, 1998, *ibid.*, no. 6 (1998), pp. 5–9, English translation in *Statutes and Decisions*, no. 5 (2001).

[106] Morshchakova, "Voprosy vzaimodeistviia...", p. 58; and Morshchakova, "Konstitutsionnye (ustavnye) sudy subektov Rossiiskoi Federatsii," in Igor Petrukhin, ed., *Sudebnaia vlast*, p. 388.

[107] RCC decision 1-P of January 25, 2001, *VKS RF*, no. 3 (2001), pp. 11–22. For the subsequent disobedience on the part of the Supreme Court, see Sergei Zhdakaev, "Za volokitu: Orlovskii advokat Liubov Samoilova possorila Verkhovnyi sud Rossii s Konstitutsionnym," [For the Red Tape: Orel's Advocate Liubov Samoilova Caused the Supreme Court to Quarrel with the Constitutional Court] *Izvestiia*, October 14, 2003, available at http://www.izvestia.ru/conflict/article39695.

[108] RCC decision 210-O of May 27, 2004, *VKS RF*, no. 6 (2004), pp. 83–85.

sentences, a very rare occurrence (four in 2002, three in 2003, one in 2004, four in 2005, and five in 2006) because most Russian judges are usually removed from office without criminal charges being brought against them.[109] The Russian judges admit long delays in handling caseloads. They blame the parties and their counsel for not showing up for court cases, experts for the slow processing of judicial requests, and law-enforcement agencies for poor investigation and lack of convoy guards to escort the accused.[110] Thus, the issue of judicial impunity remains controversial. Judges do not want to sacrifice their independence but citizens want fair and speedy trials. Politicians do not want to set aside funds for compensating aggrieved citizens and, at the same time, Russia's rulers do not want citizens to turn to the ECHR in Strasbourg.[111]

In summary, the resistance of other courts and law-enforcement agencies to obeying the Constitutional Court decisions has limited the revolutionary impact of the 2nd RCC in the area of due process rights. Both the judicial branch and the executive have tended to disobey the RCC when the tribunal limited their discretion and powers in criminal procedure, in questioning the binding nature of RCC judgments, and in demanding the return of these prerogatives to them.[112] Moreover, the rise to power of *siloviki*, a cadre of professionals from the military, security services, and law-enforcement agencies, in Putin's Russia further undermined the efforts of the RCC to liberalize criminal justice.[113] The saga of the delayed adoption of the 2001 Criminal Procedure Code and its subsequent numerous amendments shows that *siloviki* focus on showing loyalty to Vladimir Putin, on fighting crime, and on their economic and institutional interests

---

[109] Statistics on the dismissals of and criminal cases against judges are available at the Web site of the Russian Higher Judicial Qualification Commission, available at http://www.vkks.ru.

[110] Alexei Trochev, "Lack of Guards in St. Petersburg Threatens Criminal Court Reform," *Russian Regional Report*, vol. 7, no. 12 (2002), March 27, p. 4.

[111] In August 2005, the RCC had to publicly complain about noncompliance with the January 2001 judgment. See Elena Getman, "Chinovnik glavnee Konstitutsii. Kto i pochemu ne vypolniaet resheniia glavnogo suda strany," [Officer Is Above the Constitution. Who and Why Does not Carry out Decisions of the Highest Court of the Land] *Rossiiskaia gazeta*, August 9, 2005.

[112] Konstantin Katanian, "KS protiv vsekh ostalnykh sudov," [RCC Is Against All Other Courts] *Nezavisimaia gazeta*, February 13, 1996.

[113] For more on the phenomenon of *siloviki*, see, for example, Olga Kryshtanovskaya and Stephen White, "Putin's Militocracy," *Post-Soviet Affairs*, vol. 19, no. 4 (2003), pp. 289–306; Bettina Renz, "'Putin's Militocracy'? An Alternative Interpretation of the Role of Siloviki in Contemporary Russian Politics," *Europe-Asia Studies*, vol. 18, no. 6 (2006), pp. 903–924; and Sharon Werning Rivera and David W. Rivera, "The Russian Elite under Putin: Militocratic or Bourgeois?" *Post-Soviet Affairs*, vol. 22, no. 2 (2006), pp. 125–144.

Rights Revolutions Unfulfilled

instead of following RCC guidelines.[114] Needless to say, enforcing the constitutional rights of the accused in criminal cases is also unpopular with the public in the context of surging crime rates. There is no doubt that the Constitutional Court felt both the pressure from *siloviki*, who pursued their frequently changing short-term power needs, and the backlash from the public that demanded a tougher stance on fighting crime.

Rights of Bona Fide Taxpayers

Regrettably, this pattern of noncompliance with RCC decisions appears in other rights areas as well. Consider the fate of the taxpayer rights revolution, which should be popular among voters and, therefore, among elected politicans. As I have discussed in Chapter 5, taxation cases occupied a central place on the docket of the 2nd RCC, partly because the Court had to defend its vision of fair taxation against the rest of the government. To be sure, budgetary considerations compelled the RCC to weaken the protection of taxpayers by granting the legislature up to 11 months to amend the tax statutes, which allowed the tax authorities to collect taxes even after they were declared unconstitutional as if there was no RCC judgment on the matter![115] Here, the Russian Court was not unique – constitutional courts in other countries often suspend the enforcement of their judgments so that governments can bring their policies in line with judicial orders.

But what happened to the judge-made, abstract constitutional principles of fair taxation? The series of cases dealing with the concept of the bona fide taxpayer illustrates how difficult it is to make judge-made concepts work in practice. In October 1998, just a few months after a nationwide financial crisis brought down Sergei Kirienko's Cabinet, the Constitutional Court boldly ruled that the taxpayer's obligation to pay taxes ended at the moment that the tax amount was deducted from the account of the taxpayer in good faith.[116] On paper, this legally sound judgment overruled the practice of the federal Tax Ministry and the Higher *Arbitrazh* Court, which believed that the tax obligation ended only after the tax amount had been deposited in the state coffers. In the context

---

[114] See Solomon, "The Criminal Procedure Code of 2001."

[115] See, for example, Oleg Kokorin, "Konstitutsionnyi printsip ravenstva," [Constitutional Principle of Equality] *EZh-Iurist: Sudebnoe prilozhenie*, no. 26 (June 2003), pp. 6–7.

[116] RCC decision 24-P of October 12, 1998, *VKS RF*, no. 1 (1999), pp. 10–17, English translation in *Statutes and Decisions*, no. 5 (2000).

of widespread "bank runs," this unconstitutional practice meant that if, for any reason, the tax payment did not reach the state coffers on time it was OK for the revenue agency to deduct the same tax again in a single tax period. The RCC disagreed and ruled that the taxpayers could not be held responsible for the illegal behavior of banks that delayed the transfer of tax payments to the state budget. Moreover, Article 45 of the Russian Tax Code, which entered into force in January 1999, copied the wording of the RCC decision: "the tax obligation ends when the tax amount is deducted from the account of the taxpayer."

On the ground, however, this RCC judgment made little difference. Although the federal Pension Fund and several federal ministries reimbursed those who paid their taxes twice, the State Customs Committee in February 1999 issued a secret letter that banned customs officers from clearing goods unless the customs duties have been deposited in the state budget. The Russian Supreme Court approved this noncompliance by ruling that the clearance of goods through customs should be done only after the "real payment of customs duties," that is, after the payment had been deposited in the state coffers. Thus, the deduction of customs duties from the account of the payer ends the obligation to pay the duties, but it does not bind the customs officials.[117] Moreover, in May 1999, the Russian Tax Ministry issued a secret letter in which it banned tax officers from applying this RCC judgment retroactively. In practice, this meant that all taxpayers who were taxed twice before October 12, 1998, the date of the RCC decision, would not receive a refund. The Higher *Arbitrazh* Court upheld the legality of this secret letter and consistently refused all lawsuits in which taxpayers sought to recover taxes paid twice.[118]

As expected, aggrieved taxpayers flooded the RCC with complaints, trying to recover their taxes, and in July 1999, the RCC defended their right to fair taxation by ruling that its October 1998 decision applied to all payments of taxes, fees, and duties to the state budget.[119] At the same time, the Enforcement Department of the RCC contacted the legal office of the Tax Ministry, but to no avail. The Procuracy also refused to act on behalf of these taxpayers. Numerous publications in the mass media about this unconstitutional behavior of the bureaucracy and the judicial branch did not help either. In May 2000, the RCC again clashed with the

---

[117] Sergei Pepeliaev, "Kommentarii," in Boris Ebzeev, ed., *Kommentarii k postanovleniiam Konstitutsionnogo Suda RF. T. 2* (Moskva: Iurist, 2000), pp. 515–516.

[118] *Ibid.*, pp. 518.

[119] RCC decision 97-O of July 1, 1999, *VKS RF*, no. 5 (1999), pp. 37–39, English translation in *Statutes and Decisions*, no. 1 (2002).

arbitrazh courts by ruling that its October 1998 decision was to be applied retroactively to remedy the rights of the "good faith" taxpayers.[120] All in all, by March 2001, the RCC, in twenty-three decisions, insisted on its own definition of the timing of tax payments, which, of course, the aggrieved taxpayers used extensively in trying to recover taxes paid unconstitutionally between 1994 and 1998. The *arbitrazh* courts, however, launched a unified front to defend the budget against this flood of lawsuits.[121] These courts had the support of the federal Tax Ministry, which complained that by mid-2001, the Russian budget had lost 31 billion rubles as a result of the October 1998 RCC decision.[122]

In July 2001, the RCC appeared to have given up its "taxpayer rights" revolution. As Justice Gadzhiev recalls, his colleagues asked the Tax Ministry to petition the Court to "clarify" its October 1998 decision.[123] The Tax Ministry could not refuse such a tempting offer from the guardians of constitutional order, and the RCC promptly issued a "clarification" ruling in which it restricted the application of its October 1998 judgment to taxpayers "in good faith" and essentially gave a freehand to the revenue agencies to determine the "good faith" element.[124] According to the RCC, instead of assuming that taxpayers behave "in good faith," revenue agencies have to check the "good faith" of both the taxpayers and the banks that delay the transfer of tax payments from the payer's account to the state budget. In a sign of clear deference to the executive, the Court held that the tax authorities had to impel the "good faith" taxpayers to pay their taxes in full and on time. Moreover, in the Court's view, the "good faith" taxpayers ought to pay their taxes through banks that are "approved" by local branches of the Tax Ministry. It should be noted that the Russian Tax Code does not define "good faith" behavior – it presumes that all taxpayers are bona fide, and, therefore, street-level tax authorities faced virtually no checks on the abuse of their authority to separate "reliable" banks from "bad" ones and "good" taxpayers from "malicious" ones. The Higher *Arbitrazh* Court developed its own test to identify "good faith" taxpayers: they had to ask tax authorities

---

[120] RCC decision 101-O of May 4, 2000, *VKS RF*, no. 6 (2000), pp. 21–25.

[121] See Boikov, "Postanovleniia," pp. 51–54.

[122] van den Berg, "Constitution of the Russian Federation Annotated," p. 471, fn. 16.

[123] "G. A. Gadzhiev: 'U nas ogromnyi potok zhalob nalogoplatelshchikov, i on vriad li umenshitsia v obozrimom budushchem,'" [G. A. Gadzhiev: We Have A Huge Stream of Complaints of Taxpayers, and This Is Unlikely to Subside in the Foreseeable Future] *Rossiiskii nalogovyi kurer*, no. 24 (December 2004).

[124] RCC decision 138-O of July 25, 2001, *VKS RF*, no. 2 (2002), pp. 27–30.

if their bank was reliable and efficient in transferring payments to the state budget.[125] The flood of complaints against the abuse of this authority, by and large protected by the *arbitrazh* courts, prompted the RCC to issue yet another decision in October 2003. Here, the Court changed its July 2001 decision by ruling that government agencies, including the *arbitrazh* courts, had to presume the "good faith" behavior of taxpayers and could not impose on them obligations not authorized by tax statutes.[126] In essence, the RCC required the tax authorities to behave "in good faith," thus, inserting the "good faith" principle in the Russian tax law.[127] Following this decision, the Russian Tax Ministry still resisted presuming that all corporations whose tax payments did not reach the state coffers on time were innocent and, throughout 2004, attempted to change the Tax Code in its favor.[128]

The Kremlin-approved 'tax collection' campaign against YUKOS, at the time Russia's largest private oil exporter, only strengthened this stance of the Tax Ministry and the *arbitrazh* courts. As expected, the YUKOS lawyers complained to the RCC against a whopping 99.4 billion ruble (US$3.4 billion) tax bill imposed by the tax authorities for back taxes for the year 2000 and approved by the Moscow *Arbitrazh* Court in 2004. In January 2005, the RCC responded with a Solomonic judgment. The Constitutional Court blasted the Moscow *Arbitrazh* Court judge for abusing the concept of a "good faith" taxpayer and upheld the 3-year statute of limitations on back tax claims, as provided by Article 113 of the Tax Code. Yet the RCC stopped short of ordering the rehearing of the YUKOS case and dismissed the complaint.[129] But just a few months later, in another Solomonic decision involving the same back tax claims against YUKOS and the same legal issues, the RCC changed its position. In a 16–3 vote, the Court changed the meaning of the 3-year statute of limitations on back tax claims by allowing tax authorities to pursue claims indefinitely if they can prove "obstruction" on the part of the taxpayer.[130]

---

[125] Irina Skliarova, "Posmotri v moi chestnye glaza," [Look in My Honest Eyes] *Vremia novostei*, May 17, 2004.

[126] RCC decision 329-O of October 16, 2003, unpublished, available at http://www.ksrf.ru.

[127] See "G. A. Gadzhiev: 'U nas ogromnyi potok zhalob...'"

[128] See, for example, Marina Gradova, "MNS vystupaet za zakonodatelnoe reshenie problemy s 'zavisshimi platezhami,'" [Tax Ministry Stands for the Legislative Solution to the Problem of 'Stuck Tax Payments'] *RIA Novosti*, February 12, 2004; and Skliarova, "Posmotri v moi chestnye glaza."

[129] RCC decision 36-O of January 18, 2005, *VKS RF*, no. 3 (2005), pp. 108–112.

[130] RCC decision 9-P of July 14, 2005, *VKS RF*, no. 4 (2005), pp. 67–102 (Gadzhiev, Iaroslavtsev, and Kononov, dissenting).

The RCC ruled that the statute did not apply to "dishonest taxpayers," who acted illicitly for the purpose of dragging out tax audits. Court observers agreed that the full impact of the ruling would hinge on how the *arbitrazh* courts and the tax authorities interpret what constitutes proof of obstruction.[131] Deferring to the executive and other courts again proved dangerous to the Constitutional Court. In October 2006, after a prolonged debate, the Higher *Arbitrazh* Court rejected the good faith concept stated previously by the RCC and established a brand new concept of unjustified tax benefit. This innovation is binding on all *arbitrazh* courts and targets good faith taxpayers, who may be accused of tax optimization or utilization of tax planning schemes or interaction with bad faith taxpayers. For example, any tax benefit related to transactions with a shady business or any incomplete, inaccurate, or inconsistent information in primary or supportive documents may mean a tax benefit is unjustified. A taxpayer must justify a business rationale for the questioned operation and its consistency with true economic intent.[132]

In summary, just as occurred with landmark decisions in the area of due process rights, the judgments of the 2nd RCC created a "quiet revolution" in Russian taxation. These judgments repeatedly surprised both tax authorities and taxpayers, as the head of the Russian Tax Ministry Legal Department delicately put it in August 2004.[133] Yet, on the ground, short-term political campaigns against oligarchs and the defiance of the bureaucracy and the rest of the judiciary have mitigated the impact of this "taxpayer rights" revolution and forced the RCC to change its mind in its approach to fair taxation.

Something similar happened with RCC decisions on the confiscation of goods by customs. Under pressure from the customs authorities, the RCC frequently changed its stance against unconstitutional takings by the state.[134] At the same time, customs officials skillfully used

---

[131] Alex Fak, "Uncertainty Lingers Despite Tax Ruling," *Moscow Times*, July 18, 2005, p. 6.

[132] Ivan Smirnov, "New Taxpaying Realities – Unjustified Benefits," *St. Petersburg Times*, December 26, 2006.

[133] "VAS i KS – ukaz MNS. Nalogoviki o nalogovykh sporakh," [The Higher *Arbitrazh* Court and RCC Must be Obeyed by the Tax Ministry. Tax Officials about Tax Disputes] *Dvoinaia zapis*, August 3, 2004.

[134] Compare the following RCC decisions: 8-P of May 20, 1997, *VKS RF*, no. 4 (1997), pp. 55–63 (Kononov, dissenting), English translation in *Statutes and Decisions*, no. 2 (2000); 8-P of March 11, 1998, *ibid.*, no. 3 (1998), pp. 52–65 (Vitruk, dissenting), English translation in *Statutes and Decisions*, no. 4 (2000), p. 11; 201-O of December 3, 1998, *ibid.*, no. 3 (1999), pp. 2–4, English translation in *Statutes and Decisions*, no. 6 (2001);

240   *The 2nd Russian Constitutional Court (1995–2007)*

contradictions among the three high courts and kept on confiscating improperly cleared goods under their standard operation procedures of dubious legality.[135] Even when President Putin's "dictatorship of law" campaign was well underway, the Deputy Head of the State Customs Committee issued an internal memo to all customs officers to disregard all judicial decisions that enforced the April 2001 RCC decision on the unconstitutionality of confiscating goods not cleared through customs.[136]

Social Rights: (Not) Compensating the Victims of Stalin's Purges

The political branches and regular courts also persistently defied Constitutional Court decisions on social rights. Recall from Chapter 5 that the majority of the 2nd RCC justices focused on protecting the positive rights of the most vulnerable groups in the population, such as victims of Stalin's purges, pensioners, disabled persons, and so on. Protecting their rights on the ground usually requires more public spending, and the lack of money is the usual excuse of governments around the world when they do not want to carry out a certain policy (not necessarily Court-mandated). Thus, according to Justice Nikolai Vitruk, it took many years to implement the RCC decisions that called for the payment of compensation to injured parties – for example, illegally discharged employees, children of people who were purged under Stalin's regime, workers who cleaned up the 1986 Chernobyl radiation leak, and individuals suffering from illegal judicial decisions.[137] Such delayed implementation of Court-ordered generosity is understandable in Yeltsin's Russia with its deep economic crisis of the 1990s. But this is less justifiable in Putin's Russia, which enjoyed stable economic growth and boasted record-level, high gold reserves at the beginning of the millennium. If in early 2001 the RCC officially blamed the State Duma for the failure to pass statutes that were necessary to carry out ten judgments of the Court, by mid-2007, Chairman Zorkin publicly complained that the State Duma failed to adopt laws necessary to implement twenty-five judgments of his Court. Many of them required

---

8-P of May 14, 1999, *ibid.*, no. 4 (1999), pp. 50–61, English translation in *Statutes and Decisions*, no. 6 (2000); 7-P of April 27, 2001, *ibid.*, no. 5 (2001), pp. 46–67 (Kononov, dissenting); and 3-O of January 10, 2002, *ibid.*, no. 4 (2002), pp. 4–13.

[135] See the "Letter 01–07/9187 of January 13, 2001," by Mikhail Vanin, the Head of the RF State Customs Committee, in Mitiukov et al., *Problemy ispolneniia . . .*, pp. 307–314.

[136] Igor Popov, "Snachala arest, potom obvinenie," [First – Arrest, Then – Accusation] *Finansovye izvestiia*, June 25, 2002.

[137] Nikolai Vitruk, "Ispolnenie reshenii Konstitutsionnogo Suda Rossiiskoi Federatsii," [Implementation of Decisions of the RF Constitutional Court] *Konstitutsionnoe pravo: vostochnoevropeiskoe obozrenie*, no. 3 (2002), pp. 53–63.

Rights Revolutions Unfulfilled

the Russian government to bring its welfare reform in line with the constitutional requirement of *Sozialstaat*.[138] For example, Zorkin blasted the Duma for the failure to amend pension laws, previously found unconstitutional, that would entitle tens of thousands of retired military officers to higher pensions.[139]

Consider the fate of the 1995 RCC decision in which the Court ordered the Russian parliament to amend the 1991 statute on compensating children whose parents vanished during Stalin's purges.[140] In effect, the Court wanted the legislature to compensate these orphans for their damages and suffering in full, and then Chairman Tumanov wrote a detailed letter to the State Duma on how to achieve this fair compensation. However, the Duma placed the drafting of this bill on the backburner, and President Yeltsin was unwilling and unable to intervene. Only in March 2000, when President Putin came to power and almost 5 years after the RCC decision on the matter, did the liberal Duma members introduce a bill that met the guidelines of the Court. The federal Cabinet, however, criticized the bill on the grounds that expanding compensation for orphans/victims of Stalin's purges would create social tension (!) and require significant public spending.[141] The RCC immediately stepped in and, in April 2000, reiterated that such orphans should be treated and compensated in full, the same way as other victims of Stalin's purges.[142] The State Duma, however, agreed with the federal Cabinet and in October 2000 buried the bill on compensating the orphans. Similarly, law-enforcement bodies, which are responsible on the ground for issuing certificates to the victims of the purges, refused to enforce both RCC decisions on the orphans. Officials claimed that they could recognize orphans as victims only after the 1991 law on the rehabilitation of victims of Stalin's purges was amended accordingly.[143] Finally, the regular courts consistently refused to

---

[138] Data for 2001 are published in Mitiukov et al., *Problemy ispolneniia...*, pp. 330–331. Data for 2007 come from Vladimir Ivanov, "Neuvazhaemyi Konstitutsionnyi sud," [Disrespected Constitutional Court] *Gazeta*, July 19, 2007, available at http://gzt.ru/wallet/2007/07/18/220222.html.

[139] Zorkin complained about the nonimplementation of the RCC decision 187-O of May 11, 2006, *VKS RF*, no. 5 (2006), pp. 22–28, in which the Court ordered the passage of the law on the pensions for retired military personnel.

[140] RCC decision 6-P of May 23, 1995, *VKS RF*, nos. 2–3 (1995), p. 51.

[141] Sheinin, "Problemy ispolneniia," pp. 110–111.

[142] RCC decision 103-O of April 18, 2000, *VKS RF*, no. 6 (2000), pp. 13–17.

[143] Sheinin, "Problemy ispolneniia reshenii," pp. 111–112; Vladimir Davydov, "Uchastie organov prokuratury v realizatsii reshenii Konstitutsionnogo Suda Rossiiskoi Federatsii," [Participation of the Procuracy in Carrying out the Decisions of the RF Constitutional Court] in Mitiukov et al., *Problemy ispolneniia...*, p. 65.

compensate victims of Stalin's terror in full, contrary to the RCC decisions.[144] Needless to say, hundreds of victims of the purges flooded the Court, complaining at such open sabotage by courts and bureaucrats, and the RCC justices repeatedly criticized, in private, this disobedience. Only in the fall of 2001 did the Procuracy, the police, and the Labor Ministry give up their resistance and start to recognize children as victims, according to the RCC guidelines.[145] The fact that these federal ministries, which are usually fighting among each other, reversed their resistance simultaneously, secretly, and in a concerted fashion indicates that they did so according to orders from the Kremlin, but not out of respect for the Court and the rule of law.

In summary, fearing no punishment for noncompliance, politicians, bureaucrats, and regular courts applied secret government instructions instead of RCC judgments. Stalin's victims began to feel the impact of the landmark 1995 RCC decision only after President Putin chose to intervene in the fall of 2001. This (still unfinished) saga of dealing with the past clearly shows that RCC decisions lack binding force in the operational legal hierarchy, and they acquire this force only after powerful political actors choose to make judicial decisions binding. Ignoring the 2001 "implementation" amendments to the 1994 RCC Act, the Russian parliament amended the 1991 law on the rehabilitation of victims of Stalin's purges to include orphans only in early 2003.[146] Meanwhile, the federal Cabinet routinely failed to disburse funds to regional governments to provide benefits for victims of Stalin's terror, thus rendering meaningless

---

[144] See, for example, RCC decision 19-O of February 5, 1998, *VKS RF*, no. 3 (1998), pp. 24–26.

[145] See Letter of the Russian Procuracy General "O poriadke ispolneniia Opredeleniia Konstitutsionnogo Suda Rossiiskoi Federatsii ot 18.04.2000 N 103-O" of August 3, 2000, no. 13r, [On the Procedure of Implementing the RCC Decision 103-O of April 18, 2000] unpublished document; Order of the Russian Minister of Internal Affairs "O vnesenii izmenenii i dopolnenii v instruktsiiu, utv. Prikazom MVD Rossii ot 22 iunia 2000 g. N 675" of October 25, 2001, no. 938, [On Amending the Instruction As Confirmed by the Order 675 of June 22, 2000] *Rossiiskaia gazeta*, November 28, 2001; and Directive of the Russian Ministry of Labor "O realizatsii Opredeleniia Konstitutsionnogo Suda Rossiiskoi Federatsii ot 18.04.2000 N 103-O" of September 18, 2001, no. 2294–14, [On Implementing the RCC Decision 103-O of April 18, 2000] unpublished document.

[146] Although President Putin signed the amendments in February 2003, the bill entered into force on January 1, 2003. See Federalnyi zakon 26-FZ "O vnesenii izmenenii i dopolnenii v Zakon Rossiiskoi Federatsii 'O reabilitatsii zhertv politicheskikh repressii,'" of February 9, 2003, [Federal Law 26-FZ on Amending the RF Law on the Rehabilitation of the Victims of the Political Repression] *SZ RF*, 2003, no. 6, item 509.

Rights Revolutions Unfulfilled

the efforts of the RCC to compensate the victims.[147] However, the welfare reform of 2004, the so-called monetization of social benefits, converted compensatory benefits for all victims of Stalin's purges into "social assistance" benefits and delegated the responsibility for providing these benefits to the regions.[148] As a result, victims of Stalin's purges receive a meager 300 rubles (US$10) per month from regional governments and can no longer claim compensation for moral harm caused by the purges.[149] Not surprisingly, victims of Stalin's terror came back to the Constitutional Court and asked for the overturn of the abolition of their benefits. In July 2005, the Court agreed with petitioners and ordered the federal Cabinet to reinstate the amount of benefits to the victims in a "full and speedy" fashion.[150] But the Court stopped short of striking down the transformation of compensatory benefits into "social assistance" as unconstitutional. To be sure, the executive branch senses the deference of the RCC and may find ways to disobey this and other RCC decisions in the area of welfare reforms, unless there is strong political pressure from the chief executive.

Regional Defiance: Land, Elections, and Propiska

Finally, the 2nd RCC also fought hard for regional compliance with its judgments in the area of basic rights. To be sure, even during President Putin's second term, some regions still defy RCC decisions, and the postdecision implementation games will likely continue in recalcitrant regions. For example, it took 2 years to implement a December 2001 RCC decision that struck down the 1994 Moscow city land fees statute and ordered the Moscow city government to return the plot of land to the complainant.[151] The Moscow mayor obeyed this decision only after

---

[147] See, for example, RCC decision 282-O of July 10, 2003, *VKS RF*, no. 6 (2003), pp. 76–78.

[148] For analysis of welfare reform under Putin, see Linda J. Cook, *Postcommunist Welfare States: Reform Politics in Russia and Eastern Europe* (Ithaca, NY: Cornell University Press, 2007), pp. 145–192.

[149] Natalia Biianova, "450 rublei na odnogo repressirovannogo," [450 Rubles for One Victim of Repressions] *Gazeta*, March 28, 2005. Also, see justice Kononov's dissenting opinion in RCC decision 462-O of December 1, 2005, *VKS RF*, no. 2 (2006), pp. 74–82; and no. 3 (2006), pp. 125–128.

[150] RCC decision 246-O of July 5, 2005, *VKS RF*, no. 6 (2005), pp. 104–108.

[151] Interestingly, the Mexican Supreme Court also faced regional noncompliance both in electoral matters and land regulations. Jeffrey K. Staton, "Judicial Activism and Public Authority Compliance: The Role of Public Support in the Mexican Separation-of-Powers System" (Ph.D. diss., Washington University, 2002), p. 170, chapter 7.

Putin's envoy personally asked him to return the land to the 89-year-old Muscovite, who won the case in the RCC after regular courts repeatedly refused to intervene.[152] Meanwhile, other regions that had enacted similar land-use statutes and took away plots of land from private owners continued to insist, well into 2004, that this RCC decision did not apply to them.[153]

Recall from Chapter 5 that the Court consistently held that constitutional rights could be limited only by federal statutes and repeatedly struck down regional statutes infringing on electoral and mobility rights. On the ground, the Court achieved far more in the area of electoral rights. Although President Yeltsin tolerated chronic regional restrictions on voting rights, his successor, Vladimir Putin, did not wish to do so, as he distrusted the regional elites. Electoral rights figured highly in Putin's campaign to bring regional laws in line with federal standards, as he tried to ensure that his "Unity" party dominated regional legislatures. For example, following the March 2000 decision in which the RCC struck down a gerrymandering scheme in the Orenburg region, Putin's staff in Moscow and in Orenburg stepped in quickly to overcome the resistance of the local procurator and the local electoral commission. Orenburg amended its electoral law in August 2000 only as a result of this swift action on the part of federal officials.[154] Even Tatarstan, a region that publicly denounced RCC decisions throughout the 1990s, promptly changed its electoral district scheme according to the RCC decision in the 2002 *Saliamov* case. Still, in a clear effort to deter more litigation in Moscow, Tatarstan complied only after local police held Saliamov, the complainant, who was a local businessman and a Communist Party member, in jail for 10 hours right after he returned from the Court's session.[155]

---

[152] RCC decision 16-P of December 13, 2001, *VKS RF*, no. 2 (2002), pp. 3–9. See Mariia Zheleznova, "Moskvichka otsudila u merii zemliu predkov," [Muscovite Won the Lawsuit Against the Mayor in the Case of Her Ancestors' Land] *Gazeta*, November 11, 2003.

[153] See, for example, Konstantin Katanian, "Prokuror podderzhal pozitsiiu 'Rodnoi gazety,'" [Procurator Supported Position of 'Rodnaia gazeta'] *Rodnaia gazeta*, August 13, 2004, p. 10.

[154] RCC decision 4-P of March 23, 2000, *VKS RF*, no. 3 (2000), pp. 21–28. Amended Orenburg electoral law was published in *Iuzhnyi Ural*, August 26, 2000.

[155] RCC decision 2-P of January 22, 2002, *VKS RF*, no. 3 (2002), pp. 14–23. Tatarstan constitution and Elections Act were amended in April and November 2002, respectively. On detaining the complainant Saliamov, see Vera Postnova, "Kutuzka za konstitutsionnye prava," [Jailed for Constitutional Rights] *Nezavisimaia gazeta*, November 22, 2001, p. 4.

In an effort to reduce the power base of regional governors, Putin's local government reform of 2003 also aspires to carry out RCC judgments in the area of local self-government – the switch to direct election of city mayors (who used to be appointed by the governors in most regions) and the introduction of elected councils for small municipalities across Russia.[156] Throughout his presidency, Vladimir Putin repeatedly blocked all attempts to abolish direct election of city mayors.[157] But he did so not because of obedience to the RCC but because the Kremlin (and most governors) had sufficient resources to "persuade" any recalcitrant mayor to follow through. In short, the Court is winning this battle against the regions, in part, because the federal center pays closer attention to the regional political process in an effort to bring federal power closer to the people. But the introduction of uniformity and regularity in electoral processes at the local level is good for Russia, as formal procedures gradually replace the whim of the powers-that-be.

The fate of RCC decisions on freedom of movement is a different story. These judgments required the complete overhaul of the national migration control system. Here, the RCC was taking a stand against both regional and federal executive branches that did not want to change their practices of social control.[158] Regions openly defied these judgments as they limited their ability to control the influx of migrants and to charge exorbitant fees for residence permits. Under Yeltsin, the regions frequently overrode RCC judgments on this matter and suffered no punishment for noncompliance.[159] To the disappointment of the RCC judges, the Procuracy and the police supported this regional defiance.

---

[156] For an overview of Putin's local self-government reform, see Tomila Lankina, "President Putin's Local Self-Government Reforms," in Peter Reddaway and Robert W. Orttung, eds., *The Dynamics of Russian Politics: Putin's Reform of Federal–Regional Relations, Volume 2* (Lanham, MD: Rowman and Littlefield, 2005), pp. 145–177.

[157] The latest such attempt occurred in the fall of 2006 when the pro-Kremlin "United Russia" party sponsored a bill that would give regional governors the option of eliminating the post of mayor in their regional capitals. See, for example, Aleksei Makarkin, "Mery: borba za nezavisimost," [Mayors: Battle for Independence] *Pro et Contra*, vol. 11, no. 1 (2007), pp. 19–29, available at http://www.carnegie.ru/en/pubs/procontra/Vol11num1-02.pdf.

[158] Aleksei Kirpichnikov, "Est takie mekhanizmy!" [There Are Such Mechanisms!] *Segodnia*, April 11, 1996.

[159] For a passionate defense of regional noncompliance, see Petr Kurdiuk, "O praktike ispolneniia Konstitutsionnogo Suda Rossiiskoi Federatsii Zakonodatelnym Sobraniem Krasnodarskogo kraia," [On the Practice of Implementing the RF Constitutional Court Decisions by the Legislative Assembly of the Krasnodar Territory] in Mitiukov et al., *Problemy ispolneniia . . .*, pp. 165–167.

Law-enforcement agencies resisted any attempts to allow judicial oversight of refusals to issue residence permits and to punish local bureaucrats for noncompliance with RCC decisions. Instead, as the head of the Enforcement Department of the RCC publicly complained, local police officials argued that they followed a secret directive that contradicted the RCC decisions.[160] In summer 2007, Federal Migration Service officials claimed that there was no discrimination on the basis of residence permits even though the Russian Human Rights Ombudsman admitted that such discrimination "penetrated numerous spheres of everyday life" and experts from the Russian Academy of Sciences estimated that at least 3 million Russians were discriminated against on this basis.[161] The Russian Supreme Court has also proved inconsistent in fighting against regional attempts to restrict mobility rights. In summary, Soviet-era residence permits restricting freedom of movement still play a vital role in the life of ordinary Russians, regardless of several landmark decisions by the RCC and repeated complaints by it justices about the sabotage of these decisions on the ground.[162]

Vladimir Putin's efforts to enforce the supremacy of federal laws (not the federal constitution) in all regions seem to focus on building a certain kind of legal hierarchy.[163] In practice, though, this hierarchy aspires to achieve the compatibility of all regional laws with presidential decrees and directives of the federal Cabinet. President Putin had his own needs in mind: less than half of his orders were implemented in 2002, and,

---

[160] Tatiana Bolshakova, "Realizatsiia reshenii Konstitutsionnogo Suda," [Implementation of the Constitutional Court Decisions] in S. Gannushkina and Iu. Chardina, eds., *Problemy zhertv voennykh deistvii v Chechenskoi Respublike. Mekhanizm realizatsii reshenii sudov i mer prokurorskogo reagirovaniia* (Moskva: NIPTs Memorial, 2000), chapter 8, available at http://www.memo.ru/hr/refugees/sem8rus/Chapter10.htm.

[161] Alexandr Naumov and Alexandr Kolesnichenko, "Ves registratsii," [Weight of Registration] *Novye izvestiia*, 6 June 2007, available at http://www.newizv.ru/print/70549.

[162] See, for example, Interview of RCC Chairman Valerii Zorkin, December 1, 2006, *Konsultant Plius*, at http://www.consultant.ru/law/interview/zorkinbd.html; "Vot takie pravila bespraviia," [Here Are the Rules of Rightlessness] *Rodnaia gazeta*, March 12, 2004, p. 20; and "Pasportnye stoly Moskvy pridumyvaiut svoi 'pravila registratsii'" [Passport Offices in Moscow Make up Their Own Registration Rules], *Izvestiia*, September 21, 2004, http://www.izvestia.ru/capital/article420094.

[163] Speaking to a conference of Russian judges and law-enforcement officials in January 2003, then RCC Chairman Baglai declared that "the Rule-of-Law State is the one in which judges govern!" Sitting next to him, President Vladimir Putin could not help replying that he always thought, "the Rule-of-Law State is the one in which laws govern!" Yuri Feofanov, "Zakony i sud'i," *Vremya MN*, February 6, 2003, p. 6.

in 2003, 935 legal acts of federal departments violated federal law.[164] Therefore, it is unclear whether Constitutional Court decisions would end up at the top of this legal hierarchy, given that, as I have shown in this chapter, the federal center under both presidents failed to implement numerous RCC decisions on basic rights. Moreover, the supremacy of federal laws makes the constitution flexible. According to many observers, federal laws that were passed by pliant parliament during Putin's presidency allowed Vladimir Putin to "transform the scope of basic constitutional definitions and the hierarchy of their values."[165] Finally, the short-term power needs of rulers and their subordinates and the instrumental use of courts in politically motivated campaigns against regional bosses, political opponents, or billionaires undermine the image of the judiciary and entrench arbitrary implementation of court decisions. RCC Justice Gadis Gadzhiev aptly summed up the campaigns against the oligarchs, "It is impossible in a law-based state to single out a particular business firm, pull it out like a bunch of radishes in the garden, and scream: 'caught red-handed!' While other businesses continue to operate in the same way. This is not a law-based state, this is pure arbitrariness!"[166]

The Public Image of the Russian Constitutional Court

As should be clear by now, many landmark decisions of the 2nd RCC did not reach the average Russian due to sometimes open, sometimes secret, defiance by political branches, federal and regional bureaucracies, and other courts. Because of this defiance, the groundbreaking potential of the human rights jurisprudence was buried under secret executive directives, which in turn were covered up by other courts. The Russian voters thus lacked any capacity to monitor the implementation of RCC judgments and could punish neither elected officials nor nonelected judges and bureaucrats. Year after year, hundreds of petitioners complained to the RCC about this noncompliance, while the Court responded with decisions with so-called positive content, which were often ignored by the rest of the government and went unnoticed by the rest of Russian society.

---

[164] "Kontrol nad glavnym," [Control over Chief] *Izvestiia*, May 15, 2003, p. 3; Sabir Kekhlerov, Deputy Procurator-General, speech at the conference on the Monitoring of Legal Space, Moscow, May 20, 2004, http://www.garant.ru/files/audio/kehlerov01.mp3.
[165] See, for example, Andrey N. Medushevsky, *Russian Constitutionalism: Historical and Contemporary Development* (New York: Routledge, 2006), pp. 216–217.
[166] "Konstitutsiia vam v pomoshch," [Let the Constitution Help You] *Dvoinaia zapis*, no. 12 (December 2003).

248   *The 2nd Russian Constitutional Court (1995–2007)*

This chronic nonenforcement of RCC decisions in the area of human rights explains why the "rights revolution," Russian-style still has not occurred and why the politicization of rights litigation was not prominent, as is the case in other countries with active judicial review.[167] Moreover, this sabotage on the part of the bureaucracy and other courts explains why, when asked to evaluate the work of the RCC, Russians consistently give it a failing grade. According to one survey by the authoritative All-Russian Center for the Study of Public Opinion (VTsIOM), between February 2001 and September 2002, the RCC, like other Russian courts, received a 2.77–2.91 mark on a five-point scale, trailing behind the president, the federal Cabinet, the army, the security services, and the law-enforcement agencies.[168] The same pattern of weak public approval of the Court seems to continue. According to one poll, only 14 percent of St. Petersburg residents reported that the RCC "worked well" in 2002–2003. In February 2006, only 20 percent of Russians surveyed by VTsIOM reported that that the Court "worked well."[169] Throughout the past decade, Russians also consistently distrusted political parties and the parliament, which means that voters in Russia (as in the case of Hungary, which I discussed in Chapter 2) are unlikely to use elections as a weapon against officials who disobey Constitutional Court decisions.

Note that these low levels of satisfaction with the RCC were recorded during Putin's presidency, precisely when the Court became bolder in its decisions regarding federalism and human rights cases, and when politicians amended the 1994 RCC Act to strengthen punishment for defiance of the Court. Paradoxically, when it comes to particular RCC decisions, Russians tend to approve of them, as happened in 2002 with the speedy introduction of judicial arrest warrants or with presidential powers to remove regional governors, discussed above. But when it comes to the general evaluation of the RCC, citizens are so critical of this tribunal that even

---

[167] See, for example, Charles R. Epp, *The Rights Revolution* (Chicago: University of Chicago Press, 1998); and Ran Hirschl, *Towards Juristocracy* (Cambridge, MA: Harvard University Press, 2004).

[168] Russian schools use a five-point scale that ranges from one (fail) to five (excellent), where three is a passing grade. See L. A. Sedov, "Obshchestvennoe mnenie v sentiabre 2002 goda," [Public Opinion in September 2002] *VTsIOM*, October 7, 2002, available at http://www.levada.ru/press/2002100700.html, accessed December 17, 2007.

[169] "Bolshinstvo peterburzhtsev dovolny rabotoi Prezidenta Rossii za poslednii god," [Most Petersburgers Are Satisfied with the Performance of the Russian President in the Last Year] *300online.Ru*, July 1, 2003, http://www.300online.ru/articleso/5969.html; VTsIOM, "Constitutional Court: An Important Yet Little-Known Institution," *Press-vypusk no. 395*, February 16, 2006.

Rights Revolutions Unfulfilled

Putin's administration has chosen to comment in public only on favorable RCC judgments. As one official in the presidential administration admitted, "We do not criticize Constitutional Court decisions – we either approve of them or keep silent."[170] Explaining this paradox of simultaneous public support of landmark judgments and disapproval of the Court's work in general is beyond the scope of this book. But the pattern of chronic noncompliance clearly damages the reputation of the Court in the eyes of ordinary Russians.

One could improve the Court's reputation if the citizens knew more about it. Research on public attitudes with respect to the U.S. Supreme Court has clearly shown that those who know the court tend to view it more favorably, even if individuals disagree with particular judgments. Public approval of the Court comes, in part, from belief in "principled decision making" of judges, fair and legalistic procedures in the court, and other ideals of judicial neutrality, impartiality, and independence.[171] By the middle of its second decade, the RCC, however, confronts a serious challenge in public ignorance. Unlike politicians, bureaucrats, and the judicial community, ordinary Russians do not know much about their federal Constitutional Court. In fact, two out of three residents of St. Petersburg, the second largest city in Russia, surveyed in June 2003, reported that they knew nothing about the work of the RCC. By February 2006, the same proportion of Russians reported the same lack of knowledge about the work of the tribunal, and 95 percent of them could not name even a single case decided by the 14-year-old Constitutional Court.[172] This widespread ignorance explains why, for example, Russians simply ignored the landmark RCC decision banning the death penalty, even though four out of five Russians consistently favor capital punishment.[173] Similarly, although 80 percent of Russians reported that

---

[170] Interview with an official of the presidential administration, Moscow, May 25, 2001. Indeed, observers noted that the Kremlin kept quiet about the July 2002 RCC decision on the extension of term limits of regional governors. See, for example, Stoner-Weiss, *Resisting the State*, p. 152.

[171] See, for example, Tom Tyler and Gregory Mitchell, "Legitimacy and Empowerment of Discretionary Legal Authority: The United States Supreme Court and Abortion Rights," *Duke Law Journal*, vol. 43, no. 4 (1994), pp. 703–815; and Vanessa A. Baird, "Building Institutional Legitimacy: The Role of Procedural Justice," *Political Research Quarterly*, vol. 54 (2001), pp. 333–354.

[172] "Bolshinstvo peterburzhtsev"; "Constitutional Court: An Important Yet Little-Known Institution."

[173] RCC decision 3-P of February 2, 1999, *VKS RF*, no. 3 (1999), pp. 12–24, English translation in *Statutes and Decisions*, no. 4 (2001).

they felt unprotected from crime in the past decade, they voiced no objections to dozens of groundbreaking decisions by the Court on the due process rights of the suspects, the accused, and prisoners.[174]

In judgment after judgment, the RCC ordered regular courts to enforce the Russian constitution, yet public trust in the judicial branch remains low.[175] In the fall of 2000, according to the nationwide Russian Citizen Survey of 1,804 persons, 71.4 percent of Russians had low, or no trust at all, in Russian courts as compared to 50.7 percent who distrusted the Constitutional Court. However, 8 percent of respondents said that they had very strong trust in the RCC, while only 4 percent reported very strong trust in courts in general.[176] According to the New Russia Barometer, between 2001 and 2003, about 25 percent of Russians trusted the Constitutional Court as compared to 55 percent of respondents who reported no trust in the tribunal. A similar level of distrust is reported for courts, in general. Despite knowing much about the RCC, 29 percent of Russians surveyed in 2001 thought that the tribunal had a "big influence" on their lives, while 44 percent thought that it had a "small influence." Russians accorded similar low levels of importance to political parties, the State Duma, police, and newspapers, while President Putin, regional governors, and magnates were believed to be much more important.[177] Five years later, the public perception did not change much: one out of three Russians thought the RCC played a big role in the life of the nation, another third believed otherwise, and another third had no opinion. When asked whether they thought the RCC was completely independent, 12 percent of Russians answered positively as compared to 18 percent who thought the opposite. Meanwhile, 28 percent thought that the Court "aspired to act independently but it was not

---

[174] "Rossiiane stali individualistami," [Russians Became Individualistic] *IA MiK*, January 9, 2003.

[175] Due to the lack of reliability of polling data in Russia, which is recognized by both Western and Russian experts and RCC justices, I provide survey data on courts from both Western and Russian sources. On the challenges of conducting reliable public opinion research in Russia, see, for example, Theodore P. Gerber and Sarah E. Mendelson, "Research Addendum," *Post Soviet Affairs*, vol. 19 (2003), pp. 187–188; and Natalia Konygina, "Obshchestvennoe mnenie vozmut pod kontrol," [Public Opinion Will Be Taken under Control] *Izvestiia*, August 6, 2003.

[176] One-fifth of Russians were undecided about their trust in the RCC as compared to only 9 percent of Russians who were undecided about their trust in courts in general. Jonsson, "The Constitutional Court . . . " p. 20.

[177] Richard Rose, "New Russia Barometer XI: The End of Term Report," *Studies in Public Policy*, no. 378 (2003), p. 29 and Richard Rose, "New Russia Barometer 10: Russians under Putin," *Studies in Public Policy*, no. 350 (2001), pp. 34, 39.

Rights Revolutions Unfulfilled

always possible."[178] A survey of 102 well-placed jurists in Moscow in the summer of 2004 also suggested a stronger respect for the Constitutional Court than any other court in Russia. Legal elites perceived the RCC as the court least likely to experience attempts by political and economic actors to influence judges.[179]

The social demand for independent and powerful courts is present, even if it is hidden under cynicism about the current state of the judicial system. After all, every year the Russian courts hear thousands of cases against the government and often side with private litigants.[180] Moreover, since the beginning of the 1990s, three-quarters of Russians have believed that a "judicial system that treats everyone equally" is important for democracy, and that the right to judicial protection is a "very important" right.[181] Similarly, surveys of normative attitudes of ordinary Russians reveal a consistent respect for the rule of law in the past decade, on a par with other European nations.[182] This is why two out of three Russians consistently supported judicial reform as a way to get rid of corruption and the Soviet-era legal system.[183] This abstract support for judicial independence spills over to the Russian Constitutional Court. According to one survey, excluding those with no opinion, 77 percent of Russians surveyed

---

[178] Forty-two percent had no opinion. VTsIOM, "Constitutional Court: An Important Yet Little-Known Institution."

[179] Russian Axis, *The Judicial System of the Russian Federation: A Systemic Crisis of Independence* (London: Russian Axis, 2004), available at http://www.russianaxis.org.

[180] For an insightful analysis of the lack of correlation between attitudes towards the law and litigation behavior, see Kathryn Hendley, "'Demand' for Law in Russia – A Mixed Picture," *East European Constitutional Review*, vol. 10, no. 4 (2001), pp. 72–77, at 74. For analysis of the actual state of administrative justice in Russia, see Peter H. Solomon, "Judicial Power in Russia: Through the Prism of Administrative Justice," *Law and Society Review*, vol. 38, no. 3 (September 2004), pp. 549–581.

[181] James R. Millar and Sharon L. Wolchik, "Introduction: The Social Legacies and the Aftermath of Communism," in James R. Millar and Sharon L. Wolchik, eds., *The Social Legacy of Communism* (New York: Cambridge University Press, 1994), p. 8. Inga Mikhailovskaia, Evgenii Kuzminskii, and Iurii Mazaev, *Prava cheloveka i sotsialno-politicheskie protsessy v postkommunisticheskoi Rossii* [Human Rights and Sociopolitical Processes in Postcommunist Russia] (Moskva: Proektnaia gruppa po pravam cheloveka, 1997), pp. 54–57.

[182] James L. Gibson, "Russian Attitudes towards the Rule of Law: An Analysis of Survey Data," in Denis J. Galligan and Marina Kurkchiyan, eds., *Law and Informal Practices: The Post-Communist Experience* (New York: Oxford University Press, 2003), pp. 77–91.

[183] "Otnoshenie rossiian k sudebnoi reforme ostaetsia ustoichivo pozitivnym," [Attitudes of Russians Towards Court Reform Remain Firmly Positive] *Strana.Ru*, November 15, 2001.

during Yeltsin's presidency believed that their government should obey the RCC.[184] Similarly, surveys of Russian elites, carried out under both Yeltsin and Putin in 1998 and 2000, show overwhelming support for strong constitutional review: only 3–4 percent of elites in Moscow and the regions agreed with the statement that "the president shall be able to overrule the Constitutional Court."[185] Moreover, according to a 2007 nationwide poll, 49 percent of Russians surveyed reported that the term "fairness," which the RCC uses so often in its judicial reasoning, aroused positive feelings in them.[186]

This is good news for the RCC because it can adjust its own approach toward disseminating its jurisprudence. This task of spreading reports about judicial neutrality, impartiality, and independence is daunting in the context of low public confidence in this tribunal as well as in the rest of the judicial system. Repairing the reputation of the RCC as well as other courts involves both supplying positive information about the Court and increasing public demand for strong legal accountability of political branches.

Indeed, the experience of the 1st RCC in 1992–1993 clearly shows that its members understood the necessity of popularizing the Court in the eyes of the public as they advertised their decisions (and dissenting opinions) in the mass media on a regular basis. Following the Court's suspension, its members continued advocating their views in the media. The revival of the RCC in 1995 and its avoidance of controversial cases, except the infamous *Chechnya* decision, which allowed the use of federal troops to prevent the secession of Chechnya, were also accompanied by active coverage of the tribunal in the press. Facing a bitterly divided bench, then Chairman Tumanov could not simply ban the anti-Yeltsin justices from venting their opposition in the mass media, and he often spoke publicly on the Court's work, the relations among justices, and Russian constitutional reforms. At the same time, Tumanov chastised the mass media for mounting a "large-scale unfounded criticism of state institutions."[187]

---

[184] William L. Miller, Stephen White, and Paul Heywood, *Values and Political Change in Postcommunist Europe* (New York: St. Martin's Press, 1998), pp. 151–152, as quoted in Gibson, "Russian Attitudes," p. 81.

[185] Anton Steen, *Political Elites and the New Russia* (New York: Routledge, 2003), p. 55.

[186] Fifty-eight percent reported the same about the term "order" and 37 percent about the term "freedom." "Poriadok i spravedlivost – glavnye tsennosti rossiian," [Order and Fairness – Chief Values of Russians] *VTsIOM*, March 27, 2007, available at http://wciom.ru/arkhiv/tematicheskii-arkhiv/item/single/4271.html.

[187] See Tumanov's bitter remarks on the role of the media in V. P. Kazimirchuk, ed., *Konstitutsiia i zakon: stabilnost i dinamizm* [Constitution and Law: Stability and Dynamics](Moskva: IGP RAN, 1998), p. 24.

Rights Revolutions Unfulfilled 253

Tumanov's successor, Chairman Baglai, however, preferred to use private and informal channels and gradually restricted the freedom of individual judges to use the mass media. He also appeared to disapprove of the justices and Court clerks commenting on RCC judgments.[188] This lack of visibility of the RCC, together with hundreds of unpublished decisions and secret defiance of these decisions by federal and local politicians, bureaucrats and courts, led one respected legal commentator to complain at the 10-year anniversary of the RCC that the "work of the RCC remains unknown to the society. The TV does not show sessions of the Court, and Chairman Marat Baglai does not give interviews and vigorously refuses to comment on the judgments of the Court."[189] This "shyness" of the Baglai Court is not random. As I have shown in Chapter 5, several RCC decisions clearly deviated from the political mood of the powers-that-be. But Chairman Baglai may have also wanted to protect the young Court's "due process rights revolution" from public backlash.

In any case, by 2001, his colleagues clearly abandoned the view that the "invisible" Court could achieve much and launched a massive PR campaign to mark the 10-year anniversary of the Court. President Putin's tinkering with the 1994 RCC Act and his decision to ship the Court to St.Petersburg, described in Chapter 3, provoked even more of an outcry from the bench. The fact that the judges elected Valerii Zorkin in early 2003 to head the Court, despite his "peacemaking" mission in the constitutional crisis of 1993, was a clear signal for a more visible Court. Indeed, by 2005 the RCC was publishing a larger share of its judgments, which previously would have been buried in the Court's archives, and posting them on its official Web site. Moreover, the judges or their clerks provide brief commentaries on judgments to the electronic and the print media on a regular basis. The press service of the RCC is one of the most open ones in Moscow, according to journalists, and is instrumental in both advertising the work of the Court as well as doing damage control for unpopular judicial decisions. This openness, however, has its own costs. As Chairman Zorkin summed up in early 2004, judicial empowerment requires "transparency, openness, high competence, honesty and many other elements of speedy and fair administration of justice from the RCC and judicial system as whole."[190] But it also involves monetary costs

---

[188] Interview with the clerk of the RCC, Moscow, June 15, 2001.

[189] Iurii Feofanov, "Konstitutsiia – to, chto govorit o nei sudia," [Constitution Is What Judge Says It Is] *Izvestiia*, November 1, 2001, p. 4.

[190] "Valerii Zorkin: Ia uveren, chto vlast sudebnykh reshenii okrepnet," [Valerii Zorkin: I am Confident That the Power of Court Decisions Will Become Stronger] *Kollegiia*, no. 2 (2004), pp. 2–4.

for the media outlets that publish RCC decisions. As Zorkin publicly complained to President Putin in March 2006, "Russia's Gazette," which publishes RCC judgments and federal legislation, was not on sale in Moscow and beyond, and, as a result, average Russians could not read these judgments. Zorkin insisted that the government had to find ways of printing extra copies of the Gazette to make it accessible to ordinary citizens.[191] In short, currently, the RCC appears to realize the value of public opinion and attempts to change it not only by issuing judgments and insisting on their compliance but also by advertising the work of the Court among the masses. And if the Court manages to convert the complicated language of its decisions into a message that is easily understood by ordinary Russians, the RCC may eventually receive a passing grade from its citizens.

CONCLUSION

Just as securing compliance with judicial decisions is a challenge for any court in any country, studying behavioral compliance with high court decisions is a daunting task for researchers.[192] Usually, a widespread perception of the weak role of the post-Soviet judiciary in public policy making leads to the quick conclusion that even if courts are independent decision makers, they still lack sufficient authority to compel the government to comply with judicial decisions. What happens after the Constitutional Court issues an antigovernment decision? It depends. It depends on the authoritativeness of the judgment and the Court itself in the "power map" of a polity. My analysis of the young RCC supports the argument that "the authoritativeness of judicial decisions or the readiness of government officials and members of the public to comply stems from a mixture of ingrained attitudes toward courts and short-term calculations."[193] As I have shown in this book, Russian political actors have had a wide range of responses to Constitutional Court decisions (from suspension of the Court in 1993–1994 to prompt compliance) and have only begun to learn to cooperate in an uncertain institutional environment. Although a few academics still advocate the abolition of the RCC or merging it

---

[191] Anna Zakatnova, "Pravovoi barer," [The Legal Barrier] *Rossiiskaia Gazeta*, March 15, 2006.

[192] On both of these challenges in the U.S. context, see Tyler and Mitchell, "Legitimacy and Empowerment," p. 721.

[193] See, for example, Solomon, "Judicial Power in Russia," p. 553.

Conclusion

with the Supreme Court,[194] political actors widely use judicial review to pursue their policy preferences and obey the Court. Similarly, recalcitrant regions no longer suspend the jurisdiction of this Court on their territories, as was the case in 1992. On the contrary, they flood this tribunal with their petitions against the federal center. President Putin's efforts to streamline the mechanisms of Russian governance may further contribute to this cohabitation of the RCC with the rest of government actors, who are slowly learning to use court decisions as political resources. In short, the last decade of Russia's competitive authoritarianism, to use the term coined by Lucan Way and Steven Levitsky, generated demand for judicial review among rival elites. But it was not enough to compel rulers to obey the Constitutional Court.

Beneath Putin's efforts to formalize Russian governance, there lies a structure of informal sanctions and incentives that influences the extent to which bureaucrats and the rest of the judiciary are willing and able to carry out the decisions of the Russian Constitutional Court. Unlike the increasing willingness of political actors to obey the Court, this informal structure has been largely successful in defying the Court and blocking the implementation of its landmark rulings. This is why the judicial strategy of concentrating on individual rights cases did not result in higher public trust in the Court. As I have shown in this chapter, street-level bureaucrats obeyed the RCC in large part only after their superiors ordered them to do so. Still, the hierarchy and discipline within the Russian bureaucracy cannot be taken for granted. Both Yeltsin's and Putin's Russia show the inability of rulers to concentrate political control over large segments of the bureaucracy in the center and in the provinces.[195] Many other factors, like corruption, business interests, pressure from local politicians, a hostile public mood, and even familial ties, prevail in the everyday life of public administration.[196] This means that the

---

[194] See, for example, S. V. Borodin and V. N. Kudriavtsev, "O sudebnoi vlasti v Rossii," [On Judicial Power in Russia] *Gosudarstvo i pravo*, no. 10 (2001): 21–27, at 23; and Vladimir Popondopulo, "Zachem Femide tri ruki?" [Why Themis Needs Three Arms?] *Parlamentskaia gazeta*, October 19, 2004.

[195] See, for example, Smith, *State-Building in Russia*; Lucan A. Way, "Authoritarian State Building and the Sources of Regime Competitiveness in the Fourth Wave: The Cases of Belarus, Moldova, Russia, and Ukraine," *World Politics*, vol. 57, no. 2 (January 2005), pp. 231–261; and Stoner-Weiss, *Resisting the State*.

[196] For more on the practice of Russia's public administration, see Alena V. Ledeneva, *How Russia Really Works: The Informal Practices That Shaped Post-Soviet Politics and Business* (Ithaca, NY: Cornell University Press, 2006). For comparative perspectives on this issue, see Marc Hertogh and Simon Halliday, eds., *Judicial Review and Bureaucratic Impact* (Cambridge, UK: Cambridge University Press, 2004).

elite competition works against the successful enforcement of Constitutional Court decisions. As this chapter makes clear, it was not the "legitimate" power of the Court, flowing from judgments about the Court's authority, that guided government officials in deciding whether to obey the RCC. On the contrary, it was the "coercive" power of department heads or other important figures that compelled bureaucrats to obey the Court.[197]

The RCC judges acutely felt this prevalence of coercive power. In 1992, the first year of the RCC, Justice Vitruk complained that government officials often disregarded the constitution and defied RCC decisions due to low levels of respect for the law and the constitution.[198] In 1996, Justice Morshchakova still complained that street-level bureaucrats blocked the implementation of RCC decisions. In her view, the Court, together with the political branches, would have to "break the psychology" of officials to make them obey judicial decisions.[199] In 2001, the "implementation" amendments to the 1994 RCC Act reinforced this view that Constitutional Court decisions meant something in practice only after the federal center or the regional governments amended or repealed the norm that had been declared void by the Court. In mid-2004, retired Justice Morshchakova still complained that "inquisitorial thinking of the local judges and the law-enforcement officers" blocked groundbreaking RCC judgments in the area of due process rights. And by mid-2007, Chairman Zorkin still complained about problems in implementing judgments of his Court.[200] Therefore, new rights and unwritten constitutional principles that were created by the RCC still have to find their niche in the law on the ground.

---

[197] For the distinction between "coercive" power, contingent on external negative outcomes, and "legitimate" power, internalized by the voluntary acceptance of the legitimate authority, see John R. P. French, Jr. and Bertram H. Raven, "The Bases of Social Power," in Dorwin Cartwright, ed., *Studies in Social Power* (Ann Arbor, MI: Research Center for Group Dynamics, Institute for Social Research, University of Michigan, 1959), pp. 150, 156–161, as quoted in Tyler and Mitchell "Legitimacy and Empowerment," p. 721, fn. 54.

[198] "Esli vas uvolili po starosti, otkazalis propisat ili lishili liubimoi gazety . . . Konstitutsionnyi sud Rossii v gostiakh u 'Literaturnoi gazety,'" *Literaturnaia gazeta*, March 4, 1992, p. 11.

[199] Maslennikov, "Konstitutsionnyi sud."

[200] Leonid Nikitinskii, " . . . I suda net. Diagnoz doktora Morshchakovoi," [. . . And No Court. Diagnosis by Doctor Morshchakova] *Novaia gazeta*, July 19, 2004; and Ivanov, "Neuvazhaemyi Konstitutsionnyi sud."

Conclusion 257

Making a difference in the lives of ordinary Russians, however, is impossible without informing them about judicial decisions and cultivating ideals about judicial independence and impartiality. This is yet another challenge for the RCC as well as for the rest of the judiciary, in addition to changing the mentality of the bureaucracy. More and more Russians win against the government in courts, yet public confidence in the judicial system is steadily low year after year, contrary to mainstream judicial legitimacy theories.[201] Only the courts themselves can narrow this gap between the practice of administrative and constitutional justice and the low levels of public trust in the judiciary. Drawing on widespread normative respect for the rule of law and abstract support for the RCC, the Court can surely do more in educating the public about proportionality and fairness so that an average Russian understands the importance of the "quiet" judge-made revolutions in her life.[202] Making citizens aware that the Court rules on the basis of a kind of constitutional philosophy can only improve the reputation of judges in the eyes of the wider society.[203] Only then will this internalization of judicial legitimacy, together with greater public interest in holding government officials accountable via the threat of litigation, be likely to strengthen judicial power in Russia.

[201] See, for example, James Gibson, Gregory Caldeira, and Vanessa Baird, "On the Legitimacy of National High Courts," *American Political Science Review*, vol. 92, no. 2 (June 1998), pp. 343–358.

[202] On the "quiet revolutions," engineered by the RCC, see Stoner-Weiss, *Resisting the State*, pp. 151–152; V. Bozhev, "Tikhaia revoliutsiia Konstitutsionnogo Suda v ugolovnom protsesse Rossiiskoi Federatsii," [Quiet Revolution of Constitutional Court in the RF Criminal Procedure] *Rossiiskaia iustitsiia*, no. 10 (2000), p. 9; and A. Pavlushina, "Sudebnyi normokontrol: 'tikhaia revoliutsiia' v grazhdanskom protsesse," [Judicial Review of Laws: 'Quiet Revolution' in Civil Procedure], *ibid.*, no. 7 (2002), p. 17.

[203] For a similar argument made in the study of the Mexican Supreme Court, see Staton, "Judicial Activism and Public Authority Compliance."

8

"Tinkering with Judicial Tenure" and "Wars of Courts" in Comparative Perspective

Judging Russia's trials and tribulations with constitutional review is impossible without comparing them against the experiences of constitutional courts in other countries. Is Russia's nonlinear judicial empowerment unique? To answer this question, we need to look at actual judicial politics elsewhere in order to detect whether judicial empowerment is a dynamic and nonlinear process. This chapter explores how other countries dealt with the two most controversial issues that arose in making and remaking the Russian Constitutional Court. One of them was the role of politicians who repeatedly tinkered with judicial tenure attempting to create a friendlier bench, as I discussed in Chapter 3. In the process of this tinkering, judges had to become politicians and lobby the political branches to either lengthen their tenure or leave their Court alone. As a result of this tinkering, Justice Morshchakova, for example, overstayed her term on the bench – a fact that generated conflict within the Court. If my argument that short-term power needs prevail in the business of creating constitutional courts is correct, we should at least examine the attempts (successful or failed) at changing judicial tenure in other countries.

The second main controversy involved the repeated clashes between the constitutional court and other top courts. As I demonstrated in Chapters 3 through 7, the Russian Supreme Court correctly foresaw these clashes, tried its best to prevent the RCC from reviewing verdicts of ordinary courts, and, when that failed, staunchly defended its appellate jurisdiction from invasion by the RCC and even fiercely competed for the power to police Russian federalism. Are these controversies yet more proof of Russian exceptionalism: the lack of rule-of-law traditions, a totalitarian legal culture, low popularity of the constitutional court, and so on? If my argument that the intercourt rivalries are systemic is correct, then we

"Tinkering with Judicial Tenure" in Comparative Perspective 259

should witness such rivalries beyond Russia, in democracies and non-democracies alike.

"TINKERING WITH JUDICIAL TENURE" IN COMPARATIVE PERSPECTIVE

Surveying the age of judicial empowerment reveals that during the period of 1967–2003 more than a dozen countries, in addition to Russia, attempted to modify the terms of judicial tenure *de jure* or *de facto* (see Table 8.1).[1] Most of these attempts involved extensive bargaining between politicians and justices and resulted in changes in the actual length of judicial tenure. This shows that political majorities continue to keep the judiciary accountable even though the "global diffusion of judicial power" limits the range of choices available to political branches of government in their efforts to influence judicial decision making.

In some countries, justices of newly created constitutional courts overstayed their terms. In Albania, justices of the 3-year-old Constitutional Court refused to submit to rotation in 1995 and to retire after their first 3 years on the bench.[2] In Spain, Constitutional Tribunal magistrates overstayed their terms 4 to 6 months when political wrangling delayed the election of new members of the Tribunal in 1983 and 1992.[3] To address this problem, the tenure of Italian Constitutional Court justices was changed in 1967 to make them retire exactly after the expiry of their 9-year term on the bench.[4] Prior to this amendment, the rules of the Court established that a justice should remain in office until the date on which the justice called to replace him or her was sworn in.[5] In Portugal, the wrangling of political parties prior to the 1997 constitutional amendments and the very process of revising the constitution effectively delayed the reappointment of the Constitutional Tribunal justices for two

---

[1] This section draws on Alexei Trochev, "'Tinkering with Tenure': The Russian Constitutional Court in Comparative Perspective," in Ferdinand Feldbrugge, ed., *Russia, Europe, and the Rule of Law* (The Hague: Martinus Nijhoff, 2006), pp. 47–78.

[2] "Albania Update," *East European Constitutional Review*, vol. 4, no. 3 (1995), p. 3.

[3] Heidi Ly Beirich, "The Role of the Constitutional Tribunal in Spanish Politics (1980–1995)," (Ph.D. diss., Purdue University, 1998), pp. 184–189.

[4] Forty years later, exactly the same change of judicial tenure was made in Bulgaria by the decision of the Bulgarian Constitutional Court that declared unconstitutional this tenure clause in Article 5 of the Law on the Bulgarian Constitutional Court. See Decision No. 1 of March 7, 2006, *Darzhaven Vestnik*, no. 23, March 17, 2006.

[5] Annibale Marini, "Regarding the Guarantees of Independence of the Italian Constitutional Court," *Konstitutsionnoe pravosudie*, no. 3 (2001), p. 141.

TABLE 8.1. *Tinkering with the tenure of high courts in comparative perspective*

Country	When	Term of office on paper	Changed term of office
		JUDGES OVERSTAY	
Albania	1995	3-year rotation	Judges refuse to retire
Spain	1983, 1992	3-year rotation of one-third of the court	overstayed 4–6 months
Portugal	1995–1998	6-year term	overstayed 2.5 years
Russia	2001–2002	retire at age sixty-five	overstayed 1 year
		TENURE AMENDMENTS	
Italy	1967	9 years until replaced	calendar 9-year term
Bulgaria	2006	9 years until replaced	calendar 9-year term
South Africa	1996	7-year nonrenewable term	12-year nonrenewable term, retire at age seventy
Portugal	1997	6-year, renewable term	9-year, nonrenewable term
Poland	1997	8-year term, with rotation of one-half of the Court every 4 years	9-year term, no rotation
Taiwan	1997	9-year term	8-year term, with rotation of one-half of the Court every 4 years
Egypt	2001	retire at age sixty-four	retire at age sixty-six
Slovakia	2001	7-year term	12-year term
Kyrgyzstan	2003	15-year term	10-year term
Kyrgyzstan	2007	10-year term	life tenure, retire at age seventy
Azerbaijan	2003	10-year, once renewable	15-year, nonrenewable
		FAILED TENURE AMENDMENTS	
Israel	1965	retire at age seventy	retire at age seventy-five
Hungary	1998	9-year, once renewable	12-year, nonrenewable
Armenia	2002	life tenure, retire at age seventy	12-year, retire at age sixty-five
Ukraine (draft)	2003	9-year nonrenewable, retire at age sixty-five	9-year, once renewable, retire at age seventy-five

"Tinkering with Judicial Tenure" in Comparative Perspective 261

and a half years (October 1995–March 1998)! The revised constitution increased the tenure of Portuguese Constitutional Tribunal justices from 6-year, renewable terms to 9-year, nonrenewable terms. Justices hailed this constitutional revision as a move to reduce the dependence of individual justices on political parties that appointed them.[6]

But there were also cases of extending judicial tenure where political wrangling over judicial appointments was not at issue. In the 1996 South African constitution, the tenure of sitting judges of the 2-year-old constitutional court was extended from 7-year to 12-year terms subject to the requirement that they retire at age seventy.[7] The new constitution of Poland, which entered in force in October 1997, extended the tenure of Constitutional Tribunal justices from 8 to 9 years and abolished the rotation of justices every 4 years.[8] In February 2001, the Slovak constitution was amended to extend the tenure of Constitutional Court justices from 7 to 12 years on the bench.[9] Nondemocratic regimes also tinkered with judicial tenure. The mandatory retirement age of the Egyptian Supreme Constitutional Court justices was extended from 64 to 66 years of age in 2001. The timing of this extension was made with the appointment of a new chief justice who proved to be loyal to the president and who was expected to "tame" the growing power and independence of the constitutional review tribunal.[10] In Azerbaijan, in 2003, the tenure of the justices of the 6-year-old Constitutional Court was extended from a ten-year, renewable term to a 15-year, nonrenewable term, but the new terms of office did not apply to the sitting justices.[11]

However, there were also "tenure" amendments that decreased the length of tenure. In 1997, Taiwan's constitution was amended to achieve what the Polish constitution makers did away with in their new 1997 constitution. Taiwan's constitutional reform shortened the terms of the

---

[6] Pedro C. Magalhães, "The Limits to Judicialization: Legislative Politics and Constitutional Review in the Iberian Democracies," (Ph.D. diss., Ohio State University, 2003), pp. 220–221, 313, 360, endnote 37.

[7] Heinz Klug, *Constituting Democracy: Law, Globalism and South Africa's Political Reconstruction* (New York: Cambridge University Press, 2000), p. 141.

[8] Article 194(1), 1997 Constitution of the Republic of Poland.

[9] "Constitution Watch: Slovakia," *East European Constitutional Review*, vol. 10, no. 1 (2001), available at http://www.law.nyu.edu/eecr/vol10num1/constitutionwatch/slovakia.html.

[10] Tamir Moustafa, *The Struggle for Constitutional Power: Law, Politics, and Economic Development in Egypt* (New York: Cambridge University Press, 2007), p. 198, fn. 53.

[11] The Law of Azerbaijan Republic on Constitutional Court of December 23, 2003, *Azerbaijan*, January 8, 2004. See the text of the law in English at http://www.legislationline.org/legislation.php?tid=112&lid=3320.

Council of Grand Justices from 9 to 8 years and provided for staggered appointments that coincide with the 4-year presidential election cycle. This set of "tenure" amendments serves to "ensure that each president can appoint roughly half the Council."[12] The February 2003 amendments to the Kyrgyzstan constitution reduced the tenure of the Constitutional Court justices from 15 to 10 years on the bench (Article 80(5)).[13] This reduction was a clear sign of dissatisfaction of then President Askar Akaev with the existing constitutional review tribunal. Moreover, the Tulip Revolution of 2005 that ousted Akaev from office failed to induce new political leaders to protect judicial tenure. In late 2005, current President Bakiev sponsored wholesale constitutional reform that sought to abolish the Constitutional Court altogether. Experts from the Venice Commission blasted Bakiev's plans and insisted on preserving the tribunal. They, together with Constitutional Court judges, seemed to convince President Bakiev to preserve a separate Constitutional Court.[14] But the chief justice had to physically stand between Bakiev and the opposition to ensure that whatever constitutional reform transpired it would keep the Constitutional Court operational. The latest constitutional amendments of October 2007 abolished the 10-year term for Constitutional Court judges and introduced life tenure with a mandatory retirement age of seventy.[15]

To be sure, there are examples of how tinkering with judicial tenure failed. Consider pre-Orange Revolution Ukraine. A presidential draft of the Ukrainian constitution that was published in early March 2003 raised the mandatory retirement age of Constitutional Court justices from sixty-five to seventy-five (Article 126), allowed justices to sit for a second 9-year term in a row (Article 148), and deleted the 3-year limit of the chief justice's term (Article 148). The then Chief Justice of the Ukrainian Constitutional Court, Mykola Selivon, publicly hinted that he would speed up the review of these amendments by his Court to clear the way for

---

[12] Tom Ginsburg, *Judicial Review in New Democracies: Constitutional Courts in Asian Cases* (Cambridge, UK: Cambridge University Press, 2003), p. 120.

[13] These provisions do not apply to the current Constitutional Court justices who continue to serve until the expiration of their 15-year terms (Article V-12).

[14] Bermet Malikova, "Chto mne zakony, kol sudi znakomy!" [Why Respect Laws If Judges Are My Buddies!] *Vechernii Bishkek*, December 1, 2005; Leila Saralaeva, "Kyrgyzstan: Saving the Constitutional Court," *Institute for War and Peace Reporting Central Asia*, no. 424, November 29, 2005, available at http://www.iwpr.net/?p=rca&s=f& o=258356&apc_state=henh.

[15] Articles 83.5 and 84.1 of the constitution of the Kyrgyz Republic.

"Tinkering with Judicial Tenure" in Comparative Perspective   263

their ratification at a nationwide referendum.[16] However, these proposals met serious opposition from political forces who expected to replace the majority of justices in September 2005 when their nonrenewable term would end. Socialist Party leader Oleksandr Moroz accused the Ukrainian president of bribing the justices and argued against extending their terms in office.[17] This time the opposition won, and President Kuchma withdrew these changes from the text of constitutional amendments that were approved by Ukrainian lawmakers a few weeks before the Orange Revolution of December 2004.

One of the constitutional reform proposals in Armenia limited the Constitutional Court members' term in office to 12 years and lowered the mandatory retirement age to sixty-five from the previous seventy. However, these proposals were not included in the text of the constitutional amendments decided by the constitutional referendum of May 2003, in which the majority of voters rejected any amendments to the 1995 Armenian Constitution.[18]

Among failed attempts to extend the judicial tenure of incumbent chief justices are the Israeli and Hungarian cases. In Israel in 1965, several members of the Knesset proposed to extend the age of retirement from seventy to seventy-five to keep soon-to-retire Supreme Court President Izhak Olshan in office. The legal argument for this was similar to the Russian case, namely, to equalize the retirement age for the Supreme Court president with that of the head of the rabbinical court, seventy-five. The timing of this initiative left a strong impression that supporters of Olshan wanted to prolong his stay at the Court. Similar to the Russian case, this attempt fueled suspicions of a plot between the legislators and Olshan, who denied any involvement in this proposal.[19]

In contrast, the first Hungarian Constitutional Court President, Laszlo Solyom, openly proposed in 1998 to amend the constitution to extend

---

[16] "Konstitutsionnyi sud obeshchaet 'v operativnom poriadke' pomoch provesti politicheskuiu reformu," [Constitutional Court Promises Speedy Help in Pursuing Political Reform] *ForUm*, 26 February 2003, available at http://rus.for-ua.com/news/2003/02/26/111318.html.

[17] Aleksandr Moroz, "Meniat sistemu vlasti neobkhodimo segodnia," [The Change of the System of Power Is Needed Today] *Zerkalo nedeli*, April 12–18, 2003, available at http://www.zerkalo-nedeli.com/nn/show/439/38263.

[18] The Draft of the Constitution of the Republic of Armenia (a copy was kindly provided to the author by Kristina Galstyan).

[19] Shimon Shetreet, *Justice in Israel: A Study of the Israeli Judiciary* (The Hague: Martinus Nijhoff, 1994), p. 409.

the tenure of all incumbent justices from 9-year, once renewable terms to 12-year, nonrenewable terms. Here, the argument was practical rather than legal, namely, to prevent the total overhaul of the Court's composition and facilitate a smooth transition between incumbent and incoming members of the Constitutional Court. The timing of this initiative was very close to the 1998 parliamentary elections, and, of course, politicians had other priorities. Under the existing rules, in 1998–1999 the remaining members of the Court faced the risk of not being reappointed. Although Justice Solyom was sure that he would be reappointed, the new 1998 government announced that none of the incumbent justices would be reappointed. Needless to say, new rulers did not want to lose a chance to appoint their own preferred nominees and used it to their fullest advantage. Meanwhile, public support for the Constitutional Court was failing, due to efforts by Solyom to remain on the bench and due to inactivity of the post-Solyom Court.[20] But Solyom honed his lobbying skills and became Hungary's president in 2005, thus taking the meaning of "juristocracy" to a whole new level.

A careful observer may note that the majority of these attempts to change the top justices' terms of office occurred in so-called late democratization countries and may be attributed to weak or undeveloped political commitment to judicial independence. However, this assessment depends on the criteria used to evaluate this commitment. Comparing it with the stability of the life tenure of the U.S. Supreme Court justices is one thing. However, comparing it with the wholesale impeachment of the Argentinean Supreme Court would produce a different result, especially if one remembers that these "tenure" amendments were enacted in the 1990s, during the era of the "global diffusion of judicial power."[21] This means that politicians had to deal with a much more powerful constitutional judiciary, yet they still could "tinker" with the terms of office for justices they liked or disliked. What would stop rulers from "fine tuning" judicial tenure in the future? As Table 8.1 makes clear, most tinkering with judicial tenure resulted in lengthening the stay of justices on the bench. Perhaps governing coalitions liked the judges they had and derived important benefits from constitutional review. Indeed, as the next section of

---

[20] Kim Lane Scheppele, "Democracy By Judiciary. Or Why Courts Can Sometimes Be More Democratic Than Parliaments," in Adam W. Czarnota, Martin Krygier, and Wojciech Sadurski, eds., *Rethinking the Rule of Law After Communism* (Budapest: Central European University Press, 2005), pp. 25–60.

[21] C. Neal Tate and Torbjorn Vallinder, eds., *The Global Expansion of Judicial Power* (New York: New York University Press, 1995).

this chapter shows, new constitutional tribunals often picked their fights carefully – they battled with weaker political actors, namely, other courts.

"WARS OF COURTS" IN COMPARATIVE PERSPECTIVE

Why do courts collide in the process of constitutional revolutions? Why does constitutional entrenchment of individual rights and independent judiciary generate rivalries among high courts? Finally, why should we care about these seemingly narrow and technical issues of interactions between constitutional courts and the rest of the judiciary?

Although some tend to portray the conflict among high national courts as an unexpected "paradox of acceptance and rejection of constitutional courts," or as birth pangs, or as a fight between progressives and hard-liners,[22] I argue that intercourt rivalries ought to be expected in constitutional revolutions because all courts gain power to uphold constitutional supremacy, to enforce constitutional norms, and to interpret statutes in light of new constitutional principles. Constitutional courts as new political institutions have to carve out their own place in the political system and have no choice but to compete with other domestic courts for the primary role in building the rule-of-law system. New constitutions with bills of rights elevate the role of judicial precedents and invite competition among courts to make "judge-made" law in an already hostile environment of civil law systems. This competition for "judge-made" law, however, complicates the entrenchment of the "rule-of-law" regime. On the one hand, intercourt conflicts weaken the protection of individual rights and may provide incentives for political branches to stifle the process of judicial empowerment. On the other hand, vibrant judicial rivalries may improve the international image and enhance the quality of the public debate in these countries. Just as democracy is born or built of conflicts among various political and economic interests, the rule of law grows out of the struggles for power among various interests and institutions, including top courts. Therefore, one should care about the politics within judicial systems in order to understand the process of entrenching the rule of law.

The first decade and a half of postcommunist constitutional justice shows that various patterns of intercourt conflicts have emerged in the

---

[22] Bostjan Zupancic, "From Combat to Contract or: What Does the Constitution Constitute?" *Pravnik* 6 (1998), pp. 476–510; and Pavel Hollander, "The Role of the Constitutional Court for the Application of the Constitution in Case Decisions of Ordinary Courts," *Archiv fur Rechts- und Sozialphilosophie*, vol. 86 (2000), pp. 541–552.

process of designing the powers of these new courts, in the process of constitutional adjudication, and in the struggles over the enforcement of constitutional court decisions. Indeed, the problems of "peaceful coexistence" of postcommunist constitutional courts with other branches of the judicial system have been so acute that European constitutional court judges addressed them at numerous meetings.[23] Clearly, judges are concerned about the really existing judicial pluralism.[24] This pluralism can take the form of simple disagreements between judges, of resistance and noncompliance with the decisions of the constitutional court, or judicial pluralism can degenerate into "wars of courts." Constitutional court judges lament that their judgments are not enforced because of the resistance and sabotage from the rest of the judiciary. But ordinary judges complain that constitutional courts routinely usurp the function of judicial review of legislation and intrude in the traditional domain of the regular judiciary. This intrusion may take the form of annulling court decisions, of interpreting statutes, and even of defining the boundaries of judicial institutions.

However, at the beginning of the new millennium, the relationship between constitutional and ordinary courts remains "a crucial and understudied issue for comparative constitutional studies."[25] Even though judges in many countries from Spain to Belgium to Italy to Russia to Korea to Colombia have lived through this uneasy relationship, scholars are still in the early stages of theorizing this phenomenon.[26] For example,

---

[23] See, for example, the meetings of the European Commission for Democracy through Law (Venice Commission), available at http://www.venice.coe.int/site/dynamics/N_Seminar_ef.asp?L=E&TID=5. Also, the theme of the 12th Congress of the Conference of European Constitutional Courts held in Brussels (May 2002) was "The relations between the Constitutional Courts and the other national courts, including the interference in this area of the action of the European courts," at http://www.confcoconsteu.org. The Czech Republic and Russia submitted their reports, available at http://www.confcoconsteu.org/en/reports/reports.html.

[24] Judicial pluralism may also arise from legal pluralism, the coexistence of different legal systems within one state. Here, I discuss how judicial pluralism may exist without legal pluralism.

[25] Ginsburg, *Judicial Review in New Democracies*, p. 134.

[26] See, for example, Leslie Turano, "Spain: Quis Custodiet Ipsos Custodes?: The Struggle for Jurisdiction Between the Tribunal Constitucional and the Tribunal Supremo," *I-CON: International Journal of Constitutional Law*, vol. 4, no. 1 (2006), pp. 151–162 (Spain); John H. Merryman and Vincenzo Vigoriti, "When Courts Collide: Constitution and Cassation in Italy," *American Journal of Comparative Law*, vol. 15, no. 4 (1967), pp. 665–686 (Italy); Lech Garlicki, "Constitutional Courts Versus Supreme Courts," *I-CON: International Journal of Constitutional Law*, vol. 5, no. 1 (2007), pp. 44–68 (Germany, Italy, and Poland); Radoslav Procházka, *Mission Accomplished: On Founding Constitutional Adjudication in Central Europe* (Budapest: Central European

"*Wars of Courts*" in Comparative Perspective   267

as one astute observer of Eastern European constitutional review notes, "the confrontation between the Polish and Czech constitutional courts on one side and the ordinary courts on the other was as significant an element of their countries' constitutional discourses as was" the interaction between constitutional tribunals and parliaments in Hungary and Slovakia.[27] Certainly, the positive role of the supreme courts (and negative or neutral role of the constitutional courts) in the electoral or "colored" revolutions in Serbia (2000), Georgia (2003), Ukraine (2004), and Kyrgyzstan (2005) has attracted the attention of international observers and pointed out the need to take the issue of judicial pluralism more seriously.[28]

Those who pay attention to judicial pluralism usually offer two kinds of explanations for its existence.[29] The first one is legalistic, and it belongs to the widespread view that postcommunist politics was a mess, and that constitution makers there did not really know what they were doing. This view blames legislators for the failure to distribute properly the judicial powers between supreme and constitutional courts: judicial pluralism would disappear if only politicians adopted clearer laws on the division of labor between high courts. Depending on which court the proponents of this legalistic view support, they may demand to codify the power

---

University Press, 2002), pp. 159–167 (Czech Republic); Renate Webber, "The Romanian Constitutional Court: In Search of Its Own Identity," in Wojciech Sadurski, ed., *Constitutional Justice, East and West* (The Hague: Kluwer Law International, 2002), pp. 283–308 (Romania); Jiri Priban, "Judicial Power vs. Democratic Representation: The Culture of Constitutionalism and Human Rights in the Czech Legal System," in Wojciech Sadurski, ed., *Constitutional Justice, East and West* (The Hague: Kluwer Law International, 2002), pp. 373–394 (Czech Republic); "Interview with Jan Drgonec," *East European Constitutional Review*, vol. 6, no. 1 (Winter 1997), p. 89 (Slovakia); Ginsburg, *Judicial Review in New Democracies* (Korea and Taiwan); Herve Bribosia, "Report on Belgium," in Anne-Marie Slaughter et al., eds., *The European Courts and National Courts – Doctrine and Jurisprudence* (Oxford: Hart Publishing, 1998), pp. 3–39 (Belgium); David Landau, "The War of the Courts: Inter-Court Conflict and the Failure of the European Model of Constitutional Review in Latin America," (January 2007) unpublished manuscript, on file with author (Colombia); and William Burnham and Alexei Trochev, "Russia's War between the Courts: The Struggle over the Jurisdictional Boundary between the Constitutional Court and Regular Courts," *American Journal of Comparative Law*, vol. 55, no. 3 (2007), pp. 381–452 (Russia).

[27] Procházka, *Mission Accomplished*, p. 274.

[28] Alexei Trochev, "Fragmentation? Defection? Legitimacy? Explaining Judicial Behavior in Post-Communist 'Colored Revolutions.'" Paper presented at the annual meeting of the American Political Science Association, Philadelphia, September 1, 2006.

[29] Certainly, personal animosity between judges of different top courts can help to fuel even more intercourt conflicts. Judges are humans, and have personal friends and enemies, as Lawrence Baum argues in *Judges and Their Audiences* (Princeton: Princeton University Press, 2006).

of constitutional courts to review the judgments of the other courts or to abolish judicial review of judicial decisions. Indeed, as one Bulgarian Constitutional Court judge told the author, Bulgaria's top courts have good relations because the Constitutional Court there is very well designed. This is despite the fact that this court shares many institutional features with the Romanian (absence of individual access) and the Italian constitutional courts (one-third of justices are appointed by the judicial community). But both Romania and Italy have witnessed severe judicial pluralism, while Bulgaria has not. Thus, institutional design alone does not determine intercourt relations.[30] Moreover, this legalistic view conveniently forgets that top judges can manipulate seemingly clear laws in their favor. Russian and Czech constitutional court judges repeatedly proved this point by saying that they did not know what exactly a "constitutional question" was, so they could not guarantee that they would never invade the domain of other courts. Moreover, constitutional courts could easily strike down any limits on their jurisdiction.

The second explanation of judicial pluralism is also popular, as it argues that ordinary judges disobey new and progressive constitutional courts because the former come from the old authoritarian regime, they are reactionary hardliners and supporters of parliamentary supremacy, they are conservative, and they cannot champion rights as trumps, to use Dworkin's expression. This view simplistically portrays judicial pluralism as a fight between good guys (constitutional courts) and bad guys (supreme courts). For example, to constitutional judges in Slovenia and in the Czech Republic (both consolidated democracies by now), the negative reaction of ordinary courts to constitutional court judgments is an unexpected "paradox of the acceptance and rejection of constitutional courts," where highly popular constitutional courts face rejection and hostility among ordinary judiciary and political elites.[31] They base this paradox on the thesis that "democratizing" political elites and the voters

---

[30] More research is needed on the reasons for the absence of judicial pluralism in Bulgaria. I can only speculate that Bulgarian judges have amicable relationships because of two factors: one is that in the mid-1990s, Bulgarian judges had to stand together to resist repeated attacks from the former Communist Party-led government on the judicial system. And second is that members of Bulgarian top courts frequently trade places – Constitutional Court judges retire and serve on the bench of the Supreme Court and vice versa – which means that judges know each other well, mingle in the same circles and have a pretty clear idea of how to avoid intercourt battles. I know of no other country in which the constitutional court judges served on the bench of the supreme court after they retired.

[31] On Slovenia, see Zupancic, "From Combat to Contract"; on the Czech Republic, see Hollander, "The Role of the Constitutional Court...."

"Wars of Courts" in Comparative Perspective 269

prefer new, progressive constitutional courts rather than old, reactionary and conservative ordinary judges.[32] This vision explains the origins of judicial pluralism in postwar Italy and in post-Franco Spain. However, it does not explain the persistence of these intercourt wars in these countries: both countries have had a generational change in the legal profession, yet they still have these conflicts. This view cannot explain the war of courts in the Czech Republic, as will be shown in this chapter, which had the fastest and the most thorough cleansing of the judicial corps after the fall of Communism. Nor does this vision explain well the enthusiasm of Russian regular courts to exercise judicial review of local law making (discussed in Chapter 7). This view also fails to explain why "democratizing" elites appointed some of these distrusted judges to the bench of new constitutional courts and entrusted all distrusted judges with the right (or an obligation) to refer cases to new constitutional courts.[33]

There is nothing unexpected and paradoxical about old (ordinary) courts fighting to protect their turf from the jurisdiction of assertive new (constitutional) courts. High courts collide because they want to use their constitutionally derived powers to uphold constitutional supremacy, to enforce constitutional norms, and to interpret statutes in light of new constitutional principles. This, in turn, provides fertile ground for an inherent tension between supreme courts and constitutional courts. In practice, constitutional courts, as new political institutions, have to carve out their own place in the political system and have no choice but to compete with other domestic courts for the primary role in building a rule-of-law system.[34] Postcommunist constitutional review bodies routinely intrude in what used to be the traditional domain of the regular judiciary. This is particularly true of constitutional courts in nondemocratic regimes: there, judges know that powerful executives would not tolerate recalcitrant tribunals. But new constitutional courts also have to build their own

---

[32] Louis Favoreu, "American and European Models of Constitutional Justice," in David S. Clark, ed., *Comparative and Private International Law: Essays in Honor of John Henry Merryman on His Seventieth Birthday* (Berlin: Duncker u. Humblot, 1990), p. 110. Herman Schwartz, *The Struggle for Constitutional Justice in Post-Communist Europe* (Chicago: University of Chicago Press, 2000), p. 23; John Ferejohn and Pasquale Pasquino, "Constitutional Courts as Deliberative Institutions: Towards an Institutional Theory of Constitutional Justice," in Wojciech Sadurski, ed., *Constitutional Justice, East and West* (The Hague: Kluwer Law International, 2002), pp. 31–32.

[33] For criticism of this thesis, see Wojciech Sadurski, "Legitimacy and Reasons of Constitutional Review after Communism," in Sadurski, *Constitutional Justice, East and West*, p. 175.

[34] Lech Garlicki, "Constitutional Courts Versus Supreme Courts."

jurisdiction, and they do it by grabbing power away from the other courts. This intrusion may take the form of annulling court decisions, of issuing a statutory interpretation and even of defining the boundaries of judicial power. Similar to the constitutional courts in Germany, Italy, and Spain, which are behaving "increasingly as supreme courts and appear as a fourth level of jurisdiction . . . overseeing the decisions of ordinary jurisdictions,"[35] the postcommunist constitutional courts check the constitutionality of other top court decisions. In some cases, constitutional tribunals do it consciously to avoid heavyweight fights with political branches. For example, the Kyrgyzstan Constitutional Court has been consistently accepting appeals against the rulings of the Supreme Court and the Supreme Commercial Court and overturning their judgments.[36] More than two-thirds of all cases heard by this constitutional court dealt with appeals of these courts' decisions. As I will show in this chapter, intense intercourt conflict occurred in the Czech Republic over the power of the constitutional court to supervise the constitutionality of judgments issued by other top national courts.

The postcommunist constitutional courts also overrule established statutory interpretations[37] that were issued previously by other top national courts. Instead of striking down the statutes, constitutional courts interpret them in a way that is consistent with postcommunist constitutional norms and declare this interpretation to be binding on all other courts. Constitutional courts can even give retroactive effect to this new statutory interpretation. This means that other courts, including the highest national courts, have to review their previously decided cases according to new constitutional court guidelines. Naturally, they do not like to see their decisions overturned and protest such constitutional court orders.[38]

Every time a constitutional court tells other courts to readjudicate a case, issues a statutory interpretation contrary to established judicial doctrine, and creates other obligations for other courts without increasing

---

[35] Favoreu, "European and American Modes of Constitutional Justice," pp. 105, 117. Cited in Schwartz, *The Struggle for Constitutional Justice*, p. 256, fn. 26

[36] As a result of the constitutional amendments of 2003, the Supreme Commercial Court of Kyrgyzstan was abolished and its functions were transferred to the Supreme Court.

[37] This category includes both direct and indirect interpretations of the statutes produced by the Constitutional Court in all abstract and concrete review cases.

[38] On Poland, see Schwartz, *The Struggle for Constitutional Justice*, p. 73; on Slovakia, see Schwartz, *The Struggle for Constitutional Justice*, p. 223; "Interview with Jan Drgonec, Judge of the Slovakia Constitutional Court," *East European Constitutional Review*, vol. 6, no. 1 (Winter 1997), p. 89.

"Wars of Courts" in Comparative Perspective 271

their power, one can reasonably expect a certain degree of judicial resistance to such constitutional court orders. In the postcommunist context this degree of resistance is likely to be high because of the novelty of constitution and constitutional courts and the continual struggle over the nature of top political institutions. The nature of the political regime does not appear to matter in overcoming this resistance. The very powerful Hungarian Constitutional Court had a much easier time persuading the parliament to obey its judgments than compelling the town court to follow through. Political branches complied but the Hungarian Supreme Court repeatedly accused the Constitutional Court of intrusion in the Supreme Court's jurisdiction. And until mid-1999, the ordinary courts refused to reopen civil and administrative cases on the basis of landmark judgments of the Hungarian Constitutional Court and interpreted these judgments contrary to the intent of the Constitutional Court.[39] The same pattern persists in nondemocratic Belarus: the relations between the pliant Constitutional Court and other no less pliant courts were far from being friendly. Regular judges are less likely to disobey the constitutional court if their superiors (appellate courts and supreme courts) are telling them to comply with the constitutional court ruling. However, most often it is the high national courts that contest either the exclusive nature of the constitutional review powers of constitutional courts or the binding force of constitutional court orders.

Consider the experience of the Romanian Constitutional Court, which some view as the strongest postcommunist constitutional court[40] and others tend to treat as the weakest one.[41] Romanian criminal courts, including the Supreme Court, refused to comply with a Constitutional Court decision on limiting the length of pretrial detention to 1 month as prescribed by Article 23 of the Romanian constitution. The Romanian Constitutional Court invalidated the norms of the Criminal Procedure Code that allowed virtually unlimited detention of arrested persons. Romanian ordinary judges responded that "the legislature alone was bound by the decisions of the Constitutional Court . . . while judges, who are subject only to

---

[39] Peter Paczolay, "Effects, Enforceability, and the Execution of the Decisions of the Constitutional Court – The Hungarian Experience," report presented at the Seminar on the Execution of Decisions of the Constitutional Court, Kyiv, Ukraine, October, 28–29, 1999, available at http://www.venice.coe.int/docs/1999/CDL-JU(1999)026-e.asp.

[40] Shannon Ishiyama-Smithey and John Ishiyama, "Judicious Choices: Designing Courts in Post-Communist Politics," *Communist and Post-Communist Studies*, vol. 33, no. 1 (2000), pp. 163–182.

[41] Schwartz, *The Struggle for Constitutional Justice*, pp. 226–227.

the law, cannot directly apply the provisions of the Constitution or dispositions of the Constitutional Court, unless incorporated" in a statute.[42] The Romanian Supreme Court openly opposed the Constitutional Court decision upholding the nationalization decrees of the postwar Communist government. The Supreme Court questioned the power of the Constitutional Court to tell regular courts what to do and ordered the subordinate courts to hear cases on nationalization decrees, thus ignoring this Constitutional Court decision.[43] Moreover, Romania lost fifty-eight cases over these decrees in the European Court of Human Rights (ECHR) between 2002 and 2004, and the prospects of enforcing these ECHR judgments remained bleak.[44] By the end of 2002, it was still difficult to predict how an open confrontation between the Romanian high courts would end.[45] As we will see from the Czech "war of courts" discussion, Romanian judges are not alone in their attitude toward judicial review.

The postcommunist constitutional courts also define the constitutional boundaries of judicial power by interpreting constitutional norms directly or by checking the constitutionality of legislation. These courts engage in creative "positive" law making under the disguise of "clarifying" vague constitutional provisions. In general, their constitutional interpretation favors the expansion of judicial power as an extension of the "due process" constitutional clauses. For example, postcommunist constitutional courts broadened the jurisdiction of the courts to hear all sorts of complaints previously heard solely by executive bodies. In Russia, Moldova, and Kyrgyzstan, constitutional courts essentially revolutionized criminal procedure and expanded the power of courts to cover various phases of criminal prosecution.

However, constitutional courts also have to preserve their own exclusive jurisdiction and to limit attempts by other courts to conduct

---

[42] Gabor Koszokar, "The Effects of the Constitutional Court Decisions with a Special View on the Ordinary Courts Jurisprudence," *Konstitutsionnoe pravosudie*, no. 3 (2001), pp. 165–166 (in English).

[43] Mihaela Serban, "Resheniia rumynskogo Konstitutsionnogo Suda kak istochnik prava," [Decisions of the Romanian Constitutional Court as a Source of Law] *Konstitutsionnoe pravosudie v postkommunisticheskikh stranakh* (Moskva: MONF, 1999), April 25–26.

[44] Lavinia Stan, "The Roof over Our Head: Property Restitution in Romania," *Journal of Communist Studies and Transition Politics*, vol. 22, no. 2 (2006), pp. 180–205. Stan estimates that in these cases alone the ECHR ordered the Romanian state to pay damages totaling more than 4.6 million Euros.

[45] Renate Weber, "The Romanian Constitutional Court: In Search of Its Own Identity," in Sadurski, *Constitutional Justice, East and West*, p. 308. See also an article by the chief justice of the Romanian Constitutional Court Ioan Vida, "The Obligatory Force of Decisions of the Constitutional Court for Other Courts as a Stabilizing Factor," *Konstitutsionnoe pravosudie*, no. 2 (2004), pp. 78–90.

constitutional review. So far constitutional courts have preserved the monopoly of conducting constitutional review by requiring ordinary courts to request a decision of the constitutional court if the issue of unconstitutionality of an applicable statute has been raised in litigation. The core logic behind monopolizing judicial review of laws in the hands of the constitutional court is this: if an ordinary judge is convinced that a certain statute violates the constitution, and the judge lacks the power to check the constitutionality of such statute and the power to set such statute aside, he then has a duty to suspend the case and to petition the constitutional court, and, finally, has to decide the case following the constitutional court orders.

As will be shown below, the Czech ordinary judges responded to these new obligations without enthusiasm and petitioned constitutional courts rather rarely. Instead, regular judges either followed the Supreme Court's guidelines or attempted to apply constitutional norms directly. Both options, therefore, represented attempts at "judicial law making" by the regular courts contrary to the case law of the Constitutional Court. Indeed, the new postcommunist constitutions elevate the role of judicial precedents and invite competition among courts to make "judge-made" law. However, continental legal systems do not recognize court decisions as sources of domestic law. According to the traditional legal doctrine inspired by the French jurist Charles Montesquieu, judges are subservient to the will of the legislature with its monopoly to make laws. Therefore, the competition for "judge-made" law among national high courts aims to break this traditional approach in a hostile environment of legislative supremacy.

Judicial pluralism understood as a struggle for judicial power via legal reasoning carries significant costs for the entrenchment of constitutionalism in postcommunist states. High courts that work at cross-purposes impede the entrenchment of both legal certainty and legal predictability – the core elements of a rule-of-law regime. Intercourt confrontations weaken the protection of individual rights, a main pillar of a new constitutional order.[46] Individuals who bring constitutional complaints and obtain a judgment of the constitutional court in their favor are unable to win in ordinary courts. These individuals are forced to complain to the constitutional court again, and this "ping-pong" between courts may last several years, as the Czech and Russian experience demonstrates.

---

[46] Renata Uitz, "Konstitutsionnye i verkhovnye sudy – partnery ili soperniki?" [Constitutional and Supreme Courts – Partners or Rivals?] *Konstitutsionnoe pravo: vostochnoevropeiskoe obozrenie*, no. 1 (2003), pp. 109–122.

Naturally, such intercourt rivalries undermine the reputation of courts and the public trust in the effectiveness of the judicial system and of law in general. When these quarrels among high courts become intense, politicians may find it useful to reduce the powers of the judiciary. Also, they may abolish certain courts to minimize infighting in judicial quarters. Therefore, judicial empowerment may produce judicial hyperpluralism, which, in turn, may prove fatal for the weaker courts.

Fortunately, the current international human rights regime supports more courts, not less, and views any attempts to curb judicial power with suspicion. Close international scrutiny, however, still leaves great latitude of action for judges to sort out their conflicts and for politicians to enhance the accountability of judges, for example, by changing their terms of office, as I discussed in this chapter. This means that each country is likely to attempt to overcome intercourt conflicts on its own by balancing the costs and benefits of particular measures, such as constitutional amendments, judicial reform, accession to the European Union, turnover of judicial personnel, bargaining among judges, or an unwritten "peace treaty" among "belligerent" courts. Clearly, formal and informal arrangements aimed at resolving conflicts among high national courts may prove more durable than simple replacement of recalcitrant judges on the bench. To be sure, constitutional courts will not hesitate to review the constitutionality of these intercourt peace-building arrangements; and supreme courts will interpret these arrangements on their own.

However, having more courts means that judicial pluralism is likely to flourish. As I argued in this chapter, in nondemocratic regimes constitutional courts are likely to focus their energies on grabbing power from the supreme courts because the former would hesitate to challenge the powerful executive. But the same may be true of democratic regimes with vibrant electoral markets, as the decades-long persistence of judicial pluralism in postwar Italy and post-Franco Spain shows. The current parliamentary crisis of post-Orange Revolution Ukraine also shows that in the context of severe political competition, rival political parties may capture different courts and fuel intercourt rivalries.[47] So, under certain conditions, political fragmentation goes hand in hand with judicial pluralism.

---

[47] "Ukrainians will become witnesses of war of courts soon," *IA REGNUM*, May 4, 2007, available at http://www.regnum.ru/english/823094.html; "The Victory of Tymoshenko May Launch a New War of Courts," (in Russian) *Korrespondent.Net*, August 14, 2007, available at http://www.korrespondent.net/main/203068.

Paradoxically, judicial pluralism may also be beneficial for the development of the rule of law. One benefit of the struggles between constitutional courts and other domestic courts is the cultivation of peaceful and reasoned dialogues among "warring" judges, lawyers, bureaucrats, and politicians. When the supreme court disobeys a decision of the constitutional court, the former has to provide persuasive reasons for noncompliance. When the constitutional court admonishes ordinary courts for noncompliance, it also has to use legal arguments to assure compliance and to behave like a court rather than a "third legislative chamber." Lawyers have to strengthen their claims so that their clients (individuals, corporations, and government agencies) can succeed in the "war of courts." Competition for "judge-made" law enhances the deliberative character of democracy because constitutional litigation often concerns serious political controversies over separation of powers, federalism, and the limits of government interference with private lives. Finally, rivalries among high national courts may stimulate debates among politicians on how to secure the implementation of constitutional court decisions. These debates may produce an adjustment of public policies toward meeting constitutional standards. Eventually, this may contribute to the subordination of government to the constitution and the rule-of-law order.

Learning to argue about the law and sharpening legal arguments in contemporary Europe is impossible without referring to the decisions of the European Court of Human Rights (ECHR), which have the force of precedents and bind the member states of the Council of Europe. Domestic high courts draw on the reasoning and binding force of ECHR decisions to claim the binding force of their own judgments vis-à-vis the legislature. Using the arguments of the ECHR in their own decision making, constitutional court judges and ordinary judges compete with each other and learn to argue their own standpoints. So far, postcommunist constitutional courts have fared better in learning and using the decision making of the Strasbourg Court. No doubt, the frequent citing of European human rights law has contributed to the survival and successes of the new postcommunist constitutional judiciary. Postcommunist constitutional courts are perceived as the "engines" that drive their nations toward European legal order. The rulers in former Eastern bloc countries like the fact that their courts cite ECHR judgments – it makes them look good in the family of European nations.[48] This benefit works as long as postcommunist rulers agree to enforce the judgments of the Strasbourg Court. They do

---

[48] Recall President Putin's remarks on the positive role of the ECHR from Chapter 7.

not always agree, however, as the saga over property restitution in Romania shows.[49] Moreover, with time, ordinary courts will eventually learn ECHR case law and their understanding of ECHR judgments may differ from that of the constitutional courts. No doubt, these differences will generate more battlefields for judicial pluralism. And as Lech Garlicki, a former judge of the Polish Constitutional Tribunal, notes, supreme courts may prevail over constitutional courts.[50]

The war of courts in the Czech Republic illustrates the dynamics of judicial pluralism nicely. By September 1993, all Czech judges "who have been found guilty of active collaboration with the Communist regime have been purged" or left the bench voluntarily.[51] This radical lustration campaign achieved its goals: by mid-2001, 40 percent of judges (out of 2,500 active judges) had been trained in Communism times.[52] This is the lowest figure in Eastern Europe, which contributed to the optimistic expectations of speedy "perestroika" in the mindset of the judiciary. In fact, in mid-1993 many government officials and observers believed that public support for the reformed judiciary was on the rise and expected that it would take a couple of years before the image of the Czech judiciary would dramatically improve.[53]

In the midst of this euphoria, the Czech Constitutional Court (CCC) ruled in 1993 (the first year of the Court's existence) that it had jurisdiction over final decisions of the Supreme Court because courts, including the Supreme Court, fall under the category of "public authorities."[54] The Supreme Court repeatedly objected to this "arrogation" of competence by the CCC by arguing that Supreme Court decisions were final, with no appeal to the CCC because the latter was outside of the ordinary court system. Moreover, according to the Supreme Court, ordinary courts were not "public authorities" in the sense of Article 87(1d) of the 1992 constitution. This defiance prompted the Constitutional Court to elaborate its reasoning in greater detail. On November 13, 1997, the CCC invoked both the legal doctrine and the letter of the Constitutional

---

[49] Stan, "The Roof over Our Head: Property Restitution in Romania."

[50] Garlicki, "Constitutional Courts Versus Supreme Courts," pp. 66–68.

[51] Jiri Pehe, "Changes in the Czech Judiciary," *RFE/RL Report*, September 17, 1993, pp. 54–57.

[52] James Pitkin, "And Justice for All," *Prague Post*, May 9, 2001, available at http://www.praguepost.cz/sprt050901a.html.

[53] Pehe, "Changes in the Czech Judiciary." By mid-2001, 65 percent of Czechs said they did not trust the courts; Pitkin, "And Justice for All."

[54] CCC decision No. I. US 131/93.

"Wars of Courts" in Comparative Perspective 277

Court Act to reaffirm its power to review the constitutionality of Supreme Court decisions. In the Constitutional Court's view, the term "public authority" encompasses all state bodies, including the ordinary courts and the Supreme Court.[55]

Although the Supreme Court had little ability to stop the Constitutional Court from taking up complaints against judicial decisions, it continued to contest the binding force of the CCC's guidelines. The Supreme Court repeatedly reopened cases following the orders of the CCC, only to criticize the Constitutional Court's opinions, and instructed lower courts to do the same. Instead of rehearing such a case, the Supreme Court simply stated its disagreement with the Constitutional Court's reasoning, accused the CCC of exceeding authority, declared its nonbinding character, and sometimes even proposed that the CCC to change its opinion!

Most often, the Supreme Court refused to comply with the Constitutional Court's intrusion in the traditional domains of judicial law making, such as the procedural rights to a public hearing in land restitution cases, criminal law standards of lifting the statute of limitations in the lustration cases, counting time in imprisonment, or imposing punishment in cases of conscientious objectors to military service. All of these issues were hotly debated across Central and Eastern Europe in the context of correcting the injustice of the Communist regimes and dealing with surging crime rates. The Czech Constitutional Court also took part in these debates. Facing consistent disobedience by the ordinary courts, the Court invalidated numerous provisions of contested laws and offered extensive statutory interpretations in seemingly technical matters. Moreover, the CCC, while preaching judicial self-restraint, repeatedly annulled judicial decisions because it found that the ordinary court failed to examine relevant evidence (an appellate jurisdiction of the Supreme Court) and even engaged in the fact-finding mission itself (original jurisdiction of the ordinary court)![56]

Not surprisingly, ordinary judges disagreed with these forays of the Constitutional Court in civil or criminal procedure. Moreover, in the context of the "war of courts," ordinary courts petitioned the CCC rather rarely. In addition, Article 95(2) of the Czech constitution required ordinary judges to explain the reasons for the unconstitutionality of law in such petitions. This requirement left a great deal of discretion to the

---

[55] CCC decision No. III. US 337/97.

[56] Radoslav Prochazka, *Mission Accomplished: On Founding Constitutional Adjudication in Central Europe* (Budapest: Central University Press, 2002), pp. 159–167.

judges in deciding not to refer statutes to the CCC, even though the latter insisted that ordinary courts must refer in cases of patently unconstitutional provisions.[57] The CCC, on the other hand, is not bound by the arguments of potential unconstitutionality in judicial referrals. Therefore, the only way to monitor the enforcement of Constitutional Court judgments is through the constitutional complaint procedure. Individuals, dissatisfied with the ping-pong between the ordinary courts and the CCC, petitioned the latter again and again in hopes of protecting their fundamental rights. The CCC reviews constitutional complaints in three-member panels; therefore, it is able to deal with numerous complaints in an expeditious manner.

The most visible "war" between Czech courts occurred in handling the cases of refusal to perform military service (see Table 8.2 for the chronology of this intercourt conflict). Ordinary courts routinely applied Article 269 of the Criminal Code (the failure to report for military service with the intention to evade it permanently) and sentenced conscientious objectors every time the latter avoided the draft.[58] In September 1995, the Constitutional Court heard the complaint of one of the objectors and interpreted the word "permanently" in light of the constitutional "double jeopardy" clause that nobody may be prosecuted or punished repeatedly for the same act. Accordingly, the CCC annulled these court decisions as violating the constitution and Protocol No. 7 of the European Convention on the Protection of Human Rights and Basic Freedoms. Moreover, the Court expected that this decision would "serve for the ordinary courts' future decision making as a guideline concerning the length of punishment for those who permanently refuse to perform military service, or civilian service."[59]

However, only a handful of criminal courts followed this guideline. The majority of ordinary courts quietly ignored this interpretation. The Supreme Court adamantly opposed this decision of the CCC as invading its authority to guide the lower courts in the uniform application of Czech laws. In April 1996, the Supreme Court flatly refused to apply

---

[57] Ivana Janu, "Relations of the Constitutional Court to the Ordinary Courts." Report presented at the Workshop on Eurasian Constitutional Courts, Istanbul, May 22–23, 1998. See para. 12 of the *Report of the Constitutional Court of Czech Republic.*

[58] For an overview of these court cases, see the compilation of materials on the freedom of religion and belief in the Czech Republic, *Human Rights Without Frontiers,* available at http://www.hrwf.net/religiousfreedom/news/1999PDF/czech_1999.pdf.

[59] CCC decision No. IV. US 81/95, of September 18, 1995, available at http://angl.concourt.cz/angl_verze/doc/4-81-95.php.

"Wars of Courts" in Comparative Perspective

TABLE 8.2. *The "War of Courts" in the Czech Republic: Joseph Chodera's case, 1993–1999*

July 10, 1991 – The District Court in Kolin sends Chodera (military service objector) to prison for 6 months.

August 27, 1991 – The Regional Court changes Chodera's sentence to conditional punishment.

April 10, 1992 – Chodera is sentenced again for avoiding civilian service to 8 months to prison.

November 7, 1992 – The District Court in Kolin changes the conditional sentence to an unconditional one.

1993 – The Constitutional Court asserts its power to review the decisions of the Supreme Court.

September 18, 1995 – The Constitutional Court rules that nobody should be punished repeatedly for the same offence.

January 4, 1996 – Minister of Justice Jirí Novák requests the Supreme Court to annul Chodera's sentence.

April 25, 1996 – The Supreme Court refuses this request.

March 20, 1997 – The Constitutional Court cancels the decision of the Supreme Court.

October 9, 1997 – The Supreme Court rejects the opinion of the Constitutional Court and confirms its previous decision.

April 2, 1998 – The Constitutional Court cancels the decision of the Supreme Court again.

September 10, 1998 – Two Supreme Court judges excuse themselves from reopening Chodera's case.

December 21, 1998 – Minister of Justice Otakar Motejl proposes to impeach both Supreme Court judges.

February 12, 1999 – Supreme Court Chair Eliska Wagnerová publicly reprimands both judges. Vice-Premier Pavel Rychetský hurries to assure the citizens that a "war of law courts does not immediately threaten us."

February 18, 1999 – The Supreme Court discusses the impeachment proposal and refuses to impeach both judges.

April 2, 1999 – Constitutional Court Justice Milos Holecek complains to the media: "We have had the Czech Constitutional Court here for 6 years, but still some judges aren't able to accept that and uphold its decisions."

August 25, 1999 – The Supreme Court submits to the Constitutional Court ruling and repeals its decision in Chodera's case.

the Constitutional Court's interpretation of Article 269 of the Criminal Code and confirmed the legality of repeated sentences for conscientious objectors.[60] The unfortunate objector appealed to the Constitutional Court. The CCC cancelled the sentence as unconstitutional in March 1997

---

[60] Czech Supreme Court decision of April 25, 1996, file no. 2 Tzn 10/96.

and sent the case back to the Supreme Court. In October 1997, the Supreme Court reopened the case and confirmed its earlier decision. The Supreme Court announced that the CCC had issued an "untenable" and "legally unfounded" decision. The Supreme Court suggested that the Constitutional Court change its interpretation of the Criminal Code to overcome "the situation of stalemate, one which ... it has not proved possible to resolve even in joint meetings of representatives of all interested ministries (justice, defense, and labor and social affairs), with Deputies and Senators present, as well as Justices of the Supreme Court and of the Constitutional Court, present."[61] In April 1998, a frustrated CCC struck down this Supreme Court decision and sent the case back to the Supreme Court. The Constitutional Court argued that its statutory interpretation was binding on all courts, including the Supreme Court, and that several panels of the Supreme Court had already followed the guidelines of the CCC.[62] In July 1998, the CCC threatened that noncompliance of ordinary courts with its statutory interpretations would result in violation of the constitutional principle of equality of rights.[63] In response to this threat, in October 1998 two Supreme Court judges claimed bias and excused themselves from reopening the case of the conscientious objector. In earlier times, both judges could have gotten away with open defiance or quiet ignorance of the CCC directives, but by October 1998, the Supreme Court was split on the issue of the binding force of these directives.[64] In February 1999, the Supreme Court chairman publicly scolded both recalcitrant judges, stopping short of their dismissal. Finally, after repeated interventions by the Minister of Justice, on August 25, 1999, the Supreme Court submitted to the CCC ruling and repealed its decision in the case.[65] Note that in May 1999, the Czech Constitutional Court enjoyed a 63 percent

---

[61] Czech Supreme Court decision of October 9, 1997, file no. 2 Tzn 10/96.

[62] CCC decision No. III. US 425/97 of April 2, 1998, available at http://angl.concourt.cz/angl_verze/doc/3-425-97.php.

[63] CCC decision No. III. US 139/98 of July 9, 1998, cited in Hollander, "The Role of Constitutional Court," pp. 546–547.

[64] The lower courts sensed this split and in some cases refused to follow the orders of the Supreme Court to reopen cases and to decide them according to the Supreme Court guidelines. Anna Makova, "The Constitutional Court of the Czech Republic and the Legal Force of Its Decisions," *Konstitutsionnoe pravosudie*, no. 4 (1999), pp. 41–55.

[65] See pt. 292 of the "Initial Report of the Czech Republic on the Implementation of the International Covenant on Civil and Political Rights for the Period 1993–1999" (March 3, 2000), Office of the United Nations High Commissioner for Human Rights. However, the courts continued to deny Joseph Chodera the compensation for nonpecuniary damages arising from this illegal sentencing. The CCC struck down this denial as unconstitutional in 2006. See decision No. I. US 85/04 of June 13, 2006, available at http://angl.concourt.cz/angl_verze/doc/1-85-04.php.

"Wars of Courts" in Comparative Perspective 281

approval rating while the public trust in other government institutions was in decline.[66]

To sum up this particular case, clashes between the Czech Constitutional Court and the Supreme Court lasted almost 4 years. A popular Constitutional Court defended its own interpretation of the Criminal Code and received backing from the media, parts of the judiciary, and three ministers of justice. The Supreme Court defended its own long-settled vision of the Criminal Code and received backing from the military, the police, and certain political elites. During this "war of courts," appeals from both sides to amend the Criminal Code or to narrow the powers of the CCC were fruitless, and the impasse between high courts was resolved only after months of negotiations between judges and government officials in the context of media outrage. The Constitutional Court has won this battle but it is unclear how durable its victory will be because of two major changes:

1. The new Supreme Administrative Court in charge of resolving election disputes and reviewing administrative actions entered the Czech judicial system in 2003.[67]
2. The 10-year term of the Czech Constitutional Court justices expired in 2003.

Therefore, the Czech Republic planned to start the year 2004 with two new high courts, but the heightened political competition further damaged both the Constitutional Court and the Supreme Court. It took almost 3 years for President Vaclav Klaus and the Senate to agree on the names of new justices for the Constitutional Court.[68] At the same time, the Supreme Court was distracted and bitterly divided by President Klaus's attempt to unseat its chairwoman, Iva Brozova, who in turn complained against Klaus to the Constitutional Court and won.[69] Meanwhile, the Constitutional Court repeatedly overturned the decisions of the Supreme Administrative Court, which in turn has been in no hurry to refer issues

---

[66] Reported in Schwartz, *The Struggle for Constitutional Justice*, p. 320, fn. 22.

[67] The CCC "helped" to create this new court by invalidating the whole section 5 of the Civil Procedure Code (on administrative court system) in 2001, although petitioners did not ask for it. CCC decision No. Pl. US 16/99, *Sbirka zakonu* 276/2001 Sb. For criticism of this decision of the CCC, see Petr Mikulovsky, "Ústavnost rozhodování Ústavního soudu," *Vase Prava*, December 12, 2002.

[68] Zdenek Kühn and Jan Kysela, "Nomination of Constitutional Justices in Post-Communist Countries: Trial, Error, Conflict in the Czech Republic," *European Constitutional Law Review*, vol. 2 (2006), pp. 183–208.

[69] CCC decision No. Pl. US. 18/06 of July 11, 2006, available at http://angl.concourt.cz/angl_verze/doc/p-18-06.php; and Kieran Williams, "The Growing Litigiousness of Czech Elections," *Europe-Asia Studies*, vol. 59, no. 6 (September 2007), pp. 937–959.

of constitutionality to the Constitutional Court.[70] To be sure, the distribution of power between the three top Czech courts will again have to be worked out through "judge-made" law rather than through the will of the legislature. This is because the cease-fire between the Constitutional Court and the Supreme Court was based on personalities rather than institutional arrangements within the judicial system. Still, the "war of courts" helped to cultivate the sense of constitutional supremacy among ordinary judges albeit at the cost of ineffective protection of individual rights and a damaged reputation of the Supreme Court.[71]

CONCLUSION

Judging Russia's experimentation with judicial review through comparative lenses makes it plain that Russia's difficulties in building judicial power are not unique to that polity. Just like in Russia, rulers and judges in other countries have fought to ensure a loyal bench by tinkering with the rules of judicial tenure. In the current global, "judicialization of politics" era, politicians do not quietly swallow court orders and also demand more accountability from judges.[72] My preliminary survey of "tinkering" with judicial tenure revealed one aspect of these pressures on judges: how political actors attempt to shape court decisions by "fine-tuning" the judicial tenure rules because, after all, courts consist of judges who issue those decisions.[73] Politicians realize the link between judicial tenure and the degree of judicial independence, but they also want to recruit loyal judges. My analysis of tinkering with the tenure of judges of the highest national courts in a number of countries beyond Russia shows that the degree of judicial independence depends not only on the legislative texts, but also on the reputation of the courts and judges and on the commitment of political elites to an independent judiciary. How long judges stay

[70] See, for example, CCC decision No. III US. 252/04 of January 25, 2005, available at http://angl.concourt.cz/angl_verze/doc/3–252–04.php; Williams, "The Growing Litigiousness of Czech Elections," p. 942.

[71] Jiri Priban, "Judicial Power vs. Democratic Representation: The Culture of Constitutionalism and Human Rights in the Czech Legal System," in Sadurski, *Constitutional Justice, East and West*, pp. 373–394, esp. pp. 380–381.

[72] See, for example, Peter H. Russell and David M. O'Brien, eds., *Judicial Independence in the Age of Democracy: Critical Perspectives from around the World* (Charlottesville, VA: University of Virginia Press, 2001).

[73] Kate Malleson and Peter Russell, eds., *Appointing Judges in an Age of Judicial Power: Critical Perspectives from around the World* (Toronto: University of Toronto Press, 2006).

Conclusion

on the bench does not depend on the letter of the law alone. The bargaining among politicians and judges may also determine the actual length of judicial tenure. On the one hand, successful and failed attempts to adjust the terms of office of incumbent justices, which I discuss in this book, may infect politicians in other countries with the virus of "tinkering" with judicial tenure. On the other hand, it shows that politicians realize that the judiciary is slowly gaining power. Therefore, we are likely to witness more political struggles not only over judicial nominations, but also over the institutional features of high courts that will determine the balance between an independent – and an accountable – bench. What can prevent rulers from adjusting the terms of judicial tenure in the future? More research is needed to see whether "the global diffusion of judicial power" constrains the reign of Joseph Stalin's famous dictum: "Cadres decide everything!"

Similar to Russia, constitutional judges in other countries have had to fight with other courts to implement their own constitutional visions and to *matter* in the law on the ground. We usually think that judicial pluralism is bad for the rule of law: courts that work at cross-purposes and issue contradictory decisions on the same issue undermine legal certainty and predictability, make rights revolutions hollow, and undermine public trust in the legal system. But if we look at the legal history of England, the birthplace of the rule-of-law doctrine, we also notice that the four major courts of England, the Court of Common Pleas, the Kings Bench, the Exchequer, and the Chancery, actively competed with each other for centuries even though all four had their distinct jurisdictions clearly defined at the time of their creation. Moreover, the royal courts actively competed for power (and income) with religious courts and merchant courts. Arguably, this jurisdictional competition among courts played a crucial role in the development of common law.[74]

The intercourt conflicts in postcommunist countries demonstrate that the vagueness of constitutions and laws invites creative use of judicial decision making. High courts compete for "judge-made" law and behave like courts rather than "quasilegislative chambers." This competition is a struggle for power via judicial reasoning and legal discourse. Unless this

---

[74] See, for example, Daniel Klerman, "Jurisdictional Competition and the Evolution of the Common Law: A Hypothesis," *Australian Journal of Legal History*, vol. 77 (2004), p. 1; Harold J. Berman, *Law and Revolution: The Formation of the Western Legal Tradition* (Cambridge, MA: Harvard University Press, 1983), pp. 165–294; and Theodore F. T. Plucknett, *A Concise History of the Common Law* (Rochester, NY: The Lawyers Cooperative Publishing, 1929), pp. 144–145, 248–249, 382–383, 394, 405–411.

struggle is so severe that it leads to the abolition of courts, judges learn to argue about the law and the constitution. They eventually learn to coexist and settle for some kind "temporary peace agreement" that can be later codified in legislation on judicial power. The rule of law, then, emerges as a by-product of these creative intrajudicial struggles, similar to the process of entrenching democratic regimes, in which rival political and economic interests clash until they agree that democracy is "the only game in town." In short, we should study patterns of conflicts among high courts in order to understand how to consolidate the rule-of-law regime.

The second reason why we should care about intercourt conflicts concerns the effective protection of individual rights.[75] The Czech and Russian experiences show that constitutional complaints became a mechanism for monitoring the implementation of constitutional court decisions. The Czech and Russian cases also demonstrate that implementation of constitutional court decisions on individual rights depends on the compliance of the ordinary courts. For example, the invalidation of the death penalty by many postcommunist constitutional courts was unpopular among the citizenry and depended on the willingness of criminal courts to impose such punishment. Enforcing the constitutional rights of the accused in criminal cases is also unpopular with the public in the context of high crime rates and is dependent on the willingness of criminal courts to protect these rights. Protecting social and economic rights as mandated by constitutional courts also requires the obedience of regular courts. In short, effective protection of constitutional rights is impossible without cooperation among different branches of the judiciary. And if we want to learn more about the process of instilling rule-of-law regimes, we need to account for changes in judicial behavior. Fortunately for scholars (but unfortunately for plaintiffs), the "wars of courts" in postcommunist countries provide fertile ground for comparative research on the role of law and courts in social change.

---

[75] Uitz, "Konstitutsionnye i verkhovnye sudy – partnery ili soperniki," pp. 118–119.

9

Conclusion: Zigzagging Judicial Power

This study of the 16-year-old Russian Constitutional Court provides several insights for scholarship on the "black box" of judicial empowerment. Although these insights, learned from a three-case study within one state, may not travel successfully across other times and places, this learning may provide a context for future systematic comparisons and may illuminate the puzzles to be addressed in future research. Understanding the turbulent emergence of Russian constitutionalism and judicial review in the post-Soviet era informed us about several puzzles of judicial empowerment:

1. why the same powerful political actors who created the judicial review tribunal in 1991 nearly disbanded it after 2 years of its operation, and then revived the court shortly thereafter;
2. why the RCC exercised its judicial powers broadly yet inconsistently; and
3. why government officials, including judges on other courts, promptly carried out RCC decisions in some cases, delayed implementation in other cases, and sometimes simply ignored RCC orders.

My short answer to all three puzzles is that a mix of domestic and international legal, political, and psychological factors accounts for this zigzag behavior on the part of politicians, judges, and bureaucrats. Those who pay attention to judicial review (politicians, judges, bureaucrats, and legal elites) can attempt to influence the impact of the constitutional courts by changing the design of these courts, their jurisprudence, and levels of compliance with their judgments. This may generate the following nonlinear trajectories of judicial empowerment.[1]

---

[1] On nonlinear dynamics of judicial empowerment in Latin America, see, for example, Rebecca Bill Chavez, *Rule of Law in Nascent Democracies: Judicial Politics in Argentina*

286   *Conclusion: Zigzagging Judicial Power*

PUZZLE 1: ZIGZAGS IN DESIGNING RUSSIAN CONSTITUTIONAL REVIEW

As I discussed in Chapter 3, the protracted birth story of the 1st RCC in 1991, its near-death experience in the fall of 1993, and the slow rebirth of the Court in 1994, clearly show that the legal elites were instrumental in pushing through their agenda of a separate Constitutional Court only because they were able to convince the political actors that judicial review had useful political potential. In 1991, the "founding fathers" of the RCC established the Court in the context of constitution-making euphoria and in a strong legislature–weak presidency arrangement. Upon reaching a hard-fought consensus over the Court's powers and its justices, the politicians approved the 1st RCC even though they failed to fill two of the seats on the bench. In 1993–1994, the legal elites, together with the members of the 1st RCC, overcame Yeltsin's distaste for the Court and managed to convince him that this tribunal would be capable of protecting the semipresidential system, enshrined in the 1993 constitution. The fact that Yeltsin's circle was unable to purge the Court of his staunch opponents also shows the power of persuasion the legal elites had in the Kremlin. To guarantee a pro-Yeltsin majority on the bench, political leaders activated the 2nd RCC only in 1995, after all the justices were appointed.

In summary, both birth stories of this Court clearly show that its designers succeeded both in using the momentum of Gorbachev's campaign for the rule-of-law state and in tailoring foreign constitutional arrangements to the needs of their political superiors. Russia's rulers improved their reputation as "civilized" and law-abiding in the eyes of the international community, while some of the RCC designers went to sit on the bench of the Court. This means that, in addition to exploring the impact of domestic political competition and local demand for constitutionalism,[2] national-level comparative studies of judicial empowerment must

---

(Palo Alto, CA: Stanford University Press, 2004); and Pilar Domingo, "Judicialization of Politics or Politicization of the Judiciary? Recent Trends in Latin America," *Democratization*, vol. 11, no. 1 (2004), pp. 104–126.

[2] On the issue of demand for law in Russia, see Cheryl W. Gray and Kathryn Hendley, "Developing Commercial Law in Transition Economies: Examples from Hungary and Russia," in Jeffrey Sachs and Katharina Pistor, eds., *Rule of Law and Economic Reform in Russia* (Boulder: Westview Press, 1997), pp. 139–164; Kathryn Hendley, "Rewriting the Rules of the Game in Russia: The Neglected Issue of the Demand for Law," *East European Constitutional Review*, vol. 8, no. 4 (1999), pp. 89–95; Kathryn Hendley, "'Demand' for Law in Russia – A Mixed Picture," *ibid.*, vol. 10, no. 4 (2001), pp. 72–77; and Katharina Pistor, "The Demand for Constitutional Law," *Constitutional Political Economy*, vol. 13 (2002), pp. 73–87.

Puzzle 2: Russian Constitutional Review in Action

take into account the influence of international pressures and opportunities that result in a certain institutional arrangement.[3]

Politicians, on the other hand, revealed their short-term goals and concerns with the selection of judges in the processes of making and remaking the RCC (and of amending the 1994 RCC Act twice in 2001 for this purpose). Thus, another lesson for judicial empowerment theories is that politicians are as concerned about the individuals who compose the courts as they are about the scope of judicial review.[4] Finally, both the 1st and the 2nd federal constitutional courts in Russia shared similar dynamics of heavy and lengthy legislative scrutiny of their design and judicial recruitment, yet the tribunals had remarkably different life stories. Hence, the third finding of my study is that, by itself, strong parliamentary support and involvement in both designing constitutional review and in selecting the justices does not guarantee the success of the constitutional court. More broadly, *Judging Russia* shows that courts, like other political institutions, rarely act in the ways envisioned by their creators and produce unintended consequences. What really matters is judicial behavior and the reaction of the rest of the government apparatus to the judgments of the court.

PUZZLE 2: RUSSIAN CONSTITUTIONAL REVIEW IN ACTION

This brings us to the second puzzle: what accounts for the way in which the RCC judges formulated their rulings. As Chapters 4 and 5 demonstrate, the newly minted RCC justices used the euphoria of constitution making and deference of the rulers to the expertise of legal professionals to immediately navigate Russia's transition between the Scylla of totalitarianism and the Charybdis of territorial disintegration. Clearly, they had their own preferences for where Russia should be heading in terms of its democratization and federalization.[5] This is why the 1st RCC devoted a lot of

---

[3] Radoslav Procházka, *Mission Accomplished: On Founding Constitutional Adjudication in Central Europe* (Budapest: Central European University Press, 2002); Wojciech Sadurski, ed., *Constitutional Justice, East and West* (The Hague: Kluwer Law International, 2002); Herman Schwartz, *The Struggle for Constitutional Justice in Post-Communist Europe* (Chicago: University of Chicago Press, 2000).

[4] See, for example, Kate Malleson and Peter H. Russell, eds., *Appointing Judges in an Age of Judicial Power: Critical Perspectives from Around the World* (Toronto: University of Toronto Press, 2005).

[5] Russian judges are not alone in this practice. Supreme Court judges in Canada, most notably Bora Laskin, superimposed their views of what Canadian federalism should be within the text of their judgments. See, for example, Katherine E. Swinton, *The Supreme*

attention to the separation of powers and federalism disputes, and did not hesitate to rule against the powers-that-be even after they threatened individual justices. At the same time, this Court exercised a significant degree of discretion and stayed away from numerous political debacles. As I have shown, the 1st RCC quickly ran into trouble not because it focused on political heavyweights and not because Chairman Zorkin tried to make peace between President Yeltsin and the parliament. The Court failed because it overestimated its own ability to persuade fighting politicians who, in the context of the all-or-nothing war between Yeltsin and the Supreme Soviet, questioned the legitimacy of the constitutional rules and of the tribunal charged with protecting these rules. Thus, the severe diffusion of political power resulted in the overthrow of the constitutional order, not in the institutionalization of judicial review, as *strategic* theories, which link electoral uncertainty with judicial empowerment, predict.[6]

According to many observers, the 2nd RCC fared much better than its predecessor due to its cautious avoidance of bitter disputes between politicians and its greater attention to the protection of individual rights. My analysis of the published and the unpublished decisions of this Court partially confirms this judicial strategy. Indeed, the Court appears to have some sort of political question doctrine. For example, it refuses to review the constitutionality of electoral rules during an electoral campaign and never disbands legislatures elected according to rules that are later declared unconstitutional. Moreover, by engaging in the transnational "rights talk" with other high courts from abroad, this Court

1. created numerous rights, for example, the freedom of contract, and designed a hierarchy of rights, something the German Federal Constitutional Court chose not to do;
2. made constitutional review more accessible: now foreigners, corporations and state-owned enterprises, municipalities and the Procurator-General can petition the Court, although the 1994 RCC Act does not grant them standing to bring claims; and
3. elaborated unwritten constitutional principles of governmental interference with fundamental rights, such as proportionality and fairness.

Court and Canadian Federalism: The Laskin-Dickson Years (Toronto: Carswell, 1990). I am indebted to Jacqueline Krikorian for bringing this to my attention.

[6] See, for example, Tom Ginsburg, *Judicial Review in New Democracies: Constitutional Courts in Asian Cases* (New York: Cambridge University Press, 2003).

However, justices could not simply abandon their own vision of Russian governance. This is why they chose many politically salient cases for review and did not hesitate to overrule the president or the parliament. As I have shown in Chapter 5, four justices' votes were sufficient to strike down a statute. The political actors knew about this minimal threshold, and this is why they continued to litigate in hopes that the Court would invalidate the majoritarian policies. At the same time, justices skillfully used petitions to impose their own vision of the separation of powers and of a strong federal supremacy as opposed to Yeltsin's bargaining approach to Russian federalism. Unlike its predecessor, the 2nd RCC manipulated the timing of adjudicating politically sensitive cases and usually delayed the hearings and the publication of judgments in order to pacify the litigants. Moreover, in the fluidity and inconsistency of the short-term power needs of the rulers, judges could not be consistent in their decision making. The zigzag-like changes in the Court's doctrine on the fiscal powers of the executive branch and on the constitutionality of regional law making clearly show that constitutional judges could not engage in principled decision making precisely at the time when they were expected to do so.

There is no doubt that the RCC is a constrained court, yet this Court has frequently surprised the powerful players and anticipated crucial public policy changes. For example, the jurisprudence of the 2nd RCC in the federalism cases cannot be said to have reflected preferences of President Yeltsin. Moreover, many RCC decisions paved the way for Putin's reforms of Russian governance. In summary, Russian constitutional review has produced unintended consequences because the judges frequently ruled against the wishes of the powerful politicians. Whether these consequences have really changed the behavior of the politicians and other government officials is an empirical question, and it is also the core of the third element of judicial review power.

PUZZLE 3: SUCCESSES AND FAILURES IN IMPLEMENTING RUSSIAN CONSTITUTIONAL COURT DECISIONS

As many scholars and judges have argued, the implementation of judicial decisions depends on the cooperation of the political branches of government, the bureaucracy, and the judicial system. Moreover, the political branches have the capacity to reduce the institutional powers of the courts, impeach judges or abolish the court altogether. The experience of Russian constitutional review, as I have shown in Chapters 6 and 7, provides ample evidence for this argument, as Russia's rulers tried all three options yet they succeeded only in reducing the powers of the Court and packing it in 1994–1995. A good sign for judicial empowerment in Russia is that the 1st RCC was not abolished and its justices were not impeached (a result of both international pressures and domestic lobbying by the justices).

Some have argued that fledgling constitutional courts are more likely to secure compliance in separation-of-powers disputes by exploiting the rivalries between the legislature, the prime minister and the president. Others disagree about whether this would be a safe course for young judicial review bodies. Instead, strategic accounts of judicial behavior suggest that courts would achieve higher levels of compliance in individual rights jurisprudence. Yet another safe way to achieve compliance is to uphold central authority vis-à-vis that of the subnational governments. Russia's experiments with constitutional review, which dealt with all three categories of cases, provide contradictory evidence to these claims. The 1st RCC both succeeded and failed in securing compliance with its judgments in all three categories of cases. In 1992, the federal political branches obeyed the RCC in the separation-of-powers cases while the regional governments openly defied the centralist decisions of the Court. In 1993, an embittered President Yeltsin carried out the Court's order on how to count votes in the nationwide referendum. Yet, a few months later, Yeltsin almost abolished the Court for its "politicized and biased" decision making. The same year, Yeltsin both obeyed and disobeyed decisions of the Court in federalism disputes. Finally, the regular courts and the bureaucracy refused to carry out the judgments of the RCC in individual rights cases.

The 2nd RCC fared better in getting the government officials to obey its rulings. This Court succeeded in the separation-of-powers cases: currently, the federal legislative process proceeds based on the guidelines established by the Court. The Russian president does not use his "implied" powers beyond the limits as set out by the RCC. However, the compliance of the Russian Supreme Court and the Higher *Arbitrazh* Court with the orders of the RCC remains an issue. Placing the RCC decisions above the "guiding explanations" of both high courts in the operational legal hierarchy is not easy, as all three top courts vie to build their jurisdiction. The readiness of the regional governments to comply with RCC decisions has also significantly improved: the most recalcitrant regions no longer question the legitimacy of the Court and, instead, flood the Court with petitions against the federal center, while the federal center is actively using RCC judgments in reforming federalism through law. This is a remarkable change from Yeltsin's regime, which enforced centralist RCC decisions against the regions in an inconsistent manner, thus largely forgiving the regional defiance of the Court.

Finally, as I have shown in Chapter 5, the RCC is acclaimed for its many "rights" revolutions. Yet here the Court has encountered fierce resistance from the federal and the regional bureaucracies and the rest of the judicial system even though the political branches have largely agreed with its rights jurisprudence. Russia's rulers largely obeyed because the RCC justices have managed to convince them that compliance is their only option in order to avoid an international embarrassment, as Russians are increasingly petitioning the European Court of Human Rights in Strasbourg. However, this obedience rarely spilled over to the street-level bureaucrats and other courts. My analysis shows that these actors carried out the RCC directives only when their superiors ordered them to do so. Thus, coercion and threats of punishment motivate compliance on the ground. And, where these threats from above are lacking, noncompliance ensues. As a result, the RCC produces many "quiet" rights revolutions that do not reach ordinary Russians and have little impact on the "law in action." For example, landmark judgments of the Court on freedom of movement remain unimplemented because here the Court sided with individuals against the federal and the regional bureaucracies, law-enforcement agencies and regular courts. Moreover, the RCC is unlikely to break this resistance in the future as Russia attempts to control migration flows and prevent terrorism threats.

This secret sabotage of the Court-ordered rights revolution did not go unnoticed by the public. Although Russians, just as other European nations, value judicial independence, they increasingly distrust their courts, including the RCC. Having learned that a police officer or tax inspector can openly disobey judicial decisions without being punished, Russians appear to consider litigation as an inefficacious option to defend their rights. Meanwhile, the RCC redirects the majority of individual complaints to these distrusted regular courts. Naturally, it breeds even more disappointment with the judicial system regardless of the fact that the Russian courts have been consistently ruling on behalf of individual complainants against state officials.[7] Moreover, bureaucrats exploit this public distrust and further refuse to obey judicial decisions. Breaking this vicious circle is an arduous task that should begin with informing

[7] Peter H. Solomon, Jr., "Judicial Power in Russia: Through the Prism of Administrative Justice," *Law and Society Review*, vol. 38, no. 3 (2004), pp. 549–581.

the public about the essence of constitutional court decisions in plain language. This is an important educational responsibility of judges in those societies with thin constitutional traditions.[8]

In summary, this power of the Court to compel other actors to obey its judgment is what makes judicial review real. The constitution makers may design a weak judicial review power, yet the judges may creatively expand the power of their Court. Judges may independently exercise judicial review of governmental actions but they may stay away from politically sensitive cases. But if the government officials ignore and disobey constitutional court decisions on a regular basis, then it does not really matter how much power this court has or how many human rights cases it decides or how independently judges behave. Here, Russia provides an important addition to Epp's theory of the rights revolution.[9] In addition to a bills of rights, actual judicial independence, and a "support structure" for legal mobilization in civil society, real rights revolutions occur only when the effective infrastructure of public governance is there to support them.

Therefore, studies of judicial politics have to measure the actual impact of judicial review (judgments and their enforcement) on the political process, the capacity of the state, and the well-being of ordinary citizens. Without studying the postdecision implementation games, scholars will not know how societies move towards constitutionalism, whether the courts serve as veto points or insurance mechanisms, and whether government officials (dis) obey judicial decisions out of respect for the rule of law or other less noble reasons. The first decade of the RCC shows that politics plays a large role in creating, conducting, and enforcing judicial review. Thus, it appears that the rule of law may become entrenched as a by-product of political struggles overseen by constitutional courts.

PUZZLE 3.1: THE "WAR OF COURTS" IN THE RUSSIAN FEDERATION

Theories of comparative politics have yet to come up with a plausible explanation of the "wars among courts" that flare up from the Atlantic

---

[8] Wojciech Sadurski, "Review of *The Struggle for Constitutional Justice in Post-Communist Europe* by Herman Schwartz" (Chicago: The University of Chicago Press, 2000)," *I-CON: International Journal of Constitutional Law*, vol. 1, no. 1 (2003), p. 160.

[9] Charles R. Epp, *The Rights Revolution: Lawyers, Activists, and Supreme Courts in Comparative Perspective* (Chicago: University of Chicago Press, 1998).

Puzzle 3.1: The "War of Courts" in the Russian Federation   293

to the Pacific. The implementation of constitutional court decisions on individual rights depends entirely on the compliance of the rest of the judicial system, yet, regretfully, the dynamics of interaction between ordinary and constitutional courts remain a "crucial and understudied issue in comparative constitutional studies."[10] A "veto points" approach does not account for the high courts repeatedly vetoing each other, since it assumes that the same dominant political elites influence judicial decision making via judicial recruitment and ideological propensities.[11] Why would the high courts incessantly quarrel among each other, if the judges are appointed by the same elites and share the same values? Some might argue that the rulers separated the constitutional court from the rest of the judicial branch in order to control the judicial system according to the Roman maxim of "divide and rule." But is it easier to control three high courts instead of one? This is an empirical question, and a subject for future research of the "judicialization of politics."

The *strategic* judicial review thesis argues that intercourt conflicts occur as all courts pursue the important goal of expanding their power, yet this theory does not predict how this conflict will be resolved.[12] My analysis also suggests that this intercourt competition over judge-made law is inevitable; yet, in the European context, the constitutional courts have usually won this race by drawing on the decisions of the European Court of Human Rights. So far, constitutional courts have been the locomotives of revolutionizing due process rights according to the guidelines of the Strasbourg court, and they have largely succeeded. Thus, the intercourt rivalry in the area of basic rights is resolved by appealing to international human rights standards, not by the dynamics of domestic politics. Here, the interests of the constitutional court judges and the political leaders were similar: both groups wanted to join the "civilized West," and gave each other mutual support in getting their countries closer to Europe.

Intercourt rivalry in the area of federalism is a different story because it touches upon the actual distribution of power within the federation. Russia's federal elites, including the RCC judges, seemed to agree on only one basic notion, namely, not to repeat the collapse of the USSR or Yugoslavia. However, there was little interelite consensus on how to

---

[10] Ginsburg, *Judicial Review in New Democracies*, p. 134.
[11] George Tsebelis, *Veto Players: How Political Institutions Work* (Princeton: Princeton University Press, 2002).
[12] Ginsburg, *Judicial Review in New Democracies*, p. 255.

prevent Russia's breakup. Persistent rivalries between the RCC and the Russian Supreme Court over the power to review regional laws, explored in Chapter 6, show how deeply the federal actors were divided in restraining the separatist tendencies in the regions. Here, the RCC lacked the ability to draw on international legal standards, first, because domestic political bargaining was crucial in handling federalism disputes, and, second, because of "a relative dearth of comparative judicial exploration of issues of federalism" around the globe.[13] The RCC appears to win its battles against the Russian Supreme Court on this front, in large part, due to the support of President Putin. How durable his support is, and how Putin responds to increasing constitutional litigation over his federalism reforms is not yet clear. What is clear, however, is that the intercourt rivalries in the politically sensitive areas of federalism or separation-of-powers disputes are likely to be resolved by compromise, reflecting the larger political struggles and interests of powerful actors. Given the institutional freshness of judicial review in an uncertain transition, this compromise solution, depending on the degree of political polarization, may range from merging the top courts into one body to the peaceful "cohabitation" of top courts Italian-style, in which both tribunals respect each other's jurisprudence.

SUMMARY

My answers to the three puzzles show that the power of the RCC is growing (albeit in a nonlinear fashion) both in terms of its judicial discretion and the authoritativeness of its judgments. On one hand, the Court creatively expands its own jurisdiction and increasingly "surprises" all branches of government with its judgments despite its unpopularity among ordinary Russians. On the other hand, federal and regional political actors, corporations, and ordinary citizens actively use constitutional review and increasingly comply with its judgments. Moreover, a fragile interelite consensus appears to avoid public criticism of this teenaged tribunal in public, a frequent problem for the Court throughout the 1990s. This is a remarkable achievement for an institution that rebuilt itself from a near-death experience in 1993. In summary, following Tom Ginsburg's criteria for judicial power: by and large, the RCC independently decides

---

[13] Vicki C. Jackson, "Comparative Constitutional Federalism and Transnational Judicial Discourse," *I-CON: International Journal of Constitutional Law*, vol. 2, no. 1 (2003), p. 93.

Alternative Explanations of Russian Experiments 295

politically significant issues and compels others to obey most of its judgments.[14] However, this successful institutionalization of the 2nd RCC has not resulted in *juristocracy* in Russia, to use Hirschl's term.[15] More research is needed to see whether my thesis of nonlinear judicial empowerment may explain the current global trend towards *juristocracy* as a temporally (second half of the twentieth century) and spatially (new and old democracies) limited turn in the zigzag-like history of world constitutionalism.

ALTERNATIVE EXPLANATIONS OF RUSSIAN EXPERIMENTS WITH CONSTITUTIONAL REVIEW

A growing number of theories provide competing explanations for the origins and the performance of constitutional review. Some theories suggest that *international* pressures and opportunities have a strong impact on constitutional revolutions. They view the proliferation of new constitutional review tribunals in the ex-Soviet region as an extension of a "global diffusion of judicial power" or of a post–World War II hegemony of human rights agenda. By subjecting their choices to judicial scrutiny, post-Communist rulers demonstrate their commitment to democracy and the rule of law to the voters and to the rest of the world. Constitutional courts, then, uphold democratic values, protect individual rights, and serve as a bulwark against the return to a totalitarian past.

Russia's experiments with judicial review involved the *international* context in both designing and exercising this institution. "Peer pressure" within the ex-Soviet world also played a role: everyone else has a constitutional court, why can't we? However, Russia's rulers appealed to the Western concepts of "democracy" and "higher law" in making, breaking, and remaking the constitutional court. Similarly, the RCC judges defended their human rights decisions by appealing to European legal doctrine yet their jurisprudence lacks a coherent framework on many issues. By relying on European legal principles the RCC also won its battles with the Supreme Court. In summary, "the rise of world constitutionalism" to use Bruce Ackerman's phrase, provides tangible political resources to the rulers and to the judges.[16]

---

[14] Ginsburg, *Judicial Review in New Democracies*, p. 252.

[15] Ran Hirschl, *Towards Juristocracy: The Origins and Consequences of the New Constitutionalism* (Cambridge, MA: Harvard University Press, 2004).

[16] Bruce Ackerman, "The Rise of World Constitutionalism," *Virginia Law Review*, vol. 83, no. 4 (1997), pp. 771–797.

The experience of the RCC refutes the view of Russian exceptionalism. Just as the citizens of other European nations do, Russians consistently praise judicial independence and actively petition the Court. The RCC systematically engages in transnational judicial dialogues with other constitutional courts from abroad. Moreover, Russia's top courts actively compete for the judge-made law among themselves, just as constitutional and regular courts in Europe and Asia do. However, the relatively successful RCC does not appear to prevent Russia from transiting back to authoritarianism under Putin's presidency. This is why the importance of the *international* context is limited by *domestic* power struggles.

Other scholars propose *institutionalist* explanations regarding the need for strong judicial review. According to them, a powerful judiciary provides efficient ways to govern a polity (and even to promote prosperity), and, therefore, strong courts have to be created. For example, various separation-of-powers schemes (bicameralism, strong presidencies, and a divided executive branch between the president and the prime minister) demand constitutional review to resolve intragovernmental conflicts.[17] Federalism, as an arrangement to share power between the central government and the subnational units, also appears to require an independent umpire to resolve federal–regional and interregional conflicts and to promote the common market by punishing recalcitrant regions.[18] As the best cure for overcoming ungovernability, powerful courts are also prescribed for polities facing political polarization and polities with an expanding administrative state. Here, having an independent judiciary is presented as an efficient way to monitor distrusted politicians and bureaucrats.[19]

Russian experiments with constitutional review provide evidence that creating the constitutional court was inextricably linked to the separation

[17] See, for example, Ackerman, "The Rise of World Constitutionalism," pp. 771–797; and Martin Shapiro, "The Success of Judicial Review and Democracy," in Martin Shapiro and Alec Stone Sweet, *On Law, Politics, and Judicialization* (Oxford: Oxford University Press, 2002), pp. 149–183.

[18] See Ginsburg, *Judicial Review in New Democracies*, p. 59, and accompanying notes therein.

[19] See, for example, Carlo Guarnieri and Patrizia Pederzoli, *The Power of Judges: A Comparative Study of Courts and Democracy* (New York: Oxford University Press, 2002), pp. 150–183; Malcolm Feeley and Edward Rubin, *Judicial Policy Making and the Modern State: How the Courts Reformed America's Prisons* (Cambridge, UK: Cambridge University Press, 1998); Matthew D. McCubbins, Roger G. Noll, and Barry R. Weingast, "Administrative Procedures as Instruments of Political Control," *Journal of Law, Economics, and Organization*, vol. 3, no. 2 (1987), pp. 243–277.

of powers and the presidency. In 1991, the 1st RCC was set up together with a weak presidency. In contrast, in 1993, the 2nd RCC was adopted alongside a superpresidential system. Throughout the first decade of post-communism, Russia's subnational political elites did not simply follow the prescriptions of the federalist rationale for creating one federal judicial body to review the federal–regional disputes. Instead, subnational constitution makers decided to have their own courts to police Russian federalism.[20] Also, *institutionalist* theories do not explain well why the federal center failed to enforce the highly centralist decisions of the 1st RCC or why the bureaucrats, who simply forgot the RCC judgments, got away with not being punished. Similarly, the distribution of power between the RCC and other courts does not function smoothly. Here, the unwillingness and incapacity of the federal center to coerce autonomy-minded regions and bureaucrats at all levels of the administrative state limited the extent to which the Court managed to improve public governance in the course of the Russian transition. In sum, these explanations (and justifications) are correct in focusing on the demand for strong constitutional review. Without such a demand (domestic or international), the rulers would not create constitutional courts. Yet these theories, according to Hirschl, "overlook the human agency and the fact that legal innovations require legal innovators – people who make choices as to the timing, scope, and extent of legal reforms."[21]

Note that this category of "legal innovators" includes both constitution makers, political and legal elites who decide when and how to empower the court and when and how to obey judicial decisions, and judges, who decide when and how to uphold, overturn or give a new "constitutionally acceptable" interpretation to a particular government policy. *Strategic* approaches to judicial empowerment explore the dynamics of these choices on the part of judges and politicians, and, therefore, help account for the timing and extent of the institutionalization of constitutional review. According to these approaches, which correctly assume that judicial review power is part and parcel of political struggles, politicians choose to empower the judiciary when they

1. want to signal their long-term commitment to certain policy preferences: empowered courts, then, guard these preferences, while the

---

[20] Alexei Trochev, "Less Democracy, More Courts: A Puzzle of Judicial Review in Russia," *Law and Society Review*, vol. 38, no. 3 (2004), p. 519.

[21] Hirschl, *Towards Juristocracy*, p. 37.

298   *Conclusion: Zigzagging Judicial Power*

legislators derive significant benefits from the interest groups – beneficiaries of the judicially protected policies;[22] and/or

2. fear losing elections: strong and independent courts, then, protect policies adopted by the outgoing legislative majorities.[23]

Thus, the politicians agree to subject their own policy-making flexibility to judicial review now in exchange for the protection of their interests by powerful courts in the future. This future, according to numerous studies, is bright, enhancing legal stability and even democratic consolidation.[24] This future of judicial empowerment is so bright because the constitutional courts also act strategically, that is, judges strike down laws only when they are confident that the political branches will comply with their rulings.[25] This is because judicial review tribunals are "constrained" actors, for they can have their judgments implemented only if the political branches cooperate. In sum, the constitution makers and the constitutional judges "lose the battle in order to win the war": they forego short-term gains in order to score victories against their opponents in the long-term, be it locking-in preferred policies or entrenching judicial review.

The turbulent childhood of the RCC has not escaped the attention of *strategic* approaches.[26] According to them, the 1st RCC failed in 1993 because it was not sensitive enough to the problem of compliance, while its

[22] See, for example, William Landes and Richard Posner, "The Independent Judiciary in an Interest Group Perspective," *Journal of Law and Economics*, vol. 18, no. 3 (1975), pp. 875–901; Eli Salzberger and Paul Fenn, "Judicial Independence: Some Evidence from the English Court of Appeal," *Journal of Law and Economics*, vol. 42, no. 2 (1999), pp. 831–847.

[23] See, for example, J. Mark Ramseyer, "The Puzzling (In) Dependence of Courts: A Comparative Approach," *Journal of Legal Studies*, vol. 23, no. 2 (1994), pp. 721–748; Ginsburg, *Judicial Review in New Democracies*; Pedro C. Magalhães, "The Limits To Judicialization: Legislative Politics and Constitutional Review in the Iberian Democracies" (Ph.D. diss., Ohio State University, 2003); Pilar Domingo, "Judicial Independence: The Politics of the Supreme Court of Mexico," *Journal of Latin American Studies*, vol. 32, no. 3 (2000), pp. 705–735; and Jodi Finkel, "Judicial Reform in Argentina in the 1990s: How Electoral Incentives Shape Institutional Change," *Latin American Research Review*, vol. 39, no. 3 (2004), pp. 56–80.

[24] See, for example, Lee Epstein, Jack Knight, and Olga Shvetsova, "The Role of Constitutional Courts in the Establishment and Maintenance of Democratic Systems of Government," *Law and Society Review*, vol. 35, no. 1 (2001), pp. 117–163.

[25] Georg Vanberg, *The Politics of Constitutional Review in Germany* (Cambridge, UK: Cambridge University Press, 2005).

[26] *Strategic* accounts that focus on electoral uncertainty have yet to come up with plausible explanations of the "birth stories" of subnational constitution making in Russia. See Trochev, "Less Democracy."

successor survives through its second decade because the Court chooses to be sensitive to avoid backlash from political branches.[27] Yet *strategic* accounts of a constrained RCC ignore the international context of judicial decision making that enable this judicial review tribunal to issue landmark decisions in the area of fundamental rights. As many observers of European judicial empowerment have argued, an exclusive focus on domestic political struggles (electoral markets or credible commitments) cannot adequately explain the dynamics of the judicialization of politics at the national level.[28] For example, my analysis clearly shows that the aggressive reliance on European human rights standards was crucial for the RCC in waging its battles against the Supreme Court and the Higher *Arbitrazh* Court.[29] Similarly, *strategic* approaches fail to explain the sheer volume of nonimplemented RCC judgments and provide little guidance in predicting the probability of their implementation. To be sure, the RCC has been a constrained court. But my analysis goes deeper and shows how and why the Russian rulers and the street-level bureaucrats dealt with constitutional review, sometimes by obeying the RCC orders and sometimes by simply ignoring them.

Unlike the *institutionalist* and *strategic* approaches, which focus mainly on the elites, the *public support* approach to judicial empowerment insists that the fate of judicial review depends on its acceptance by the broader society, not just by the elites. According to this approach, which draws upon judicial politics in developed democracies, courts, like any other public institution, depend on public support in order to survive. Newly created constitutional courts must gain the support of citizens by ruling in line with the majority will; otherwise courts will be viewed as illegitimate or redundant government institutions. Over time, the mass of popular judgments will create a shield, which constitutional

---

[27] Epstein et al., "The Role of Constitutional Courts"; Anna Jonsson, "The Constitutional Court of the Russian Federation, 1997–2001," *Working Papers of the Department of East European Studies, Uppsala University*, no. 73 (October 2002); Ginsburg, *Judicial Review in New Democracies*, pp. 101–104.

[28] See, for example, Trochev, "Less Democracy," pp. 520–521 (noting that domestic politics determine the institutionalization of judicial review only at the local level, not at the national level); and Nancy Maveety and Anke Grosskopf, "'Constrained' Constitutional Courts as Conduits for Democratic Consolidation," *Law and Society Review*, vol. 38, no. 3 (2004), pp. 464–469 (arguing that the "international context serves to enable, rather than constrain, courts to promote social change and policy reform").

[29] In fact, frequent intercourt conflicts, which have flared up from the Atlantic to the Pacific in the past several decades, have yet to be explained by the *strategic* approaches of judicial behavior.

court judges can use later to issue controversial decisions and to compel others to enforce them.

The core idea behind this *public support* approach is the accountability of governments to the voters but, as I have shown in my studies, neither the rulers nor the rest of the Russian state are accountable to the citizenry. Although ordinary Russians have had consistent respect for judicial independence and the rule of law in the past decade, on a par with other European nations, public officials have been unwilling and unable to carry out RCC decisions. Needless to say, votes do not matter much when two (or three in the case of Russia) high national courts refuse to respect each other. Also, the *public support* approaches have yet to explain why fewer and fewer voters in societies as diverse as Russia and Mexico approve of their high courts despite their groundbreaking jurisprudence in the area of human rights.

In summary, by analyzing the human agency of constitution makers and judges, by paying attention to their policy choices as well as the legal rules, and by exploring the actual impact of the RCC decisions on the ground, I have been able to explain why many of these decisions remain unenforced, contrary to the predictions of *strategic* accounts of judicial behavior. Future studies of the RCC will also have to probe how this Court was able to solidify its power under the hostile conditions of the growing public disapproval of the Court and entrenched authoritarianism of President Putin.

CONCLUSION

Although the business of studying judicial review is a booming industry in comparative politics, *Judging Russia* has attempted to explain the growing pains of Russian constitutional review in the past decade by looking at the following paradoxes:

1. Why and how the Russian rulers and their legal advisers chose to create a powerful Russian Constitutional Court in 1991, then nearly destroy it in 1993, only to reactivate it in 1994.
2. Why and how the RCC failed in 1993 only to recover and succeed by 2003.
3. Why government officials, including judges on other courts, promptly carried out RCC decisions in some cases, delayed the implementation in other cases, and sometimes simply ignored RCC orders.

Conclusion 301

A complex blend of internal and external politico-legal factors accounts for this seemingly confusing behavior of politicians, judges, and bureaucrats. Short-term considerations in place of strategic calculations on the part of politicians and bureaucrats appear to provide answers to Puzzles 1 and 3. This is why the RCC may have been unable to gauge the potential responses from political branches to adverse judgments. An ad hoc coalition of political and legal elites succeeded in making the RCC operational in 1991 before adopting a new constitution. The RCC was not abolished in 1993 only because the RCC justices and some presidential advisers managed to convince Boris Yeltsin that his archrivals would leave the bench. Short-term calculations of political elites appear to be everywhere: in the debates over the powers of the Court and its financial independence, and over the selection of judges and their tenure. The Russian bureaucrats also appear to obey unfavorable Court judgments only when their bosses order them to do so.

In short, the momentary solutions chosen by the constitution makers, which are inextricably linked to the overwhelming pressures of the post-communist transition,[30] rather than commitments to the rule of law and democracy, drove the dynamics of creating constitutional review. Therefore, a constitutional court emerges as a possible but not an inevitable and not necessarily efficient by-product of these political struggles. Because these are short-term interests in the context of a "quadruple" transition to a new mode of governance (and even new statehood for former members of socialist federations),[31] they are fluid and "subject to change without notice," that is, politicians can easily change their minds about making the constitutional courts operational or about dissolving them or about impeaching already appointed justices.[32] This means that the severe diffusion of political power may result in the overthrow of the constitutional order, but not in the institutionalization of judicial review, particularly given the ease with which new democrats reject "unjust" laws.

How does a constitutional court build its own judicial power among these gigantic waves of political expediency in the tumultuous sea of post-communist transition? Partly, by catering to the interests of the powers-that-be, and, partly, by expanding its own jurisdiction under the veils

---

[30] See, for example, Martin Horak, *Governing the Post-Communist City: Institutions and Democratic Development in Prague* (Toronto: University of Toronto Press, 2008).

[31] Taras Kuzio, "Transition in Post-Communist States: Triple or Quadruple?" *Politics*, vol. 21, no. 3 (2001), pp. 168–177.

[32] For a similar argument about Latin American judicial reforms, see Domingo, "Judicialization of Politics or Politicization of the Judiciary?" p. 120.

of judicial independence and the rule of law. Which part prevails in this undoubtedly conscious judicial strategizing depends on the politico-legal context that surrounds the court and on the aspirations of judges. The rise and fall of the 1st RCC in 1992–1993 clearly shows that the aspirations of its justices prevailed over the short-term interests of the Russian rulers, and eventually provoked a political backlash against the young Court. The slow recovery of the RCC since 1995, on the other hand, shows that the Court has been able to restore its own power by catering to the interests of the powers-that-be. The 2nd RCC, then, used this power to impose its own policy agenda, particularly in areas of criminal procedure, taxation, and federalism reforms.

To be sure, other powerbrokers do not easily share their power with a constitutional review tribunal. Similar to the early years of the U.S. Supreme Court,[33] the RCC faced surges of subnational defiance of its judgments, which gradually became accepted by the most recalcitrant regions. Similar to the early years of Italian, Korean, and Spanish constitutional courts, the RCC led the battles against the rest of the Russian judiciary. The federal bureaucracy, including the law-enforcement agencies, continues to resist numerous RCC decisions in the area of individual rights. This is why the impact of Russian constitutional review on the lives of ordinary citizens, who courageously keep suing the state, has been limited. And this is why the successful institutionalization of the 2nd RCC has not resulted in *juristocracy*.

Therefore, in the context of the instrumental use of courts by ever-myopic Russian elites and the ensuing decline in the reputation of courts in the eyes of the public, the Constitutional Court cannot afford to be isolated from the public. Its judges have to maintain the link between the Olympus of unwritten constitutional principles and the everyday needs of broad groups of Russian society. As Jennifer Widner reminds us, to secure and to maintain an independent judiciary, it is vital for the judges "to find more permanent allies" at home and abroad.[34] However, the desire of judges to be popular may damage their independence. In other words, the constitutional court must turn its numerous "quiet" revolutions into concrete and widely known tools for social change so that ordinary Russians, who hold abstract commitments to the rule of law, can learn the

---

[33] Leslie Goldstein, *Constituting Federal Sovereignty* (Baltimore: Johns Hopkins University Press, 2001), pp. 22–33.

[34] Jennifer Widner, *Building the Rule of Law* (New York: W. W. Norton & Company, 2001), p. 394.

Conclusion 303

benefits of having a powerful and independent constitutional review. The "global diffusion of judicial power" may help judges to cultivate constitutional rights consciousness among the citizenry, and comparative judicial politics scholars may also help them by measuring the actual impact of judicial review (judgments and their enforcement) on the political process, the capacity of the state, and on the well-being of ordinary citizens.

Appendix

RCC Justices

Ernest Ametistov	01/11/1991– 07/09/1998[†]
Marat Baglai	07/02/1995 – 25/02/2005*
Nikolai Bondar	16/02/2000 –
Iurii Danilov	15/11/1994 –
Boris Ebzeev	30/10/1991 –
Gadis Gadzhiev	30/10/1991 –
Vladimir Iaroslavtsev	24/10/1994 –
Sergei Kazantsev	29/03/2002 –
Olga Khokhriakova	25/10/1994 –
Mikhail Kleandrov	12/02/2003 –
Anatolii Kononov	30/10/1991 –
Larisa Krasavchikova	12/02/2003 –
Viktor Luchin	01/11/1991 – 25/02/2005*
Sergei Mavrin	27/02/2005 –
Nikolai Melnikov	25/02/2005 –
Tamara Morshchakova	30/10/1991 – 29/03/2002*
Vladimir Oleinik	30/10/1991 – 17/02/1999[†]
Nikolai Seleznev	30/10/1991 –
Anatolii Sliva	14/10/1998 –
Vladimir Strekozov	06/12/1994 –
Iurii Rudkin	30/10/1991 –
Oleg Tiunov	30/10/1991 – 12/02/2003*
Vladimir Tumanov	25/10/1994 – 20/02/1997*
Nikolai Vedernikov	30/10/1991 – 16/02/2000*
Nikolai Vitruk	30/10/1991 – 12/02/2003*
Liudmila Zharkova	11/06/1997 –
Gennadii Zhilin	18/05/1999 –
Valerii Zorkin	30/10/1991 –

[†] passed away while in office
* reached mandatory retirement age

Bibliography

SUMMARY

1. Documents
2. Interviews with the Author
3. Published Interviews and Speeches
4. Russian Sources on Russia and the USSR
5. English Language Sources on Russia, Eastern Europe, and the USSR
6. Judicial and Democratic Theory

1. DOCUMENTS

a. Constitutions

"Konstitutsiia Respubliki Dagestan." *Dagestanskaia pravda*. July 26, 2003.

Konstitutsiia (Osnovnoi zakon) Soiuza Sovetskikh Sotsialisticheskikh Respublik. Moskva: Izvestiia Sovetov narodnykh deputatov SSSR, 1977.

Konstitutsiia (Osnovnoi zakon) Rossiiskoi Sovetskoi Federativnoi Sotsialisticheskoi Respubliki. Moskva: Sovetskaia Rossiia, 1978.

Konstitutsiia (Osnovnoi zakon) Rossiiskoi Federatsii – Rossii: priniata na vneocherednoi sedmoi sessii Verkhovnogo Soveta RSFSR deviatogo sozyva 12 aprelia 1978 goda, s izmeneniami i dopolneniami. . . . Moskva: Izd. Verkhovnogo Soveta Rossiiskoi Federatsii, 1993.

Konstitutsiia Rossiiskoi Federatsii. Moskva: Iuridicheskaia literatura, 1994.

b. Constitutional Drafts

Proekt Konstitutsii Rossiiskoi Federatsii. Podgotovlen Konstitutsionnoi komissiei Sezda narodnykh deputatov Rossiiskoi Federatsii [Supreme Soviet draft]. Moskva: Respublika, 1993.

"Proekt Konstitutsii Rossiiskoi Federatsii. Predstavlen Prezidentom Rossiiskoi Federatsii" [President Yeltsin's draft], *Moskovskaia pravda*. May 5, 1993.

"Proekt Konstitutsii Rossiiskoi Federatsii, odobrennyi Konstitutsionnym soveshchaniem" [Constitutional Convention draft], *Rabochaia tribuna*. July 21, 1993.

307

308   *Bibliography*

"Proekt Konstitutsii Rossiiskoi Federatsii, vynosimyi na vsenarodnoe golosovanie 12.12.1993" [Constitutional draft to be approved by popular vote on December 12, 1993], *Rossiiskaia gazeta*. November 10, 1993.

c. Stenographic Records and Hansards

Gosudarstvennaia Duma: Stenogramma zasedaniia. Vesenniaia sessiia. T. 4. 6–27 aprelia 1994 g. Moskva: Respublika, 1995.
Gosudarstvennaia Duma: Stenogramma zasedaniia. Vesenniaia sessiia. T. 6. 8–24 iuniia 1994 g. Moskva: Respublika, 1995.
Iz istorii sozdaniia Konstitutsii Rossiiskoi Federatsii. Konstitutsionnaia Komissiia: stenogrammy, materially, dokumenty (1990–1993 gg.) [On the History of Creating the RF Constitution. Constitutional Commission: Stenographic Reports, Materials, Documents (1990–1993)] Moskva: Wolters Kluwer, 2007.
Konstitutsionnoe soveshchanie. Stenogrammy. Materialy. Dokumenty. 29 aprelia–10 noiabria 1993 g. v 20 tomakh. [Constitutional Convention. Stenographic Reports. Materials. Documents. April 29–November 10, 1993] Moskva: Iuridicheskaia literatura, 1995–1996.
Materialy XIX vsesoiuznoi konferentsii Kommunisticheskoi partii Sovetskogo Soiuza. Moskva: Politicheskaia literatura, 1988.
Piatyi (vneocherednoi) Sezd narodnykh deputatov RSFSR: Stenogr. Otchet. T.2. Moskva: Respublika, 1992.
Sovet Federatsii. Zasedanie 8. 12–14 iiuliia 1994 g. Stenograficheskii otchet. Moskva: Sovet Federatsii, 1995.
Sovet Federatsii. Zasedanie 11. Biulleten no. 1 (38). Chast 1. 24 oktiabria 1994 g. Stenograficheskii otchet. Moskva: Sovet Federatsii, 1995.
Sovet Federatsii. Zasedanie 12. Biulleten no. 1 (42). Chast 1. 15 noiabria 1994 g. Stenograficheskii otchet. Moskva: Sovet Federatsii, 1995.
Sovet Federatsii. Zasedanie 13. Biulleten no. 1 (45). 6 dekabria 1994 g. Stenograficheskii otchet. Moskva: Sovet Federatsii, 1995.
Sovet Federatsii. Zasedanie 16. 7–10 fevralia 1995 g. Stenograficheskii otchet. Moskva: Sovet Federatsii, 1996.

d. Other Documents and Compilations

Avakian, Suren. *Konstitutsiia Rossii: priroda, evoliutsiia, sovremennost.* Moskva: RIuID, 2000. (Constitutional drafts by Sergei Shakhrai, Andrei Sakharov, Communist Party of the RF, and Russian Movement for Democratic Reforms [RDDR]).
Batkin, L. M., compiler. *Konstitutsionnye idei Andreia Sakharova.* Moskva: Novella, 1990.
van den Berg, Ger P., compiler. "Constitution of the Russian Federation Annotated with Summaries of Rulings and Other Decisions of Constitutional (Charter) Courts: 1990–2001," *Review of Central and East European Law*, vol. 27 (2001): 175–488.
Gosudarstvennoe Sobranie-Kurultai Respubliki Bashkortostan. Zapros o proverke sootvetstviia p. 3 st. 6, pp. 6 i 7 st. 6.1 Zakona RF "O statuse sudei v RF" Konstitutsii RF." May 17, 2003. Unpublished document.

Bibliography

Materialy dela o proverke konstitutsionnosti Ukazov Prezidenta RF, kasaiushchikhsia deiatelnosti KPSS i KP RSFSR, a takzhe o proverke konstitutsionnosti KPSS i KP RSFSR. Moskva: Spark, 1996–1997.

Morshchakova, Tamara, ed. *Konstitutsionnyi Sud Rossiiskoi Federatsii. Postanovleniia. Opredeleniia. 1992–1996.* Moskva: Novyi Iurist, 1997.

―――. *Konstitutsionnyi Sud Rossiiskoi Federatsii. Postanovleniia. Opredeleniia. 1997–1998.* Moscow: Iurist, 2000.

―――. *Konstitutsionnyi Sud Rossiiskoi Federatsii. Postanovleniia. Opredeleniia. 2000.* Moskva: Iurist, 2001.

―――. *Konstitutsionnyi Sud Rossiiskoi Federatsii. Postanovleniia. Opredeleniia. 2001.* Moskva: Iurist, 2002.

Strekozov, Vladimir, ed. *Konstitutsionnyi Sud Rossiiskoi Federatsii. Postanovleniia. Opredeleniia. 2002.* Moskva: Iurist, 2003.

―――. *Konstitutsionnyi Sud Rossiiskoi Federatsii. Postanovleniia. Opredeleniia. 2006.* Moskva: Norma, 2007.

2. INTERVIEWS WITH THE AUTHOR (2001–2005)

a. Justices, Russian Constitutional Court

Nikolai Bondar
Iurii Danilov
Boris Ebzeev
Gadis Gadzhiev
Vladimir Iaroslavtsev
Olga Khokhriakova
Anatolii Kononov
Viktor Luchin
Tamara Morshchakova
Nikolai Seleznev
Vladimir Strekozov
Vladimir Tumanov
Nikolai Vitruk
Liudmila Zharkova
Valerii Zorkin

b. Staff, Russian Constitutional Court

Elena Abrosimova (Clerk, Justice Khokhriakova)
Tatiana Bolshakova (Head of the Implementation Control Department)
Vladislav Iastrebov (Clerk, Justice Seleznev)
Viacheslav Ivanov (Head of the Private Law Department)
Rozalia Ivanova (Head of the Labor Law Department)
Petr Kondratov (Head of the Criminal Justice Department)
Elena Kravchenko (Chief of Staff of the Chairman of the Court)
Vladimir Kriazhkov (Adviser, the Analytical Center)
Viktor Maksimov (Clerk, Justice Bondar)
Anna Malysheva (Head of the Press Service)
Evgenii Pyrikov (Head of the International Relations Department)

310   *Bibliography*

Peter Sedugin (Consultant, Private Law Department)
Khiil Sheinin (Head of the Human Rights Department)
Vladimir Sivitskii (Consultant, Constitutional Law Department)
Boris Strashun (Head of the Analytical Center)

c. Presidential Administration

Vera Bobrova (Chief of Staff of the Counsel to the Russian President)
Mikhail Mitiukov (Counsel to the Russian President)
Tatiana Shubert (Assistant to the Counsel to the Russian President)

d. Other officials, journalists, and scholars

Liudmila Batmanova (Justice of the Komi Constitutional Court, Syktyvkar)
Dmitri Bedniakov (Member of the Federation Council)
Larisa Chetverikova (Head of the Legal Department, State Council of the Komi Republic, Syktyvkar)
Olga Doronina (Russian Academy of State Service, Moscow)
Iulia Dultseva (Federal Judge, Syktyvkar)
Iurii Gavriusov (Chief Justice of the Komi Constitutional Court, Syktyvkar)
Konstantin Katanian (Journalist, *Moskovskie novosti*, Moscow)
Igor Kravets (Law Professor, Novosibirsk State University, Novosibirsk)
Pavel Punegov (Justice of the Komi Constitutional Court, Syktyvkar)
Alexandr Pitiulin (City Procurator, Syktyvkar)
Olga Shwarts (Russian Foundation for Legal Reform, Moscow)
Sergei Tolstov (Justice of the Komi Constitutional Court, Syktyvkar)
Oleg Vokuev (Assistant City Procurator, Syktyvkar)

3. PUBLISHED INTERVIEWS AND SPEECHES

Alekseev, Sergei. "What Is the Constitution?" *Moscow News.* May 6–13, 1990, p. 6.

Baglai, Marat. Interview to *RTR 'Vesti'*. June 4, 1998.

———. "Konstitutsionnoe pravosudie v Rossii: stanovlenie i razvitie," [Constitutional Justice in Russia: Formation and Development]. *Zhurnal rossiiskogo prava*, no. 10 (October 2001): 3–11.

"Beseda s Valeriem Zorkinym: Zhit po pravu." *Sovetskaia Rossiia.* October 5, 1996, pp. 1–2.

"Delo suda – ne politika, a pravo. Vladimir Tumanov." *Rossiiskie vesti.* August 2, 1995.

"Diktatura Chubaisa ili zakona? Interviu s Gadisom Gadzhievym." *Patriot*, no. 50 (December 1996), p. 11.

Dorofeev, Nikolai. "Vladimir Tumanov: Ia ne liubliu gromkikh protsessov." *Trud.* June 28, 1995.

"Dva goda nazad nachala deistvovat Rossiiskaia Konstitutsiia. Marat Baglai." *Nezavisimaia gazeta.* December 26, 1995.

Ebzeev, Boris. Speech. *Vserossiiskoe soveshchanie rukovoditelei organov gosudarstvennoi predstavitelnoi i ispolnitelnoi vlasti respublik v sostave Rossiiskoi*

Bibliography

Federatsii, kraev, oblastei, avtonomnoi oblasti, avtonomnykh okrugov, gorodov Moskvy i Sankt-Peterburga. Moskva: Respublika, 1992, pp. 73–75.

"Esli vas uvolili po starosti, otkazalis propisat ili lishili liubimoi gazety... Konstitutsionnyi sud Rossii v gostiakh u 'Literaturnoi gazety': T. Morshchakova, V. Luchin, Iu. Rudkin, O. Tiunov, E. Ametistov, N. Vitruk." *Literaturnaia gazeta*. March 4, 1992, p. 11.

Feofanov, Iurii. "Interviu s S. S. Alekseevym." *Izvestiia*. June 17, 1990, p. 2.

"G. A. Gadzhiev: Konstitutsiia vam v pomoshch," *Dvoinaia zapis*, no. 12 (December 2003).

"G. A. Gadzhiev: 'U nas ogromnyi potok zhalob nalogoplatelshchikov, i on vriad li umenshitsia v obozrimom budushchem.'" *Rossiiskii nalogovyi kurer*, no. 24 (December 2004).

Gligich-Zolotareva, Milena. Report at the Roundtable "International Experience of Federal Democracies." Moscow, April 8, 2003. *Analiticheskii vestnik 'Mezdunarodnyi opyt federativnoi demokratii'*, no. 23 (2003): 13–19, available at http://www.council.gov.ru/inf_sl/bulletin/item/37/index.html, accessed December 16, 2007.

"Internet press-konferentsiia s Valeriem Zorkinym." *Garant-Internet*. November 26, 2003, available at http://www.garweb.ru/conf/ks/20031126/index.htm, accessed December 17, 2007.

Interview with the chief justice of the Russian Constitutional Court, Valerii Zorkin. *Komsomolskaia pravda*. January 15, 1992, p. 1.

Interview with RCC Chairman Valerii Zorkin. *Konsultant Plius*. December 1, 2006, available at http://www.consultant.ru/law/interview/zorkinbd.html, accessed December 17, 2007.

Kamakin, Andrei. "'Kolybel' Konstititutsii. Interview with Vladimir Kozhin," *Itogi*. December 2, 2007, available at http://www.itogi.ru/paper2007.nsf/Article/Itogi_2007_12_02_01_4914.html

Katanian, Konstantin. "Sud – ne pozharnaia komanda. Marat Baglai." *Vremia MN*. August 16, 2002.

Kekhlerov, Sabir. Speech at the conference on the Monitoring of Legal Space. Moscow, May 20, 2004, available at http://www.garant.ru/files/audio/kehlerov01.mp3.

Kievskii, Pavel. "Sergei Filatov: Yeltsin pravil Konstitutsiiu." *Trud*. December 10, 2003.

Kovler, Anatolii. "Interviu Predsedatelia KS RF V. A. Tumanova." *Gosudarstvo i Pravo*, no. 1 (1995): 5.

Maslennikov, Valentin. "Khvatit zhdat, pora dogoniat. Nikolai Vedernikov." *Rossiiskaia gazeta*. March 16, 1995.

Maslennikov, Valentin. "Konstitutsionnyi sud – ne dekorativnyi bantik v rossiiskoi demokratii. Tamara Morshchakova." *Rossiiskaia gazeta*. August 2, 1996.

"My daleko ushli ot vsiakoi tainstvennosti i zakrytosti. M. Baglai, Iu. Danilov, G. Gadzhiev, O. Khokhriakova." *Rossiiskaia gazeta*. November 1, 2001.

"Nelzia byt sudiei v sobstvennom dele. Nikolai Vitruk." *Rossiiskaia gazeta*. July 29, 1992.

Nikitinskii, Leonid. "Interview with Boris Ebzeev, Justice of the Constitutional Court of the Russian Federation." *East European Constitutional Review*, vol. 6, no. 1 (1997): 83–88.

312   *Bibliography*

Nikitinskii, Leonid. "...I suda net. Diagnoz doktora Morshchakovoi." *Novaia gazeta*. July 19, 2004.

Orlov, Dmitrii. "Reshenie po 'delu KPSS' narushaetsia kompartiei i ne vypolniaetsia chinovnikami. Tamara Morshchakova." *Rossiiskie vesti*. July 16, 1996.

Ostapchuk, Anna. "Prezident skazal, chto ego bespokoit 'moia druzhba s Khabulatovym.' Valerii Zorkin o situatsii v Konstitutsionnom sude." *Nezavisimaia gazeta*. November 12, 1993, pp. 1–2.

"Poslednii shans – diktatura zakona. Interviu s Valeriem Zorkinym." *VEK*, no. 43 (October 22, 1996).

Putin, Vladimir. "Novoi Rossii nuzhna silnaia i nezavisimaia sudebnaia sistema," *Rossiiskaia gazeta*, January 26, 2000, pp. 1–2.

Shakhrai, Sergei. Speech at the meeting of the Political Consulting Council. Moscow, February 20, 1998. *Materialy zasedaniia Politicheskogo konsultativnogo soveta 20.02.1998 g.* Moskva: PKS, 1998, pp. 21–26.

"Valerii Zorkin: Glavnaia nasha zadacha – zashchitit konstitutsionnyi stroi." *Rossiiskaia iustitsiia*, nos. 7–8 (April 1992): 18.

"Valerii Zorkin: Ia uveren, chto vlast sudebnykh reshenii okrepnet." *Kollegiia*, no. 2 (2004): 2–4.

"Valery Zorkin: Russia's President Has His Mandate, Not an Indulgence." *Moscow News*, no. 5 (February 1992): 16.

"Zatovarilis. Nikolai Vedernikov." *Rossiia*. February 24–March 2, 1993.

Zhirnov, Oleg. "Konstitutsionnyi sud predlagaet zabyt Konstitutsiiu? Gadis Gadzhiev." *Moskovskaia pravda*. September 17, 1996, p. 8.

"Zhizn posle zhizni. Vladimir Strekozov." *Ogonek*, no. 23 (June 1995): 38.

Zhukov, Maksim. "Vladimir Tumanov: 'Nyneshnee izbiratelnoe zakonodatelstvo ne adaptirovano k rossiiskim usloviiam.'" *Kommersant-daily*. October 20, 1995, p. 3.

4. RUSSIAN SOURCES ON RUSSIA AND THE USSR

The following periodicals, online sources and legal databases were frequently consulted. Specific citations are in the footnotes.

Periodicals:	*Gazeta*	*Pravda*
	Izvestiia	*Rodnaia gazeta*
	Kommersant-daily	*Rossiiskaia gazeta*
	Literaturnaia gazeta	*Rossiiskie vesti*
	Moskovskie novosti	*Segodnia*
	Moskovskii komsomolets	*Sovetskaia Rossiia*
	Nezavisimaia gazeta	*Trud Vedomosti*
	Novaia gazeta	*Vremya MN*
	Obshchaia gazeta	*Vremya novostei*
Online Sources:	*Gazeta.Ru*	*Regions.Ru*
	IAMiK.Ru	*Regnum.Ru*
	Intertat.Ru	*Rosbalt.Ru*
	Lenta.Ru	*Strana.Ru*
	Polit.Ru	
Legal Databases:	*Garant,*	*Konsultant Plius,*
	http://www.garant.ru	http://www.consultant.ru

Bibliography

Abova, T. "Vysshii Arbitrazhnyi Sud Rossiiskoi Federatsii. Sistema arbitrazhnykh sudov," in Igor Petrukhin, ed., *Sudebnaia vlast*. Moskva: Prospekt, 2003, pp. 372–384.

Ametistov, Ernest. "Zashchita sotsialnykh prav cheloveka v Konstitutsionnom Sude Rossiiskoi Federatsii: pervye itogi i dalneishie perspektivy," *VKS RF*, no. 4 (1995): 13–33.

Baglai, Marat. "Problemy ukrepleniia konstitutsionnoi zakonnosti," in V. P. Kazimirchuk, ed., *Konstitutsiia i zakon: stabilnost i dinamizm*. Moskva: IGP RAN, 1998, pp. 25–33.

Barry, Donald D. "Konstitutsionnyi sud Rossii glazami amerikanskogo iurista," *Gosudarstvo i pravo*, no. 12 (1993): 84–87.

Balutenko, Maksim S., Grigorii V. Belonuchkin, and Konstantin A. Katanian. *Konstitutsionnyi Sud Rossii. Spravochnik*. Moskva: IEG "Panorama," 1997.

Belkin, Alexandr. *Kommentarii k resheniiam Konstitutsionnogo Suda Rossiiskoi Federatsii. 1992–1993*. S.-Peterburg: Izd-vo S.-Peterburgskogo un-ta, 1994.

Blankenagel, Alexander. *"Detstvo, otrochestvo, iunost" Rossiiskogo Konstitutsionnogo Suda*. Moskva: TsKI MONF, 1996.

Boikov, Oleg. "Postanovleniia Konstitutsionnogo Suda Rossiiskoi Federatsii v deiatelnosti arbitrazhnykh sudov," in Mikhail Mitiukov, Sergei Kabyshev, Vera Bobrova, and Sergei Andreev, eds., *Problemy ispolneniia federalnymi organami gosudarstvennoi vlasti i organami gosudarstvennoi vlasti subektov Rossiiskoi Federatsii reshenii Konstitutsionnogo Suda Rossiiskoi Federatsii i konstitutsionnykh (ustavnykh) sudov subektov Rossiiskoi Federatsii*. Moskva: Formula prava, 2001, pp. 50–55.

Bolshakova, Tatiana. "Realizatsiia reshenii Konstitutsionnogo Suda," in S. Gannushkina and Iu. Chardina, eds., *Problemy zhertv voennykh deistvii v Chechenskoi Respublike. Mekhanizm realizatsii reshenii sudov i mer prokurorskogo reagirovaniia*. Moskva: NIPTs Memorial, 2000, chapter 10; available at http://www.memo.ru/hr/refugees/sem8rus/Chapter10.htm.

Bondar, Nikolai. "Rossiiskaia Federatsiia," in *Konstitutsionnoe pravosudie i sotsialnoe gosudarstvo: Sbornik dokladov*. Moskva: IPPP, 2003, pp. 160–187.

———. "Konventsionnaia iurisdiktsiia Evropeiskogo Suda po pravam cheloveka v sootnoshenii s kompetentsiei Konstitutsionnogo Suda RF," *Zhurnal rossiiskogo prava*, no. 6 (2006): 113–128.

Borodin, Stanislav V., and Vladimir N. Kudriavtsev. "O sudebnoi vlasti v Rossii," *Gosudarstvo i pravo*, no. 10 (2001): 21–27.

Bozhev, Viacheslav "Tikhaia revoliutsiia Konstitutsionnogo Suda v ugolovnom protsesse Rossiiskoi Federatsii," *Rossiiskaia iustitsiia*, no. 10 (2000): 9.

Burkov, Anton. "Borba za vlast mezhdu Konstitutsionnym Sudom RF i Verkhovnym Sudom RF: postradaiut li prava cheloveka?" *Grazhdanin i pravo*, no. 5 (2003): 33–38.

Byzov, Leontii "Rossiiane o khode ekonomicheskikh i politicheskikh reform nakanune VII Sezda," *Konstitutsionnyi vestnik*, no. 13 (November 1992): 213–220.

Chernenko, Aleksandr. "Budet zashchishchat! Ia skazal!" *Iuridicheskaia praktika*, no. 48, November 30, 2000.

Chetverikova, Larisa. "Resheniia Konstitutsionnogo Suda Rossiiskoi Federatsii: kak ikh ispolniat?" *Zakonodatelnye (predstavitelnye) organy vlasti subektov RF. Praktika, mneniia, problemy*, no. 1 (1999): 49–52.

Bibliography

Chetvernin, Vladimir A., ed. *Konstitutsiia Rossiiskoi Federatsii: Problemnyi kommentarii*. Moskva: MONF, 1997.

Danilov, Aleksandr, and Aleksandr Pyzhikov. "Neizvestnyi konstitutsionnyi proekt." *Gosudarstvo i pravo*, no. 1 (2002): 84–89.

Davydov, Vladimir. "Uchastie organov prokuratury v realizatsii reshenii Konstitutsionnogo Suda Rossiiskoi Federatsii," in Mikhail Mitiukov, Sergei Kabyshev, Vera Bobrova, and Sergei Andreev, eds., *Problemy ispolneniia federalnymi organami gosudarstvennoi vlasti i organami gosudarstvennoi vlasti subektov Rossiiskoi Federatsii reshenii Konstitutsionnogo Suda Rossiiskoi Federatsii i konstitutsionnykh (ustavnykh) sudov subektov Rossiiskoi Federatsii*. Moskva: Formula prava, 2001, pp. 63–67.

"Deiatelnost Konstitutsionnogo Suda RF v tsifrakh (noiabr 1991 g. – iiul 2001 g.)," *Rossiiskaia iustitsiia*, no. 10 (2001): 43–45.

Durdenevskii, Vsevolod N. "Sudebnaia proverka konstitutsionnosti zakona," *Voprosy prava. Zhurnal nauchnoi iurisprudentsii*, vol. 11, no. 3 (1912): 89.

Ebzeev, Boris. *Konstitutsiia. Pravovoe gosudarstvo. Konstitutsionnyi Sud*. Moskva: Zakon i pravo "IUNITI," 1997.

———, ed. *Kommentarii k postanovleniiam Konstitutsionnogo Suda Rossiiskoi Federatsii. T. 1*. Moskva: Iurist, 2000.

———, ed. *Kommentarii k postanovleniiam Konstitutsionnogo Suda Rossiiskoi Federatsii. T. 2*. Moskva: Iurist, 2000.

———, ed. *Kommentarii k postanovleniiam Konstitutsionnogo Suda Rossiiskoi Federatsii. T. 3*. Moskva: Iurist, 2002.

———. "Zashchita prav cheloveka v Konstitutsionnom Sude Rossiiskoi Federatsii," *Konstitutsionnoe pravosudie*, no. 1 (2003): 91–99.

Federalnyi konstitutsionnyi zakon "O Konstitutsionnom Sude Rossiiskoi Federatsii." Kommentarii. Moskva: Iuridicheskaia literatura, 1996.

Gadzhiev, Gadis. "Osnovnye konstitutsionno-pravovye problemy ekonomicheskoi reformy v Rossii," in Natalia Varlamova and Tatiana Vasileva, eds., *Rossiiskii federalizm: konstitutsionnye predposylki i politicheskaia realnost*. Moskva: MONF, 2000, pp. 112–120.

———. *Konstitutsionnye printsipy rynochnoi ekonomiki*. Moskva: Iurist, 2002.

———. "Publikatsiia osobogo mneniia sudi, Ili Istoriia normy, kotoraia iavliaetsia kamertonom sudebnoi reformy v Rossii," *Zakonodatelstvo i Praktika Mass-Media*, no. 12 (December 2005), available at http://www.medialaw.ru/publications/zip/136/5.htm.

Geliakhov, Abdullakh. "Pozitsii Konstitutsionnogo Suda Kabardino-Balkarskoi Respubliki po sovershenstvovaniiu zakonodatelstva v sfere konstitutsionnoi iustitsii," in Mikhail Mitiukov, Sergei Kabyshev, Vera Bobrova, and Sergei Andreev, eds., *Problemy ispolneniia federalnymi organami gosudarstvennoi vlasti i organami gosudarstvennoi vlasti subektov Rossiiskoi Federatsii reshenii Konstitutsionnogo Suda Rossiiskoi Federatsii i konstitutsionnykh (ustavnykh) sudov subektov Rossiiskoi Federatsii*. Moskva: Formula prava, 2001, pp. 211–217.

Gorbachev, Mikhail. *Life and Reforms. Volume 1*. Moscow: Novosti, 1995.

Gurvich, Isaak "Severo-Amerikanskie Soedinennye Shtaty," in *Gosudarstvennyi stroi v Zapadnoi Evrope i Soedinennykh Shtatakh.T.3*. S.-Pb., 1907.

Bibliography

"Iuridicheskaia nauka i praktika v usloviiakh perestroiki," *Kommunist*, no. 14 (1987): 42–50.

Karpovich, V. D., ed. *Kommentarii k Konstitutsii RF*. Moskva: Iurait-M, 2002.

Kazimirchuk, V. P., ed. *Konstitutsiia i zakon: stabilnost i dinamizm*. Moskva: IGP RAN, 1998.

Kerimov, D. A., and A. I. Ekimov. "Konstitutsionnyi nadzor v SSSR," *Sovetskoe gosudarstvo i pravo*, no. 9 (1990): 3–13.

"Konstitutsionnyi nadzor – shag k pravovomu gosudarstvu," *Kommunist*, no. 4 (1990): 68–76.

Kotliarevskii, Sergei A. "Umy i palaty." *Poliarnaia zvezda, 1906*. Reprinted in *Novoe vremia*, nos. 19–20 (1995): 59.

Khokhriakova, Olga. "Rossiiskaia Federatsiia," *Konstitutsionnoe Pravo: vostochnoevropeiskoe obozrenie*, no. 1 (2003): 90–95.

Kokorin, Oleg. "Konstitutsionnyi printsip ravenstva," *EZh-Iurist: Sudebnoe prilozhenie*, no. 26 (June 2003), pp. 6–7.

Kononov, Anatolii. "Konstitutsionnyi printsip svobody peredvizheniia i praktika Konstitutsionnogo Suda Rossiiskoi Federatsii," in *Rossiia i Sovet Evropy: perspektivy vzaimodeistviia*. Moskva: IPPP, 2001, pp. 172–181.

———. "Pravo na Osoboe Mnenie," *Zakon*, no. 11 (November 2006).

Kriazhkov, Vladimir. *Konstitutsionnoe pravosudie v subektakh Rossiiskoi Federatsii*. Moskva: Formula prava, 1999.

———, and Leonid Lazarev. *Konstitutsionnaia iustitsiia v Rossiiskoi Federatsii*. Moskva: BEK, 1998.

Kurdiuk, Petr. "O praktike ispolneniia Konstitutsionnogo Suda Rossiiskoi Federatsii Zakonodatelnym Sobraniem Krasnodarskogo kraia," in Mikhail Mitiukov, Sergei Kabyshev, Vera Bobrova, and Sergei Andreev, eds., *Problemy ispolneniia federalnymi organami gosudarstvennoi vlasti i organami gosudarstvennoi vlasti subektov Rossiiskoi Federatsii reshenii Konstitutsionnogo Suda Rossiiskoi Federatsii i konstitutsionnykh (ustavnykh) sudov subektov Rossiiskoi Federatsii*. Moskva: Formula prava, 2001, pp. 165–167.

Lazarev, Boris. "Komitet konstitutsionnogo nadzora SSSR (Podvodia itogi)," *Gosudarstvo i pravo*, no. 5 (1992): 21–34.

Lazarev, Leonid. *Pravovye pozitsii Konstitutsionnogo Suda Rossii*. Moskva: Gorodets, 2003.

Lebedev, A. N. *Status subekta Rossiiskoi Federatsii*. Moskva: IGP RAN, 1999.

Lebedev, Viacheslav. "Praktika primeneniia reshenii Konstitutsionnogo Suda Rossiiskoi Federatsii sudami obshchei iurisdiktsii pri osushchestvlenii pravosudiia," in Mikhail Mitiukov, Sergei Kabyshev, Vera Bobrova, and Sergei Andreev, eds., *Problemy ispolneniia federalnymi organami gosudarstvennoi vlasti i organami gosudarstvennoi vlasti subektov Rossiiskoi Federatsii reshenii Konstitutsionnogo Suda Rossiiskoi Federatsii i konstitutsionnykh (ustavnykh) sudov subektov Rossiiskoi Federatsii*. Moskva: Formula prava, 2001, pp. 46–49.

Luchin, Viktor. *Konstitutsiia Rossiiskoi Federatsii: problemy realizatsii*. Moskva: IUNITI, 2002.

———, and Olga Doronina. *Zhaloby grazhdan v Konstitutsionnyi Sud RF*. Moskva: Zakon i Pravo. IUNITI, 1998.

Bibliography

Makarkin, Aleksei. "Mery: borba za nezavisimost," *Pro et Contra*, vol. 11, no. 1 (2007), pp. 19–29, available at http://www.carnegie.ru/en/pubs/procontra/Vol11num1-02.pdf

Mikhailovskaia, Inga, Evgenii Kuzminskii, and Iurii Mazaev. *Prava cheloveka i sotsialno-politicheskie protsessy v postkommunisticheskoi Rossii.* Moskva: Proektnaia gruppa po pravam cheloveka, 1997.

Mikhalevich, Igor V. "O praktike prokurorskogo reagirovaniia na nesootvetstvie federalnomu zakonodatelstvu pravovykh aktov subektov Rossiiskoi Federatsii," in Suren Avakian, ed., *Konstitutsionnoe zakonodatelstvo subektov RF: problemy sovershenstvovaniia i ispolzovaniia v prepodavanii.* Moskva: Izdatelstvo MGU, 1999, pp. 251–256.

Mitiukov, Mikhail. *K istorii konstitutsionnogo pravosudiia Rossii.* Moskva: ATSO, 2002.

―――. "Konstitutsionnye sudy postsovetskikh gosudarstv: problemy ispolneniia reshenii," in *Ispolnenie reshenii konstitutsionnykh sudov: sbornik dokladov.* Moskva: IPPP, 2003, pp. 210–23.

―――. *Sudebnyi konstitutsionnyi nadzor 1924–1933 gg.: voprosy istorii, teorii i praktiki.* Moskva: Formula prava, 2005.

―――. *Predtecha konstitutsionnogo pravosudiia: vzgliady, proekty i institutsionalnye predposylki (30 – nachalo 90-h gg. XX v.).* Moskva: Formula prava, 2006.

―――, and Aleksandr Barnashov. *Ocherki konstitutsionnogo pravosudiia.* Tomsk: Izd-vo Tomskogo un-ta, 1999.

Mizulina, Elena. "Problemy realizatsii reshenii Konstitutsionnogo Suda Rossiiskoi Federatsii v deiatelnosti Gosudarstvennoi Dumy Federalnogo Sobraniia – parlamenta Rossiiskoi Federatsii," in Mikhail Mitiukov, Sergei Kabyshev, Vera Bobrova, and Sergei Andreev, eds., *Problemy ispolneniia federalnymi organami gosudarstvennoi vlasti i organami gosudarstvennoi vlasti subektov Rossiiskoi Federatsii reshenii Konstitutsionnogo Suda Rossiiskoi Federatsii i konstitutsionnykh (ustavnykh) sudov subektov Rossiiskoi Federatsii.* Moskva: Formula prava, 2001, pp. 68–73.

Morshchakova, Tamara. "Rol Konstitutsionnogo Suda RF v protsesse demokraticheskikh preobrazovanii," *Konstitutsionnoe pravosudie*, no. 2 (1998): 22–33.

―――. "Primenenie mezhdunarodnogo prava v konstitutsionnom pravosudii: itogi i perspectivy," *Konstitutsionnoe pravosudie*, no. 4 (2001): 114–123.

―――. "Voprosy vzaimodeistviia Konstitutsionnogo Suda Rossiiskoi Federatsii i sudov inykh vidov iurisdiktsii," in Mikhail Mitiukov, Sergei Kabyshev, Vera Bobrova, and Sergei Andreev, eds., *Problemy ispolneniia federalnymi organami gosudarstvennoi vlasti i organami gosudarstvennoi vlasti subektov Rossiiskoi Federatsii reshenii Konstitutsionnogo Suda Rossiiskoi Federatsii i konstitutsionnykh (ustavnykh) sudov subektov Rossiiskoi Federatsii.* Moskva: Formula prava, 2001, pp. 56–62.

―――, ed. *Kommentarii k zakonodatelstvu o sudebnoi sisteme Rossiiskoi Federatsii.* Moskva: Iurist, 2003.

―――. "Konstitutsionnye (ustavnye) sudy subektov Rossiiskoi Federatsii," in Igor Petrukhin, ed., *Sudebnaia vlast.* Moskva: Prospekt, 2003, pp. 385–396.

Moskva. Osen'-93: Khronika protivostoianiia. Moskva: Respublika, 1995.

Bibliography

Orzikh, Mark, Mark Cherkes, and Anatolii Vasilev. "Pravovaia okhrana Konstitutsii v sotsialisticheskom gosudarstve," *Sovetskoe gosudarstvo i pravo*, no. 6 (1988): 3–10.

Ovsepian, Zhanna. *Stanovlenie konstitutsionnykh i ustavnykh sudov v subektakh Rossiiskoi Federatsii (1990–2000 gg)*. Moskva: IKTs 'MarT', 2001.

Pashin, Sergei. "Sudia 'sudit' zakony," *Narodnyi deputat*, no. 12 (1991): 69–72.

———. "Pora stanovleniia," *Iuridicheskaia gazeta*, no. 12 (1993): 5.

Pavlushina, Alla. "Sudebnyi normokontrol: 'tikhaia revoliutsiia' v grazhdanskom protsesse," *Rossiiskaia iustitsiia*, no. 7 (2002): 17.

Pershutov, Anatolii. "Problemy vzaimodeistviia Federalnogo Sobraniia i Konstitutsionnogo Suda RF v protsesse zakonotvorchestva," *Pravo Sibiri*, no. 1–2 (2001).

Petrov, Alexei. "O nekotorykh neopublikovannykh opredeleniiakh Konstitutsionnogo suda Rossiiskoi Federatsii," *Akademicheskii iuridicheskii zhurnal*, no. 1 (2002), available at http://advocat.irk.ru/aum.

Petrukhin, Igor, ed. *Sudebnaia vlast*. Moskva: Prospekt, 2003.

Rabinovich, Igor, and Sergei Fufaev. "Respublika Bashkortostan," *Konstitutsionnoe pravo: vostochnoevropeiskoe obozrenie*, no. 4–1 (2000–01): 198–200.

Radchenko, Vladimir. "Kompetentsiia administrativnykh sudov nam poniatna," *Rossiiskaia iustitsiia*, no. 6 (2001): 9–11.

Rudnev, Valerii. "Administrativnye sudy: byt ili ne byt?" *Rossiiskaia iustitsiia*, no. 9 (2002): 20.

Serban, Mihaela. "Resheniia rumynskogo Konstitutsionnogo Suda kak istochnik prava," *Konstitutsionnoe pravosudie v postkommunisticheskikh stranakh*, Moskva: MONF, 1999.

Shablinskii, Ilia. *Predely vlasti: borba za rossiiskuiu konstitutsionnuiu reformu: 1989–1995 gg*. Moskva: TsKI MONF, 1997.

Shalland, Lev A. "Verkhovnyi sud i konstitutsionnoe gosudarstvo," in *Konstitutsionnoe gosudarstvo: Sbornik statei*. 2nd ed. Saint Petersburg: Tip. T-va "Obshestvennaia polza," 1905, pp. 412–421.

Sheinin, Khiil. "Problemy ispolneniia reshenii Konstitutsionnogo Suda Rossiiskoi Federatsii," in Mikhail Mitiukov, Sergei Kabyshev, Vera Bobrova, and Sergei Andreev, eds., *Problemy ispolneniia federalnymi organami gosudarstvennoi vlasti i organami gosudarstvennoi vlasti subektov Rossiiskoi Federatsii reshenii Konstitutsionnogo Suda Rossiiskoi Federatsii i konstitutsionnykh (ustavnykh) sudov subektov Rossiiskoi Federatsii*. Moskva: Formula prava, 2001, pp. 107–113.

Sliva, Anatolii. "Rol Prezidenta Rossiiskoi Federatsii v ukreplenii konstitutsionnoi zakonnosti," in *Problemy ukrepleniia konstitutsionnoi zakonnosti v respublikakh Rossiiskoi Federatsii*. Ufa: RIO BAGSU, 1998, pp. 6–11.

"Spravka ob ispolnenii reshenii Konstitutsionnogo Suda Rossiiskoi Federatsii, priniatykh v oktiabre-dekabre 2001 goda." April 3, 2002. Unpublished document.

Titkov, Alexei. "Konstitutsionnyi sud v otnosheniiakh Tsentra s regionami," in Nikolai Petrov, ed., *Regiony Rossii v 1999 g.: Prilozhenie k "Politicheskomu almanakhu Rossii."* Moscow: Carnegie Center, 2001, pp. 260–265.

Tiunov, Oleg. "O roli Konventsii o zashchite prav i osnovnykh svobod i reshenii Evropeiskogo suda po pravam cheloveka v praktike Konstitutsionnogo Suda

318 Bibliography

Rossiiskoi Federatsii," in *Rossiia i Sovet Evropy: perspektivy vzaimodeistviia*. Moskva: IPPP, 2001, pp. 75–88.

Tumanov, Vladimir. "Sudebnyi kontrol za konstitutsionnostiu normativnykh aktov," *Sovetskoe gosudarstvo i pravo*, no. 3 (1988): 14.

———. "Piat let konstitutsionnoi iustitsii v Rossii: uroki, problemy, perspektivy," *VKS RF*, no. 6 (1996): 10–15.

Uitz, Renata. "Konstitutsionnye i verkhovnye sudy – partnery ili soperniki?" *Konstitutsionnoe pravo: vostochnoevropeiskoe obozrenie*, no. 1 (2003): 109–122.

Umnova, Irina. "Konstitutsionno-pravovye aspekty biudzhetno-finansovogo federalizma," *Federalizm*, no. 1 (1999): 135–46.

Vasileva, Tatiana. "Razreshenie pravovykh kollizii mezhdu Federatsiei i subektami Federatsii," *Konstitutsionnoe pravo: vostochnoevropeiskoe obozrenie*, no. 1 (2002): 105–118.

Vinogradov, Vladimir A. "O konstitutsionnoi deliktnosti zakonodatelstva subektov Rossiiskoi Federatsii," in Suren Avakian, ed., *Konstitutsionnoe zakonodatelstvo subektov RF: problemy sovershenstvovaniia i ispolzovaniia v prepodavanii*. Moskva: Izdatelstvo MGU, 1999, pp. 256–270.

Vishnevskii, Boris. "Arbitr, udalennyi s polia," *Rossiiskaia Federatsiia segodnia*, no. 24 (2001): 24–26.

Vitruk, Nikolai. *Konstitutsionnoe pravosudie v Rossii: 1991–2001 gg.: ocherki teorii i praktiki*. Moskva: Gorodets-izdat, 2001.

———. "Ispolneniie reshenii Konstitutsionnogo Suda Rossiiskoi Federatsii," *Konstitutsionnoe pravo: vostochnoevropeiskoe obozrenie*, no. 3 (2002): 53–63.

Zhilin, Gennadii. "Problemy povysheniia effektivnosti konstitutsionnogo sudoproizvodstva v Rossiiskoi Federatsii," *Konstitutsionnoe pravosudie*, no. 4 (2000): 14–22.

Zhuikov, Viktor. "Konstitutsionnyi Sud RF vypolniaet istoricheskuiu rol," *Rossiiskaia iustitsiia*, no. 10 (October 2001): 18.

Zykova, Valeriia. "O politicheskoi situatsii v Cheliabinskoi oblasti," *Politicheskii monitoring IGPI*, (October 1993), available at http://www.igpi.ru/monitoring/1047645476/oct_93/1058172872.html.

5. ENGLISH LANGUAGE SOURCES ON RUSSIA, EASTERN EUROPE, AND THE USSR

The following periodicals and online sources were frequently consulted. Specific citations are in the footnotes.

Newspaper:	*Eurasia Daily Monitor*	*RFE/RL Russia Report*
	Moscow News	*St. Petersburg Times*
	Moscow Times	
Online Sources:	*Russian Regional Report*	*Johnson's Russia List*
Translation Services:	*Current Digest of the Soviet Press*	*Current Digest of the Post-Soviet Press*

Andrews, Josephine T. *When Majorities Fail: The Russian Parliament, 1990–1993*. Cambridge, UK: Cambridge University Press, 2002.

Ashwin, Sarah, and Simon Clarke. *Russian Trade Unions and Industrial Relations in Transition*. London: Palgrave Macmillan, 2003.

Bibliography

Barry, Donald D. "Trial of the CPSU and the Principles of Nuremberg," *Review of Central and East European Law*, vol. 22, no. 3 (1996): 255–262.

———. "Decision-Making and Dissent in the Russian Federation Constitutional Court," in Roger Clark, Ferdinand Feldbrugge, and Stanislaw Pomorski, eds., *International and National Law in Russia and Eastern Europe: Essays in Honor of George Ginsburgs*. The Hague: Kluwer Law International, 2001, pp. 1–17.

Baudoin, Marie-Elisabeth. "Is the Constitutional Court the Last Bastion in Russia against the Threat of Authoritarianism?" *Europe-Asia Studies*, vol. 58, no. 5 (July 2006): 679–700.

Blankenagel, Alexander. "The Court Writes its Own Law, Roundtable: Redesigning the Russian Constitutional Court," *East European Constitutional Review*, vol. 3, no. 4 (Summer–Fall 1994): 74–79.

———. "Eyes Wide Shut: Displaced Cultural Objects in Russian Law and Adjudication," *East European Constitutional Review 8*, no. 4 (1999): 75–80.

Bunce, Valerie. "Comparative Democratization: Big and Bounded Generalizations," *Comparative Political Studies*, vol. 33, nos. 6–7 (2000): 703–734.

———. "Rethinking Recent Democratization: Lessons from the Postcommunist Experience," *World Politics*, vol. 55, no. 2 (2003): 167–192.

———, and Maria Csanadi. "Uncertainty in the Transition: Post-Communism in Hungary," *East European Politics and Society*, vol. 7, no. 2 (Spring 1993): 240–275.

Burnham, William, Peter Maggs, and Gennady Danilenko. *Law and Legal System of the Russian Federation*. New York: Juris Publishing, 2004.

———, and Alexei Trochev. "Russia's War between the Courts: The Struggle over the Jurisdictional Boundary between the Constitutional Court and Regular Courts," *American Journal of Comparative Law*, vol. 55, no. 3 (Summer 2007): 381–452.

Collins, Kathleen. *Clan Politics and Regime Transition in Central Asia*. New York: Cambridge University Press, 2006.

Colton, Timothy J. *Transitional Citizens: Voters and What Influences Them in the New Russia*. Cambridge, MA: Harvard University Press, 2000.

"Comparative Text of the 1977 USSR Constitution with Draft and Final Amendments," *Review of Socialist Law*, vol. 15 (1989): 75.

Cook, Linda J. *Postcommunist Welfare States: Reform Politics in Russia and Eastern Europe*. Ithaca, NY: Cornell University Press, 2007.

Daniels, Richard W. *The End of Communist Revolution*. London: Routledge, 1993.

Desai, Padma, and Todd Idson. *Work Without Wages: Russia's Non-Payment Crisis*. Cambridge, MA: MIT Press, 2000.

Domrin, Alexander N. "'Trophy Art Law' as an Illustration of the Current Status of Separation of Powers and Legislative Process in Russia," in Norman Dorsen and Prosser Gifford, eds. *Democracy and the Rule of Law*. Washington, DC: Congressional Quarterly Press, 2001, pp. 283–288.

Dragneva, Rilka O., and William B. Simons. "Rights, Contracts and Constitutional Courts: The Experience of Russia," in Ferdinand Feldbrugge and William Simons, eds., *Human Rights in Russia and Eastern Europe: Essays in Honor of Ger P. van den Berg (Law in Eastern Europe, No. 51)*. The Hague: Kluwer Law International, 2002, pp. 35–63.

Bibliography

Dupre, Catherine. *Importing the Law in Post-Communist Transitions: The Hungarian Constitutional Court and the Right to Human Dignity.* Portland, OR: Hart Publishing, 2003.

Epstein, Lee, Jack Knight, and Olga Shvetsova. "The Role of Constitutional Courts in the Establishment and Maintenance of Democratic Systems of Government," *Law and Society Review,* vol. 35, no. 1 (March 2001): 117–164.

Fogelklou, Anders. "Interpretation and Accommodation in the Russian Constitutional Court," in Ferdinand Feldbrugge, ed., *Russia, Europe, and the Rule of Law.* Leiden: Martinus Nijhoff, 2007, pp. 29–46.

Foglesong, Todd S. "*Habeas Corpus* or 'Who Has the Body?' Judicial Review of Arrests and Detention in Russia," *Wisconsin International Law Journal,* vol. 14 (1996): 541–578.

———. "The Dynamics of Judicial (In) Dependence in Russia," in Peter H. Russell and David O'Brien, eds., *Judicial Independence in the Age of Democracy: Critical Perspectives from around the World.* Charlottesville, VA: University Press of Virginia, 2001, pp. 62–88.

Gadzhiev, Gadis. "Power Imbalance and Institutional Interests in Russian Constitutional Engineering," in Jan Zielonka, ed., *Democratic Consolidation in Eastern Europe.* New York: Oxford University Press, 2001, pp. 269–292.

Galligan, Dennis J., and Marina Kurkchiyan, eds. *Law and Informal Practices: The Post-Communist Experience.* Oxford: Oxford University Press, 2003.

Ganev, Venelin I. *Preying on the State: The Transformation of Bulgaria After 1989.* Ithaca, NY: Cornell University Press, 2007.

———. "The Bulgarian Constitutional Court, 1991–1997: A Success Story in Context," *Europe-Asia Studies,* vol. 55, no. 4 (2003): 597–611.

———. "The Rise of Constitutional Adjudication in Bulgaria," in Wojciech Sadurski, ed., *Constitutional Justice, East and West.* The Hague: Kluwer Law International, 2002, pp. 247–264.

Gelman, Vladimir, Sergei Ryzhenkov, and Michael Brie. *Making and Breaking Democratic Transitions: The Comparative Politics of Russia's Regions.* Lanham, MD: Rowman and Littlefield, 2003.

Gerber, Theodore P., and Sarah E. Mendelson. "Research Addendum," *Post Soviet Affairs,* vol. 19 (2003): 187–188.

Gibson, James L. "Russian Attitudes towards the Rule of Law: An Analysis of Survey Data," in Denis J. Galligan and Marina Kurkchiyan, eds., *Law and Informal Practices: The Post-Communist Experience.* New York: Oxford University Press, 2003, pp. 77–91.

Gray, Cheryl W., and Kathryn Hendley. "Developing Commercial Law in Transition Economies: Examples from Hungary and Russia," in Jeffrey Sachs and Katharina Pistor, eds., *The Rule of Law and Economic Reform in Russia.* Boulder: Westview Press, 1997, pp. 139–164.

Haspel, Moshe, Thomas F. Remington, and Steven S. Smith. "Lawmaking and Decree Making in the Russian Federation: Time, Space, and Rules in Russian National Policymaking, *Post-Soviet Affairs,* vol. 22, no. 3 (July 2006): 249–275.

Hausmaninger, Herbert. "From the Soviet Committee on Constitutional Supervision to the Russian Constitutional Court," *Cornell International Law Journal,* vol. 25, no. 2 (Spring 1992): 305–237.

Bibliography

———. "Towards a 'New' Russian Constitutional Court," *Cornell International Law Journal*, vol. 28 (1995): 349–386.

Hendley, Kathryn. "Rewriting the Rules of the Game in Russia: The Neglected Issue of the Demand for Law," *East European Constitutional Review*, vol. 8, no. 4 (1999): 89–95.

———. "'Demand' for Law in Russia – A Mixed Picture," *East European Constitutional Review*, vol. 10, no. 4 (2001): 72–77.

———. "Suing the State in Russia," *Post-Soviet Affairs*, vol. 18, no. 2 (April–June 2002): 148–181.

Henderson, Jane. "The First Russian Constitutional Court: Hopes and Aspirations," in Rein Müllerson, Malgosia Fitzmaurice, and Mads Andenas, eds., *Constitutional Reform and International Law in Central and Eastern Europe*. The Hague: Kluwer Law International, 1998, pp. 105–121.

———. "Reference to International Law in the Decided Cases of the First Russian Constitutional Court," in Rein Müllerson, Malgosia Fitzmaurice, and Mads Andenas, eds., *Constitutional Reform and International Law in Central and Eastern Europe*. The Hague: Kluwer Law International, 1998, pp. 59–77.

———. "The Russian Constitutional Court and the Communist Party Case: Watershed or Whitewash?" *Communist and Post-Communist Studies*, vol. 40, no. 1 (March 2007): 1–16.

Herron, Erik S., and Kirk A. Randazzo. "The Relationship Between Independence and Judicial Review in Post-Communist Courts," *Journal of Politics*, vol. 65 (2003): 422–438.

Hollander, Pavel. "The Role of the Constitutional Court for the Application of the Constitution in Case Decisions of Ordinary Courts," *Archiv fur Rechts- und Sozialphilosophie*, vol. 86 (2000): 541–552.

Horak, Martin. *Governing the Post-Communist City: Institutions and Democratic Development in Prague*. Toronto: University of Toronto Press, 2007.

Ishiyama Smithey, Shannon, and John Ishiyama. "Judicious Choices: Designing Courts in Post-Communist Politics," *Communist and Post-Communist Studies*, vol. 33, no. 1 (2000): 163–182.

———. "Judicial Activism in Post-Communist Politics," *Law and Society Review*, vol. 36, no. 4 (2002): 719–741.

Janu, Ivana. "Relations of the Constitutional Court to the Ordinary Courts." Report presented at the Workshop on Eurasian Constitutional Courts, Istanbul, May 22–23, 1998.

Jonsson, Anna. "The Constitutional Court of the Russian Federation, 1997–2001." *Uppsala University Working Papers*, no. 73 (October 2002).

Jordan, Pamela. *Defending Rights in Russia: Lawyers, the State, and Legal Reform in the Post-Soviet Era*. Vancouver: University of British Columbia Press, 2005.

Jowitt, Kenneth. *The New World Disorder: The Leninist Extinction*. Berkeley: University of California Press, 1992.

Kahn, Jeffrey. *Federalism, Democratization and the Rule of Law in Russia*. Oxford: Oxford University Press, 2002.

Kitchin, William. "Legal Reform and the Expansion of Judicial Power in Russia," in C. Neal Tate and Torbjörn Vallinder, eds., *The Global Expansion of Judicial Power*. New York: New York University Press, 1995, pp. 421–440.

Bibliography

Koszokar, Gabor. "The Effects of the Constitutional Court Decisions with a Special View on the Ordinary Courts Jurisprudence," *Konstitutsionnoe pravosudie*, no. 3 (2001): 158–166.

Krug, Peter. "Departure from the Centralized Model: The Russian Supreme Court and Constitutional Control of Legislation," *Virginia Journal of International Law*, vol. 37, no. 3 (1997): 725–787.

———. "The Russian Federation Supreme Court and Constitutional Practice in the Courts of General Jurisdiction: Recent Developments," *Review of Central and East European Law*, vol. 26, no. 2 (February 2000): 129–146.

———. "Glasnost as a Constitutional Norm: The Article 29 Jurisprudence of the Constitutional Court and Other Courts in the Russian Federation." Paper presented at the annual convention of the American Association for the Advancement of Slavic Studies, November 2001, Arlington, VA.

———. "Assessing Legislative Restrictions on Constitutional Rights: The Russian Constitutional Court and Article 55(3)," *Oklahoma Law Review*, vol. 56, no. 3 (Fall 2003): 677–696.

———. "Strasbourg Review: Russia and the European Court of Human Rights." Paper presented at the annual convention of the American Association for the Advancement of Slavic Studies, November 2003, Toronto.

Kryshtanovskaya, Olga, and Stephen White. "Putin's Militocracy," *Post-Soviet Affairs*, vol. 19, no. 4 (2003): 289–306.

Kühn, Zdenek, and Jan Kysela. "Nomination of Constitutional Justices in Post-Communist Countries: Trial, Error, Conflict in the Czech Republic," *European Constitutional Law Review*, vol. 2 (2006): 183–208.

Kurmanov, Midkhat. "Judicial System in Russia: A Perspective from Tatarstan," in Thomas Fleiner and Rafael Khakimov, eds., *Federalism: Russian and Swiss Perspectives*. Kazan: Kazan Institute of Federalism, 2001, pp. 65–68.

Kuzio, Taras. "Transition in Post-Communist States: Triple or Quadruple?" *Politics*, vol. 21, no. 3 (2001): 168–177.

———, Robert S. Kravchuk, and Paul D'Anieri. *State and Institution Building in Ukraine*. New York: St. Martin's Press, 1999.

Lankina, Tomila. *Governing the Locals: Local Self-government and Ethnic Mobilization in Russia*. Lanham, MD: Rowman and Littlefield, 2004.

———. "President Putin's Local Government Reforms," in Peter Reddaway and Robert W. Orttung, eds., *The Dynamics of Russian Politics: Putin's Reform of Federal-Regional Relations, Volume 2*. Lanham, MD: Rowman and Littlefield, 2005, pp. 145–177.

Ledeneva, Alena V. *How Russia Really Works: The Informal Practices That Shaped Post-Soviet Politics and Business*. Ithaca, NY: Cornell University Press, 2006.

Linz, Juan, and Alfred Stepan. *Problems of Democratic Transition and Consolidation*. Baltimore: Johns Hopkins University Press, 1996.

Ludwikowski, Rett R. "'Mixed Constitutions' – Product of an East-Central European Melting Pot," *Boston University Journal of International Law*, vol. 16, no. 1 (Spring 1998): 1–70.

Lukin, Alexander. *The Political Culture of the Russian 'Democrats.'* Oxford: Oxford University Press, 2000.

Bibliography

Magalhães, Pedro C. "The Politics of Judicial Reform in Eastern Europe," *Comparative Politics*, vol. 32 (1999): 43–62.

Maggs, Peter B. "Enforcing the Bill of Rights in the Twilight of the Soviet Union," *University of Illinois Law Review*, vol. 4, no. 4 (1991): 1049–1063.

Makova, Anna. "The Constitutional Court of the Czech Republic and the Legal Force of Its Decisions," *Konstitutsionnoe pravosudie*, no. 4 (1999): 41–55.

Maveety, Nancy, and Anke Grosskopf. "'Constrained' Constitutional Courts as Conduits for Democratic Consolidation," *Law and Society Review*, vol. 38, no. 3 (September 2004): 463–488.

McAuley, Mary. *Russia's Politics of Uncertainty*. Cambridge, UK: Cambridge University Press, 1997.

McFaul, Michael. "Institutional Design, Uncertainty, and Path Dependency during Transitions: Cases from Russia," *Constitutional Political Economy*, vol. 10, no. 1 (1999): 27–52.

Medushevsky, Andrey N. *Russian Constitutionalism: Historical and Contemporary Development*. New York: Routledge, 2006.

Millar, James R., and Sharon L. Wolchik. "Introduction: The Social Legacies and the Aftermath of Communism," in James R. Millar and Sharon L. Wolchik, eds., *The Social Legacy of Communism*. New York: Cambridge University Press, 1994, pp. 1–28.

Miller, William L., Stephen White, and Paul Heywood. *Values and Political Change in Postcommunist Europe*. New York: St. Martin's Press, 1998.

Mishler, William, and Richard Rose. "What Are the Origins of Political Trust? Testing Institutional and Cultural Theories in Post-Communist Societies," *Comparative Political Studies*, vol. 34 (2001): 30–62.

Offe, Claus, Jon Elster, and Ulrich Preuß. *Institutional Design in Post-Communist Societies: Rebuilding the Ship at Sea*. New York: Cambridge University Press, 1988.

Orttung, Robert W. "Key Issues in the Evolution of the Federal Okrugs and Center-Region Relations under Putin," in Peter Reddaway and Robert W. Orttung, eds., *The Dynamics of Russian Politics. Volume 1*. Lanham, MD: Rowman and Littlefield, 2004, pp. 19–52.

Osiatynski, Wiktor. "Paradoxes of Constitutional Borrowing," *I-CON: International Journal of Constitutional Law*, vol. 1 (2003): 244–268.

Paczolay, Peter. "Effects, Enforceability, and the Execution of the Decisions of the Constitutional Court – The Hungarian Experience." Report presented at Seminar on the Execution of Decisions of the Constitutional Court, Kyiv, Ukraine, October, 28–29, 1999, available at http://www.venice.coe.int/docs/1999/CDL-JU(1999)026-e.asp.

Pastukhov, Vladimir. "Law under Administrative Pressure in Post-Soviet Russia," *East European Constitutional Review*, vol. 11, no. 3 (Summer 2002): 66–74.

Pehe, Jiri. "Changes in the Czech Judiciary," *RFE/RL Report*, September 17, 1993, pp. 54–57.

Pistor, Katharina. "The Demand for Constitutional Law," *Constitutional Political Economy*, vol. 13 (2002): 73–87.

Polishchuk, Leonid. "Legal Initiatives in Russian Regions: Determinants and Effects," in Peter Murrell, ed., *Assessing the Value of Law in the Economic*

Transition from Socialism. Ann Arbor: University of Michigan Press, 2001, pp. 330–368.

_____. "Should the Legal Foundations of a Federal State be Flexible or Rigid? Canadian Experience and Russian Dilemmas," in Peter H. Solomon, Jr., ed., *Making Federalism through Law: Canadian Experience and Russian Reform under Putin.* Toronto: CREES, University of Toronto, 2003, pp. 43–64.

Pomeranz, William. "Judicial Review and the Russian Constitutional Court: The Chechen Case," *Review of Central and East European Law,* vol. 23 (1997): 9–48.

_____. "The Russian Constitutional Court's Interpretation of Federalism: Balancing Center-Regional Relations," *Parker School Journal of East European Law,* vol. 4, no. 4 (1997): 401–443.

Priban, Jiri. "Judicial Power vs. Democratic Representation: The Culture of Constitutionalism and Human Rights in the Czech Legal System," in Wojciech Sadurski, ed., *Constitutional Justice, East and West.* The Hague: Kluwer Law International, 2002, pp. 373–394.

Procházka, Radoslav. *Mission Accomplished: On Founding Constitutional Adjudication in Central Europe.* Budapest: Central European University Press, 2002.

Rabinovich, Igor. "Bashkortostan Ignores Court Ruling," *EastWest Institute Russian Regional Report,* vol. 5, no. 36, October 4, 2000.

_____. "Bashkortostan, Tatarstan Weaken Putin's Reforms," *Russian Regional Report,* vol. 8, no. 13, July 23, 2003.

Rakowska-Harmstone, Teresa. "Communist Constitutions and Constitutional Change," in Keith Banting and Richard Simeon, eds., *The Politics of Constitutional Change in Industrial Nations: Redesigning the State.* London: Macmillan, 1985, pp. 203–231.

Reisinger, William M. "Legal Orientations and the Rule of Law in Post-Soviet Russia," in Sally J. Kenney, William M. Reisinger, and John C. Reitz, eds., *Constitutional Dialogues in a Comparative Perspective.* New York: Palgrave Macmillan, 1999, pp. 172–192.

Remington, Thomas F. *The Russian Parliament: Institutional Evolution in a Transitional Regime, 1989–1999.* New Haven, CT: Yale University Press, 2001.

_____. "Taming Vlast: Institutional Development in Post-Communist Russia," in Donald R. Kelley, ed., *After Communism: Perspectives on Democracy.* Fayetteville, AR: The University of Arkansas Press, 2003, pp. 89–118.

Renz, Bettina. "'Putin's Militocracy'? An Alternative Interpretation of the Role of Siloviki in Contemporary Russian Politics," *Europe-Asia Studies,* vol. 18, no. 6 (2006): 903–924.

Rivera, Sharon W., and David W. Rivera. "The Russian Elite under Putin: Militocratic or Bourgeois?" *Post-Soviet Affairs,* vol. 22, no. 2 (2006): 125–144.

Rose, Richard. "New Russia Barometer 10: Russians under Putin," *Studies in Public Policy,* no. 350 (2001).

_____. "New Russia Barometer XI: The End of Term Report," *Studies in Public Policy,* no. 378 (2003).

Rudden, Bernard. "Civil Law, Civil Society, and the Russian Constitution," *Law Quarterly Review,* vol. 110, no. 1 (January 1994): 56–83.

Russian Axis. *The Judicial System of the Russian Federation: A Systemic Crisis of Independence.* London: Russian Axis, 2004, available at http://www. russianaxis.org/publications/10.html.

Sadurski, Wojciech, ed. *Constitutional Justice, East and West.* The Hague: Kluwer Law International, 2002.

———. "Legitimacy and Reasons of Constitutional Review after Communism," in Wojciech Sadurski, ed., *Constitutional Justice, East and West.* The Hague: Kluwer Law International, 2002, pp. 163–188.

———. "Review of *The Struggle for Constitutional Justice in Post-Communist Europe* by Herman Schwartz (Chicago: The University of Chicago Press, 2000)," *I-CON: International Journal of Constitutional Law*, vol. 1 (2003): 159–162.

Sajó, András. "The Judiciary in Contemporary Society: Hungary," *Case Western Reserve Journal of International Law*, vol. 25 (1993): 293–301.

———. "How the Rule of Law Killed Hungarian Welfare Reform," *East European Constitutional Review*, vol. 5, no. 1 (1996): 31–41.

———. "The Roundtable Talks in Hungary," in Jon Elster, ed., *Roundtable Talks and the Breakdown of Communism.* Chicago: University of Chicago Press, 1996, pp. 69–98.

———. "Rule by Law in East Central Europe," in Volkmar Gessner, Armin Hoeland, and Csaba Varga, eds., *European Legal Cultures.* Aldershot: Dartmouth, 1996, p. 472.

Schedler, Andreas, Larry Diamond, and Marc F. Plattner, eds. *The Self-Restraining State: Power and Accountability in New Democracies.* Boulder, CO: Lynne Rienner, 1998.

Scheppele, Kim Lane "Declarations of Independence: Judicial Reactions to Political Pressures," in Stephen B. Burbank and Barry Friedman, eds., *Judicial Independence at the Crossroads.* Thousands Oaks, CA: SAGE Publications, 2002, pp. 227–279.

———. "Constitutional Negotiations: Political Contexts of Judicial Activism in Post-Soviet Europe," *International Sociology*, vol. 18, no. 1 (March 2003): 219–238.

———. "A Realpolitik Defense of Social Rights," *University of Texas Law Review*, vol. 82, no. 7 (2004): 1921–1961.

———. "Democracy By Judiciary. Or Why Courts Can Sometimes Be More Democratic Than Parliaments," in Adam W. Czarnota, Martin Krygier, Wojciech Sadurski, eds., *Rethinking the Rule of Law After Communism.* Budapest: Central European University Press, 2005, pp. 25–60.

———. "Guardians of the Constitution: Constitutional Court Presidents and the Struggle for the Rule of Law in Post-Soviet Europe," *University of Pennsylvania Law Review*, vol. 154, no. 6 (2006): 1757–1851.

Schiemann, John W. *The Politics of Pact-Making: Hungary's Negotiated Transition to Democracy in Comparative Perspective.* New York: Palgrave Macmillan, 2005.

Schwartz, Herman. *The Struggle for Constitutional Justice in Post-Communist Europe.* Chicago: University of Chicago Press, 2000.

Shandarov, Maksim. "Siberian Federal Okrug," in Peter Reddaway and Robert W. Orttung, eds., *The Dynamics of Russian Politics: Putin's Reform of Federal-Regional Relations, Volume 1*. Lanham, MD: Rowman and Littlefield, 2004, pp. 211–242.

Sharlet, Robert. "Russian Chief Justice as Judicial Politician," *East European Constitutional Review*, vol. 2, no. 2 (1993): 32–37.

———. "The Russian Constitutional Court: First Term," *Post-Soviet Affairs*, vol. 9, no. 1 (January–March 1993): 1–39.

———. "Russian Constitutional Crisis: Law and Politics under Yeltsin," *Post-Soviet Affairs*, vol. 9 (1993): 314–336.

———. "Transitional Constitutionalism: Politics and Law in the Second Russian Republic," *Wisconsin International Law Journal*, vol. 14 (1996): 495–521.

———. "The Role of the West in the Transformation of the Post-Soviet Legal Systems," in Karen Dawisha, ed., *The International Dimension of Post-Communist Transitions in Russia and the New States of Eurasia*. (Armonk, NY: M. E. Sharpe, 1997), pp. 322–349.

———. "Legal Transplants and Political Mutations: The Reception of Constitutional Law in Russia and the Newly Independent States," *East European Constitutional Review*, vol. 7, no. 4 (1998): 59–68.

———. "Russia's Second Constitutional Court: Politics, Law, and Stability," in Victoria E. Bonnell and George W. Breslauer, eds., *Russia in the New Century: Stability or Disorder?* Boulder: Westview Press, 2001, pp. 59–77.

———. "Russia in the Middle: State Building and the Rule of Law," in Donald R. Kelley, ed., *After Communism: Perspectives on Democracy*. Fayetteville, AR: The University of Arkansas Press, 2003, pp. 143–159.

———. "The Russian Constitutional Court's Long Struggle for Viable Federalism," in Gordon B. Smith and Robert Sharlet, eds., *Russia and Its Constitution: Promise and Political Reality*. Leiden: Martinus Nijhoff, 2007, pp. 23–50.

Shterin, Marat. "Legislating on Religion in the Face of Uncertainty," in Denis J. Galligan and Marina Kurkchiyan, eds., *Law and Informal Practices: The Post-Communist Experience*. New York: Oxford University Press, 2003, pp. 113–134.

Smilov, Daniel. "The Character and Legitimacy of Constitutional Review: Eastern European Perspectives," *I-CON: International Journal of Constitutional Law*, vol. 2 (2004): 177–193.

Smith, Gordon B. *Reforming the Russian Legal System*. New York: Cambridge University Press, 1996.

———. "State-Building in a New Russia: Assessing the Yeltsin Record," in Gordon B. Smith, ed., *State-Building in Russia: The Yeltsin Legacy and the Challenge of the Future*. Armonk, NY: M. E. Sharpe, 1999, pp. 3–16.

———, ed. *State-Building in Russia: The Yeltsin Legacy and the Challenge of the Future*. Armonk, NY: M. E. Sharpe, 1999.

Smith, Kathleen E. *Mythmaking in the New Russia: Politics and Memory during the Yeltsin Era*. Ithaca, NY: Cornell University Press, 2002.

Solnick, Steven. *Stealing the State: Control and Collapse in Soviet Institutions*. Cambridge, MA: Harvard University Press, 1998.

Bibliography

Solomon, Peter H., Jr. "Gorbachev's Legal Revolution," *Canadian Business Law Journal*, vol. 17, no. 2 (1990): 184–194.

———. "The U.S.S.R. Supreme Court: History, Role, and Future Prospects," *American Journal of Comparative Law*, vol. 38 (1990): 127–142.

———, ed. *Reforming Justice in Russia: 1864–1994: Power, Culture and the Limits of Legal Order*. Armonk, NY: M. E. Sharpe, 1997.

———. "Putin's Judicial Reform: Making Judges Accountable as well as Independent." *East European Constitutional Review*, vol. 11, nos. 1–2 (2002): 117–124.

———, ed. *Making Federalism through Law: Canadian Experience and Russian Reform under Putin*. Toronto: CREES, University of Toronto, 2003.

———. "Judicial Power in Russia: Through the Prism of Administrative Justice," *Law and Society Review*, vol. 38, no. 3 (September 2004): 549–581.

———, ed. *The Dynamics of "Real Federalism": Law, Economic Development, and Indigenous Communities in Russia and Canada*. Toronto: CREES, University of Toronto, 2004.

———. "The Criminal Procedure Code of 2001: Will It Make Russian Justice More Fair?" in William Pridemore, ed., *Ruling Russia: Law, Crime, and Justice in a Changing Society*. Lanham, MD: Rowman and Littlefield, 2005, pp. 77–98.

———. "Threats of Judicial Counterreform in Putin's Russia," *Demokratizatsiia*, vol. 13, no. 3 (Summer 2005): 325–345.

———. "Informal Practices in Russian Justice: Probing the Limits of Post-Soviet Reform," in Ferdinand Feldbrugge, ed., *Russia, Europe, and the Rule of Law*. Leiden: Martinus Nijhoff, 2007, pp. 79–91.

———, and Todd S. Foglesong. *Courts and Transition in Russia: The Challenge of Judicial Reform*. Boulder, CO: Westview Press, 2000.

Sólyom, László. "The First Year of the Constitutional Court," *Acta Juridica Hungarica*, vol. 33, nos. 1–2 (1991): 5–22.

Stan, Lavinia. *Leaders and Laggards: Governance, Civicness and Ethnicity in Post-Communist Romania*. New York: Columbia University Press, 2003.

———. "The Roof over Our Head: Property Restitution in Romania," *Journal of Communist Studies and Transition Politics*, vol. 22, no. 2 (2006): 180–205.

Steele, Jonathan. *Eternal Russia: Yeltsin, Gorbachev, and the Mirage of Democracy*. Cambridge, MA: Harvard University Press, 1995.

Steen, Anton. *Political Elites and the New Russia*. London: Routledge Curzon, 2003.

Stoner-Weiss, Kathryn. *Local Heroes: The Political Economy of Russian Regional Governance*. Princeton, NJ: Princeton University Press, 1997.

———. *Resisting the State: Reform and Retrenchment in Post-Soviet Russia*. New York: Cambridge University Press, 2006.

Thomas, Cheryl A. "The Attempt to Institute Judicial Review in the Former USSR," in C. Neal Tate and Torbjörn Vallinder, eds., *The Global Expansion of Judicial Power*. New York: New York University Press, 1995, pp. 441–459.

Thorson, Carla. "Constitutional Courts as Political Actors: Russia in Comparative Perspective." Ph.D. diss., University of California at Los Angeles, 2003.

Trochev, Alexei. "Implementing Constitutional Court Decisions," *East European Constitutional Review*, vol. 11, nos. 1–2 (2002): 95–103.

_____. "Lack of Guards in St. Petersburg Threatens Criminal Court Reform," *Russian Regional Report*, vol. 7, no. 12, March 27, 2002, p. 4.

_____. "Ukraine: Constitutional Court Invalidates the 1991 Ban on the Communist Party," *I-CON: International Journal of Constitutional Law*, vol. 1, no. 3 (2003): 534–540.

_____. "Less Democracy, More Courts: The Puzzle of Judicial Review in Russia," *Law and Society Review*, vol. 38, no. 3 (September 2004): 513–548.

_____. "Fragmentation? Defection? Legitimacy? Explaining Judicial Behavior in Post-Communist 'Colored Revolutions.'" Paper presented at the annual meeting of the American Political Science Association, Philadelphia, September 1, 2006.

_____. "Judicial Selection in Russia: Towards Accountability and Centralization," in Peter H. Russell and Kate Malleson, eds., *Appointing Judges in an Age of Judicial Power: Critical Perspectives from Around the World*. Toronto: University of Toronto Press, 2006, pp. 375–394.

_____. "'Tinkering with Tenure': The Russian Constitutional Court in Comparative Perspective," in Ferdinand Feldbrugge, ed., *Russia, Europe, and the Rule of Law*. Leiden: Martinus Nijhoff, 2006, pp. 47–78.

_____. "Russia's Constitutional Spirit: Judge-Made Principles in Theory and Practice," in Gordon Smith and Robert Sharlet, eds., *Russia and Its Constitution: Promise and Political Reality*. Leiden: Martinus Nijhoff, 2007, pp. 51–75.

_____, and Peter H. Solomon, Jr. "Courts and Federalism in Putin's Russia," in Peter Reddaway and Robert W. Orttung, eds., *The Dynamics of Russian Politics, Volume 2*. Lanham, MD: Rowman and Littlefield, 2005, pp. 91–121.

Verdery, Katherine. *The Political Lives of Dead Bodies: Reburial and Postsocialist Change*. New York: Columbia University Press, 1999.

Vereshchagin, Alexander. "Dissents in Russian Courts," in Natalia Iu. Erpyleva, Mayann E. Gashi-Butler, and Jane E. Henderson, eds., *Forging a Common Legal Destiny: Liber Amicorum in Honour of William E. Butler*. London: Wildy, Simmonds, and Hill Publishing, 2005, pp. 314–326.

Vida, Ioan. "The Obligatory Force of Decisions of the Constitutional Court for Other Courts as a Stabilizing Factor," *Konstitutsionnoe pravosudie*, no. 2 (2004): 78–90.

Wagner, William. "Tsarist Legal Policies at the End of the Nineteenth Century: A Study in Inconsistency," *Slavonic and East European Review*, vol. 14 (1976): 371–394.

Walker, Edward W. "Sovietology and Perestroika: A Post-Mortem," in Susan Gross Solomon, ed., *Beyond Sovietology: Essays in Politics and History*. Armonk, NY: M. E. Sharpe, 1993, pp. 226–247.

Ware, Robert, and Enver Kisriev. "Russian Recentralization Arrives in the Republic of Dagestan: Implications for Institutional Integrity and Political Stability," *East European Constitutional Review*, vol. 10, no. 1 (2001): 68–75.

Way, Lucan A. "Authoritarian State Building and the Sources of Regime Competitiveness in the Fourth Wave: The Cases of Belarus, Moldova, Russia, and Ukraine," *World Politics*, vol. 57, no. 2 (January 2005): 231–261.

Webber, Renate. "The Romanian Constitutional Court: In Search of Its Own Identity," in Wojciech Sadurski, ed., *Constitutional Justice, East and West*. The Hague: Kluwer Law International, 2002, pp. 283–308.

White, Stephen, and Ian McAllister. "Dimensions of Disengagement in Post-Communist Russia," *Journal of Communist Studies and Transition Politics*, vol. 20 (2004): 81–97.

Williams, Kieran. "The Growing Litigiousness of Czech Elections," *Europe-Asia Studies*, vol. 59, no. 6 (September 2007): 937–959.

Wolczuk, Kataryna. *The Moulding of Ukraine: The Constitutional Politics of State Formation*. Budapest: Central European University Press, 2001.

Woodruff, David M. "Rules for Followers: Institutional Theory and the New Politics of Economic Backwardness in Russia," *Politics and Society*, vol. 28, no. 4 (2000): 437–482.

Yeltsin, Boris. *The Struggle for Russia*. New York: Random House, 1994.

Zupancic, Bostjan. "From Combat to Contract or: What Does the Constitution Constitute?" *Pravnik* 6 (1998): 476–510.

6. JUDICIAL AND DEMOCRATIC THEORY

Ackerman, Bruce. "The Rise of World Constitutionalism," *Virginia Law Review*, vol. 83, no. 4 (May 1997): 771–797.

Baird, Vanessa A. "Building Institutional Legitimacy: The Role of Procedural Justice," *Political Research Quarterly*, vol. 54 (2001): 333–354.

Bartole, Sergio. "Conclusions: Legitimacy of Constitutional Courts: Between Policy Making and Legal Science," in Wojciech Sadurski, ed., *Constitutional Justice, East and West*. The Hague: Kluwer Law International, 2003, pp. 409–432.

Baum, Lawrence. *Judges and Their Audiences: A Perspective on Judicial Behavior*. Princeton: Princeton University Press, 2006.

Beirich, Heidi Ly. "The Role of the Constitutional Tribunal in Spanish Politics (1980–1995)." Ph.D. diss., Purdue University, 1998.

Bell, John. *Judiciaries within Europe: A Comparative Review*. New York: Cambridge University Press, 2006.

Berman, Harold J. *Law and Revolution: The Formation of the Western Legal Tradition*. Cambridge, MA: Harvard University Press, 1983.

Bickel, Alexander. *The Least Dangerous Branch: The Supreme Court at the Bar of Politics*. Indianapolis: Bobbs-Merrill Co., 1962.

Breyer, Stephen G. "Judicial Independence in the U. S.," *Issues of Democracy*, vol. 1, no. 18 (December 1996): 6–11, available at http://www.usia.gov/journals/journals.htm.

————. "Comment: Liberty, Prosperity, and a Strong Judicial Institution," *Law and Contemporary Problems*, vol. 61, no. 3 (Summer 1998): 3–6.

Bribosia, Herve. "Report on Belgium," in Anne-Marie Slaughter et al., eds., *The European Courts and National Courts – Doctrine and Jurisprudence*. Oxford: Hart Publishing, 1998, pp. 3–39.

Brugger, Winfried. "European Integration and the Ideal of the Common Good," in Vicki C. Jackson and Mark Tushnet, eds., *Defining the Field of Comparative Constitutional Law*. Westport, CT: Praeger, 2002, pp. 93–106.

Burbank, Stephen B., and Barry Friedman, eds. *Judicial Independence at the Crossroads: An Interdisciplinary Approach*. Thousands Oaks, CA: SAGE Publications, 2002.

Canon, Bradley C., and Charles A. Johnson. *Judicial Politics: Implementation and Impact*. Washington, DC: CQ Press, 1999.

Carothers, Thomas, ed. *Promoting the Rule of Law Abroad: In Search of Knowledge*. Washington, DC: Carnegie Endowment for International Peace, 2006.

_____. "The Rule of Law Revival," *Foreign Affairs*, vol. 35 (1997): 1–23.

Chavez, Rebecca Bill. *Rule of Law in Nascent Democracies: Judicial Politics in Argentina*. Palo Alto, CA: Stanford University Press, 2004.

Comella, Victor F. "The European Model of Constitutional Review of Legislation: Toward Decentralization?" *I-CON: International Journal of Constitutional Law*, vol. 2 (2004): 461–491.

Domingo, Pilar. "Judicial Independence: The Politics of the Supreme Court of Mexico," *Journal of Latin American Studies*, vol. 32, no. 3 (2000): 705–735.

_____. "Judicialization of Politics or Politicization of the Judiciary? Recent Trends in Latin America," *Democratization*, vol. 11, no. 1 (February 2004): 104–126.

Dotan, Yoav, and Menahem Hofnung. "Legal Defeats – Political Wins: Why Do Elected Representatives Go to Court?" *Comparative Political Studies*, vol. 38, no. 1 (2005): 75–103.

Dworkin, Ronald. "Rights as Trumps," in Jeremy Waldron, ed., *Theories of Rights*. Oxford: Oxford University Press, 1984, pp. 153–167.

Elster, Jon. *Ulysses and the Sirens: Studies in Rationality and Irrationality*. Cambridge, UK: Cambridge University Press, 1979.

Engel, Christoph. "The Constitutional Court – Applying the Proportionality Principle – as a Subsidiary Authority for the Assessment of Political Outcomes," *Preprints aus der Max-Planck-Projektgruppe Recht der Gemeinschaftsgüter*, no. 10 (October 2001), available at http://www.coll.mpg.de/pdf_dat/2001_10.pdf, accessed December 17, 2007.

Epp, Charles R. *The Rights Revolution: Lawyers, Activists, and Supreme Courts in Comparative Perspective*. Chicago: University of Chicago Press, 1998.

Epstein, Lee, and Jack Knight. *The Choices Justices Make*. Washington, DC: CQ Press, 1998.

_____. "Towards a Strategic Revolution in Judicial Politics: A Look Back, A Look Ahead," *Political Research Quarterly*, vol. 53, no. 3 (September 2000): 625–661.

_____. "Constitutional Borrowing and Nonborrowing," *I-CON: International Journal of Constitutional Law*, vol. 1 (2003): 196–223.

Fabre, Cecile. *Social Rights under the Constitution*. Oxford: Oxford University Press, 2000.

Favoreu, Louis. "American and European Models of Constitutional Justice," in David S. Clark, ed., *Comparative and Private International Law: Essays in Honor of John Henry Merryman on His Seventieth Birthday*. Berlin: Duncker u. Humblot, 1990, pp. 105–120.

Feeley, Malcolm, and Edward Rubin. *Judicial Policy Making and the Modern State: How the Courts Reformed America's Prisons*. Cambridge, UK: Cambridge University Press, 1998.

Bibliography

———. *Federalism: Political Identity and Tragic Compromise*. Ann Arbor: University of Michigan Press, 2008.

Ferejohn, John, and Pasquale Pasquino. "Constitutional Courts as Deliberative Institutions: Towards an Institutional Theory of Constitutional Justice," in Wojciech Sadurski, ed., *Constitutional Justice, East and West*. The Hague: Kluwer Law International, 2003, pp. 21–36.

Filippov, Mikhail, Peter C. Ordeshook, and Olga Shevtsova. *Designing Federalism: A Theory of Self-Sustainable Federal Institutions*. New York: Cambridge University Press, 2004.

Finkel, Jodi. "Judicial Reform in Argentina in the 1990s: How Electoral Incentives Shape Institutional Change," *Latin American Research Review*, vol. 39, no. 3 (2004): 56–80.

———. "Judicial Reform as Insurance Policy: Mexico in the 1990s." *Latin American Politics and Society*, vol. 47, no. 1 (Spring 2005): 87–113.

Fiss, Owen M. "Objectivity and Interpretation," *Stanford Law Review*, vol. 34, no. 4 (1982): 739–763.

Fletcher, Joseph F., and Paul Howe. "Public Opinion and Canada's Courts," in Paul Howe and Peter H. Russell, eds., *Judicial Power and Canadian Democracy*. Montreal: McGill University Press, 2001, pp. 255–296.

French, John R. P., Jr., and Bertram H. Raven. "The Bases of Social Power," in Dorwin Cartwright, ed., *Studies in Social Power*. Ann Arbor, MI: Research Center for Group Dynamics, Institute for Social Research, University of Michigan, 1959, pp. 150–167.

Gagnon, Alain-G. "The Political Uses of Federalism," in Michael Burgess and Alain-G. Gagnon, eds., *Comparative Federalism and Federation*. Toronto: University of Toronto Press, 1993, pp. 15–44.

Garlicki, Lech. "Constitutional Courts Versus Supreme Courts," *I-CON: International Journal of Constitutional Law*, vol. 5, no. 1 (2007): 44–68.

Garrett, Geoffrey. "The Politics of Legal Integration in the European Union," *International Organization*, vol. 49 (1998): 171–181.

Gibson, James, Gregory Caldeira and Vanessa Baird. "On the Legitimacy of National High Courts," *American Political Science Review*, vol. 92, no. 2 (June 1998): 343–358.

Gillman, Howard. "Elements of a New 'Regime Politics' Approach to the Study of Judicial Politics." Paper presented at the annual meeting of the American Political Science Association, Chicago, IL, September 2004.

Ginsburg, Tom. *Judicial Review in New Democracies: Constitutional Courts in Asian Cases*. New York: Cambridge University Press, 2003.

Goldstein, Leslie. *Constituting Federal Sovereignty: The European Union in Comparative Context*. Baltimore: Johns Hopkins University Press, 2001.

Goldwin, Robert A., and Art Kaufman, eds. *Constitution Makers on Constitution Making*. Washington, DC: American Enterprise Institute for Public Policy Research, 1988.

Grosskopf, Anke. "A Supranational Case – Comparing Sources of Support for Constitutional Courts." Ph.D. diss., University of Pittsburgh, 2000.

Guarnieri, Carlo, and Patrizia Pederzoli. *The Power of Judges: A Comparative Study of Courts and Democracy*. Oxford: Oxford University Press, 2002.

Bibliography

Hammergren, Linn A. *Envisioning Reform: Improving Judicial Performance in Latin America*. University Park, PA: Pennsylvania State University Press, 2007.

Hertogh, Marc, and Simon Halliday, eds. *Judicial Review and Bureaucratic Impact*. Cambridge, UK: Cambridge University Press, 2004.

Hirschl, Ran. *Towards Juristocracy: The Origins and Consequences of the New Constitutionalism*. Cambridge, MA: Harvard University Press, 2004.

Horowitz, Donald L. "Constitutional Courts: A Primer for Decision Makers," *Journal of Democracy*, vol. 17, no. 4 (October 2006): 125–137.

Howe, Paul, and Peter H. Russell, eds. *Judicial Power and Canadian Democracy*. Montreal: McGill University Press, 2001.

Jackson, Vicki C. "Comparative Constitutional Federalism and Transnational Judicial Discourse," *I-CON: International Journal of Constitutional Law*, vol. 2 (2004): 91–138.

Jacob, Herbert. "Courts and Politics in the USA," in Herbert Jacob et al., *Courts, Law and Politics in Comparative Perspective*. New Haven, CT: Yale University Press, 1996, pp. 16–80.

Klerman, Daniel. "Jurisdictional Competition and the Evolution of the Common Law: A Hypothesis," *Australian Journal of Legal History*, vol. 77 (2004): 1–19.

Klug, Heinz. *Constituting Democracy: Law, Globalism and South Africa's Political Reconstruction*. New York: Cambridge University Press, 2000.

Kommers, Donald. *The Constitutional Jurisprudence of the Federal Republic of Germany*. Durham, NC: Duke University Press, 1997.

Landau, David. "The War of the Courts: Inter-Court Conflict and the Failure of the European Model of Constitutional Review in Latin America," (January 2007), unpublished manuscript, on file with author.

Landes, William, and Richard Posner. "The Independent Judiciary in an Interest-Group Perspective," *Journal of Law and Economics*, vol. 18, no. 3 (December 1975): 875–901.

Lane, Jan-Erik, and Svante Ersson. *The New Institutional Politics: Performance and Outcomes*. London: Routledge, 2000.

Lasser, William. *The Limits of Judicial Power*. Chapel Hill, NC: University of North Carolina Press, 1988.

Levi, Margaret. *Of Rule and Revenue*. Berkeley, CA: University of California Press, 1988.

Long, John M. "The Geography of Spain's Constitutional Court." Ph.D. diss., University of South Carolina, 2001.

Magalhães, Pedro C. "The Limits to Judicialization: Legislative Politics and Constitutional Review in the Iberian Democracies," Ph.D. diss., Ohio State University, 2003.

Malleson, Kate, and Peter H. Russell, eds. *Appointing Judges in an Age of Judicial Power: Critical Perspectives from Around the World*. Toronto: University of Toronto Press, 2005.

Marini, Annibale. "Regarding the Guarantees of Independence of the Italian Constitutional Court," *Konstitutsionnoe pravosudie*, no. 3 (2001): 137–145.

McCloskey, Robert, and Sanford Levinson. *The American Supreme Court*. Chicago: University of Chicago Press, 1994.

Bibliography

McCubbins, Matthew D., Roger G. Noll, and Barry R. Weingast. "Administrative Procedures as Instruments of Political Control," *Journal of Law, Economics, and Organization*, vol. 3 (1987): 243–277.

McCubbins, Matthew D., and Thomas Schwartz. "Congressional Oversight Overlooked: Police Patrols versus Fire Alarms," *American Journal of Political Science*, vol. 28 (1984): 165–179.

Merryman, John H., and Vincenzo Vigoriti. "When Courts Collide: Constitution and Cassation in Italy," *American Journal of Comparative Law*, vol. 15 (1967): 665–686.

Moore, Barrington, Jr. *Social Origins of Dictatorship and Democracy: Lord and Peasant in the Making of the Modern World*. Boston: Beacon Press, 1966.

Morton, F. L. "Dialogue or Monologue?" in Paul Howe and Peter H. Russell, eds., *Judicial Power and Canadian Democracy*. Montreal: McGill University Press, 2001, pp. 111–117.

Moustafa, Tamir. *The Struggle for Constitutional Power: Law, Politics, and Economic Development in Egypt*. New York: Cambridge University Press, 2007.

———. "Law Versus the State: The Judicialization of Politics in Egypt," *Law and Social Inquiry*, vol. 28 (2003): 883–930.

North, Douglass C., and Barry R. Weingast. "Constitutions and Commitment: The Evolution of Institutions Governing Public Choice in Seventeenth-Century England," in Lee J. Alston, Thrainn Eggertsson, and Douglass C. North, eds., *Empirical Studies in Institutional Change*. Cambridge, UK: Cambridge University Press, 1996, pp. 134–165.

O'Brien, David. *Storm Center*. New York: Norton, 2000.

O'Donnell, Guillermo. "Why the Rule of Law Matters," *Journal of Democracy*, vol. 15, no. 4 (2004): 32–46.

Orren, Karen, and Stephen Skowronek. *The Search for American Political Development*. New York: Cambridge University Press, 2004.

Plucknett, Theodore F. T. *A Concise History of the Common Law*. Rochester, NY: The Lawyers Co-operative Publishing, 1929.

Provine, Marie, and Antoine Garapon. "The Selection of Judges in France: Searching for a New Legitimacy," in Kate Malleson and Peter H. Russell, eds., *Appointing Judges in an Age of Judicial Power: Critical Perspectives from Around the World*. Toronto: University of Toronto Press, 2006, pp. 176–195.

Przeworski, Adam. *Democracy and the Market*. Cambridge, UK: Cambridge University Press, 1991.

———, and Henry Teune. *The Logic of Social Inquiry*. New York: John Wiley, 1970.

Putnam, Robert. *Making Democracy Work: Civic Traditions in Modern Italy*. Princeton, NJ: Princeton University Press, 1993.

Rakove, Jack. *Original Meanings*. New York: Alfred Knopf, 1997.

Ramseyer, Mark J. "The Puzzling (In) dependence of Courts: A Comparative Approach," *Journal of Legal Studies*, vol. 23 (1994): 721–747.

Roca, Javier Garcia. "Effects, Enforceability and the Execution of the Decisions of the Spanish Constitutional Court." Paper presented at the Workshop on the Execution of the decisions of the Constitutional Court. Kyiv, October 28–29, 1999, available at http://www.venice.coe.int/docs/1999/CDL-JU(1999)028-e.asp.

Rosenberg, Gerald N. *The Hollow Hope: Can Courts Bring About Social Change?* Chicago: University of Chicago Press, 1991.

Rubin, Edward L. "Independence as a Governance Mechanism," in Stephen B. Burbank and Barry Friedman, eds., *Judicial Independence at the Crossroads: An Interdisciplinary Approach*. Thousands Oaks, CA: SAGE Publications, 2002, pp. 56–100.

Rupp, Hans G. "Some Remarks on Judicial Self-Restraint," *Ohio State Law Journal*, vol. 21, no. 4 (Autumn 1960): 503–515.

Russell, Peter H. "The Supreme Court in Federal-Provincial Relations: The Political Use of Legal Resources," *Canadian Public Policy*, vol. 11, no. 2 (1985): 161–170.

———. "Toward a General Theory of Judicial Independence," in Peter H. Russell and David O'Brien, eds., *Judicial Independence in the Age of Democracy: Critical Perspectives from Around the World*. Charlottesville, VA: University of Virginia Press, 2001, pp. 1–24.

———, and David O'Brien, eds. *Judicial Independence in the Age of Democracy: Critical Perspectives from Around the World*. Charlottesville, VA: University of Virginia Press, 2001.

Salzberger, Eli, and Paul Fenn. "Judicial Independence: Some Evidence from the English Court of Appeal," *Journal of Law and Economics*, vol. 42 (1999): 831–847.

Scheppele, Kim Lane. "Constitutional Ethnography: An Introduction," *Law and Society Review*, vol. 38, no. 3 (September 2004): 389–406.

Shapiro, Martin. *Courts: A Comparative and Political Analysis*. Chicago: University of Chicago Press, 1981.

———. "The Success of Judicial Review," in Sally J. Kenney, William M. Reisinger, and John C. Reitz, eds., *Constitutional Dialogues in Comparative Perspective*. New York: St. Martin's Press, 1999, pp. 193–219.

———. "The Success of Judicial Review and Democracy," in Martin Shapiro and Alec Stone Sweet, eds., *On Law, Politics, and Judicialization*. Oxford: Oxford University Press, 2002, pp. 149–183.

———. "Some Conditions for the Success of Constitutional Courts: Lessons from the U. S. Experience," in Wojciech Sadurski, ed., *Constitutional Justice, East and West*. The Hague: Kluwer Law International, 2003, pp. 37–60.

———, and Alec Stone Sweet. *On Law, Politics, and Judicialization*. Oxford: Oxford University Press, 2002.

Shetreet, Shimon. *Justice in Israel: A Study of the Israeli Judiciary*. The Hague: Martinus Nijhoff, 1994.

Silverstein, Gordon. "Why Judicial Review Happens? Towards a Theory of Evolution and Acceptance of Judicial Review." Paper presented at the annual meeting of the American Political Science Association, Boston, August 2002.

Skolnick, Jerome H. *Justice Without Trial: Law Enforcement in Democratic Society*. New York: Wiley, 1966.

Slaughter, Anne-Marie. *A New World Order*. Princeton, NJ: Princeton University Press, 2004.

Bibliography

"Symposium: The Chief Justice and the Institutional Judiciary," *University of Pennsylvania Law Review*, vol. 154, no. 6 (June 2006): 1323–1930.

Staton, Jeffrey K. "Judicial Activism and Public Authority Compliance: The Role of Public Support in the Mexican Separation-of-Powers System." Ph.D. diss., Washington University, 2002.

———, and Mark Strahan. "The Emergence of an Effective Constitutional Court." Paper presented at the annual meeting of the American Political Science Association, Boston, August 2002.

Stone, Alec. *The Birth of Judicial Politics in France*. Oxford: Oxford University Press, 1992.

Sweet, Alec S. *Governing with Judges: Constitutional Politics in Europe*. Oxford: Oxford University Press, 2000.

Swinton, Katherine E. *The Supreme Court and Canadian Federalism: The Laskin–Dickson Years*. Toronto: Carswell, 1990.

Tate, Neal C., and Torbjörn Vallinder, eds. *The Global Expansion of Judicial Power*. New York: New York University Press, 1995.

Tilly, Charles. "Reflections on the History of European State-Making," in Charles Tilly, ed., *The Formation of National States in Western Europe*. Princeton, NJ: Princeton University Press, 1975, pp. 3–83.

Toharia, Jose, "Judicial Independence in an Authoritarian Regime: The Case of Contemporary Spain." *Law and Society Review* 9 (1975): 475–496.

Tsebelis, George. *Veto Players: How Political Institutions Work*. Princeton, NJ: Princeton University Press, 2002.

Turano, Leslie. "Spain: Quis Custodiet Ipsos Custodes?: The Struggle for Jurisdiction Between the Tribunal Constitucional and the Tribunal Supremo," *I-CON: International Journal of Constitutional Law*, vol. 4, no. 1 (2006): 151–162.

Tyler, Tom, and Gregory Mitchell. "Legitimacy and Empowerment of Discretionary Legal Authority: The United States Supreme Court and Abortion Rights," *Duke Law Journal*, vol. 43, no. 4 (1994): 703–815.

Vanberg, Georg. *The Politics of Constitutional Review in Germany*. Cambridge, UK: Cambridge University Press, 2005.

———. "Establishing Judicial Independence in West Germany: The Impact of Opinion Leadership and the Separation of Powers," *Comparative Politics*, vol. 32 (2000): 333–353.

Volcansek, Mary L. *Constitutional Politics in Italy: The Constitutional Court*. New York: St. Martin's Press, 1999.

Waldron, Jeremy. "Precommitment and Disagreement," in Larry Alexander, ed., *Constitutionalism: Philosophical Foundations*. Cambridge, UK: Cambridge University Press, 1998, pp. 271–299.

Widner, Jennifer. *Building the Rule of Law*. New York: W. W. Norton & Co., 2001.

Wilson, Richard. *Compliance Ideologies: Rethinking Political Culture*. New York: Cambridge University Press, 1992.

Yamanishi, David S. "Rule of Law, Property Rights, and Human Rights: An Informal Theory of the Effects (and Non-Effects) of Legal Institutions." Paper presented at the annual meeting of the American Political Science Association, Washington, DC, September 2000.

Statutes and Decrees

STATUTES AND BILLS

-1988-

Zakon SSSR of December 1, 1988 "Ob izmeneniiakh i dopolneniiakh Konstitutsii SSSR." *Vedomosti Verkhovnogo Soveta SSSR*, 1988, no. 49, item 727. [Constitutional amendments establishing the USSR Constitutional Supervision Committee.]

-1989-

Zakon SSSR of December 23, 1989 "O konstitutsionnom nadzore v SSSR." *Vedomosti Verkhovnogo Soveta SSSR*, 1989, no. 29, item 572. [Law on the USSR Constitutional Supervision Committee.]

-1991-

Zakon RSFSR of May 6, 1991 "O Konstitutsionnom sude RSFSR." *VSND i VS RSFSR*, 1991, no. 19, item 621. [Law on the Russian Constitutional Court.]
Zakon RSFSR of May 24, 1991 "Ob izmeneniiakh i dopolneniiakh Konstitutsii (osnovnogo zakona) RSFSR." *VSND i VS RSFSR*, 1991, no. 22, item 776. [Constitutional amendments establishing the Russian Constitutional Court.]

-1992-

Zakon RSFSR of April 21, 1992 "Ob izmeneniiakh i dopolneniiakh Konstitutsii (osnovnogo zakona) RSFSR." *VSND i VS RSFSR*, 1992, no. 20, item 1084. [Constitutional amendments empowering the Russian Constitutional Court to review the constitutionality of political parties.]

-1994-

Federalnyi konstitutsionnyi zakon "O Konstitutsionnom Sude Rossiiskoi Federatsii" of July 21, 1994. *SZ RF*, 1994, no. 13, item 1447. [Law on the Russian Constitutional Court.]

338   *Statutes and Decrees*

-1996-

Federalnyi konstitutsionnyi zakon "O sudebnoi sisteme Rossiiskoi Federatsii" of December 31, 1996. *SZ RF*, 1997, no. 1, item 1. [Law on the judicial system of the Russian Federation.]

-1997-

Federalnyi zakon "O vnesenii izmenenii i dopolnenii v KZoT RF" of March 17, 1997. *SZ RF*, 1997, no. 12, item 1382. [Law implementing the 1993 RCC decision on the full compensation of employees for wrongful dismissal.]

-1998-

Federalnyi zakon "O poriadke priniatiia i vstupleniia v silu popravok k Konstitutsii Rossiiskoi Federatsii" of March 4, 1998. *SZ RF*, 1998, no. 10, item 1146. [Law implementing the 1995 RCC decision on the constitutional amendment procedure.]

-2000-

Federalnyi zakon "O vnesenii izmenenii i dopolnenii v Federalnyi zakon 'Ob obshchikh printsipakh organizatsii zakonodatelnykh (predstavitelnykh) ispolnitelnykh organov gosudarstvennoi vlasti subektov Rossiiskoi Federatsii'" of July 29, 2000, *SZ RF*, 2000, no. 31, item 3205. [Law authorizing the president to dismiss regional governors and disband regional legislatures for violation of constitution and federal law.]

Gosudarstvennaia Duma Federalnogo Sobraniia RF. "Postanovlenie no. 824-III GD 'O federalnykh admnistrativnykh sudakh v Rossiiskoi Federatsii.'" *Legal database SPS "Konsultant Plius: Zakonoproekty."* November 22, 2000. [Bill on the creation of administrative courts, approved in the first reading.]

-2001-

Federalnyi konstitutsionnyi zakon "O vnesenii izmenenii i dopolnenii v federalnyi konstitutsionnyi zakon 'O Konstitutsionnom Sude Rossiiskoi Federatsii'" of February 8, 2001. *SZ RF*, 2001, no. 7, item 607. [Law abolishing the mandatory retirement age for RCC justices.]

Ugolovno-protsessualnyi kodeks RF of December 18, 2001 no. 174-FZ. *SZ RF*, 2001, no. 52 (Part I), item 492. [RF Criminal Procedure Code.]

Federalnyi konstitutsionnyi zakon "O vnesenii izmenenii i dopolnenii v federalnyi konstitutsionnyi zakon 'O Konstitutsionnom Sude Rossiiskoi Federatsii'" of December 15, 2001. *Rossiiskaia gazeta*, December 20, 2001, p. 9. [Law reinstating the mandatory retirement age for RCC justices and improving the implementation of the RCC decisions.]

-2002-

Federalnyi zakon "O vnesenii izmenenii i dopolnenii v Federalnyi Zakon 'O vvedenii v deistvie Ugolovno-protsessualnogo kodeksa Rossiiskoi Federatsii'" of

Statutes and Decrees

May 29, 2002. *Rossiiskaia gazeta*, June 1, 2002. [Law implementing the March 2002 RCC decision on judicial arrests.]

-2003-

Federalnyi zakon 26-FZ "O vnesenii izmenenii i dopolnenii v Zakon Rossiiskoi Federatsii 'O reabilitatsii zhertv politicheskikh repressii'" of February 9, 2003. *SZ RF*, 2003, no. 6, item 509. [Law implementing the May 1995 RCC decision on the compensation of children-victims of Stalin's purges.]

-2005-

Federalnyi konstitutsionnyi zakon "O vnesenii izmenenii i dopolnenii v federalnyi konstitutsionnyi zakon 'O Konstitutsionnom Sude Rossiiskoi Federatsii'" of April 5, 2005. *Rossiiskaia gazeta*, April 9, 2005. [Law introducing life tenure for all RCC justices and setting the mandatory retirement age at 70.]

-2007-

Federalnyi konstitutsionnyi zakon "O vnesenii izmenenii i dopolnenii v federalnyi konstitutsionnyi zakon 'O Konstitutsionnom Sude Rossiiskoi Federatsii'" of 5 February 2007. *Rossiiskaia gazeta*, February 9, 2007. [Law on the relocation of the seat of the RCC from Moscow to Saint Petersburg.]

DECREES AND EXECUTIVE REGULATIONS

-1993-

Presidential Decree no. 1612 "O Konstitutsionnom sude Rossiiskoi Federatsii" of October 7, 1993. *SAPP*, 1993, no. 41, item 3921. [Suspension of the Russian Constitutional Court.]

Presidential Decree no. 2289 "O zameshchenii vakantnykh dolzhnostei federalnykh sudei" of December 25, 1993. *SAPP*, 1994, no. 4, item 698. [Submission of judicial nominations.]

-1997-

Presidential Decree no. 193 "O merakh po realizatsii postanovleniia Konstitutsionnogo Suda RF ot 24 ianvaria 1997 g. N 1-P" of March 10, 1997. *SZ RF*, 1997, no. 10, item 1130. [Implementation of the RCC decision 1-P of January 24, 1997 in the *Udmurtiia* local self-government reform.]

-2001-

Letter 01–07/9187 of January 13, 2001, by Mikhail Vanin, the Head of the RF State Customs Committee, in Mitiukov et al., *Problemy ispolneniia . . .*, pp. 307–314. [Implementation of the RCC decisions on the confiscation of imported goods.]

340   *Statutes and Decrees*

Letter of the Russian Procuracy General "O poriadke ispolneniia Opredeleniia Konstitutsionnogo Suda Rossiiskoi Federatsii ot 18.04.2000 N 103-O" of August 3, 2001, no. 13r, unpublished document. [Implementation of the May 1995 RCC decision on the compensation of children-victims of Stalin's purges.]

Directive of the Russian Ministry of Labor "O realizatsii Opredeleniia Konstitutsionnogo Suda Rossiiskoi Federatsii ot 18.04.2000 N 103-O" of September 18, 2001, no. 2294-14, unpublished document. [Implementation of the May 1995 RCC decision on the compensation of children-victims of Stalin's purges.]

Order of the Russian Minister of Internal Affairs "O vnesenii izmenenii i dopolnenii v instruktsiiu, utv. Prikazom MVD Rossii ot 22 iunia 2000 g. N 675" of October 25, 2001, no. 938. *Rossiiskaia gazeta*, November 28, 2001. [Implementation of the May 1995 RCC decision on the compensation of children-victims of Stalin's purges.]

-2002-

Presidential Decree no. 671 "O vnesenii izmenenii v obshchevoinskie ustavy Vooruzhennykh Sil Rossiiskoi Federatsii" of June 30, 2002. *Rossiiskaia gazeta*, 3 July 2002. [Implementation of the March 2002 RCC decision on judicial arrests in the military.]

Presidential Decree no. 1413 "Ob utverzhdenii perechnia dolzhnostei, periody sluzhby (raboty) v kotorykh vkliuchaiutsia v stazh gosudarstvennoi sluzhby dlia naznacheniia pensii za vyslugu let federalnykh gosudarstvennykh sluzhashchikh" of December 17, 2002. *Rossiiskaia gazeta*, December 20, 2002. [Increase of the retirement benefits for the former Communist Party officials.]

-2004-

Presidential Decree no. 151 "O priznanii utrativshim silu Ukaza Prezidenta Rossiiskoi Federatsii ot 2 noiabria 1993 g. N 1815 'O merakh po preduprezhdeniiu brodiazhnichestva i poproshainichestva'" of February 6, 2004. *SZ RF*, 2004, no. 6, item 412. [Implementation of the March 2002 RCC decision on judicial arrests with regard to vagrancy.]

-2007-

Letter of the RF Ministry of Finance No. 03-02-07/2-138 of August 7, 2007, unpublished. English translation is available at http://subscribe.ru/archive/law.kodekseng/200708/16121843.html.

Presidential Decree no. 1740 "O meste postoiannogo prebyvaniia Konstitutsionnogo Suda Rossiiskoi Federatsii." *Rossiiskaia gazeta*, December 27, 2007, p. 2. [On the Location of the Permanent Sojourn of the RF Constitutional Court.]

Court Decisions

Bulgaria
Constitutional Court decisions:
No. 12 of July 23, 1996, *Darzhaven Vestnik*, no. 67, August 6, 1996 (Todorov, Danailov, Penev, and Arabazhiev, dissenting), available at http://www.constcourt.bg/re12_96.htm.
No. 3 of February 8, 2001, *Darzhaven Vestnik*, no. 15, February 16, 2001 (Markov, Gochev, Beronov, Gotsev, and Neikov, dissenting), available at http://www.constcourt.bg/re3_2001.htm.
No. 1 of March 7, 2006, *Darzhaven Vestnik*, no. 23, March 17, 2006 (Gruev, Drumeva, Pavlova, Stoianova, Tanchev, and Iankov, dissenting), available at http://www.constcourt.bg/r1_2006.htm.

Canada
Reference re Secession of Quebec, 2 S.C.R. 217 (1998).

Czech Republic
Supreme Court decisions:
No. 2 Tzn 10/96, of April 25, 1996.
No. 2 Tzn 10/96, of October 9, 1997.

Constitutional Court decisions:
No. I. US 131/93
No. IV. US 81/95 of September 18, 1995, available at http://angl.concourt.cz/angl_verze/doc/4-81-95.php.
No. III. US 337/97
No. III. US 425/97 of April 2, 1998, available at http://angl.concourt.cz/angl_verze/doc/3-425-97.php.
No. III. US 139/98
No. Pl. US 16/99, *Sbirka zakonu* 276/2001 Sb.
No. III. US 252/04 of January 25, 2005, available at http://angl.concourt.cz/angl_verze/doc/3-252-04.php.
No. I. US 85/04 of June 13, 2006, available at http://angl.concourt.cz/angl_verze/doc/1-85-04.php.
No. Pl. US 18/06 of July 11, 2006, available at http://angl.concourt.cz/angl_verze/doc/p-18-06.php.

341

Latvia

Constitutional Court decision 2002–06–01 of February 4, 2003, available at http://www.satv.tiesa.gov.lv/Eng/spriedumi/06–01(02).htm.

Lithuania

Constitutional Court conclusion of March 31, 2004, Case No. 14/04, available in English at http://www.lrkt.lt/dokumentai/2004/c040331.htm.

Spain

Constitutional Tribunal decisions:
23/1988
158/1993
18/2003

Ukraine

Constitutional Court decision 13-rp of November 16, 2000, *Visnyk Konstytutsijnogo Sudu Ukrainy*, 2000, no. 5, 24.

United States

Texas v. White, 74 US 700 (1869).
Majors v. Abell 361 F3d 349 (7th Cir. 2004).
McConnell v. Federal Election Commission 124 SCt 619 (2003).

Russia

Bashkortostan Constitutional Court decisions:
14-P of October 4, 2000. Van den Berg, compiler, "Constitution of the Russian Federation Annotated,"494–497.
17-P of December 28, 2001. Van den Berg, compiler, "Constitution of the Russian Federation Annotated," 494–497.
Dagestan Constitutional Court decision of October 3, 2000. *Digest 'Akty konstitutsionnogo pravosudiia subektov Rossiiskoi Federatsii,'* 2000, no. 10, 44.
Tatarstan Constitutional Court decisions:
10-O of November 28, 2001.
11-O November 28, 2001.
8-P of February 7, 2003. *Respublika Tatarstan*, February 14, 2003.
Tiumen Regional Court (Presidium) decision of November 15, 2002, *Biulleten Verkhovnogo Suda RF*, 2003, no. 4.
Russian Supreme Court decisions:
Decision of February 17, 1998, *Biulleten Verkhovnogo Suda RF*, 1998, no. 6, 1–2.
Determination of the Russian Supreme Court No. 53-Go1–9 of August 17, 2001, unpublished, available at the Web site of the Russian Supreme Court, at http://www.vsrf.ru/vs_docs.php.
"Review of Judicial Practice of the RF Supreme Court in the 4th Quarter of 2003," *Biulleten Verkhovnogo Suda RF*, 2004, no. 7, 28.
Decision of the Presidium No. 8pvo4 of July 14, 2004, *Biulleten Verkhovnogo Suda RF*, 2005, no. 2, 2–4.
Russian Constitutional Court decisions:

Court Decisions

-1992-

1-P of January 14, 1992, *VKS RF*, 1993, no. 1, 11–19 (Ametistov, concurring).

2-P of February 4, 1992, *VKS RF*, 1993, no. 1, 29–37 (Gadzhiev, concurring).

3-P of March 13, 1992, *VKS RF*, 1993, no. 1, 40–52 (Ametistov, dissenting).

5-P of May 19, 1992, *VKS RF*, 1993, nos. 2–3 (Ebzeev, dissenting).

7-P of June 9, 1992, *VKS RF*, 1993, nos. 2–3, 29–36.

8-P of June 23, 1992, *VKS RF*, 1993, nos. 2–3, 41–52.

8-R of September 24, 1992, *VKS RF*, 1993, no. 1, 38–39.

9-P of November 30, 1992, *VKS RF*, 1993, nos. 4–5, 37–64, and no. 6, 1–48 (Ebzeev, Kononov, and Luchin, dissenting).

-1993-

1-P of January 27, 1993, *VKS RF*, 1993, nos. 2–3, 56–64.

3-P of February 12, 1993, *VKS RF*, 1994, no. 1, 12–24 (Kononov, dissenting).

1-Z of March 23, 1993, *VKS RF*, 1994, no. 1, 47–63 (Ametistov, Morshchakova, and Vitruk, dissenting).

6-P of April 2, 1993, *VKS RF*, 1994, nos. 2–3, 8–19.

7-P of April 16, 1993, *VSND i VS RSFSR*, 1993, no. 29, item 1141 (Morshchakova, dissenting).

8-P of April 21, 1993, *VKS RF*, 1994, nos. 2–3, 33–52 (Ametistov and Morshchakova, dissenting).

9-P of May 11, 1993, *VKS RF*, 1994, nos. 2–3, 54–59.

11-P of May 27, 1993, *VKS RF*, 1994, nos. 2–3, 75–95 (Kononov, dissenting).

12-P of May 31, 1993, *VKS RF*, 1994, nos. 4–5, 12–16.

13-P of June 3, 1993, *VKS RF*, 1994, nos. 4–5, 21–36 (Kononov and Vitruk, dissenting).

14-P of June 7, 1993, *VKS RF*, 1993, nos. 4–5, 40–53 (Kononov, dissenting).

70-R of July 12, 1993, unpublished, available at the Web site of the Russian Constitutional Court, http://www.ksrf.ru.

15-P of September 10, 1993, *VKS RF*, 1994, nos. 4–5, 64–78 (Kononov and Morshchakova, dissenting).

73-O of September 16, 1993, *Konstitutsionnyi Sud Rossiiskoi Federatsii. Postanovleniia. Opredeleniia. 1992–1996*, ed., Tamara Morshchakova, 652–654.

17-P of September 17, 1993, *VKS RF*, 1994, no. 6, 18–25.

2-Z of September 21, 1993, *VKS RF*, 1994, no. 6, 40–56 (Ametistov, Kononov, Morshchakova, and Vitruk, dissenting).

18-P of September 30, 1993, *VKS RF*, 1994, no. 6, 29–39.

88-R of December 1, 1993 (Ebzeev, dissenting). In Boris Ebzeev, *Konstitutsiia. Pravovoe gosudarstvo. Konstitutsionnyi Sud*, 137–143.

-1995-

1-P of March 23, 1995, *VKS RF*, 1995, nos. 2–3, 3–16 (Gadzhiev, Luchin, Morshchakova, and Rudkin, dissenting).

2-P of April 12, 1995, *VKS RF*, 1995, nos. 2–3, 17–31 (Gadzhiev and Ebzeev, dissenting).

4-P of May 3, 1995, *VKS RF*, 1995, nos. 2–3, 42–44.

62-O of May 17, 1995, unpublished, available at http://www.ksrf.ru.

63-O of May 17, 1995, unpublished, available at http://www.ksrf.ru.

5-P of May 17, 1995, *VKS RF*, 1995, nos. 2–3, 45–50.

6-P of May 23, 1995, *VKS RF*, 1995, nos. 2–3, 51–56.

29-O of June 15, 1995, *VKS RF*, 1995, nos. 2–3, 67.

8-P of June 23, 1995, *SZ RF*, 1995, no. 27, item 2622 (Danilov, dissenting).

9-P of July 10, 1995, *VKS RF*, 1995, no. 4, 2–12 (Vitruk, dissenting).

10-P of July 31, 1995, *VKS RF*, 1995, no. 5, 3–64 (Ametistov, Ebzeev, Gadzhiev, Kononov, Luchin, Morshchakova, Vitruk, and Zorkin, dissenting).

11-P of October 16, 1995, *VKS RF*, 1995, no. 6, 5–9.

12-P of October 31, 1995, *VKS RF*, 1995, no. 6, 10–17 (Morshchakova, dissenting).

99-O of November 2, 1995, *Konstitutsionnyi Sud RF. Postanovleniia. Opredeleniia. 1992–1996*, ed., Tamara Morshchakova, 658–660.

77-O of November 20, 1995, *VKS RF*, 1995, no. 6, 22–30 (Ametistov, dissenting).

16-P of November 30, 1995, *VKS RF*, 1995, no. 6, 42–47.

104-O of December 4, 1995, *Konstitutsionnyi Sud Rossiiskoi Federatsii. Postanovleniia. Opredeleniia. 1992–1996*, ed., Tamara Morshchakova, 498–500.

17-P of December 20, 1995, *VKS RF*, 1995, no. 6, 48–63 (Kononov and Vitruk, dissenting).

-1996-

1-P of January 16, 1996, *VKS RF*, 1996, no. 1, 2–12 (Vitruk, dissenting).

2-P of January 18, 1996, *VKS RF*, 1996, no. 1, 13–30 (Gadzhiev, Rudkin, and Vitruk, dissenting).

3-P of February 1, 1996, *VKS RF*, 1996, no. 1, 34–47 (Vitruk, dissenting).

4-P of February 2, 1996, *VKS RF*, 1996, no. 2, 2–11.

8-O of March 11, 1996, unpublished, available at http://www.ksrf.ru.

17-O of March 11, 1996, unpublished, available at http://www.ksrf.ru.

7-P of March 11, 1996, *VKS RF*, 1996, no. 2, 26–33 (Gadzhiev, dissenting).

8-P of March 27, 1996, *VKS RF*, 1996, no. 2, 34–41.

20-O of April 1, 1996, unpublished, available at http://www.ksrf.ru.

9-P of April 4, 1996, *VKS RF*, 1996, no. 2, 42–61 (Baglai, dissenting).

32-O of April 19, 1996, unpublished, available at http://www.ksrf.ru.

10-P of April 22, 1996, *VKS RF*, 1996, no. 3, 5–14.

11-P of April 30, 1996, *VKS RF*, 1996, no. 3, 15–28 (Luchin, dissenting).

59-O of May 22, 1996, *Konstitutsionnyi Sud Rossiiskoi Federatsii. Postanovleniia. Opredeleniia. 1992–1996*, ed., Tamara Morshchakova, 181.

13-P of May 30, 1996, *VKS RF*, 1996, no. 3, 37–47 (Ametistov, dissenting).

14-P of June 13, 1996, *VKS RF*, 1996, no. 4, 2–13 (Vitruk, dissenting).

53-O of June 21, 1996, *VKS RF*, 1996, no. 4, 20–22.
77-O of July 11, 1996, unpublished, available at http://www.ksrf.ru.
17-P of October 24, 1996, *VKS RF*, 1996, no. 5, 2–10 (Ebzeev, dissenting).
19-P of November 28, 1996, *VKS RF*, 1996, no. 5, 15–21.
20-P of December 17, 1996, *VKS RF*, 1996, no. 5, 22–29.
103-O of December 26, 1996, unpublished, available at http://www.ksrf.ru.
105-O of December 26, 1996, unpublished. Van den Berg, compiler, "Constitution of the Russian Federation Annotated," 265.

-1997-

1-O of January 23, 1997, unpublished, available at http://www.ksrf.ru.
1-P of January 24, 1997, *VKS RF*, 1997, no. 1, 2–24 (Gadzhiev and Vitruk, dissenting).
2-P of January 28, 1997, *VKS RF*, 1997, no. 1, 25–42 (Ametistov, Luchin, Oleinik, and Vedernikov, dissenting).
13-O of February 4, 1997, unpublished. Van den Berg, compiler, "Constitution of the Russian Federation Annotated," 269–270.
16-O of April 1, 1997, *VKS RF*, 1997, no. 4, 18–19.
23-O of February 4, 1997, unpublished. Van den Berg, compiler, "Constitution of the Russian Federation Annotated," 270.
3-P of February 18, 1997, *VKS RF*, 1997, no. 1, 43–53 (Morshchakova, dissenting).
4-P of March 4, 1997, *VKS RF*, 1997, no. 1, 54–63 (Zorkin, dissenting).
20-O of March 19, 1997, unpublished, available at http://www.ksrf.ru.
56-O of March 19, 1997, *VKS RF*, 1997, no. 4, 2–4.
5-P of March 21, 1997, *VKS RF*, 1997, no. 4, 5–12.
6-P of April 1, 1997, *VKS RF*, 1997, no. 4, 13–17.
7-P of April 30, 1997, *VKS RF*, 1997, no. 4, 24–54 (Ebzeev, Gadzhiev, and Vitruk, dissenting).
8-P of May 20, 1997, *VKS RF*, 1997, no. 4, 55–63 (Kononov, dissenting).
59-O of June 6, 1997, *VKS RF*, 1997, no. 5, 7–10.
9-P of June 24, 1997, *SZ RF*, 1997, no. 26, item 3145 (Vitruk, dissenting).
10-P of July 2, 1997, *VKS RF*, 1997, no. 5, 20–24.
88-O of October 7, 1997, *VKS RF*, 1997, no. 5, 44–48.
13-P of October 8, 1997, *VKS RF*, 1997, no. 5, 49–56.
14-P of October 16, 1997, *VKS RF*, 1997, no. 5, 57–64.
15-P of November 3, 1997, *VKS RF*, 1997, no. 6, 2–8.
16-P of November 11, 1997, *VKS RF*, 1997, no. 6, 9–22 (Kononov and Vitruk, dissenting).
18-P of December 1, 1997, *VKS RF*, 1997, no. 6, 41–63 (Morshchakova and Vitruk, dissenting).
20-P of December 16, 1997, *VKS RF*, 1998, no. 1, 17–22.
21-P of December 23, 1997, *SZ RF*, 1997, no. 51, item 5878 (Kononov, dissenting).

346   *Court Decisions*

-1998-

1-P of January 9, 1998, *VKS RF*, 1998, no. 2, 5–18.

2-P of January 15, 1998, *VKS RF*, 1998, no. 2, 19–27 (Ebzeev and Vitruk, dissenting).

3-P of January 15, 1998, *VKS RF*, 1998, no. 2, 28–43.

4-P of February 2, 1998, *VKS RF*, 1998, no. 3, 3–10.

22-O of February 5, 1998, *VKS RF*, 1998, no. 3, 30–34.

19-O of February 5, 1998, *VKS RF*, 1998, no. 3, 24–26.

6-P of February 17, 1998, *VKS RF*, 1998, no. 3, 35–40.

7-P of February 24, 1998, *VKS RF*, 1998, no. 3, 41–57.

32-O of March 12, 1998, *VKS RF*, 1998, no. 3, 66–70.

8-P of March 11, 1998, *VKS RF*, 1998, no. 3, 52–65 (Vitruk, dissenting).

9-P of March 16, 1998, *VKS RF*, 1998, no. 3, 71–78.

11-P of April 6, 1998, *VKS RF*, 1998, no. 4, 11–20 (Ametistov, dissenting).

12-P of April 17, 1998, *VKS RF*, 1998, no. 4, 21–35 (Strekozov and Vitruk, dissenting).

13-P of April 29, 1998, *VKS RF*, 1998, no. 4, 35–40.

14-P of May 12, 1998, *VKS RF*, 1998, no. 4, 41–50.

16-P of May 29, 1998, *VKS RF*, 1998, no. 5, 10–13.

17-P of June 10, 1998, *VKS RF*, 1998, no. 5, 28–41(Vitruk, dissenting).

19-P of June 16, 1998, *VKS RF*, 1998, no. 5, 51–66 (Gadzhiev and Vitruk, dissenting).

88-O of July 1, 1998, unpublished, available at http://www.ksrf.ru.

93-O of July 1, 1998, *VKS RF*, 1998, no. 5, 67–69.

86-O of July 14, 1998, *VKS RF*, 1998, no. 6, 10–57 (Gadzhiev, Kononov, Morshchakova, and Oleinik, dissenting).

20-P of July 2, 1998, *VKS RF*, 1998, no. 5, 70–80.

21-P of July 6, 1998, *VKS RF*, 1998, no. 6, 5–9.

22-P of July 17, 1998, *VKS RF*, 1998, no. 6, 58–67 (Kononov, dissenting).

23-P of July 17, 1998, *VKS RF*, 1998, no. 6, 68–73.

116-O of October 7, 1998, *VKS RF*, 1998, no. 6, 74–79.

24-P of October 12, 1998, *VKS RF*, 1999, no. 1, 10–17.

147-O of November 5, 1998, *VKS RF*, 1999, no. 1, 35–40.

144-O of November 26, 1998, *VKS RF*, 1999, no. 2, 2–8 (Kononov, dissenting).

26-P of November 17, 1998, *VKS RF*, 1999, no. 1, 48–67 (Vedernikov, dissenting).

28-P of December 11, 1998, *SZ RF*, 1998, no. 52, item 6447 (Luchin, Oleinik, and Vitruk, dissenting).

201-O of December 3, 1998, *VKS RF*, 1999, no. 3, 2–4.

167-O of December 25, 1998, *VKS RF*, 1999, no. 2, 40–47.

-1999-

11-O of January 26, 1999, *VKS RF*, 1999, no. 2, 62–63.

2-P of January 27, 1999, *VKS RF*, 1999, no. 3, 5–11.

3-P of February 2, 1999, *VKS RF*, 1999, no. 3, 12–24.

4-P of February 23, 1999, *VKS RF*, 1999, no. 3, 49–56.

Court Decisions

18-O of February 4, 1999, *VKS RF*, 1999, no. 3, 38–48 (Kononov, dissenting).

19-O of March 4, 1999, *SZ RF*, 1999, no. 15, item 1928.

7-P of April 20, 1999, *VKS RF*, 1999, no. 4, 41–49.

8-P of May 14, 1999, *VKS RF*, 1999, no. 4, 50–61.

9-P of May 28, 1999, *VKS RF*, 1999, no. 5, 2–13 (Vitruk, dissenting).

97-O of July 1, 1999, *VKS RF*, 1999, no. 5, 37–39.

98-O of July 1, 1999, unpublished, available at http://www.ksrf.ru.

11-P of July 15, 1999, *VKS RF*, 1999, no. 5, 48–56.

12-P of July 20, 1999, *VKS RF*, 1999, no. 5, 57–80.

14-P of October 28, 1999, *VKS RF*, 1999, no. 6, 8–15.

16-P of November 23, 1999, *VKS RF*, 1999, no. 6, 21–36 (Zharkova, dissenting).

17-P of December 1, 1999, *SZ RF*, 1999, no. 51, item 6364 (Luchin, dissenting).

209-O of December 9, 1999, *VKS RF*, 2000, no. 2, 41–43.

18-P of December 23, 1999, *VKS RF*, 2000, no. 1, 2–24.

-2000-

6-O of January 13, 2000, *VKS RF*, 2000, no. 2, 44–48.

10-O of January 13, 2000, *Konstitutsionnyi Sud Rossiiskoi Federatsii: Postanovleniia. Opredeleniia. 2000*, ed., Tamara Morshchakova, 206.

1-P of January 14, 2000, *VKS RF*, 2000, no. 2, 49–64 (Ebzeev and Vitruk, dissenting).

9-O of February 3, 2000, *VKS RF*, 2000, no. 3, 57–59.

41-O of February 3, 2000, *VKS RF*, 2000, no. 3, 60–64.

2-P of February 14, 2000, *VKS RF*, 2000, no. 3, 9–12.

3-P of February 18, 2000, *VKS RF*, 2000, no. 3, 13–20.

4-P of March 23, 2000, *VKS RF*, 2000, no. 3, 21–28.

6-P of April 10, 2000, *VKS RF*, 2000, no. 4, 15–29 (Zhilin, dissenting).

43-O of April 13, 2000, in *Konstitutsionnyi Sud Rossiiskoi Federatsii: Postanovleniia. Opredeleniia. 2000*, ed., Tamara Morshchakova, 262.

46-O of April 13, 2000, *VKS RF*, 2000, no. 4, 58–64.

103-O of April 18, 2000, *VKS RF*, 2000, no. 6, 13–17.

7-P of April 25, 2000, *VKS RF*, 2000, no. 4, 30–37.

101-O of May 4, 2000, *VKS RF*, 2000, no. 6, 21–25.

8-P of May 16, 2000, *VKS RF*, 2000, no. 4, 38–45.

9-P of June 6, 2000, *VKS RF*, 2000, no. 4, 46–53.

10-P of June 7, 2000, *VKS RF*, 2000, no. 5, 2–45 (Luchin and Vitruk, dissenting).

91-O of June 8, 2000, *VKS RF*, 2000, no. 5, 53–58.

134-O of June 8, 2000, *VKS RF*, 2000, no. 6, 26–29.

147-O of June 23, 2000, *VKS RF*, 2000, no. 6, 33–38.

176-O of June 23, 2000, *Konstitutsionnyi Sud Rossiiskoi Federatsii. Postanovleniia. Opredeleniia. 2000*, ed., Tamara Morshchakova, 375.

11-P of June 27, 2000, *VKS RF*, 2000, no. 5, 46–52.

92-O of June 27, 2000, *VKS RF*, 2000, no. 5, 59–80, and no. 6, 10–12 (Luchin, dissenting).

150-O of July 5, 2000, *VKS RF*, 2000, no. 6, 46–49.

133-O of July 6, 2000, *Konstitutsionnyi Sud Rossiiskoi Federatsii. Postanovleniia. Opredeleniia. 2000*, ed., Tamara Morshchakova, 420.

191-O of July 6, 2000, *VKS RF*, 2001, no. 1, 35–37.

198-O of October 5, 2000, *VKS RF*, 2001, no. 1, 60.

204-O of October 5, 2000, unpublished, available at http://www.ksrf.ru.

13-P of October 24, 2000, *VKS RF*, 2001, no. 1, 3–9.

217-O of October 27, 2000, *VKS RF*, 2001, no. 2, 8–10.

233-O of October 27, 2000, *VKS RF*, 2001, no. 2, 10–13.

244-O of December 14, 2000, *VKS RF*, 2001, no. 2, 50–55.

14-P of November 22, 2000, *VKS RF*, 2001, no. 1, 10–17.

258-O of December 14, 2000, *VKS RF*, 2001, no. 2, 46–49.

239-O of December 15, 2000, *VKS RF*, 2001, no. 2, 56–58.

251-O of December 15, 2000, *Konstitutsionnyi Sud RF. Postanovleniia. Opredeleniia. 2000*, ed., Tamara Morshchakova, 540.

252-O of December 21, 2000, *VKS RF*, 2001, no. 2, 62–65.

290-O of December 21, 2000, *VKS RF*, 2001, no. 2, 74–77.

-2001-

7-O of January 18, 2001, *VKS RF*, 2001, no. 3, 64.

1-P of January 25, 2001, *VKS RF*, 2001, no. 3, 11–22.

14-O of February 8, 2001, *Konstitutsionnyi Sud Rossiiskoi Federatsii. Postanovleniia. Opredeleniia. 2001*, ed., Tamara Morshchakova, 239–242.

33-O of February 8, 2001, *VKS RF*, 2001, no. 3, 70–78 (Khokhriakova and Zhilin, dissenting).

67-O of March 1, 2001, *VKS RF*, 2001, no. 4, 36–39.

4-P of March 12, 2001, *VKS RF*, 2001, no. 5, 2–19.

65-O of April 19, 2001, *Rossiiskaia gazeta*, May 16, 2001, 10.

70-O of April 19, 2001, *VKS RF*, 2001, no. 4, 63–65.

6-P of April 25, 2001, *VKS RF*, 2001, no. 5, 31–45 (Kononov, dissenting).

7-P of April 27, 2001, *VKS RF*, 2001, no. 5, 46–67 (Kononov, dissenting).

9-P of June 25, 2001, *VKS RF*, 2001, no. 6, 6–21.

10-P of July 3, 2001, *VKS RF*, 2001, no. 6, 15–27 (Ebzeev, dissenting).

11-P of July 5, 2001, *VKS RF*, 2001, no. 6, 28–41.

130-O of July 5, 2001, *VKS RF*, 2002, no. 1, 64–69.

138-O of July 25, 2001, *VKS RF*, 2002, no. 2, 27–30.

182-O of October 4, 2001, *VKS RF*, 2002, no. 2, 30–32.

260-O of November 13, 2001, *SZ RF*, 2002, no. 7, item 741.

229-O of November 20, 2001, unpublished, available at http://www.ksrf.ru.

15-P of November 22, 2001, *VKS RF*, 2002, no. 1, 12–23 (Kononov and Vitruk, dissenting).

228-O of December 6, 2001, *VKS RF*, 2002, no. 2, 71–76.

249-O of December 6, 2001, *SZ RF*, 2002, no. 4, item 374.

250-O of December 6, 2001, unpublished, available at http://www.ksrf.ru.

255-O of December 6, 2001, *VKS RF*, 2002, no. 2, 80–83.

297-O of December 6, 2001, *VKS RF*, 2002, no. 2, 77–80.

Court Decisions

310-O of December 6, 2001, *VKS RF*, 2002, no. 3, 85–89.
216-O of December 7, 2001, *VKS RF*, 2002, no. 2, 87–89.
16-P of December 13, 2001, *VKS RF*, 2002, no. 2, 3–9.
17-P of December 25, 2001, *VKS RF*, 2002, no. 2, 10–16.

-*2002*-

3-O of January 10, 2002, *VKS RF*, 2002, no. 4, 4–13.
1-P of January 15, 2002, *VKS RF*, 2002, no. 3, 3–13 (Bondar, dissenting).
2-P of January 22, 2002, *VKS RF*, 2002, no. 3, 14–23.
3-P of January 24, 2002, *VKS RF*, 2002, no. 3, 24–31.
7-O of February 7, 2002, *VKS RF*, 2002, no. 4, 28–34.
5-P of February 19, 2002, *VKS RF*, 2002, no. 3, 40–51.
48-O of February 20, 2002, *VKS RF*, 2002, no. 4, 67–70.
26-O of February 21, 2002, *VKS RF*, 2002, no. 4, 70–73.
6-P of March 14, 2002, *VKS RF*, 2002, no. 3, 51–56.
7-P of April 2, 2002, *VKS RF*, 2002, no. 3, 57–71 (Vitruk, dissenting).
8-P of April 4, 2002, *VKS RF*, 2002, no. 5, 3–37 (Gadzhiev, Iaroslavtsev, Morshchakova, and Vitruk, dissenting).
105-O of April 10, 2002, *VKS RF*, 2002, no. 6, 64–66.
88-O of May 14, 2002, *VKS RF*, 2002, no. 6, 75–80.
94-O of May 14, 2002, *VKS RF*, 2002, no. 6, 81–88.
112-O of May 14, 2002, unpublished, available at http://www.ksrf.ru.
115-O of June 6, 2002, *VKS RF*, 2003, no. 1, 61–67.
133-O of June 6, 2002, unpublished, available at http://www.ksrf.ru.
10-P of June 11, 2002, *VKS RF*, 2002, no. 5, 51–63.
11-P of June 19, 2002, *VKS RF*, 2002, no. 5, 69–84 (Vitruk, dissenting).
200-O of July 4, 2002, *VKS RF*, 2003, no. 1, 77–81.
12-P of July 9, 2002, *VKS RF*, 2002, no. 6, 3–15.
13-P of July 17, 2002, *SZ RF*, 2002, no. 31, item 3160.
14-P of July 22, 2002, *VKS RF*, 2002, no. 6, 29–41; and *VKS RF*, 2003, no. 1, 3–6 (Iaroslavtsev, dissenting).
228-O of October 1, 2002, *VKS RF*, 2003, no. 2, 3–6.
258-O of October 10, 2002, *VKS RF*, 2003, no. 2, 13–16.
15-P of November 21, 2002, *VKS RF*, 2003, no. 1, 7–12.
283-O of December 10, 2002, *VKS RF*, 2003, no. 2, 57–66.
284-O of December 10, 2002, *VKS RF*, 2003, no. 2, 66–79; and no. 3, 68–71 (Gadzhiev, dissenting).
293-O of November 10, 2002, *VKS RF*, 2003, no. 2, 38–41.
314-O of November 10, 2002, *VKS RF*, 2003, no. 2, 45–48.

-*2003*-

30-O of February 6, 2003, unpublished, available at http://www.ksrf.ru.
1-P of February 27, 2003, *VKS RF*, 2003, no. 3, 3–9.
2-P of March 4, 2003, *SZ RF*, 2003, no. 12, item 1176.
103-O of March 6, 2003, *VKS RF*, 2003, no. 4, 81–85.

350

3-P of March 19, 2003, *VKS RF*, 2003, no. 3, 17–40 (Vitruk and Kononov, dissenting).

4-P of April 1, 2003, *VKS RF*, 2003, no. 3, 41–53.

132-O of April 9, 2003, *VKS RF*, 2003, no. 5, 65–68.

5-P of April 10, 2003, *VKS RF*, 2003, no. 3, 48–53.

6-P of April 21, 2003, *VKS RF*, 2003, no. 3, 54–61.

7-P of April 24, 2003, *VKS RF*, 2003, no. 4, 3–11.

8-P of May 14, 2003, *VKS RF*, 2003, no. 4, 12–23 (Kononov, dissenting).

10-P of June 11, 2003, *VKS RF*, 2003, no. 4, 30–51 (Iaroslavtsev and Luchin, dissenting).

270-O of July 10, 2003, *VKS RF*, 2003, no. 5, 91–93.

282-O of July 10, 2003, *VKS RF*, 2003, no. 6, 76–78.

13-P of July 18, 2003, *VKS RF*, 2003, no. 5, 15–29.

272-O of September 26, 2003, unpublished, available at http://www.ksrf.ru.

347-O of October 2, 2003, unpublished, available at http://www.ksrf.ru.

318-O of October 16, 2003, unpublished, available at http://www.ksrf.ru.

329-O of October 16, 2003, unpublished, available at http://www.ksrf.ru.

387-O of November 6, 2003, *VKS RF*, 2004, no. 1, 95–99.

15-P of October 30, 2003, *VKS RF*, 2003, no. 6, 3–30 (Gadzhiev, Iaroslavtsev and Kononov, dissenting).

16-P of November 11, 2003, *VKS RF*, 2003, no. 6, 31–45.

17-P of November 12, 2003, *VKS RF*, 2003, no. 6, 46–53.

428-O of December 4, 2003, *VKS RF*, 2004, no. 3, 20–23.

19-P of December 15, 2003, *VKS RF*, 2004, no. 1, 26–37.

-2004-

1-P of January 27, 2004, *VKS RF*, 2004, no. 2, 3–21 (Kononov, dissenting).

2-P of January 29, 2004, *VKS RF*, 2004, no. 2, 22–31.

103-O of February 19, 2004, unpublished, available at http://www.ksrf.ru.

4-P of February 25, 2004, *VKS RF*, 2004, no. 2, 47–56.

138-O of March 4, 2004, *VKS RF*, 2004, no. 5, 81–85.

7-P of April 6, 2004, *VKS RF*, 2004, no. 4, 3–18 (Bondar and Kononov, dissenting).

132-O of April 9, 2003, *VKS RF*, 2003, no. 5, 65.

9-P of April 23, 2004, *VKS RF*, 2004, no. 4, 30–49 (Bondar, concurring).

10-P of May 13, 2004, *VKS RF*, 2004, no. 4, 50–60.

210-O of May 27, 2004, *VKS RF*, 2004, no.6, 83–85.

12-P of June 17, 2004, *VKS RF*, 2004, no. 4, 74–91 (Gadzhiev, concurring).

303-O of July 8, 2004, *VKS RF*, 2005, no. 1, 112–115.

-2005-

36-O of January 18, 2005, *VKS RF*, 2005, no. 3, 108–112.

17-O of February 15, 2005, *VKS RF*, 2005, no. 5, 13–25 (Gadzhiev, concurring).

58-O of February 15, 2005, unpublished, available at http://www.ksrf.ru.

224-O of June 9, 2005, unpublished, available at http://www.ksrf.ru.

246-O of July 5, 2005, *VKS RF*, 2005, no. 6, 104–108.

8-P of July 14, 2005, *VKS RF*, 2005, no. 4, 46–66 (Bondar, dissenting).

9-P of July 14, 2005, *VKS RF*, 2005, no. 4, 67–102 (Gadzhiev, Iaroslavtsev, and Kononov, dissenting).

351-O of October 20, 2005, unpublished, available at http://www.ksrf.ru.

366-O of November 8, 2005, *VKS RF*, 2006, no. 2, 31–33.

10-P of November 14, 2005, *VKS RF*, 2006, no. 1, 3–24 (Bondar, Gadzhiev, Krasavchikova, and Mavrin, dissenting).

365-O of December 1, 2005, *SZ RF*, 2006, no. 5, item 634.

462-O of December 1, 2005, *VKS RF*, 2006, no. 2, 74–82, and no. 3, 125–128 (Kononov, dissenting).

13-P of December 21, 2005, *VKS RF*, 2006, no. 1, 49–75 (Kononov and Iaroslavtsev, dissenting).

-2006-

2-P of February 28, 2006, *VKS RF*, 2006, no. 3, 15–36 (Kleandrov, dissenting).

16-O of March 2, 2006, *VKS RF*, 2006, no. 3, 112–117.

187-O of May 11, 2006, *VKS RF*, 2006, no. 5, 22–28.

5-P of May 15, 2006, *VKS RF*, 2006, no. 3, 68–81.

8-P of June 30, 2006, *VKS RF*, 2006, no. 4, 24–34.

137-O of July 17, 2006, *VKS RF*, 2006, no. 5 (Bondar, Ebzeev, and Kononov, dissenting).

485-O of October 17, 2006, unpublished, available at http://www.ksrf.ru.

540-O of November 2, 2006, *VKS RF*, 2007, no. 2, 80–88.

9-P of November 26, 2006, *VKS RF*, 2007, no. 1, 26–47 (Bondar and Gadzhiev, concurring, and Kononov, dissenting).

542-O of December 7, 2006, *VKS RF*, 2007, no. 2, 123–128.

-2007-

3-P of March 21, 2007, *Rossiiskaia gazeta*, March 30, 2007 (Kazantsev, dissenting).

6-P of May 16, 2007, *VKS RF*, 2007, no. 3, 62–77 (Kazantsev, dissenting).

9-P of July 10, 2007, *VKS RF*, 2007, no. 4, 23–37 (Gadzhiev, dissenting).

Index

Accommodation approach to federalism, 109–110, 197–198, 200
Accountability, lack of, 39–40, 300
Ackerman, Bruce, 295, 296
Adenauer, Konrad, 116
Administrative acts, judicial review of, 113–114
Adygei, 226
Age discrimination cases
  First RCC and
    damages, 203–204
    judicial review,
    Russian constitution, under, 112
  judges, retirement age for (*See* Tenure of judges)
Akaev, Askar, 262
Albania, constitutional court in, 2, 259
Alcohol license fees, 211–212
Alekseev, Sergei, 60, 95, 98–99
All-Russian Center for the Study of Public Opinion, 248
All-Russian Congress of Judges, 133, 212
Ambiguity, constitutional rights and, 177–178
Ametistov, Ernest
  Constitutional Convention of 1993, role at, 73, 74
  impeachment of Yeltsin, on, 108
  individuals, on petitions by, 114
  retirement age cases, on, 203
Amnesty, suits against acts of, 159–160
Argentina
  nonlinear judicial empowerment in, 24
  tenure of judges in, 264

Armenia
  constitutional court in, 263
  CSC and, 96
Arrest power
  Russian constitution, under, 213
  Second RCC and, 133–134, 213–214
Audit Chamber, 131–132
Australia, federalism in, 142
Austria, constitutional court in, 28
Azerbaijan
  constitutional court in, 261
  CSC and, 96

Baglai, Marat
  appointment of, 118
  chair of Second RCC, as, 119
  Chechnya, on, 119
  constitutional rights, on, 158
  mass media, on, 252–253
  presidential decrees, on, 222
  social justice, on, 181
  Tatarstan referendum, on, 197
  tenure of judges and, 86
Bakiev, Kurmanbek, 262
Bankruptcy, Second RCC and, 169
Bashkortostan, 168, 196, 206, 219, 224, 225–227
Belarus, constitutional court in, 2, 23, 271
Breyer, Stephen, 8, 36
Brozova, Iva, 281
Bulgaria
  constitutional court in, 1, 2, 40
  judicial review in, 190
  "War of the Courts" in, 268

353

354   *Index*

Cabinet
  alcohol license fees, 211–212
  Stalinist purges, and victims of, 241,
    242–243
  taxation and, 154
Canada
  federalism in, 142, 287
  impact of jurisprudence, 176
  judicial review in, 50
Capital punishment, Second RCC and, 163
Central Elections Commission, 137–138,
  171, 172
Chavez, Rebecca, 24, 285
Chechnya
  public opinion regarding, 197
  Second RCC and
    federalism, 142, 144, 221
    mass media, in, 252
    separation of powers, 128–129
  short-term policy making and, 8
Chelyabinsk, 198–199
Chernobyl, 178–179, 240
Chernomyrdin, Viktor, 212, 221
Civil Procedure Code, 153
Civil rights, CSC and, 97–98
Coexistence of courts, 283–284
Collective complaints, 161
Communist Party
  First RCC and
    ban of party, case regarding, 103,
      106–107, 192–193
    opposition to, 66–68
    support for, 64
  referendum process and, 137–138, 172
  Second RCC, support for, 80
Communist Russia. *See* Soviet Union
Comparison of Russian courts, 10–11
Compliance
  capacity of state machinery, 41
  CSC, with (*See* Constitutional
    Supervision Committee (CSC))
  decision making, effect on, 23, 33
  design, effect on, 22–23
  executive decree, and rule by, 36–37
  First RCC, with (*See* First Russian
    Constitutional Court)
  institutional uncertainty, impact of, 189
  judicial appointments and, 223–225
  judicial empowerment and problems in,
    8
  overview, 188

presidential decrees, importance of,
  222–223
problems in, 33–34
prosecutors, problems with, 232
routine obedience, ensuring, 36–37
Second RCC, with (*See* Second Russian
  Constitutional Court)
short-term policy making and, 301
strategic approach, under, 49–50
strategies for success, 188–189
threat to vital interests, impact of, 34–35
trial procedures, problems with, 232–233
unpopular decisions, 34–35
values of ruling authorities, impact of, 34
Conference of European Constitutional
  Courts, 229
Conflict of laws, 136
Congress of People's Deputies
  dissolution by Yeltsin, 74–75, 108
  First RCC and
    opposition to, 66–68
    role in establishing, 61–62
    separation of powers, 106
  referendum regarding, 193–195
Constitutional/charter courts, 218–219
Constitutional Commission, 61–62, 63–64
Constitutional Convention of 1993
  appointments to RCC at, 75–77
  compromise at, 79
  convening of, 73–74, 193–195
  expansion of judicial review at, 78–79
  jurisdiction of RCC at, 77
  limits on authority of RCC at, 75, 77–78
  new draft by Yeltsin, 73
  preservation of RCC at, 75–77
  tenure of judges, changes in, 75
  threats to authority of RCC at, 73–74
Constitutional courts. *See also specific state*
  authoritarian states, in, 2
  comparison of Russian courts, 10–11
  Constitutional Supervision Committee
    (*See* Constitutional Supervision
    Committee (CSC))
  First Russian Constitutional Court (*See*
    First Russian Constitutional
    Court)
  hybrid states, in, 2
  international context, 12–13
  judicial pluralism (*See* "War of the
    Courts")
  legal *versus* ethical authority, 35–36

Index

355

nondemocratic states, in, 2
other states, Russian courts compared
    with courts in, 12–13
overview, 1–2
purposes of, 19
scholarly debate regarding Russian
    experience, 12
Second Russian Constitutional Court
    (*See* Second Russian
    Constitutional Court)
tables, 3
toleration by authoritarian rulers, 6
uniqueness of Russian experience, 10,
    296
"War of the Courts" (*See* "War of the
    Courts")
Constitutional review. *See* Judicial review
Constitutional rights. *See also specific right*
ambiguity and, 177–178
CSC, compliance with, 190
fairness and (*See* Second Russian
    Constitutional Court)
First RCC and (*See* First Russian
    Constitutional Court)
proportional restrictions on (*See* Second
    Russian Constitutional Court)
Second RCC and (*See* Second Russian
    Constitutional Court)
vagueness and, 177–178
"War of the Courts," effect of, 284
Constitutional Supervision Committee
    (CSC)
civil rights cases in, 97–98
compliance with
    constitutional rights, in, 190
    First RCC compared, 191
    judicial heteronomy theory, 190–191
    lessons from failure of, 191
    poor performance, 190–191
    republics, resistance from, 189–190
consumer rights cases in, 97
decision making by, 95–99
dissolution, 61
establishment of, 58
extrajudicial behavior of, 98–99
First RCC compared
    compliance, 191
    decision making, 99–100
    extrajudicial behavior, 98–99
    statutory authorization, 64–66
    strength of, 63–64

Gorbachev and, 58
judicial review, weakness of, 59, 95–96
labor cases in, 97
legal elites in, 59–61
political weakness of, 99
Procuracy and, 68
propiska and, 97–98
proposals for, 57
purposes of, 58
radical political change, impact of, 58–59
republics and, 58–59, 95–97
residence permits and, 97–98
Soviet Union, effect of weakness of, 61
strategic behavior of, 98
wrongful dismissal cases in, 97
Consumer rights, CSC and, 97
Contract rights, Second RCC and, 166–168
Council of Europe, 43, 44, 228
Coup of August 1991, 60–61
Court design. *See* Design
Criminal procedure
arrest power
    Russian constitution, under, 213
    Second RCC and, 133–134, 213–214
First RCC and, 111–112
judges, complaints for damages against,
    233–234
prosecutors, compliance problems, 232
search and seizure, Second RCC and,
    133–134
sentencing, fairness in, 180–181
separation of powers, Second RCC and,
    133–134, 213–214
siloviki, power of, 234–235
trial procedures, compliance problems,
    232–233
Criminal Procedure Code, 204, 213–214,
    230–232
Croatia, constitutional court in, 176
CSC. *See* Constitutional Supervision
    Committee (CSC)
Customs officials, confiscation of property
    by, 239–240
Czechoslovakia, constitutional court in,
    28, 190
Czech Republic
constitutional court in, 40
"War of the Courts" in
    assumption of jurisdiction by
        constitutional court, 270,
        276–277

356   *Index*

Czech Republic (*cont.*)
  criticism of constitutional court, 277
  judicial appointments and, 281–282
  lack of referrals to constitutional
    court, 277–278
  legalistic explanation, 268
  military service cases, 278–280
  noncompliance with constitutional
    court, 277
  overview, 51, 52, 220
  progressive/reactionary explanation,
    268, 269
  purge of Communists and, 276
  resolution of, 281
  timeline, 279

Dagestan, 144, 158, 226
Decision making
  authoritativeness of, 37–38
  compliance, effect on, 23
  CSC, in, 95–99. (*See also* Constitutional
    Supervision Committee (CSC))
  design, effect on, 21–22
  discretion in, 31
  extrajudicial behavior
    CSC, of, 98–99
    First RCC, of, 115
    politics and, 31–32
  First RCC, in (*See* First Russian
    Constitutional Court)
  institutional uncertainty, impact of,
    40–41
  overview, 93–94
  political context, 30–31
  Second RCC, in (*See* Second Russian
    Constitutional Court)
  short-term policy making and, 301
Delegation of power, 47–49
Democratization and nonlinear judicial
  empowerment, 52
Design
  compliance, effect on, 21
  Constitutional Convention of 1993 (*See*
    Constitutional Convention of
    1993)
  CSC, of (*See* Constitutional Supervision
    Committee (CSC))
  decision making, effect on, 21
  difficulties in, 90–91
  First RCC, of (*See* First Russian
    Constitutional Court)

legal elites, significance of, 286
overview, 54–55
rule of law, effect on, 21
Russian Constitutional Court Act of
  1994 (*See* Russian Constitutional
  Court act of 1994)
Second RCC, of (*See* Second Russian
  Constitutional Court)
short-term policy making and, 54–55,
  91–92, 301
Disability payments, Second RCC and,
  178–179
Discretion in decision making, 31
Duma. *See* State Duma
Dynamic analysis of judicial
  empowerment, 19–21

Ebzeev, Boris
  chair of First RCC, on, 100
  Constitutional Convention of 1993, role
    at, 73, 74
  constitutional rights, on, 163
  European Court of Human Rights, on,
    176
  federalism, on, 109
  regional law making, on, 151
Economic rights, Second RCC and, 178
Egypt
  constitutional court in, 261
  judicial independence in, 33
  nonlinear judicial empowerment in, 24
Elections
  electoral rights, 244
  gerrymandering, 244
  local officials, of, 149–150, 152–153,
    155–156
  proportional restrictions on rights
    campaigning, 172–173
    dispute resolution, 171–172
    mass media and, 172–173
    referendum process, 172
    State Duma, 170–171
  referendum process
    Communist Party and, 137–138, 172
    Congress of People's Deputies,
      regarding, 193–195
    Tatarstan referendum, 109, 195–197
Employment Act, 182
Enforcement of decisions. *See* Compliance
Epp, Charles R., 292
Epstein, Lee, 11

Index

Ersson, Svante, 42
Estonia, constitutional court in, 2
European Convention on Human Rights, 163, 174–176, 233, 278
European Court of Human Rights
  appeals to, 162
  avoidance of, 234
  effect of litigation on reputation of Russia, 187
  encouragement of human rights, 158
  increase in petitions to, 291
  Putin on, 229
  Romania in, 272
  Second RCC and
    citation of decisions by, 174–176
    study of decisions by, 228
  speedy trial requirements, 125
  "War of the Courts" and, 275–276, 293
European Union, 43
Extension of terms of judges, 261, 262–264
Extrajudicial behavior
  CSC, of, 98–99
  First RCC, of, 115
  politics and, 31–32

Fairness. *See* Second Russian Constitutional Court
Federal Budget Code, 154
Federalism. *See also* Regions (Russia)
  First RCC and (*See* First Russian Constitutional Court)
  fiscal federalism
    First RCC and, 199–200
    Second RCC and, 145–146, 154–155
  historical context of, 139–140
  local self-government, 155–156, 244–245
  matryoshka federalism, 140
  Russian constitution and, 140
  Second RCC and (*See* Second Russian Constitutional Court)
  symmetrical federalism, 221
  "War of the Courts" and, 293–294
Federal Migration Service, 246
Federation Council
  composition of, 210
  relocation of Second RCC, resistance to Putin proposals regarding, 89–90
  retirement and tenure of judges, resistance to Putin proposals regarding, 86
  Second RCC and

  appointments to, 81, 82–85
  conflict with, 209
  separation of powers and, 209
  State Duma, disputes with, 130–131
  taxation and, 154
Federation Treaty, 109
Feeley, Malcolm, 141
Filatov, Sergei, 76
First Russian Constitutional Court. *See also specific justice*
  administrative acts, judicial review of, 113–114
  age discrimination cases
    damages, 203–204
    judicial review,
    Russian constitution, under, 112
  appointments to
    Constitutional Convention of 1993, at, 75–77
    initial appointments, 69–71
    Yeltsin, by, 69–70, 75–77
  authority of, 66
  avoidance of political cases, 103–104
  caseload, 103
  Communist Party, case regarding ban of, 103, 106–107, 192–193
  compliance with
    constitutional rights, 200–205
    cost–benefit analysis, 195
    CSC compared, 191
    federalism, 195–200
    obstacles to, 202, 205
    overview, 205–206, 290
    political willingness, importance of, 200
    selective political reaction, 195
    separation of powers, 191–195
    strategies for success, 290
  Constitutional Convention of 1993 (*See* Constitutional Convention of 1993)
  constitutional rights and
    compliance, 200–205
    decision making, 111–115
    monetary obligations of government to individuals, 200–202
    Second RCC compared, 158
  criminal procedure and, 111–112
  CSC compared
    compliance, 191
    decision making, 99–100

358   *Index*

First Russian Constitutional Court (*cont.*)
   extrajudicial behavior, 98–99
   statutory authorization, 64–66
   strength of, 63–64
  decision making by
   constitutional rights and, 111–115
   CSC compared, 99–100
   federalism and, 109–111
   Second RCC compared, 185
   separation of powers and, 104–109
  difficulties in establishing, 90–91
  dissenting opinions, 104
  dissolution of Soviet Union and, 103
  extrajudicial behavior of, 115
  federalism and
   accommodation approach, 109–110,
    197–198, 200
   Chelyabinsk case, 198–199
   compliance, 195–200
   decision making, 109–111
   fiscal federalism, 199–200
   Irkutsk case, 110, 199–200, 206
   joint jurisdiction issues, 110
   Kabardino-Balkaria case, 110, 223
   Mordovia case, 198
   Moscow privatization case, 199
   overview, 110–111
   Second RCC compared, 227–228
   subfederal units, 109
   Tatarstan referendum, 109, 195–197
  impeachment and
   power of, 78
   Yeltsin, of, 108, 193–195
  individuals, petitions by, 111, 113, 114
  innovation in, 92
  judicial activism in, 92, 100
  judicial review in
   limitations on, 200
   strength of, 100, 105
   struggle for, 115
  jurisdiction, 77
  labor law cases, 112–114
  law-application practice and, 68–69, 111,
   137, 202–203
  legal elites and, 286
  legitimacy of, 64
  limits on authority of, 75, 77–78
  lobbying by, 101
  nonbinding decisions by, 101
  opposition to
   Communist Party, from, 66–68

   Congress of People's Deputies, from,
    66–68
   law enforcement, from, 68–69
   Procuracy, from, 68–69
  other states compared, 72, 115–116
  overestimation of power, 287–288
  political fragmentation and, 116–117
  political struggles regarding, 72
  politicization of, 115–116
  president and, 63–64
  press, relationship with, 101
  privatization and, 103
  proactive nature of, 99–100
  proposals for, 62–63
  publication of decisions, 101–102
  Referendum of 1991 and, 66
  retirement age cases
   damages, 203–204
   judicial review, Russian constitution,
    under, 112
  Russian constitution and, 61–62, 71–72
  Russian sovereignty and, 63–64
  Russian Supreme Court, conflict with
   age discrimination cases, 203–204
   constitutional rights, over, 114–115
   labor law cases, in, 112–114
   reasons for, 204–205
   retirement age cases, 203–204
   wrongful dismissal cases, 202–203
  Second RCC compared
   constitutional rights, 158
   decision making, 185
   federalism, 227–228
   separation of powers, 138–139
  separation of powers and
   Communist Party, case regarding ban
    of, 106–107, 192–193
   compliance, 191–195
   Congress of People's Deputies,
    authority of, 106
   decision making, 104–109
   impeachment of Yeltsin, 108
   implied powers of president, 108–109
   intraexecutive disputes, 106
   intralegislative disputes, 106
   joint executive–legislative decrees,
    105–106
   overview, 104–105
   Second RCC compared, 138–139
   special governance regime, 107–108,
    193–195

short-term policy making and, 91–92
statutory authorization, difficulties in,
    64–66
suspension of, 1, 74–75, 108–109,
    193–195
tenure of judges, changes in, 75
threats to authority of, 73–74
timelines, 65
wrongful dismissal cases
    compensation, 202–203
    damages, 113
    judicial review, 112–113
Fiscal federalism
    First RCC and, 199–200
    Second RCC and, 145–146, 154–155
Fradkov, Mikhail, 151
France
    constitutional court in
        First RCC compared, 72
        impact of jurisprudence, 176
        judicial review, 186
    judicial review in, 26
    legal elites in, 27
Fundamental rights. *See* Constitutional
    rights

Gadzhiev, Gadis
    constitutional rights, on, 174
    economic rights, on, 178
    federalism, on, 142, 156, 247
    problems in compliance, on, 49
    separation of powers, on, 128
    taxation cases, on, 183, 237
Ganev, Venelin, 190
Garlicki, Lech, 276
General Procurator, 153–154
Georgia
    constitutional court in, 2, 22
    "War of the Courts" in, 267
Germany
    constitutional court in
        caseload, 159
        constitutional rights and, 288
        dissenting opinions, 121–122
        establishment of, 28
        financial independence of, 22
        hierarchy of rights, 186
        impact of jurisprudence, 176
        individuals, petitions by, 126
        interpretative decisions, 122
        intrajudicial disputes, 134

politicization of, 116
politics and, 31
public support for, 50
sessions and chambers, 122
judicial review in, 26
legal elites in, 27
nonlinear judicial empowerment in,
    24
Russian Constitutional Court Act of
    1994 compared, 79
"War of the Courts" in, 270
Gerrymandering, 244
Ginsburg, Tom, 294
Gorbachev, Mikhail
    Coup of August 1991 and, 60–61
    CSC and, 58
    dissolution of Soviet Union, on, 98
    joint police/military patrols, on, 96
    judicial review and, 56–58
    legal elites and, 26–27
    mass meetings and demonstrations, on,
    95
    retirement age, on, 112
    rule of law and, 286
Govorin, Boris, 200
Gusliannikov, Vasilii, 198

Higher *Arbitrazh* Court
    financial independence of, 212
    guiding explanations, 215
    reopening of cases, 214–215
    Second RCC, conflict with
        continuing problems, 290
        guiding explanations, 215
        regional law making, 216
        reopening of cases, 214–215
        statutory interpretation, 134–135
        taxpayer rights and, 235, 236, 237
Hirschl, Ran, 295, 297
Hobbes, Thomas, 29
Human rights law
    judicial review, impact on, 295–296
    Second RCC, impact on, 174–176
Human Rights Ombudsman, 78, 246
Hungary
    constitutional court in, 1, 40, 51,
        116
    extension of terms of judges, 263–264
    judicial independence in, 33
    judicial review in, 202
    "War of the Courts" in, 271

Impeachment
 First RCC, powers of, 78
 Yeltsin, of, 1, 103, 108, 193–195
 Zorkin, of, 206
Implementation of decisions. *See*
  Compliance
Individual rights. *See* Constitutional rights
Ingushetia, 110, 224–225
Institutional conflict as strengthening
  courts, 45–47
Institutionalist approach
 judicial empowerment, to, 5, 45–46
 judicial review, to, 296–297
International Covenant on Civil and
  Political Rights, 174, 204
International Covenant on Economic,
  Social and Cultural Rights, 174
International Labor Organization, 112
International pressure
 judicial review, impact on, 295–296
 nonlinear judicial empowerment, effect
  on, 43–44
 Second RCC, impact on, 228–229,
  286–287
Interpretative decisions, 122–123
Irkutsk, 110, 199–200, 206
Israel
 constitutional court in, 263
 judicial review in, 50
Italy
 constitutional court in, 36, 122, 176
 overstaying of terms of judges, 259
 "War of the Courts" in, 51, 269, 270,
  274, 302

Judicial activism
 First RCC, in, 92, 100
 Second RCC, in, 92, 122–125
Judicial behavior. *See* Decision making
Judicial empowerment
 compliance (*See* Compliance)
 decision making (*See* Decision making)
 democratization and, 4–5, 6
 design (*See* Design)
 domestic context, 5
 dynamic analysis, 19–21
 effectiveness of, 8–9
 failures of, 11–12
 feedback in, 19–21
 institutionalist approach to, 5, 45–46,
  296–297
 institutional uncertainty, impact of, 9

international context, 4–5
judicial independence compared, 32
"juristocracy" and, 302
linear analysis, 19
nonlinear judicial empowerment (*See*
  Nonlinear judicial empowerment)
overview, 2–4, 9–10
political context, 41–42
political struggles, in context of, 6–7
public support approach to, 5–6, 50–52
questions regarding, 2–4, 285, 300
resistance to, 302
short-term policy making, impact of, 7–8
strategic approach to, 5, 7, 47–50,
  297–299
strategies for survival, 301–302, 303
successes of, 11–12
toleration by authoritarian rulers, 6
Judicial heteronomy theory, 190–191
Judicial independence
 judicial empowerment compared, 32
 Second RCC, public support for, 251–252
 tenure of judges and political
  commitment to, 264–265
 Tsarist Russia, in, 33
 variation in, 32–33
Judicial pluralism. *See* "War of the Courts"
Judicial review
 administrative acts, of, 113–114
 Constitutional Convention of 1993,
  expansion at, 78–79
 CSC, weakness in, 59, 95–96
 democratization and, 6
 dynamic analysis, 19–21
 First RCC, in
  limitations on, 200
  strength of, 100, 105
  struggle for, 115
 Gorbachev and, 56–58
 human rights law, impact of, 295–296
 institutionalist approach to, 296–297
 international pressure, impact of,
  295–296
 legal elites, role of, 25–26
 legitimacy of, 28–30
 monopolizing by constitutional courts,
  272–273
 overview, 28
 perestroyka and, 56–58
 political struggles, arising from, 292
 psychological power of, 28–30
 public support approach to, 299–300

Russian exceptionalism and, 295–296
Second RCC, in
  growth of, 186
  intrajudicial disputes, 137
  limitations on, 120–121
  proportional restrictions on rights,
    development of standard via, 169
  theories of, 219–220
Soviet Union, in, 56
strategic approach to, 297–298, 299, 300
Tsarist Russia, in, 55–56
uniqueness of Russian experience, 10
"Juristocracy," 11–12, 294–295, 302

Kabardino-Balkaria, 110, 223
Kalmykia, 143, 225
Kasianov, Mikhail, 89
Kazakhstan, constitutional court in, 2,
  23
Kazantsev, Sergei, 138, 184
KGB, 105, 192
Khakassia, 143
Khokhriakova, Olga, 181
Khasbulatov, Ruslan, 71, 101, 102–103,
  193–195, 196
Kirienko, Sergei, 212, 235
Klaus, Vaclav, 281
Komi, 223
Kononov, Anatolii
  Communist Party, on ban of, 107
  Constitutional Convention of 1993, role
    at, 74
  constitutional rights, on, 176
  impeachment of Yeltsin, on, 108
  sentencing, on, 181
Korea
  constitutional court in, 159, 166,
    176
  "War of the Courts" in, 51, 220, 302
Krasnodar, 168
Krug, Peter, 166
Kuchma, Leonid, 263
Kyrgyzstan
  constitutional court in, 2, 40, 61
  criminal procedure in, 272
  shortening of terms of judges, 262
  "War of the Courts" in, 267, 270

Labor Code, 203
Labor law
  CSC and, 97
  First RCC, in, 112–114

Labor Ministry, 242
Labor Pensions Act, 184
Land use statutes, 243–244
Lane, Jan-Erik, 42
Latvia
  constitutional court in, 2, 46, 61
  CSC and, 96
  "War of the Courts" in, 215
Law-application practice, 68, 111, 137,
  202–203
Lebed, Alexandr, 221
Legal elites
  CSC, in, 59–61
  design, significance in, 286
  First RCC and, 286
  Gorbachev and, 26–27
  influence of, 26–27
  judicial review, role in rise of, 25–26
  other states compared, 27–28
  rule of law and, 25–26
  Second RCC and, 286
Legislature. See Congress of People's
    Deputies; State Duma
Levitsky, Steven, 255
Linear analysis of judicial empowerment,
  19
Lithuania
  constitutional court in, 1, 2
  CSC and, 96
Local self-government, 155–156,
  244–245
Luchin, Viktor
  Communist Party, on ban of, 103
  dissolution of Soviet Union, on,
    103
  resignation of, 77
  retirement age cases, on, 203
  Second RCC, on, 119
  separation of powers, on, 128
Lukianov, Anatoliy, 96
Luzhkov, Yuri, 199

Mass media, Second RCC and,
  252–253
Matryoshka federalism, 140
Matvienko, Valentina, 88
Mexico, constitutional court in, 8, 31, 34,
  52, 300
Ministry of Internal Affairs, 105, 192
Mitchell, Gregory, 23
Mitiukov, Mikhail, 62, 63, 71
Mizulina, Elena, 231

Index

Moldova
  constitutional court in, 2, 23
  criminal procedure in, 272
Montesquieu, Charles, 273
Mordovia, 198, 206
Moroz, Oleksandr, 263
Morshchakova, Tamara
  compliance, on problems with, 256
  Constitutional Convention of 1993, role
      at, 73, 74
  criminal procedure, on, 158
  impeachment of Yeltsin, on, 108
  individual rights, on, 133
  overstaying of term, 258
  retirement age cases, on, 203
  Second RCC, on, 119
  separation of powers, on, 128
  tenure of judges and, 86
Moscow privatization case, 199
Moustafa, Tamir, 24

Nagorno-Karabakh, 96
National Salvation Front, 107
Nonlinear judicial empowerment
  accountability, and lack of, 39–40
  assumptions regarding, 38–39
  compliance (*See* Compliance)
  decision making (*See* Decision making)
  democratization and, 52
  design (*See* Design)
  feedback in, 19–21
  "good guys" *versus* "bad guys," 44–45
  institutional conflict as strengthening
      courts, 45–47
  international pressure, effect of,
      43–44
  legal elites in
    influence of, 26–27
    judicial review, role in rise of, 25–26
    other states compared, 27–28
  other states compared, 23–24
  overview, 19, 38–39
  prior elites, and commitment to
      democratization and rule of law,
      42–45
  public support approach to
    objection to nonlinear theory, as,
        50–52
    other states, in, 50–52
    problems with, 52
  separation of powers and, 45–46

short-term policy making and, 39–41,
    52–53
Soviet experience, rejection of, 24–25
strategic approach to
  compliance under, 49–50
  delegation of power and, 47–49
  objection to nonlinear theory, as,
      47–50
  strength of constitutional courts under,
      49
  Ulysses metaphor, 47–49
variation in, 52
Normative decrees, 130
North Ossetia, 110

Olshan, Izhak, 263
Orenburg, 244
Orphans Benefits Act, 182
Overstaying of terms of judges, 259–261
Overview, 15–18

Pension cases, Second RCC and, 161, 184
Perestroyka
  judicial review and, 56–58
  retirement age and, 112
Poland, constitutional court in, 2, 22, 261
Pomeranz, William, 139
Portugal
  constitutional court in, 116
  overstaying of terms of judges, 259–261
Positive content decisions, 123–125, 208
Positive law making, 272, 273
President. *See also* Putin, Vladimir; Yeltsin,
    Boris
  compliance, importance of presidential
      decrees to, 222–223
  implied powers of
    First RCC and, 108–109
    Second RCC and, 128–130
  law making power, 211
  Russian constitution, powers under, 128
  separation of powers and, 209
  veto power, 129–130, 211
Prior elites, commitment to
    democratization and rule of law,
    42–45
Privatization, 103
Procuracy
  CSC and, 68
  detention of accused by, 213–214
  establishment of, 56

Index 363

harmonization of laws and, 218–219
opposition to First RCC, 68–69
regional law making and, 217–218
residence permits and, 245
Stalinist purges, and victims of, 242
taxpayer rights and, 236
Procurator General, 78, 213
Property rights, Second RCC and, 166
Propiska
  CSC and, 97–98
  Second RCC and
    compliance, 245–246
    proportional restrictions on rights, 168
Proportional restrictions on rights. *See*
    Second Russian Constitutional
    Court
Prosecutors, compliance problems with,
    232
Przeworski, Adam, 116
Public support approach
  judicial empowerment, to, 5–6
  judicial review, to, 299–300
  nonlinear judicial empowerment, to
    objection to nonlinear theory, as,
      50–52
    other states, in, 50–52
    problems with, 52
Putin, Vladimir
  Criminal Procedure Code, on, 213–214
  dissolution of regional governments and,
    147–148
  electoral rights and, 244
  European Court of Human Rights, on,
    229
  federalism and, 150, 246–247,
    293–294
  Irkutsk case and, 199–200
  judicial appointments by, 225
  local self-government and, 155–156,
    244–245
  monetary obligations of government to
    individuals and, 201–202
  referendum against, 137–138
  Russian Constitutional Court Act of
    1994, amendments to
    binding nature of rulings, regarding,
      87–88
    proposals, 85
    relocation of court, 88–90
    tenure of judges, regarding, 85–87
  siloviki and, 234–235

sovereignty clauses, on, 226
Stalinist purges, and victims of, 240–243
subnational sovereignty and, 146–147
Tatarstan referendum, on, 197

Rakhimov, Murtaza, 227
RCC. *See* First Russian Constitutional
    Court; Second Russian
    Constitutional Court
Referendum process
  Communist Party and, 137–138,
    172
  Congress of People's Deputies, regarding,
  Tatarstan referendum, 109, 195–197
Regions (Russia). *See also* Federalism;
    specific region
  accommodation approach, 109–110
  constitutional/charter courts, 218–219
  dissolution of regional governments,
    147–148
  election of local officials, 149–150,
    152–153, 155–156
  federal preemption of regional law,
    145–146
  fiscal policy, federal control over,
    148–149
  harmonization of laws, 218–219
  joint jurisdiction issues, 110
  judicial appointments, 223–225
  regional law making, 142–143, 151–152,
    153–154, 215–216, 218
  relative strength of, 150–151
  Second RCC, use of, 127
  sovereignty clauses, 225–227
  subfederal units, 109
  subnational sovereignty, 146–147
  Tatarstan referendum, 109
  uniformity in regional governments,
    144–145
  Yelstin, relationship with, 142–143
Religious freedom, Second RCC and,
    178
Remington, Thomas, 129
Republics (Soviet Union), CSC and, 58–59,
    95–97, 189–190
Residence permits
  CSC and, 97–98
  Second RCC and
    compliance, 245–246
    proportional restrictions on rights,
      168

Index

Retirement age cases
  First RCC and
    damages, 203–204
    judicial review,
      Russian constitution, under, 112
    judges, retirement age for (*See* Tenure of
      judges)
Right to counsel, Second RCC and, 163
Romania
  constitutional court in, 2
  "War of the Courts" in, 220, 268,
    271–272
Rubin, Edward, 141
Rudkin, Iurii
  First RCC, role in establishing, 62, 63
  retirement age cases, on, 203
Rule of law
  coexistence of courts and, 283–284
  design, effect of, 21
  fiscal policy and, 169–170
  Gorbachev and, 286
  legal elites and, 25–26
  political struggles, arising from, 2–4
  prior elites, commitment of, 42–45
  public support for, 251–252
  United Kingdom, in, 283
  "War of the Courts" and, 265, 274–275
Rupp, Hans G., 35
Russian Academy of Sciences, 246
Russian Central Bank, 149
Russian constitution
  age discrimination cases under, 203–204
  amendment process, 209–210
  arrest power under, 213
  Constitutional Convention of 1993 (*See*
    Constitutional Convention of
    1993)
  federalism and, 140
  First RCC and, 61–62, 71–72
  presidential powers under, 128
  retirement age cases under, 203–204
  Yeltsin, new draft by, 73
Russian Constitutional Court. *See* First
    Russian Constitutional Court;
    Second Russian Constitutional
    Court
Russian Constitutional Court Act of 1994
  draft of bill, 79–80
  Putin, amendments under
    binding nature of rulings, regarding,
      87–88

    proposals, 85
    relocation of court, 88–90
    tenure of judges, regarding, 85–87
  State Duma, debate in, 80
Russian Council of Judges, 133, 212
Russian exceptionalism, 295–296
Russian Orthodox Church, 178
Russian Supreme Court
  financial independence of, 212
  First RCC, conflict with
    age discrimination cases, 203–204
    constitutional rights, over, 114–115
    labor law cases, in, 112–114
    reasons for, 204–205
    retirement age cases, 203–204
    wrongful dismissal cases, 202–203
  reopening of cases, 214–215
  residence permits, on, 246
  Second RCC, conflict with
    continuing problems, 290
    harmonization of laws, 218–219
    judicial review, 137
    regional law making, 215–216, 217
    reopening of cases, 214–215
    statutory interpretation, 134–135
  taxpayer rights and, 236
  tenure of judges and, 85

Scholarly debate regarding Russian
    experience, 12
Search and seizure, Second RCC and,
    133–134
Second Russian Constitutional Court. *See*
    also specific justice
  alcohol license fees, 211–212
  appointments to
    Federation Council, by, 81, 82–85
    Yeltsin, by, 80–81, 82–85
  binding nature of rulings, amendments
    regarding, 87–88
  capital punishment cases, 163
  caseload, 123, 126–127
  Central Elections Commission, conflict
    with, 137–138
  chambers, 122
  Chechnya and
    federalism, 142, 144, 221
    mass media, in, 252
    separation of powers, 128–129
  Chernobyl and, 178–179
  compliance with

binding nature of rulings, amendments
regarding, 87–88
complaints of justices regarding, 256
constitutional rights, problems with,
229–230, 291
decision making, relationship with, 150
distrust of courts, impact of, 291–292
effective governmental infrastructure,
necessity of, 292
executive branch resistance, 211
federalism, 221–228
financial independence and, 212–214
judicial appointments and, 223–225
monitoring, difficulty in, 208–209
overview, 207–208, 254–255, 290–291
presidential decrees, importance of,
222–223
problems with, 81–82
prosecutors, problems with, 232
reasons for problems with, 255–256
residence permits, 245–246
separation of powers, 209–214
trial procedures, problems with,
232–233
constitutional rights and
access to court, 288
ambiguity and, 177–178
amnesty, suits against acts of, 159–160
binding nature of international laws,
174–176
caseload, 158–159
collective complaints, 161
compliance problems, 229–230, 291
creation of, 288
distrust of courts, impact of, 291–292
effective governmental infrastructure,
necessity of, 292
equality of outcome, 178
expansion of access to court, 160–161
First RCC compared, 158
focus on, 228, 288–289
hidden principles, 173–174, 288
hierarchy of rights, 163–165
human rights law, effect of, 174–176
importance of, 158
institutions, suits against, 159–160
international pressure, impact of,
228–229
jurisprudence from other states, effect
of, 176
legitimate restrictions, 165–166

overview, 185–187
strategic behavior of, 161–163
vagueness and, 177–178
contract rights, 166–168
criminal procedure and
Criminal Procedure Code, 230–232
judges, complaints for damages
against, 233–234
prosecutors, compliance problems,
232
sentencing, fairness in, 180–181
separation of powers, 133–134,
213–214
siloviki, power of, 234–235
trial procedures, compliance problems,
232–233
customs officials, confiscation of
property by, 239–240
decision making by
compliance, relationship with, 150
First RCC compared, 185
overview, 120, 127
difficulties in establishing, 90–91
disability payments and, 178–179
dissenting opinions, 121, 122
distrust of all courts, effect of, 250–251
economic rights and, 178
education of public, need for, 256–257
electoral rights and, 244
European Court of Human Rights and
citation of decisions by, 174–176
study of decisions by, 228
fairness in
deference to political branches,
183–184
legal formalism contrasted, 180
overview, 179–180, 184–185
pension cases, 184
sentencing, in, 180–181
social justice and
balancing individual rights, 181–182
overview, 181
taxation cases, 182–183
vulnerable groups, 182
wage cases, 182–183
federalism and
caseload, 139
Chechnya and, 142, 144, 221
compliance, 221–228
dissolution of regional governments,
147–148

Second Russian Constitutional (*cont.*)
  election of local officials, 149–150,
    152–153, 155–156
  First RCC compared, 227–228
  fiscal federalism, 145–146, 154–155
  growing role of, 156–157
  historical context of, 139–140
  judicial reluctance, 143–144
  Komi, 223
  local self-government, 155–156,
    244–245
  preemption of regional law, 145–146
  presidential decrees, importance of,
    222–223
  regional fiscal policy, federal control
    over, 148–149
  regional law making, 142–143,
    151–152, 153–154, 215–216,
    218
  relationship between decision making
    and compliance, 150
  sovereignty clauses in regional
    constitutions, 225–227
  subnational sovereignty, 146–147
  symmetrical federalism, 221
  taxation cases, 154–155
  Udmurtia case, 144, 149, 221–222
  unification approach, 140–141
  uniformity in regional governments,
    144–145
financial independence of, 82, 133,
  212–214
First RCC compared
  constitutional rights, 158
  decision making, 185
  federalism, 227–228
  separation of powers, 138–139
growth in power of, 294–295
Higher *Arbitrazh* Court, conflict with
  continuing problems, 290
  guiding explanations, 215
  regional law making, 216
  reopening of cases, 214–215
  statutory interpretation, 134–135
ignorance regarding, 249–250
individuals, petitions by, 126
innovation in, 92
international pressure and, 228–229,
  286–287
interpretative decisions, 122–123
judicial activism in, 92, 122–125

judicial independence, public support
  for, 251–252
judicial review in
  growth of, 186
  intrajudicial disputes, 137
  limitations on, 120–121
  proportional restrictions on rights,
    development of standard via, 169
  theories of, 219–220
"juristocracy" and, 294–295
lack of information regarding rulings,
  247
land use statutes and, 243–244
legal elites and, 286
mass media and, 252–253
opinion polls regarding, 247–248,
  250–251
political bodies, petitions by, 126–127
political disputes, avoidance of, 288–289
political problems in, 118–120
politicization of, 157
positive content decisions, 123–125, 208
property rights, 166
proportional restrictions on rights
  bankruptcy cases, 169
  election cases
    campaigning, 172–173
    dispute resolution, 171–172
    mass media and, 172–173
    referendum process, 172
    State Duma, 170–171
  fiscal penalties, 169–170
  judicial review, development of
    standard via, 169
  malicious intent standard, 173
  overview, 165–166, 168–169
  residence permits and, 168
  statutory requirement, 168
  taxation cases, 169–170
public hearings, lack of, 125–126
public image of, 247–254
public policy changes and, 289
public relations efforts, 253–254
regions and
  constitutional/charter courts, 218–219
  dissolution of regional governments,
    147–148
  election of local officials, 149–150,
    152–153, 155–156
  federal preemption of regional law,
    145–146

Index

fiscal policy, federal control over,
148–149
harmonization of laws, 218–219
judicial appointments, 223–225
regional law making, 142–143,
151–152, 153–154, 215–216, 218
relative strength of, 150–151
sovereignty clauses, 225–227
subnational sovereignty, 146–147
uniformity in regional governments,
144–145
use by, 127
religious freedom and, 177–178
relocation of, 88–90
reopening of cases, 214–215
residence permits and
compliance, 245–246
proportional restrictions on rights, 168
right to counsel, 163
Russian Constitutional Court Act of
1994 (*See* Russian Constitutional
Court act of 1994)
Russian Supreme Court, conflict with
continuing problems, 290
harmonization of laws, 218–219
judicial review, 137
regional law making, 215–216, 217
reopening of cases, 214–215
statutory interpretation, 134–135
separation of powers and
arrest power, 133–134, 213–214
Audit Chamber, 131–132
Cabinet decrees, 211–212
Chechnya and, 128–129
compliance, 209–214
conflict of laws, 135–137
constitutional amendment process,
209–210
criminal procedure, 133–134, 213–214
executive branch resistance, 211
Federation Council, conflict with, 209
First RCC compared, 138–139
implied powers of president, 128–130
intrajudicial disputes, 134–135
intralegislative disputes, 130–131
normative decrees, 130
president and
law making power, 211
veto power, 211
referendum process, 137–138
search and seizure, 133

stability in, 127–128
State Duma and
conflict with, 209
second reading, fundamental
changes introduced in, 210–211
subconstitutional disputes, 135–137
taxation cases, 132–133
veto power, 129–130, 211
sessions, 122
short-term policy making and, 91–92,
287
specific rulings, public support for,
248–249
Stalinist purges, and victims of,
240–243
strategies to enhance reputation of,
252
surveillance cases, 163–165
taxation cases
bank deposits and tax obligations,
235–237
double taxation, 235–237
fairness in, 182–183
federalism and, 154–155
good faith taxpayers, 237–238
overview, 235
proportional restrictions on rights,
169–170
resistance to rulings, 239
separation of powers and, 132–133
YUKOS case, 238–239
tenure of judges, amendments regarding,
85–87
timelines, 83
transparency, lack of, 125–126
Yeltsin and
appointments by, 80–81
conflict with, 209
relationship with, 118–120
Selivon, Mykola, 262
Sentencing, fairness in, 180–181
Separation of powers
Federation Council and, 209
First RCC and (*See* First Russian
Constitutional Court)
nonlinear judicial empowerment and,
45–46
president and, 209
Second RCC and (*See* Second Russian
Constitutional Court)
State Duma and, 209

Serbia
  constitutional court in, 2
  "War of the Courts" in, 267
Shakhrai, Sergei, 68, 70, 126
Shortening of terms of judges, 261–262, 263
Short-term policy making
  Chechnya and, 8
  compliance and, 301
  decision making and, 301
  design and, 54–55, 91–92, 301
  judicial empowerment, impact on, 7–8
  nonlinear judicial empowerment and, 39–41, 52–53
  Second RCC and, 287
Shulzhenko, Iurii, 57
Shumeiko, Vladimir, 84
Siloviki, power of, 234–235
Skuratov, Yuri, 213
Slaughter, Anne-Marie, 176
Slobodkin, Yuri, 67, 68
Slovakia, constitutional court in, 2, 261
Slovenia, "War of the Courts" in, 268
Social justice, Second RCC and
  balancing individual rights, 181–182
  overview, 181
  vulnerable groups, 182
Soloviev, Vadim, 198
Solyom, Laszlo, 263–264
Sources of data
  interviews, 14
  primary sources, 13–14
  secondary sources, 14
South Africa, constitutional court in, 261
Sovereignty clauses in regional constitutions, 225–227
Soviet Union
  Central Executive Committee, 56
  Congress of People's Deputies (See Congress of People's Deputies)
  CSC (See Constitutional Supervision Committee (CSC))
  dissolution of, 98, 103
  judicial review in, 56
  Procuracy (See Procuracy)
  republics, CSC and, 58–59, 95–97, 189–190
  Supreme Court, 56

Supreme Soviet (See Supreme Soviet)
  Union Treaty, 60–61
Spain
  constitutional court in
    caseload, 159
    compliance problems, 34
    impact of jurisprudence, 176
    impeachment power, 8
    individuals, petitions by, 126
    legal hierarchy, 36
    overstaying of terms, 259
    politicization of, 116
    politics and, 31
    public support for, 50
  federalism in, 142
  judicial independence in, 33
  "War of the Courts" in, 51, 269, 270, 274, 302
Special governance regime, 107–108
Stalin, Joseph, 283
Stalinist purges, victims of, 240–243
State Duma
  binding nature of judicial rulings, resistance to Putin proposals regarding, 87–88
  dissolution power, 78
  election cases, proportional restrictions on rights, 170–171
  Federation Council, disputes with, 130–131
  relocation of Second RCC, resistance to Putin proposals regarding, 89–90
  retirement and tenure of judges, resistance to Putin proposals regarding, 86
  Russian Constitutional Court Act of 1994, debate on, 80
  Second RCC, conflict with, 209
  second reading, fundamental changes introduced in, 210–211
  separation of powers and, 209
  Stalinist purges, and victims of, 241
  taxation and, 154
Stepankov, Valentin, 68, 72
Strategic approach
  judicial empowerment, to, 5, 7
  judicial review, to, 297–298, 299, 300
  nonlinear judicial empowerment, to compliance under, 49–50
  delegation of power and, 47–49

Index

objection to nonlinear theory, as, 47–50
strength of constitutional courts under, 49
Ulysses metaphor, 47–49
"War of the Courts" and, 293, 299
Subfederal units, 109
Subnational sovereignty, 146–147
Sumin, Petr, 198, 199
Supreme Soviet
CSC and, 59
dissolution by Yeltsin, 74–75, 108
First RCC, role in establishing, 61–62
Surveillance cases, Second RCC, 163
Symmetrical federalism, 221

Taiwan
constitutional court in, 34
shortening of terms of judges, 261–262
"War of the Courts" in, 52
Tajikistan, constitutional court in, 2
Tatarstan
constitutional/charter courts and, 219
electoral rights in, 244
judicial appointments in, 224
judicial review, resistance to, 206
referendum, 109, 195–197
residence permits in, 168
sovereignty and, 225–227
Taxation
Cabinet and, 154
Federation Council and, 154
Second RCC and
bank deposits and tax obligations, 235–237
double taxation, 235–237
fairness in, 182–183
federalism, 154–155
good faith taxpayers, 237–238
overview, 235
proportional restrictions on rights, 169–170
resistance to rulings, 239
separation of powers, 132–133
YUKOS case, 238–239
State Duma and, 154
Tax Code, 236, 237
Tax Ministry, 235–237, 239
Tenure of judges
comparative perspective, 282–283

Constitutional Convention of 1993, changes at, 75
extension of terms, 261, 262–264
overstaying of terms, 259–261
overview, 258, 259
political commitment to judicial independence and, 264–265
Russian Supreme Court and, 85
Second RCC, amendments regarding, 85–87
shortening of terms, 261–262, 263
tables, 87, 260
Teune, Henry, 116
Tilly, Charles, 37
Tiunov, Oleg, 203
Trial procedures, compliance problems, 232–233
Tsarist Russia
judicial independence in, 33
judicial review in, 55–56
Tumanov, Vladimir
chair of Second RCC, as, 119
Chechnya, on, 221
civil rights, on, 158
compliance, on problems with, 81
mass media, on, 252
Stalinist purges, on victims of, 241
Zorkin, on, 77
Tyler, Tom, 23
Tyva, 225

Udmurtia, 144, 149, 155, 221–222
Ukraine
constitutional court in, 2, 61
extension of terms of judges, 262–263
"War of the Courts" in, 52, 267, 274
Union Treaty, 60–61
Uniqueness of Russian experience, 10
United Kingdom
legal elites in, 27
"War of Courts" in, 283
United States
compliance in, 302
federalism in, 142
First RCC compared, 72
judicial review in, 27–28, 50
tenure of judges in, 264
Universal Declaration of Human Rights, 174

USSR. *See* Soviet Union
Uzbekistan, constitutional court in, 2, 46

Vagueness, constitutional rights and, 177–178
Vanberg, Georg, 24
Vedernikov, Nikolai
  monetary obligations of government to individuals, on, 200, 201
  regional law making, on, 152
Venice Commission for Democracy through Law, 229, 262
Verdery, Katherine, 39
Veto points approach, 292–293
Veto power, 129–130, 211
Vitruk, Nikolai
  appointments to Second RCC, on, 81
  compensation of victims, on, 240
  compliance, on problems with, 82, 256
  conflict of laws, on, 136
  Constitutional Convention of 1993, role at, 73, 74
  decision making, on, 80
  dissolution of First RCC and, 75
  financial independence of Second RCC, on, 82
  impeachment of Yeltsin, on, 108
  joint executive–legislative decrees, on, 105
  retirement of, 227
  Russian Constitutional Court Act of 1994, on, 79
  sentencing, on, 181
  sovereignty clauses, on, 226
  Udmurtia case, on, 222
Voronezh, 168

"War of the Courts." *See also specific state*
  assumption of jurisdiction by constitutional courts, 269–270
  coexistence of courts and, 283–284
  competition among courts, necessity of, 265, 269–270
  constitutional rights, effect on, 284
  Czech Republic, in (*See* Czech Republic)
  European Court of Human Rights and, 275–276
  federalism and, 293–294
  Higher *Arbitrazh* Court, conflict with Second RCC

    continuing problems, 290
    guiding explanations, 215
    regional law making, 216
    reopening of cases, 214–215
    statutory interpretation, 134–135
  judicial resistance to constitutional courts, 270–271
  legalistic explanation, 267–268
  monopolizing of judicial review by constitutional courts, 272–273
  nature of disputes, 265–266
  overview, 258–259, 265
  political causes of, 274
  positive law making and, 272, 273
  postcommunist states, in, 270
  problems arising from, 273–274
  progressive/reactionary explanation, 268–269
  rule of law and, 265, 274–275
  Russian Supreme Court
    First RCC, conflict with
      age discrimination cases, 203–204
      constitutional rights, over, 114–115
      labor law cases, in, 112–114
      reasons for, 204–205
      retirement age cases, 203–204
      wrongful dismissal cases, 202–203
    Second RCC, conflict with
      continuing problems, 290
      harmonization of laws, 218–219
      judicial review, 137
      regional law making, 215–216, 217
      reopening of cases, 214–215
      statutory interpretation, 134–135
  scholarly attention, lack of, 266–267
  strategic approach and, 293, 299
  strategies for resolving, 274, 276
  table, 216
  veto points approach, 292–293
Way, Lucan, 193, 255
Widner, Jennifer, 302
World Bank, 43
Wrongful dismissal
  CSC and, 97
  First RCC, in
    compensation, 202–203
    damages, 113
    judicial review, 112–113

Index

Yeltsin, Boris
Chelyabinsk case and, 198–199
Communist Party, ban of, 106–107,
192–193
Congress of People's Deputies,
dissolution of, 108
constitutional amendment process and,
209–210
Constitutional Commission, as head of,
61–62
Constitutional Convention of 1993,
convening of, 73–74
First RCC and
appointments to, 69–70, 75–77
legal elites and, 286
resistance to, 290
support for, 64
suspension of, 1, 74–75, 108–109
impeachment of, 1, 103, 108
Irkutsk case and, 199
judicial appointments by, 223–225
Khasbulatov, relationship with,
monetary obligations of government to
individuals and, 201
Mordovia case and, 198
Moscow privatization case and, 199
new draft of Russian constitution by, 73
regions, relationship with, 142–143
Second RCC and
appointments to, 80–81, 82–85
conflict with, 209
legal elites and, 286
relationship with, 118–120
special governance regime, 107–108
Supreme Soviet, dissolution of, 108
Tatarstan referendum, on, 196–197
Udmurtia case and, 222

veto power, on, 129
Zorkin and
impeachment of, on, 206
relationship with, 101, 102–103, 115,
288
Yugoslavia, constitutional court in, 190
YUKOS case, 238–239

Zadornov, Mikhail, 212–213
Zorkin, Valerii
chair of First RCC, as, 100–101
chair of Second RCC, as, 119–120
compensation of victims, on, 240–241
compliance, on problems with, 256
constitutional rights, on, 158
"court packing," on, 77
dissolution of First RCC and, 75
federalism, on, 141–142
impeachment of, 206
institutional conflict, on, 46
judicial review, on, 105
Khasbulatov, relationship with, 101,
102–103
monetary obligations of government to
individuals, on, 201
political strength of, 100–101
public hearings, on, 125
public relations efforts, 253–254
regions, on petitions by, 157
resignation from First RCC, 104
Second RCC, on, 119
separation of powers, on, 63, 104–105,
192
Yeltsin and
impeachment of, on, 108
relationship with, 101, 102–103, 115,
288

For EU product safety concerns, contact us at Calle de José Abascal, 56–1°,
28003 Madrid, Spain or eugpsr@cambridge.org.

www.ingramcontent.com/pod-product-compliance
Ingram Content Group UK Ltd.
Pitfield, Milton Keynes, MK11 3LW, UK
UKHW010857060825
461487UK00012B/1190